PERSONALITY

Christopher Peterson

University of Michigan

Harcourt Brace Jovanovich, Publishers
San Diego   New York   Chicago   Austin   Washington, D.C.
London   Sydney   Tokyo   Toronto

Lisa M. Bossio is a writer of style and substance. Her generous and thoughtful help made *Personality* much better than it otherwise could have been.

This book is dedicated with much love to my parents, Duane C. Peterson and Leota F. Peterson.

Thank you. Thank you. Thank you.

PREFACE

One of the most important realizations of this century is that each of us sees the world from a particular perspective. Numerous assumptions, both acknowledged and unacknowledged, filter our observations, shape our conclusions, and dictate our future activities. Thomas Kuhn introduced the term *paradigm* to describe such perspectives within the history of science. Kuhn and others persuasively argue that even "objective" observation is theory-laden.

Unlike the physical sciences, however, in which a single perspective dominates at any given time, the social sciences usually have several perspectives flourishing simultaneously. Individual social scientists adopt one of these views and pose their questions accordingly: What constitutes an adequate theory? How should research be conducted? What applications are sensible? Within a particular group of social scientists, answers to these questions are consensual and coherent; but across different groups, we sometimes see indifference, disagreement, and even outright hostility.

Some debate whether the social sciences can even be described in terms of overarching paradigms, but I have found the possibility so compelling that I used the notion of paradigm to organize *Personality*. As I view the field, the psychology of personality is characterized by three major paradigms: the psychoanalytic, the trait, and the cognitive. Within each, there are three major concerns: theory, research, and application. Simple multiplication gives us the nine core chapters of this fifteen-chapter book.

What makes up the rest of *Personality*? I begin with a four-chapter introduction that addresses those concerns that cut across the major paradigms: the meaning of personality, the nature of personality psychology, the history of the field, and the notion of paradigm itself. Chapters 5 through 13 present the paradigms, in the order they appeared over the last century. In Chapter 14, I discuss behaviorism and how it relates to personality psychology. Behavioral approaches represent a coherent approach to psychology, but I argue that they do not simply represent another paradigm of personality psychology. Rather, behaviorism should be viewed in light of the criticisms it raises about the whole of personality psychology. Finally, in Chapter 15, I consider what the future of personality psychology might bring—how a single paradigm integrating the current diversity of perspectives may be just out of sight.

How does *Personality* differ from other textbooks in the field? There are really only two types of personality textbooks. The first models itself after the traditional Hall and Lindzey text, which describes in successive chapters the major personality theorists. The second, and more recent, type focuses on research topics currently of interest to personality psychologists.

In using paradigms as the means of organization, *Personality* accomplishes what these other textbooks do not. It allows us to have it both ways: theory and research in the same package. *Personality* does not force instructors to choose between a book that stresses theory and a book that stresses research. Theory and research both matter, and once the field of personality psychology is organized in terms of its dominant paradigms, the relationship between them becomes clear.

In contrast to the "theorist" texts, my book shows that personality psychology is a somewhat coherent field. There is a reason that Freud and Jung and Adler seem to be saying similar things. It's because they are saying similar things! I don't devote separate chapters to theorists who can be sensibly placed within the same paradigm. And in contrast to the "research" texts, my book shows that personality psychology is not a perfectly coherent field defined by a monolithic view of the scientific method. Researchers within the psychoanalytic, trait, and cognitive paradigms work from drastically different assumptions. I've tried to make these assumptions clear.

A further dividend of using paradigms to organize *Personality* is that I could cover the range of applications that make the field so intriguing. Readers will find not just standard discussions of how personality pertains to psychopathology; they will also find discussions of advertising, cognitive maps, education, personnel selection, surrealism, health promotion, political polls, psychohistory, television, short-circuiting the SAT, and criminality, among other topics. I locate none of these discussions in traditional textbook "boxes" because I think they are more than mere "tickles." Applications are an integral part of personality psychology, yet most other textbooks find no easy way to describe them. *Personality* does so by integrating applications with theory and research.

So, I see personality psychology as comprising theory, research, and application. As a teacher of personality psychology courses, I looked for an undergraduate textbook true to this characterization. I couldn't find such a book, so I wrote it. Writing occupied me from April 1984 to April 1987. (I assume that a number of textbooks are similarly bracketed by 1040 forms.) I wrote first at Virginia Tech, then at the University of Pennsylvania, then back at Virginia Tech, and finally at the University of Michigan.

At each school, I was fortunate to have friends and colleagues who helped me see how I might capture personality psychology between two covers. I was also fortunate to have students who were fully engaged in learning. They were curious about the big picture, and they demanded that it be fleshed out with compelling detail. They managed to teach me something about teaching—in general and as it pertains to personality. I hope that some of what I have learned from them shines through in *Personality*.

I obviously approached the book as a teacher (this is, after all, a textbook), but I also wore the hats of the clinician, the researcher, and the writer. I tried to strike a balance between the intellectual and the experiential, the abstract and the concrete, the pedagogical and the personal. You may find it bothersome that I've used the first person exclusively and that I've drawn on my own life for illustrations. But this is how I teach. For better or worse, I've shown my true colors, and *Personality* is literally part of my personality. So be forewarned. I have a quirky sense of humor. I have opinions about right and wrong. And I like to start sentences with "and" while ending them with prepositions, because this is the style that my writing has evolved into.

In writing *Personality*, I've tried to be engaging—entertaining as well as enlightening. I believe that playful humor and serious purpose need not trip over each other. But, if at times I seem to be hopping heedlessly along on one leg, bear with me until my full stride is regained.

Several people were kind enough to review chapters of the book, both in an official capacity and as personal favors to me. I'd like to thank the following:

- James Austin—Virginia Polytechnic Institute & State University
- Cynthia Baum—Catholic University
- Daniel Cervone—University of Illinois: Chicago
- David Funder—University of Illinois: Urbana-Champaign
- Lester Luborsky—University of Pennsylvania
- Beth Meyerowitz—Vanderbilt University
- Thomas Monson—Florida Atlantic University
- Susan Nolen-Hoeksema—Stanford University
- Wayne Osgood—University of Nebraska
- Leonard Rorer—Miami University
- Abigail Stewart—University of Michigan
- Peter Villanova—Northern Illinois University
- Stephen Zaccaro—Virginia Polytechnic Institute & State University

I appreciate the time and energy they devoted to the reviews. The proof of my appreciation is that I incorporated all of their suggestions into the final manuscript.

The folks at Harcourt Brace Jovanovich were consistently enthusiastic about this project, and I enjoyed working with each of them. Everyone's contribution was praiseworthy. Candace Young put together the art package. Martha Gilman designed the page layout. Lynne Bush oversaw production. Karen Davidson and Anthony Maddela patiently saw the book through its later stages.

In particular, I'd like to thank Kenneth Cherry for his humor, intelligence, and skill as an editor. Ken was committed to maintaining the integrity of the book's style and substance. *Personality* owes much to his understanding and support of my purpose as teacher, psychologist, *and* writer.

Finally, let me acknowledge my special gratitude to Lisa M. Bossio. She helped me write this book by being characteristically herself, which means she rolled up her sleeves and pitched in. She read and reread every sentence of every draft of every chapter: writing, rewriting, criticizing, and praising, always with grace and always with intelligence.

Christopher Peterson

CONTENTS

1

WHAT IS PERSONALITY?

"She has a good personality."

"He has no personality."

"Well, she has a good personality."

"Well, he doesn't have much personality."

"She has personality."

"He has personality plus."

"He has too much personality."

"She is a personality."

"He was a personality; now he's on 'Hollywood Squares'."

"He's got personality, plus a brand new car."

"It's just her personality."

"She has her mother's personality."

"He and I have a personality conflict."

T hese opening quotes are all statements about **personality** that I have heard people say recently. You've probably heard or said similar things yourself, and you might decide from these statements that personality has no simple or single meaning. We understand what each conveys, but we have trouble seeing what is common to all of their meanings. Personality psychologists have the same difficulty, only more so; which brings me to the purpose of this book: to discuss personality and how psychologists attempt to understand it.

First, let's consider how psychologists define personality. As scientists, psychologists greatly value a precise definition of their subject matter. But, while the following definitions are precise, you might question whether they capture the various meanings of personality contained in the above quotations.

> A stable set of characteristics and tendencies that determine those commonalities and differences in the psychological behavior (thoughts, feelings, and actions) of people that have continuity in time and that may not be easily understood as the sole result of the social and biological pressures of the moment. (Maddi, 1980, p. 10)

> The governing organ of the body, an institution, which, from birth to death, is ceaselessly engaged in transformative functional operations. (Murray, 1951, p. 436)

The dynamic organization within the individual of those psychophysical systems that determine his characteristic behavior and thought. (Allport, 1961, p. 28)

That which permits a prediction of what a person will do in a given situation. (Cattell, 1950, p. 2)

These definitions sound scientific, and they seem precise, but they fall short of capturing what we mean by personality when we talk about it in ordinary life. Perhaps a dictionary definition comes closer:

3 a: the complex of characteristics that distinguishes an individual or a nation or group; b (1): the totality of an individual's behavioral and emotional tendencies; (2): the organization of the individual's distinguishing character traits, attitudes, or habits. (*Webster's New Collegiate Dictionary*, 1977, p. 855)

Again, this seems to fall short. But, when all else fails, we can turn on the radio and hear this definition of personality: "All you need are looks and a whole lot of money."

Billy Joel's definition is certainly the easiest to understand, and it contains enough truth for us to smile at it. But like the more formal definitions proposed by psychologists, it fails to capture the whole of what we mean by personality (I hope).

Since I don't seem to be getting around to defining personality, you may be feeling a bit frustrated. Maybe that's just the way you are—easily frustrated—but that's the way psychology is. It wrestles with definitions because it is concerned with everyday life. Psychology's topics are not exotic occurrences. Rather, they stem from central questions and issues about being a person. What am I? Why do I do what I do? What will I be like in the future? How can I get along with others? Why do some people lie, cheat, and kill? Why are other people thrifty, reverent, kind, and brave? How do people change? Can we make them change in ways that we want them to?

PERSONALITY IS A FUZZY TERM

These questions and issues were raised long before there were psychologists or any scientists at all. They were phrased in terms of everyday language, and they continue to be phrased in these terms. Everyday language is rich. It is colorful. It is emotional. With it, we can express contradictions and nuances, subtle contrasts and bizarre comparisons. This is all well and good, and it keeps poets and songwriters busy, but it complicates the task of the psychologist. Because ordinary language terms resist precise definition, they do not lend themselves to scientific theories and research. Some psychologists

"*Might I point out, sir, that that one goes particularly well with your tie?*"

SOURCE: Drawing by Gahan Wilson; © 1982 The New Yorker Magazine, Inc.

have therefore argued against any scientific attempt to understand topics as long as they are phrased in terms of everyday language.

Personality is one of these inherently *fuzzy* terms that eludes precise definition. It is not the sort of term for which one can specify critical characteristics that unambiguously and exactly define it. Prior definitions have probably been too narrow, and, in their exactness, have failed to depict what is meant by personality.

So what? Well, as I see it, the imprecise nature of personality terminology must be explicitly recognized. But this does not mean that a scientific psychology of personality is impossible. Rather, it means that personality psychologists must look to the use of such terms for precision, not to the terms themselves. Otherwise, the science of personality psychology will have an unsound foundation.

One of the lessons psychologists can well learn from the past is that precision for its own sake can be dangerous. A timely example comes from psychology's approach to *punishment* and its application to child-rearing. Psychologists study punishment in carefully controlled laboratory experiments where they define it as *any stimulus following some behavior that decreases the future probability of that behavior.* For purposes of laboratory research, this is a perfectly fine definition: exact and unambiguous.

This research finds that punishment is not always an effective way to change behavior, since it is accompanied by negative emotions, a finding that has led some to conclude that punishment has no place in the rearing of children. Thus, parents should not spank, scold, or restrict their kids. According to these well-intentioned individuals, parents should ignore misbehavior instead of punishing it, since the consequences (negative emotions) may be worse than the original misbehavior. However, this recommendation has a problem—it proves to be wrong! Children who are punished by their parents do not grow up to have emotional problems. If anything, a lack of punishment during childhood appears to be associated with emotional difficulties later on.

The inconsistency between the laboratory findings and the facts about child-rearing is not really an inconsistency at all. Do you see that the term punishment is being used in two very different ways? The way in which experimental psychologists define and study punishment has little pertinence to the way in which parents actually punish their children: with a mostly symbolic rebuke accompanied by an explanation to the child of what was done wrong in the past and what should be done right in the future.

The term may be used in both these ways as well as others. But when these uses are considered collectively, punishment loses exact meaning. Personality is similarly imprecise, because people use it to refer to a variety of things. Since personality psychologists also use the term in a variety of ways, they should not expect there to be a simple and single definition.

There is a branch of philosophy known as **ordinary language philosophy,** conducted by such philosophers as Ludwig Wittgenstein (1953) and Gilbert Ryle (1949), which is concerned with *the meaning of concepts.* I have found the approach of ordinary language philosophy useful in understanding the language of personality and how personality psychologists might reasonably use it.

One of the most important ideas from ordinary language philosophy is that *the meaning of concepts is inherent in the way people use them.* To understand the meaning of specific terms, ordinary language philosophers attend to the manner in which people use these terms in conversations. What distinctions do they make? What distinctions do they ignore?

These philosophers liken language to a game, where the meaning of a given concept resides in how the rules of the language game allow it to be used. For instance, slang is fun because we have to learn how to use it. We feel superior to people who have not quite mastered the rules of the games that govern expressions like "totally," "awesome," "dirtbag," and "it's not love, but it's not bad."

In contrast to this view that meanings of concepts lie in their use, psychologists often treat meanings as if they reside within the concepts themselves. Psychologists may propose **operational definitions** for particular concepts, *specifications of how to identify the presence or absence of a concept in terms of necessary and sufficient conditions.* A **necessary condition** is *some characteristic or attribute found in all instances of a given concept.* For example, a necessary condition for "triangle" is three sides. A **sufficient condition** is *some characteristic or attribute found only in instances of a given concept.* So, a sufficient condition for "American car" is having been manufactured in Detroit (and hopefully not on a Monday or Friday).

Let me say this in a different way. A necessary and sufficient condition is some characteristic or attribute found in all instances of a given concept and only in instances of this concept. When psychologists propose operational definitions, they specify how these necessary and sufficient conditions can be identified. So, if intelligence is operationally defined as what is measured by an IQ test, then intelligence only means an IQ score, and IQ scores only mean intelligence.

Now let's return to the different view of ordinary language philosophers. They believe that most ordinary language concepts lack necessary or sufficient characteristics and so do not admit to operational definitions. In a famous illustration of this point, Wittgenstein asked if there were necessary and sufficient conditions for the concept of *game.* Is there some characteristic or attribute that games possess, and only games? He considered a number of likely candidates in turn, rejecting each as he found a counter-example.

Perhaps games must involve two or more people—except solitaire. Maybe games must have winners or losers—except war games. Let's suppose games must have explicit rules—except make-believe. And so on. The point here is that *game* is like many ordinary language terms. We have no difficulty using the term. We recognize examples and nonexamples, but we don't do so by identifying some critical attribute that makes some things games and other things nongames.

Maybe you're persuaded that this is a reasonable idea for games. Appreciate that many of the terms we use in everyday conversation are just as fuzzy. Follow Wittgenstein's example and analyze some other concept, like fruit, dog, joke, aggression, fun, or life. Is there some specific characteristic that all fruits have, and only fruits—like sweetness, seeds, or Vitamin C? Is there something that makes all dogs canine—like fur, a bark, or Paul McCartney eyes? Is there something common to all jokes, to all types of fun, to each instance of life? I think not, but if you're game, why don't you try to convince yourself otherwise.

Regardless, many psychology terms don't have necessary and sufficient conditions. Since psychologists have often specified operational definitions for these terms, you can see why confusion has occurred within the field. Consider again the example of intelligence operationally defined as an IQ score. We all know intelligent people who scored poorly on the SAT, as well as unintelligent people who scored well. Our bafflement at this state of affairs evaporates when we realize that a high SAT score is neither a necessary nor a sufficient condition for intelligence.

Personality is just as complex a notion as intelligence, and so we shouldn't be surprised that personality psychologists have been unable to propose a fully satisfactory definition of their subject matter. After all, they have often proceeded by specifying necessary and sufficient conditions for personality.

DEFINING FUZZY TERMS: THE FAMILY RESEMBLANCE APPROACH

Where does this leave us? Luckily, the situation is not as bleak as it seems, since there is an alternative to defining concepts with necessary and sufficient conditions. Just because instances of psychological concepts do not possess critical characteristics does not mean that they cannot be defined. Wittgenstein suggested a way to regard ordinary language concepts and their instances. This view has come to be known as the **family resemblance approach.** According to Wittgenstein, concepts are indeed characterized by attributes, but it is a set of *pertinent attributes* that is important rather than a single one. *A pertinent attribute is one that many instances of a concept possess, and that few instances of other concepts possess.* However, a pertinent attribute is neither necessary nor sufficient.

The term *family resemblance* comes from a once popular procedure of superimposing photographs of individuals from the same family upon one another. Characteristics like a jutting jaw or curly hair, possessed by many

Members of this family share distinctive characteristics.

family members, were exaggerated in the composite picture, while other characteristics, possessed by only a few family members, were blurred and lost. The resulting picture was a summary of how the family looked, so to speak, but not an exact facsimile of how any one family member looked. Still, it was usually apparent that two individuals belonged to the same family since they possessed some characteristics in common.

Ordinary language philosophers suggest that instances of ordinary language concepts share a similar family resemblance. A set of attributes characterizes the various instances of a concept, but any two instances may have few of these attributes in common. So, in order to identify the family of pertinent characteristics, we have to examine a large number of instances.

Indeed, if you want to identify the family resemblance that characterizes the instances of a concept, you need to look at many *striking instances* of the concept. Striking instances are good examples because they tend to possess many of the pertinent attributes that characterize the concept.

Your mother's spaghetti? *That* is a great meal.

I don't know much about art, but *that* is a great painting.

That is love; Chuckie's even combed his hair.

You did what? *That* is crazy.

Ordinary language philosophers call these striking instances **ostensive definitions,** *pointing-to definitions.* These are quite different from operational definitions, but nonetheless quite common and quite effective.

If you think for a minute, you can see that children mostly learn the meanings of concepts through ostensive definitions provided by adults:

That is a doggie.

That is creamed bananas with oatmeal, and you are going to eat it and like it.

That is naughty.

That is good for you.

Most parents wear out their index fingers pointing to instances of concepts and identifying them for their children. Kids eventually grasp the concepts exemplified by the instances, and do so quite easily. In fact, some psychologists feel that this process entails the essence of how people learn, remember, and employ abstract concepts.

Psychologist Eleanor Rosch has studied the relationship between concepts and their examples extensively (see, for example, Rosch & Mervis, 1975). She follows Wittgenstein in believing that everyday concepts like "dog" or "fruit" are characterized by a set of attributes. Rosch calls these sets of attributes **prototypes.** And any given example of an everyday concept may have few or many of these attributes.

One of the interesting aspects of Rosch's work involves asking people to identify good versus bad examples of various concepts. People show high agreement. It turns out that good examples have a large number of pertinent attributes, while poor examples do not. So, good examples resemble the prototype of a concept, while poor examples do not.

Lassie is a better example of "dog" than is a basenji, since this latter creature, though certainly a canine, does not bark. Apples are better examples of "fruit" than are kumquats or kiwi fruits. To an American observer, baseball is a better example of "sport" than is Australian rules football, since we expect referees to wear dark colors, not white tuxedoes! And, to most people Tom Selleck is a better example of "man" than Boy George. Within psychology, schizophrenia is a better example of "mental illness" than is alcoholism, since it more closely resembles our prototype of illness.

I have discussed these ideas in detail because they help to explain the nature of the term personality and the ways that it is used. Like most ordinary language concepts, personality is a fuzzy term. It is applied to a number of

Tom Selleck and Boy George represent, for many of us, two disparate characterizations of "Man."

instances that may not greatly overlap each other. Does this make a science of personality impossible? Not at all, because fuzzy terms are not capricious. The relationship between concepts and their examples is not exact, but neither is it incoherent. We can precisely describe the way in which nonprecise terms are used, but, in doing so, we must remember several things.

First, there is a difference between an abstract concept and its concrete examples. Concepts are prototypes—pure cases—dwelling in the realm of theories and ideas. Examples are "real" things, residing in the world of "real" things, where there is little that is either simple or pure. *Science is the business of using concepts to predict and explain examples,* but the examples are found in reality, not the concepts.

I earlier criticized operational definitions for assuming that instances of concepts are always unambiguous. Psychologists are mistaken if they say without hesitation that everything on *this* side of the line is "intelligence" while everything on *that* side is not. Still, operational definitions are absolutely necessary in the business of science, since research is done in the world of real things, and we have to know how to draw conclusions about abstract concepts based on what we have learned about real things. To assess the real things, we need operational definitions. But, although operational definitions help us draw conclusions about abstract concepts, we must remember that they are merely aids for making our inferential leaps. They do not guarantee success.

Second, the path from abstract concepts to concrete examples is neither a straight road nor a limited-access highway. We can sometimes go astray or even be broadsided. These accidents will most likely occur if we forget the difference between concepts and examples. Conclusions about personality per se will generally apply to specific examples of personality, but they will rarely fit perfectly. Occasionally, conclusions will be completely incorrect, as in the earlier example about punishment. *Science is the business of making probabilistic statements:* generalizations but not truisms. The science of personality is no exception.

While you read about the psychological studies I describe in this book, think about the ways various abstract concepts are measured. Do you see why the researcher has chosen a particular *operationalization* (measure)? Do you agree or disagree with what has been done? For instance, one common operationalization of aggression is used in research with children: noting how many times a child punches or strikes a Bobo doll (which always bounces off the floor for more "aggression"). Is this a good operational definition of aggression? For some purposes, yes, but I for one would be reluctant to draw conclusions about the causes of war from such research, despite the striking similarity between Bobo dolls and some politicians.

You may find that you disagree with a particular idea or research result, but this is not necessarily a reason to dismiss what you have read. You may have found one of the places where the path from concept to example is interrupted. Science attempts to keep these detours to a minimum, but some will always exist. Try to find a better route before dismissing a theory or finding.

THE FAMILY RESEMBLANCE OF PERSONALITY: GENERAL, CHARACTERISTIC, ENDURING, INTEGRATED, AND FUNCTIONAL PROPERTIES OF THE INDIVIDUAL

Now that I've described some ideas from ordinary language philosophy that help us understand the meaning and use of everyday terms like personality, let's look at some ways the word is used in everyday conversation. Remember the quotes that opened this chapter? Each statement was an ostensive definition of personality, since the speaker was pointing to something and saying that it embodied one sense or another of the term. What is the family resemblance shared by these senses?

She has a good personality. Most simply, this statement is a positive evaluation. There is something about this woman that you like, and it is not her looks, her possessions, her connections, or her status. Rather, there is something about her that makes you feel good: her way of acting, her beliefs, style, flair, or character, the "way" she has about her, quirks, kinks, virtues and vices, and what she brings to a situation that someone else does not. You enjoy being with this woman and would clone her if possible since others would probably enjoy being with her as well.

He has no personality. Again, this statement is an evaluation, but a negative one. You do not like this guy. You don't dislike him either, unless you happen to be trapped in an elevator or a two-person office with him for forty hours a week. Dislike is an active emotion, and someone with no personality arouses no emotions. This man has nothing that stamps him as different from others: no passion, character, strange hobby or peculiar ability, and no desire to be anything except there. He neither likes nor dislikes the New York Giants. He can take or leave Chinese food, Richard Simmons, and video games. He has no strange but endearing pet, no mismatched socks, no bumper stickers on his car. This man just is, like a piece of furniture.

Well, she has a good personality. This is an ambivalent statement. Back in the days when we had blind dates, if this was the best thing that was *said* about your heretofore unknown partner, it was *heard* as the worst thing. There is nothing about her that is commendable or distinct: no good looks, no hard-to-find LP's, no phony I.D., no crazy sense of adventure, no parents who are away for the weekend, no bottles of Scotch, and no jive. On the bright side, she has no obvious scars, no communicable diseases, no sadistic tendencies, no overbearing opinions, and only a few annoying habits. She has what everybody has: a personality, a self, an identity, chromosomes, and a social security number. Ho hum.

Well, he doesn't have much personality. Here's another ambivalent evaluation, but it's not too ambivalent because the additional message tucked between the lines is quite positive: "But he doesn't need much personality; he's got something else going for him." You tend to like this man, not for who he is, but for what accompanies him. Here we see that personality is not everything associated with a person.

She has personality. You might well be pointing to someone's most distinct characteristic. Some people ride unicycles, others ride the E train, and some ride umpires at baseball games. Some people run marathons, run drugs, and/or run scared. Some have freckles or Lithuanian ancestors or chronic bad moods. And then there are those who have personality: spunk, sparkle, pizzazz—an ability to be themselves against all odds. This woman is characteristically herself regardless of where she is or who she is with. You may or may not like who she is, but you admire the fact that she is herself. You may even be a bit afraid that she will rub off on you; you know that you won't rub off on her.

He has personality plus. This statement embodies the above sentiments, only more so, and there is even a hint of criticism in the description. This man is always on: big smile, big ideas, big energy; cool, calm, collected, and larger than life. You are describing the class president, starting quarterback, and valedictorian. He does volunteer work and never has wrinkled clothes. He has never had a cavity, a parking ticket, constipation, or a broken heart. You want to like him, but can't quite believe in his perfection. You also want to dislike him, but can't quite find any reason to do so.

He has too much personality. You believe that this person is overbearingly himself, making every situation his own, even if he doesn't pay the rent. This is someone who expands to fill every enclosure, even if it is someone else's wedding, surprise party, or funeral. If he is a vegetarian, then don't eat lunch with him unless you want to feast on spinach salad. If he smokes cigarettes, have the nurse disconnect your oxygen when he visits you in the hospital. And if he doesn't smoke, don't accompany him to Winston-Salem, North Carolina, because he may get the War Between the States started up again. He's a damn Yankee, an ugly American, and a wild and crazy guy. Everyone should have some personality, but they should know when to leave it in the holster.

She is a personality. According to Andy Warhol, in the future everyone will be famous for about ten minutes. Then it will be someone else's turn. Until such a time, though, there are some people who are celebrities and others who are not. *People* magazine and *The National Enquirer* write about celebrities so noncelebrities can read about them. And the most notable type of celebrity is the personality. Rodney Dangerfield, Jackie Kennedy Onassis, George Steinbrenner, Martha Quinn, and R2-D2 are celebrities who are also personalities, since they are famous in part for being themselves. They are important, not just for what they do but for how they do it. In this sense, a personality is an individual who plays a role in our culture in such a way that the role becomes identified with what the personality brings to the role. (Pia Zadora, Evel Knievel, Nastassia Kinski, Bruce Jenner, and Tom Landry are celebrities who are not personalities, since we have no idea who they are apart from their fame.)

He was a personality; now he's on "Hollywood Squares." This is merely a reflection of the fact that fame is fleeting for some celebrities. They cease being a personality and instead become a former personality, famous in a left-handed way because they used to be famous, although no one quite remembers the reason for their former fame. This man has something sad about him, and what it is reveals something interesting about the way in which the term personality may be used. He can no longer play the role that he once played, perhaps because he played it so well there is nothing he can do to rival that role. Former athletes, former child movie stars, and former rock-and-roll musicians sometimes hold on to their past personalities, and we feel sorry for them because personality exists in the present and extends into the future. Personality is not a scrapbook, a memory, or a Bob Uecker commercial.

He's got personality, plus a brand new car. This statement about personality, unlike the previous ones, doesn't make a distinction between personality and some other characteristic of a person. It describes a man, saying that who he is and what he has somehow fit together nicely. You like the package, so there is no need to distinguish his good personality from his new car. The point is that a person's characteristics usually fit together in a coherent way, and this leads us to another way that the term is used: to refer to the entire person, above and beyond specific personality characteristics.

It's just her personality. You are offering an excuse, attempting to explain why a woman did something that was annoying or offensive. Her personality is blamed for the action, and the woman herself is excused, since she doesn't have much control over the sort of person she is. We expect people of a given sort to do those things that people of their sort do. Crude people shock our sensibilities, shy people tiptoe around us, and crazy people defy our understanding. When their actions impinge upon us, we may get upset, but we don't take it personally. Their personality may be accorded a role independent of their intentions, and it's only an accident that we happen to be in the path of such a personality. Anyone else in the situation would have been treated the same way.

She has her mother's personality. Many statements about personality point to distinguishing characteristics, what makes each of us different in some way. But personality is also used to make comparisons among people, pointing to commonalities and similarities. For most of us, it is second nature to catalogue how people remind us of others we have known. They may have similar mannerisms. When she laughs, she may shake her hair just like her mother does. And maybe they have similar temperaments. She cries easily over sad movies just like her mother does. The similarity may even be global: the entire personality. If you are a member of a large family, you have played an endless game your entire life with other members of your family:

> Well, you may have Aunt Gloria's pretty blue eyes, but you also have Daddy's stubbornness. I'd rather be me. No blue eyes but also no stubbornness. Plus, I'm glad I have Mommy's way with children and animals. You're just a doofus like Cousin Ichabod.

He and I have a personality conflict. Here, you are explaining why you don't get along with this man. Further, you are also predicting that you two will never get along, unless one of you changes who you are. Personalities are sometimes regarded as inherently incompatible, conflicting with each other regardless of how each person acts. Personality conflicts may erupt over the most trivial instance: how to arrange the office furniture, what television channel to watch, which ingredients should be ordered for the pizza.

We believe that certain types of people simply do not mix well, like oil and water, and that bad feelings will ensue for all involved, including bystanders, when these natural enemies come into contact.

On the brighter side, there is an opposite belief about how other types of people naturally mesh. We may call it "love at first sight" or "bosom buddies" or "kindred spirits." Regardless, the idea here is that personality is what makes us get along well with certain types of people.

I've discussed these different statements about personality in detail to try to draw out the specific senses in which people use the term. I could go on and discuss another dozen or so, but I believe these capture the family resemblance of the concept. Like superimposed photographs, these juxtaposed sentences reveal several of the pertinent attributes of the concept personality.

Personality is something that is a property of the individual; psychological in nature; general in its manifestation; characteristic of the individual; enduring over time; integrated with itself and with other aspects of the individual; and related to how the individual functions in the world, or fails to function.

Personality as a Property of the Individual   Personality usually refers to something that a person has, does, or is; it is attached to a specific person. We do not refer to personality apart from people. When we attribute personality to other entities, like groups, nations, animals, or machines, we imply that these entities are like people, not that people are like them. Personality is also usually brought to a situation and taken away from it. When we speak of personality, we mean a quality that transcends the momentary demands and pressures of a particular time and place.

Personality as Psychological   As we have seen, personality is rarely used to describe the material attributes, possessions, and status of a person. Personality usually refers to the person, to his or her behavior—thoughts, actions, and feelings. Accordingly, personality is the province of the psychologist, not the biologist, the economist, or the historian.

Personality as General   Not every aspect of a person's psychological makeup is typically classified as personality. Most uses of personality point to general properties of a person—thoughts, actions, and feelings painted with a broad brush. And it usually refers to pervasive properties of an individual, those evident in a variety of domains. Personality is not how you cut your toenails, unless that is also how you cut your fingernails, trim your moustache, mow your lawn, trim your steak, cut your losses, sever your romances, and purge your computer files. In this sense, personality describes the whole person, not just the fine print.

Personality as Characteristic   Personality is frequently used to describe those properties of an individual that distinguish him or her from others. When we call someone aggressive or introverted or energetic, we mean that the person is exceedingly so, more than others. In this sense, personality means a person's psychological signature or fingerprint. Psychologists sometimes call the study of personality the field of individual differences, meaning the ways in which people differ from each other.

Personality as Enduring   As we have seen, we use personality to point to lasting properties of the individual. A headache is not considered part of someone's personality, unless it is a chronic migraine. Bad moods, fleeting thoughts, temporary fatigue, or broken arms are also not classed as part of personality. Personality may of course change throughout one's life, and it may even do so suddenly. However, we generally reserve the term for the relatively enduring characteristics of a person; when they do change, we expect them to do so quite gradually or in response to a profound event.

Personality as Integrated   Personality is also frequently used to mean that which is unitary about the person. In other words, one's *self* is an excellent example of personality, since most of us regard our self as singular. We acknowledge facets of who we are, and we are vaguely aware of inconsistencies among our thoughts, actions, and feelings. However, we believe that a singular self lurks behind our various facets and integrates the surface inconsistencies. We commonly ask others to explain who they really are, and we often want to reveal to them who we really are. This "who" is the integrated aspect of personality.

Personality as Functional or Dysfunctional   Finally, personality sometimes means the way people get along in the world. Do we survive in good fashion? Then we have a healthy or strong personality. Do we seem destined to join the dodo and the carrier pigeon? Then we have a disordered or weak personality. We frequently use personality characteristics to explain how and why we are happy or sad, successful or failing, fully functional or just getting by. We have to be careful not to treat a description of health as its explanation, that is, to invoke a happy personality to explain happiness, when our only evidence for a happy personality is the observed happiness. Nevertheless, personality is often defined as the source of a person's success or failure at life.

In sum, we can define personality by using a family of pertinent attributes. To repeat, none of these attributes is necessary or sufficient to call something personality. However, we do expect each instance to possess at least some of these attributes, and we expect some instances to at least somewhat resemble other instances of personality.

A GOOD EXAMPLE OF PERSONALITY: TRAITS

Are there any particularly good examples of personality? Remember, a good example is one that closely resembles the prototype of a concept, one that possesses a number of the pertinent attributes that comprise the family resemblance of the concept. Is there anything in the real world that is a psychological property of a person that is also general, characteristic, enduring, integrated, *and* functional?

Most ordinary language speakers point to such things every time they attribute a personality **trait** to an individual. Traits like stinginess, curiosity, assertiveness, or laziness are virtually perfect examples of personality. They are properties of the individual that belong in the psychological realm. By definition, they are evident in a variety of areas of a person's life and characterize some individuals but not others. Traits are enduring because we believe that we can see continuity in them across an individual's entire lifespan. "Oh, I remember. He was always such a well-behaved baby. He became the all-American boy, and now he's a minister. I'm not at all surprised."

In the personality psychology courses I teach, I ask my students on the first day of class to write a one-page essay about themselves, in which they describe "whatever is general, characteristic, enduring, integrated, and functional" about themselves. I do this mainly as an informal exercise that gets them to think about what we mean by personality. Based on my reading of hundreds if not thousands of these essays, I believe that most of my students most of the time describe these aspects of themselves with personality traits.

Here is an example of one of these essays:

> The most important thing about me is my friends and how we treat each other. We never let each other down. If they need anything, then I drop whatever I'm doing, and I'm always there. And they're just as loyal to me as I am to them. People are real important to me; I'm a social person, and I need to be around others.
>
> My friends and I have a lot of fun together. I have a crazy sense of humor, and I'm always doing things to make people laugh, like hiding their notebooks for school or pretending to be someone else on the telephone. Most of the time, at least, my friends get a kick out of what I do.
>
> When I'm by myself, I like to play my guitar or listen to my tapes. I've always been a fan of rock-and-roll. In high school, I used to play in a band. I haven't hooked up with one here yet, but I will. And I must have almost a thousand

different cassettes. I never get tired of listening to them. But I don't have a Walkman. I always go out with other people, and those things are rude when you're with others.

What else? It may not seem like it, but I'm pretty close with my family, and that's a strength for me. I can always turn to them for support and encouragement. If school is tough, or if I get worried about my future, I know that my family will be there.

When I was growing up, my parents and I never had any of those big fights like other families did. We talk about most things, and even now when I'm away at school, we talk on the phone a couple of times a week. I really respect my father. He had to sacrifice a lot to raise the family, and I never heard him complain about it once. And the same with mom—she had wanted to go to college, but there wasn't enough money, so she never went. But she never has complained about that, and I respect her for it.

The writer has assigned to himself a number of traits: sociability, loyalty, humor, musical ability, and respect for his parents. These traits are psychological properties. They are general: note that he has used words like "never" and "always" to describe the way he acts. The assigned traits are also characteristic because they set him apart from others. Sometimes this is implied, as with his "crazy sense of humor." Sometimes this is explicitly stated, as with his extreme closeness to his family. His traits are enduring; he has traced several of them to early in his life. Also, they are integrated. They belong together. After describing himself as a wild and crazy guy who is close to his friends, the writer felt obliged to point out that his good relationship with his parents might seem a bit inconsistent with his other characteristics, but that it really wasn't. Finally, the traits he described are importantly related to how he gets along in the world—with other people, with his schoolwork, and with his future plans.

In 1936, Gordon Allport and Henry Odbert published the results of a massive undertaking. They read through the entire 1925 *Webster's New International Dictionary,* approximately 400,000 entries, and extracted all the words that describe personality. They found 17,953 such terms. That's about 4.5 percent of the total English vocabulary!

I've listed just a small number of these trait terms in Table 1-1. I tried to choose words that have obscure meanings because they're fun to read. Maybe you'll feel inspired enough to try and find some of these words in the current Webster's dictionary. You might learn that you're nothing but a *quipsome panglot,* a *nittering nabob,* or a *habile quidnunc.* Then again, you may just recognize yourself as an old-fashioned *gurl.*

And trait language evolves. As some of these words go out of fashion, new ones are invented. So, Allport and Odbert did not include some of the traits that have since become familiar to us: freaked out, all-American, preppy, and punk. And some of the familiar types of people who live in our present

Table 1-1
Trait Terms

abstemious	gleamy	nabob	techy
accendible	gurl	nash	twazzy
accumbrous	habile	nittering	ugging
adamantean	hagiolatrous	nympholeptic	ugsome
bestiarian	handersome	obdurating	ultrapurist
bibacious	hyppish	olent	umbrageous
bibliophagic	iconological	omissible	virose
bibulous	implastic	orective	vomitory
consentient	impuissance	pantoglot	votary
consuetudinary	inchoate	parvipotent	vulnific
contumelious	jiggish	paughty	wally
cormorant	jocose	pound-foolish	wandy
delitescent	joskin	quavery-mavery	wanless
demonic	jovish	queromonious	wordmonger
demophil	kim-kam	quidnunc	Xanthippe
dumpish	Kiwanian	quisby	xanthous
earthbred	kleptic	rackety	xenomania
earwiggish	knaggy	rogatory	xerantic
ebrious	lickerish	rudas	yabbering
ebullient	lickpenny	rumpscuttle	yegg
fenny	limpsy	sonsy	yeuky
fiducial	lithy	soothfast	yirring
fikie	macabre	sop	zany
fizgig	macaronic	spalpeen	zebrine
giggish	missikin	tarloch	zesting
gimcrack	mogilalia	tearmouth	zooid

SOURCE: Allport & Odbert, 1936.

world were also absent from their era: computer hack, MBA, superstar, Dead Head, Trekkie, company man, Moonie, jock, and young Republican.

CONTROVERSY: DO TRAITS EXIST?

Granted the extensive vocabulary we have available to us to describe these good examples of personality, you may find it surprising that some contemporary personality psychologists are skeptical about the existence of traits.

Just because we have words doesn't mean that there are things in the real world to which we can apply them. People may not think, act, or feel in ways that are general, characteristic, and enduring. There may be nothing in their behavior that we can point to in assigning a personality trait. As you will see, the possibility that people cannot be described in terms of personality traits has been an overriding issue in personality psychology.

Every time we ascribe a personality trait to someone, we assume that this person will show at least some consistency across situations. This assumption is embodied in each of the 17,953 trait terms that Allport and Odbert identified. Someone who is *rogatory* is expected to act in a rogatory fashion in a variety of settings. *Fiducial* folks are expected to be frequently so. But in 1968, Stanford psychologist Walter Mischel surveyed the personality research literature to see if people indeed acted consistently in different situations. It was an extreme blow to common sense and to personality psychology when he concluded that there was little evidence for cross-situational consistency in people's thoughts, actions, and feelings. Children who acted dishonestly in one situation did not necessarily act dishonestly in a different situation. Adults who respected authority in one setting, such as the army, did not always respect authority in another setting, such as the workplace.

What's going on here? If personality traits aren't really reflected in the real world, then why do trait terms exist? According to Mischel, the popularity of trait terms may in part result from a cognitive illusion—a trick of the mind, so to speak. When we watch a person doing something, we assume that the action originates from within, caused by a pervasive trait. We neglect to consider the possibility that we are observing a product of the situation that the person happens to be in.

Consider, for example, Stanley Milgram's (1963) experiments on destructive obedience. In these studies, research subjects were asked to deliver what seemed to be exceedingly painful electric shocks to another person. Despite the protests of this person, who actually was an actor in cahoots with the experimenter, approximately 60 percent of the research subjects complied, a surprisingly high figure.

The important point of these studies is that situational demands (in this case a psychology experimenter urging a research subject to continue with the experiment) may have a tremendous effect on what people do, regardless of who they are. These experiments have been repeated frequently enough so that we know it is the situational demand that is mostly responsible for the compliance.

When I explain this point to my students, I tell them several times, "Odds are you'd do exactly the same thing in that situation." But some of them insist that there was really something wrong with Milgram's research subjects. "They were wimpy, spineless, sadistic, or confused. That's why they complied with the request. The situation was not the cause of their behavior." These students are making an error, just as you would if you ever asked "What's a nice person like you doing in a place like this?" That's because the answer is, "The same thing that you're doing, since that's what everybody does in places like this."

Are we always guilty of such errors when we talk about personality? Should personality psychology be relegated to the scrapheap of science along with alchemy, astrology, and phrenology? No, of course not, and the idea of family resemblances helps explain why.

I've suggested that personality traits are particularly good examples of what personality means, since they possess all of the pertinent attributes that comprise the family resemblance of this term. However, perhaps we should be skeptical that traits could perfectly describe what people actually do. If a trait is a perfect example of what is meant by personality, then it is a proto-type, and prototypes do not exist in the real world.

When Mischel (1968) criticized the notion of traits, he was really arguing that people don't show perfect consistency across situations. This argument doesn't mean that personality isn't real, only that traits are not perfect descrip-tions of what people do. But we knew this from the start. Ordinary language analyses convince us that personality has no necessary or sufficient condi-tions, only a set of pertinent attributes. No instance of personality in the real world is apt to have all of these attributes, but that doesn't mean that we cannot sensibly use the term to describe things in the real world. And it doesn't mean that the science of personality psychology has no subject matter.

SO WHAT? IMPLICATIONS OF PERSONALITY'S FUZZINESS

The family resemblances approach is a powerful tool that we can use to under-stand the meaning of terms. I will refer to it throughout this book, which is why I have spent so much time developing and illustrating the idea. In par-ticular, family resemblances help us understand several characteristics of personality and personality psychology that might otherwise seem puzzling.

Why It Is Difficult to Define Personality Terms Precisely   As we have seen, personality is a fuzzy term without necessary or sufficient conditions. It resists precise operationalizations. The same holds true for specific per-sonality terms. Consider any of a number of trait names, such as timid, inde-pendent, anxious, or energetic. Each of these is used in a variety of senses, and there are probably no critical elements that cut across all of these senses.

Like the general term personality, the specific terms that we choose to describe personality are captured by a family resemblance, a set of pertinent attributes, with no single attribute being necessary or sufficient.

When we refer to specific personality traits, types, states, and so on, we must remember that these are *idealizations.* They do not exist in the real world any more than our prototype of personality does. Our use of personality language can be precise, however, as long as we recognize the discrepancy between the pure concept and its concrete instances. We must also remember that neither the concepts nor the examples themselves are precise.

Why Some Characteristics of a Person Are Ambiguously Classified as Part of Personality   I have stated that personality traits are good—perhaps even perfect—examples of what we mean by personality. But there are also poor examples, aspects of a person that seem to be somewhat part of her personality and somewhat not. The family resemblances idea helps resolve this ambiguity. These borderline instances of personality characteristics are precisely that: characteristics that possess some of the pertinent attributes, but not many. Whether we regard them as part of personality or not depends on our purpose.

Attitude is an example of borderline personality characteristics, possessing only some of the pertinent elements of personality. Social psychologists usually employ attitudes to predict and explain prejudiced behavior. Let's look at Gordon Allport's definition of attitude:

> A mental and neural state of readiness to respond, organized through experience and exerting a directive and dynamic influence on behavior. (1968, p. 63)

Defined in this way, an attitude is a *psychological property of an individual, an evaluation that dictates behavior.* It follows that we all differ with respect to our attitudes: I may hate reruns of "I Love Lucy" while you love them, and a third person may be indifferent. An attitude is therefore characteristic. It is also functional or dysfunctional, since it channels how a person interacts with the world.

But when we compare attitudes to personality traits, we usually regard the former as less general, less enduring, and less integrated. In other words, when we speak of attitudes, we usually treat them as less central than personality traits in defining who a person is. But there are exceptions. Someone who has an extreme attitude is apt to be importantly characterized by it. A member of the Ku Klux Klan, for instance, might be described merely as someone with a negative attitude toward religious and ethnic minorities, but this description doesn't really capture him very well. His personality certainly includes this negative attitude, and we would expect it to be generally apparent, long-lasting, and related to much of what he thinks, does, and feels. For some people at least, attitudes are part of their personality, while for other people, they are not.

A similar point can be made about intelligence. Here is a representative definition:

Intellectual ability: the ability to solve problems, master concepts, and deal rationally with the environment. (Freedman, 1982, p. 391)

As with attitude, intelligence has some of the pertinent attributes of personality. It is a psychological property that is characteristic of the individual. Indeed, when looking for procedures with which to measure personality differences, psychologists employed a number of the techniques already developed to measure differences in intelligence. Also, intelligence is functional; lack of it is dysfunctional.

But is intelligence general, enduring, and integrated? Here we find considerable and legitimate controversy. I used an abstract definition of intelligence which accords the term considerable generality, even more than the term personality. However, intelligence is usually operationalized or measured with an intelligence test, and people are less willing to believe that one's IQ score is related broadly to behavior. IQ scores do a good job of predicting a student's grade in a traditional academic course, but they are less relevant to other aspects of what an individual thinks, does, and feels.

Similarly, there is controversy regarding the stability of intelligence across one's lifespan. IQ scores are somewhat enduring, but this finding does not necessarily imply that intelligence is an enduring characteristic. Furthermore, IQ scores sometimes prove to be notably malleable. And finally, intelligence as measured by IQ scores may or may not be well-integrated with the rest of a person's characteristics. Whether or not one wishes to regard intelligence as part of personality is an ambiguous decision. So, intelligence is a borderline example of personality.

Physical characteristics also fall along the edge of what we mean by personality. Our physical appearance—general, characteristic, and enduring—is certainly part of our personal identity. I have never been in someone's house or apartment without seeing at least one mirror. Hair color, skin color, height, and weight distinguish us from others, and we all have strong opinions about our best and worst features (not to mention those of others).

Perhaps to our dismay, research by social psychologists shows that the way a person looks can be overwhelmingly important in determining how others react. Doors open or close, people smile or frown, dates are made or broken, all in accord with physical characteristics. Clearly, physical characteristics are seen as functional or dysfunctional.

However, in everyday conversation, we usually don't consider physical characteristics as part of personality, since they are physical properties of the

There is a fuzzy line between the physical and the psychological.

individual rather than psychological ones. This may be erroneous, though, since the idea of family resemblances suggests that the physical realm and the psychological realm are fuzzier than we often believe. And people can exercise considerable control over their appearance. They color their hair, tattoo their skin, and pierce their ears. They restrict calories and take laxatives to become emaciated, or they lift weights and ingest steroids to become muscle-bound. And people adorn themselves in various costumes: bangles and beads, leather and lace, Lacoste shirts and Top-siders. So when does the physical start to become the psychological?

Answer: there is a fuzzy line between the physical and the psychological properties of an individual. In many ways, physical characteristics are part of personality, although both everyday people and personality psychologists have usually neglected them as such. Consider the big men in basketball: Al McGuire's aircraft carriers. According to sports stories I have read, many seven-foot tall men have the same personality, regardless of their race, their athletic ability, or the particular circumstances in which they grew up. For example, both Jack Sikma and Kareem Abdul-Jabbar seem shy, quiet, introspective, and gentle.

While there are, of course, exceptions to this generalization, it seems at least plausible when we imagine ourselves in the tall man's large shoes, so to speak. If any of us grew up and up, towering over others, we would hear the same jokes and comments, have the same difficulties in finding clothes that fit, and face the same expectations of maturity and physical prowess as Sikma and Abdul-Jabbar. Our stature would become an important part of our personality, perhaps the most important part.

In a series of interesting studies, McGuire and McGuire (1981) asked young people to respond in their own words to questions like "Tell us about yourself," much as I have done with college students in my personality psychology classes. These researchers were concerned with the aspects of this "spontaneous self-concept" that were most salient. They found that physical characteristics figure predominantly in the self-concepts of children. So, in one study, height was spontaneously mentioned by 19 percent of the sample, weight by 11 percent, hair color by 14 percent, and eye color by 11 percent.

McGuire and McGuire were even able to predict which kids would or would not mention a given physical characteristic in their spontaneous self-concept by taking into account how distinctive the characteristic was within the child's classroom. Children who were taller or shorter than their peers were more likely to include height in their descriptions than were children of average

Physical characteristics can be a "big" part of our personalities.

height. Children who were heavier or lighter than their peers were more likely to mention weight than were the other children. And so on. Physical characteristics define who we are to the degree that they stamp us as different from those around us. For some people with certain physical characteristics in certain situations, physical characteristics are part of personality.

Another instance of a borderline personality characteristic is ethnicity or race. Most everyday people and personality psychologists do not consider these part of personality, maybe because it seems prejudiced to suggest that different groups of people are comprised of different sorts of people. Nevertheless, an individual's racial or ethnic group possesses some of the attributes of personality. Group membership is a property of the individual that is usually general, enduring, integrated, and functional. Is it psychological? Well, to the degree that we can speak of ethnic identity or racial consciousness, of course ethnicity and race are psychological.

But are these characteristics part of personality? According to the family resemblances idea, they sometimes are and sometimes are not. It depends in part on how characteristic they are. If someone is the only black in an otherwise white classroom, or the only Jew in an otherwise Roman Catholic town, or the only Vietnamese in an otherwise Hispanic neighborhood, then ethnicity or race are clearly instances of personality. In a segregated society, ethnicity and race are not part of personality. But in the complex world where most of us live, they are ambiguously characteristics of personality.

Finally, gender is another ambiguous personality characteristic. It is a property of the individual that is usually general, enduring, integrated, and functional. Although we regard maleness or femaleness as biological, they are probably more psychological than anything else. Gender is sometimes part of personality, and sometimes not. In an all-girl school, being female is irrelevant. And, the fact that the current President of the United States is a male is of no interest to anyone trying to contrast his personality with those of his predecessors.

When I use the term personality, I am applying it to both good and ambiguous examples. Both importantly define who a person is, and both possess at least some of the attributes that comprise the family resemblance of personality.

Why the Field of Personality Psychology Is Diverse and Diffuse   I haven't described what personality psychology is all about because that's the subject for the rest of my book. However, the idea of family resemblances will help me explain to you why the field is like a smorgasbord. In a typical day, two personality psychologists may have little to do with each other's work. They may be interested in different questions, employ different research methods, study different samples of people, and publish their findings in different journals. If they teach courses, they might use different textbooks, and they certainly choose different lecture topics. At the same time, however, these two personality psychologists can and do speak to each other. They have enough in common that they cannot afford to ignore each other's work. Even if personality psychology is a smorgasboard, it is still served on the same table.

The reason for the considerable but not total diversity of personality psychology is the diversity of instances of personality. Different fields have developed different approaches to study, respectively, those instances which are general, those which are characteristic, those which are enduring, and so on. I'll describe some of these approaches in Chapter 2, where you'll see how they bear a family resemblance to each other.

Why the Field of Personality Psychology Embraces a Variety of Theoretical Perspectives   We use theories to predict and explain occurrences in the real world. Since personality is applied to so many different instances in the real world, which bear only a family resemblance, personality psychology must employ a variety of theories. Although it's a tempting goal, no theorist has been able to develop an all-inclusive theory of personality. Granted the way that I have defined personality, no theorist is likely to do so in the future, since the topic is not unitary. As a student, you may be dismayed by the variety of theoretical perspectives, and you may assume that personality psychologists are incapable of agreeing on things. However, I think the real reason for the field's diversity is its subject matter.

Any given theory attempts to explain several things about personality, and indeed, most theories try to be generally applicable. Unfortunately, it turns out that any given theory does a particularly good job explaining some aspects of personality while doing a particularly poor job at others. Think of a theory as an explicitly stated language game, and you can see why it works well in some domains of the real world and not so well in others. Numerous games can be played with bats and balls, but if we were limited to this equipment, baseball would be one of the most sensible. If we had rackets and shuttlecocks at our disposal, baseball would be an unwieldy "theory" to apply, and we had best search for a different game. If we are fortunate, we'll come across badminton.

The same is true within the field of personality psychology. We should try to match up the theory with that part of the real world it best fits. I'll describe a number of personality theories in the remainder of this book, and in each case, part of my description will entail a sketch of where it fits and where it doesn't. So, Freud's theory of personality does a good job of explaining our dark and passionate side, but it doesn't have much to say about how we learn to do long division.

Why the Field of Personality Psychology Employs a Variety of Research Methods   Because the different instances of personality are diverse, they can't be studied in the same way. We have already seen that no single operational definition captures the whole of personality. Similarly, no single research approach is always appropriate for the study of personality. Sometimes personality psychologists work in experimental laboratories, studying people or even rats. Sometimes they spend half a lifetime talking to the same individual about her dreams, fears, and fantasies. Sometimes they pass out questionnaires to half of a campus, half of a town, or half of the world. The research method they choose depends on what they want to know about whatever aspect of personality interests them.

Why the Findings of Personality Psychology Have Been Applied to Such an Array of Topics   Many personality psychologists have applied what they know about personality to the real world. Psychotherapists, for instance, attempt to help people solve their problems so they can get along better with themselves and others. Other personality psychologists choose to work in schools, trying to predict which students will do well or poorly in which courses. Still other personality psychologists work for private businesses, attempting to make products like Captain Crunch, Cabbage Patch Dolls, or Chryslers look more attractive to the consumer. Others devote time to basketball players, helping them make free throws; to defense lawyers, helping them select lenient jurors; or to interior decorators, helping them choose appropriate colors and textures.

I will describe a number of the applications of personality psychology. They are diverse, but no more diverse than the meanings of personality. Although these applications bear a family resemblance to each other, they never perfectly overlap. Successful marketing does not involve the same ingredients as successful psychotherapy. Both involve the creative application of theories and findings from personality psychology, but the particular theory and the particular findings usually differ from application to application.

Why Prediction and, Ultimately, Explanation Are Bounded   One of the important topics in personality psychology is measurement—how to assess an individual's personality characteristics, how to assign an individual to a personality category, how to ascertain the manner in which an individual functions. Once measurement is complete, psychologists employ the scores to predict future behavior—instances of thinking, acting, and feeling. To the disappointment of many, predictions are far from perfect. Usually, measurement-based forecasts improve upon mere chance, but not to the degree that Big Brother is keenly interested in them.

One reason for these very real boundaries on prediction is compelled by the family resemblances idea. Prediction is based on a theory, *an abstract account of the interrelationships among prototypes,* but it is applied to the real world of concrete particulars. In the course of measurement, different instances are classed together, and it is inevitable that this classification is sometimes erroneous, since measurement treats particulars as identical when they are not. The upper limit to one's accuracy in predicting future behavior cannot be 100 percent. It will always be lower. Explanation is also bounded. We cannot give a full theoretical account of what occurs in the real world, because the real world will always bear an imperfect relationship to our theories.

Why This Textbook Meanders at Times   It is customary for authors to be modest about their books and to take responsibility for all manner of short-comings. Most of the time, I'm pretty good at being flawed, but I'll apologize for this book only up to a point. There are certain shortcomings in this book that have nothing to do with me. Rather, these flaws are inherent in the field of personality psychology, flaws that result from the attempt to grapple sci-entifically with topics phrased in ordinary language terms. These attempts have been successful enough that we understand personality better than before they were made, but they have not been so successful that the book is closed, complete, or even neat. Personality psychology is a fuzzy field, dynamic and evolving. To the degree that this textbook accurately covers personality psy-chology, it will reflect these characteristics.

SUMMARY

This chapter discusses what is meant by the term **personality.** I first consid-ered a number of the ways that personality is used in everyday conversation, then I presented some of the standard psychological definitions. These fall short in accounting for the everyday uses of personality. To explain why, I suggested that personality is a *fuzzy* term, resisting a precise definition in regard to **necessary** and **sufficient conditions.** Rather, like many **ordinary language terms,** personality is defined by a set of **pertinent attributes,** no one of which need be present in a particular instance of personality.

Taken together, these pertinent attributes define a **family resemblance** that embodies what we mean by personality. An analysis of the way we use the term in everyday conversation suggests that these attributes include psy-chological properties of the individual that are *general, characteristic, endur-ing, integrated,* and/or *functional.* Just remember that no given instance of personality need possess all these attributes.

A good example of personality defined in this way is a **personality trait.** The English language abounds in trait terms, and new ones appear all of the time. Indeed, a personality trait is probably a perfect example of what is meant by personality, since it embodies the entire set of attributes within the family resemblance. However, recent opinions call into question the actual existence of personality traits. There may be little about what a person thinks, does, and feels that is general, characteristic, and enduring. Perhaps personality traits should be regarded more as idealizations than realities.

The family resemblance idea is a powerful one. With it, one can explain a great deal about personality and the field of personality psychology: why it is difficult to define personality in precise terms; why some characteristics of a person are ambiguously classified as part of personality; why the field of personality psychology is diverse and diffuse; why the field embraces a variety of theoretical perspectives; why the field employs a variety of research methods; why its findings have been applied to an array of topics; and why prediction and, ultimately, explanation are bounded.

2

WHAT IS
PERSONALITY
PSYCHOLOGY?

ccording to the family resemblances idea, concepts are characterized by a set of pertinent attributes, with no single one being necessary or sufficient. Any given instance of a concept may or may not have one of the pertinent attributes. In Chapter 1, I suggested that this idea is a powerful one that helps us understand personality and personality psychology. One way it does so is by explaining why personality psychologists pursue different but related activities. In this chapter, I'll describe two of the most important activities of personality psychologists. They are also two of the most disparate. I think you'll be impressed by the diversity they represent.

MODELS OF HUMAN NATURE: POPULAR AND NUMEROUS

I first want to describe how personality psychologists propose models or metaphors for human nature. Those who work with models attempt to suggest some essence that lies at the core of being human. They phrase this essence in metaphorical language and use the metaphor to understand what people think, do, and feel.

The use of models has been common throughout the history of science. The early Greeks believed that the earth was held aloft by a giant who stood on the back of a turtle. I suspect that they did not literally believe that a large man was squeezing the planet. They did not fear, for instance, that he would lose his grip on Italy and crush Egypt as he juggled the earth or that federal regulations would require him to wear a hard hat and allow him to take frequent coffee breaks. Rather, the vision of Atlas and his heroic task was a metaphor for understanding the world and its secure place in the physical universe.

The French philosopher René Descartes reportedly used the mechanical fountains of fifteenth century Paris, in which streams of water activated moving parts, as the basis for his theory of the nervous system and how it worked. Descartes argued that fluid was transmitted from one part of the body to another through nerves, where it pushed the body into activity (Boring, 1950). This model is not far removed from current beliefs about how the nervous system works, except that the fluid is now called a neurotransmitter, and its mode of activation is chemical rather than mechanical.

A **model** is a simple version of some more complex phenomenon. It includes those characteristics of the actual phenomenon that are essential in

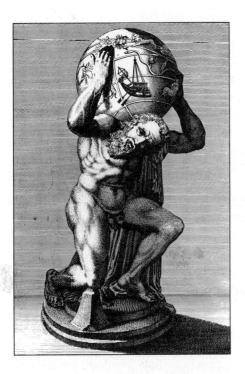

defining it, leaving out less important ones. If you built model cars when you were little, you knew even then that a model was not an exact copy. It was "realistic" not because it reproduced the literal Ford Edsel, but because it included some of the details that comprised your prototype of a car.

When personality psychologists propose some model of human nature, some metaphor with which to understand why people behave, we also should not take these models literally. What is important is whether a model aids our understanding of personality, not whether it exactly replicates people in the real world. From our ordinary language analysis of personality, we have good reason to believe that there is no single essence to being human. Any attempt to specify such an essence is never going to be 100 percent successful, regardless of the metaphor. Still, some metaphors for human nature resemble our various behaviors enough so that they often ring true. Let us consider some of them.

People as Animals

Darwinian ideas have influenced all branches of psychology, including personality psychology. Perhaps the most basic of these ideas is that human beings are members of the animal kingdom, in some ways best understood as animals. Throughout the twentieth century, this model of people as animals has been quite popular.

Sigmund Freud's personality theory, which we'll examine in detail later, proposes that one key to understanding human beings lies in recognizing their sexual and aggressive instincts—biologically based drives that demand satisfaction. Although society may coerce a person into expressing these instincts indirectly, they are always present, close to the surface and waiting to erupt, like David Banner turning into the Incredible Hulk.

This metaphor is presently undergoing a resurgence with the advent of **sociobiology**—*an extension of evolutionary theory to social behavior* (Wilson, 1975). Sociobiology successfully addresses the problem of the selfish gene. Since evolution works by survival of the fittest, those individuals that survive can pass on their genes. But social behavior often requires the sacrifice of individuals, at least in a reproductive sense. So how can social behavior evolve? And how can sacrifice be advantageous to the individual if it involves not passing on one's genes?

Sociobiology argues that there can be an evolutionary advantage in sacrificing your reproductive potential for that of another, if that other individual shares genes in common with you. In sacrificing yourself for a close relative, you are assuring that your genes are passed on to future generations, since close relatives share these genes.

The ideas of sociobiology apply most directly to the social insects, like ants and termites, most of whom are sterile. These creatures "altruistically" serve and protect the few members of their society who do reproduce, but their altruism is self-serving. The queen and her consorts share genetic material with them.

This argument has been applied to the social behavior of human beings as well. Altruism and cooperation among close relatives may be genetically predisposed, since they further the survival of one's genes. For instance, suppose you decide not to have a family, but you contribute large amounts of time and money to your brother's family. Your generosity has the effect of perpetuating some of your own genes—those you share with your brother (and thus with his children). As you might imagine, sociobiology applied to people is controversial. No one wants to conclude that genetic predispositions are all-important in determining social behavior. Despite the controversy, sociobiology lends a fresh legitimacy to the metaphor of people as animals, suggesting that the search for a genetic basis to certain personality traits may be productive.

People as Energy Systems

Another popular metaphor likens people to energy systems. Again, Sigmund Freud championed this idea, proposing that human functioning involves the transformation of psychological energy, what he called *libido*. Like real energy, libido obeys the laws of thermodynamics: it can neither be created nor destroyed, and once present, demands to be used.

Freud believed that if one's psychological energy is used for one purpose, then it cannot be used for another. There is only so much libido available, and emotional problems are literally exhausting. They are like bad investments, tying up your psychological assets and precluding their more productive use.

The therapy technique of *catharsis* brings about emotional well-being by encouraging a person to talk about his problems. An outpouring of emotion might occur as the problem is discussed, a "Thanks, I needed that" reaction followed by a sense of relief. The energy metaphor holds that catharsis works because it releases psychological energy, making it available for other purposes.

Konrad Lorenz (1966), a noted expert on animal behavior, proposes in his book *On Aggression* that human violence is caused by our instinctive energy demanding to be discharged. Other animals vent their aggressive drives harmlessly through ritualized displays. They butt their heads together, hiss, puff up their fur, or beat their chests with their fists. But people do not vent their energy in harmless rituals; and often murder and warfare are the results.

In some ways, people are best understood as animals.

People as White Rats

Psychologists and everyday people sometimes joke that psychology is the scientific investigation of what the white rat *(Rattus norwegicus)* and the college sophomore *(Homo sophomorus)* have in common. They refer mainly to white rats being used in laboratory experiments concerned with learning. However, they also refer to the tendency to view human beings as if they were white rats. Although this metaphor is not usually acknowledged, it has nonetheless played an important role in psychology as a model of human nature.

What are the essential characteristics of a white rat? If you are squeamish, when you think of white rats, visions occur and recur of beady red eyes and naked tails. If you are dispassionate, you see them as domesticated animals living under highly confined and controlled conditions. They follow a life of routine and are keenly responsive to rewards and punishments—Purina Rat Chow and electric shock. Think of them as the consummate hedonists, pursuing pleasure and avoiding pain.

So, in looking at the white rat, we can see that part of us produced by the rewards and punishments imposed from without, the part that utterly depends upon the world. The white rat metaphor explains why we "run the rat race" and why we "play the game." An important tension within personality psychology is whether our behavior is caused by forces within ourselves or by forces from outside. Those who adopt the rat metaphor favor the view that we behave as we do because of outside forces.

People as Machines

Most psychologists are materialists, believing that—ultimately—human action will be fully explained by referring to chemical and physical forces. This materialistic assumption can be reflected in a model of people as machines—systems of physical parts related by simple cause-and-effect processes.

What does it mean to assume that people are like machines? First of all, a psychologist becomes interested in the parts of this machine. A common way to introduce psychology, in a textbook or in a course, is by enumerating these parts, starting with the most basic and working up to the most complex. A section on the nervous system is followed by one on the five senses, a section on learning and memory, then sections on motivation, language, development, and so on. Finally, the book gets around to personality, the most complex cog in the machine, and to psychopathology, the ways in which the cog can break or malfunction.

Also, a psychologist who believes that people are like machines is committed to the view that our understanding of the complex aspects of the machine must be grounded in an understanding of the more basic aspects. This means that psychological aspects of the person, such as personality, are best understood after an introduction to the biological aspects. Such an assumption is termed **reductionism.**

Reductionism is not the only strategy available for understanding complex systems. Critics of psychology have taken to task this approach to understanding what people think, do, and feel, arguing that a science of people is not the same as a science of the parts of people. Our ordinary language analysis of personality suggests that this is often a valid criticism, since personality is not simply a part of a person, and it certainly is not just a biological part.

Another aspect of the mechanistic model is a concern with simple cause and effect relationships among the parts of this machine. Much of psychology is an attempt to specify which environmental events (causes) lead to which behaviors (effects). *Classical conditioning* is a good example of this concern with cause and effect. Remember the last time you drank too much alcohol and became ill? The next day, if you were awake, the mere smell of alcohol, even in your perfume or cologne, made you feel nauseated. Why? According to the principles of classical conditioning, the smell of alcohol was paired with your sickness the day before. Through an automatic process, the smell now elicits nausea. It has become a cause.

One popular way to interpret a personality trait is in mechanistic terms, as a device that channels the effects of environmental events into thoughts, actions, and feelings. Since we often believe that each person has several personality traits, the particular combination of these traits stamps the individual as unique, just as how you arrange your furniture makes your house characteristically your own (even if you shop at department stores and live in a tract house).

Psychopathology can be viewed as some sort of damage to an essential part of the human machine. Sometimes this conceptualization of human difficulties is literal, as when damage to brain tissue results in amnesia, paralysis, or confusion. Other times, it is metaphorical. In a nervous breakdown, nerves are not broken, at least not in the sense that your car throws a rod or your cassette deck makes pasta of your tapes. Psychotherapy is not a literal tuneup or a major overhaul.

People as Fields

You may be less familiar with what scientists mean by a **field,** so I'll start by contrasting a field with a machine. Machines are systems of parts in which changes in a given part only influence a small number of other parts, those that are physically connected. In contrast, a field is a system of parts in which changes in one part influence all other parts. Compare a lawn mower with a waterbed. The lawn mower is composed of a number of parts attached to each other by nuts and bolts. If you run over a large stone which bends the blades of the mower, you have broken blades and perhaps a twisted axle. The handle, the wheels, and the grass catcher are undisturbed by the accident.

What happens, though, if this same stone is propelled by the lawn mower blades through your bedroom window, where it hits your waterbed? It doesn't hit the bed hard enough to break it, thank goodness, but it arrives with some velocity. In contrast to the lawn mower, where few parts were affected by the stone, the entire waterbed responds. The bed pushes up everywhere that the stone doesn't hit. Once the stone rebounds, the bed again responds as a whole. It sloshes up and down, and if someone were on it, he too would slosh up and down.

The point is that the entire waterbed is responsive to changes in each of its parts. This is the defining characteristic of a field in contrast to a machine. If you have studied ecology, you understand this point in terms of *ecosystems.* The displacement of a single species from its niche in the ecosystem affects all other species. The hue and cry some years ago about whether a dam should be built that might endanger the snail-darter was not born of any great concern with these fish, but rather from a worry that the well-being of other species, including our own, was tied to the fate of this creature.

Some psychologists feel that people should be described in field terms instead of mechanistic terms. Remember, personality often refers to that which is integrated about an individual. Machines have no overall unity, no guiding principle. They are simply a set of parts. In contrast, fields are unified. They are defined by the interrelation of their parts, and there is a wholeness to them.

Another characteristic of fields that makes this model attractive to personality psychologists is that fields are self-regulating. Recall your waterbed. It was sloshing around when we left it, but it has now restored itself to its prior condition. It has returned to an equilibrium. Similarly, magnetic fields, gravitational fields, and ecosystems return to their original states: *homeostasis.* Unlike machines, fields can survive dramatic disturbances like a forest fire. Fields heal themselves. Machines do not.

Can people heal themselves of psychological distress? Yes, by all means, although psychologists have only recently come to appreciate how prevalent and successful self-help is. For instance, many people who stop smoking cigarettes do not do it through nicotine tablets, hypnotism, acupuncture, psychotherapy, or voodoo. Instead, they do it from within, by simply stopping (Schacter, 1982). Nothing from without occurred; it is in the nature of a field— and perhaps in the nature of a person—to reach an equilibrium.

The field metaphor has several limitations however. First and foremost, most people some of the time and some people most of the time do not respond as a whole. They have different sides to themselves which may act independently. Second, people do not always reachieve equilibrium after a disturbance. Individuals confined to concentration camps during World War II may still show symptoms of distress decades later (Dor-Shav, 1978). The field metaphor does not deal well with this fact. Third, and perhaps this is a clue about people's occasional failure to right themselves after a wrong, there are aspects of a person that are mechanistic. In emphasizing how a person is like a field, one must not forget that sometimes a person is not.

People as Information Processors

With the advent of the computer age, a new metaphor was developed to understand human nature: man as computer. This model attributes properties of both machines *and* fields to people. From the middle 1960s through the present, psychologists have explored the limits of this metaphor. Does the essence of a person lie in her ability to process information according to rules and strategies?

One reason for the popularity of this metaphor is that computers are sufficiently complex to do justice to the complexity we attribute to people. Most of the models I am discussing in this section are simplistic; this model is not. A second reason for its popularity is the ease with which it can be assimilated to ways of thinking already established within psychology. Thus, information or data readily correspond to stimuli in the environment. Output is analogous to behavior. Hardware has its counterpart in the neurons and organs that comprise our physical body, while software is akin to what we learn—attitudes, opinions, beliefs, values, and so on.

This metaphor is extremely rich, since the computer age involves a new vocabulary as much as a new technology. *Programming* is learning; *feedback loops* are trial-and-error; *user friendly* is social facility; *glitches* are minor character flaws; *consultants* are psychotherapists; *infinite do-loops* are self-defeating habits; and so on. Recall the idea of language game that I discussed in the first chapter. The computer model provides psychology with a host of new rules, new ways to express the meaning of concepts.

Stereotyping—the attribution of undesirable characteristics to some group of individuals—has often been discussed in connection with prejudice, with the assumption that stereotyping springs from undesirable emotions. But the vantage provided by the computer metaphor suggests that stereotyping may not be due to hatred. Instead, it may be a natural consequence of the way people process information from the social world.

In a provocative discussion, Hamilton and Gifford (1976) argued that people remember striking information better than mundane information. So, typical white adults in our society may remember that a black man acted rudely more readily than they remember a white man doing so. Even if black men are no more likely to act rudely than white men, the stereotype of black male rudeness may nonetheless arise because of these differences in recall.

This view suggests that stereotyping is not motivated. It leads to prejudice, but it does not result from it. What is particularly intriguing about this idea, should it prove generally valid, is that stereotyping may be combatted with information. People can *learn* not to be prejudiced. The stereotyper is thus not to be villified but rather corrected. The computer metaphor makes possible this benign view of what is otherwise an irrational action.

Although this metaphor has been helpful in demystifying a number of otherwise inexplicable actions, it can be carried too far. It may render us a species of Vulcans: cool, calm, and collected caricatures of ourselves. Mr. Spock of "Star Trek" is one of the most beloved contemporary characters, and we enjoy his detached and rational view of matters. However, we like his character precisely because he sometimes departs from his computer-like mode. He certainly teases Dr. McCoy more than an information-processing system would, and his loyalty and bravery transcend what is merely "reasonable." We like Spock because he is part Vulcan; we love him because he is part human.

I find it helpful to remember Mr. Spock in evaluating the computer metaphor. Metaphors are useful both when applied and when not applied; in other words, part of using a metaphor in a productive fashion is knowing its limitations. Robert Burns did not liken his love to a red, red rose to emphasize her need for sunshine or occasional pruning. So far, psychologists captivated with the computer metaphor have been guilty of over-applying its perspective.

Mr. Spock has become a modern-day archetype for many of us, representing the fusion of computer-like rationality and human emotion.

Later in the book, as you read about information-processing approaches to personality, keep in mind the need to be judicious when using this metaphor.

People as Scientists

A metaphor of human nature similar to the computer model is one that likens people to scientists. George Kelly (1955) forcefully stated this model in his *personal constructs* theory, which I'll discuss in some detail later. Kelly argues that everyday people are engaged in much the same business as the scientist—trying to understand the world. They represent this understanding in terms of theories about the world, and they undertake various tests of their theories.

Sometimes the tests confirm one of their theories, and the theory is regarded with confidence: "I knew he was a schmuck all along. I gave him a chance to do something nice, and he just acted in the same old selfish way!" Other times the tests prove a theory wrong: "Well, my first impression was a mistake. I didn't think she could handle the job I gave her, but she did it twice as well as anybody else ever has!"

Personality psychologists have been interested both in the contents of people's metaphorical scientific theories as well as in the manner in which they test them. Peterson and Seligman (1984), for instance, propose that individuals have a characteristic way of explaining why bad events happen to them. They call these characteristic theories *explanatory style* and are particularly concerned with a style that blames pervasive aspects of the self for bad events: "I failed the test because I'm just no good at anything." As you might imagine, such a theory has been linked to depression. In contrast, people who attribute the causes of bad events to outside factors ("I failed the test because the teacher doesn't know what he's doing") or to more circumscribed aspects of the self ("I failed because I didn't get a good night's sleep") are unlikely to be depressed (Peterson, Schwartz, & Seligman, 1981).

The person-as-scientist metaphor has been popular in contemporary psychology for the same reasons that the computer metaphor has been popular. Both characterize people as rational and orderly, making sense of environmental information. Both suggest new ways of looking at seemingly irrational actions and intervening to change them. Depressed people might be suffering not because they are crazy, but because they are entertaining incorrect theories about themselves. Indeed, depression may be a rational and logical response, granted certain beliefs and opinions. One supposes that the depressed person's theories are sometimes wrong, but they persist because people are always looking for evidence to support their theories.

What are the limits of this metaphor? One important limitation is shared by the computer model: people are not always as logical as this view implies.

Psychotherapy is not always a matter of correcting erroneous beliefs because people may hold to their personal theories more tenaciously than science holds to its favored hypotheses.

People as Actors

"All the world's a stage, and all the men and women merely players." If Shakespeare's well-known expression is true, then there are personality psychologists who are drama critics. Yet another popular metaphor of human nature is the actor model, which proposes that the essence of a person lies in the roles that he or she plays.

The term **role** is borrowed directly from the theater. When we apply it to a person's everyday life, we suggest that behavior is due to parts or positions assigned by society and not the person who is playing the role. Viewing people as actors does not mean regarding them as shams or fakes. Rather, it means that everything we do is the result of one or more roles. There is no person behind all of these roles; instead, the person is the sum of the roles played.

Where do the roles come from? In most cases, society assigns them. All cultures make distinctions among their members based on gender, age, status, and occupation. These distinctions involve *scripts* that a person is expected to more-or-less follow when assigned to a particular set of roles. For instance, forty-five-year-old male college professors at Harvard University act differently than thirteen-year-old female tennis players at Wimbledon. This difference no doubt results from their different gender roles, age roles, job roles, and so on.

The actor model is sometimes linked to the branch of sociology known as microsociology, a field associated with Erving Goffman (1959). His book *The Presentation of Self in Everyday Life* is a brilliant application of this model. Goffman borrows not just the notion of role to explain how people act in the world, but other theater terminology and concepts as well. In discussing individuals in work settings, for instance, Goffman distinguishes between the behavior seen "onstage" and that seen "backstage."

Think about a fancy restaurant. When a waiter is taking orders, opening bottles of wine, refilling water glasses, and so on, his actions are likened to a performance for the benefit of the audience, his customers. The waiter is poised, sophisticated, and polite. And then he goes into the kitchen, out of sight from his audience. A cigarette dangles from his lips, and its ashes fall into the soufflé. The soufflé itself falls onto the floor, only to be scraped up and plopped onto a plate. The waiter may then engage in crude banter with the cook. He berates the customers for their atrocious taste. "Catsup with prime rib? Gag me with an American Express Card!" Without doubt, he is no longer playing the role he was playing in front of the customers.

Society assigns us roles based on our gender, age, and status.

The actor metaphor allows people to be interchangeable, and there is a certain truth to this. I once worked as a psychologist in a mental health clinic. Patients had a lot of trouble remembering which twenty-eight-year-old therapist saw them the week before. "He had a moustache, I think." Well, we all did, just as we had innumerable other characteristics in common. But eventually, distinctions were made. Is this at odds with the model? Not really, because the model allows for variations in the way that a role is played. Indeed, variation is expected, since people play their roles differently.

Theodore Sarbin and Vernon Allen (1968) describe several ways that role enactment varies. For instance, there is **role appropriateness.** Is the right role being played for a particular setting? The "ugly American" stereotype refers to an American tourist in a foreign country acting as if he were at Yankee Stadium. His role is inappropriate for the setting.

For another instance, actors differ in terms of **role propriety.** How well do they play a given role? Are their performances up to standards? Some actors are better than others, both in movies and real life. The skill with which someone enacts a given role is a distinguishing characteristic. Every once in a while you may read that someone was arrested for impersonating a medical doctor, and that he had "passed" successfully for years. All of his patients were shocked. "He was a perfect doctor." I assume that such a ruse can work because the phony doctor played his role with consummate skill, that his bedside manner compensated for his lack of knowledge.

Sarbin and Allen (1968) describe still other dimensions along which the enactment of roles may differ. For instance, how many roles are played at the same time? Do multiple roles result in role conflict—contradictory demands— as often experienced by someone who tries to combine career and family? Of a person's various roles, which are pre-emptive; which take precedence? To what degree does the role involve the person? There is a difference, for instance, between being the secretary of a high school class that has a reunion every ten years, and being the target of a voodoo hex (Sarbin & Allen, 1968). Both are roles, but the former is much less involving than the latter. How specific is an actor's script? How formal is it? How big is the part? And so on.

When we contrast the actor metaphor with other models of human nature, we see that it lends itself poorly to the purposes of psychology. It is primarily a sociological account. Society provides the roles, not the individual. People differ in the manner they play a role, but the actor metaphor leaves little room for improvisation. Perhaps this metaphor would be more useful if it were combined with another model. It can be used to explain the public part of personality, while an additional metaphor can explain what is private or personal about personality.

People as Pilots

The pilot model is one such metaphor that can be combined with the actor model. It is an explicit attempt to understand what lies behind the roles that we play. By this view, a person is the ghost in the machine of the body—the pilot of the airplane. Have you ever asked someone who he or she *really* is? You were asking for the identity of the pilot, for an acknowledgment and description of what personality psychologists call the **self.**

The self has had a long and difficult history in psychology. William James (1890), the first American psychologist, regarded the concept of the self as essential for psychological explanation. Theorists thereafter have similarly invoked the pilot metaphor to explain various facts about people (Wylie, 1968). Clearly, one cannot perfectly predict what a person will do by just observing external conditions and overt characteristics of the person. Perhaps the self will improve prediction.

Relatedly, people often pursue goals. I presume you are attending college in order to graduate, in order to obtain a certain sort of job, in order to live a certain style of life, in order to be happy, maybe even to gain wisdom. What allows you to pursue these goals? Machines have no destinations; neither do fields, animals, or computers. Something has to be added to these models to account for the purposive nature of behavior. That something is often identified as the self.

As shown by our ordinary language analysis of personality, people's thoughts, actions, and feelings are often seen as integrated. Individuals may protect themselves from hurt feelings by avoiding information that questions their competence. What provides the integration or plays the role of protector? Who's in charge here anyway? Again, personality psychologists frequently suggest the self.

Since the notion of a self seems helpful in explaining several facts about people, and since we are all aware that we have a self, two questions arise. First, why have I called the self a metaphor? Second, why have I described the history of this metaphor as difficult?

The answers to these questions are the same: it is all but impossible to define or characterize the self in such a way that psychologists can use it in their theories and research. Despite our awareness of a self within us, it is not a real thing. It has no location, no height, no weight. If we are aware of a self, then what in us is having this awareness? Can the self be aware of the self, as if it is looking in a mirror?

Similarly, if we do things that protect our self from slights, then what is doing the protecting? Can the self protect itself without being aware that it is doing so? Finally, if the self is the pilot of our aircraft, who pilots the self? Does the concept of the self merely push the problem of explanation back one step, acknowledging the need for explanation without accomplishing it?

Some of the problems with the notion of the self are avoided if the self is regarded not as a literal thing but as a metaphor, a hypothetical entity that proves useful in explaining the integrated and purposive aspects of a person. Like any metaphor, the pilot model only applies up to a point. As you will see throughout this book, most personality psychologists include the self in their theories, but problems with definition and assessment inherently plague their attempts.

People as People

By now you may be sick of my discussion about models and metaphors. But it is necessary since they all figure in personality psychology. A major activity of personality psychologists is to propose and scrutinize models of human nature. Nevertheless, you may be skeptical about this approach to understanding personality.

If so, you are not alone. After all, from the start, we knew the best we could say about a model is that it sometimes applies and sometimes doesn't. All metaphors run the risk of the map-territory problem: confusing the map of a territory with the territory itself; expecting the two to be identical.

Each model proves useful for a particular purpose. Yet no model or set of models will be useful in understanding everything about human nature because people are not animals, machines, computers, or scientists. People are people.

In an enlightening book, Rom Harré and Paul Secord (1973) suggest that psychologists adopt a new model of human nature: the **anthropomorphic model.** If we look at what the word roots mean, we recognize their proposal as tongue-in-cheek, a model of people that accords them the general form (-morphic) of people (anthropo-). In other words, Harré and Secord propose that psychologists base their theories of people on what is known to be the case about people, not on what is known to be the case about white rats, actors, or pilots.

These authors undertake an ordinary language analysis of the concept of person and suggest that psychological theories attend to the pertinent attributes revealed by the analysis. First, *the term person is applied to entities that have the power to initiate change.* People don't have to wait to be prodded into action by external events or internal occurrences. People not only respond to the world, but also make the world respond to them.

Second, *the term person is applied to entities that have the power of speech.* People communicate. None of the metaphors accord much importance to language. Harré and Secord find this a glaring deficiency of the typical models entertained by psychologists.

Third, *the term person is applied to entities that have the capacity of awareness, including self-awareness.* People attend to the world in which they live, and they are aware of their attention. Again, most metaphors proposed by personality psychologists fail to grapple with this inherent characteristic of a person.

Taken together, these three attributes capture Harré and Secord's "model" of people as *conscious* agents capable of reporting on the reasons for their behavior, both before and after the fact. This characterization of human nature is radically different from other models. Harré and Secord do not regard the other models as useless, but caution psychologists not to rely on them exclusively.

In sum, one of the important activities of personality psychologists is to explore models of human nature. They present us not with a single view, but rather with multiple possibilities. While no single model is likely to capture all that is meant by personality, if put together, they paint the family portrait of our species.

Is an integrated view possible—the personality psychology equivalent of a medley of greatest hits? Yes, but the suggestion for a model that partakes of all models should not be made glibly. After all, there is a reason that a given model has cohered in the way it has, and some models are largely incompatible with others. We don't play cops-and-robbers with bows and arrows, we don't serve Chinese vegetables over Spanish rice—and we don't combine a model of people as wild animals with a model of them as information processors. The Incredible Hulk and Mr. Spock are different men, and a composite—the Incredible Spock—is not a credible creation.

However, an integrated model could be developed in one of two ways. First, it could specify which people are best described by which model. Some individuals are indeed like scientists, while other individuals are indeed like actors, or white rats, or machines. One way to integrate the various models proposed by personality theorists is to regard them as a system of pigeon-holes; a given individual can be classified in one of the categories.

Second, an integrated model could specify which aspects of people are best described by which model. Each model applies to all people, but only to some aspect of them. The person-as-scientist metaphor could be invoked to explain how people cope with problems. The person-as-wild-animal metaphor, in contrast, could explain how people express their biological needs. And so on.

Unfortunately, no personality psychologist has proposed a fully accepted integration of the models. If this model is ever to exist, I suspect it will be composed of new ingredients, models not yet proposed. As we enter the age of information, we might look toward *interactive computing, self-correcting programs,* and *networks* to find new models that depict the essence of a human being.

To conclude, when personality psychologists propose models of human nature, they focus on what is general and enduring about people. Specific models may additionally be sensitive to what is characteristic, integrated, and/or functional about an individual. As such, models help personality psychologists explain and predict what people think, do, and feel. We judge models not as accurate or inaccurate, but rather as useful or not. Of course, what is useful depends on one's purpose.

INDIVIDUAL DIFFERENCES AND PERSONALITY ASSESSMENT

Another important activity of personality psychology addresses the characteristic aspect of personality: *how are people consistently like themselves and different from others?* Personality psychologists pursuing this end have two related concerns. First, they are interested in describing and explaining individual differences, the myriad of ways that people are different. Second, they are interested in measuring these differences.

This first concern is reflected in the traits, temperaments, types, factors, styles, habits, aptitudes, skills, motives, values, and interests that depict what is distinctive about an individual. The second concern is reflected in an equally imposing variety of tests, measures, questionnaires, batteries, and inventories that assess these distinctive aspects, often for the purpose of making educational, occupational, or clinical decisions.

It is impossible to detail this particular topic in a single chapter, or even in a single book. Instead, I'll sketch the big picture of individual differences and their assessment, filling in some representative details. More details will appear later on as I discuss specific theories and applications.

In the next chapter, where I describe the history of personality psychology, you'll see we can trace interest in individual differences to Charles Darwin. His idea that some individuals are more fit for certain environments than others has led to several important assumptions about individual differences.

Individuals Differ from Each Other   Some of us survive, while others pass into oblivion. Some of us receive A grades, while others receive D− grades. Some of us move into corner offices, while others make do with broom closets. Even the most cynical person would not suggest that such facts are always due to chance. And even the most egalitarian person would not suggest that these facts are always due to circumstance. Accordingly, the differences we observe in people's *fitness* suggest that we look to their biological and psychological makeup, including personality, to find out why.

These Differences Are General and Stable Characteristics of the Individual   Our ordinary language analysis of personality showed the importance of general and enduring attributes. For the most part, individual differences not only refer to characteristic aspects of personality, but also to long-lasting aspects manifest in much of what a person does. Otherwise, personality differences would not help explain the variation in human fitness. So, individual differences refer to intelligence, traits like introversion, and styles like sloppiness, not to circumscribed characteristics like attitudes toward pinochle, the order that toenails are clipped, or one's least favorite FM radio station. Nor do individual differences refer to transient characteristics like bad moods, swollen glands, or sunburns.

Taken together, the assumptions of generality and stability of individual differences state that behavior is consistent, across time and situations. The belief that personality is consistent has been at the center of the most important controversy in contemporary personality psychology.

This controversy has caused personality psychologists interested in individual differences and their assessment to take a closer look at their theories and measures. Rather than just assuming that a given measure of individual differences is a summary of what a person is about and will be about, researchers now test this possibility. And, in recent years, great strides have

"Yes, they're all fools, gentlemen... But the question remains, 'What KIND of fools are they?' "

SOURCE: "The Far Side" cartoon by Gary Larson is reproduced by permission of Chronicle Features, San Francisco.

been made in understanding the generality and stability of individual differences. I'll detail these advances later in the book; they have resulted from the consistency controversy and its attention to individual differences.

These Differences Are Quantitative Characteristics   Fitness is not an all-or-none occurrence; it exists in degrees. Many criteria of fitness—longevity, income, happiness, satisfaction, vacation days, grade point average, and health—rank individuals according to "how much" of the criterion they respectively possess. Similarly, individual differences in personality are also regarded as quantitative, and such differences are sometimes called *personality dimensions,* a label that captures this quantitative assumption (London & Exner, 1978).

For example, the personality characteristic of *field independence* and *dependence* refers to "the degree to which people function autonomously of the world around them" (Goodenough, 1978, p. 165). Field independent individuals have internal frames of reference and do not rely on immediate environmental cues. In contrast, field dependent individuals rely on external frames of reference. One would expect a gymnast on a balance beam to do a better back flip if she is field independent rather than field dependent. Her internal sense of up and down tells her where she is in relation to the beam.

Most people are not extreme examples of field independence or field dependence. They fall at varying points along the continuum defined by these two extremes, just as National Basketball Association players may be arranged along a dimension of height ranging from Spud Webb on one end to Manute Bol on the other.

These Differences Determine Function   Individual differences are related to the way in which a person gets along in the world. They are thought to cause a good or poor adjustment to a particular social environment, just as a particular biological characteristic like razor-sharp fangs determines survival or extinction in the jungle. Sensitivity to others leads to social success. Intelligence and the Protestant Ethic are important causes of academic and occupational success (or at least we are told that they are). And so on.

Most personality psychologists interested in individual differences study how these differences may predispose function or dysfunction. Not surprisingly, many personality psychologists work in applied settings such as schools, industries, or clinics, and attempt to encourage what is adaptive about personality in that setting.

These Differences Can Be Measured in a Straightforward Fashion
Personality assessment is intimately tied to individual differences. As already stated, an incredible array of personality assessment techniques is available, and each one purports to measure a single aspect of personality. Usually, scores are assigned to an individual, placing him or her along the quantitative dimensions of concern. Extensive norms may be available that depict the distribution of possible scores within a given group; thus, one can interpret the particular score of an individual. Finally, each technique attempts to predict success or failure with respect to some particular domain that's deemed important.

Individual Differences: How and Why People Differ

The psychology of individual differences is an academic discipline in itself. A sense of the richness of this discipline can be gained by merely surveying those psychological characteristics that are regarded as individual differences. For instance, Lee Willerman's 1979 book *The Psychology of Individual and Group Differences* includes such broad categories as intelligence, achievement, personality traits, psychopathology, handicaps, genius and talent, sex and gender, age, and race and ethnicity. From the perspective of family resemblances, all these categories are more or less personality characteristics.

Some years earlier, Gordon Allport (1961) surveyed the personality literature and catalogued the different classes of individual differences of concern to personality psychology. First, there are personality **types**—*a finite number of pigeon-holes into which people can be classified, in a mutually exclusive and exhaustive fashion.* Astrology comprises a typology, specifying twelve basic types of people, determined by the particular sign under which they were born. Astrology predicts that Aquarians (like John Travolta and me) share characteristics. To my constant puzzlement, I still can't dance. Why is this more Travolta's Age of Aquarius than it is mine?

Allport also described personality **traits**—*quantitative characteristics used to describe all people.* He introduced his own refinement here by subdividing traits into two categories: common traits and personal traits. **Common traits** refer to the typical use of trait—habitual thoughts, behaviors, or feelings that all individuals possess to different degrees. Allport thought there were few common traits, if by trait is meant a consistent behavioral tendency. He suggested instead that people are consistent with respect to only some traits, and that these differ from person to person. These are the **personal traits,** and an individual's personality is depicted not only by "how much" of a trait she possesses but more basically by whether that trait meaningfully describes what she does.

Finally, Allport described **factors.** Just as traits summarize thoughts, feelings, and behaviors that tend to co-occur, factors summarize traits that go together. Personality psychologists sometimes study just one or two traits in isolation from others. But sometimes they are interested in a large number of traits, perhaps in an attempt to capture the full range of an individual's personality. If so, they must simplify what they are doing. Suppose one hundred college students have completed one hundred personality questionnaires measuring one hundred different traits that range from "abstemiousness" to "zebriness." How can we make sense of this vast amount of information?

To summarize and simplify such data, Raymond Cattell (1950) and Hans Eysenck (1952b) use a statistical technique called **factor analysis.** Think of it as a way for determining which traits do or do not co-occur in individuals. Suppose most of the college students who score high (or low) on the questionnaire assessing abstemiousness also score high (or low) on the questionnaire assessing zebriness, as well as on questionnaires measuring three other traits. These five traits together reflect some underlying factor of personality, with interpretation depending on the meanings of the traits involved.

What Is the Origin of a Particular Individual Difference?   The *nature versus nurture* controversy—whether a characteristic results from genetic inheritance (nature) or environmental influence (nurture)—occurs repeatedly in the field of individual differences. This is not an idle academic controversy, since important social policy decisions hang in the balance.

Suppose intelligence, like hair color or eye color, is passed on through the genes. Then society would not be so concerned with assuring equal opportunity in education. Intelligent adults, identified by their prominent positions in society, would have intelligent children, who are then accorded the best education. If intelligence is a biological matter, then the status quo need not change. If anything, steps should be taken so that only the privileged are accorded future privilege.

On the other hand, suppose intelligence is mainly the result of your early experiences with learning. Then intelligence is created by providing a stimulating home environment where books are available, the television set is turned to "Sesame Street" instead of "All-Star Wrestling," and family members value education. If so, then equal opportunity in education should be a pressing societal concern, both morally and practically.

The nature versus nurture controversy rarely has a simple answer. It certainly does not have a simple one-or-the-other answer with regard to intelligence. I'm sure you're aware of the arguments surrounding this particular version of the issue. Nature versus nurture was partly at the root of the Supreme Court decision regarding segregation, and it has surfaced again in the current furor over busing, open admissions, affirmative action, and so on.

How Is a Given Characteristic Related to Good or Poor Functioning in the World?   Although researchers can readily establish a link between high intelligence and good grades in school, they are usually not satisfied with just describing this relationship. They also want to know how it is brought about. Intelligence does not leap off an IQ test onto a report card. What transpires in between? In an attempt to understand this link, some psychologists have broken intelligence into components and studied how comprehension, retention, and recall of abstract information lead to better academic performance.

Similarly, consider *psychopathy,* a personality characteristic associated with grossly inappropriate actions toward others. The classic psychopath lies, cheats, and steals. Since punishment appears ineffective in dissuading the psychopath, Prichard (1837) dubbed this characteristic "moral insanity" to convey the psychopath's seeming lack of a conscience and insensitivity to rebuke. Why such unsavory actions?

Schacter and Latané (1964) suggest that psychopathy is associated with a failure to be physiologically aroused by the threat of punishment. Try to appreciate that our conscience—our moral self—probably arises from early experiences of our parents punishing us for minor transgressions, like pulling the cat's tail. Freud and others have theorized that most children learn to anticipate punishment for certain deeds and thus refrain because they experience anxiety at the mere thought—except the future psychopath, who seems incapable of such learning. As a result, he fails to develop a conscience, and the rapacious behavior that comprises his problem (and ours) results.

How Can Dysfunctional Behavior Be Prevented or Changed?   We are familiar with individual psychotherapy, where a person with profound depression meets with a counselor to solve the problem. There are a variety of therapy techniques, most of which are based on some underlying model of man and how behavior can go awry. Biological interventions like Valium assume that the client's problems are the result of damaged or injured biology. Informational interventions like advice regarding sexual techniques assume that the client's problems are the result of insufficient or incorrect information.

Broadly defined, *psychotherapy includes education, legislation, and other forms of social influence taken for the betterment of the individual or group.* Head Start, Dale Carnegie courses, ballet lessons, Little League, public television, conventions, and Continuing Education are some examples of attempts to help people function better in the world.

Personality Assessment: The Measurement of Individual Differences

Personality psychologists are concerned with individual differences not just in the abstract, but also in the concrete. What is the best way to measure how people differ? *Personality assessment* assigns scores to people to reflect where they fall along a personality dimension. Those who are similar with respect to a personality characteristic are classified together and distinguished from those who are different. Personality assessment is usually undertaken for some purpose, like predicting future performance or diagnosing current strengths and weaknesses. For instance, one may want to predict whether or not a high school student will perform well at an exclusive university. Or one might try to ascertain whether or not a middle-aged man has suffered memory loss following a stroke.

A concept crucial to personality assessment is the **reliability** of an assessment procedure—its *ability to assign an individual the same score on different occasions.* You hope, for instance, that your speedometer is reliable: if you discover on Tuesday that driving to school at 37 miles per hour is sufficient for you to find a parking place thirty minutes after your alarm clock goes off, you want the same thing to be true on Thursday.

A second crucial concept is the **validity** of an assessment procedure— its *ability to measure what it purports to measure.* Again, you hope that your speedometer is valid: if you drive at 55 miles per hour through a speed trap on an interstate highway, you want the 55 on your speedometer to be the same 55 that appears on the digital readout of the state trooper's radar machine. (You also want both to correspond to the speed of a car that can traverse a measured mile in one minute and six seconds.)

No personality test is perfectly reliable or valid. One reason is the family resemblances idea that I introduced in Chapter 1. When personality psychologists think of individual differences, they do so in terms of prototypes, pure cases that do not exist in the real world. A test could only be 100 percent reliable and valid if people's actual behavior corresponded to prototypes, and of course it does not. People are sometimes inconsistent. Their test scores may be determined by factors other than the individual difference of concern. People classified as similar by a personality measure may in fact be quite different.

If real-world considerations can be kept to a minimum, personality assessment can be a relatively reliable and valid endeavor. On the other hand, a particular test may prove unreliable or invalid, and its usefulness thereby be compromised. As you can imagine, personality psychologists devote much energy to improving the reliability and validity of their measures.

Although everyone recognizes that perfect reliability and perfect validity are ideal standards impossible to achieve, there is considerable and legitimate controversy about how good is good enough. How reliable should a test be before it can be used? How valid should it be? The line is fuzzy, and it shifts depending upon the particular purpose of the test.

To answer such questions, personality psychologists rely on information depicted by **correlation coefficients.** You may already have encountered these in a statistics course. Their importance to personality assessment cannot be exaggerated.

To those of you unfamiliar with correlation coefficients, let me give you a brief introduction, starting with the notion of correlation. *Correlation refers to the association between two characteristics.* So, if we measured the height and weight of everyone in your class, we might be interested in how these two variables go together. We could graph them as shown at the left of Figure 2-1. On the whole, height and weight are associated because increases in one usually involve increases in the other. This is what is meant by a **positive** correlation.

Let's introduce two other characteristics of you and your fellow students. We can assess how much money each of you has in your pockets and the length of hair on your head. Again, we can graph the relationship between these two variables (see the middle of Figure 2-1). This time, we find that

Figure 2-1
Examples of Correlation Coefficients

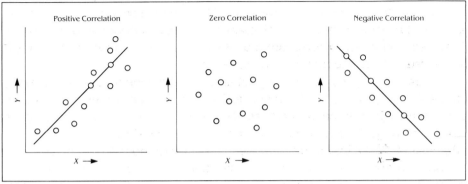

spare change and hair length do not go with each other at all. The two variables are **independent** of each other, showing a **zero** correlation.

Finally, let's assess everyone's social security number and ask everyone how many times they've been in New York City. (A background fact: social security numbers are assigned geographically and get bigger from East to West.) If we graph the relationship, we see that there is an association (right of Figure 2-1). The higher the social security number, the less frequently one has been in New York City, and vice versa. This is called a **negative** correlation.

Now you have a feel for correlation. A correlation coefficient is a mathematical expression of the degree to which two variables are associated. High correlations reflect strong associations. In other words, if the points on a graph fall tightly along a straight line, a high correlation coefficient results. If they do not fall along a line too well, we have a low correlation.

Correlation coefficients range from − 1.00 (a perfect negative association between two variables) through 0.00 (no association at all) to + 1.00 (a perfect positive association). When correlation coefficients take on these particular values, there is no difficulty interpreting the association between the variables involved—they either go together perfectly or not at all. In practice, however, correlation coefficients take on intermediate values, and considerable debate ensues about what to make of these intermediate correlations.

How strongly should two characteristics be associated before we attach importance to their correlation? This question lies at the heart of the debate over the consistency or inconsistency of personality. More generally, researchers must address this question every time they try to ascertain the reliability or validity of a personality measure.

After calculating a particular correlation coefficient, researchers usually compute further statistics to determine whether the two variables are correlated to a degree that would be unlikely by chance. If this appears to be the case, the correlation coefficient is said to be statistically significant. Appreciate that **statistical significance** need not mean theoretical significance. With a large enough sample of individuals, quite modest correlations among their characteristics will yield statistically significant correlations.

Some researchers rely mainly on statistical significance to evaluate associations among variables, while other researchers rely mainly on the actual value of the correlation coefficient. In the latter case, one often finds that correlations involving personality measures rarely exceed .30. With a sufficient sample size, such correlations are statistically significant, although they strike some people as quite small in absolute magnitude.

What is the answer to this debate? I think that researchers must look to both the statistical significance of a correlation coefficient as well as to its magnitude. Both are important, telling the researcher different things. Further, I think that neither should be taken out of context, as researchers sometimes do. Statistical significance must be interpreted in light of the sample size. If one has studied thousands of individuals, a statistically significant correlation is rather trivial. And the "absolute" magnitude of a correlation coefficient must be interpreted in light of other correlation coefficients. There is a temptation to judge a particular correlation against the anchors of -1.00, 0.00, or $+1.00$, but this is misleading.

A correlation of .30 is "low" only if most other correlations in a particular domain are considerably higher. The fact that .30 seems closer to 0.00 than to $+1.00$ is irrelevant in making this judgment call. The magnitude of correlations in different domains varies markedly. If you correlate temperature with the amount that a bridge expands, the correlation coefficient crowds $+1.00$. If you correlate habits like smoking with length of life, the correlation coefficient is greater than 0.00, but barely so. Yet we treat both these correlations as important by placing them in their respective contexts. The same must be done for correlation coefficients that describe relations among personality variables.

Now let's return to personality assessment. Psychological tests for various purposes are coming under increasing criticism, including lawsuits from Ralph Nader's group. In my opinion, the actual tests are neither good nor bad. It is how one uses the tests that should be scrutinized. Given a test's reliability and validity, what sorts of errors are expected? What does inaccuracy cost? What is the benefit of accuracy?

The most intuitive way to gauge the reliability of a psychological test is to give it to the same group of individuals on two occasions. Do they receive the same scores each time? If so, then the measure has **test-retest reliability.** But it may be impractical to test people twice. Or the fact that people have already taken the test once may render the second testing suspect. Consider the last midterm examination you took. If your instructor wanted to show that her midterm examination was reliable, she probably would not let you take it twice. Presumably, everybody would score higher the second time.

A more common way to investigate the reliability of a test is to employ one that has several different items, each attempting to measure the same thing, like your knowledge of European history. If you answer one item correctly or incorrectly, is the same true for the other items? If so, then the test has **internal reliability,** or **consistency.**

Most personality tests use multiple items, so that their internal reliability can be calculated. The more items employed to measure the dimension of concern, the more likely the extraneous determinants of scores will cancel out. For instance, depression is often measured using the Beck Depression Inventory or BDI (Beck, 1967). This questionnaire asks individuals to report on the severity of twenty-one different thoughts, behaviors, or feelings associated with depression. The individual chooses statements that describe recent behavior and receives the score associated with it. Here is a sample:

0   I can sleep as well as usual.
1   I don't sleep as well as I used to.
2   I wake up 1–2 hours earlier than I used to and cannot get back to sleep.
3   I wake up several hours earlier than I used to and cannot get back to sleep.

Sleep disturbance is a common depressive symptom, and your score on the BDI is increased to the degree that you have trouble sleeping.

However, sleep disturbance can also result from factors other than depression. Suppose you sprained your wrist. It throbs when you don't keep it elevated, and you have trouble sleeping more than a few hours at a time. Your BDI score would increase, even though you are not at all depressed. For this reason, the BDI asks about twenty other symptoms of depression: feelings of guilt, thoughts of suicide, loss of interest in other people, and so on. Although each of these measures may also be incorrectly affected by extraneous factors, it is unlikely that all twenty-one items will be distorted in the same way by the same factors.

The validity of a personality test is more difficult to ascertain than its reliability, because of the problems in making what a test is really measuring concrete. As I have emphasized, there is a difference between the abstract notions used in personality theories and what people do in the real world. The goal of personality assessment is to describe people's actual behavior in terms of abstract personality dimensions, and this endeavor isn't always a simple one.

It is simple to judge a personality test's validity if there is an unambiguous measure of the real characteristic of interest. The degree to which the personality test yields scores that correlate with this measure is its validity. However, most personality characteristics do not have a single and true manifestation against which a test can be calibrated. Remember, personality and personality characteristics tend not to have necessary and sufficient conditions. Fuzzy concepts are difficult to measure, and the measures—once created—are problematic to evaluate.

Theorists have devised many ways of ascertaining the validity of personality assessment techniques. **Face validity** refers to whether the test looks like it measures what it is supposed to measure. This is a primitive criterion of validity, relying on the researcher's intuition and nothing else. But face validity has some value. For instance, exit interviews conducted outside polling places in which voters are asked which candidate they voted for seem to be a reasonable way to predict who will win an election. But exit interviews conducted outside high school graduations in which college-bound students are asked how well they will do in college seem to be an unreasonable way to predict who will do well.

Content validity tells us whether the assessment technique contains a representative sample of the behavior of interest. A test to assess one's ability to work long-division problems possesses content validity if it includes such problems. However, a test need not possess content validity to be useful. A test that includes only multiplication problems may well distinguish how well people can work long division.

Criterion validity tells us how well a test predicts the particular behavior being studied. Intelligence tests have criterion validity, at least to the degree that they predict academic performance. Within work settings, personality assessment devices can be validated against work performance. Most applications for secretarial positions include the results of a typing test that assesses how many words per minute an individual can type, as well as how many errors he or she makes. Such tests predict how many acceptable letters a secretary can type in a typical day; they have criterion validity.

Clinical psychologists frequently use tests for diagnosing a psychiatric patient, predicting prognosis, and recommending treatment. At their best, such tests have been validated against previous clinical observations. Patients in the past who have scored in such-and-such a way have met this psychiatric diagnosis, showed this course of improvement, and responded best to this type of therapy.

One such test is the Minnesota Multiphasic Personality Inventory (MMPI), which consists of 550 statements written in the first person like "I am worried about sex matters" and "I used to like playing drop the hanky." (These may be related behaviors, especially if you don't know what "drop the hanky" means.) Someone's yes or no answers yield scores that place him along a number of personality dimensions. As the result of extensive research with the MMPI, particular profiles of scores are associated with specific diagnoses, prognoses, and effective treatments.

Suppose we have two groups that we know to be different with respect to some characteristic. If a test measuring this characteristic distinguishes between the two groups, then the test has **known-group validity.** Julian Rotter's (1966) locus of control questionnaire, for instance, tries to measure the degree to which individuals feel that important outcomes in life are due to their own actions (internal locus of control) or to factors outside their personal control (external locus of control). It has been validated in part with the known-group approach; groups of convicts, paraplegics, ethnic minorities, and students indeed score more in the direction of external locus of control than do other people.

Construct validity tells us whether scores from a test measuring a particular personality dimension are related to scores from other tests attempting to measure related dimensions. Suppose you create a measure of creativity based on the assumption that creativity involves the ability to form diverse associations between words. Your test consists of pairs of words like lightbulb and razor, and asks the respondent to list as many similarities between the two words as possible. The number of similarities listed is the creativity score.

If your test possesses construct validity, then test scores ought to be related to the scores on the vocabulary subtest of the SAT. The greater someone's vocabulary, the greater their creativity should be, at least as you have defined it and attempted to measure it.

Psychologists Donald Campbell and Donald Fiske (1959) emphasized that construct validity is established in two related ways. **Convergent validity** is demonstrated when a test yields scores that correlate with those from theoretically relevant tests. **Discriminant validity** occurs when a test's scores do not correlate with those from theoretically irrelevant tests. To return to the creativity example, you would expect your creativity scores to be largely independent of people's shoe size, since there is no obvious theoretical rationale that links them.

Let me summarize these ideas about reliability and validity by describing the steps involved in creating a useful measure of individual differences. I'll describe an actual questionnaire that my students developed in a personality class that I taught some years ago. First, one must have a clear picture of the individual difference to be assessed. You cannot measure something without knowing what it is. My class decided to measure the degree to which someone was a jester: someone who always makes a joke out of serious matters, who pokes fun at the status quo, who makes others laugh in spite of the situation.

To understand the notion of a jester, we talked about people we knew who were like this, as well as people who were not. What did these folks do?

In what situations did they perform? Who or what were their typical targets? When we had a good feeling for this personality dimension, we were ready for the second step: creating face-valid measures of the dimension. We decided to use a questionnaire where people would report whether or not they typically acted in ways that reflected our notion of a jester. For each statement, a "yes" answer was scored 2, while a "no" answer was scored 1. Someone's total jester score was the sum of these scores, and the higher the score, the more jester-like the person was.

We used statements like the following on the questionnaire:

I wear blue jeans to church.

I sit in the back of classrooms and make fun of the teacher.

I have a bumper sticker that reads: "I support the right to arm bears" or "Warning, I brake for unicorns."

I read *National Lampoon*.

I respect John Belushi more than I do William F. Buckley, Jr.

I think I'm ridiculous.

Letters to Ann Landers make me laugh.

I have at least two pairs of mismatched socks.

I'd rather have people notice me than like me.

I know the first names of Cheech and Chong.

I think this questionnaire is fun to complete.

I had my secretary, who was definitely not a jester, type the questionnaire, and we asked various students around campus to complete it.

Once we had a lot of completed questionnaires, we undertook the third step in creating a measure of individual difference: ascertaining reliability. We had decided to assess internal reliability, so we looked at how answers to one question were related to answers to the other questions. According to the mentality behind our test, someone should consistently answer like a jester or consistently not. In other words, in answering our questions, a given respondent should provide a lot of endorsements or very few. Such proved to be the case: our questionnaire was reliable.

We now had to take the fourth step: estimating validity. The questionnaire seemed to possess content validity, in that some of the items poked fun at the questionnaire itself, and by implication, at those completing the questionnaire. This is exactly what is meant by content validity: including behaviors that reflect a jester-like character. (We also looked at which students wrote nasty comments in the margins of the questionnaire—"This is the stupidest thing I've ever done" was a representative comment—and ascertained that they endorsed few items indicating a jester-like approach to life.)

To establish criterion validity, we looked up the students who had completed the questionnaires and asked to look at their college identification cards, which had their pictures on them. Was the picture silly or not? In other words, did the student pose in some strange way, like with a feather boa, or a lizard, or a Grateful Dead headband? Did the student ham it up in the picture, by sticking out his tongue, rolling his eyes to the top of his head, or picking his nose? Some of you reading this may be horrified that someone might have an ID card that looks this way. You're probably not a jester. A fair number of the folks in our research project did indeed have silly photos, and as we had hoped, they also scored higher on our jester questionnaire than folks with standard pictures. So, our questionnaire had criterion validity.

Finally, we evaluated the validity of the questionnaire with the known-groups strategy. We compared the scores of students who were drama majors with the scores of students who were in the pre-medical curriculum. It seemed reasonable, at least on this particular campus, to assume that the first group of students was more likely to contain jesters than the second group. Again, this proved true.

We did not evaluate the construct validity of the jester questionnaire, but by now, you should be able to see how this could be done. What other individual differences should be related to the underlying construct of jester-hood? Do measures of these dimensions relate to scores from the jester questionnaire? If so, then the measure has a degree of construct validity.

"Jesters? I'm sure! Gag me with a spoon!"

Nor did we investigate whether this individual difference was adaptive or maladaptive. Common sense suggests that its relationship to function depends on the particular situation. Parties, vacations, or long bus rides would make a jester a popular companion, whereas weddings, funerals, or job interviews would not bring rewarding consequences to a jester.

To conclude, an important activity of personality psychologists is to conceive and assess individual differences. This activity addresses the characteristic aspect of personality: that which makes people distinctly themselves, different from all others. Contrast this interest in individual differences with the interest in human nature, and you will see that personality psychology is indeed a broad field.

SO WHAT? COMMON THREADS IN PERSONALITY PSYCHOLOGY

Because it is such a diverse field, personality psychology cannot be precisely defined. Personality psychologists may be interested in genetics and historical factors, in unconscious motivation and computer models of the mind, in child-rearing and nuclear threat. Although fuzzy, personality psychology is not incoherent. Any given activity of a personality psychologist represents some of the pertinent attributes that characterize personality as a whole, but none of these particular attributes are necessary or sufficient. Here is the family resemblance of personality psychology.

First, *personality psychology is concerned with describing and explaining what the individual does*—not with parts of people or with statistical generalizations about "average" folks bearing no similarity to concrete individuals.

Second, *personality psychology acknowledges the importance of the social world.* The attention is placed on the person, but the person is not lost in space. Rather, personality is tied to the world, with the most important aspect of the world being other people.

Third, *personality psychology is practical.* Those working in this field wish to apply its theories and findings to the real world. Clinical psychology, educational psychology, and industrial/organizational psychology are examples of fields with roots in personality psychology.

Fourth, *personality psychology is controversial.* A particular personality approach takes a strong stance on several issues, contradicting those of other approaches. What units should be used to describe personality? Is personality fixed or static? Are the determinants of personality biological or environmental?

SUMMARY

This chapter describes two of the major activities of personality psychologists. In each case, I have identified its important issues and concerns, and used a variety of examples to illustrate them. My goal was to impress upon you that personality psychology is fully as diverse as the instances of personality itself.

Models of human nature are attempts to specify some essence that lies at the core of being human. This essence is phrased in *metaphorical language,* and the *metaphor* is used to understand what people think, do, and feel. Among the models of human nature that have been popular within personality psychology are those that liken people to animals, energy systems, white rats, machines, fields, computers, scientists, actors, and pilots. One metaphor compares people to people, of all things!

Individual differences and *personality assessment* comprise an activity addressing how people are consistently like themselves and different from others. Workers here attempt to describe and explain individual differences. As part of their endeavor, they are greatly concerned with how best to measure these differences. Several issues crosscut this activity: What is the origin of a particular individual difference? How is a given characteristic related to good or bad functioning in the world? How can dysfunctional behavior be prevented or changed? Measuring individual differences requires that assessment techniques be **reliable** and **valid.**

Together, these activities suggest a family resemblance for personality psychology, one that parallels the family resemblance defining personality itself. Personality psychology is concerned with the concrete individual, describing and explaining personality against the background of the social world. It is a practical field of psychology. And, of course, it houses a number of controversies.

3

THE
HISTORY OF
PERSONALITY
PSYCHOLOGY

Personality psychology was born in the twentieth century, the offspring of such ancestors as experimental psychology, psychiatry, and the psychological testing tradition. These ancestors in turn resulted from a productive nineteenth century marriage between philosophy and science. In this chapter, I will describe the three immediate ancestors of personality psychology, and then sketch the field's history throughout the twentieth century.

I want to give you a historical perspective on personality psychology to place it in a social context. Then perhaps I can dispel the mistaken notion you may have that scientific theories simply appear out of thin air. Newton did not invent physics just because an apple fell on his head. Scientific theories emerge from a particular cultural and intellectual setting. To describe this interdependence of scientific theory and the real world in which the theorist lives, historians have introduced two concepts.

Zeitgeist is a German word which translates as "spirit of the times," conveying the notion that scientific ideas reflect the given time in which they are proposed. The history of science is filled with examples of simultaneous discoveries, each making the point that discoveries come from someplace. When the raw ingredients for a theory are present and when the time is right, then the discoveries appear. For instance, Charles Darwin proposed the theory of evolution at about the same time as Alfred Russell Wallace did, in 1859.

Ortgeist is another German word which translates as "spirit of the place"—scientific theories reflect the given place in which they are proposed. Thus, explanations from different cultures have a characteristic stamp upon them. Personality psychology originated in several nations, and the spirit of each nation is still evident. The German approach to psychology emphasizes the mind, possibly because the German language allows the expression of great subtleties among mental states. Influenced by evolutionary theory, the English approach stresses classification. Thus, the testing tradition first appeared in England. An emphasis on emotion and irrationality characterizes a French approach, creating great breakthroughs in how to conceive psychopathology. And, finally, the American approach is pragmatic: What's the consequence? What works? Can you get it for me wholesale? And so what? Applied psychology is a characteristically American endeavor.

The history of personality psychology is also the history of personality psychologists. A handful of creative and charismatic theorists created the field. Their work reflected who they were, and who they were was a product of a given time and place. Sigmund Freud may have created psychoanalytic theory, but it was Victorian Europe that created Sigmund Freud.

IMMEDIATE ANCESTOR 1: EXPERIMENTAL PSYCHOLOGY

E. G. Boring wrote the definitive history of experimental psychology in 1950. He placed the origin of this field in Europe, during the 1800s, when different scientific and philosophical trends came together to form the Zeitgeist from which psychology emerged. Most historians point specifically to the establishment of Wilhelm Wundt's experimental psychology laboratory in 1879 at the University of Leipzig as the culmination of these trends and the beginning of experimental psychology. Soon after, psychology branched into different approaches, and from each stemmed a particular way of regarding personality.

The Psychology of Wundt: What Are the Elements of Consciousness?

Ideas and discoveries emerge from a social and cultural context, but they do not automatically appear without the talents of a particular individual. In experimental psychology, this individual was Wilhelm Wundt, a German who lived from 1832 to 1920, a period which spanned great cultural and scientific change. As a young man, Wundt studied and specialized in physiology. He taught at several universities and in 1875 was appointed professor of philosophy at the University of Leipzig. Then in 1879, he received permission to establish a laboratory for his experiments, and the Psychologische Institut was founded, as a single room.

Why is Wundt considered the first experimental psychologist? Well, unlike his intellectual predecessors who might be given this title, Wundt considered himself a psychologist. He discarded earlier definitions of psychology as too philosophical and instead defined the field as *the science of consciousness,* regarding experimentation as the beginning point (Wertheimer, 1979).

The goal of Wundt's psychology, now called **structuralism,** was *to understand experience as it is immediately given to the individual.* Following the examples of chemistry and physics, he tried to specify the basic elements of experience using techniques pioneered in the investigations of physiology and sensation. Wundt felt that once the basic elements of consciousness had been identified, the exact manner in which they combined to form complex mental phenomena could be ascertained.

The elements of consciousness were discovered through a form of observation called **introspection,** a literal "in-looking" in which the research subject observed his immediate experience and discovered the constituent units, presumably different types of sensations and feelings. The **stimulus error,** confusion of one's interpretation of experience with the immediate experience itself, had to be avoided. So, in examining a guava, the research subject would describe his experience in terms of sensations like color, shape, and weight. He would not make the mistake, however, of interpreting these sensations as an edible fruit.

Wundt's structuralism flourished for decades. As we will see, though, its details were controversial, and ultimately structuralism passed on, leaving little direct influence on personality psychology. However, it marked the beginning of experimental psychology, paving the way for other approaches that did directly influence personality psychology.

Why was Wundt's system controversial? In a nutshell, structuralism attempted to discover via introspection the mental elements of the normal, adult European male. As such, it was a static and abstract endeavor, with no relevance to pragmatic concerns. Further, the method of introspection proved less objective than the structuralists believed.

Three major alternatives to structuralism developed in response to the different shortcomings of Wundt's approach. **Gestalt psychology** took issue with the assumption that mental elements were fundamental, proposing instead that *relationships were the basis of mental phenomena.* **Functionalism** took issue with the static character of structuralism, suggesting that *the consequences of mental activity were more important than its elements.* This approach concerned itself with individual differences, extending psychology to include animals, children, the mad, and so on. In short, *functionalism was applied psychology.* Finally, **behaviorism** took issue with the technique of introspection, branding it subjective and unreliable. More profoundly, behaviorism also disagreed with Wundt's definition of psychology as the study of consciousness, decreeing instead that *psychology's subject matter was observable behavior.*

Gestalt Psychology: Relationships Are Fundamental

Max Wertheimer, a German psychologist, created Gestalt psychology following his discovery of the **phi phenomenon:** *the illusion of apparent movement* that all of us experience if we sit still in a train next to another train that begins to move. We have the momentary experience that it is our train that has moved, when in actuality, the experience was illusory, caused by the movement of the other train. Do you see how the phi phenomenon challenged the assumption that conscious experience can be understood by breaking it into constituent elements? There is nothing in the person's constituent sensations that correspond to the experience of the train moving. So, *immediate experience cannot be created from the building blocks of individual sensations.*

The German word **gestalt** means whole, or pattern, or configuration; thus, the basic stance of gestalt psychology is that *immediate experience itself is patterned.* The whole (of experience) is not equal to the sum of its parts (sensations). Gestalt psychology contends that structuralism's distrust of the stimulus error is itself an error, a profound mistake that misdirects psychology's attention to parts rather than wholes.

A melody exemplifies the notion of a gestalt. One can play a tune at the left end of a piano keyboard, where the notes are deep. Then one can scoot up to the right end and play the same tune, where the notes are high. Assuming that one's fingers do not slip, the tunes are recognizable as the identical melody, even though none of the notes are the same. Why? Because the pattern—the gestalt—is fundamental.

The first gestalt psychologists—Max Wertheimer, Kurt Koffka, and Wolfgang Kohler—were concerned with such psychological processes as *perception, learning,* and *thinking.* They stressed the importance of relationships and interpreted psychological phenomena as fields, as interdependent with their context. In the process of perception, irregularities and asymmetries are smoothed out. Percepts seek **good gestalts,** *examples of the self-regulating nature of a field and its inherent movement toward homeostasis.*

Gestalt psychologist Wolfgang Kohler (1924) described learning in terms of relationships. In a well-known study, conducted when he was trapped on an island during World War I, Kohler investigated the ability of chimpanzees to achieve insight into learning situations. Let me describe one of these experiments. A banana or similar treat was suspended from the top of a cage, beyond the chimp's grasp. A box and a stick were placed in the cage. Kohler wanted to know if the chimp could see how to use the different objects to get the banana. (In case you don't see the point, the chimp has to push the box directly under the banana and climb on it with the stick in hand. Then the banana can be reached, and chimpanzee bliss ensues.) This task requires insight, grasping the whole of the task in terms of a useful relationship among its parts—the banana, the box, and the stick—before action is taken. Perhaps surprisingly, the chimp managed the task with relative ease.

The gestalt approach was influential, and other psychologists applied its basic tenets to a variety of topics: psychopathology, group processes, and personality. Kurt Lewin is the giant figure among those applying gestalt ideas to complex human behavior. His 1935 book *A Dynamic Theory of Personality* examined the person in field terms, paying particular interest to self-regulating processes. Lewin termed the psychological field in which behavior occurred the **life space,** and studied how the equilibrium of the life space was restored following a disturbance. He posited psychological forces called *vectors* that worked to establish a good gestalt in the life space.

"The Far Side" cartoon by Gary Larson is reproduced by permission of Chronicle Features, San Francisco.

In 1932, Lewin came to the United States, where he taught at Stanford, Cornell, Iowa, and MIT, attracting scores of students who have gone on to make their own mark in social and personality psychology. All share several Lewinian emphases. First is a concern with the concrete person in the concrete situation. Lewin disagreed with generalizations like these:

He is psychotic because of his heredity.

The rigidity of his problem-solving behavior is due to his ethnocentrism.

Friends work better together than do strangers.

A highly cohesive group will be more productive than a less cohesive group. (Deutsch, 1968, p. 418)

These statements pull apart the person and the situation. In contrast, Lewin believed that psychology should address particulars, and particulars involved individual people in immediate situations. As you have seen, this idea still thrives in contemporary personality psychology.

A second Lewinian emphasis is a recognition of the importance of reality *as it is perceived.* Behavior occurs within a psychological field, not a physical one. When people behave, they do so according to what is psychologically real for them, and psychological reality may include ghosts and demons, or the military-industrial complex, or the necessity for getting straight A's. Clearly, psychological reality varies from individual to individual, and the personality psychologist must see the world as his or her research subject sees it.

Finally, a third emphasis is Lewin's belief that psychology can and should be used to solve social problems. He advocated **action research:** the *explicit blurring of pure and applied investigation.* How can effective leadership styles be cultivated? How can prejudice be eliminated? How can marital conflict be resolved? Again, we see Kurt Lewin's approach foreshadowing personality psychology as I characterized it in Chapter 2.

In sum, gestalt psychology has influenced contemporary personality psychology in several ways. First, it is an early example of a field theory, an increasingly popular way of explaining personality. Second, in its emphasis on relationships and good gestalts, gestalt psychology provides a framework for regarding the unity and integrity of personality. Third, gestalt psychology, particularly the work of Lewin, led personality psychologists to attend to the particular manner in which the individual sees reality. The numerous cognitive theories in contemporary personality psychology attest to the importance of this emphasis.

Functionalism: The Mind in Use

Just as gestalt psychology reacted against an aspect of Wundt's structuralism, so too did functionalism. In this case, functionalism was concerned not with the structure of the mind, as was Wundt's psychology, but instead with its function. The structuralists asked *what* and *how;* the functionalists asked *why.*

Functionalism can be traced to Darwinian thought, and in particular to how the Englishman Herbert Spencer applied it to human action in the late 1800s. Sir Francis Galton, whose contribution to the testing tradition will be discussed later in this chapter, can also be described as a functionalist. However, functionalism was primarily an American endeavor, and its story starts with two important figures, William James of Harvard and John Dewey of Chicago and Columbia.

William James was the first American psychologist. The brother of novelist Henry James, William completed a Harvard medical degree in 1869 and stayed on to teach physiology and later philosophy. In 1890, he published his two-volume *Principles of Psychology,* a brilliant textbook that touches on a variety of topics: habit, emotion, will, memory, consciousness, and so on. This book paved the way for a functional psychology, one that emphasizes the mind meeting the demands of everyday living. So, James argued that memory is not an abstract and general property of the mind but rather a task-specific skill, used in particular activities with particular consequences.

James founded the first psychology laboratory in the United States, but he was never much of an experimentalist. Instead, he taught a number of men and women who went on to perform important psychology experiments. And the students who first learned about psychology through his textbook are beyond count.

In his later years, James turned his attention from psychology per se to matters of philosophy, where he is well-known for his contributions to **pragmatism,** the only wholly American philosophy. Pragmatism stresses the relativity of knowledge and the necessity for evaluating knowledge in terms of its applications. Again, James professed a functional point of view. Murphy and Kovach (1972) describe James as America's greatest psychologist, "in the judgment of scholars and of laymen alike, any second to him was a poor second" (p. 206).

The other significant figure in the history of functionalism is John Dewey, who won fame not just as a psychologist, but also as a philosopher and educational theorist. (If you've ever wondered where the Dewey Decimal System came from, you need look no further.) After appointments at Michigan and Minnesota, Dewey went to the new University of Chicago in 1894, where he founded the Laboratory School, also known as the Dewey School, as a natural setting in which to test his ideas about education. After ten years at Chicago, he went to Columbia where he was associated with the famous Teachers College.

Like James, Dewey influenced psychology not just by his particular contributions but also by his general attitude of pragmatism. He was a champion of progress, of experiment, of use, and of innovation (Boring, 1950, p. 553). He opposed what he saw as artificial categories imposed upon thought and action by the structuralists and others. His most influential paper, "The Reflex Arc Concept in Psychology," attacks the familiar stimulus-response dichotomy (Dewey, 1896). Dewey believed there can be no stimulus without a response, no response without a stimulus. Speaking of them as if they were separate entities misses the important point that human activity is a whole, a means of coordinating the person with the world.

He cites an example of a child who burns his finger by touching a lighted candle. One might say that being burned was the stimulus, and pulling the finger away was the response. Dewey objects to this description because it makes it seem that the child's action involved two steps: burning his finger

One of the central tenets of John Dewey's educational philosophy was that children should "learn by doing."

and pulling it away. Instead, according to Dewey, these steps are the same action, one best understood in terms of its result: stopping the pain.

The influence of Dewey on the form of American education is still felt. *Learning by doing* captures his approach to education and reflects his belief that the developing child is active and curious. Education should neither drill information into a passive observer nor let the child run rampant through the halls and the curriculum. Instead, education should encourage the child's natural tendencies through guided opportunities that put these lessons into practice.

This approach to education embodies the functional approach by emphasizing not the formal properties and contents of the mind so much as the consequences of the mind when used. Dewey believed in habit, and felt that virtue and intelligence followed from habits of fair-mindedness, objectivity, imagination, and courage. Dewey himself was a social critic, an advocate of democracy and academic freedom.

Functionalists made important inroads into what we now recognize as personality psychology. In keeping with Darwinian thought, they examined all manner of populations, not just adult European males. They also maintained the Darwinian emphasis on fitness, examining individual differences in thought and action. For instance, Robert Woodworth (1918) emphasized the role of motivation, particularly drives. A person's actions could be understood in terms of what drove them, and different individuals have different ⌐ ⌐ ⌐ hence, different personalities.

Functionalism stimulated a number of applied psychologies still around today: child psychology, educational psychology, abnormal psychology, industrial psychology, animal psychology, cross-cultural psychology, psychology of women, and so on. But as a discrete approach to psychology, functionalism rather quickly gave way to behaviorism, which is as much a descendant of functionalism as a reaction against structuralism. But the legacy of functionalism is still with psychology and particularly with personality psychology. First, functionalism forced psychology to attend to *action*, stressing that action should be understood in terms of its consequences. Second, functionalism leads to the contemporary interest in *adaptation*. And third, functionalism—along with the testing tradition—stimulated interest in *individual differences*, one of the characteristic concerns of personality psychology.

Behaviorism: An Emphasis on Overt Actions

The final reaction to Wundt's structuralism was behaviorism, which objected not just to the use of introspection to discover the elements of consciousness but also to the very definition of psychology as the study of consciousness. Instead, according to John B. Watson, the first behaviorist, psychology should study observable behavior.

Watson was an animal psychologist and, at first, a functionalist. As I have mentioned, the functionalists saw the study of animals as legitimate for psychology, since Darwin stressed the continuity between animals and people. At the turn of the century, animal psychology was concerned with the mind of animals. Not surprisingly though, this field was just as concerned with what animals did, interpreting their behavior in terms of *tropisms*, reflexive movements toward or away from objects in the environment.

The time was right for John Watson to take these ideas one step further and apply them to people. While at Johns Hopkins University in 1913, he published his famous paper "Psychology as the Behaviorist Views It," laying out his criticisms of psychology and proposing his solutions to the problems. More basically, he criticized introspection as the structuralists employed it. According to Watson, the major problem with this supposedly objective research technique was that different observers saw different things when they peered within their minds. So, consciousness was an inappropriate subject matter for psychology, one that should not be studied. Instead, psychology should deal with observable behavior.

Consciousness has since returned to a respectable position within psychology, along with more acceptable ways of investigating it, but it was lost for quite a while in the wake of Watson's arguments. In the meantime, Watson made a positive contribution to the field as well. He proposed that *condition-ing,* as described by the Russian physiologist Ivan Pavlov, should be the cornerstone of his new *objective psychology* of animal and human behavior.

In a famous study with an infant known as Little Albert, Watson and Rayner (1920) demonstrated that fear of furry animals could be brought about by clanging a metal bar with a hammer when Little Albert viewed a white rat. Though just a demonstration, this example of a conditioned fear has become important to psychology, particularly to behaviorism, suggesting that psychopathology, in this case a phobia, might be brought about by mundane processes of learning.

If phobias can be learned, then so too can more productive ways of behaving. Watson's emphasis on conditioning led to an optimism about what psychology could accomplish, an optimism that still characterizes behavioral approaches to psychology:

> Give me a dozen healthy infants, well-formed, and my own specified world to bring them up in, and I'll guarantee to take any one at random and train him to become any type of specialist I might select—doctor, lawyer, artist, merchant-chief, and, yes, even beggar-man and thief, regardless of his talents, penchants, tendencies, activities, vocations and race of his ancestors. (1930, p. 65)

America at the turn of the century responded well to this promise of a better world through conditioning theory, and Watson's influence spread as he further extended his ideas to people. Other behaviorists soon followed his example.

An extremely rare photograph of John Watson (in Santa mask) with assistant, Rosalie Rayner, as they conditioned Little Albert.

SOURCE: Courtesy Dr. Ben Harris.

Some emphasized Pavlov's classical conditioning approach, while others made use of **operant conditioning,** the Law of Effect studied by Edward Lee Thorndike (1911), a Columbia functionalist who studied at Harvard with William James. Thorndike devised puzzle-boxes from which cats and other animals could escape if they performed some response like clawing at a rope. Thorndike showed that such learning proceeded slowly as the animal learned through trial-and-error which responses led to good outcomes (escape) and which did not.

Although behaviorism has influenced personality psychology, there is a noticeable tension between the two. Much of what is meant by personality cannot be well explained by behaviorism. Rather than focusing on the individual, behaviorism focuses on the environment. Rather than looking at someone's general characteristics, behaviorism concerns itself with highly specific habits. Although able to explain individual differences in terms of different histories of conditioning, behaviorism regards individual differences as arbitrary and easily subject to modification. Similarly, rather than expecting behavior to endure, behaviorism views it as transient, under the sway of the particular rewards and punishments in the immediate environment.

However, behaviorism does a spectacular job of explaining what is functional or dysfunctional about behavior, and one of the success stories of modern psychology is **behavior modification,** the application of conditioning theory within psychotherapy. For a number of problems, behavior modification is the treatment of choice. To Watson's catalogue of doctor, lawyer, beggar-man, and thief can be added another type of person made possible by conditioning: the individual free of needless worry and fear.

Thus, behaviorism has left its mark on contemporary personality psychology in several ways. First, it legitimized the application of theories and findings from the animal learning laboratory to people. Second, it elevated the experimental method to the most respected position among the research techniques of psychologists, an occurrence that has not always served personality psychology well. Third, and most important, behaviorism and its distrust of superfluous explanation have helped curb the occasionally extravagant and muddled theories sometimes invoked to explain personality.

IMMEDIATE ANCESTOR 2: PSYCHIATRY

Modern medicine appeared on the scene about the same time as experimental psychology. Although the medical profession has been practiced since the time of the early Greeks, the 1800s marked the most important medical breakthrough to date: the **germ model** of disease was formulated. Today, we are so familiar with this model that it is a bit sobering to realize that the world had printing presses, steam engines, soccer, bicycles, and *The New York Times* before it had the idea that germs caused illness.

As summarized by Maher and Maher (1979), the germ model consists of five related assumptions:

1. For each disease there is a specific germ.

2. Successful identification of the germ depends on careful description and classification of the clinical syndrome of the disease.

3. The germ is necessary and sufficient for the disease.

4. Any treatment that removes or prevents the germ from entering the body will cure the disease.

5. Immunization to the disease results from prior infection with small intensities of the germ.

The germ model was soon elaborated to propose that illness also resulted from defects in the body or from injuries to the body.

The Medical Model: From Physical Illness to Psychopathology

Taken together, these views that illness results from germs, or from defects, or from injuries are termed the **medical model.** As Bursten (1979) observes, the medical model assumes that illness is a biologically based dysfunction that the patient does not choose. When employed in psychiatry, the medical model means, "whenever you see mental illness, look to biology for the significant etiological data" (p. 662).

The medical model was brought about by some of the same trends that influenced experimental psychology. Although the histories of these two fields diverged considerably until personality psychology reunited them in the twentieth century, they have in common the intellectual ancestor the theory of evolution. That experimental psychology took one path while modern medicine took another is largely due to the differing demands of the university versus the clinic.

Stimulated by discoveries about the nervous system, the entirely new medical field of neurology developed between 1840 and 1900.

> The advent of the specialty of neurology raised the "nervous" patient to a status that demanded and received dignified recognition. Symptoms attributable to the brain and the spine standing upon an objective footing were subject to therapeutic enterprise. With increasing accent on nervous symptoms, hitherto impatiently dealt with by physicians, or treated by hypnotists or faith-healers, came a new series of descriptive terms. . . . As medical men gladly relinquished their troublesome hysterics, neurologists accepted the burden. (Bromberg, 1959, p. 151)

In short fashion, neurology merged with the primitive psychiatry then in practice, and by the turn of the century, researchers like Adolph Meyer were attempting to find the basis of mental disorders like senility, epilepsy, general paresis, and mania within defects of the nervous system. Sigmund Freud's original medical training was in neurology, and much of psychoanalytic theory can be viewed as a straightforward translation of neurological concepts into the realm of mind and behavior.

The medical model represented a unifying perspective on disease, allowing physicians to share a common viewpoint on the causes of various illnesses and how to prevent and treat them. This perspective was extended to supposed diseases of the nervous system, and, in the 1800s, medicine began to treat a whole new class of patients, folks we now recognize as suffering from psychological problems. The physicians who treated these "mental" patients increasingly recognized the importance of psychological factors, but they continued to use the vocabulary and perspective of the medical model in their explanations and treatments.

Freud's theory of abnormality formed the basis for his theory of personality, one that is couched in the language of the medical model, even though early in his career Freud abandoned his attempts to find specific neurological equivalents of the processes he hypothesized.

Of great importance in psychoanalytic theory is the mental conflict, which plays the role of a metaphorical germ. It rests within the person, producing a host of observable symptoms for him. The analyst must work backward from these symptoms to discover the particular conflict at work. More often than not, the conflict was implanted early in life, where it attacked a vulnerable part of the mind. Problems are cured by removing the conflict through any of a number of techniques. Problems can be prevented, however, by metaphorical immunization—exposing the ego to small frustrations and difficulties which thereby strengthen it.

The medical model is inherent not just in psychoanalytic theories of personality, but in other approaches as well. Cognitive theories sometimes assign the role of germ to low self-esteem (Rogers, 1951), unrealistic assumptions (Beck, 1976), or irrational beliefs (Ellis, 1962). And, in his *learned helplessness theory of depression,* Seligman (1975) attributes depressive symptoms to the belief that one cannot control important outcomes in one's life. He speaks explicitly about "curing" a depressive of this belief and of "immunizing" someone against it through early mastery of outcomes.

Similarly, behavorial approaches to abnormality sometimes embody aspects of the medical model. Although behaviorists have often been vociferous critics of the model (for example, Ullmann & Krasner, 1975), they hold faulty learning responsible for abnormal behavior. Faulty learning creates bad habits such as conditioned fear, which bear a family resemblance to germs. Behavior modification techniques are thought to remove these bad habits as surely and as automatically as antibiotics remove germs. My aim here is to illustrate how influential the reductionist medical model has been, mainly because it leads to the successful treatment of problems, both physical and psychological.

The Emergence of Modern Psychiatry: Mesmer to Charcot to Janet to Freud

In contrast to experimental psychology, which originated mainly in Germany and England, psychiatry's important roots lie in France. The French were more attuned to the subject matter of psychiatry: abnormality, irrationality, emotion, and the unconscious. In fact, French medicine stressed the clinical study of the patient, making French hospitals and asylums for the mentally ill among the most advanced in the world. They provided a setting for research and the training of psychiatrists. However, because the reality of the clinic forced attention upon the specific problems of the individual, the theories developed to explain these problems of necessity embraced the entire person. They were personality theories in the modern sense of the term.

Among the patients who attracted the attention of French psychiatrists were women suffering from **hysteria,** an inexplicable paralysis of some part of the body accompanied by a host of other symptoms:

> She had been ill for some months. . . . She had paralysis of the right arm, both legs were paralyzed, and she could move only the fingers of her left hand. She was unable to feed herself, and she was barely able to turn her head because of what appeared to be a paralyzed neck muscle. She complained of visual difficulty, so that she could neither write nor read. . . .
>
> Bertha spoke in half or broken sentences and complained that "black snakes" and "death's heads" were present in the room . . . most of the time Bertha did not appear to hear what was being said to her. She appeared very weak and sickly and refused to eat any food that was given to her. (Rosenbaum, 1984, p. 2)

Since the time of Hippocrates, hysteria was thought to be a disease peculiar only to women, the result of a wandering uterus, which had become dislodged and had travelled through the body causing the symptoms that comprise the disorder.

Freud's first patients were hysterics, and his first important contribution to psychiatry was his psychological interpretation of hysteria and its effective treatment. But the thinkers of the 1800s mostly viewed hysteria in physical terms, quite literally applying the medical model.

One such figure was Franz Anton Mesmer, who lived from 1734 to 1815 and is best known for developing the technique of **mesmerism,** now called hypnotism. Mesmer was a Viennese physician who used magnets to treat various illnesses including hysteria. He held that living beings were influenced by *animal magnetism,* a fluid that fills the universe. (Perfume and cologne advertisements still adhere to this belief in modified form; animal magnetism now resides in a spray bottle, available for a modest price.) An imbalance of animal magnetism resulted in illness, and cures involved redistributing the fluid.

Magnets were one way to achieve this redistribution, but eventually Mesmer relied only on his own being, dressing in a magician's robe and inducing a state of hypnosis. Although Mesmer's techniques seemed to be effective, his therapy aroused great opposition, probably because of its resemblance to magic and its trappings of quackery. In 1778 he moved to Paris, where he continued to cure hysterics and attract great public attention. Again, he was discredited, this time in 1784 by a scientific commission that included as members Benjamin Franklin, Lavoisier (who discovered oxygen), and Guillotin (who discovered the ultimate cure for headaches).

Still, hypnosis techniques survived Mesmer's decline and fall, becoming a tool for French psychiatrists. One well-known user of hypnosis was Jean Martin Charcot, a Parisian physician who established the famous Salpêtrière neurological clinic in the middle of the nineteenth century. Charcot made the important observation that the symptoms of hysteria corresponded to the expectations of the patient and not to what was known about the nervous system. For instance, cases of glove paralysis, a type of hysteria in which all feeling is lost in the hand from the wrist down, were seen as anatomically

The professional use of hypnosis was widespread during the nineteenth century.

impossible, since nerves aren't distributed that way in the hand. Nevertheless, Charcot adhered to a physical interpretation of hysteria and its treatment by hypnosis.

Charcot's famous student, Pierre Janet, who lived from 1859 to 1947 (spanning Darwin and Hiroshima, if you care to marvel at what some individuals have seen), proposed a psychological interpretation of hysteria. Janet suggested that the problem resulted from personality splitting, with consciousness concentrating in one part and retracting from the other. Hypnosis restored the balance. This view of hypnosis, introducing the role of the unconscious in abnormality, was similar to that proposed by Freud, who went one step further to explain why hysteria occurred in the first place.

The most important student of the French approach to psychiatry was the young Sigmund Freud, who spent 1885 in Paris learning the techniques of hypnosis. Upon Freud's return home to Vienna, he began work with Joseph Breuer, an older physician who had discovered the technique of *catharsis* to treat hysteria, a procedure similar to hypnosis except that it didn't involve a trance state. From this early work on hysteria, psychoanalysis was born, bringing to an end my brief account of the early history of psychiatry.

In sum, psychiatry has influenced personality psychology in several ways. First, it introduced the medical model to the field, a perspective on problems and how to treat them that is still the benchmark against which other approaches are measured. Second, psychiatry is concerned with clinical phenomena, concrete individuals with concrete problems of adaptation; much of personality psychology focuses on the abnormal case, and several of the most influential personality theorists have been clinicians.

IMMEDIATE ANCESTOR 3: PSYCHOLOGICAL TESTING

The **psychological testing** tradition is the story of particular tests of individual differences, the statistical procedures developed to interpret them, and their applications. When psychological testing began, the tests measured intelligence and ability. These tests subsequently influenced personality psychology by providing a model for assessing individual differences. The giant figures in the story of psychological testing include Sir Francis Galton in England (who originated psychological testing), James McKeen Cattell in the United States (who popularized testing), and Alfred Binet in France (who provided the first great success of testing with his IQ measure).

Some of the main characters in the history of psychological testing also played important roles in the history of experimental psychology. However, the two fields are distinct in that mainstream experimental psychology was concerned with basic psychological processes in the average adult, while psychological testing was concerned with individual differences. Consequently, like functionalism, psychological testing was extended to a variety of populations, often for practical purposes. What was regarded as error by experimental psychologists was essence to psychological testers: "One's man ceiling is another man's floor."

Francis Galton: Mental Testing

The psychological testing tradition begins with the Englishman Sir Francis Galton, a cousin of Darwin who lived from 1822 to 1911. He's known for leaving his mark on psychological testing in innumerable ways. In Chapter 2, I described the assumptions of personality psychology's approach to individual differences and personality assessment:

- Individuals differ from each other.
- These differences are general and stable characteristics of the individual.
- These differences are quantitative characteristics.
- These differences determine function.
- These differences can be measured in a straightforward fashion.

By the turn of the century, Galton had already established these tenets in his investigations of intelligence.

One of Galton's best-known works is the book *Hereditary Genius* (1869), a biographical study of the tendency of genius to run in families. Galton quantified the degree of genius and assumed it was distributed in the general population according to a bell-shaped curve. Like eggs, movies, or restaurants, geniuses were rated *A, B, C,* and so on through *X,* with *A* meaning "just above average" and *X* meaning "one in a million." Genius (or intelligence) determined eminence, and so on.

Other important books by Galton included *English Men of Science* (1874) and *Natural Inheritance* (1889). In 1876 Galton published a paper on twins and how resemblances between them might be used to disentangle the effects of nature and nurture, terms first introduced in this paper. What has come to be known as the *twin method* is now a standard research procedure for investigating the role of genetics in personality and intelligence.

Galton invented the **mental test,** a procedure characterized by its brevity and emphasis on performance. In contrast to the elaborate techniques of *psychophysics,* the mental test does not attempt to reveal everything about mental functioning but rather tries to show individual differences in the consequences of functioning (Boring, 1950). Galton developed several tests for measuring imagery, pitch, visual judgment, muscular sense, reaction time, and so on. Many of these tests are still part of standard laboratory procedures in psychology.

Galton believed that intelligence could be measured with simple tests of sensory capacities, such as the ability to discriminate among tones or weights. Such tests proved of little value, but they influenced the course of psychological testing until Alfred Binet showed that intelligence was better measured with tests reflecting complex mental operations (Freeman, 1962).

Galton also introduced the earliest version of the **personality questionnaire** (Freeman, 1926). To measure vividness of mental imagery, he asked people to report what they remembered their breakfast to have looked like that morning. Although my imagery is poor, I remember that I was asked to respond to such a questionnaire when I was an introductory psychology student at the University of Illinois in 1969. (I hadn't eaten any breakfast, so I left it blank.) No doubt, the researcher was interested in the same thing that Galton was: quantifying the vividness of an individual's visual imagery.

Fully a century ago, Galton laid out the basic assumptions for the study of individual differences and the assessment of personality. Further, he believed that individual differences had a biological basis, determined by evolution and perhaps amenable to enlightened manipulation by modern science. In 1883, he even proposed a field called **eugenics** to "improve the race" by encouraging intelligent selection.

As you might imagine, eugenics was and is controversial. It assumes a biological basis to eminence and achievement that is hardly as well-established as Galton believed. In *Hereditary Genius*, for instance, insufficient attention was given to the very real possibility that the sons of famous fathers have greater opportunities than do other people. Their "genius" may reflect these opportunities and nothing more.

Finally, Galton (1888) contributed the concept of **correlation,** discussed in Chapter 2. He sought a way to quantify the strength of relations between variables (the link between fathers' genius and that of their sons, for example) since some pairs show a stronger relationship than do others. The index of *co-relation* was thus developed, soon to be rechristened the correlation coefficient.

Galton's colleague Karl Pearson (1896) worked out the mathematics of the correlation coefficient, and Pearson's computational procedures are still employed by statisticians today. Once the procedure for computing correlations was developed, other statistics for describing individual differences soon followed. Charles Spearman (1904) noted that most measures of performance and ability showed positive correlations. He proposed that all such measures reflected a general factor g, and some people came to believe that *g* was intelligence. Further, others came to believe that *g* was a biologically based characteristic that was inherited. However, the assumption that intelligence is a unitary characteristic with a tangible reality is at best dubious (Gould, 1981). Nevertheless, this assumption has usually been adopted within the testing tradition. As this tradition gave rise to personality tests, Spearman's assumption came along for the ride, often to the detriment of the endeavor.

The technique of **factor analysis** came about through the efforts of Godfrey Thompson, Cyril Burt, and L.L. Thurstone to understand a pattern of correlation coefficients in terms of the underlying factors that they reflect. Factor analysis has been applied not just to measures of performance and ability but also to personality tests.

James McKeen Cattell: Psychological Testing

James McKeen Cattell was a student of William Wundt. Indeed, the American Cattell was Wundt's first research assistant. As the story goes, Cattell brashly introduced himself to Wundt, "Herr Professor, you need an assistant, and I will be your assistant" (Boring, 1950, p. 324)! And indeed he was. But despite his central role in Wundt's experimental laboratory, Cattell was always more of a functionalist than a structuralist. He was interested in individual differences in reaction time, a concern eventually transformed into a concern with psychological testing, the term that Cattell himself coined.

Cattell taught at Pennsylvania, then Bryn Mawr, then briefly at Cambridge where he met Galton, again at Pennsylvania, and finally at Columbia, were he stayed the longest, from 1891 to 1917. Even after his dismissal from Columbia because of his pacifism in the face of World War I, Cattell remained active in psychology, leaving his mark in a number of ways.

Cattell maintained his interest in individual differences and their measurement throughout his career. In 1890, he published one of the first test batteries, which included ostensible measures of intelligence and personality. Like Galton, Cattell assumed that tests of simple reactions would give information about more complex processes. As I said earlier, this assumption has since been abandoned by mental testers, who now favor complex tests, often those with content validity. Also like Galton, Cattell was interested in eminence. He started the series *American Men of Science,* a ranking of men in the scientific professions with stars after the names of the most distinguished.

But Cattell's importance to the psychological testing tradition goes far beyond his specific contributions. He was a tireless advocate of psychology, particularly its study of individual differences. He edited numerous psychology journals, served on national committees for the American Psychological Association, and was active in the Psychological Corporation, an organization that made psychological services available to industry and the general public

(Boring, 1950). Indeed, the Psychological Corporation is still one of the primary sources for psychological tests.

According to Boring (1950), Cattell was in the right place at the right time. Because he was in tune with the American Zeitgeist, people listened to him, and he was able to shape American psychology in fundamental ways:

> Cattell's psychology is, however, something more than mental tests and reaction times and statistical methods and the resultant objective judgments that are not introspections. . . . It is motivated by a desire to determine how well men can do in this or that situation. . . . It seeks a description of human nature in respect of its range and variability. . . . It is important to realize the significance of the movement, because it, almost more than any other school, has been typical of the American trend. (pp. 539–540)

Alfred Binet: Intelligence Testing

The tests that Galton and Cattell employed came from the laboratories of experimental psychologists. But, as I have already mentioned, these tests did not prove useful in predicting the achievement outcomes that psychological testers were interested in. At best, there were modest correlations between scores on sensory and motor tests and academic performance (Freeman, 1926). Since the tests were intended to measure intelligence, and since intelligence is presumably reflected in academic performance, something was amiss.

Alfred Binet solved the problem. Instead of borrowing simple tasks from experimental psychology with which to test intelligence, Binet devised measures that tapped the higher mental functions—memory, imagery, attention, comprehension, and so on. And they proved useful in predicting academic achievement, so much so that tests like the SAT and the ACT still embody the belief that achievement is best predicted from performing complex tasks.

At about the turn of the century, Binet was commissioned by the Minister of Public Instruction in France to develop a procedure for separating dull children from those having difficulty at school for nonintellectual reasons (Murphy & Kovach, 1972). Modern intelligence tests were thus born, since Binet (in collaboration first with Victor Henri and then with Theodore Simon) devised tests with complex tasks like the following:

CHILDREN OF EIGHT YEARS

I. Compares Two Remembered Objects. This is a valuable test because it does not depend in the least on instruction, and brings into play the natural good sense of the subject. It consists in investigating whether the subject can, in thinking of two objects, distinguish a difference between them. . . .

II. Counts from 20 to 0. This is partly a test of school knowledge; one must have learned to count to be able to reverse the process. . . .

III. Indicates Omissions in Pictures. Four pictures are shown successively . . . in one an eye is lacking, in one the nose, in one the mouth, in one the arms. The child is asked each time: "What is missing in this picture?" (Binet & Simon, 1913)

Similar tasks were given to children of different ages, and scoring is relative to other children of the same age.

Binet introduced a number of ideas still important in psychological testing. First, test items were kept or deleted in accordance with what has come to be known as the known-group validity procedure, described in the last chapter. The very best and the very worst students were selected from a classroom and given a variety of potential test items. Only those questions where the brains outscored the sweathogs were retained for the test.

Second, Binet introduced the idea of scoring intelligence tests on a relative basis. The term **mental age** refers to the average performance by a child of a particular age. A mental age of six corresponds to the average score of a six-year-old child. Mental age may or may not correspond to chronological age, a fact that led to William Stern's (1904) suggestion that intelligence be represented as the quotient of mental age and chronological age. So, IQ is just shorthand for **intelligence quotient.**

Third, Binet recognized that the bottom line for such tests was the degree to which they served their intended purpose. Galton and Cattell's tests were developed and administered for quite some time before their limited usefulness was recognized. In contrast, Binet's tests proved useful from the start in identifying intellectually deficient students.

Several revisions of Binet's measures were made before he died in 1911. Since that time, his tests have been translated into a number of languages, and the revisions continue. In 1912, Lewis Terman at Stanford University developed an English-language version of the test that still exists as the Stanford-Binet.

World War I provided the impetus for group-administered intelligence tests. Because modern war had become so complicated, it was desirable to separate bright from dull soldiers. Intelligence tests seemed a good way to accomplish this purpose, but up to this time, they had only been administered individually. The necessity of testing some two million American recruits demanded another procedure. So psychologists developed the Army Alpha Examination, a pencil-and-paper test that could be taken by large groups of individuals at the same time. Army Alpha was the forerunner of the group testing that all of us have been subjected to: *Do not mark the test booklet!*

By the 1920s, the limitations of intelligence testing had come to be recognized. The fact that the Stanford-Binet and the Army Alpha were culture-bound became apparent. They favored native speakers of English and those from a bookish or verbal environment (Boring, 1950). Plus, the assumption

WWI recruits were among the first to have to "sit through" intelligence testing.

that intelligence was some unitary and fixed characteristic of the individual was also challenged. Special abilities and talents unrelated to general intelligence were documented, and more specific aptitude tests were developed to measure these.

Throughout the twentieth century, psychologists have suggested culture-fair tests: measures of intelligence unbiased by a person's particular social and educational background. So far, none of these tests have proven satisfactory, probably because they are impossible. Culture-fair tests are based on the doubtful assumption that one can speak of adaptation (intelligence) apart from a particular setting. Most intelligence tests are validated against the criterion of academic performance, and this criterion clearly favors certain cultural and social backgrounds over others. That poor people and minorities sometimes score poorly on standard intelligence tests says more about bias in academic institutions than anything else.

Intelligence testing has influenced personality testing by providing an example of how an individual difference can be reliably measured and used to predict subsequent behavior. However, the success of intelligence testing stems from the unambiguous criterion (school grades) against which they have been continually validated. This criterion is typically the behavior to be predicted. In contrast, personality tests are validated against an ambiguous criterion, and the behavior which they attempt to predict may be different than this criterion. No wonder personality tests have sometimes been unsuccessful.

The Emergence of Personality Testing

Intelligence tests dominated early psychological testing, but personality tests followed closely on their heels, using the procedures exemplified by measures of intelligence. For instance, in 1919, Eleanor Morgan, Helen K. Mull, and Margaret W. Washburn described a measure of cheerfulness versus depression validated by the known-groups method. The researchers presented subjects with a list of fifty words on each of five successive days. For each word, the subject thought of some experience that was then classified as either pleasant or unpleasant. Later, subjects were asked to remember the words in the lists and were given a score reflecting the proportion of pleasant to unpleasant words they recalled. These scores were compared to reports by friends on whether the subjects were generally optimistic or pessimistic. As you might expect, cheerful (optimistic) subjects recalled a greater proportion of pleasant words than the depressed (pessimistic) subjects, who showed the opposite pattern (see Bower, 1981).

Also early in the century, at the request of General Pershing, Robert Woodworth created the first personality measures that asked subjects to describe their own personality, the Personal Data Sheet, which was used with army recruits in World War I and published in 1919. The Personal Data Sheet attempted to identify men who were unfit for military service because of personality maladjustment. Individuals were asked to respond to such questions as:

- Does the sight of blood make you sick or dizzy?
- Do you sometimes wish that you had never been born?
- Are you happy most of the time?
- Do people find fault with you much?

If a person gave a sufficient number of undesirable answers, he had a personal interview. Because the Personal Data Sheet attempted to assess a variety of personality characteristics, it is also the first example of a personality inventory, foreshadowing such later tests as the MMPI.

Other early personality measures included tests of temperament (Downey, 1923), emotion (Pressey, 1921), moral judgment (Fernald, 1912), aesthetic sensitivity (Thorndike, 1916), and so on. Each measure regarded some aspect of personality as an individual difference and assigned scores to subjects reflecting how much of the aspect they possessed. Methods included self-report questionnaires, ratings by observers, word-association tasks, and analyses of behaviors such as handwriting.

More and more tests of personality appeared as the result of attempts to measure the individual differences suggested by an ever-increasing number of personality theories. Psychoanalytic theory inspired measures of individual differences in needs and drives, and Gestalt theory gave rise to measures of individual differences in tendencies to tolerate uncertainty and ambiguity. In other cases, personality measures appeared in response to practical demands. Remember how World War I led to group intelligence testing? The more settings that applied psychologists worked in, the more measures of individual differences they devised in response to the practical questions posed in these settings (Freeman, 1926).

When should children enter school? Once there, are they performing up to their ability? Which applicants should be chosen for professional school? For what job is a person best suited? What abilities are needed to perform a particular task? Who commits crime? Which individuals should be allowed to immigrate to the United States?

To date, the clinic has been the most important setting for applied psychologists. In the early days of clinical psychology, psychologists did not do psychotherapy, Bob Newhart notwithstanding. Rather, clinical psychologists administered psychological tests to patients under the care of psychiatrists (Korchin, 1983). These tests were used to diagnose particular problems, to understand their causes, to recommend treatments, and to forecast outcomes. (World War II created an urgent demand for more therapists, a need filled by clinical psychologists; but that is a different story.)

Chief among the tests administered to mental patients by clinical psychologists are **projective tests,** so named because they present ambiguous stimuli which allow subjects to project their personality in responding to them. The best-known projective measure is Hermann Rorschach's Inkblot Test:

> The subject is given one plate after the other and asked, "What might this be?" He holds the plate in his hand and may turn it about as much as he likes. The subject is free to hold the plate near his eyes or as far away as he chooses. . . . An attempt is made to get at least one answer to every plate, though suggestion in any form is, of course, avoided. . . .

> The test has proven to be of diagnostic value. In normals it makes possible differential diagnosis of personality; in patients, the diagnosis of illness. Furthermore, it presents an intelligence test almost completely independent of previous knowledge, memory, practice, and degree of education. It is possible by means of the test to draw conclusions concerning many affective relationships. The test has the advantage of almost unlimited applicability making possible without further data comparison of the results in the most heterogeneous subjects. (1942, pp. 14–18)

The popularity of the Inkblot Test stems from its compatibility with psychoanalytic theory, which holds that an individual's underlying needs and drives affect all spheres of functioning. The basic premise of the Rorschach Inkblot Test is that individual responses reveal personality characteristics as readily as do dreams, free associations, and slips of the tongue.

Another well-known projective test is the Thematic Apperception Test, developed by Christina D. Morgan and Henry Murray at the Harvard Psychological Clinic in 1935. The TAT, as it is known, presents subjects with ambiguous pictures. The subject tells a story about the characters in the picture. She tells any sort of story she wants, so long as it has a beginning, middle, and end. Again, the individual reveals her personality by projecting it upon the pictures she sees. Murray and his colleagues were particularly interested in individual differences in needs, such as the need for achievement or the need for recognition, and they devised ways to score these needs from TAT stories.

The Minnesota Multiphasic Personality Inventory is yet another widely used clinical test (see Chapter 2). Starke R. Hathaway and his collaborators (1943) created this test during World War II by presenting a number of statements to individuals with known psychiatric diagnoses. They determined the pattern of responses associated with a particular diagnosis, just as Binet determined which of his test items accompanied good versus poor academic achievement. The MMPI is widely used to make initial diagnoses of emotional difficulty. Further, because it measures a number of ways that people can differ from each other, it is considered an *inventory:* a collection of personality measures that attempts to be exhaustive, if not exhausting. The MMPI has also been extensively used with normal subjects.

The personality testing field thrives today, with new discoveries in statistics and the technological revolution of computers allowing ever-sophisticated attempts to measure individual differences and predict subsequent functioning. Despite this sophistication, personality testing still suffers from validity problems. Of special concern is that the criterion of a particular test is ambiguous, since the individual difference of concern usually bears no simple relation to a particular aspect of the world.

PERSONALITY PSYCHOLOGY DURING THE LAST FIFTY YEARS

When did modern personality psychology first appear? I have described its three immediate ancestors—experimental psychology, psychiatry, and psychological testing—but the field has no specific date of birth. As various researchers and theorists began to weave together the ideas, methods, and applications provided by these ancestors, personality psychology began in many ways at many times. But, as we look backward, we see that something significant was taking place in the early decades of the twentieth century.

Once established, personality psychology followed a course that parallels the history of psychology in general (Wertheimer, 1979). First, in the 1930s and 1940s, there was a flourishing of great schools promoted by charismatic theorists. Next, in the 1950s, there followed a breakdown of these schools and the creation of a second generation of theories more closely linked to research findings. Then, in the 1960s, personality psychology suffered a crisis of confidence and began a period of intensive self-scrutiny that continued into the 1970s. Finally, we see today a new era in personality psychology, one marked by creativity and growth in which personality psychologists are responding to the years of self-criticism. Today, personality psychology attempts to resolve the crisis in the field while remaining true to the earlier vision of a scientific account of individual lives.

Great Schools (1930–1950)

When he first proposed his theories at the turn of the century, Freud was controversial and unpopular. However, by the 1930s, his ideas had gained acceptance and respect, and Freud was recognized as a towering intellectual figure. A school of psychoanalytic thought had developed around him, one with notable advocates and dissenters.

Psychoanalytic theory during the 1930s was extended by Freud and others in agreement with his position, as well as by the neoFreudians, theorists who emphasized the role of the environment to a greater degree than did the orthodox Freudians. Anna Freud in 1935, Karen Horney in 1937, Harry Stack Sullivan in 1947, Erich Fromm in 1941, as well as others contributed importantly to psychoanalytic thought.

At the same time, other schools of thought proposing general theories of personality flourished. Carl Jung (1924) and Alfred Adler (1927), who had broken with Freud some time earlier, elaborated their *psychodynamic* theories, attracting many followers. Henry Murray (1938) of TAT fame published *Explorations in Personality,* describing a personality theory based on motivation. He called his approach **personology** to emphasize his interest in understanding the individual person.

Gordon Allport of Harvard University also made numerous contributions to personality psychology during the 1930s. He reported his *Studies in Expressive Movement* (Allport & Vernon, 1933), an investigation into the consistency of behavioral styles, and published a still-used questionnaire that measures *values* (Allport & Vernon, 1931). Most important, *Personality: A Psychological Interpretation* (1937) contained Allport's argument that personality psychology must recognize and study the uniqueness of the individual person. Personality psychology thus stands apart from all other sciences, which are concerned with the general case. This was the first phrasing of the **idiographic-nomothetic** issue, a debate still alive today over whether personality psychology entails understanding the unique (idiographic) or the general (nomothetic).

Other personality schools reflected Gestalt orientations. Kurt Lewin (1935) and Kurt Goldstein (1939) applied gestalt ideas to personality. Goldstein coined the term **self-actualization,** the idea that *people have a drive to fulfill their inner potential, to seek the good gestalt inherent in their personality.* Self-actualization became a central aspect of later theories in humanistic psychology. The idea has even surfaced in television advertisements for the Army: "No one knows that helicopter like you do. . . . Be all that you can be!" Also, Murray and Allport used gestalt ideas in their personality theories, emphasizing that people must be understood as coherent wholes, not in terms of disconnected parts.

Other personality theories of this era were William Sheldon's (1940) *constitutional approach,* a theory of personality based on physique, and Gardner Murphy's (1947) *biosocial approach,* an integration of biological and cultural determinants. Edward C. Tolman (1932) at Berkeley, B.F. Skinner (1938) at Harvard, and Clark L. Hull (1943) at Yale offered influential views about behaviorism. And what else? Lewin and Murray introduced experimentation to the study of personality. And the first textbooks in personality psychology appeared, written by Ross Stagner (1936) and Gordon Allport (1937).

This was an exciting era in personality psychology: bold theories were proposed by bold theorists; students debated their pros and cons; and pioneering applications of personality psychology were made in the classroom, the workplace, and the clinic. Although disagreement characterized the field, so too did great expectations. The use of scientific psychology to answer questions about human nature promised much.

Nevitt Sanford was one noteworthy participant in this age of great schools, a student at Harvard in the 1930s and a faculty member at Berkeley in the 1940s. He writes of this time:

> The most important expectation was that all hands should have intellectual interests. When scholars said to one another, "That's interesting," the reference, almost always, was to ideas, theoretical issues, or research findings that had significance within a theoretical framework.
>
> As to *what* a person was interested in, there was a great diversity, and broad tolerance for the diversity. The spirit of William James walked abroad. People remembered with what satisfaction he had said, after successfully recruiting a philosophical opponent, that now *all* points of view were represented in his department.

Given this value for diversity, which was based on the conviction that no pathway to the truth should be neglected, professors and students had to learn how to differ; they had to familiarize themselves with their opponents' positions and accord them respect, while forthrightly expressing their own views. (1976, p. 757)

The spirit of the time and the university allowed grand theories of personality to be proposed. But, as universities became more specialized, professors and students no longer devoted time and energy to such activities. Instead, research (gathering and publishing data) became more important than theory (proposing general accounts of human nature). Nevertheless, personality psychology continued to attract more than its share of brilliant contributors.

Second Generation Theories (1950–1960)

During the 1950s, important empirical research gave rise to a second generation of personality theories. Each of these theories flowed from one of the grand approaches of the preceding decades, but they were more tied to research findings and somewhat more narrow in scope. One well-known study resulted in *The Authoritarian Personality* (Adorno, Frenkel-Brunswik, Levinson, & Sanford, 1950), an attempt to understand the phenomenon of European Fascism. What was the appeal of such dictators as Mussolini and Hitler? Why had their message been so popular? Why did six million die in concentration camps?

Susceptibility to Fascism was explained with an individual difference called **authoritarianism** comprised of rigid conventionality, submission to authority, prejudice, preoccupation with dominance and submission, coupled with an exaggerated concern with sexual matters (Dillehay, 1978). This personality variable was measured with the F Scale (F = Fascism), which asks respondents to agree or disagree with such statements as:

- Obedience and respect for authority are the most important virtues children should learn.
- An insult to our honor should always be punished.
- People can be divided into two distinct classes: the weak and the strong.
- Homosexuals are hardly better than criminals and ought to be severely punished.

"Yes" answers count toward a high authoritarianism score in each case. The authors of *The Authoritarian Personality* used psychoanalytic and gestalt ideas to explain how certain forms of child-rearing produced the rigid and intolerant authoritarian.

Another important line of personality research beginning in the 1950s was David McClelland's (1961, 1965, 1971) investigations of **achievement**

motivation. Starting with the TAT, McClelland refined techniques for scoring individual differences in the motive to achieve. Applying his techniques to all sorts of material—folk stories, Greek vases, even Dick-and-Jane readers—he was able to predict the subsequent success or failure of individuals as well as societies!

Raymond B. Cattell (1950) and Hans Eysenck (1952b) applied factor analysis to personality measures and proposed theories to interpret the factors of personality they discovered. In both cases, they interpreted these factors in terms of learning theory.

John Dollard and Neal E. Miller (1950) applied Clark Hull's learning theory to personality, particularly to the way that individuals resolved conflicts. We now sprinkle our ordinary conversations with the phrase *approach-avoidance conflict,* first introduced by Dollard and Miller. Harry Harlow's (1958) famous studies of infant monkeys began as an investigation of the claim by Dollard and Miller that love results from satisfying the hunger drive. Harlow disproved this reductionist hypothesis by showing that infant monkeys preferred a cuddly mother surrogate to one that provided nourishment. The way to someone's heart may not always lie through the stomach (but don't tell my mother that).

A number of important personality theories were also proposed by psychotherapists moving beyond their original psychoanalytic training. Erik Erikson (1950) extended psychoanalytic theory to include development across the entire life span. At Ohio State, Julian B. Rotter (1954) articulated his *social learning theory,* which casts principles of learning in field terms and assigns central importance to an individual's expectations about the world. Another Ohio State professor, George Kelly (1955) drew on his years of clinical practice to write his two-volume *Psychology of Personal Constructs,* a theory of personality based on the person-as-scientist metaphor. Carl R. Rogers published *Client-Centered Therapy* in 1951, in which he presented his *cognitive theory of personality and psychotherapy.* According to Rogers, a positive perception of the self is needed for health and happiness: abnormality results from low self-regard; psychotherapy tries to boost self-regard.

Cross-cultural psychology took form as John Whiting and Irving Child (1953) began to use data from various cultures to test explicit hypotheses. Of particular interest were psychoanalytic predictions relating child-rearing practices to adult personality types. Correlations were computed not on the scores of individuals but on the scores of entire societies. For instance, high rates of alcohol use in a society are associated with strong pressures on children to achieve (Child, 1968).

In addition to new personality theories, this era also saw the intensive investigation of specific individual differences measured by particular personality tests. These variables usually originated in some general theory of personality, but in keeping with the increasing specialization of psychology, they often took on a life of their own as the focus of circumscribed research. Herman A. Witkin and his colleagues (1954) studied field dependence and independence; Donn Byrne (1961) investigated repression; Julian Rotter (1966) looked at locus of control; and so on.

My final note about personality psychology in the 1950s concerns Calvin S. Hall and Gardner Lindzey's (1957) exemplary textbook, *Theories of Personality*. This book provided "compact yet comprehensive summaries of the major contemporary theories of personality written at a level of difficulty that is appropriate for undergraduate or graduate instruction" (Hall & Lindzey, 1970, p. ix). The book presents theories successively, and makes comparisons and contrasts in a concluding chapter. *Theories of Personality* proved so popular that most subsequent textbooks in the field acknowledge themselves as pale imitations.

Self-criticism, Doubt, and Crisis (1960–1975)

The 1960s and 1970s were times of turmoil and doubt, in society as a whole as well as in personality psychology. Perhaps the self-criticism reflected some aspect of the Zeitgeist, a realization that the American Dream did not always come true, that science did not hold all the answers for human problems, that the old maps did not describe the new territories. Bob Dylan was right: the times, they were a'changing.

Psychological testing was criticized as a tool of the establishment, a way to rationalize prejudice and preserve the status quo. It had been recognized for years that intelligence tests were culture-bound, but the 1960s brought recommendations that tests therefore be abandoned, and consumer advocate groups instituted lawsuits to bring this about.

Related skepticism surfaced about the wisdom of researchers relying on personality questionnaires. Some feared that personality psychology was becoming the scientific study of questionnaire completion. And questionnaire completion itself might reflect merely a collection of response biases, such as tendencies to answer in socially acceptable ways, to answer extremely (or moderately), even to lie and conceal. "Where's the person in personality research?" asked Rae Carlson (1971) in a well-known review of questionnaire studies.

Psychotherapy was branded ineffective, as critics like Hans Eysenck (1961) marshalled evidence that it did not work. More profoundly, other critics led by Thomas Szasz (1961) attacked the very notion of mental illness, calling it a myth. Perhaps the medical model had nothing to say about problems in living; perhaps the personality theories that embody the medical model, in part or whole, were irrelevant to understanding why people think, feel, and act as they do.

Humanists took issue with the overly mechanistic theories that dominated psychology. Influential approaches like psychoanalysis and behaviorism were seen as relegating people to the role of passive victims, pulled and pushed about by internal drives or external stimuli. Inspired by existential thought, humanistic psychologists called for a psychology broad enough to incorporate what they deemed critical to being human: experience, freedom, choice, meaning, and will. Traditional personality theories were seen as lacking, and psychotherapies based on these theories were branded inevitable failures.

But Stanford psychologist Walter Mischel struck the most telling blow in his 1968 book *Personality and Assessment*. As he describes in the preface to this important work, it began in an attempt to write a textbook on personality psychology, "to survey six or seven equally viable alternative theoretical approaches to personality and to examine the implications of each for personality assessment, psychotherapy, and research" (p. vii). In the course of his library research, though, something unsettling occurred. Mischel concluded from the studies he read that one of the basic assumptions of personality psychology—that people act consistently across situations—was contradicted by the facts.

Personality and Assessment turned into a presentation of these facts and the far-reaching conclusion that people could not be described sensibly in terms of pervasive personality traits. Instead, personality was better understood in terms of the situation in which the person was found, a position fully consistent with the social learning orientation that Mischel espoused. Of course, a situational account of personality is really not personality psychology. Mischel's critique of personality traits therefore went far beyond traits per se and struck at the entire field. To some, the conclusion from *Personality and Assessment* was that personality psychology was dead.

Contemporary Personality Psychology

Was personality psychology really dead? Mischel's (1968) book at first attracted heavy and widespread criticism. The basic data upon which he relied, his strategy of selecting studies, the inferences he made from them, and his social learning alternative to traditional personality psychology were all attacked. However, once the smoke cleared, the book's contributions were recognized, and theorists and researchers began to accommodate them within the field. In 1983, Stephen West wrote:

> From the vantage point of 15 years, it appears that Mischel's *Personality and Assessment* has provided a valuable corrective for the field of personality. It helped precipitate a much needed critical reexamination of the field out of which has emerged a number of genuine contributions and a generally more cautious and precise approach to the prediction of behavior. . . . Personality research has

achieved considerable vitality and a number of researchers are actively addressing these important issues. Far from being a moribund field as some earlier
critics maintained, personality has emerged from its crisis period to become
one of the most exciting areas of research in psychology. (p. 283)

Today, far from being regarded as the individual who did away with personality psychology, Mischel is regarded as one of the field's most important
contributors. He shook things up, and as they settled, they were put together
in new and exciting ways.

Assessment is now approached with more sophistication. The fuzzy nature
of personality has been recognized, so questionnaires are now validated against
a number of behaviors instead of a single criterion (Epstein, 1980). Personality measures that are highly specific are more successful in predicting relevant outcomes than highly general measures (Jaccard, 1974). New techniques for combining the results of different studies—called **meta-analysis**—
have uncovered relationships not otherwise obvious. For instance, meta-
analysis suggests that psychotherapy is effective after all (Smith & Glass,
1977), so millions of psychotherapists can breathe easier (and so can their
clients).

Another reaction to Mischel's book is *interactionism,* a rediscovery of
Lewin's dictum that behavior is the joint product of the person and the situation (Bowers, 1973; Ekehammar, 1974; Endler & Magnusson, 1976a, 1976b).
From this view, personality traits per se do not explain what a person thinks,
says, or does. Neither do situational factors. We must consider the concrete
person in the concrete situation.

Daryl Bem and Andrea Allen (1974) similarly resurrected one of Gordon
Allport's ideas: that people differ in terms of the traits best used to describe
them. Since a trait, by definition, is shown only when a person acts consistently, then it follows that some traits only apply to some people. Said another
way, different people have different traits. These researchers demonstrated
that impressive consistency in behaviors reflecting a trait like conscientiousness does indeed exist for folks nominating themselves as consistent, but
not for others.

New ways to study individual lives with *psychobiography* and *psychohistory* appeared (Runyan, 1982), and several ambitious longitudinal studies
found impressive coherence in personality over decades (Block, 1971; Vaillant, 1977). Henry Murray's (1938) vision of a scientific personology again
took form.

In the last decade, personality psychology has become increasingly cognitive. In his 1968 review, Mischel did find evidence for consistency of cognitive characteristics like field dependence-independence. Kelly's (1955) *personal construct theory* is now more popular than ever, as are newer formulations
like Albert Bandura's (1977a) *self-efficacy theory* that regard personality as
the way people think about themselves and the world. Mischel (1979) calls

these cognitive characteristics **person variables** to distinguish them from traits, but they still refer to individual differences that are general and enduring.

Finally, textbooks are being written that describe the personality psychology renaissance. From 1954 until just a few years ago, the Hall and Lindzey book defined all that a personality text should be: a systematic comparison and contrast of traditional personality theories. However, such a presentation of the field no longer reflects the reality. Gerald Mendelsohn (1983) believes that "A text on theories of personality will provide an inadequate and, more important, distorted picture of the field; the course in theories of personality . . . is an anachronism" (p. 435).

I hope to convey what personality psychologists actually do in the 1980s. Matters of theory are still important, but so too are research and applications. Current activities in personality psychology follow from past activities, and so the traditional theories remain important for understanding the field as it currently stands. However, personality psychology is now much more than a catalogue of theories from the 1930s. The great theories have evolved into general orientations that influence the particular activities of present personality psychology. These orientations—or paradigms— are the subject of my next chapter.

To conclude the present chapter, I believe that the complexity of personality psychology stems in part from its diverse ancestors, so the contemporary personality psychologist must master many skills: design a laboratory experiment; interview a patient; be conversant with human neurology and physiology; administer a Rorschach test; compute a correlation coefficient; work in academic and applied settings; implement a vocational training program; and most important, integrate these skills into the scientific investigation of what is general, characteristic, enduring, and functional about the individual person. The history of personality psychology explains where the need for each of these skills originated.

SUMMARY

Although personality psychology made its earliest appearance in age-old classifications of types of people, the history of the field clearly begins in the 1800s when three fields emerged: experimental psychology, psychiatry, and psychological testing. These fields were the immediate ancestors of personality psychology as we now know it. In this chapter, I described the histories of these ancestors, which partly overlap and partly do not. All began as scientific and philosophical trends that came together in nineteenth century Europe.

In 1879, Wilhelm Wundt founded the first experimental psychology laboratory. His approach to psychology, now called **structuralism,** has since
passed into disfavor, but it stimulated vigorous opposition in the form of
three approaches that still affect the field, including its approach to personality. **Gestalt psychology** was concerned with the patterns inherent in experience. **Functionalism** stressed mind-in-use; its focus on the consequences
of behavior gave rise to applied psychology. Finally, **behaviorism** called for
a study of what was observable—overt behavior rather than subjective experience—thus popularizing theories of learning.

Psychiatry resulted from the application of the **medical model** to problems in living. According to this model, illness and disease result from mal-
functions of the body, so perhaps mental difficulties are similarly produced.
Jean Charcot and Pierre Janet studied hysteria and devised ways to treat it.
The young Sigmund Freud, studying in France, kindled an interest in hysteria
that resulted in psychoanalytic theory, a metaphorical neurology of the mind.

The testing tradition started in England with the work of Darwin's cousin,
Sir Francis Galton, who was interested in intelligence and interpreted it in
evolutionary terms. He invented psychological tests and pioneered statistical
techniques with which to interpret their results. Psychological testing was
given further boosts by James McKeen Cattell in the United States and Alfred
Binet in France. Tests of personality characteristics followed the example of
intelligence tests.

Personality psychology as a discrete field cohered in the 1930s in the
work of charismatic theorists like Freud, Allport, Murray, and Lewin. Additional personality theories were proposed throughout the 1950s in conjunction with a variety of studies and applications. In the 1960s, personality psychology began a period of intensive self-criticism marked by Walter Mischel's
1968 critique of personality traits as useless fictions. Personality psychology
recovered from this attack by accepting Mischel's arguments and making
breakthroughs in theory, measurement, and research. Today personality psychology is a thriving endeavor.

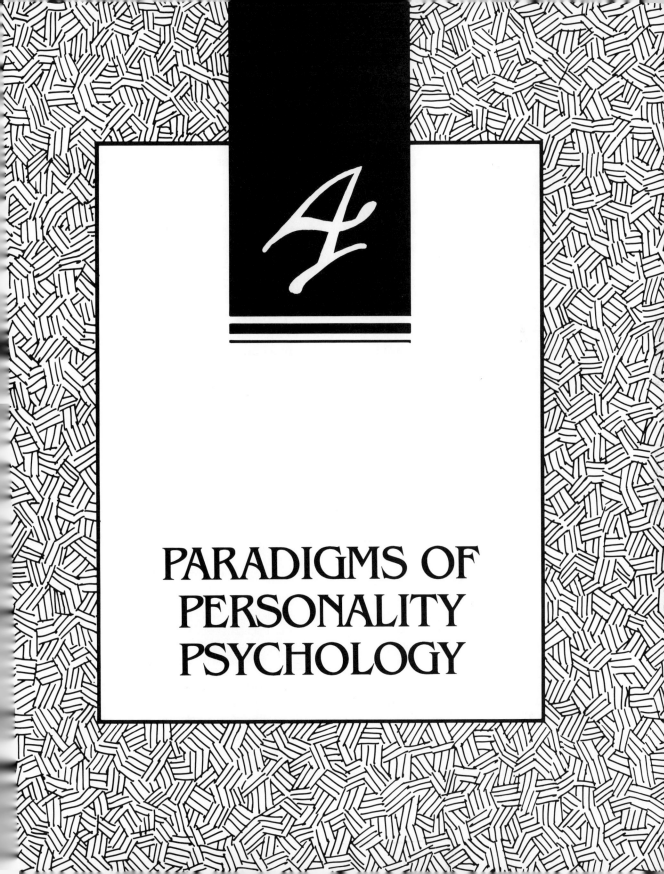

4

PARADIGMS OF
PERSONALITY
PSYCHOLOGY

Some activities are highly prescribed; by consensus, there is one and only one way to go about them. Making a hamburger at McDonald's, filling out a loan application, and performing long division are invariably done the same way by almost all people. In contrast, other activities are quite loosely prescribed. Again by consensus, there are dozens of ways to go about them. Shopping for groceries, packing a suitcase, and decorating an apartment are done in different ways by almost all people. So, activities can be classified along a dimension of uniformity versus idiosyncrasy.

So too can we classify the sciences. In some cases, scientists agree about the best way to propose a theory, conduct a study, and apply the results. In other cases, they disagree. Theory, research, and application are almost a matter of taste. Where does personality psychology fall along this continuum?

As I see the field, it's someplace in the middle. There is neither high nor low agreement regarding the best way to go about it. More than one perspective in personality psychology exists, but not an infinity of them. Indeed, the number is quite small—three to be exact, and they are the subject of the remainder of this book. In this chapter, I will present an overview of the important concerns of the three personality perspectives with regard to theory, research, and application.

SCIENTIFIC PARADIGMS: WEBS OF BELIEF

In science, what I have been calling a perspective is referred to as a **paradigm.** This term has various meanings, captured by such synonyms as procedure, framework, and approach applied in the broadest sense to a science.

> "Scientific paradigm" . . . refers to the total complex of a science. It includes the language, theories, conceptual schemas, methods, and limits of the science. It determines which aspects of the world the scientist studies and the kinds of explanations he considers. Most important, it includes the way the scientist sees the data, laws, and theories of his science. (McCain & Segal, 1973, p. 81)

In other words, a scientific paradigm is a *worldview,* a set of related assumptions and values that the scientist uses while going about scientific activities.

The gestalt psychologists introduced the ideas of **figure and ground** to convey that we perceive objects (figures) against backdrops (grounds). These terms can aid our understanding of a scientific paradigm. A given theory, study, or application is the figure which holds our attention, while the paradigm is the ground against which it makes sense. We attend more to the figure than to the ground, but only because the ground allows us to do so. In essence, *scientific paradigms are the background assumptions that dictate the particulars of a science and allow us to understand them.*

A scientific paradigm is usually implicit, in that the scientist is mostly unaware of it in day-to-day activities. Indeed, scientists may not even be able to articulate all that is involved in the paradigm within which they work. That doesn't really matter. What is important is that the paradigm underlies what is done. Consider the grammar of the English language. When we speak, or listen, or read, or write, we are usually not aware of grammar. And if called upon, most of us cannot be explicit about the particular rules. However, with little trouble, we can say about a particular sentence, "Gee, that sounds wrong" or "Yeah, that sounds alright to me." So, we use grammar to understand what is grammatical. And the scientist uses a paradigm to understand what is scientific.

The assumptions that comprise a scientific paradigm are coherent. They are related to each other, so that the paradigm as a whole has a given character. One's theory of personality, for instance, tells one to use certain research techniques, and not others. One's research in turn results in certain findings to be accommodated by a certain theory, and not others.

Mechanistic explanations of personality, like social learning theory, often rely on experiments, and this makes sense in terms of the paradigm involved. Experiments manipulate situational factors (causes) and measure the consequences (effects). Mechanistic theories demand experimental research, since no better way exists to investigate them. At the same time, experiments yield results pointing to the importance of situational causes. As a necessary consequence of experimentation, internal determinants of behavior are overlooked, as are individual differences. Experimental research demands mechanistic theories.

Philosophers W. V. Quine and J. S. Ullian (1978) describe the interrelatedness of any system of beliefs, including scientific paradigms, as a web. Particular beliefs are woven together with other beliefs, and we judge a given fact in terms of how well it fits within the entire web of beliefs. Some beliefs are more central than others, because they bear upon a large number of other beliefs. We are reluctant to give these up because doing so would entail an overhaul of our entire system:

> When our system of beliefs supports our expectation of some event and that event does not occur, we have the problem of selecting certain of our interlocking beliefs for revision. This is what happens when an experiment is made to check a scientific theory and the result is not what the theory predicted. The scientist then has to revise his theory somehow; he must drop some one or another, at least, of the beliefs which together implied the false prediction. (p. 20)

The scientific paradigm tells one which beliefs are to be revised in the face of contrary evidence. The paradigm itself is rarely changed. It is where you stand to paint the floor. You can't very well paint the same place on which you are standing.

Thomas Kuhn (1970), a historian of science, uses the notion of scientific paradigm to explain change. According to Kuhn (1970), science does not evolve slowly and surely. Instead, it changes in leaps and bounds, in what he calls *paradigm shifts,* as if the channel selector on your television set were suddenly spun. Kuhn describes these rapid changes as *revolutions,* since they entail the replacement of one paradigm with another.

Most of the time, scientists work within a given paradigm, conducting research, making slight corrections in theory, and so on. The basic paradigm is unaffected by these activities, which Kuhn calls *ordinary science.* But it may happen that anomalous findings occur, or that theoretical contradictions surface. Kuhn believes the science then enters a *crisis state.* Problematic findings or deductions are either ignored or swept away, or a new paradigm emerges to accommodate them. If the new perspective wins out, then a revolution has occurred, as surely as the Bolsheviks replaced the Czar of Russia in 1917.

You might compare the process of scientific revolution described by Kuhn to the more familiar phenomenon of religious conversion. Perhaps a friend or family member (or even you) have made a dramatic change in the way that religion (or politics or sexuality) is regarded. Whether this involved taking on new beliefs, discarding old ones, or both, the conversion was a radical change in perspective. All thought, actions, and feelings were affected. A paradigm shift occurred, no doubt precipitated by some event or belief that could not be accommodated within the old way of thinking about things.

Kuhn based his theory of scientific change on the physical sciences, using physics as his primary example. The Copernican paradigm gave way to the Newtonian paradigm, which in turn gave way to the new physics of Einstein (for a readable history of this process, see Zukav, 1979). Kuhn hesitates to extend his ideas to the social sciences, which he considers *pre-paradigmatic.*

In other words, the social sciences—including psychology—have not matured to the point where a single paradigm dominates scientific activity. I have to agree with Kuhn on this point, since I see at least three major perspectives regarding proper science within personality psychology alone. However, I think that Kuhn's ideas are still quite useful in the social sciences, because they help make sense of what otherwise seems a hodgepodge of theories, methods, and applications.

It is not an accident that personality psychologists who favor a particular theory also favor a particular research method, nor is it an accident that they make only certain applications of their ideas. The activities of personality psychologists are clustered together, and these clusters seem pretty much what Kuhn calls paradigms.

At the same time, they are not exactly what he means by a paradigm because several of them exist at the same time, overlapping in some ways (but not in others). Consider Kuhn's paradigm a prototype of the way science is conducted, and consider the personality paradigms that I will discuss here as fuzzy examples of this prototype.

Paradigm shifts occur among the fuzzy perspectives of personality psychology, as well. These may not always supplant earlier perspectives, but they arise in response to anomalies, and they represent a profoundly different way to regard personality. When Freud introduced the idea of childhood sexuality, he did so to explain some puzzling aspects of hysteria. Personality psychology has not been the same since. And hysteria has all but vanished! Ideas are powerful.

Why are there only three paradigms of personality psychology? If a paradigm is a point of view, there surely can be more than three of them. Hypothetically, I'm sure this is the case. But the history of personality psychology provided only so many raw ingredients to combine into points of view about how to conduct personality psychology.

Additionally, remember that personality psychology tries to explain personality. There are only so many paradigms for personality psychology because there are only so many ways to explain what is general, characteristic, enduring, and functional about an individual.

ROOT METAPHORS: BASIC FORMS OF EXPLANATION

History shows that explanations change. When they do, it is not just in their details, but also in their very nature. Consider the question "Why did you leave the room?" It requires an explanation, but several are possible. Thus

"I left the room because it was too hot."

"I left the room because I wanted to."

"I left the room because I wasn't interested in what was being said."

"I left the room because I'm not the sort of person who can sit still too long."

"I left the room because it was time to leave."

"I left the room because I was afraid."

"I left the room because I was thirsty."

"I left the room because my business there was through."

"Why did I leave the room? You really should ask why I stayed as long as I did."

These all might be perfectly reasonable explanations in response to the question, but they answer it in different ways. One explanation points to a characteristic of personality ("I'm not the sort of person who can sit still . . ."), and another to a cause in the situation ("It was hot . . ."). Yet another points to a developmental factor ("It was time . . .") or to an interaction between the person and the situation ("My business was through . . ."). And still another "explanation" may even be the denial that anything needs to be explained.

In *World Hypotheses,* the philosopher Steven Pepper (1942) formally catalogued the different forms that explanation takes, and his system helps us identify the paradigms of personality psychology. Pepper argues that a coherent explanation has at its basis a *root metaphor,* a format that must be satisfied. Four of these root metaphors are particularly relevant to personality psychology. Past and present explanations of personality have used these root metaphors, usually individually but sometimes in combination, adding—once again—to the fuzziness of the endeavor.

Formism is *explanation by categorization, specifying some form that captures the essence of the phenomenon.* When the category into which something falls is specified, then the explanation is done. Personality typologies are good examples of formist explanation, as are some of our most crass stereotypes. "Oh, he's a mesomorph . . . what more do you need to know?" "She's a Sagittarius and a vegetarian . . . that explains it all, doesn't it?" "He's Jewish . . . can't you tell?

Mechanism is *explanation in terms of causes, necessary and sufficient conditions that precede the phenomenon of concern.* Once the causes are

Formism

Mechanism

specified, then the phenomenon has been explained, since it is the "effect" of the cause. In Chapter 2, I described the mechanistic model of human nature, and theories that embrace such a model are good examples of mechanistic explanation. For instance, learning theories attribute our current behavior to our past experience. We feel nauseated when we smell Southern Comfort (effect) because two weeks ago we drank too much and vomited (cause).

Organicism, Pepper's third category of root metaphor, is *explanation in terms of the unfolding of an inherent nature*. When the particular stage in this process has been specified, then a satisfactory explanation has been provided for the phenomenon that is undergoing the process. Many biological theories of development fall within this category. Remember the discussion of mitosis from your high school biology class? Cells divide in a certain sequence because it is in their nature to develop in such a way, to unfold in keeping with their genetic blueprint. Psychological theories of development, particularly stage theories that assume discontinuities in development, are good examples of organicist explanation. Piaget's theory of cognitive development posits stages through which individuals pass in an invariant sequence.

Finally, **contextualism** is *explanation in terms of the interdependence of a phenomenon and its context*. Once this give-and-take has been specified, explanation is done. Field theories are good examples of contextualist explanation, since the notion of a field explicitly assumes that a phenomenon is defined by its context. Also, certain cognitive theories of personality embody

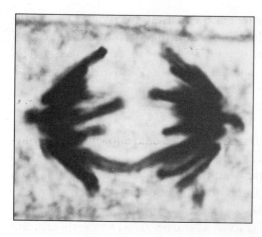

Organicism

SOURCE: Photograph by Carolina Biological Supply
Company.

this type of explanation, since they propose that the person is embedded in a social context. One cannot speak of people apart from their social world, and one cannot speak of the social world apart from people. Neither is assigned priority—one is not the cause of the other. Instead, people and the social world reciprocally define each other.

Contextualism

SOURCE: M. C. Escher, *Realitivity*, 1953. National Gallery of Art, Washington, D.C.

It's not always obvious that equally good explanations may take the radically different forms that Pepper describes, and this accounts for some of the quarrels within personality psychology. Disagreements between two points of view occur not just over the details of an explanation, but additionally over what qualifies as a good explanation. Unfortunately, this latter disagreement can be unstated, and arguments occur at cross-purposes.

Proponents of trait approaches to personality often conflict with those who favor learning approaches. Each side produces data showing that behavior can be well-explained by properties of the person or of the situation, respectively. Each side then concludes that the other side is wrong. What this particular argument misses is that the bottom line is not always dictated by data. Rather, the bottom line may be the favored root metaphor. Trait theorists usually endorse formist explanations, which learning theorists criticize because they neglect the situation (that is, causes). Conversely, learning theorists usually go with mechanistic explanations, which trait theorists criticize for neglecting the person (that is, forms).

Which side is right? Well, it depends on what you are trying to do. There is no one best explanation for all purposes. As you have already seen, personality psychology has many purposes, demanding different root metaphors. And each of the major paradigms of personality emphasizes one of the root metaphors that prescribes a satisfactory explanation.

First, the **psychoanalytic paradigm** employs the organicism metaphor. As I described in the last chapter, psychoanalysis emerged from psychiatry, and psychiatry in turn resulted from the application of the medical model to problems in living. Throughout this historical process, theorists used biological explanations. Freud's theory of psychosexual development describes the unfolding of an inherent nature, as the individual passes through stages defined by the part of the body that provides gratification. More generally, the psychoanalytic paradigm assumes that people are complex energy systems. The way that this energy seeks discharge is determined by the person's stage of development.

Research within the psychoanalytic tradition tends to favor the **case history** method, intensive examination of a single individual over time. Case histories are derived from medical records, which in turn are similar to the early descriptions of naturalists. What better way to understand the unfolding of inner nature than to describe this process as it occurs to an individual in a natural habitat?

Most applications stemming from the psychoanalytic paradigm attempt to reroute an individual's instinctive energy. Psychoanalytic therapy aims at freeing the energy devoted to neurotic symptoms. Once released, it becomes available for other—presumably healthier—purposes. Other psychoanalytic applications provide outlets for people's sexual and aggressive drives. Your college no doubt has an extensive intramural program. Part of the rationale for sports is to cultivate sportsmanship and the like, but the rest of the rationale is to divert your not-so-nice instincts into harmless outlets. No one ever got pregnant from a high five.

Other applications use the organicism metaphor to interpret all manner of cultural products—art, literature, music, religion, even graffiti and television commercials ("All my men wear English leather, or they wear nothing at all . . .")—as reflecting the incessant striving of our inner drives for satisfaction. Some artists, such as Salvador Dali, have self-consciously used psychoanalytic theory to help them choose symbols.

Second, the **trait paradigm** makes use of the formist metaphor. Whether the category where a person is placed is defined by a type, a trait, or a factor, proponents of this paradigm assume that satisfactory explanation resides in such placement. In Chapter 3, I showed how the trait paradigm developed from functionalism and the psychological testing tradition, the purpose being to identify stable and enduring individual differences. Whatever the difference, it determined adaptation, and success or failure was explained by pointing to the individual's score—whether on an intelligence test, the F Scale, or the MMPI.

Research within the trait paradigm centers on personality tests, usually questionnaires. Large numbers of subjects are studied at a given time to obtain considerable variation in characteristics. Success or failure at adaptation is also measured in this research, and correlations between the individual difference of concern and the measure of adaptation are computed. Of relatively minor concern within the trait paradigm is change, since traits—by definition—are thought not to vary.

Accordingly, applications of the trait approach try to describe and predict how individuals behave more than they try to change people. The goal of psychological testing in the workplace, the school, and the clinic is to tell it like it is, under the assumption that how it is is how it will be. *Amelioration* consists of matching the person to the right setting. Placement in a job, a school, or a therapy program is a typical application within the trait paradigm.

Third, the **cognitive paradigm** uses contextualism as its root metaphor. The basic concept of this paradigm is that a person's thoughts and beliefs provide the key to understanding behavior. Remember, these thoughts and beliefs have specific reference to the world. One does not simply have an attitude; one has an attitude about something: authority, motherhood, the Democratic Party, cable television, and so on. If you were told in high school that you had an attitude problem, I think the person who told you that meant that you didn't like him, and he didn't like that. At any rate, your thoughts and beliefs are a product not just of you but also of the world. The cognitive paradigm grew out of the gestalt psychology tradition, which regarded perception as the joint product of the world (stimuli) and the perceiver (tendencies to seek good gestalts).

Research within the cognitive paradigm relies on an individual's self-report, since the best way to understand perceived reality is to ask the person who perceives it. Sometimes these perceptions are assessed with a questionnaire, like Rotter's (1966) locus of control scale, which I described earlier. Sometimes these perceptions are measured with an interview. And sometimes they are inferred from the way a person has acted: "Since she gave up at the task she probably believes it has no solution." Of particular interest to the cognitive paradigm is the way a person establishes congruence among beliefs.

Consider, for a moment, Leon Festinger's (1957) cognitive dissonance theory. Festinger studied with Kurt Lewin, and the theory of cognitive dissonance is merely a special case of the Lewinian assumption that people restore equilibrium to their life space after a disturbance, in this case, the realization that attitudes and actions are discrepant.

Within the cognitive paradigm, applications of theory and research try to change the way that a person sees things. Let me emphasize that this does not involve telling someone that problems are just in his mind. Instead, the cognitive paradigm proposes that one's point of view reflects the way the world is just as much as it reflects the way a person's head works. Cognitive therapy attempts to change the person-in-the-world. Therapy for depression, for instance, encourages a person to think better of himself while also advising him to seek out friends who will confirm this belief (Beck, Rush, Shaw, & Emery, 1979).

The root metaphor of mechanism may be introduced into all of these paradigms, although it is most comfortable within experimental psychology and especially behaviorism. Psychoanalytic approaches, trait approaches, and cognitive approaches may invoke causes, and when they do, they reflect the cause-effect thinking of mechanism. They also end up mixing their metaphors. In some cases, this is fine and adds a level of understanding to what the particular paradigm provides.

An individual's passage through the psychosexual stages can be thwarted by environmental events, for instance, and subsequent functioning might thereby be disrupted. Similarly, a trait might have an environmental cause, as internal locus of control appears to in certain forms of childrearing that employ suggestion more than direction: "Why don't you try it like this" versus "Do it this way" (Loeb, 1975). And a general belief about a group of people may be caused by a particular experience with a representative of this group (Cook, 1969).

In other cases, mixing mechanism with another metaphor is confusing, since it creates circular explanations. At their worst, psychoanalytic theory, trait theory, and cognitive theory all fall prey to the same shortcoming: they employ their favored explanation as a cause of some behavior, and use the behavior as evidence for the cause. Nothing is accomplished by such an exercise. To say that a psychosexual stage is the cause of compulsive behavior is to say nothing if the only sign of the stage is compulsivity. Ditto for traits and cognitions.

Mechanism requires that one specify a causal sequence, not a causal circle. Usually, this sequence travels outside the individual, so that the cause itself is not part of his or her personality. The root metaphor of mechanism seems most useful in personality psychology as an adjunct to the other metaphors, not as a replacement. A wholly mechanistic account of personality is unwieldy, since personality means more than environmental causes.

THEORY IN PERSONALITY PSYCHOLOGY

The root metaphor of a personality paradigm is the essence of the paradigm's theory. However, I want to say more about theory in personality psychology, since a root metaphor is not the same thing as a personality theory. Scientific theories are much more complex than the metaphors they embrace. Theories are sets of conventions created by theorists; these conventions involve assumptions about the real world, interrelations among these assumptions, and explicit definitions (or operationalizations) about how one moves from observations about the world to theoretical assumptions (Hall & Lindzey, 1970, pp. 10–12).

Whether theories are strictly true or false is not a reasonable criterion by which to judge them. Instead, theories are useful or not, and any particular theory must be regarded as tentative, to be used until a better theory—for the purpose at hand—comes along. And what are the purposes of a personality theory? As I discussed in the last chapter on the history of personality psychology, the field has served various masters. Let me enumerate some of the more important of these.

A Personality Theory Must Account for Known Facts   We know a lot about personality: general, characteristic, enduring, and functional aspects of a person. A personality theory must speak to what we know. I sometimes suggest to my students that they start to read the *Washington Post* or the *Chicago Tribune* from front to back, attempting to explain each fact they encounter from the perspective of some psychological theory. When they get stuck on some particular fact, they should stop and note the page number. This is a quantitative measure of how well the theory accounts for miscellaneous facts.

Personality theories almost always get someone a lot farther than do other psychological theories. What can a theory of memory do for the reader of the *Post* or the *Tribune?* In the days of Watergate, it could explain—after a fashion—the lapses of recall that made headlines. But, most of the time, theories of memory don't explain too many facts in the paper. How about a theory of psychophysiology? It depends on the particular news stories. Maybe someone climbed a tower and shot at passersby. Maybe this madman had a brain tumor.

In contrast, theories of personality explain the headlines in Section A: politics, war, murder, arson, Sean Penn punching this, that, or whatever; they account for the human interest topics in Section B: Ann Landers, popular adventure movies, exercise books by celebrities, another craze from California; they explain the business facts in Section C: interest rates up, building rates down, Christmas spending steady, Tylenol not selling at all; they help us account for facts in the sports pages of Section D: Dwight, George, and Ted in the summer—Magic, Bird, and the Great One in the winter—and so on.

Why are theories of personality so general? Unlike other psychological theories, personality theories apply to people, not to parts of people. As you saw in Chapter 1, most things that people do fall under the heading of personality. Personality theories must be applicable to the whole spectrum of human activities. And these theories often originated in the attempt to explain abnormal behavior. Why do the symptoms of hysteria co-occur? Why do alcoholics drink to the point of violent illness? Why do depressed people kill themselves? A personality theory must be able to explain a lot.

As if this were not enough, the theory is expected to work in a simple fashion. Brevity of explanation, or **parsimony,** is one of the virtues to which a theory aspires. Consider this saying among doctors attempting a diagnosis: "When you hear hoofbeats, think horses, not zebras." They remind themselves to attempt explanation in a mundane fashion before reaching for an exotic account.

Watson's behaviorism was so popular in psychology because it promised to account for all sorts of facts with a few simple principles of learning. Of course, there is often a tradeoff between the scope of a theory and its simplicity, and some argue that comprehensiveness and efficiency require an inevitable compromise (Thorngate, 1976). Psychoanalysis is the most comprehensive personality theory; it is also the most complex.

A Personality Theory Must Generate New Facts   Scientists do more than look backwards to rationalize what has already happened. Important as post-diction may be, the true test of any scientific theory is prediction. Can the theory tell the future? Can it specify what will happen granted the fulfillment of certain conditions? All personality theories involve a number of assumptions about how to predict future thoughts, feelings, and actions. The most general forecast relies on *psychological inertia:* past behavior predicts future behavior. Most personality theories make this prediction, although we have already seen that it is far from universally true. More precise predictions specify when the past is continuous with the future, and when it is not.

Personality psychology research allows a test of how well a particular theory can predict the future. Will the new facts gathered in research (data) be accommodated within the theory? Different theories emphasize different sorts of data, but in each case, they are explicit about how the theory is supported or denied by new facts.

A Personality Theory Must Be Useful to the Practitioner   Personality psychology is pragmatic, and theories must not wilt outside the ivory tower. Can they be used by personality psychologists who work in clinics, schools, or industries to make concrete decisions about specific individuals? If personality theories were used only to account for esoteric facts or to adjudicate hair-splitting debates, considerable latitude could be exercised in choosing among theories.

However, applications of personality psychology bear critically upon the lives of individuals and upon the course of society. A personality theory must be explicit about assessment procedures. Are psychological tests reliable and valid? Anyone who wants to go to college, medical school, or law school should care about the answers to these questions. So should anyone who seeks help from a psychotherapist. Applications of personality psychology affect your life, and you should hope that reasonable theories dictate them.

Most personality theories are also explicit about development and change. How and why do they occur? Can they be facilitated by parents, teachers, or other responsible adults? Can they be thwarted by poverty, ignorance, or prejudice? Can they be corrected by therapy or other social interventions? A personality theory needs to answer these questions.

Within these general guidelines, personality theories show considerable variability. Even theories classified within the same paradigm differ. What are the individual differences among personality theories? Consider that every personality theory has to provide an answer to the following questions.

What Aspect of Personality Is Explained?

Personality refers to a variety of human activities. Although most personality theories attempt to be general, each invariably does a better job explaining some of the things meant by personality than it does explaining other things.

George Kelly (1955) calls this aspect of a theory its **range of convenience.** In other words, to what behaviors is it most applicable? These comprise the theory's range of convenience. To what behaviors is the theory awkward or irrelevant? These fall outside the range.

In the era of the great schools of psychological thought, theories mostly had wide ranges of convenience. They aspired to be general theories of behavior, and most therefore accounted for personality as a special case of general behavior. In recent years, psychology has moved away from general theories to more circumscribed explanations. Only in personality psychology do we still find theories attempting broad applicability.

However, even among personality theories, there is variation in the range of convenience. Not surprisingly, most cognitive theories best explain conscious thoughts and beliefs, while emotions fall outside their range. Some writers call emotions *hot cognition* to distinguish them from the cool, calm, and collected thought best explained by the typical cognitive theory (Abelson, 1963).

Behavioral theories do their best job explaining discrete behaviors that occur at a *rate,* since the rate of an activity is under the sway of environmental rewards and punishments. More diffuse and more covert actions, for which a rate is unimportant or nonsensical, fall outside the range of convenience. Fear of avocadoes can easily be explained within the behavioral paradigm, since a person with such a fear shows varying degrees of fear-related activities, like walking fast or slow in the presence of guacamole. In contrast, existential dread—the sense that life is meaningless—cannot be accommodated within the behavioral paradigm since it is not a discrete behavior, and it hardly occurs at a rate.

One of the most impressive things about psychoanalytic theory is the range of topics that it can explain. Indeed, almost all things human admit to explanation within the psychoanalytic paradigm: jokes, Marilyn Monroe, art, music, Richard Nixon, religion, slips of the tongue, the Goodyear Blimp, leaders, followers, Prince, masochism, Carol Doda, fear of flying, cigarette smoking, nose picking, love, hate, ambivalence, even the fear that avocadoes have no meaning.

But the broad range of convenience possessed by the psychoanalytic paradigm does not automatically lend it preferred status. Indeed, this paradigm is often criticized because it achieves breadth at the cost of simplicity. Mundane behaviors that are quite easily explained by more circumscribed theories are attacked with the same complexity that psychoanalytic theory brings to bear on diffuse and unusual behaviors.

In sum, the different personality paradigms have different ranges of convenience. Each paradigm does a better or worse job explaining specific aspects of personality. Once again, we see why we must evaluate personality theories in light of particular goals and purposes.

What Units Are Employed?

Gordon Allport (1961) regards this as the most fundamental question for personality psychology. Let us examine what he means by a *unit* in personality theory:

> Man's nature, like all of nature, is composed of relatively stable structures. The success of psychological science, therefore, as of any science, depends in part upon its ability to identify the significant units of which its assigned portion of the cosmos is composed. Without its table of elements chemistry could not exist. Where would physics be without its quanta, or biology without the cell? All science is analytic, and *analysis* means "to loosen or unbind" . . . .
>
> It is often said that personality is "far behind" other sciences because psychology cannot discover its fundamental units. . . . Something must account for the *recurrences* and *stabilities* in personal behavior. Although we admit that units cannot exist in a "pure state" . . . , still we do find that personality is relatively stable over time and in different situational fields. How can we account for this fact unless we search for some sort of structures? (pp. 311–312)

Units therefore explain the recurrence and stability of personality.

The history of personality psychology could well be told in terms of the rise and fall of different units of explanation. Humours, faculties, instincts, drives, needs, values, sentiments, temperaments, traits, habits, and factors have all had their champions as the best way to describe and explain personality. But none of these units has won general acceptance.

Perhaps the problem in finding the basic units of personality lies in the multiplicity of candidates, and their variation in complexity and generality. Contrast the narrow habit with the general trait. Even more global units include the fundamental project of existential thought and the lifestyle of common vernacular. Why are there so many units of personality? I think because we can sensibly describe personality in terms of them all, with no description more fundamental than any other.

The purpose at hand usually dictates the choice of units. Each of the personality paradigms therefore has a set of terms to describe and explain what people do, and these units range from general to specific. Take, for example, the psychoanalytic paradigm. It proposes instincts and drives as units of personality, but also invokes specific defense mechanisms as well as general character types. And the trait paradigm describes and explains with personal dispositions, but also with more specific habits and more general factors. Finally, the cognitive paradigm invokes thoughts and beliefs, which go from specific ideas ("I like to stick my hand in fans") to general styles of processing information.

What Model of Human Nature Is Assumed?

Remember the models of human nature that I described in Chapter 2? Articulating such metaphors is a common activity of personality psychologists. A particular paradigm relies on one or more of these metaphors, using them to help predict and understand what people actually do.

The psychoanalytic paradigm uses a host of related biological metaphors (people as animals, people as energy systems); the cognitive paradigm is fond of different metaphors (people as fields, people as computers, people as scientists); while the trait paradigm uses the largest array of metaphors, each in accordance with the particular trait being studied.

A model of human nature explicitly states what people are like. Just as importantly, a model implicitly conveys a statement about what is irrelevant to human nature. Models preclude as well as include, and thus serve the paradigm in its role as a filter or template for the personality psychologist.

What Stance Is Taken on Fundamental Issues?

What are the basic issues that separate the personality paradigms (Wertheimer, 1972)? First, the paradigms differ in regarding individuals as *masters of their fate versus victims.* How much control do people have over their thoughts, actions, and feelings? The psychoanalytic paradigm and the trait paradigm accord less purposiveness to people than does the cognitive paradigm. Only in this latter personality approach is choice given serious consideration.

Second, the paradigms differ in their view of people as *good versus evil.* Although a given personality theory usually won't employ such straightforward moral language, these evaluations are implied by most. The psychoanalytic paradigm paints a dark picture of human nature. People have inherently selfish drives, held in check by a coercive society. The trait paradigm characterizes people as amoral, playing out the cards dealt to them by fate. And the cognitive paradigm regards people as inherently well-intentioned; as described in Chapter 2, an ostensible evil like prejudice is explained as confusion.

Third, the paradigms take different positions with respect to emphasizing the *mind versus the body.* Explanations tend to be phrased in either mental or physical terms. The psychoanalytic paradigm explains mental events, but it does so with the metaphor of neurology. As you will see in the next chapter, Freud's (1950) "project for a scientific psychology" was a bold attempt to explain mind in terms of body. Although unfinished, this project stamped the psychoanalytic paradigm with the materialism that still characterizes it. Similarly, the trait paradigm, derived from evolutionary thought, favors a physical explanation. Allport (1961) described personal traits as neurologically based, and more contemporary trait theories look for a genetic basis to these characteristics (Buss & Plomin, 1975; Loehlin & Nichols, 1976). Finally, the cognitive paradigm, not surprisingly, is *mentalistic.* If its proponents were to solve the mind-body problem of philosophy, they would not do so by sacrificing the reality of mental events (Lewontin, Rose, & Kamin, 1984).

Fourth, personality paradigms differ in their orientation toward *subjectivity versus objectivity.* What is the best way to understand someone, from the inside or the outside? Both the psychoanalytic paradigm and the cognitive paradigm opt for the inside view, under the assumption that psychological reality is not the same thing as physical reality. Different people live in different worlds defined by their varying needs, drives, thoughts, beliefs, and values. In contrast, the trait paradigm takes the outside view. Psychological tests were never really interested in the processes involved in test performance. Instead, the pragmatic emphasis was on the observable consequences of these hidden processes, the actual test performance.

Fifth, personality paradigms explain behavior by *factors in the past versus factors in the immediate present.* This then-now distinction is of course one of relative emphasis, but both the psychoanalytic and trait paradigms lean toward the then and away from the now. Psychoanalysts trace current actions to early childhood experiences, and some versions of psychoanalytic theory assume that personality is fixed by adolescence. (Now that's a chilling thought if you weren't the starting quarterback or the head cheerleader in high school!) Trait theorists also regard adult dispositions as originating in childhood, or even in the moment of conception. The cognitive paradigm, in contrast, takes a nonhistorical view of behavior. What a person does is determined by the psychological field as it immediately exists. If one runs from a burning building, it might simply be that it is hot; information about past events adds little to the explanation.

Sixth, the paradigms of personality psychology take different positions with respect to the *nature versus nurture* controversy. The trait paradigm clearly embraces the genetic determination of behavior, while the cognitive paradigm chooses the opposite view. The psychoanalytic paradigm often embraces both notions. In explaining the obsessional neurosis of a patient known as the Rat Man (because of his fears of rats), Freud (1909b) enumerated various experiential factors that produced the problem and additionally pointed to a constitutional weakness that allowed the environmental events to do damage.

Finally, the different personality paradigms vary in terms of *simplicity versus complexity.* How many principles are suggested? How many terms are introduced? The psychoanalytic paradigm is the most complex. (Some of my students complain that psychologists oversimplify things—except Freud, who makes them more complicated than they really are.) Trait theories are much more simple and, in the case of personality typologies, epitomize simplicity. Cognitive theories vary. Some propose but a single law governing personality, such as a drive toward consistency, while others suggest many more.

There are no right or wrong answers to these issues. However, realize that the paradigms take a position with respect to each, and that these are consonant with the rest of the paradigm—theoretically, methodologically, and practically. Additionally, they help place the three paradigms in their historical and intellectual context, linking them to like-minded movements in science and philosophy and distinguishing them from ideological opponents. Table 4-1 shows how the three approaches stand on Wertheimer's (1972) fundamental issues. Can you see how the psychoanalytic paradigm stems from medicine, the trait paradigm from functionalism and psychological testing, and the cognitive paradigm from gestalt psychology?

If you read the Dr. Dolittle books when you were young, or just last week as I did, you might recall the pushmi-pullyu, a fanciful animal that was a gazelle on each end (see Figure 4-1). Every time this creature walked forward, it also walked backward. And vice versa. The two parts of the pushmi—pullyu are in obvious conflict, but neither would have much of an existence without

Table 4-1
Stances with Respect to Fundamental Issues

Issue (see text)	Personality Paradigm		
	Psychoanalytic	Trait	Cognitive
Masters versus Victims	Victim	Victim	Master
Good versus Evil	Evil	Neither	Good
Mind versus Body	Body	Body	Mind
Subjectivity versus Objectivity	Subjectivity	Objectivity	Subjectivity
Past versus Present	Past	Past	Present
Nature versus Nurture	Both	Nature	Nurture
Simplicity versus Complexity	Complexity	Simplicity	Both

Figure 4-1

Dr. Dolittle's Pushmi-Pullyu

" 'Lord save us!' cried the duck. 'How does it make up its mind?'"

SOURCE: From Lofting, H. (1968). *Doctor Dolittle: A treasury.* London: Jonathan Cape, p. 27.

the other. I think of the fundamental issues of personality psychology in the same way. Each stance needs the opposite to make any sense. More generally, each paradigm needs the other paradigms as well. This might mean that personality psychology will not be dominated by a single paradigm until basic questions about human nature are answered.

What Is the Relationship of Theory and Research?

In the ideal of science, theory and research are symbiotic—one uses a theory to make a prediction about the world and then conducts research to check one's prediction against the facts. If the facts confirm the prediction, then the theory remains as is. If the facts contradict the prediction, then the theory is changed to accommodate them.

This ideal somewhat captures the business of science, but it overlooks the role of paradigms in determining whether research findings are "true" facts or not. As Kuhn (1970) argues, theories are not changed simply by facts.

Indeed, their fundamentals are rarely changed at all. They flourish, and then they die, replaced by another theory.

In Kuhn's view of science (which I believe), research and theory can have relationships other than simple calibration. In some cases, research dominates theory. The facts are of more interest to scientists than their abstract meaning. Description precedes explanation. Theory is cursory, perhaps just a summary of findings or a restating of observed relationships. Remember Spearman's g, the general factor characterizing the positive correlations among tests of performance? This has been interpreted as general intelligence, and several theories have been proposed regarding g. However, correlation coefficients preceded the theory, and they still take precedence.

In other cases, theory is more important than research. Explanation precedes description, coloring it to such a degree that research doesn't test theory as much as it illustrates it. A common criticism of Freudian theory is that it is nonfalsifiable. The theory provides such a powerful explanation for all sorts of facts that nothing can ever count against it. An annoying aspect of psychoanalytic theory has been the fact that some psychoanalysts interpret disagreement with their position as proof of their theory's validity.

If I say that people guard themselves against threatening ideas, and that this defense is unconscious, then when you disagree with this idea, you are merely employing the very process with which you take issue, even though you don't know it! Hmmm. There may be some truth to this line of logic, and I would not object if it were used to explain someone who burned Freud's books. But I wouldn't like to see this reasoning used to dismiss thoughtful and sincere criticism of the psychoanalytic paradigm. At any rate, my point is that the psychoanalytic paradigm accords more importance to theory than to research, while the trait paradigm does the opposite. The cognitive paradigm sometimes has research dominating, sometimes theory.

I've sketched extreme views of the relationship between theory and research. But research never proceeds in complete independence of theory. Otherwise, the facts of the Manhattan phone book would be considered scientific data, and that's not so. And never does theory exist oblivious to the facts. Otherwise, any ideology would be considered a scientific theory, and that's not so either. Though the extremes don't exist, they define a real continuum along which the paradigms may be placed.

Because of behaviorism's great influence, experiments are a favored research method within psychology, even personality psychology. As I noted earlier in this chapter, **experiments** do a great job of investigating mechanistic theories. But, to the degree that a theory embraces a metaphor other than mechanism, it is apt to be estranged from data produced by experiments. Don't be surprised when I say that one relationship between personality theory and research is one of mutual disinterest. Sometimes theorists and researchers don't have much to say to each other because they choose different root metaphors for their activities.

What Is the Relationship of Theory and Application?

A final question that each personality paradigm needs to answer regards the proper relationship of theory and application. On the simplest level, applied personality psychology simply takes a theory and extrapolates to the real world to accomplish a particular purpose. However, nothing is ever so simple, and the practitioner must look to her paradigm for guidance in how to regard an application, not just in how to go about it.

The applied psychologist may take on different roles, and the different paradigms regard some as more legitimate than others. The most fundamental distinction comes from the question of who the applied psychologist serves: the individual, the group, or the society? Consider the case of a convicted criminal ordered by the court to start psychotherapy. You are the therapist. Who are you trying to make happy? Your answer may be a glib, "I'm trying to make the client happy by helping him fit into society, which will also be happy. And then I'll be happy." But when the situation is made concrete, your answer is seen as an empty, "Have a nice day" uttered on "The Day After." Suppose your client is a child molester. Suppose he is a champion of religious freedom. Suppose he is a public drunk. Suppose he is a murderer, whose victim was a would-be mugger. Who are you trying to make happy?

A personality theory will not contain all that is needed to answer questions about proper roles for the applied psychologist. However, it often steers the practitioner in one direction or another. Remember the fundamental issues? Many are related to those classic political positions of liberal versus conservative. If a theory assumes the goodness of people, subjectivity, choice, and so on, it leads to a liberal perspective in that problems are viewed as solvable. The status quo should be changed so that people can be happy within it. In contrast, if a theory assumes the opposite, it leads to a more conservative approach. Problems are inherent, and so people should be changed to fit the status quo.

By and large, the psychoanalytic and trait paradigms involve conservative applications. According to Freud (1930), people may be doomed to accept an unhappy compromise between their instinctive drives and the dictates of a repressive society. Psychoanalytic therapy, therefore, should help the individual adjust. Similarly, those who administer psychological tests use them to match people to the world, not vice versa. The cognitive paradigm may also give rise to conservative applications, if intervention is directed at the individual. But if intervention is directed at the world, then the cognitive paradigm gives rise to liberal applications.

METHOD IN PERSONALITY PSYCHOLOGY

In personality psychology, method varies as much as theory. Although certain methodological concerns cut across the paradigms, each has its favored research strategy. Any strategy has inherent strengths and weaknesses, and is better suited for some purposes than others. A researcher makes his or her choice of a method of investigation according to the broader perspective of a personality paradigm.

Crosscutting Research Issues

Regardless of the paradigm in which one works, one must address issues common to all personality research: operationalization; reliability and generality; validity; emphasis on pure versus applied research; and nomothetic versus idiographic goals. Additionally, one must decide how tightly or loosely one wishes to bind research and theory.

Operationalization   In Chapter 1, I discussed the need to operationalize, or measure, a personality characteristic. Let me repeat some of the points I made. First, operationalizations are absolutely necessary for science. Without explicit rules about what facts in the real world correspond to what assumptions in the scientific theory, the whole scientific endeavor comes to a halt. Second, at the same time, operationalizations are imperfect translations of reality into theory. Particularly in the case of personality, where terms do not have necessary and sufficient conditions, measures of concepts are fuzzy. Third, it follows that operationalizations are not the same thing as the concepts they purport to measure. Intelligence is not the same thing as an IQ score, despite a casual way of speaking that equates them. Whenever a personality researcher makes conclusions about intelligence, or authoritarianism, or whatever, you should fill in what has not been specifically stated: intelligence as I have operationalized it (with the Stanford-Binet), authoritarianism as I have operationalized it (with the F-scale), and so on.

Research within each of the different personality paradigms needs to be explicit about operationalization. The basis for going from facts to theory, or from theory to facts, should be clear so that the research can be evaluated by the careful consumer. Psychoanalysis has sometimes been criticized because the links between constructs and observations are numerous, tenuous, and unstable. This makes research difficult, but it need not preclude investigations. As you will see, the psychoanalytic researcher often uses case studies because they provide rich information and allow these links to be disentangled.

The trait paradigm is the most straightforward in terms of its operationalizations, but this can be a misleading impression. Questionnaires in which research subjects choose "like me" or "unlike me" are objective in that the researcher can easily and reliably score them, but objectivity in scoring is not the same as precision and simplicity in operationalization. An objective questionnaire may or may not be a good measure.

Finally, the cognitive paradigm also uses straightforward operationalizations, assessing thoughts and beliefs by asking people to report them. But remember John Watson's distrust of introspection. Some of this legitimate skepticism spills over onto contemporary operationalizations that rely on self-report. Respondents may distort, lie, or simply not know the answer.

Most insidiously, respondents may sincerely answer questions even though they don't know the answer. In an article entitled "Telling More Than We Can Know," Richard Nisbett and Timothy Wilson (1977) argue that subjects in a psychological investigation will hazard an answer to any question asked, even questions that make no sense. For instance, subjects will report why they like their roommate, or why they prefer pretzels over potato chips, or why they have a Mohawk haircut and a pierced nose. Nisbett and Wilson caution that these attributed causes should not be confused with the "real" causes of these behaviors, since folks may not really know why they do these things. What they report may provide a clue, but the report is not the same thing as the real motive. This is just another way of saying that measures are not theoretical constructs. Motivation exists in a psychological theory, not on the tip of a research subject's pen or tongue.

For reasons like these, researchers within the cognitive paradigm are currently developing different ways to measure thoughts and beliefs. Rather than asking people to report directly on their cognitions, researchers provide memory and decision-making tasks for people to perform. They then make inferences about cognitions from how subjects do.

Reliability and Generality   As I described in Chapter 2, reliability is the degree to which measures repeatedly give the same answer. Generality is the degree to which investigations repeatedly give the same conclusion. Lack of reliability and generality undercut a science, and psychology has had its share of false alarms: exciting findings that could not be replicated (Greenwald, 1976).

For instance, at one time it seemed that functions of the autonomic nervous system—involuntary responses like dilation of blood vessels—could be controlled with biofeedback (Miller, 1969). The prospect that people could cure difficulties like hypertension by learning to regulate their bodies was discounted by subsequent investigations unable to repeat the original results (Miller & Dworkin, 1974).

Confidence in results increases with their reliability, and reliability increases with the number of observed facts that count toward results. Thus, questionnaires with many items yield more reliable scores for individual differences than do questionnaires with few items (Epstein, 1980). Remember Mischel's (1968) conclusion that behavior is inconsistent across different situations? This conclusion has in turn been criticized for relying on studies assessing but one action per situation. In contrast, if many behaviors reflecting the same personality trait are assessed in the various situations, then cross-situationality consistency is apt to increase above the low levels that Mischel (1968) reports, since behavior has been estimated more reliably (Epstein, 1983).

Reliable measures are a necessary precondition for generality of findings. Further, generality is served by increasing the number of research participants, as well as the number of independent investigations of the same question. Studies with many research subjects yield more reliable results than do studies with few subjects. Studies repeated several times yield more general conclusions than studies conducted once. Let me distinguish two sorts of **replications: exact replications,** in which *the procedure of a study is exactly repeated in a second study,* and **conceptual replications,** in which *different operationalizations of the same theoretical concepts are employed in two independent studies.*

Research within the three personality paradigms differs in terms of reliability and generality. Psychoanalytic research typically studies a small number of individuals in great depth. Because so many observations are made, reliability is great. However, generality is poor.

Trait research typically investigates a greater number of individuals in less depth. Generality is satisfactory, but not necessarily reliability. A given questionnaire is usually reliable in the sense of high internal consistency (see Chapter 2), since it contains many items. However, attempts to operationalize the same trait with different questionnaires have sometimes been disastrous; different measures may not correlate at all (see, for example, Scott, Osgood, & Peterson, 1979).

Cognitive research also studies a large number of research participants in the same investigation, strengthening generality of the results. But self-report measures of thoughts and beliefs do not always contain multiple items, so their reliabilities are unknown. Like trait research, attempts to show that different measures of presumably similar cognitive characteristics converge have sometimes been unsuccessful (Goldstein & Blackman, 1978).

Validity   My discussion of reliability and generality spills over into a discussion of validity, since the distinctions among them are vague. Measures must be reliable in order to be valid (see Chapter 2). The generality of results across different samples and different procedures argues for their validity—that the research is indeed concerned with what it purports to be.

Most of the forms of validity are easy to understand and judge: face validity, content validity, criterion validity, and known-group validity. The exception, however, is construct validity, since it relies on the theoretical framework in which the measure is regarded. To repeat my example from Chapter 2, consider a measure of creativity and its correlation with the verbal test of the SAT. Does a substantial relationship in this case count toward construct validity? Well, yes and no; it depends on whether your theory holds creativity to be related to vocabulary.

Attempts to demonstrate construct validity thus reflect as much on theory as they do on research. Accumulated evidence for construct validity is termed a *nomological net* (Cronbach & Meehl, 1955), since the entire set of results establishes validity. Like Quine and Ullian's (1978) web of belief, the nomological net usually does not rest on any single strand.

How do the three personality paradigms regard construct validity? The psychoanalytic paradigm holds that a particular fact bears on numerous theoretical concepts. Construct validity may therefore be difficult to establish. However, the psychoanalytic paradigm is also explicit that each and every fact must bear on each and every theoretical concept. Psychoanalysts do not attribute odd findings to error.

The trait paradigm relies on vast amounts of data, presented as correlations, to establish construct validity of measures. As already noted, this paradigm is open to criticism for over-reliance on a single method. Despite what seems to be a richly woven net of evidence, there is a critical thread on which it all depends. One pull and the construct validity may unravel.

The *F*-Scale is a case in point. It was used as the favored measure of authoritarianism in innumerable investigations before a factor potentially undermining it was pointed out: a high score supposedly indicating authoritarianism is obtained by answering all questions in the affirmative. Does the *F*-Scale measure the tendency to agree with statements regardless of their content, or does it measure the more specific beliefs endorsed by fascists (Cohn, 1956)? (The answer seems to be both; Goldstein & Blackman, 1978).

A factor other than the intended one that affects a measure or result is called a **confound.** Is an obtained relationship between two variables like popularity and good grades produced by a third variable like cheerfulness that causes both? If so, then the popularity-grade correlation is confounded by cheerfulness, and a researcher must be careful not to attribute good grades to popularity, or popularity to good grades. Research in the trait paradigm is not uniquely susceptible to confounds. As I describe empirical investigations throughout the book, one of my standard exercises will be considering possible third variables that might confound the results.

Problems with self-report represent the biggest threat to validity for cognitive research. Is a research participant sincere when he reports on a belief or idea? If sincere, is he accurate? Another difficulty with cognitive research is that it sometimes fails to adequately test theoretical claims that patterns of thought precede outcomes of interest. If measures of both are taken at the same time, one cannot justifiably conclude that thought precedes outcome.

Do not despair from my discussion of validity that personality research is fatally flawed. Problems of validity occur in all sciences, and what helps the personality researcher solve them is the pragmatic stamp on all three paradigms. Research always comes back to the real world, back to an application, back to the attempt to say something meaningful about function and dysfunction. The contact made with concrete individuals in concrete situations is always sobering and helps the researcher judge what is good or bad (valid or invalid) about her investigations. If it don't work, it ain't valid! In contrast to other psychology fields, where statistical significance of results is the bottom line, personality psychology additionally looks to practical significance.

Pure versus Applied Research   Within personality psychology, the line is fuzzy between investigations of theory per se and investigations of the real world. In all three paradigms, theory is about the real world, and so research is often conducted there.

However, it is true that cognitive research relies most on ivory tower investigations of college students, while psychoanalytic research relies least. Trait research varies, sometimes administering batteries of questionnaires to captives from Introductory Psychology, and sometimes not. The more applied the research, the fuzzier it is. At the same time, the more applied, the more general. A researcher has to make a hard choice in deciding where to divide the continuum of pure versus applied personality research.

Nomothetic versus Idiographic Goals   A final issue that personality researchers address is whether investigations should result in general conclusions applicable to all people (nomothetic goals) or in specific conclusions applicable only to individuals (idiographic goals). These ideals are extremes, and any researcher attempts a combination of the two. But relative emphases may be discerned.

Although psychoanalytic research studies but one individual at a time, its goal is nomothetic. Psychoanalytic theory intends to be a generally applicable theory of behavior. At the same time, conclusions should apply to each and every individual, not just to the average Joe or Josephine.

Because of its concern with statistical prediction, trait research is largely nomothetic (Eysenck, 1954), although trait theorist Gordon Allport (1937) first phrased the nomothetic-idiographic distinction, making a case for the idiographic goal. Some recent research within the trait paradigm is exploring a modified version of Allport's extreme position, expecting conclusions to apply to groups of like individuals but not to all folks (see, for example, Bem & Allen, 1974).

The cognitive paradigm is generally sympathetic to idiographic research, although like most sympathy, it lies more in word than deed. Research tools relying on self-report are equipped to capture the unique constellation of a person's thoughts and beliefs (Kelly, 1955), and are praised for this sensitivity (Mischel, 1973). However, they are rarely used to offer conclusions about a single individual. Instead, nomothetic conclusions are advanced.

Binding Research and Theory   Although personality research never proceeds without a theoretical rationale, there is wide latitude with regard to how tight a leash theory holds on research. Does the paradigm frown upon innovative methods? Does it encourage exploratory investigations, studies in which specific hypotheses have not yet been formulated? Does the paradigm respond quickly, sluggishly, or not at all to seemingly anomalous results?

In short, what is the relationship of research to theory? Many of these questions complement those discussed earlier in this chapter about the relationship of theory to research. The researcher must decide the degree to which research versus theory will lead. She must decide how closely to bind the two together.

Psychoanalytic theory developed from Freud's clinical observations, and he repeatedly revised his ideas in response to these observations. Thus, Freud himself was not rigid about the relationship of research to theory. Subsequent workers within the psychoanalytic paradigm have become more dogmatic, however, so that appropriate research activities are highly prescribed by the theory, which has been accorded a much-more-than tentative status.

> Instead of leading in the development of new concepts, as was true during the early part of the century, psychoanalysis has entrenched itself behind concepts that it is largely prepared to defend rather than lay on the line for scholarly scrutiny. (Fisher & Greenberg, 1977, p. 7)

(In this regard, it is interesting to note Freud's reported comment, "Moi, je ne suis pas un Freudiste." [I myself am not a Freudian.])

In the trait paradigm, exploratory research is common, since the computer revolution has made it possible to sift through the incredible amounts of data gathered in the course of trait research. Researchers nickname this kind of exploration: sifting, snooping, fishing, skimming, data massaging, even data mugging! Most of these terms are pejorative, since the procedure can uncover "results" simply by chance. On the other hand, all trait research-ers explore their data somewhat independently of their theory, hoping to uncover an intriguing finding that might be parlayed into a theory.

For instance, I recently read that schizophrenic patients from lower-class families are more apt to be born during the winter months than their coun-terparts from the middle class (Meer, 1984). What does this mean? Perhaps lower-class mothers have a nutrient-poor diet during the winter, lacking fresh fruits and vegetables. Perhaps brain development during the last trimester of pregnancy has something to do with schizophrenia. Or perhaps not. Future research will tell, but my point is that this interesting fact was probably uncov-ered in the course of exploring some large set of data, in particular, by cor-relating month-of-birth with psychiatric diagnosis.

Research in the cognitive paradigm is bound somewhat tightly to theory in terms of the questions investigated, but not so tightly with respect to par-ticular methods. Personality researchers interested in thoughts and beliefs are mindful of the difficulties of self-report, and devote considerable attention to the development of more valid procedures. Of current interest are research procedures developed within experimental psychology to study perception, memory, and cognition. Personality psychologists are borrowing these pro-cedures and adapting them to the study of personality (Taylor & Fiske, 1982).

Research Strategies: Pros and Cons of Case Histories, Correlational Studies, and Experiments

Our discussion of personality research has been pretty abstract so far. Although the issues I've discussed are critical, they only come into play when an actual investigation is conducted. And the most important consideration in con-ducting an actual investigation is which strategy of research will be followed. In general, three alternatives are available—case histories, correlational stud-ies, and experiments. Pros and cons exist for each strategy, and the researcher makes her choice within the context of the personality paradigm she's oper-ating under.

Case Histories A case history is "the presentation and interpretation of detailed information about a single subject: whether an event, a culture, or . . . an individual life" (Runyan, 1982, p. 121). Usually, the case history coheres around a particular problem that its subject suffers, and the goal of this method is to understand this problem and devise a solution. Case histories have been critical in the development of psychoanalytic theory and clinical thinking in general. As the most obvious way to study individual lives, they have seen considerable use as a research strategy in personality psychology (White, 1966).

At the same time, case histories are the most controversial research strategy employed to investigate personality. Some researchers dismiss them entirely as nonscientific, useful perhaps for suggesting ideas to be investigated in appropriate ways, but so plagued by threats to reliability and validity that they cannot yield scientific data (Campbell & Stanley, 1966).

One way to resolve these polar opinions about the usefulness of case histories is to distinguish between their in-principle shortcomings and the avoidable shortcomings that occur as some employ them. This distinction shows the case history strategy to be a properly scientific strategy, although not a perfect approach (since none exists).

What are the in-principle difficulties in studying only one individual? First, in an intensive study, some information is second-hand or retrospective, perhaps distorted in the process. Second, because a case history is just one shot, it is difficult to separate factors critical for subsequent outcomes from irrelevant factors that just happen to be there. Third, even if valid conclusions are drawn about the individual under study, they are best limited only to this individual; generality is severely bounded.

These shortcomings are illustrated in one of Freud's (1909a) most famous case histories, that of Little Hans, who was afraid of horses. Here is William Runyan's (1982) brief summary of this case:

> Little Hans was the child of a musicologist and his wife; the latter a onetime patient of Freud's. Little Hans' parents were among Freud's "closest adherents," and regularly reported observations of their child to Freud. In January 1908, when Hans was four and three-quarters years old, his father reported that a problem had developed. "My dear Professor, I am sending you a little more about Hans—but this time, I am sorry to say, material for a case history. . . . He is afraid *that a horse will bite him in the street.* Apart from his being afraid of going into the street and from his being depressed in the evening, he is in other respects the same Hans, as bright and cheerful as ever" . . . .

> In one of the first days of January, Little Hans woke up crying in the morning and reported that he had had a bad dream in which he thought his Mummy was gone and that he had no one to cuddle with. Several days later while the nurse was taking him to the park, he began to cry in the street, saying that he wanted to go home to Mommy and to cuddle with her. The next day he went out with his mother, yet still appeared frightened, and told her that he was afraid a horse would bite him. That evening, he grew frightened again, and wanted to caress his mother. "He said, crying, 'I know I shall have to go for a walk again tomorrow.' And later, 'The horse'll come into the room'" . . . .

> Freud's interpretation of Little Hans' horse phobia is that it stems from the Oedipal conflicts, which erupted during a period of intensified sexual attraction toward his mother. "Hans was really a little Oedipus who wanted his father 'out

of the way,' to get rid of him, so that he might be alone with his handsome mother and sleep with her". . . . Little Hans transferred his fear of his father onto horses, and . . . he was most afraid of horses with muzzles and blinkers, which may have resembled his father's moustache and eyeglasses. (pp. 139–140)

Freud's interpretation has been challenged by various critics (for example, Wolpe & Rachman, 1960), but let's use it to illustrate the in-principle difficulties with the case history research strategy.

First, Freud did not meet with Little Hans, relying instead on the reports of the child's father. Even if Freud had spoken with the child directly, he would still need to rely on retrospective reports about past incidents, such as being afraid in the street. Second, it seems critical to Freud's interpretation that the father had a moustache, but how could Freud know that this wasn't just a coincidence? Third, suppose Little Hans indeed feared horses because he desired his mother sexually and therefore anticipated the anger of his father. Can the same be said of Little Albert, Jim Morrison, Prince, and Howdy Doody? Probably not—conclusions are best limited to Little Hans, who may or may not be typical. (By the way, Silverman, 1980, reports that Little Hans supposedly grew up to be the story director of the New York Metropolitan Opera.)

Are these shortcomings sufficient to void the use of case histories in personality research? Contemporary opinion says no, that they are analogous to problems with reliability and validity that potentially threaten any strategy of investigation. The task of the researcher is to minimize these threats so that firm conclusions result. Case histories should be judged as good or bad on an individual basis, since this judgment can be made.

Runyan (1981) proposed a number of questions to be asked about conclusions made from case histories:

1. Are they logically sound?
2. Are they comprehensive, accounting for all of the available information?
3. Do they survive attempts to prove them wrong?
4. Are they consistent with all of the available evidence?
5. Are they consistent with what is known about people in general?
6. Are they more credible than alternative conclusions?

(Note that these questions could be asked about conclusions from any study of personality, regardless of the strategy of investigation.)

The researcher who uses a case history strategy must operationalize his concepts, and he must ascertain their reliability and validity. This probably involves independent confirmation of second-hand and retrospective information, not an impossible undertaking. Conclusions must be evaluated against

alternatives, and confounds must be ruled out. Finally, the criterion of parsimony must be applied. Is the phobia of Little Hans more easily explained
in terms of the Oedipal conflict or in terms of conditioned fear occasioned
by a frightening experience with a horse (Wolpe & Rachman, 1960)?

The issue of generality remains a real one. Freud himself argued that
conclusions had to be established on the basis of repeated case studies; those
he published seem intended as illustrations. Since psychoanalytic theory aspires
to be universally applicable, a single case study can carry considerable weight
if it disproves a prediction of the theory. This is why Margaret Mead's (1928)
anthropological observations in Samoa attracted so much attention. She
reported that early sexual experience among Samoan youngsters was not
associated with later neurosis, an instance in which Freud's pronouncements
about the universality of the sexual conflicts were wrong.

So, let me turn to the virtues of the case history method. First, as just
explained, case histories can serve as existence proofs or disproofs, challenges to theories that say this or that can never be, or that they always are.
The well-known studies of chimpanzee language are, after all, case studies,
since a single ape is studied at one time (Premack, 1971). But the importance
of these case histories is incredible since they challenge long-established
beliefs about the uniqueness of language to human beings.

Second, case histories are the only way rare phenomena can be investigated. Personality psychology in particular is often concerned with abnormality, and some instances of abnormality are so rare as to be encountered
only once or twice in the lifetime of a researcher. You may be aware of C. H.
Thigpen and H. Cleckley's description of a multiple personality, the well-known
individual of *The Three Faces of Eve* (1957). No personality psychologist wishes
to dismiss these descriptions as nonscientific just because they are only based
on one research subject (or on three).

Third, case histories provide the rich detail conspicuously lacking from
other research strategies. If one's research goal is to study the complexity of
an individual's personality, then case histories are the strategy of choice. They
are well-suited for psychoanalytic research which intends a careful description
of the development of personality within a social context. Detail is needed for
such a description, under the psychoanalytic assumption that facts are related
to theoretical constructs in diverse and diffuse ways. Only the intensive approach
of a case study allows these tenuous links to be specified.

Correlational Studies   The second major research strategy of personality
psychologists is the **correlational** approach. This strategy measures pertinent variables and calculates correlations reflecting the degree of association among these variables. It is the basic research strategy of personality

psychologists interested in how people are characteristically themselves and different than others (Cronbach, 1957).

Nevertheless, this research strategy is problematic, for two related reasons. First, if it is deployed to answer questions about the sequence of two factors, it may lead to erroneous conclusions, since both factors are measured at the same time. Correlational research is sometimes used to answer questions about causes, but the identified "cause" may not precede the "effect" of concern.

For instance, schizophrenia is sometimes attributed to disordered patterns of communication within the family (see, for example, Bateson, Jackson, Haley, & Weakland, 1956; Laing, 1965; and Lidz, 1975). One way in which this hypothesis could be tested is for the researcher to visit the homes of a number of individuals, some with diagnosed schizophrenia and some without. She could sit quietly in the corner and watch while the family members interacted, noting whether they encourage each other to doubt their own experiences. A count of exchanges like this could be made:

Father: Have you chosen your college courses yet?

Son: Yes, I've thought about taking biology, calculus, and English, then maybe something else.

Father: That sounds pretty difficult. Are you sure you can handle it?

Son: Gee, I think so. Anyway, those are courses that I have to take to go pre-med.

Father: You know you're going to get overwhelmed by those courses. You get so carried away.

Son: Maybe I should postpone taking calculus. I could take photography. I understand the college has a great introductory course in that.

Father: How can we afford to buy you a camera? You must think I'm made out of money. You're going to college to make something of yourself, not to snap pictures.

Son: But Dad . . .

Mother: Now, son, you listen to your father. You know he loves you and wants what's best.

Father: The most important thing is for you to be happy. Whatever you want is fine with me.

In this conversation, both Mother and Father seem to deny what has been communicated to their son. He is criticized first as a marginal student and then as a frivolous one; the summary of these criticisms, however, is that he is loved and can do what he wishes.

(Do not be too upset if this conversation is typical of your dinner table, since it may not be disordered communication at all. Your family members may recognize these exchanges as fussing on the part of a father who is reluctant to see his son grow up and leave home. As long as everyone recognizes your father's motives, then communication is perfectly clear. The schizophrenia researcher is, however, interested in the case where the dynamics of the conversation are obscure and only the surface meanings are recognized. In this case, the son is apt to feel like a tennis ball going back-and-forth, back-and-forth, after which he is told that everybody left their rackets at home.)

If the researcher visits one hundred homes, and stays at each for an hour, she will have a set of scores to correlate with the diagnosis of schizophrenia (1) or not (0). Suppose she finds that the two variables are substantially correlated, so that schizophrenics tend to come from families with a great deal of disordered communication, while nonschizophrenics do not. What can be concluded? The researcher may be tempted to believe that disordered communication leads to schizophrenia. Her data are after all consistent with this conclusion.

However, cause and effect may be entangled here because of the correlational research strategy (Mischler & Waxler, 1968). No one established that disordered communication preceded schizophrenia, as it must if it is to be considered a cause. Perhaps the schizophrenic family member preceded the disordered communication, perhaps even causing it by frustrating, disappointing, or confusing the parents. The researcher cannot distinguish between this possibility and the first one she considered.

Besides its insensitivity to the sequence of variables, the correlational research strategy has another shortcoming: possible confounding by third variables. Consider again the example of disordered communication and schizophrenia. The researcher must hesitate not only in assigning one of these factors a causal role but also in concluding that they bear any direct relationship at all. Some theorists believe that schizophrenia is biologically based and that it may be genetically transmitted. Suppose that the "gene" for schizophrenia causes disordered communication in some family members and full-blown schizophrenia in others. If so, then the same correlation is expected, except in this case because of an underlying variable. (The actual cause of schizophrenia remains as elusive as this extended example suggests.)

All personality researchers recognize these in-principle difficulties with the correlational research strategy. Why then do they continue to employ it? Like the case history method, the correlational method also possesses several virtues, so the choice to use it reflects a decision that the benefits outweigh the shortcomings.

One benefit of the correlational research strategy is that it allows prediction, often with great accuracy. One variable may be highly related to a second variable, whether or not it is a cause. If a researcher wishes to predict this second variable, as often happens in applied psychology, then it may be irrelevant that the causal relationship is unclear. Perhaps you are familiar with the highly successful attempts by lawyers to choose sympathetic jurors for a given case. These rely on the correlational strategy. The community from which jurors are drawn is canvassed, and it is established with correlations that citizens who favor acquittal also tend to read certain magazines but not others, say, *Rolling Stone* instead of *Soldier of Fortune*. In screening jurors, then, the lawyer can ask about magazine preferences and in effect be asking about attitudes toward acquittal. Reading preference may not directly cause these attitudes, but knowledge of it makes for an accurate prediction.

Another benefit of the correlational strategy is that it allows the relationships among variables to be characterized numerically. In contrast to the case history method, the correlational strategy yields conclusions about the relative strength or weakness of associations. Personality psychologists use this research strategy to discover types of people. What characteristics frequently go together?

Fisher and Greenberg (1977) summarized a number of studies investigating Freud's (1908b) proposed anal character type, an individual who is excessively orderly, greedy, and obstinate. In a number of studies, operationalizations of individual differences with respect to these three characteristics indeed correlate with each other, as proposed. No attempt is made to point to one factor as the cause of another, or even to specify the sequence in which these characteristics might appear. These questions are of concern from the perspective of mechanism, but not from that of formism. If the researcher works within the trait paradigm, he usually adopts the root metaphor of formism, and he usually favors the correlational strategy, which is well-suited for categorization.

Still, causal questions frequently enter all paradigms, even the trait paradigm. For this reason, correlational researchers have refined their basic strategy so that causal conclusions can be drawn. The simplest refinement is to use a longitudinal design. If factors at Time One correlate with factors at Time Two, then one can certainly rule out the possibility that the latter variables cause the former. Causes do not work backwards in time. With a longitudinal design, the researcher therefore eliminates one alternative to the causal explanation she favors. This strategy lies at the basis of *epidemiology research*, which correlates variables of concern with possible outcomes known to follow them in time. Smoking cigarettes is correlated with heart disease. But the circulation difficulties suffered by a sixty-year-old cannot reach backwards in time to cause the fifteen-year-old adolescent to sneak a smoke in the school bathroom. If the two are directly related, then smoking has to be the cause, since it precedes heart disease.

More sophisticated attempts to use the correlational strategy for conclusions about causes are called experiments of nature or **quasi-experiments** (Campbell & Stanley, 1966). These strategies use various control groups to rule out possible third variables. True experiments eliminate third variables explicitly, by randomly assigning research participants to different groups where the experiment imposes different events upon them. Quasi-experimentation arose within educational settings where true experimentation was unwieldy or impossible.

Let me give an example of a quasi-experiment. I recently completed an investigation of "burnout" among counselors at a camp for multiply handicapped individuals. Such counselling can be emotionally taxing, and the counselor may end up tired, depressed, and disillusioned. The Department of Recreation at Virginia Tech runs a brief camp for the multi-handicapped, using undergraduate students as the counselors. They spend the first eight weeks of a school term in a classroom, learning about counselling. Then they spend a week at the camp with handicapped campers putting what they have learned into practice.

I wished to see if the counselors would experience burnout, so I devised a self-report questionnaire measuring the feelings that accompany burnout and administered it to the 120 counselors during the first week of class and again right after the week-long camp. Scores were quite a bit higher the second time. The counselors were burned out.

However, I could not conclude that counselling per se was the culprit. Maybe all undergraduate students get tired and depressed as the school term progresses. In fact, this seems quite plausible. I couldn't definitely attribute the increase in burnout to what happened at camp. I had anticipated this difficulty, however, and had administered the questionnaire at the same times to another group of students who did not participate in the camp. Although these students showed some increase in bad feelings from Time One to Time Two, the magnitude of increase was nowhere near that of the counselors.

With these data available, I could conclude more confidently that counselling produces burnout. If you are reading this carefully, you see that my conclusion should still be tentative. Other third variables might be present. Maybe students who are likely to sign up to be counselors are also likely to feel emotional fatigue as the school term goes on, regardless of what happens. The week-long camp may have been irrelevant in producing burnout. I could not rule out this possibility, but I think that you see how other controls might be introduced to do so. Suppose that only half of the 120 volunteers actually went to camp, and that only these showed burnout. This fact would further strengthen my causal conclusion.

Experiments   The third major research strategy for personality psychologists is the experiment. As noted, experiments have been favored within psychology since the time of Wundt and Watson because of their notable ability to isolate causes. Many important psychological questions ask about causes and effects, and the experiment is the best way to go about answering them. Even in personality psychology, where root metaphors other than mechanism define the three major paradigms, causal questions are frequently raised.

The researcher's control over which research participants experience which events defines an experiment, and the very language used to describe experiments conveys the importance of this control. Research participants are called subjects, because they are "subject to" whatever the researcher imposes upon them. Experimental groups are given different manipulations, called the independent variable. Dependent variables are measured, so termed because they "depend on" the manipulation.

In the ideal experiment, everything is held constant except the independent variable of interest. Research subjects are randomly assigned to different treatment conditions, which has the effect of cancelling out extraneous factors that the subjects may bring with them to the experiment. In my study of camp counselors and burnout, I did not control who was a counselor and who was not; therefore, I could not definitely attribute the observed burnout to the experience of the camp, as I had wished to do. Instead, burnout may have been due to uncontrolled individual differences like sensitivity that distinguished counselors from noncounselors. In a true experiment, this alternative would not be a viable one because the process of *randomization* cancels out such third variables.

Experiments are usually conducted in laboratories where control over extraneous factors is easier to exercise. However, laboratory settings are neither necessary nor sufficient for experimentation. Instead, what is important is the researcher's control, and this may be exercised in nonlaboratory settings. (These are called *field studies*, because the very first experiments of this nature were agriculture investigations literally conducted in fields.)

To take a more contemporary example, let's say that some applied psychologists want to know the best way to arrange the controls on a power lawn mower. They create several different configurations and randomly assign research participants to the different mowers and let them mow lawns. The researchers determine which arrangement of controls results in the fastest moving, the least confusion, the fewest accidents, the most fun, and so on. A conclusion can then be drawn that ignores the people pushing the mower, since their characteristics are cancelled out by randomization.

The primary strength of experimentation also involves its primary weakness, at least for personality psychology. Because experiments allow the

"For crying out loud, gentlemen! That's us! Someone's installed the one-way mirror in backward!"

SOURCE: "The Far Side" cartoon by Gary Larson is reproduced by permission of Chronicle Features, San Francisco.

researcher to look beyond the characteristics of research subjects to identify situational causes, they are also insensitive to individual differences. As you saw in Chapter 1, such differences often define personality, and experimentation of necessity precludes their investigation. For this reason, experimentation has never dominated personality research to the degree that it has other psychology fields.

For the personality psychologist, a second shortcoming of the experimental research strategy is that it confines study to reactions on the part of subjects. Part of what is meant by personality is what a person spontaneously does. Folks do more than just respond to stimuli in the environment. Indeed, the concept of self-actualization, prominent in many cognitive theories of personality, suggests that people may even push against the environment, transcending it by resisting its potential causes.

Field theories of personality are concerned with the give-and-take between people and their social context, what Albert Bandura (1978) calls *reciprocal determinism.* If the person and the environment indeed affect each other, then experiments make this process impossible to study. Experimenters, for instance, do not allow subjects to determine the nature of the experimental treatment. If they did, control would be relinquished, and an experiment would no longer exist.

There are several other shortcomings of experimentation in personality psychology. It may be impractical, for reasons of time or money, to study certain questions experimentally. If you are interested in the effects of different forms of childrearing on how well an individual adjusts to retirement, you could conceivably proceed with an experiment. However, few researchers would wish to wait sixty-five years or more to assess the dependent variable.

Similarly, it may be impossible to study other questions experimentally. If you are interested in gender differences on achievement, you cannot randomly assign some subjects to be males and other subjects to be females. Your independent variable walks into the laboratory, so to speak, making a true experiment impossible.

Finally, it may be unethical to investigate certain questions experimentally, even though it would be simple to do so. Personality psychology is often concerned with adjustment and maladjustment, and many theories propose potential causes of this disorder or that. One would not wish to impose these possible causes on randomly assigned subjects to see if depression, anxiety, failure, or hatred results. One might be right!

In all these cases, the researcher may opt for a case history strategy or a correlational strategy. Problems of logistics, logic, and ethics may thereby be minimized. However, if the central question is causal, then strong conclusions are also minimized.

Do not get the idea that experiments are always successful in isolating operative causes. They suffer the same problems of reliability and validity that plague all research strategies. Operationalizations are not always good ones. Experimental manipulations may be confounded by third variables. An experiment is no guarantee of good research.

Consider the well-known laboratory experiment by Stanley Milgram (1963) I mentioned earlier. Milgram studied the willingness of subjects to administer presumably painful electric shocks to another person. Whether factors like the proximity of the victim to the research subject influenced the magnitude of shocks was studied experimentally, by manipulating them.

Milgram (1963) viewed his experiment as a study of obedience, operationalized by the magnitude of shocks administered. Is this a good operationalization? It probably is, but Milgram (1974) felt obliged to argue against its interpretation as a measure of aggression. Aggression is hardly the same thing as obedience, but it might have a similar effect on this particular measure.

In an intriguing argument, Donald Mixon (1971) made the point that Milgram's experiment may have measured trust instead of obedience: trust on the part of the subject that the experimenter knew what he was doing, that the supposed victim would be alright. My point here is that operationalizations should always be scrutinized, regardless of the research strategy which employs them.

Experiments may be particularly liable to certain confounds called **experimental artifacts** (Rosenthal & Rosnow, 1969). Once a subject finds himself in an experiment, it may profoundly affect the way he responds. The subject, for instance, may experience **evaluation apprehension,** the fear that the experimenter is judging his mental health or competence (Rosenberg, 1965). "Gee, if I say that I don't like that guy, I'll seem anti-social. But if I say that I do like him, maybe that'll look like I'm superficial. I don't even know him." Whatever the subject decides to do, it will probably not reflect only the processes of concern to the experimenter.

Subtle and unintended cues from the experimenter may also bias results if subjects pick up on these and act in response to them. **Experimenter bias** has been documented in a variety of experimental settings, including some used in personality psychology (Rosenthal, 1966). The sensitivity of subjects to **demand characteristics** in the experiment that "demand" certain behavior is also well-known (Orne, 1962). The essential idea is that the relationship between an experimenter and a subject is a social one. As human beings, researchers may inadvertently communicate an expectation regarding the experiment's hypothesis. Also as human beings, research subjects may sense this expectation and act in accordance with it.

For example, studies of learned helplessness look at the effects of unsolvable problems on subjects (Seligman, 1975). Experiments usually involve an experimenter giving problems like anagrams to subjects. These problems either have solutions or not. Some experimenters feel badly about giving impossible tasks to people, and they act differently with subjects in the unsolvable condition than with subjects in the solvable condition. A factor other than the intended independent variable (unsolvable-solvable problems) is introduced.

The artificiality of experiments is sometimes cited, but I think this is misplaced criticism. What makes an experiment powerful is its simplicity. Only by holding constant as many extraneous factors as possible can an experiment be used to isolate a cause, and artificiality is the price to be paid. The researcher willingly chooses causal conclusions over rich detail about natural occurrences, and this conclusion is made on an individual basis. Artificiality per se is not a shortcoming of experimentation.

Another misplaced criticism of experimentation singles out the difficulty of generalizing from the typical experimental subjects: college sophomores recruited from Introductory Psychology classes. Certainly, college sophomores are different from some other groups, but there is no reason to believe that they are particularly unique. (No offense.) In other words, generalization from college students is no more and no less difficult than generalization from any other group that personality psychologists study. Whether generalization from one sample to another is warranted must be ascertained on an individual basis. Again, undergraduate samples per se are not a shortcoming of experimentation.

How are experiments most sensibly used in personality psychology? There are three major purposes. First, like case histories, experiments may be used as proofs or disproofs. In fact, they may be even more suited for this purpose than case histories, since the experimenter can play an active role in bringing about an informative demonstration. One of the important aspects of Milgram's (1963) experiment is that situational factors may override personality traits, which were also measured. This flies in the face of common intuition, and as such, it is a valuable fact.

Second, experiments may serve the related role of providing evidence for arguments about plausible (or implausible) determinants of some behavior. Because of difficulties in generalizing from the special circumstances of the psychology experiment, the researcher can never conclude from an experiment what is universal. However, the researcher can conclude what is possible. Granted that the causes of personality are perhaps innumerable, such a conclusion may be the strongest to which a personality researcher aspires.

Third, where a mathematical theory has been proposed, experiments may allow parameters to be estimated. The phenomenon of concern is studied under various manipulated conditions, and a precise equation results from these observations. Theories like this are rare in personality psychology, but Dollard and Miller's (1950) investigation of different conflict situations was phrased in mathematical terms buttressed by experimental results.

The Best Research Strategy   My discussion of the three major research strategies used by personality psychologists makes it clear that there is no one best research strategy. One chooses a particular strategy to answer particular questions, with one's paradigm guiding this decision by framing the initial question to be investigated. To repeat the theme of this chapter: *personality paradigms are coherent, and research issues dovetail with theoretical issues.*

APPLICATION IN PERSONALITY PSYCHOLOGY

In his famous presidential address to the American Psychological Association, George Miller (1969) exhorted psychologists to "give psychology away," to contribute to society the substantive knowledge they possessed. I was just starting college then, but had I been in that audience, I would have nudged whomever was next to me and whispered, "Personality psychologists have always done that." Indeed, applications of personality psychology predated recognition of the field itself.

From the beginning, proponents of the psychological testing tradition and functionalists in general applied their ideas. Psychoanalysts and other personality psychologists concerned with abnormality applied their ideas in the clinic and in the hospital, diagnosing and treating failures of adaptation. And I showed you in Chapter 3 how Woodworth and Yerkes helped during World War I by designing assessment procedures. Henry Murray and others did the same for the Office of Strategic Services (1948) during World War II. Contemporary personality psychologists advise the government how to prevent terrorism, resist brainwashing, and treat released hostages.

What is the difference between applied psychology and just regular psychology? As you might imagine, the distinction is fuzzy, particularly for personality psychology, an inherently pragmatic endeavor. Anne Anastasi (1979) concludes that "applied psychology does not differ in any fundamental way from the rest of psychology" (p. 6). According to her, the distinction mainly corresponds to whether the research question is phrased in theoretical or practical language: "Is the investigation concerned with the nature of learning or with the most effective method for training airplane pilots?" (p. 9). This is another statement of the difference between basic versus applied research.

In other words, the distinction roughly corresponds to whether or not a research finding challenges a theory. Compare physics with engineering. If a building collapses, one does not doubt the principles of statics (and dynamics!) that were used to design its foundation. Instead, one doubts the implementation of these principles. In plain language, your lawyer will contact the building's engineer, not the physicist with whom the engineer studied.

Similarly, applied psychological research is less likely to produce facts that call theory into question than is basic research. One of my colleagues at Virginia Tech attempts to encourage the use of seat belts through various rewards like cash, prizes, and praise (Geller, 1983), a clear application of the Law of Effect. If the efforts prove unsuccessful, he does not question the theory that rewards lead to increases in the rewarded behavior. Instead, he believes that the right reward has not been used.

However, this distinction cannot be pushed too far since we have already seen that all theories somewhat resist contrary evidence. That is the nature of a scientific paradigm. So, the way that I will identify applied personality psychology in this book is simply whether the psychologist in question happens to work outside of academia, providing a specific service.

Fields of Applied Personality Psychology

Applied personality psychologists possess highly technical skills, and their day-to-day activities may seem far removed from those of their academic counterparts. However, every personality psychologist works within a paradigm, and the three major personality paradigms have each given rise to particular applications that fall within the paradigm's range of convenience. Let me discuss the major fields of applied psychology (Anastasi, 1979), and comment on how the personality paradigms have made their impact felt.

Industrial Psychology   The term applied psychology is often used in a more narrow sense than I am using it: to refer to applications in business and industry. As early as 1913, Hugo Munsterberg defined this field, which thrives today in the form of personnel selection and classification. These applications of personality mainly involve the trait paradigm and its research procedures for assessing individual differences in job-related interest, ability, and performance (Dunnette, 1976).

Organizational Psychology   The closely related field of organizational psychology is concerned with the behavior of individuals within complex organizations, usually an industrial setting but sometimes schools, hospitals, sports teams, and the military. Organizational psychologists try to balance the demands of organizational effectiveness with worker satisfaction. Organizational psychologists often adopt a field perspective, emphasizing the interdependence of the individual and the organization (Hackman, Lawler, & Porter, 1977). As such, they apply ideas from the cognitive paradigm, particularly those of Kurt Lewin (1951) and his followers. A favorite topic of organizational psychologists is leadership, and one of the truisms regarding leadership is that the best leader depends on the task at hand and the individuals to be led.

Engineering Psychology   Also known as *human factors*, this field of applied psychology is concerned with optimizing work methods, equipment, and the work environment (McCormick 1976). For the most part, engineering psychology draws on traditional experimental psychology and its findings regarding sensation, perception, and motor behavior. However, some engineering psychologists also apply theories and research from one of the three personality

Even sports teams use psychologists to help individuals cope with complex situations.

paradigms. Their focus may be on individual differences in susceptibility to fatigue, boredom, accidents, and so on (if so, then they borrow ideas from the trait paradigm). Or their focus may be on the degree to which the work environment satisfies the needs of the worker (then the psychoanalytic paradigm is pertinent). Finally, engineering psychology presupposes a particular model of human nature, and all aspects of the field reflect the assumed model (Argyris, 1969). The different personality paradigms are consulted to help articulate these assumptions.

Environmental Psychology This field concerns itself with the relationships between people and their physical environment. Such topics as personal space, territoriality, privacy, crowding, and noise pollution may be studied by environmental psychologists, who are called upon to solve the problems associated with them (Altman, 1975). Although they focus on the physical environment, environmental psychologists find Lewin's notion of the life space useful in understanding how the physical world impacts upon the individual. For instance, crowding has negative effects to the degree that a person perceives little control over it (Schmidt & Keating, 1979). So, environmental psychology is mainly a cognitive endeavor, and environmental psychologists draw frequently upon the cognitive paradigm in designing interventions (Langer & Saegert, 1977).

Consumer Psychology   Beginning with studies of advertising (Scott, 1908), consumer psychology has grown to encompass the entire relationship between the producer of products or services and the consumer (Jacoby, 1976). All three personality paradigms give rise to applications within this field. The psychoanalytic paradigm is used to conceive consumer needs and how best to meet them. The controversial technique of subliminal advertising stems from the Freudian notion that people's motives may be aroused without their awareness. Correlational research techniques from the trait paradigm are employed in consumer surveys and the targeting of certain ads to certain segments of the population. The cognitive paradigm provides models of decision-making that may underlie product choice.

Clinical Psychology   The most familiar form of applied psychology is clinical psychology. The typical clinical psychologist is called upon to perform two major duties: assess problems in living and treat these problems. Both involve the application of personality psychology. Assessment means psychological testing, and intellectual tests and personality tests are administered. Treatment means psychotherapy, and psychoanalytic and cognitive interventions are popular.

Counselling Psychology   This field bears a strong resemblance to clinical psychology. The counselling psychologist performs the same tasks as the clinical psychologist, with the major difference residing in the clients with whom they work. Clinicians usually help profoundly troubled people change in basic ways, so that they are no longer depressed, anxious, or crazy. Counselors usually help less-troubled people muster already-existing skills to solve particular problems. Counselors often work in schools where they help students choose a course of study or decide upon a career. Or they may work in other settings where they help people adjust to difficulties encountered in work, marriage, retirement, illness, or injury.

Educational Psychology   Psychology has always been involved with education. The entire psychological testing tradition received its original impetus from the need to ascertain the intellectual abilities of students. To this day, educational psychologists design and administer tests. I'm sure that you have taken the Scholastic Aptitude Test, a product of the Educational Testing Service in Princeton, New Jersey. Other activities of educational psychologists include teacher training and the development of instructional techniques. These activities are based on theories and findings of personality psychology, and depending on the particular paradigm employed, they take radically different forms.

Community Psychology   This field of applied psychology subsumes many of the fields already described. It plays a role within psychology analogous to that of public health within medicine. Community psychologists attempt to prevent psychological difficulties by intervening at the level of the community. Like organizational psychologists, they adhere to a field orientation and emphasize the interrelation between people and their social context. Prevention of problems involves interventions that enhance well-being, such as prenatal care, sheltered workshops, community mental health centers, hot lines, and job training. These interventions embody the field theory assumption that the different aspects of personality are entwined, and strengthening of some results in strengthening of others.

Health Psychology   It has long been believed that psychological factors play a role in the origin and treatment of disease. The field of applied psychology that studies these factors is health psychology, and it draws heavily on all three personality paradigms. Psychosomatic medicine may employ psychoanalytic theory to interpret such symptoms as hypertension, constipation, asthma, and peptic ulcers in terms of underlying conflicts (Alexander, 1950). The trait paradigm provides methods to help identify individuals at risk for certain diseases because of their lifestyle. For instance, coronary problems have been linked to an individual difference called the *Type A personality,* comprised of excessive time urgency, competitiveness, and hostility (Glass, 1977). At the present time, proponents of the cognitive paradigm are examining the role played by thoughts and beliefs in mediating the effects of stressful life events on susceptibility to infectious disease. Perceived control looks important (Jemmott & Locke, 1984).

Aesthetics and Criticism   Psychologists have also been concerned with how and why people find pleasure in art, music, and literature. The person who produces beauty and the person who appreciates that beauty have been investigated from the perspective of all three personality paradigms. Of interest to personality psychologists has been how best to interpret and perhaps to cultivate aesthetic ability and sensitivity. Psychoanalysts emphasize unconscious drives and how they are expressed in creative products. Trait psychologists look to individual differences in skills and preferences. Workers within the cognitive paradigm follow the lead of gestalt psychology in emphasizing the "good" relationships among the components of an aesthetic product. Like problem-solving, aesthetic appreciation can be taught by encouraging attention to the whole. A related application of personality psychology is by art and literary critics, who find the psychoanalytic perspective particularly useful in understanding creative works. Ernest Jones (1910) interpreted Hamlet in terms of the Oedipus complex, for instance, in one of the most famous of such applications.

Psychohistory　This field uses psychological theories to illuminate historical figures and events. Although all historians and biographers make implicit assumptions about psychology, the psychohistorian uses psychology explicitly. For the most part, psychohistory is tied to the psychoanalytic paradigm. Sigmund Freud pioneered this field with his studies of Leonardo da Vinci (1910), Dostoevsky (1928), and Moses (1939). Erik Erikson further developed psychohistory by applying psychoanalytic theory to such individuals as Adolph Hitler (1950), Martin Luther (1958), George Bernard Shaw (1968), Gandhi (1969), Thomas Jefferson (1974), and others. The similarities between the life history and case history are emphasized by psychohistorians, and the criteria by which to judge a good case history are the ones with which to evaluate psychohistory (Runyan, 1982).

Boundary Conditions: When Personality Psychology Fails

Despite the numerous applications to which personality psychology has been put, limitations do exist. Not all topics are profitably explained in psychological terms. In some cases, a phenomenon falls within the **range of convenience** of psychology, but not in others. A psychological explanation may be unwieldy, awkward, or simply wrong. Personality psychologists are called upon to explain a variety of social ills and perhaps to suggest solutions. And while their efforts make sense in some cases, it is important for applied workers to recognize that nonpsychological factors sometimes swamp personality characteristics in determining a social problem.

Remember the inferential error that I described in Chapter 1—explaining everything that people do in terms of pervasive personality traits. This extends to social problems as well. We may believe that poverty exists because poor people are lazy or ignorant, that crime exists because criminals are violent or irresponsible, that prejudice exists because bigots are misinformed or hateful. Upon examination, though, we learn that larger factors play a role in many social problems.

For instance, the women's movement is struggling not just against sexist attitudes (a psychological factor) but also against economic factors (women are paid less than men for doing the same job), historical factors (women are infrequently groomed for political office), religious factors (women are not allowed to play a full role in many major religions), and so on. The issues of central concern to the women's movement do not simply involve personality characteristics of women and men.

Sociologists call such larger factors **emergent properties,** since they do not reflect individuals but arise only from human collectivities. As the gestalt psychologists emphasized, the whole may not be the same as its parts. This is true not just for perception but also for groups of people. Sometimes the group, and in particular what ails the group, may have little to do with the personalities of the group members.

The idea of institutional racism shows how an emergent property works. This idea implies that an organization has rules or procedures that in effect discriminate against people of a particular race, even though no individual in the organization is prejudiced. Consider the standard policy: "Last hired, first fired." In times of cutback, the most recently hired employees are let go. This seems pretty reasonable, doesn't it? But suppose the most recently hired employees are black, while the more senior employees are all white. What happens now in times of cutback? Something has to give, and whether it is the new or the old employees, discrimination occurs. This dilemma has no easy solution, but the cause of the problem has nothing to do with the personalities involved. If a solution is to be found, it will not involve changing personalities.

The applied personality psychologist must exercise caution in deploying her skills. They may prove irrelevant to the need at hand. My work as a clinical psychologist in a Veterans Administration Medical Center convinced me that psychological disorder may involve too few jobs and too little money as much as faulty learning, irrational beliefs, or inner conflicts.

The application of personality psychology seems an attractive way to solve social problems. First, Americans greatly emphasize the individual. The American Dream, rugged individualism, Yankee ingenuity, and the Me Generation all reflect the belief that the individual is paramount. However, this belief is sometimes unwieldy. Second, interventions against personality are easier than interventions against society. They cost less in time and money, and they are more palatable politically. However, they may not work.

Where does this leave personality psychologists? I'm not recommending that they become sociologists, economists, politicians, engineers, or revolutionaries. Rather, I'm saying that they must acknowledge the role of emergent properties in the domains in which they work. These nonpsychological factors determine the boundary conditions of applied personality psychology. Indeed, all three personality paradigms recognize these conditions, although they differ in how they are regarded.

The orthodox psychoanalytic position treats society as coercive, in conflict with people's instinctive drives, but a given against which it is futile to struggle (Freud, 1930). More contemporary versions of psychoanalytic theory suggest that society can indeed change as technology provides new ways of living, so they present a more optimistic vision (Brown, 1959; Marcuse, 1962). In either case, emergent properties are clearly in sight.

Workers within the trait paradigm usually assess and diagnose difficulties in adaptation. Since society provides the criteria against which adaptation is judged, society is often regarded as fixed. Interventions are conservative and directed at the individual. Sometimes they are not undertaken at all, since the individual's nature is attributed to his biology. Not coincidentally, few forms of psychotherapy have originated within the trait paradigm, since personality is seen as static. But like the psychoanalytic paradigm, the trait paradigm recognizes the importance of nonpsychological factors in social problems.

Finally, the cognitive paradigm acknowledges emergent properties but may ignore them in focusing on the individual's beliefs and assumptions. Cognitive theory emphasizes that one's ideas are a joint product of the person and the world, but cognitive applications sometimes overemphasize the freedom a person may exercise in viewing the world. The following are considered irrational beliefs in the sense that strict adherence to them may result in disappointment and depression (Jones, 1968):

It is important to me that others approve of me.

Everyone needs someone he can depend on for help and advice.

Too many evil persons escape the punishment they deserve.

It is almost impossible to overcome the influences of the past.

However, isn't it also the case that these so-called irrational beliefs are a pretty good mirror of the social world in which we all live?

At any rate, the three paradigms of personality psychology give rise to characteristic applications. An applied psychologist's chosen paradigm dictates the problems considered worthy of attention, the methods to be used in solving them, and the standards by which these solutions are judged. The paradigm also determines the boundary conditions of an application and how these should be regarded.

SUMMARY

A scientific **paradigm** is the worldview of the scientist. It encompasses preferred theories, methods, and applications, and it is consistent within itself. Personality psychology has three major paradigms: the **psychoanalytic paradigm,** the **trait paradigm,** and the **cognitive paradigm.** In this chapter, I discussed all three. I emphasized that each paradigm in personality psychology regards a particular way of explaining things as most satisfactory. The psychoanalytic paradigm explains by pointing to the unfolding of an inherent biological nature. The trait paradigm explains by placing people into categories. The cognitive paradigm explains by specifying the interdependence of people and the world. Each paradigm may also make use of mechanistic explanations: the analysis of causes and effects. That the different paradigms favor different explanations helps explain the conflicts that sometimes occur within personality psychology. If they work within different paradigms, two personality psychologists may play by quite different rules.

All personality theories must account for known facts, generate new facts, and be useful to the practitioner. At the same time, theories show considerable diversity with regard to which aspects of personality they explain, the units they employ, the models of human nature they assume, the stances with respect to philosophical issues they suggest, and the relationships between theory and research and between theory and application they endorse.

Methods in personality psychology must grapple successfully with operationalization of constructs, reliability, generality, and validity of results, emphasis on pure versus applied research, and adoption of nomothetic versus idiographic goals. Also, whether to bind research and theory loosely or tightly must be decided.

Three research strategies are employed in personality psychology: the **case history,** the **correlational study,** and the **experiment.** Each has its own strengths and weaknesses, and there is no best research strategy for all purposes. The researcher's paradigm directs him to the preferred approach for a given purpose.

Applications of personality psychology take a variety of forms and again are dictated by the particular paradigm from which they spring. The major fields of applied psychology are described in terms of the uses of personality psychology within each: **industrial psychology; organizational psychology; engineering psychology; environmental psychology; consumer psychology; clinical psychology; counselling psychology; educational psychology; community psychology; health psychology; aesthetics and criticism;** and **psychohistory.** Every application of personality psychology is bounded by nonpsychological factors that importantly determine the phenomenon of concern. The applied personality psychologist must be attentive to the factors that fall outside the scope of her paradigm.

In sum, the most important idea in this chapter is that each of the three major approaches to personality psychology is coherent. Theory, method, and application are mutually consistent. Choice of a theory leads one to a particular method (and vice versa). And certain applications are easier within some paradigms than others.

5

PSYCHOANALYTIC PARADIGM: THEORY

By far the best-known explanations of personality are those proposed by Sigmund Freud and his followers. Psychoanalysis originated in a medical context, from the attempts of nineteenth century psychiatrists to explain the puzzling aspects of hysteria and other emotional difficulties. Taken together, these explanations comprise the theory of the psychoanalytic paradigm. As I explained in Chapter 4, this theory embraces the root metaphors of organicism and mechanism. Among the important models of human nature adopted by psychoanalytic theorists is one that likens people to complex energy systems. Psychoanalytic explanations account for personality by describing the process by which this energy is transformed and eventually discharged.

Noteworthy in psychoanalytic explanation is the assumption that behavior is **over-determined.** Even the most trivial of actions reflect numerous processes, and a satisfactory explanation within the psychoanalytic paradigm is one that articulates all the pertinent processes. So, slips of the tongue—**parapraxes**, or Freudian slips as they have come to be called—are not treated as accidents but rather as lawfully determined actions, products of unconscious motives.

Psychoanalytic theory is different than other personality theories, so much so that many psychologists approach it with caution. Indeed, some believe that psychoanalytic explanation is not a psychological theory at all, and that the writings of Freud are best relegated to bookshelves devoted to literature or philosophy. What lies behind these negative opinions?

For one thing, psychoanalytic explanation is heavily weighted in favor of **postdiction,** explaining what has already happened. In contrast, other psychoanalytic theories attempt *prediction*, explaining what will happen.

Also psychoanalytic explanation is not quantitative. Although their theories are phrased in energy terms that might lend themselves to quantitative expression, Freud and his followers did not take the step toward quantification. As a result, psychoanalytic theory is sometimes described as literary.

And psychoanalytic explanation is not systematized. Freud himself wrote extensively over a fifty-year period, constantly revising, discarding, and extending his theories. He never presented a definitive statement of psychoanalytic theory. Further, Freud stimulated numerous other personality theorists to propose theories similar to his own. (When I refer to psychoanalytic explanation, I do not mean simply Freud's psychoanalytic theory, but rather a set of theories of which Freud's is the prototype.)

Finally, as already noted, psychoanalytic explanation assumes that behavior is over-determined. The most mundane aspect of personality is shaped by various forces, and all of these forces must be specified in a satisfactory psychoanalytic account. This assumption is diametrically opposed to the principle of parsimony honored by most psychological theorists. Where other theories of personality strive for simplicity, psychoanalytic explanation allows for complexity.

Compounding these difficulties is the fact that **psychoanalysis** is used in various senses. However, when I refer to psychoanalytic theory or to psychoanalysis, I will usually mean

a theory of personality that explains human nature in terms of the ways that psychic energy is transformed and discharged; and/or

a general psychology that looks at behavior in terms of conflict between biological needs and societal demands.

Psychoanalysis also refers to a theory of psychopathology as well as a technique of therapy.

In describing psychoanalytic theory, my strategy is to emphasize the ways in which important psychoanalytic ideas originated and developed. Several individuals figure prominently here. First there is Sigmund Freud, whose theory stresses the sexual instinct and its inherent conflict with the demands of society. Next there are Alfred Adler and Carl Jung, contemporaries of Freud who followed him at first but later broke from him to propose their own theories emphasizing other forces. Then come the **neoFreudians,** a group of theorists who worked after Freud and stressed the social nature of personality. Last there is Erik Erikson, a self-described **postFreudian,** whose theory encompasses not just childhood and adolescence, as does Freud's, but the entire lifespan.

THE FAMILY RESEMBLANCE OF PSYCHOANALYTIC EXPLANATIONS

The theories of these individuals differ in important ways, but they share a family resemblance justifying their inclusion in a single chapter. First, *most psychoanalytic theories embody an energy model.* People are thought to possess a fixed amount of psychic energy, termed **libido.** Behavior is driven by this energy in accordance with a psychological version of the laws of thermodynamics.

Second, *most psychoanalytic theories have a biological emphasis.* They tend to emphasize motivation, and are phrased in terms of drives and instincts. Although the neoFreudians expand emphasis to include social determinants of behavior, they still speak of these social factors in terms of needs that require satisfaction.

Third, *most psychoanalytic theories have been influenced by Darwin's account of evolution through natural selection.* This influence is reflected in a concern with function and dysfunction: with the consequences of past struggles and how they were resolved.

Fourth, *most psychoanalytic theories propose a conflict between the individual and society.* The theories differ with regard to the exact nature of the conflict and its inevitability. Freud (1930), for instance, sees the conflict as an unavoidable one between sexual needs and societal restrictions. The neoFreudian Erich Fromm (1941), in contrast, proposes that the conflict between individuals and their society results from alienation: separation of people from the natural world and from each other. With profound societal change, this conflict can be avoided.

Fifth, *most psychoanalytic theorists adopt a developmental perspective* (Loevinger, 1976). In keeping with their biological emphasis and their use of the root metaphor of organicism, they attempt to understand present behavior in terms of the past. How did we get here from there? What path was travelled? A number of psychoanalytic theories describe development in terms of stages: discrete periods through which people pass in a fixed sequence. One's mode of functioning differs across these stages.

Sixth, *most psychoanalytic theories have been proposed by individuals actively engaged in clinical work, usually in the role of a medical doctor.* Their explanations of personality rest upon facts about people with profound problems.

Seventh, *most psychoanalytic theories propose a single guiding principle that describes the course of development and represents the most satisfactory adjustment of a person to society.* This principle can be regarded as the criterion of a healthy personality. For Jung, a healthy person integrates, bringing together disparate aspects of the self into a coherent whole. And for Erikson, the person who is healthy is the person who creates, bringing about not just products and ideas, but the next generation of people.

SIGMUND FREUD: FOUNDING FATHER

The most important psychoanalytic figure is of course Sigmund Freud (1856–1939), the Viennese neurologist who created psychoanalysis and guided it for fifty years. Although skepticism first greeted Freud's theories, and controversy has always surrounded them, Freud is regarded as one of the

Sigmund Freud poses for the sculptor O. Newmon, September, 1931.

towering intellectual figures of all times. In terms of impact, he can be classified with Confucius, Plato, Copernicus, Darwin, Marx, and Einstein.

Sigmund Freud was born into a lower-middle-class family in what is now Czechoslovakia. He was the first child of his parents, although his father—twenty years older than his mother—had two sons from a previous marriage. When Freud was four years old, the family moved to Vienna, where he lived for the next eight decades.

The realities of anti-Semitism led him to one of the few careers open to a Viennese Jew in the 1870s: medicine. During medical school, Freud was greatly influenced by Ernest Brucke, one of his instructors who was a well-known physiologist. Brucke promoted the idea that people were dynamic energy systems obeying the laws of the physical universe. Freud took these lessons seriously and later applied them to his psychoanalytic theory to such a degree that it is sometimes regarded as a neurology of the mind (Sulloway, 1979).

In school, Freud investigated adult and fetal brains, concluding that early structures formed the basis for later ones. We can see how Freud in his later work translated this idea from the neurological realm to that of the mind. Psychoanalytic theory proposes that the infant's manner of thinking and feeling—termed **primary process**—persists into adulthood where it forms the foundation for adult mental activity—termed **secondary process.**

Primary process thinking is dominated by wishes and impulses. It disregards constraints of time, space, and logic. According to Freud, primary process embodies the **pleasure principle:** "I want candy." In contrast, secondary process thinking is oriented to the demands of the real world, operating according to the **reality principle:** "And they sent me to school where they taught me to be rational, logical." Primary process is regarded as more basic and fundamental than secondary process. In unguarded moments, those occasioned by dreams, fevers, fears, or lusts, the infantile shows through undisguised: "I want my MTV!"

To return to Freud's personal life: in 1881, he received his medical degree and began private practice in neurology with Joseph Breuer, a somewhat older physician and physiologist who had also studied with Brucke. Breuer treated cases of hysteria with the technique of **catharsis,** the so-called talking cure. If a hysterical patient could be induced under hypnosis to talk about earlier events, a full expression of the emotions accompanying these events sometimes occurred, bringing an end to the hysterical symptoms.

Breuer and Freud (1895) interpreted hysteria, hypnosis, and catharsis in terms of energy transformations. Following Brucke's teachings, they assumed that people possessed a given amount of energy. Hysterical symptoms resulted from a tying up of this energy in unexpressed emotions. Hypnosis allowed an avenue to be opened to these emotions, and catharsis was their expression.

However, limitations of hypnosis soon became apparent. Not all patients could be hypnotized, so Freud came up with the technique of **free association** as a substitute. Patients were encouraged to say anything that came to mind, and the resulting pattern of associations often led to repressed memories: emotional conflicts long unconscious.

They also discovered **transference:** patients transferred emotions from prior relationships to the relationship with the therapist. That is, the female patients of Breuer and Freud fell in love with them. Breuer was so disturbed by transference that he left the treatment of hysterics to Freud, who went on with the work alone.

In 1896, Freud delivered a paper before a Viennese meeting of neurologists and psychiatrists in which he proposed that every case of hysteria was preceded by a sexual experience in early childhood. Each female patient whom he had treated for hysteria reported a traumatic sexual event, usually an older male relative forcing his attention upon her. The language of Freud's era termed this seduction; we now call it sexual abuse. Freud was convinced that these reports were valid because his patients described them with such reluctance and emotional difficulty.

Shortly after he delivered the paper with this striking thesis, Freud discovered that his pronouncement was wrong. He became convinced that most (though not all) of these early sexual abuses could not have occurred. But, in asking why his patients had reported events which did not occur, Freud came across the importance of fantasy about sexual matters in the etiology of hysteria.

Freud rapidly published books on dreams (1900), slips of the tongue (1901b), humor (1905b), and sexuality (1905c). All of these works assumed the existence of motives unavailable to a person's conscious mind that determine behavior. That an idea could be unconscious yet still affect conscious experience and behavior was Freud's germinal observation, leading him to develop his psychoanalytic theory. And, since the notion of the unconscious is such an important idea, we'll examine it in some detail.

According to Freud, the mind has three parts: the **conscious,** the **pre-conscious,** and the **unconscious.** *What we are aware of at a given moment is the conscious. What we can voluntarily call into consciousness is the pre-conscious. What we cannot become aware of is the unconscious.*

In proposing the unconscious, Freud is not merely saying that people are sometimes unaware of what they are doing and why they are doing it. Occasional unawareness is an everyday fact incorporated into all psychological theories of the mind. Attention to one aspect of the world is simultaneously lack of attention (unawareness) to some other aspect, and the process of learning to do anything involves routinizing the activity, turning it into a habit and making it something of which we are unaware. Consider these activities: playing the piano, swinging a baseball bat, driving a car, tying a shoelace, delivering a speech, or dancing. You do not consciously direct or monitor these behaviors while performing them. In this sense, the assumption of the unconscious is not at all controversial.

What is controversial about Freud's proposal is his belief that the unconscious is motivated. According to Freud, the mental contents and processes of which we are unaware are kept unconscious because they are threatening or upsetting. Freud is not concerned with how we tie shoelaces. Instead, he is concerned with why we fail to remember the name of our first lover, with why a hysteric does not know when his symptoms began, with why a surgeon cannot describe when she first became interested in medicine.

To keep material unconscious requires an expenditure of psychic energy. If a great deal of material is to be kept unconscious, then so much energy is devoted to this end that the psychological equivalent of the energy crisis ensues. This crisis is termed a **neurosis:**

> In a neurosis . . . the (conscious mind) drew back, as it were, after the first shock of its conflict with the objectionable impulse; it debarred the impulse from access to consciousness and to direct motor discharge, but at the same time the impulse retained its full charge of energy. . . it was obviously a primary mechanism of defense. (Freud, 1925, p. 29–30)

Freud called this process **repression** and regarded it as the foundation of all neuroses.

The motivated unconscious figures prominently in Freud's theory of dreams (1900) and humor (1905b). In both cases, ideas and impulses unacceptable to the conscious mind are actively kept in the unconscious. This material is usually threatening because of its sexual or aggressive content. However, the libido invested in the unacceptable material seeks discharge. And, since direct release would be too overwhelming to the individual, indirect satisfaction occurs. In both dreams and humor, expression of sexual and aggressive instincts is disguised.

The Interpretation of Dreams (1900) is regarded as one of Freud's most impressive works. In it, he grapples with an age-old concern: the meaning of dreams. Dream interpretation had always failed because dreams so often seem meaningless: jumbled, inconsistent, elusive. Freud's insight was to regard the chaos of dreams as their defining characteristic—the meaning is hidden behind their surface content. Indeed, the purpose of the surface content is to disguise the meaning, which in most cases Freud felt was a *wish*.

Sometimes the wishful nature of a dream is clear, as when you dream that a lost friend or lover reappears in your life. But other times the wish is obscure, because its blatant statement would be unacceptable. You may be extremely angry with your brother, for instance, so much so that you would like to kill him. But if you dreamed about murdering your brother, your conscious mind would probably be so upset that you would awaken. So instead you dream that some disaster befalls him: he is hit by a car, shot by a sniper, or required to repeat the seventh grade. Your aggressive impulse is satisfied, and your conscious mind is not ruffled. Most importantly, your sleep is undisturbed.

The dreamer has various techniques available for disguising unacceptable impulses so that sleep is preserved. Among the chief techniques of what Freud calls the **dreamwork** are **condensation, displacement,** and **symbolism.** In condensation, the dreamer combines different impressions and experiences. One of my frequent dreams is of me walking through a building, the successive rooms and halls of which are from all the various places I went to school. And sometimes in my dreams I speak with a person who is both my brother and my father.

Displacement occurs when emotional significance is transferred from its actual source to another. As an example, Freud describes examination dreams, common among students, in which the dreamer finds herself lost on her way to take a test for a course. According to Freud, that course is not one in which the student is having difficulty; her fear of failing has been displaced from some other course.

In symbolism, "the dream-thoughts . . . are not clothed in the prosaic language usually employed by our thoughts, but are . . . represented . . . by means of similes and metaphors, in images resembling those of poetic speech"

(Freud, 1901, p. 659). Since dreams are mostly visual, pictorial symbols figure prominently. We are all familiar with the idea that long, pointed objects like the Washington Monument, link sausages, Louisville Sluggers, and Corvettes may symbolize male genitals. However, Freud does not believe in universal symbols. Riding a horse may symbolize sexual intercourse, but not necessarily.

Humor and Its Relation to the Unconscious (1905b) similarly analyzes humor. In fact, Freud began this book in the course of writing his book on dreams, sparked by the observation that many dreams had the form of jokes, using techniques of condensation, displacement, and symbolism. Further, jokes often disguise sexual or aggressive wishes that would shock our sensibilities if directly expressed.

In the course of doing research with children, a psychologist friend of mine was told the following riddle:

Child: "What's pink, goes in hard and dry, and comes out soft and wet?"

Adult (with trepidation):   "I'm not sure . . ."

Child: "Bubble gum!"

The riddle is funny, and the interaction between the child and my friend is even funnier. On both levels, we are allowed to express our interest and expertise in sexual matters without seeming crass. A frequent technique of jokes is to put the punchline in the mouth of a child or a fool. They innocently say what our conscious mind will not allow us to say.

Freud termed such jokes **tendentious** since they have a tendency or purpose: to satisfy indirectly our unacceptable impulses. Jokes work because their techniques obscure these impulses. A failed joke is often one in which the impulse is too blatant, just as a nightmare from which you awake is a failed dream because the impulse became too much for the dreamwork to disguise.

Consider practical jokes. They rarely strike the butt as funny, since, from his point of view, the hostility inherent in them is obvious. "I was only joking" accompanies apologies too frequently for us to doubt that Freud captures something important about humor. Or consider dirty jokes. Freud observes that they are often told within earshot of an unwilling victim, one to whom the jokers are sexually attracted. The joke conveys the impulse, engages the target in a sexual encounter, and protects the jokers from rebuke, all at the same time!

In *The Psychopathology of Everyday Life* (1901b), Freud catalogued the ways in which the unconscious makes itself known through slips of the tongue or the pen. Several years ago, I was being interviewed for a position teaching at a prestigious university. One of the faculty members who was evaluating

SOURCE: *Never Eat Anything Bigger Than Your Head & Other Drawings,* published by Workman Publishing Company. Copyright © 1976 by B. Kliban. Used with permission.

me had his office lined with pictures of movie stars inscribed with personal greetings. "Oh, yes," said I, "Alan Alda. He's one of my biggest fans." The man interviewing me did not let on that he had heard me exchange the subject and object of the sentence. Regardless, it was an embarrassing slip. From Freud's perspective, however, my error was not without meaning. I was trying to aggrandize myself and had doubts that anything I had to say would be of interest to someone who was friends with the stars. Oh well, I wasn't offered the job. I hope Alan Alda still likes me.

Freud's generalization of ideas, gleaned from his work with hysterics, to such everyday behaviors as dreams, jokes, and slips of the tongue changed psychoanalysis:

> [It] was no longer a subsidiary science in the field of psychopathology, it was rather the foundation of a new and deeper science of the mind which would be equally indispensable for the understanding of the normal. (Freud, 1925, p.47)

In short, psychoanalysis had become a personality theory.

Of Freud's early works, none were more controversial than his essays on childhood sexuality. I've already described how sexual fantasies were discovered in the childhood of hysterical patients. Freud's next step was to propose that such fantasies were not unusual but instead characterized the mental life of all children. Tsk tsk! People do not like to hear that children have a sexual life. Perhaps childhood sexuality seems so bizarre because we think Freud is saying that children are sexual in the same sense that adults are sexual. This is not what the concept means. Obviously, children and adults are different.

What Freud proposes is that both have a sexual instinct, a drive that demands satisfaction. Where many people would suggest that one's sex drive appears for the first time during puberty, proponents of childhood sexuality argue that it is present all along:

> The sexual function . . . has to pass through a long and complicated process of development before it becomes what we are familiar with as the normal sexual life of the adult. (Freud, 1925, p.35)

The process through which the child's sexuality passes is termed **psycho-sexual development,** and as I have already mentioned, Freud views this development in terms of stages. As they grow up, kids pass through different stages defined by that part of the body which is sensitive to sexual stimulation. The child is thought to pass through these stages in an invariant sequence.

First there is the **oral stage,** so named because the child's mouth provides basic gratification: sucking, eating, biting, cooing, crying, and so on. Any of you familiar with infants know that the mouth is the vehicle for becoming acquainted with the world. New parents learn quickly that Junior will put anything and everything in his mouth that will fit, including things that are bigger than Junior himself.

Next there is the **anal stage,** which occurs after weaning has been accomplished and reflects the role of the anus in providing pleasure. The young child derives sexual gratification in two ways: eliminating feces and retaining them. Again, new parents learn quickly that Junior engages in both activities with equal skill. Pediatricians have become rich answering phone calls from frantic parents who cannot understand what Junior is doing (or not doing, as the case may be). During the anal stage, the child encounters strong societal demands in the form of toilet training. Retention and elimination of feces, heretofore uninhibited activities, now must reflect realities of time and place.

Then the **phallic stage** occurs. Libido is concentrated in the genitals, and children derive pleasure from touching their genitals, playing doctor, and asking questions about storks and the like. Yet again, new parents may despair over Junior's activities in the phallic stage. However, at about the age of five, children pass into what Freud calls a **latency period,** a time marked by repression of sexual impulses and a curbing of oral, anal, and phallic activities that provide pleasure.

The child emerges from latency with the onset of puberty, passing into the **genital stage.** According to Freud, this is the last psychosexual stage, that of mature sexuality, in which pleasure is provided through the genitals in the course of heterosexual activity. Although great changes occur from adolescence to old age, Freud believed that sexuality stayed the same, set in the pattern established early in life.

A question might have occurred to you while reading about these stages: why does the child pass through them? Why doesn't Junior do the Peter Pan thing and just stay where life is simple and comfortable, with pleasure readily available and frustrations rare? The answer to this question lies in the root metaphor of organicism. According to psychoanalytic theory, *children unfold their inherent nature.* This process can be thwarted or encouraged, but its essence is a biological given. It's in the nature of people to pass through the psychosexual stages, whether they want to or not. Oak trees cannot stay twigs, cats cannot stay kittens, and people cannot stay in the oral stage.

Nevertheless, people pass through the stages with varying success. The way in which someone has traversed the psychosexual stages puts a characteristic stamp on her adult personality. Gratifications may occur too easily. Alternatively, they may be frustrated. Consider the oral stage. Children may be weaned too quickly. Or they may be overindulged. Although the child passes into the anal stage and beyond, an investment of libido is left behind, unavailable for future activities.

If enough libidinal energy has been tied up in a past stage, then **fixation** has occurred. As an adult, the fixated individual may show a **character type** that reflects the fixation. The **oral character** is one who makes incessant use of his mouth: eating, drinking, talking, smoking cigarettes, ingesting drugs. If you borrow a pen from such a character, you'll end up wiping it off, because it will be sticky, and kissing someone fixated at the oral stage is apt to be exciting, in both good and bad ways.

Karl Abraham (1927) subdivided the oral stage into **oral eroticism** (sucking and eating) and **oral sadism** (biting and chewing). Fixation at the oral eroticism stage results in someone who is cheerful, optimistic, and dependent, someone who expects the world to take care of him and reacts by overeating or overdrinking if this fails to occur. Fixation at the oral sadism stage results in someone who is cynical, pessimistic, and mean, who will "bite your head off" and "chew you out" if you cross him.

Fixation at the anal stage results in the **anal character** type, which takes one of two forms reflecting the two basic strategies available to the child who has difficulty meeting demands for toilet training: **anal compulsive** and **anal expulsive.** With the first strategy, the child may respond by retaining feces altogether. Not only is this intrinsically pleasurable, but it also allows the child to punish the parents for their difficult-to-meet demands. "Okay, I'll show you

The oral character type will almost always have something in her mouth.

just how full of crap somebody can be." The anal compulsive character is therefore a person who is excessively neat and orderly. She cannot tolerate a mess. She washes the dinner dishes before the meal is served, puts slipcovers not only on her couches but on her children, and, of course, cleans the house thoroughly before the maid arrives.

The second strategy of the child coping unsuccessfully at the anal stage is to respond by expelling feces at the worst possible times, for example, right after his diaper has been changed, when the family is on a crowded train, or when the toilet is broken. Again, this strategy is intrinsically pleasurable as well as an attack against one's parents: "Okay, I'll shit all over you then."

So the anal expulsive character is at times stubborn and stingy, at other times wasteful and messy. The chaos created by this individual punishes those who make what are seen as unreasonable demands. All teachers who ask students to type papers are periodically tortured by anal expulsive students. I've been given typed papers that are so grimy and filthy that I'm afraid to handle them, and I've read a number of papers typed with what must be the very first ribbon ever made.

Fixation at the phallic stage results in the **phallic character** type, an individual whose sexual impulses are excessively oriented toward the self. According to psychoanalytic theorist Wilhelm Reich (1933), fixation at the phallic stage is produced by too little or too much genital contact. The

The anal character type will, in some settings, appear excessively messy.

individual becomes narcissistic, preoccupied with himself or herself. Traits of the phallic character include arrogance, vanity, confidence, and aggressiveness.

The macho man of contemporary society typifies the phallic character. He needs to stand out in a group, to be the center of attention. His sexuality is exaggerated with overwhelming cologne, gold chains, and an open shirt. He may lift weights and develop his body to such an extent that his profile takes on a phallic form: rigid, upright, and bulging with veins. At the same time, his sexuality has no social reference. It doesn't connect with a romantic partner. The macho man prowls through bars alone, dancing with himself.

Insofar as adult personality is concerned, the most critical events occur during the phallic stage. According to Freud, the young child, with libido newly centered in the genitals, experiences a severe conflict: a wish to possess the parent of the opposite sex and a desire to do away with the parent of the same sex. This conflict is termed the **Oedipus complex,** after the Greek drama in which the main character unknowingly acted out this scenario by killing his father and marrying his mother.

Freud feels the Oedipus complex to be a universal fact of human development, brought about by the concentration of libido in the genitals. The child's love for the parent becomes sexually colored, and jealousy of the other parent results. The particular manner in which the child resolves this conflict shapes adult personality.

Fixation at the phallic stage may result in exaggerated masculinity (steroids help, too).

Here are some of the factors entering into the Oedipus complex. First, the child fears the retaliation of the same-sex parent. Second, the child feels guilty about these ill wishes. Third, the child typically resolves the Oedipus complex symbolically, by identifying with the same-sex parent and thereby indirectly possessing the opposite-sex parent. Freud calls this process **defensive identification** and regards it as the means by which children acquire the behaviors, attitudes, and interests that characterize them as adults. Little boys become their fathers, and little girls become their mothers, presumably as a way out of the romantic triangle they experience at an early age. And then they have their own children, and the drama is played out again.

The most important distinction affecting the course of the Oedipal conflict and its resolution is whether the child is a boy or a girl. The process for boys is more straightforward than for girls. In keeping with the sexual theme of the Oedipus complex, boys fear that their fathers will retaliate by castrating them. **Castration anxiety** results, which in turn leads to repression of the boy's desire for his mother and identification with his father. "My father can beat up your father," says one toddler to another, perhaps reflecting the more primal thought, "because my father can cut off my parts!"

What makes things more complicated for girls is that just like boys, their first object of love is mother. When the phallic stage is entered, their genital curiosity leads to the observation that boys have penises, and they do not. The little girl concludes that she once had a penis, and that it was cut off. Her mother probably had something to do with it, since she has no penis either. Annoyance with mother then leads to increased affection for father, tinged with sexuality as well as envy. After all, Dad still has his penis.

Freud proposed that girls experience **penis envy,** the desire to have male genitals. Little girls wish to have sex with their father and bear him children, as a way to deal with their penis envy. The child born from this incestuous union is equated with a penis. It eventually occurs to little girls that marrying father is impractical, helped along by the fear of mother's wrath. Identification with mother therefore occurs, along with repression of all desire for father. However, this resolution does not occur as clearly as with boys, since little girls do not experience castration anxiety. (Castration has presumably already occurred.) So, they do not have the same motivation to resolve the conflict represented by the Oedipus complex. And according to Freud, females do not resolve it as well as males do.

Everyone would agree with Freud that children are biological beings, that they pass through stages as they develop, with attention centering around different parts of their body. Everyone would agree that conflict and anxiety are no strangers to children. "But," you might ask, "why call all this sexual? Sexual is X-rated, for adults only. Or maybe in California it's R-rated. Anyway, why confuse things by explaining the facts in terms of childhood sexuality?"

Quite simply, the evidence available to Freud led him to describe development in sexual terms. His clinical work invariably pointed to sexual factors in childhood that created conflicts and became repressed. His observation of children showed that they often were greatly concerned with the hows and whys of the body, particularly the genitals, and his reading of mythology and literature revealed the theme of incest to be present in all cultures.

Furthermore, the notion of childhood sexuality allows a variety of behaviors to be explained by reference to a biological function: *pleasure.* The means in which pleasure is achieved changes, bowing to the demands of the immediate environment, but the basic instinct is present in all people, from birth to death. Freud feels that the notion of infant sexuality is not at all strange. Rather, it is the opposite belief, what he calls *the agreeable legend of the asexuality of childhood,* that should be regarded with astonishment.

In the early part of the twentieth century, as Freud's writings became known throughout Europe, he attracted several able disciples, notably Alfred Adler and Carl Jung. Both men were later to break with him over the primacy he assigned to sexual motives. But, while the departure of Adler and Jung wounded Freud, he saw their disagreement as stemming from an intolerance of the truth about sexuality and its overriding importance in human personality.

The pattern of Freud's life was soon set. He extended his ideas to both normal and abnormal behavior, until the entire range of human activity fell under his theoretical umbrella. In particular, the Oedipus complex provided a far-reaching explanation for a variety of behaviors: creativity, religion, the origin of society. Most generally, psychoanalysis allowed the symbolic aspects of human activity to be explained.

Freud and his followers to this day have applied the psychoanalytic perspective to a broad spectrum of human products, from fairy tales to graffiti, from the books of the Bible to MTV, from sadism to masochism, and from the lives of saints to the lives of the rest of us. Human behavior is inherently symbolic, and most psychology theories cannot grapple well with the numerous levels upon which behavior has meaning. In contrast, psychoanalytic theory, with its assumption of over-determined behavior and its rich vocabulary for describing people's motives, is comfortable on all of these levels. As I stressed in Chapter 4, psychoanalysis can explain exactly those topics that other psychological theories cannot.

In his later life, Freud revised psychoanalytic theory in two important ways. First, he supplanted the so-called **topographical theory of the mind** (dividing it into the conscious, preconscious, and unconscious) with what is now known as his **structural theory** (dividing the mind into the **id, ego,** and **superego**). Second, he proposed an instinct for death and destruction that worked against the libidinal instinct which had previously been the basis of his theories.

What motivated the structural theory? There were several inconsistencies in Freud's distinction between the unconscious and the conscious, so he introduced his structural theory to resolve them (Fancher, 1973). Freud had characterized the unconscious in different ways. On the one hand, the unconscious was defined as whatever is not conscious or able to be made conscious. On the other hand, the unconscious was defined in terms of the pleasure principle, operating without regard to the constraints of reality.

In many cases, these different characterizations of the unconscious peacefully coexist. What is not conscious disregards time, space, and logic; and vice versa. In other cases, however, contradiction occurs. Some of the material that is kept unconscious because it is threatening is organized, consistent, and pertinent to the real world. A number of the dreams described by Freud in *The Interpretation of Dreams* disguise wishes that do not conform to the pleasure principle. Fantasies that lurk behind dreams and neurotic symptoms may be grounded in reality and highly elaborate. The Oedipal conflict is a good example of an unconscious wish that is somewhat sensitive to reality, in particular, the revenge of the same-sex parent.

Another difficulty with dividing the mind into unconscious, preconscious, and conscious parts centers on where to locate the *censor* of the threatening thoughts. The censor cannot be in our conscious or preconscious mind, since we are not aware that we are unaware of certain impulses. We are simply unaware. At the same time, the censor cannot be in our unconscious mind either, since that would require the unconscious to be sensitive to what would upset the conscious mind, that is, to operate by the reality principle. By definition, the unconscious doesn't work that way.

Freud found a way out of these difficulties by slicing the mental apparatus in another way. He proposed that the mind was composed of three interacting systems or structures: the id, the ego, and the superego. These structures are not to be confused with the earlier divisions into unconscious, conscious, and preconscious. They are different metaphors for the mind, *methods of organization rather than places.* With his new metaphor, Freud could resolve the contradictions inherent in the previous one.

The crucial aspect of the new metaphor is the ego, that part of the mind which is reality-oriented and therefore makes use of secondary process. However, the ego is not necessarily conscious, unconscious, or preconscious. All three are represented in the ego, depending on its particular function. In resisting threatening impulses, the ego operates unconsciously. In other activities, the ego operates consciously.

The part of the mind that makes use of primary process is the id, literally the "it" in German. The id is unconscious and undifferentiated, the source of instincts and impulses. At birth, a child's mind is exclusively id. The infant is out of time and space, lost in bliss. Only through interactions with the world does the ego develop, to help the child satisfy his needs without running afoul of reality, as represented by the demands and dangers of the world beyond the cradle. Freud thus maintains the developmental emphasis of his theory. With age, the child becomes increasingly adapted to the real world. The ego is the vehicle that makes this adaptation possible. At the same time, the id is always close at hand, waiting to erupt at any opportunity.

It seemed to Freud, though, that the developing person was not solely a bundle of passions held in check by a pragmatic ego. Sometimes people act in outright opposition to both selfish need and common sense. Sometimes people acted morally or justly, sacrificing instinctive and practical considerations for what was good and right. People return wallets that they find, even with hundreds of dollars in them. Soldiers on a battlefield may give up their lives so that their fellows survive. The id and ego cannot make these sacrifices.

Freud posited another mental structure to do so: the superego, the moral sense of a person. The superego doesn't appear until late childhood, developing from the Oedipal conflict and its resolution. As the child identifies with the same-sex parent and represses his or her own impulses, the values of that parent are incorporated. The resentment toward the parent is now displaced against the self, and our all-too-familiar guilty conscience appears as the tool of the superego.

The three structures of the mind constantly interact, negotiating the ways in which libidinal energy is to be utilized. You might imagine them as little people inside your head, with the id yelling, "Go for it," the superego proclaiming, "Over my dead body," and the ego hedging, "Well, maybe when I know you better." Who wins this tug-of-war? The answer is different for every person. It depends on how much libidinal energy is present in the first place. It depends on the course of psychosexual development. It depends on the circumstances to which the ego is habitually attuned. From the point of view of psychoanalytic theory, a person's personality is characterized by the relative mix of these three systems.

The ego seems to have the toughest job, since it must adjudicate the inherent conflict between instincts and morality. Freud devoted great attention to how the ego accomplished this job. He proposed that the ego has at its disposal techniques of compromise called **defense mechanisms.** Freud's description of these techniques ranks among his most stunning achievements.

One can discern many of the defense mechanisms in prior writings: in the Bible, in Aesop's fables, and in Shakespeare's plays. However, Freud was the one who brought them together and explained them in the same way. Many of the theoretical terms he introduced to explain defense mechanisms are now part of our everyday speech.

Common to all defense mechanisms is a compromise between wishes and reality. Further, their operation is for the most part unconscious. Like dreams and jokes, defense mechanisms allow wishes and impulses to be satisfied indirectly, without ruffling the conscious mind and without bringing about retaliation from an outraged world.

Here are some of the defense mechanisms described by Freud:

- **Repression** occurs when a dangerous memory is forced from consciousness, as might happen if a person is responsible for a horrible accident where someone else gets killed. The details of the accident may not be remembered.

- **Projection** is the attribution of one's own unacceptable impulses and characteristics to someone else. You periodically read of a zealous citizen who has led battles against pornography but has then been arrested for propositioning someone in the restroom of a department store. His public criticism of sexual "perverts" may be a projection of the repugnance he feels for his own sexual drive.

- **Reaction formation** is the replacement of one impulse with its opposite, hiding love with hate or hate with love. In elementary school (and beyond), little boys are apt to splash mud on the little girls they find attractive. And little girls are apt to find some boys more creepy than others, those who are not at all creepy. You must know couples whose relationship started with instant dislike.

- **Regression** occurs when a person retreats to an earlier way of acting. She walks down the up escalator of the psychosexual stages until a comfortable place is found, one where she had earlier coped with no difficulty. Regression is acting like a child in the face of demands that cannot be met. I chew my fingernails on an airplane because I am very anxious about flying.

- **Sublimation** is the channeling of instinctive impulses into activities that are socially valued. A surgeon might be redirecting her aggressive impulses by putting people under the knife. A clinical psychologist might be satisfying his sexual needs by listening in on other people's marital problems. According to psychoanalytic thought, everyone has underlying instincts. Individuals who sublimate are to be respected, since their use of these instincts is the most generally helpful.

Of all of Freud's original concepts, none have been better elaborated by other thinkers than the notion of defense mechanism. From this extension a new branch of psychoanalysis was born, known as **ego psychology,** which goes beyond the conflict-ridden model of the mind proposed by Freud. According to the ego psychologists, the ego does more than simply react to the demands of the id. Its techniques are more than just defensive. Instead, the ego is involved in normal adaptation and is responsible for health, growth, and creativity. Among the important ego psychologists are Freud's daughter Anna Freud (1937), Heinz Hartmann (1939), and Ernest Kris (1952).

So far in my discussion, I have implied that some defenses are quite healthy. It might even be a mistake to call them a defense, since that has connotations of weakness. So some theorists prefer to call defense mechanisms *coping techniques,* with some leading to good adaptation and some not.

Psychiatrist George Vaillant (1971) gives us one of the most complete taxonomies of defense mechanisms (see Table 5-1). In keeping with the ideas of ego psychology, he calls them *ego mechanisms* and arranges them in a hierarchy from immature to mature. According to Vaillant, people use characteristic ego mechanisms, so they differ with respect to the maturity of their personality. Mature individuals are expected to show superior adaptation in a variety of domains.

The second major change in Freud's psychoanalytic theory involved his view of instincts. In his early writings, Freud emphasized the libido, under which he categorized the instinct for self-preservation and the instinct for sexual gratification. Taken together, these are called the **life instinct** or *Eros,*

Table 5-1
Ego Mechanisms

Maturity Level	General Characterization	Examples
1. Narcissistic	Strategies that alter a person's perception of reality	Delusion Denial Distortion
2. Immature	Strategies that reduce a person's distress—associated with threat of intimacy or its loss	Acting out Falling ill Fantasy Passive-aggressive behavior Projection
3. Neurotic	Strategies that change a person's private feelings or expression of instincts	Displacement Dissociation Intellectualization Reaction formation Repression
4. Mature	Strategies that integrate a person's conscience and feelings	Altruism Anticipation Humor Sublimation Suppression

SOURCE: From Vaillant, 1971.

after the Greek god of love. However, evidence from Freud's clinical work caused him to question his assumption that all instincts serve life (Fancher, 1973).

Freud found that some of his patients acted in therapy just as they acted out of it: neurotically. So what? Although the tendency to repeat past actions does not seem at odds with common sense, if those past actions are injurious, their repetition contradicts Freud's assumption of a dominant instinct directed toward preservation of self and species.

A contemporary example of the **compulsion to repeat** is the *post-traumatic stress disorder* that occurs among some Vietnam veterans. Years after a traumatic event, individuals may continue to relive its painful details. They experience anxiety during the day and bad dreams during the night, all centered around an event that occurred years ago. The life instinct cannot explain post-traumatic stress disorder.

In *Beyond the Pleasure Principle,* Freud (1920) revised his theory of the instincts, positing an instinct that worked against Eros. The **death instinct,**

The Vietnam War introduced a new psychological problem to Americans: post-traumatic stress disorder. The Vietnam Veterans Memorial in Washington reminds us that there are more victims than are immediately apparent.

or *Thanatos* (after the Greek god of death) as some call it, "*is an urge inherent in organic life to restore an earlier state of things*. . . . It is a kind of organic elasticity . . . the expression of the inertia inherent in organic life" (Freud, 1920, p. 36, italics in original). What is now living was once nonliving, and the death instinct pushes the individual back to this earlier state. The compulsion to repeat is one manifestation of the death instinct.

Like the life instinct, the death instinct may be "satisfied" in various ways. If directed inward, it may be evident in masochism, thrill-seeking, or suicide, including slow deaths like alcoholism and drug addiction. If directed outward, it may show up as sadism, aggression, or hostility, all of the profound and trivial ways that people can be mean to each other.

The death instinct has not been generally accepted, even among those who otherwise embrace psychoanalytic theory. It seems at odds with the more general biological principles on which Freud based his ideas. How could a death instinct prove helpful in meeting the challenges of the environment? How could it evolve?

Despite considerable resistance to the specifics of his ideas, acclaim came to Freud within his lifetime. So too did popular attention, which may or may not have appealed to him. He was even offered a job writing an advice column for the lovelorn in *Cosmopolitan,* a forerunner of the agony column by Irma

Kurtz, no doubt! But his later years were not always happy ones. He underwent thirty-three operations for cancer of the jaw, the illness that eventually killed him in 1939.

ALFRED ADLER: STRIVING FOR SUPERIORITY

One of the first followers of Freud, Alfred Adler (1870–1937) was a Viennese physician born the second son in a well-to-do family. Adler remembered his childhood as unhappy, since he was unfavorably compared to his older brother, a reportedly model child whose attractiveness and physical prowess Adler felt incapable of matching.

He received his medical degree in 1895 from the University of Vienna, specializing in ophthalmology and later practicing general medicine. In one of his earliest papers (1907), Adler examined the issue of **organ inferiority.** It was well-known to medicine that disease often attacked weaker organs of the body, but Adler additionally observed that disease was not the inevitable consequence of a weak organ. Under some circumstances, the body may compensate for this weakness and develop a strength.

In making this general point, Adler drew upon psychological examples as well as biological ones. History and literature provided him with apt illustrations of how inferiority could be turned to superiority under favorable environmental conditions. Teddy Roosevelt was a weakling as a child, but developed into a hearty and robust adult. He started our National Park Service, coined the term "rugged individualism," and popularized the slogan "Speak softly but carry a big stick." (He also inspired the teddy bear, which is irrelevant in the present context, but an interesting fact, nonetheless.)

In 1910, Adler furthered his ideas by proposing that organ inadequacy leads to subjective feelings of inferiority. These feelings impel the attempt at compensation in the domain of inferiority. He introduced the concept of **masculine protest,** claiming that inordinate strength and power are compensations for feelings of being unmanly. The macho man of contemporary society can be seen from this view as sexually and socially inadequate, protesting excessively against his perceived inferiority with displays of exaggerated manliness.

Striving to compensate for inferiority is seen not in just the occasional person, but in everyone, since children universally feel small and dependent compared to adults. Inferiority is a natural part of development, and striving to compensate for it is an inevitable drive. Pathology results from *overcompensation.* Adler coined the term **inferiority complex,** and proposed that everyone at one time feels inferior with respect to something. These ideas apply to women as well as men. As Adler uses the term, masculinity refers to strength—not to male sexuality. Eventually, Adler used more neutral language and talked about one's **striving for superiority** in place of his (or her) masculine protest.

During this period, while Adler's psychological theories were taking form, he came into contact with Freud. Although the details of their first meeting are not clear, it is known that they attended the same weekly discussion as early as 1902. However, a break between these two important theorists was imminent, and it occurred over the primacy which Freud assigned to sexuality. While Adler acknowledged that sexual conflicts were often significant, and that feelings of inferiority could result from inadequate sexual development, he felt that people's problems stemmed from a variety of social sources, not just sexual conflicts. So, while Freud argued that women feel inferior because they lack male genitals, Adler looked to women's interactions with society to find the source of their perceived inferiority—not to their anatomy.

At about this time, Adler read Hans Vaihinger's (1911) book, *The Psychology of "As If,"* which proposed that people live in accordance with fictional goals they set for themselves. These goals may or may not be real, but when people treat them as real, they become psychologically significant and determine thoughts, actions, and feelings. Vaihinger's ideas greatly influenced Adler because they provided a way to argue against Freud's strict determinism. According to Adler, then, man was motivated more by his future goals than by his past experiences, an explanation now called **teleology.**

People are usually not aware of their goals, argued Adler, and goals are therefore the key contents of the unconscious. Inappropriate goals result in neurotic behavior. Appropriate goals result in health and happiness. Although all people are thought to strive for superiority, the way they define superiority stamps their goals as appropriate or inappropriate. Consistent with his social emphasis, Adler felt that healthy goals were those achieved by contributing to the welfare of others. Unhealthy goals undercut those of other people.

Another important concept Adler introduced (1927) is **social interest,** emphasizing his belief that people are inherently social. They are born with a sensitivity to others and cannot be understood apart from their social ties. In contrast to Freud, who states that individuals and society are in conflict, Adler believed that the relationship among people and their larger society is at least in principle harmonious.

Adler (1927) is also responsible for the attention given to a child's place within a family. He felt one's birth order influenced treatment by others and eventually determined one's personality. The eldest child is the first to be the center of attention, only to be dethroned time and again with the birth of each subsequent brother or sister. As a result, the eldest child is thought to understand power and authority better than the later children in the family. The eldest child can compete with younger siblings for parental approval only by acting maturely. She may be thrust into the role of teacher or caregiver.

The second child in a family sees the eldest child as a rival to be overcome. As a result, he may set unrealistically high goals:

> Through his childhood he has a pacemaker. A typical second child is easy to recognize. He behaves as if he were in a race, is under full steam all of the time, and trains continually to surpass his older brother and conquer him. The Bible gives us many marvelous psychological hints, and the typical second child is beautifully portrayed in the story of Jacob. (Adler, 1931, p.148)

If you recall, Jacob and Esau were the highly competitive sons of Isaac. Jacob (the second child) induced Esau to sell his birthright to him for a meal of bread and lentils, surely an extreme reaction to sibling jealousy! In contrast, if the eldest is supportive, the second child will develop in a healthy fashion. Otherwise, resentful, the second child will develop in an insecure way.

The youngest child in a family is often spoiled and pampered. Because there are several older siblings, there are a variety of examples she may follow. Hand-me-down clothes may not be desirable, but hand-me-down roles are. So, the youngest child may be flexible and diverse. As the baby, she receives support and protection from all, while at the same time feeling particularly inferior. A good friend of mine is the youngest in a family of four. Yesterday she remarked to me that just once in her life, she would like to hear someone compare one of her older sisters to her rather than vice versa. According to Adler, this is a common complaint among the youngest in a family.

After World War II, Adler played a dominant role in the establishment of child-guidance clinics in Vienna's school system. His ideas about parent-child relationships were extended to teacher-student relationships, and he came to have a lasting effect on educational theory and practice. School disobedience was seen as an attempt to achieve superiority, and disobedient children were to be encouraged to seek more productive means of achieving their goals.

In 1926, Adler visited the United States for the first time, and he accepted appointments at Columbia University and later at Long Island College of Medicine. He made the United States his permanent home in 1934, but in 1937 died of a heart attack suffered during a strenuous European lecture tour.

How should Adler be remembered? In terms of his contribution to the psychoanalytic paradigm, his notion that people are social beings rather than sexual ones is his most notable achievement (Hall & Lindzey, 1978). This characterization paved the way for later psychoanalytic theorizing by Horney, Fromm, Sullivan, and others in which the social nature of men and women is accorded fundamental status. These later theorists are called neoFreudians, in recognition of their debt to Sigmund Freud. NeoAdlerians might be a better term, however, since their ideas were more directly fore-shadowed by Adler.

CARL GUSTAV JUNG: THE COLLECTIVE UNCONSCIOUS

Another early associate of Freud, the Swiss physician Carl Jung (1875–1961) broke with Freud to found his own school of psychoanalytic thought. By all reports, Jung was originally Freud's favorite associate. He was a man of stag-gering knowledge and intelligence, groomed by Freud to be his successor as the leader of the psychoanalytic movement. By the same token, Jung greatly admired Freud and throughout his life acknowledged the importance of Freud's ideas. The eventual break between the two men was painful on both sides.

Jung was born in Kesswyl, Switzerland, the son of a pastor. He grew up in Basel, where he entered the university intending to become a philologist and archaeologist. However, he soon became interested in the natural sci-ences and then in medicine. After receiving his medical degree from the University of Basel, he took a position in 1900 at a Zurich mental hospital.

Investigations of word associations were among Jung's first inquiries. He prepared a list of one hundred words and presented it to normal individuals as well as to psychiatric patients. "Answer as quickly as possible with the first word that occurs to your mind." Response time was calculated with a stop watch. Jung also measured the individual's breathing and perspiring during the word association task.

Although previous researchers like Francis Galton and James McKeen Cattell had studied word associations, their concern was with what they revealed about intelligence. Jung was instead concerned with what word associations said about emotions. He found that some individuals took a particularly long time to respond to certain words, and also showed increased signs of arousal. They might repeat the stimulus word several times, as if unable to think of any response at all. In such cases, the word was usually associated with some topic of emotional significance, providing Jung a clue to begin his clinical inquiry.

Sometimes, the patient was quite aware of why he had an emotional response to the word. But other times, the patient seemed unable to recog-nize its emotional significance, despite the reaction it provoked. Jung regarded the latter case as evidence of an unconscious **complex,** *an aspect of mental functioning split off from the rest of the mind and functioning on its own.*

Complexes arise because of emotional trauma or conflict; they cannot coexist with the rest of the mind.

Jung was also concerned with the possible causes of schizophrenia. He was struck by the fantasies and delusions of psychotic patients. They seemed to resemble the myths and beliefs of far-flung cultures. Jung was so impressed by these parallels that he believed the contents of schizophrenic thought transcended the patients' personal experience and reflected ideas and feelings common to the entire human race. These universal beliefs resided in the **collective** or **racial unconscious,** to Jung a more important aspect of personality than Freud's so-called personal unconscious.

Like Freud, then, Jung was grappling with the unconscious. With his word association test, Jung had a measure of the effects of unconscious emotions on behavior that paralleled Freud's methods of free association and dream analysis. But where Freud entered psychiatry through clinical work with hysterics, Jung did so through work with much more troubled individuals. And while Freud brought knowledge about the nervous system to bear on personality, Jung drew upon philosophy, religion, and anthropology.

Jung was initially attracted to Freud's ideas upon reading *The Interpretation of Dreams.* This book, with its emphasis on dream symbolism, contained many ideas that agreed with Jung's observations. In 1907, Jung published *The Psychology of Dementia Praecox,* a monograph applying Freud's ideas to psychotic patients. He drew parallels between the disintegrated word associations of schizophrenics and the dreams of hysterics. Both became meaningful when one peered beneath their surface. The apparent emotional flatness of the schizophrenic was attributed to repression.

In 1906, Freud and Jung began a correspondence, and in 1907, they met for the first time and began to work closely together. Freud sensed in Jung the ideal spokesman for psychoanalytic thought. Freud was keenly aware that in some quarters his ideas were dismissed simply because he was a Jew. Jung was a Gentile—indeed, the son of a pastor—and therefore an ideal associate for Freud. On Jung's tongue, psychoanalytic ideas might reach a broader audience.

In many ways, Freud was right about Carl Jung. He would extend psychoanalytic ideas in creative directions, he would win followers and students, he would reach a worldwide audience. However, Jung did not do so as Sigmund Freud's protégé. The break started as early as 1911 and was clearly evident in Jung's 1912 book, *Symbols of Transformation.* Jung accepted the existence of psychic energy—libido—but felt that it manifested itself in numerous ways, such as religion and power. Jung also felt that people should be viewed not just in terms of past causes but also in terms of future goals and aspirations. Like Adler, Jung favored teleological explanations: people strive toward fulfillment and unity. In 1912, Freud and Jung ceased their personal correspondence.

Jung became greatly interested in the interpretation of dreams, and began to view them not as disguised wishes but as attempts to solve current problems. To explore the significance of symbols, Jung undertook field expeditions to study the minds and myths of preliterate individuals, travelling in the 1920s to Africa (to study Kenyans) and to the Southwest of the United States (to study Pueblo Indians). Jung was impressed with the apparent universality of certain psychological symbols, and he strengthened his belief in the collective unconscious—the storehouse of these symbols.

His theory of **archetypes** took form. According to Jung, by virtue of being born into the human race, we inherit not just physical characteristics but also mental and emotional predispositions. Chief among these are archetypes, *determinants of how we experience and interpret significant events.* Because of archetypes, all people think, feel, and act similarly when confronted with similar situations. Archetypes can explain the tendency of symbols, myths, and beliefs to appear across different cultures, the tendency of even the most mundane of us to act out in our own lives the stories of Liz and Dick, Cain and Abel, Bobby and Pam, Romeo and Juliet, George and Billy, and so forth.

Consider the archetype of the **shadow**—our darker self. The image of an immoral, passionate, and evil figure lurks in many legends. Satan, Dracula, Mr. Hyde, Charlie Manson, Darth Vader, and J. R. Ewing bear a strong family resemblance to each other. The prototype defining this family is Jung's archetype of the shadow, *the representation of what is inferior, primitive, and unadapted about ourselves.* We locate the shadow outside, in nooks and crannies, in those sorts of places where nice people don't go, but the actual location of the shadow is within ourselves.

On a physical level, archetypes are at odds with what we know about biological inheritance. But, from a metaphysical perspective, the idea of archetypes makes some sense. If we accept the premise of evolution, we conclude that the mind as well as the body has evolved. This means that there should be psychological continuity across species, and some forms of continuity are indeed obvious. The Law of Effect applies alike to people and planaria, dogs and cats, aardvarks and zebras. It makes sense in evolutionary terms that living things avoid pain and seek out pleasure. For the most part, these tendencies insure survival. Granted that we live in a social world and that our ancestors evolved within a social world, it is possible that certain tendencies to get along with other people were also favored by natural selection, just as certain tendencies to form associations by classical conditioning were favored.

Archetypes may therefore be regarded as social tendencies with survival value. For example, the **anima** is the feminine aspect of a man's personality, while the **animus** is the masculine aspect of a woman's personality. The anima and animus help us understand and anticipate the opposite sex. When we fall in love with another person, our idealizations of "man" and "woman" also become involved, and the affair recreates all past loves. We overlook flaws, minor and major, and we disregard mundane reality. Like Adam and Eve, we become the first people in the world. And like Adam and Eve, we populate the earth, at least to the extent of raising 2.3 children, a dog, a cat, and some gerbils.

So, *archetypes are tendencies: structures or forms.* They are not a specific content. In my earlier example of the shadow, I was careful not to say that J.R. Ewing *is* the shadow. Rather, he *represents* the shadow, fleshed out with the details of Texas and American culture. J.R. unabashedly indulges himself in liquor, women, and power. He wheels and deals, but he never seems to work. He appeals to us because he is a case study of what is inferior in ourselves, and we of course live in the same society that he does. By scrutinizing J. R., we scrutinize ourselves, and we may come to integrate the shadow into the rest of our personality. In a different time and place, the shadow would still be apparent, but in different trappings.

One of the most important archetypes identified by Jung is the **self,** a person's striving for unity among the different components of personality. This archetype is often symbolized as a **mandala,** or magic circle (see Figure 5-1). Mandala symbolism appears in all cultures and represents wholeness and balance to Jung (Wilhelm & Jung, 1931). The self only appears late in life, if at all, since the different parts of personality must first develop themselves before they can be integrated into a coherent whole. Jung himself fashioned numerous manadala drawings, and contemporary art therapy may be traced to his belief that such drawings make our journey to wholeness a concrete one.

What are the disparate aspects of personality that the person strives to integrate throughout life? First there are the **attitudes** or orientations: *general approaches to the world.* **Extraversion** is *attention to the outer, objective world,* while **introversion** is *attention to the inner, subjective world* (Jung, 1924). In a person's makeup, one orientation is dominant and conscious. However, the opposite orientation is present in the unconscious. Throughout development, the person attempts to bring these two orientations into balance.

Also important are the **functions:** *basic psychological processes.* Jung 1924) identifies two pairs—**feeling** versus **thinking** and **sensing** versus **intuiting**—and proposes that for any given person, one function in each pair is dominant, expressing itself at the expense of the other. However, the other functions are evident in the operation of the unconscious. I see a mundane example of the four functions every Christmas, when I visit with the family of my brother's in-laws. There are several grandchildren in the family, and the

Figure 5-1
Mandala Symbolism

grandparents usually give the kids identical presents. The reactions differ markedly. Upon receiving a portable tape player, one child exclaims, "It's beautiful" (feeling); another child says, "Oh, a tape player" (sensing); yet another child takes it apart and explains the wiring to us (thinking); and finally another child breathlessly whispers, "My oh my, I just knew I'd get this for a present. I had a dream I would" (intuiting).

Attitudes and functions represent a personality typology, one that is, however, more complicated than the typical typology, since all attitudes and functions are present in all people, although in differing degrees. A person's particular type is not fixed, since the self pushes toward balance among the attitudes and functions.

In his later life, Jung continued to extend his ideas. He cultivated an interest in the occult, in flying saucers, in spiritualism—not as a believer but as a psychologist (Hall & Nordby, 1973). He felt that such subjects revealed the collective unconscious. Although continuing to live in Switzerland, he travelled and lectured widely, receiving honorary degrees at Harvard and

Oxford. He was the subject of several stories in *Time* magazine, and an interview with him appeared in an early issue of *Psychology Today*. He even appeared on television, and several interviews with him were filmed, so perhaps your instructor can arrange to have one of these shown. Jung died in 1961 at the age of eighty-five.

His place in psychology is still not clear. Several contributions are obvious: the use of word association tests to identify emotions, the notion of a complex, and the theory of psychological types. His contributions to therapy have been important, as have his ideas on art, literature, religion, and mythology.

NEOFREUDIANS: A SOCIAL EMPHASIS

Many of the psychoanalytic theorists who came after Freud, Adler, and Jung share an emphasis on the social determinants of personality. Better informed by sociological and anthropological research than their predecessors, these neoFreudian theorists refashioned psychoanalytic thought to better fit new discoveries in the social sciences (Hall & Lindzey, 1978). At the same time, they placed less emphasis on biology, instincts, and sexuality. Accordingly, the neoFreudians believe that the human condition can be modified, and social criticism is an integral part of their theorizing (Brown, 1964). Karen Horney, Erich Fromm, and Harry Stack Sullivan are among the major neoFreudians.

Karen Horney

Karen Horney (1885–1952) was born in Hamburg, Germany, She attended medical school in Berlin and was trained as a psychoanalyst. Horney's first interest was in female personality. As you saw earlier in this chapter, Freud's view of women was not positive, and Horney disagreed with his pronouncements regarding women, in particular with his idea of penis envy. More generally, Horney disagreed with the entire Oedipal conflict and with Freud's emphasis on sexuality.

Horney interprets the Oedipal conflict not in terms of sex and aggression but in terms of anxiety and insecurity. Her primary concept is **basic anxiety:** feelings of isolation and helplessness caused by disturbed relationships between people (Hall & Lindzey, 1970). Basic anxiety originates in childhood, if the child's needs are not met by the parents, if intimidation occurs, if strict prohibitions are enforced. The child responds to basic anxiety with different strategies, among them the jealousy, dependency, and ambivalence that Freud labels the Oedipal conflict.

Habitual reactions to anxiety become an important element in an individual's personality, and Horney (1945) identifies a number of such reactions which she calls **neurotic needs:** incessant striving for affection and approval, for power, for prestige, for achievement, for perfection, and so on. Because these needs are insatiable, they lead to conflicts. Notice that these derivative needs are similar to the ones that Freud, Adler, and Jung regard as primary. Horney's version of psychoanalytic theory therefore makes the bold attempt to subsume its other versions.

Horney (1937) attributes much of neurosis to the person's particular culture. For instance, contemporary American life makes contradictory demands on the individual. Many of these pertain to our treatment of others. Can we love our neighbor, and at the same time be into winning? Can we regard all people as equal, and at the same time believe that income is the sole measure of worth? Can we oppose nuclear weapons, and at the same time favor abortion? (Or vice versa?) No wonder we're all bozos on this bus. Anybody would feel helpless and insecure in the face of such contradictions.

Nevertheless, Horney is optimistic that conflicts can be prevented or resolved. If the child is raised by parents who provide security and love, then the child's basic anxiety never becomes overpowering. If society can be changed to minimize its contradictions, then many forms of neurosis can be headed off at the pass.

Erich Fromm

Erich Fromm (1900–1980) was also born in Germany, in Frankfurt. Unlike the theorists so far discussed, he was not a medical doctor. Instead, he studied psychology and sociology, receiving his doctorate in 1922. Fromm then pursued psychoanalytic training. He came to the United States in the 1930s, where he taught at a number of universities and psychoanalytic institutes. In 1976, he moved to Switzerland, where he died only a few years ago.

Fromm is primarily a social critic and theorist. His most direct contribution to personality psychology is a typology of character types resulting from his analysis of contemporary society. In his theorizing, Fromm was as much influenced by Karl Marx as by Sigmund Freud, and like other twentieth century writers, attempts a synthesis of the two, a plausible undertaking since both emphasize conflicts and their resolution. Following Freud, Fromm is concerned with neurosis. Following Marx, Fromm attributes neurosis to *alienation:* the estrangement of people from the products of their labor.

In *Escape from Freedom,* Fromm (1941) argues that only people can be alienated. Indeed, the potential for feeling alone defines our species. This means that a strictly biological interpretation of personality—one that emphasizes what people and animals share—will fail to capture our essence.

Throughout history, different forms of society have developed in an attempt to reduce alienation. Feudalism, capitalism, fascism, socialism, and communism all promise to provide the means for people to unite with each other and gain security (Hall & Lindzey, 1970). They do not necessarily promise freedom, but according to Fromm, freedom is not always attractive. It brings with it a greater potential for isolation. For this reason, totalitarian political movements like Nazism have some appeal: they provide a way to escape the alienation that freedom brings.

People's most basic needs have nothing to do with sexual and aggressive instincts. Instead, Fromm (1955) describes our needs in terms of the unique aspects of human existence. So, we have needs to become interdependent with others, to be creative, to be part of the world, to be a unique person, and to understand the world. These needs are not provided by society. Instead, they are inherent in people—the product of evolution. They only become evident in the context of a particular society. Personality is the product of the way that a given culture allows a person to manifest and satisfy his or her needs.

Consider the back-to-nature movement popular in segments of the United States. Individuals who favor environmental causes, health food, exercise, and a "small is beautiful" philosophy are attempting to satisfy the basic needs of existence. To become interdependent, they form a food cooperative, buying food in bulk and distributing it among the members. To become creative, they seek out new ways of making do with less. To be part of the world, they study ecology and backpack out whatever they have backpacked in. To be a unique person, they put their own stamp on a particular mix of granola. To have a coherent way of understanding the world, they interact with like-minded individuals and discuss their philosophy. In this context, gossip may be a useful way to articulate the way that they see the world: "Can you believe that my next-door neighbor gets drunk, eats Big Mac's, and then drives his RV down wilderness trails? How disgusting!"

Fromm (1947) identifies several character types prevalent in today's society that represent the interaction of basic needs with the opportunities allowing their expression in a materialistic, capitalistic society such as our own:

- **Receptive character types** believe that all good things come from without. They are dependent and passive, incapable of seeing the relationship between what they do and what the world provides. They are what you might call wimps.

- **Exploitative character types** take what they want from others by force or by guile. They do not produce things by their own efforts but by using others. They are what you might call ripoffs.

- **Hoarding character types** withdraw from the external world, keeping what they produce for themselves. They are aloof, selfish, and suspicious, Scrooges who only want to be left alone.

- **Marketing character types** are buyers and sellers of personality. They are interested in maintaining appearances, with making themselves attractive. When marketing types speak of keeping their options open, they don't mean stocks and bonds, but themselves. Marketing types have no real concern for others, regarding them only as a potential source for a line on their resumes. Let the buyer beware!

- **Necrophilous character types,** described more recently by Fromm (1973), are attracted to everything that is dead. They are fascinated with sickness, decay, and destruction. They worship power and technology, seeing violence as the solution to all problems. They have transformed what is living into something dead. Fromm attributes nuclear proliferation to people with this character type. They are sickies.

- **Biophilous character types** are the only healthy ones identified by Fromm. They love life and are genuinely concerned with others. They are not alienated. They are together, with themselves and with others.

Fromm argues that societies are sick to the degree that they produce sick people. Certainly, he criticizes contemporary American society, pointing to its flaws and the human toll. At the same time, though, Fromm (1968) believes that reform is possible. Society must be reworked to provide everyone a meaningful and responsible role, performing work that is attractive and enjoyable. So stay tuned.

Harry Stack Sullivan

Harry Stack Sullivan (1892–1949) takes the neoFreudian perspective to its extreme, regarding personality itself as a fiction and the relationships between people as the core subject of psychoanalysis. Sullivan was born near Norwich, New York. He received his medical degree in 1917, and was already an established clinician when he undertook psychoanalytic training in the 1930s. The Chicago School of Sociology, which embraced the perspective known as **symbolic interactionism,** strongly influenced Sullivan. In this view, people are defined by their relationships with others; these relationships in turn reflect the way that one is perceived by self and others.

Sullivan's interpersonal theory of psychiatry took its form from symbolic interactionism (Hall & Lindzey, 1970). Personality is the pattern of a person's relationships with others. Particular ways of acting reflect transformations of energy called **dynamisms** which are directed toward achieving **satisfaction** and **security.** By satisfaction, Sullivan means biological drives like those emphasized by Freud. By security, he means social needs like those that concerned Horney.

Sullivan's theory is concerned more with security than satisfaction. Development, for Sullivan, is the process by which a person comes to achieve security, and, since interpersonal disruptions threaten security by producing anxiety, development is directed toward achieving harmonious relationships with others.

Like other psychoanalytic theorists, Sullivan distinguishes stages of child development. In keeping with a social emphasis, these stages are marked by the way the child relates to other people. These relations in turn define who the child is and how he regards himself. The infant who is fed and cuddled comes to think of mother as good and himself as good. The frustrated child is led to the opposite belief. The child uses language to represent her self in coherent terms and to identify with the roles that society provides. The juvenile learns to be a social being—to be dominant and submissive, competitive and cooperative, nurturant and nurtured.

According to Sullivan, the person symbolizes his image of himself in a **personification,** which reflects past experiences with significant others. These need not be accurate, but, nevertheless, result in characteristic thoughts, actions, and feelings. Consider the child who is neglected or abused while an

Harry Stack Sullivan believed that children who are nurtured and loved will view the world as basically good.

infant. He may regard himself as bad, since that is how he was treated, and as an adult, he may engage in self-injurious behavior. Notice that Sullivan can thereby explain those actions which impelled Freud to propose a death instinct.

Sullivan published only one work during his lifetime—*Conceptions of Modern Psychiatry* in 1947. However, his followers have used recordings and notes from his lectures to produce a five-volume series detailing his position (1953, 1954, 1956, 1962, 1964). Sullivan is regarded as one of the most important of American psychiatrists, not only for his psychoanalytic theory, but also for his roles as scientific statesman, therapist, and teacher.

ERIK HOMBURGER ERIKSON: DEVELOPMENT ACROSS THE LIFESPAN

In some ways, Erik Erikson (born in 1902) is an ego psychologist, emphasizing the active role of the person in coping with the demands of the world. And in other ways, he is a neoFreudian, emphasizing the social determinants of personality. But Erikson prefers to call himself a postFreudian, supplementing the theories of Freud without replacing them.

Erikson was born in Germany to Danish parents. Before his birth, his father abandoned his mother, so Erikson never knew him. His mother subsequently married Theodor Homburger. Young Erik was not told the truth about his heritage until he was an adolescent, which precipitated an identity crisis. As an adult, he changed his surname from Homburger to Erikson. In his later theories, Erikson assigns great importance to the establishment of an identity.

After graduating from high school, he travelled about Europe attempting to settle upon a career. At age twenty-five, he was offered a job teaching at a nursery school. Through this work, he met Anna Freud, who was engaged in the psychoanalytic study of young children. Erikson was then introduced to Sigmund Freud and became a student of psychoanalysis. (At one point, he was Freud's chauffeur.) In 1933, he completed psychoanalytic training.

Erikson came to the United States in the same year and settled in Boston, where he became affiliated with Harvard University. He continued to work with children, observing the course of their development. He then moved to California and studied children of the Yurok Indian tribe. His anthropological observations led him to a social view of development, since Freud's psychosexual theory proved limited.

In 1950, Erikson presented his own theory of development in *Childhood and Society,* his major contribution to personality psychology. His theory is similar to Freud's theory of psychosexual development in that it proposes stages to be traversed in an invariant sequence. However, it differs importantly by regarding people as inherently social beings. The defining characteristic of each **psychosocial stage** is the social conflict to be resolved. Further, these stages encompass the entire lifespan of the individual—from birth to death.

Erikson identifies eight different stages (see Table 5-2), explaining each in terms of the conflict to be resolved and the virtue that results from its satisfactory resolution. Passage through the stages is not automatic. Although people have the inborn potential to move through them, the environment can help or hinder them. **Ritualizations** are socially provided aids to help resolve a conflict. **Ritualisms** are ritualizations that have gone bad and become rigid, subverting their original purpose.

Let's consider several of the latter stages in Erikson's theory. Most of you have probably just emerged from stage five and the task of establishing an identity. Who shall I be: doctor, lawyer, beggar, or thief? Out of *role confusion* comes *identity crisis;* from its resolution comes *identity* and the accompanying virtue of *fidelity,* the ability to sustain loyalties.

Now you are young adults in stage six. The major psychosocial conflict you presently face is *intimacy* versus *isolation.* Can you unite your newly created identity with that of another person? Can you get the help you need to make it through the night, through the weekend, through the rest of your life? If you can, you develop the virtue of *love,* defined by Erikson as *mutuality of devotion, caring for each other as you care for yourselves.*

Table 5-2
Erikson's Psychosocial Stages

Stage	Conflict	Virtue
1. Oral-sensory	Trust versus Mistrust	Hope
2. Muscular-anal	Autonomy versus Doubt	Will
3. Locomotor-genital	Initiative versus Guilt	Purpose
4. Latency	Industry versus Inferiority	Competence
5. Puberty and Adolescence	Identity versus Role diffusion	Fidelity
6. Young Adulthood	Intimacy versus Isolation	Love
7. Adulthood	Generativity versus Stagnation	Care
8. Maturity	Integrity versus Despair	Wisdom

SOURCE: Based on Erikson, 1950.

Are you familiar with "The Gift of the Magi," the short story by O. Henry? A young couple with absolutely no money faces the coming Christmas holiday. They desperately want to buy each other a fitting present. She has beautiful long hair, in which she takes great pride, so he wishes to buy her tortoiseshell combs for her hair. He has a beautiful gold watch, in which he takes great pride, so she wishes to buy him a chain for the watch.

The story is set before VISA or MASTERCARD, so each is faced with a dilemma. She solves it by selling her hair to a wig-maker; with the money she gets, she buys a watch chain. At the same time, he solves the problem by selling his watch to a pawnbroker; with the money he gets, he buys tortoiseshell combs. They surprise each other on Christmas Eve. If you think this is a sad story, or a funny one, then you have yet to resolve Erikson's stage six. Gifts need not be what one person gives to another, but what the two share in common.

Society attempts to help young people find a partner. Opportunities are provided by schools, churches, and other institutions in the form of dances and parties. Advice is given in magazines and newspapers. Food for thought is provided in the lyrics of many popular songs, "time after time." In general, young adulthood involves a host of affiliative activities. When these go wrong, the ritualism is *elitism,* marked by exclusive groups where who is *not* a member is more important than who is a member. A former acquaintance of mine always planned parties by drawing up a list of those people she didn't want to invite, because they were not cool.

Eventually we grow old. According to Erikson, old age presents us with a conflict between *integrity* and *despair.* Does life have meaning? Are we satisfied with the way that we have lived? Integrity is present to the degree that previous conflicts have been satisfactorily resolved. In old age, individuals may develop the virtue of *wisdom,* regarded by Erikson (1964) as a "detached concern with life itself in the face of death" (p. 133).

The ritualizations of old age involve all of the ways that someone can respect and accept others who are different but integrated in their own way. I always enjoy walking through parks in the spring and seeing old men sitting together in silent enjoyment of each other. They may be black or white, rich or poor, but they respect each other, perhaps in ways that were impossible in their youth. The ritualism of old age is *sapientism,* the pretense of wisdom, marked by endless sentences beginning with, "When I was your age."

Erikson is also well-known for using his psychosocial theory to explain the lives of historical figures: Adolph Hitler (1950), Martin Luther (1958), George Bernard Shaw (1968), Gandhi (1969), Thomas Jefferson (1974), and others. In so doing, he articulated principles of interpretation that have become central to the field of psychohistory. Most generally, to understand the person, one must understand the historical and social context in which he or she lived. You cannot rip a person's life from its time and place.

With old age may come wisdom: a respect and acceptance of others.

Erikson has had a great influence on personality psychology. In particular, his lifespan theory of development has helped psychologists take a broader (should I say longer?) view of personality. This view of personality development now predominates, even among those who do not endorse psychoanalytic theory. Erikson returned to Harvard in 1960, and from there he retired in 1970.

RAPAPORT'S SYSTEMATIZATION OF PSYCHOANALYTIC THEORY

I want to conclude this chapter with a systematization of psychoanalytic theory provided by David Rapaport (1959). Rapaport is one of the most profound of psychoanalytic scholars, and among his chief accomplishments is the following description of psychoanalytic thought. In studying the work of Freud, Adler, Jung, and others, Rapaport discerned a number of different perspectives. When juxtaposed, these perspectives result in a composite psychoanalytic theory of personality. And while no given theorist endorses all of the perspectives identified by Rapaport, they are not incompatible points of view.

Indeed, I prefer to think of Rapaport's systematization as an exhaustive catalogue of the factors that comprise an overdetermined explanation of behavior. A fully satisfactory psychoanalytic explanation partakes of each perspective. If one or more perspectives is left out of an explanation, then it may be deficient. This will be clear in the next chapter, when I describe Freud's famous case histories. In each instance, you will see how Freud weaves together these multiple perspectives to capture the complexity of each subject.

1. ***The Empirical Point of View:*** the subject matter of psychoanalysis is behavior. In studying psychoanalysis, one runs the risk of getting lost in the theoretical constructs: left to drift amid the ids and other intriguing hypotheticals. However, remember that they are explanations, a means to an end. The end is what people actually do.

2. ***The Gestalt Point of View:*** behavior is integrated and indivisible. A risk in using psychoanalytic explanation is the temptation to use different theoretical constructs to explain different behaviors. So, one might regard some action as due to the superego or some other action as due to primary process. This is not careful use of psychoanalytic ideas, and it is at odds with the idea of overdetermined behavior. All actions reflect all hypothesized determinants. A particular construct refers to a particular component of behavior—not to an entire action.

3. ***The Organismic Point of View:*** no behavior stands in isolation. This perspective repeats one of the pertinent attributes of personality that emerged from the ordinary language analysis in Chapter 1. All behavior reflects the integrated personality. In giving a psychoanalytic explanation of some behavior, one must be sure that the explanation fits with the rest of what is known about the person.

4. ***The Genetic Point of View:*** all behavior is part of a genetic (developmental) series. According to this perspective, present behavior can be understood only by studying its antecedents. The typical psychoanalytic interest in early childhood reflects this perspective.

5. ***The Topographic Point of View:*** the crucial determinants of behavior are unconscious. Further, the unconscious is motivated. Psychoanalytic theory regards people as unaware of the important contents of their mind, and they are unaware because these contents are upsetting to them.

6. ***The Dynamic Point of View:*** all behavior is ultimately determined by drives. Although controversy over the exact nature and number of these drives exists, all psychoanalytic theorists regard drives as the ultimate determinants of behavior. It is important here to realize that ultimately does not mean immediately. Sometimes the drives behind a person's actions are far-removed. Consider the example of sublimation.

7. ***The Economic Point of View:*** all behavior is regulated by psychological energy. The drives provide the energy, and the energy obeys laws of conservation. Like physical energy, psychological energy can neither be created not destroyed. Once present, it can only be transformed. A person must do something with her libidinal energy.

8. **The Structural Point of View:** all behavior has structural determinants. As you recall, these determinants refer to the division of mental processes into id, ego, and superego.

9. **The Adaptive Point of View:** all behavior is determined by reality. By reality, Rapaport (1959) means external stimuli. Here he is recognizing the important role within psychoanalytic thought of ego psychology.

10. **The Psychosocial Point of View:** all behavior is socially determined. And to follow up the previous perspective, the last point of view specified by Rapaport (1959) states that social reality is the most important reality. This of course is the thrust provided by the neoFreudians.

SUMMARY

The subject matter of this chapter was psychoanalytic theory, the product of such individuals as Sigmund Freud, Alfred Adler, Carl Jung, Karen Horney, Erich Fromm, Harry Stack Sullivan, and Erik Erikson. To introduce psychoanalytic theory, I first described some of the difficulties in mastering this way of explaining personality. It tends to account for what has already happened—not what will happen. It is not quantitative. It is not systematized. It assumes that behavior has numerous determinants. Then, I sketched the family resemblance of the theories proposed by psychoanalytic thinkers. These theories tend to embody an energy model, to have a biological emphasis, to have been influenced by Darwin, to propose a conflict between the individual and society, to adopt a developmental perspective, to have emerged from clinical work, and to endorse a single principle describing the course of development.

The bulk of the chapter described the development of the major psychoanalytic theories. Freud's theory was described in the most detail. The other theories were then covered, noting when and how they diverged from Freud's version of psychoanalytic theory. For the most part, the other psychoanalytic theorists disagree with Freud's emphasis on the sexual drive as primary and the corresponding biological nature of his theory. Instead, they pay much more attention to the social determinants of personality.

To conclude this chapter, I described Rapaport's (1959) systematization of psychoanalytic theory. Rapaport identified ten points of view that capture the whole of psychoanalytic explanation. Taken together, these points of view may be regarded as the various factors needed to fully satisfy a psychoanalytic explanation.

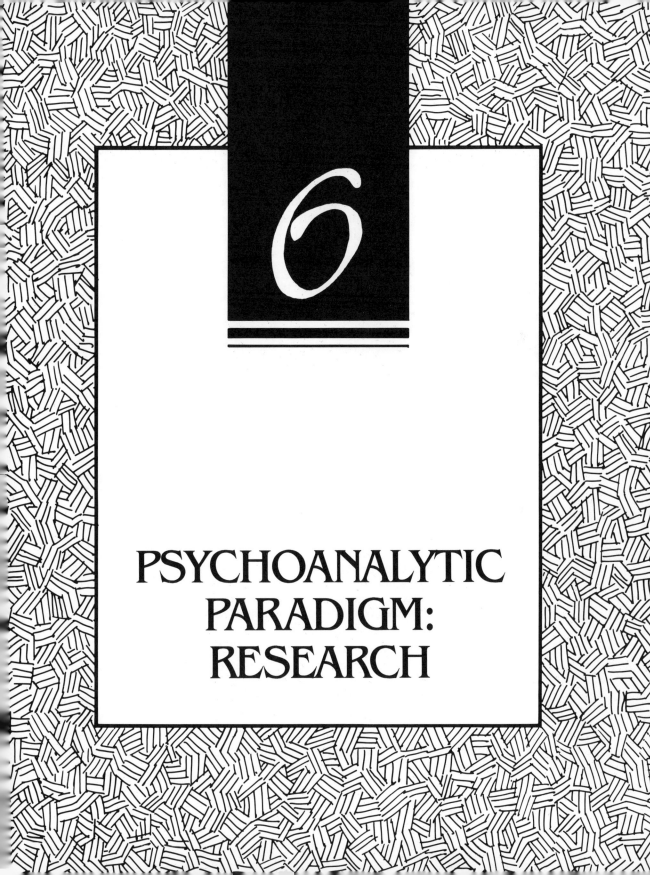

6

PSYCHOANALYTIC PARADIGM: RESEARCH

As controversial as psychoanalytic theory is, psychoanalytic research is even more controversial, at least when viewed from the perspective of traditional psychological investigations. After reading Chapter 5, you can understand why. The standard laboratory experiment cannot always be used to investigate psychoanalytic theory. Experiments typically proceed by holding all factors but one constant and then manipulating that factor to see its effects on a so-called dependent measure. Experiments are ideally suited for investigating simple cause and effect relationships. However, psychoanalytic theory does not consist of simple causal hypotheses. Instead, it consists of a variety of propositions at different levels of abstraction. Further, it assumes that behavior is overdetermined, that behaviors depend not on one factor but on many. Further, the critical determinants lie beneath the surface and therefore are difficult to manipulate—except indirectly.

It is therefore not surprising to encounter harsh indictments of psychoanalytic theory in terms of its suitability for empirical tests:

> Psychoanalytic theories were in a different class. They were simply non-testable, irrefutable. There was no conceivable human behavior which could contradict them. This does not mean that Freud and Adler were not seeing things correctly. . . . But it does mean that these "clinical observations" which analysts naively believe confirm their theory, cannot do this more than the daily confirmation which astrologers find in their practice. (Popper, 1959, p. 37)

> Freud's theory is hard to test . . . in part because his constructs are ambiguous and hard to quantify. The terms often are loose and metaphoric and convey different meanings in different contexts. Clear, observable referents for them are rarely specified. . . . Bluntly, some of these concepts do not offer the possibility of ever being disconfirmed by research. (Mischel, 1971, p. 44)

Goodness, should the chapter end right here? No, I think not. If psychoanalytic theorists are sometimes guilty of overstating the scientific case for their approach, then psychoanalytic critics are equally guilty of understating it. In this chapter, I will describe how psychoanalytic theory can be regarded so that it may be tested against the evidence. I will then describe some of its important tests. Finally, I will conclude the chapter with a revision of Rapaport's (1959) "composite" psychoanalytic theory to reflect research findings to date.

CAN PSYCHOANALYTIC THEORIES BE TESTED?

Two related themes run through the criticism of psychoanalytic theory with respect to research. To begin with, psychoanalytic constructs are regarded as ambiguous and difficult to measure. Further, psychoanalytic predictions are regarded as impossible to disconfirm.

What about these criticisms? The ambiguity of psychoanalytic constructs refers to the multiplicity of thoughts, actions, and feelings that may (or may not) reflect their presence or absence. This is sometimes referred to as the **phenotype-genotype** problem. If you recall your biology course, you remember that phenotype is the physical manifestation of an underlying genotype. But the relationship is not always one-to-one. Brown eyes, for instance, may represent several different underlying combinations of genes.

Similarly, in psychoanalytic theory, a person's behavior does not always bear a simple relationship to its underlying determinants. Someone may smoke cigarettes because she has a death wish, because she is identifying with her mother who smokes, because she is experiencing penis envy, because of all these factors, or because of none of them: she may simply enjoy smoking. Of course this is complicated, but does it mean that psychoanalytic theory is nonscientific?

Not unless we conclude that genetics is nonscientific as well. When we see a person with brown eyes, we don't see their genotype. The geneticist does not shrug her shoulders when faced with a brown-eyed phenotype. She merely proceeds to gather more information. What color eyes do the parents have? How about the children? Further information often allows a good inference about underlying genotype.

The researcher investigating psychoanalytic theory must similarly regard the relationship between overt behavior and underlying determinants as potentially ambiguous—yet not capricious. To disentangle these links, the psychoanalytic researcher must gather information above and beyond the particular behavior which she wants to explain.

Several strategies may be followed. First, the researcher may obtain a wealth of detail about an individual's life. This is the case history method, and one can use it to judge the adequacy of a psychoanalytic explanation by seeing how coherently it ties *all* the details of the case together. Second, the researcher may obtain information about a large number of different individuals, who have or have not behaved in the way of interest. This is the correlational research strategy. One can use it to judge a psychoanalytic explanation by seeing how closely the explanation corresponds to generalizations about the behavior of concern. Third, the researcher may obtain information about the behavior of interest in different conditions that she controls. This is the experimental research strategy, and one can use it to evaluate psychoanalytic explanations by seeing if they correctly predict the occurrence or nonoccurrence of behaviors under specified circumstances. As applied to psychoanalytic research, the bottom line for each strategy is to narrow the range of uncertainty in making inferences. Information is the only way to accomplish this.

The second common criticism of psychoanalytic theory with regard to research is that its predictions are impossible to prove wrong. Nothing ever counts against a psychoanalytic explanation. So, for example, suppose we are looking for evidence of the Oedipus conflict. Junior acts in a hostile way toward his father and in a loving way toward his mother. This pattern reflects the essence of Freud's ideas. Or, suppose Junior acts in a loving way toward his father and in a hostile way toward his mother. If this reflects reaction formation, then it is also consistent with the Oedipal conflict.

Is there anything that Junior does that cannot be stretched to fit Freud's theory? Probably not, if our goal is to make isolated aspects of Junior's behavior fit the Oedipal mold, but this is not the point of research. Instead, we want to evaluate a theory in light of evidence gathered in such a way that the theory has a chance to be correct as well as incorrect.

Consider the two examples. According to psychoanalytic theory, the first should appear before the second. Junior should act lovingly toward his mother before he cools to her. He should act hostilely toward his father before he disguises his resentment, and Junior's switch in overt behavior should be triggered by a real or imagined rebuke from his father.

The research supports Freud's theory to the degree that information about Junior corresponds to this line of events. The research disconfirms the theory to the degree that the facts are at odds with this scenario. If the researcher uses a case history approach, studying in great detail the life of one particular Junior, she should look for evidence about the sequencing of his feelings toward his mother and father. If she employs a correlational strategy, obtaining information on one hundred Juniors, she should look at the correlation between the age of the child and his feelings toward his parents. If she chooses experimentation, manipulating the circumstances under which different Juniors inhibit anger toward authority figures, she should look at the degree of inhibition under conditions of rebuke versus no rebuke. And so on. Psychoanalytic theory can be proven wrong if the researcher does more than look at a single behavior under a single circumstance.

On the other hand, there are aspects of psychoanalytic theory that cannot easily be proven or disproven. These are the bedrock aspects of the paradigm, and the testable theory sits on these assumptions, called **metapsychological propositions**. These are assumptions that go beyond data, such as the notion of psychic energy. I'm not sure that it is possible to prove or disprove the existence of libido. One simply assumes that people are energy systems and proceeds from there. Such bedrock assumptions also exist in everyday life, where they are called our **natural attitude**: unquestioned beliefs about the way the world is. One's natural attitude might include the notions that people are good (or bad), that miracles occur, that plants understand what is said to them, that anyone can grow up to be President, a rock star, or a guest host for the Tonight Show.

The testable aspects of psychoanalytic theory are called **clinical propositions**, since they can be checked against the actual behavior of patients in therapy. For instance, the psychoanalytic explanation of depression proposes that individuals prone to this disorder have experienced loss of love from a significant other early in life (Silverman, 1976). This proposition can be tested. Indeed, it proves true for some but not all depressives (see, for example, Lloyd, 1980).

Lloyd Silverman regards the clinical propositions of psychoanalytic theory as more important than the metapsychological propositions. Since they cannot be tested against evidence, he argues that the metapsychological propositions are nonessential and can be discarded from psychoanalysis. But, in keeping with the idea of scientific paradigms described in Chapter 4, I disagree with his line of reasoning here. The metapsychological propositions provide the background against which the clinical propositions make sense. They hold psychoanalytic theory together, just as our natural attitude holds our experience of everyday reality together.

At the same time, I find the distinction between metapsychological and clinical propositions quite useful in regarding psychoanalytic research. Investigations can only test the clinical propositions. If the majority are supported, one has faith in the bedrock assumptions. If the majority are not supported, one suspects that the metapsychological assumptions are poor ones.

So, the testing of psychoanalytic theory against evidence requires that there be a distinction between what is amenable to test and what is immune. This distinction is not always clear however. Metapsychological assumptions and clinical hypotheses are endpoints of a continuum along which actual theoretical propositions fall. In this chapter, I will focus on the aspects of psychoanalytic research more-or-less close to the ideal of clinical hypotheses.

CASE HISTORIES

Because Freud's name is almost synonymous with the case history method, you may be surprised to learn that Freud published few of them—about half a dozen in detail (Brody, 1970; Goshen, 1952). The ethics at his time prevented clinicians from disclosing details from cases. Since the assumption of over-determined behavior makes details important, it is difficult to present case histories as tests of psychoanalytic theory without revealing the identity of their subject. Nevertheless, what separates science from other ways of knowing is that its basic evidence is public.

Freud's Cases: The Original Data of Psychoanalysis

When Freud published a case study, he tried to make a theoretical point. I want to describe some of these studies and the points they make. Remember, these case histories, despite dealing with patients who suffered with serious problems, were published by Freud to test critical aspects of psychoanalytic theory.

The Case of Anna O   This first of the famous psychoanalytic cases was actually seen by Joseph Breuer, Freud's early collaborator (Breuer & Freud, 1895). Anna O. was an extremely intelligent young woman who showed a variety of hysterical symptoms. (The description of a hysterical patient quoted

The couch Freud used in his practice is now preserved in his Hampstead home museum.

in Chapter 3 is a contemporary summary of Anna O.'s symptoms.) With the active collaboration of this patient, Breuer discovered catharsis. For instance, at one time in her illness, Anna O. could not drink water, despite thirst. Under hypnosis, she described a childhood incident in which she had seen a dog drink from a glass, a scene that disgusted her. But once she had described the incident, she was able to drink water without difficulty. Anna O. referred to this procedure as *chimney sweeping*.

Anna O.'s real name was Bertha Pappenheim, and she later became famous as Germany's first social worker. Contemporary opinion suggests that she may have been more responsible for developing catharsis than Breuer (Rosenbaum, 1984). Perhaps subsequent histories of psychoanalysis will accord her the greater recognition that she seems to deserve. Regardless, the case of Anna O. is important because it marked the discovery of catharsis as a treatment for hysteria. The fact that catharsis worked in the way that it did, alleviating hysterical symptoms by bringing forgotten memories to light, points to critical psychoanalytic notions like the unconscious, psychic energy, and traumatic childhood events.

The Case of the Rat Man   Another well-known case study by Freud (1909b) is that of a young man suffering from an obsessive fear of rats. In particular, the Rat Man—as he has come to be known—experienced recurring thoughts that a horrible torture would befall those close to him. His father's or his fiancée's naked bottom would be strapped over a metal pot containing a hungry rat. The rat would then do a typical rat thing: burrow into the area of least resistance. Ahem.

The Rat Man suffered from other problems as well. Although his father was dead, he would not recognize it. And he experienced a number of internal prohibitions forbidding him to engage in certain acts for fear that disastrous consequences would befall him or someone close to him. For instance, the Rat Man was extremely fond of his niece Ella. He thought that if he made love with someone, then something bad would happen to Ella.

By now you should understand that Freud looks to the troubled individual's childhood to find the roots of the problem. In the early life of the Rat Man, critical events were unearthed. First, his sexual life began early, at about four or five, when his governess allowed him to touch her genitals. Second, he experienced a strong urge to see women naked. Third, he had been punished by his father for masturbation.

His strong sexual urges coupled with the equally strong fear of future punishment for indulging in them led to hatred of his father. At the same time, the Rat Man loved his father and felt guilty about his hatred. This conflict resulted in his various symptoms. The rat torture reflected anger toward his father and fiancée. Not recognizing the death of his father stemmed from guilt about wishing that his father would die. And so on. Freud describes his therapy with the Rat Man as successful, bringing unconscious material to light and liberating the patient from its burden.

This case is important because it includes a detailed discussion by Freud on obsessions. To Freud, recurring thoughts that an individual cannot control reflect underlying struggles. The manifest content of the obsession symbolizes what is unconscious, as do dreams and jokes, so the psychoanalyst may use it as a clue to understand the obsessive patient.

Figure 6-1 diagrams one of the Rat Man's obsessive thoughts: "If I have intercourse, then my niece will die." This seemingly irrational belief made more sense once Freud traced the Rat Man's train of thought through the unconscious. Obsessions result from a process called **distortion by omission**. As you can see in the figure, the Rat Man omits from his conscious mind the thoughts that distress him.

The Case of Schreber   Freud (1911) never met Daniel Paul Schreber. Instead, the material for this case study came from an autobiography written by Schre-

Figure 6-1
Distortion by Omission

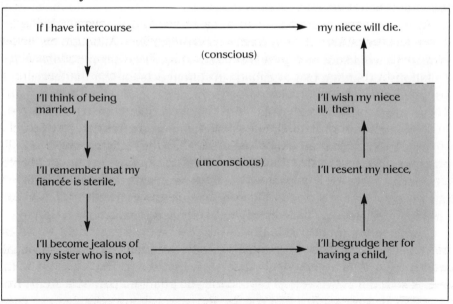

SOURCE: From Freud, 1909.

ber, a German judge of some note, following his recovery from two psychotic episodes marked by delusions of persecution. Schreber was paranoid to such a degree that everyday life became impossible and institutionalization was necessary.

In an early phase of his difficulties, Schreber felt that his physician, Dr. Flechsig, intended to harm him. In a later phase, Schreber believed that God himself wanted to harm him. For instance, God usually arranged for someone to occupy a bathroom when Schreber needed to use the facilities. (This happens to me with some frequency, right before the classes I teach, but I instead blame the university administration for making the time between classes too brief.) Additionally, Schreber held a number of unusual beliefs about bowel movements and their relationship to God. In his most severe state, Schreber believed that God intended a special purpose for him: Schreber would be the bride of God and the mother of a new race of immortal beings who would populate the earth. To prepare Schreber for his role, God would turn him into a woman.

Freud felt that Schreber's paranoia was a defense against unacceptable impulses. Specifically, Schreber was afraid of homosexual urges. Working from Schreber's statements about his childhood, Freud proposed that the young Schreber was extremely ambivalent about his father, both respecting and fearing him. The senior Schreber was a physician and writer well-known for his views on how to raise children, the Dr. Spock of his era, except that he advocated such harsh practices as forcibly restraining children so that they could not masturbate (see Chapter 7).

As a youngster, Schreber's fear of castration was so overwhelming that his sexual interest turned away from women altogether. Although on the outside Schreber showed no signs of homosexuality, Freud proposed that Schreber was indeed a homosexual with respect to his unconscious fantasy life. To guard against these unconscious fantasies ("I am attracted to this man"), Schreber turned them around ("I hate this man because he persecutes me").

Because the homosexual urges persisted despite this defense, Schreber made them more palatable by substituting God for Flechsig (who had in the first place been a substitute for Schreber's father). In this way, he could entertain his homosexual fantasies without shame, since emasculation for the purpose of marrying God could hardly be a disgrace. Needless to say, such a "solution" to unacceptable impulses doesn't work particularly well.

The case of Schreber is important in psychoanalytic thought for several reasons. First, it extended psychoanalysis to extremely troubled individuals, underscoring it as a personality theory of wide scope. Second, for the first time, it stated a controversial psychoanalytic position: paranoia stems from repressed homosexuality. I'll describe the research investigating this possibility in the next chapter.

The Case of Dora   Dora was a young woman suffering from many of the symptoms of hysteria: migraine headaches, fits of nervous coughing, loss of her voice, poor appetite. Conventional treatments failed to relieve her of her symptoms, and her family referred her to Freud (1905a) for treatment.

Information about Dora's parents and their relationship with another couple, Herr and Frau K., fills the case history. Dora's parents did not get along well with each other. Apparently, Dora's father had a long-standing affair with Frau K., of whom Dora was quite resentful. At the same time, Dora was courted by Herr K., whose attentions she seemed to have encouraged up to a point. But when he propositioned her, Dora became extremely angry and slapped him. She informed her father of the matter, and all sorts of hassles ensued with Herr K. denying the proposition altogether.

Freud interpreted Dora's hysterical symptoms in terms of her repressed sexuality. As a child, she loved her father and resented her mother, playing out the role assigned to a young girl by the Oedipal conflict. As a young woman, she continued to love her father, although now the love was repressed. It reappeared, though, in her resentment of Frau K., because her father had chosen Frau K. as his lover. Further, it appeared in her encouragement of Herr K., who represented her father.

This case is noteworthy because Dora abruptly terminated therapy, taking Freud by surprise. In retrospect, he decided that she was fleeing him just as she had fled from Herr K.: because she loved Freud and yet was angry at him. Dora's termination occasioned a fuller understanding of transference—she acted in therapy as she acted in the rest of her life. She loved Freud not for himself but because he reminded her of other men in her life, and she took revenge for the same reason. Her compulsion to repeat painful past actions inspired Freud to posit the death instinct (Chapter 5).

Evaluation   What are we to make of these case histories? Psychoanalytic theory would not exist as it does without the facts provided by them. Recall the inherent difficulties with case histories: information may be distorted; causality may be difficult to infer; and generality to other individuals may be suspect.

Each of Freud's case histories may be criticized on each of these grounds, especially that of distorted information. Not only must we accept the patient's reports of events as accurate, but we must also accept the psychoanalyst's reports as faithful. It is unreasonable to think that Freud or any psychoanalyst is unaffected by lapses in memory or biases induced by expectation.

Let's turn our attention to the question of whether Freud correctly identified causality. Here at least some of the case histories are on firmer ground, since Freud went about identifying causes by looking for patterns in what the patients did: consistencies across time and situation. To the degree that the same pattern shows up repeatedly, a cause is indicated. So, Anna O. invariably showed relief from her hysterical symptoms after talking about her problems. This occurred a number of times, leading to the conclusion that this talking was indeed a cure.

In other case histories, Freud infers causality from much more flimsy information. The fact that Dora terminated therapy is thought to be caused by a transference neurosis, but again, there is insufficient evidence for this. Maybe she stopped seeing Freud for a more mundane reason.

What about generality? Some of Freud's case histories served the purpose of existence proofs (like Dora), so this criterion is not always relevant. But other case histories are intended to show what is universally true (like Anna O.), so the question of generality is sometimes pertinent. Freud intends most of his case histories as illustrations, and he often tells the reader that his psychoanalysis of other patients is consistent with what he reports. This is problematic, raising again questions about the fidelity of Freud's information. If a case history is to be used to establish what is generally true about personality, it is essential to report replications in full detail.

To these difficulties another can be added. Although these case histories support psychoanalytic theory in general, they do not easily allow a choice among the particular theories advanced by Freud, Jung, Adler, or whomever (Farrell, 1981). Despite Freud's assertion that these cases provide unique support for his version of psychoanalysis, any of the cases can be interpreted to support any of the different theories. Schreber can be seen as attempting integration among the (extremely) disparate parts of his personality. Dora can be seen as struggling with basic insecurity. And so on.

To summarize, Freud's case histories were important sources of psychoanalytic ideas. However, the actual evidence on which the case histories are based—the raw data, so to speak—were gathered in an unscientific manner. Further, the cases do not allow a choice among the different versions of psychoanalytic theory. All in all, these cases strike me as borderline instances of research, a mix of strengths and weaknesses.

Personality research is now much more sophisticated than when Freud pioneered the case history approach. Psychoanalytic investigations, capitalizing on this increasing sophistication, have also flourished. But not all current investigations have abandoned the case history approach. After all, case histories are uniquely appropriate for testing psychoanalytic ideas. The problem with the typical case study has been mainly in its implementation. But, in the last twenty years, researchers have developed better ways of conducting and reporting case studies than did Freud.

Refinement 1: The Symptom-Context Method

Psychologist Lester Luborsky (1970) pioneered a refinement of the case history approach that he calls the **symptom-context method**. His method exploits the now widespread practice of tape recording psychotherapy sessions, which represents not only a technical advance but also changes in how the privacy of case study subjects is regarded. (Anonymity, rather than complete confidentiality, is now the rule.) The resulting tape is a permanent record of events transpiring in therapy. With the tape available, problems with the therapist's recall are avoided. Luborsky has been interested in a patient's symptoms as they appear in the course of a psychotherapy session. So problems with the patient's recall are avoided as well.

Working from the tape, the researcher determines when a given symptom does or does not occur. This determination can be checked by other researchers, and its reliability thereby ascertained. Then the researcher characterizes the context in which the symptom appears (or not). What topics were discussed? How did the patient express feelings? What did the therapist do? Again, this can be checked by others and is scientific in a way that Freud's original case histories are not.

To test psychoanalytic hypotheses linking characteristics of the context to the occurrence of symptoms, the researcher typically assesses context characteristics from four different points in the therapy session: prior to a segment in which the symptom under study appears; after such a segment; prior to a segment in which the symptom does not occur; and after such a segment. Information from such a research design allows the researcher to conclude whether a given context characteristic indeed precedes a particular symptom.

Do you see how this conclusion can be made? Suppose the hypothesis being tested proposes that incestuous thoughts lead to anxiety attacks. We can operationally define an anxiety attack in terms of shallow, rapid breathing. (Of course, there is more to anxiety than rate of respiration, but remember that no operationalization ever perfectly measures a construct.)

We have hundreds of psychotherapy sessions with a particular patient on tape. We fast-forward the tapes until we hear sounds of hyperventilation. Suppose we find ten such incidents. We run the tape back three minutes before the anxiety attack (as we have defined it) occurs, and we note whether or not the patient is discussing sexual feelings about his mother. We then run the tape forward three minutes past the anxiety attack, and again we note whether the patient is expressing sexual desire for his mother. We then choose ten incidents at random from all those in which hyperventilation does not occur, and we note the topics of the patient's conversation before and after these comparison incidents. Do they mention sexual feelings about mother?

What will we see in these data if the Oedipal hypothesis is correct? Quite simply: the greatest mention of incestuous thoughts will precede the anxiety attacks. Further, the least mention should follow the attacks, since the anxiety presumably marks the repression of the incestuous feelings. Finally, there will be little evidence of Oedipal thoughts in the comparison segments (see Figure 6-2). Other patterns of data will not support the hypothesis.

Note that the data provided by the symptom-context method are correlational in nature. Although they are often used to draw conclusions about causes, these conclusions may be derailed by confounds. Research using this method must carefully examine possible third variables.

Luborsky (1964) first used the symptom-context method to study sudden forgetting: coming up blank in the middle of a sentence. This is akin to a parapraxis, a slip of the memory rather than the tongue. According to psychoanalytic theory, momentary forgetting occurs when the topic being discussed threatens the individual. In a study of a single patient, Luborsky found that themes of rejection and feelings of helplessness preceded episodes of sudden forgetting, but not comparison episodes.

Luborsky has also used the symptom-context method to study such symptoms as asthma attacks, stomach pains, migraine headaches, and *petit-mal* seizures. For each individual, a theme of conflict preceded the symptom of concern. Common across the individuals studied, a sense of helplessness in the face of the conflict characterizes the context in which the symptom occurs. On the whole, these data are consistent with psychoanalytic theory (Luborsky, 1970; Luborsky, Sackeim, & Christoph, 1979).

What are the limitations of the symptom-context method? First, the rate of a given symptom in therapy may be low. Some symptoms may not occur at all during a session. Second, the symptom as it occurs in the therapy session may not be the same as the symptom as it appears at other times in the patient's life. Third, the provided data are correlational (linking symptoms to context), so causality can only be tentatively inferred. Fourth, even if the determinants of symptoms are correctly identified, one is limited to immediate causes. More distant determinants, including many of interest to psychoanalytic theory, cannot be investigated with this technique. Fifth, to date, the symptom-context method has been used mainly with therapy audiotapes.

On the other hand, the symptom-context method is precise and public. Within its limitations, it is reliable and valid. The method can obviously be used with therapy videotapes, so that nonverbal symptoms and contexts are thereby accessible. I imagine that it can be extended outside of therapy as well. Now that people are videotaping important events like births and weddings as readily as they once snapped Polaroids of these special times, the symptom-context method can be used to study personality in a variety of settings. Maybe the method can be used to understand why Johnny Carson

Figure 6-2
Example of Symptom-Context Method

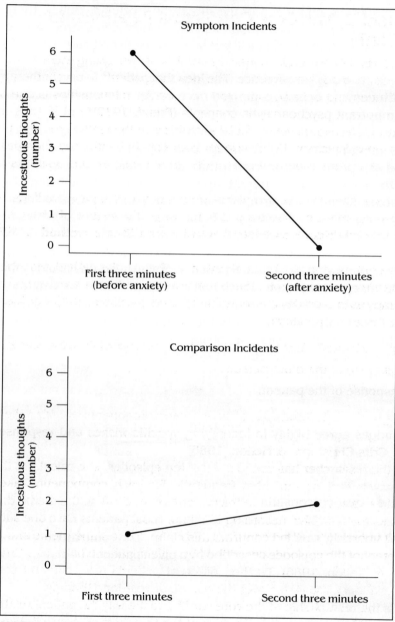

SOURCE: From Luborsky, 1970.

occasionally blows a line, why Martha Quinn occasionally becomes giddy, and why John McEnroe occasionally keeps his cool.

Refinement 2: The Core Conflictual Relationship Theme Method

Luborsky (1976, 1977) has also created a method for analyzing therapy transcripts in order to study transference. The idea that patients in psychotherapy express attitudes and behaviors derived from earlier relationships is one of the most important psychoanalytic concepts (Freud, 1912). But if the only support for transference is the therapist's intuition on the matter, you can see why this is unsatisfactory. Unintentional bias can influence the therapist, affecting what is remembered from the therapy sessions and how this is interpreted.

As we have seen for the symptom-context method, tape recordings of therapy sessions make available a public and objective record of what transpires. So, Luborsky's **core conflictual relationship theme method** (**CCRT**) starts with transcripts of one or more sessions of therapy. Independent judges read a transcript, paying particular attention to the way the patient describes episodes involving other people. (Such narrative episodes are as common in psychotherapy as in everyday conversation!) For each episode, the judge identifies these three components:

1. The patient's main wishes, needs, or intentions toward the other person.

2. The response of the other person.

3. The response of the patient.

Table 6-1 gives a brief example of how these components are identified. Different judges agree highly in identifying specific wishes and responses (Luborsky, Crits-Christoph, & Mellon, 1986).

When the researcher has coded at least ten episodes, she calculates the specific answer that occurs most frequently for each component. Taken together, these answers constitute the patient's core conflict: the theme that characterizes transference. According to Freud, most patients have one such theme, and Luborsky's method confirms this claim. The same theme shows up in 80 percent of the episodes described by a given patient (Luborsky, Crits-Christoph, & Mellon, 1986). Further, different patients have different core conflicts, and these are stable over the course of year-long therapy.

What is the relationship of the core conflict to the way the patient relates to the therapist? This after all is the crux of the transference concept. When the core conflict derived from episodes involving people other than the therapist is compared to the core conflict derived from episodes involving only

Table 6-1

The Core Conflictual Relationship Theme Method (an example)

Condensed Episode	Coding
This guy tried to dominate conversation. . . . It irritated me. . . . I repressed everything and just sank back . . . brooding . . . pissed off. . . . I had fantasies of putting him down.	Wish: to assert self Response of patient: becomes angry, withdrawn Response of other: dominates
Cop comes up and tells her to sit right. . . . They stood up to him. . . . I got really anxious. . . . I would have automatically obeyed.	Wish: to assert self Response of patient: becomes anxious, passive Response of other: dominates

SOURCE: Condensed from Luborsky, 1984, Appendix 4.

the therapist, they are essentially the same (Luborsky, Crits-Christoph, & Mellon, 1986). This is an important finding, since it confirms Freud's original proposition that patients think about and act toward their therapist as they think about and act toward other people in their lives.

Luborsky and his colleagues have also found that a patient's core conflict becomes less pervasive with successful psychotherapy. In other words, as the patient begins to solve the problems that brought him to therapy in the first place, he becomes less likely to interpret his interactions with others in the same terms. Different wishes and different responses come to characterize different relationships. Again, this is an important finding, supporting the psychoanalytic claim that a patient must "work through" transference in order for therapy to be successful. Working through transference simply means that the patient no longer conducts his life according to old patterns.

The CCRT has drawbacks. It is a laborious procedure. Further, it requires highly trained judges, usually individuals conversant with psychoanalytic theory. And the shared expertise of the judges may introduce a subtle bias in the procedure, creating agreement and confirmation for the wrong reason. For instance, suppose a patient mentions in an episode that he feels sad. Unwitting application of the psychoanalytic formula may lead the judges to infer that the patient wishes to be nurtured and that the other person is failing to do so. There is high agreement, but this is misleading. The only objective fact was the patient's sadness. Finally, the CCRT is only useful if the patient is articulate. This is often the case in psychoanalytic therapy, but the generality of the CCRT may thereby be limited.

Despite these problems, of which Luborsky is aware, the CCRT is still a powerful refinement of the case study method. By formalizing the clinician's intuition, it allows transference to be studied more objectively than was possible in Freud's era. And findings to date support psychoanalytic claims regarding transference and its central role in psychotherapy.

Refinement 3: The Natural History Method

Psychiatrist George Vaillant (1977, 1983) has made extensive use of yet another refinement of the case study approach, one that can be called the **natural history method**. This longitudinal research strategy combines the rich detail of case studies with the generality of correlational investigations. Vaillant intensively studies a large number of individuals over a significant proportion of their lives, in some cases four decades or more. Particular attention is paid to the twists and turns of a person's lifepath. Because a number of individuals are studied in the same way, strong statements can be made about the natural course of people's lives.

As you can imagine, this method is highly appropriate for the investigation of developmental theories—like psychoanalysis. Just as natural historians chronicle the lives of wild animals and birds, the personality researcher can record the lives of people. This method makes available basic facts about personality and its development that elude other research strategies, while improving upon Freud's case histories in that troubled individuals are not its exclusive focus. Generality is thereby served.

Vaillant's natural history method has mostly involved two samples of individuals. The first sample is 268 men chosen as college sophomores for their physical and psychological superiority: the most outstanding members of the 1938 through 1944 classes at a prestigious university. The average subject is now over sixty years old. The second sample is 456 men chosen as teenagers from inner-city Boston as a control group for a study of delinquency. These subjects originally joined the sample between 1940 and 1944, which means that the average subject is now about sixty years old.

Vaillant himself originated neither study. Instead, these samples have been handed down from the original investigators to other researchers and eventually to Vaillant. Each custodian of the samples has kept the available information in order and added to it. Most importantly, the custodians have kept the dropout rate to essentially zero.

What sorts of information are available? The overall focus of the original researchers was "health" broadly considered: physical, psychological, and social. Interdisciplinary investigation has been the rule, with anthropologists, social workers, psychologists, psychiatrists, and physicians making observations about each subject. These observations have been carefully recorded, and each subject's material fills several file folders to overflowing.

To investigate a particular question, the researcher reads the relevant files. Sometimes the data of concern are immediately present, such as a subject's higher level of education. In other cases, the data must be abstracted from the files. Vaillant (1983, p. 323) did this when he assigned each subject a score reflecting the degree to which they had achieved Erikson's fourth developmental stage, industry versus inferiority (see Chapter 5). He looked for evidence in each of their records for such behaviors as summer jobs held between the ages of eleven and sixteen. Several judges rated the records independently, so agreement could be checked. Further, they were blind to adult outcome, so ratings were not biased by knowledge of what happened to the subjects once the subjects became men.

How is the natural history method different than that of the typical case study? First, it is *prospective* instead of *retrospective*. Where Freud studied individuals after they had developed a problem, trying to understand which early events led up to it, Vaillant starts with the early events and sees where they lead. Second, the natural history method employs public evidence. Reliability can be checked by other individuals. Third, the method is not just intensive but also extensive. The simultaneous study of hundreds of individuals provides generalizations impossible to make from conventional case histories.

Why don't I regard the natural history method as simply a correlational research strategy employing longitudinal data? I might, since hypotheses are tested with correlation coefficients and the generic precautions for such an approach (confounding by third variables, ambiguity of causality, and so on) should be honored. However, what makes the natural history method more of a case study approach is that the original material consists of clinical details, not numerical responses to questionnaires.

Material is quantified after the fact. So, the natural history approach is both rich and—eventually—precise. Further, the approach allows longitudinal investigations of ideas not entertained by the original researchers. Vaillant coded Erikson's stage four from information obtained *before* Erikson described the psychosocial stage theory. This possibility allows efficient longitudinal research, since the original material already exists. Imagine how hard it has been to keep track of 600+ individuals for 40+ years. Many of us lose track of good friends just by moving to the other end of town. How convenient for future researchers that Vaillant and his predecessors have already done the hard work.

The natural history method is not foolproof. First, *the subjects were not randomly selected.* Women and minorities were excluded from the two samples I've described. This of course reflects the choice of the original researchers, and in retrospect, we see it as an unfortunate restriction.

Second, *a subject's lengthy participation may have affected the very course of his life.* The college sample has been interviewed on about twenty-five different occasions, with future interviews planned. Such scrutiny can create self-consciousness to an unusual degree.

Third, *information of contemporary concern may be missing from the records,* simply because the earlier researchers did not include it. Conversely, some information originally of interest may become irrelevant as theories and issues pass out of fashion. This material clogs the files and impedes their study.

Fourth, *individual interviewers obtained much of the evidence, introducing unknown bias.* Like Freud's original case histories, studies using the natural history approach are only as valuable as the accuracy of their original evidence. Although attempts were made to standardize interviews and record information accurately, the practical considerations involved put a limit on the effectiveness of these attempts.

Nevertheless, this approach to personality research is exciting, yielding conclusions of enormous practical and theoretical significance, making it possible to investigate claims of psychoanalysis as well as other theories of personality development. For instance, Vaillant (1977) investigated the long-term consequences of using immature mechanisms like projection versus mature mechanisms like sublimation.

Vaillant ascertained an individual's habitual defense mechanisms by extracting from his records descriptions of how he acted in times of crisis or conflict. Judges blind to other information about the individual categorized these extractions in terms of the defense mechanisms shown. There was good agreement among judges. Defense mechanisms were assigned scores reflecting their relative immaturity versus maturity, and each individual was then given an overall maturity score by combining the ratings of the defense mechanisms he habitually employed.

When these overall scores were correlated with long-term outcomes, the results were striking. These scores predict adult social adjustment, economic achievement, and mental health. The more mature one's defense mechanisms, the better one adapts to life. Even more strikingly, the use of mature defense mechanisms throughout one's early life predicts one's health and longevity. These results underscore the importance ego psychologists place on the way people cope with difficulties.

CORRELATIONAL AND EXPERIMENTAL RESEARCH STRATEGIES

Although case histories and their contemporary refinements are probably the best way to investigate psychoanalytic theory, they are painstaking and inefficient, particularly if embedded in therapy. Other research strategies have thus been used to address the clinical predictions of psychoanalysis. Though lacking the richness of case histories, these other strategies compensate for the shortcomings of that particular approach.

Psychoanalytic researchers employ correlational studies to investigate differences among people: in character type, in defense mechanisms, in birth order, in psychological health and illness. A number of these investigations address developmental questions. What early childhood experiences give rise to particular character types? What are the long-term consequences of certain defense mechanisms? Is it really Mom's fault that we turned out parboiled? Other researchers use experiments to study the claims of psychoanalytic theory about people's general characteristics: drives, unconscious motivation, the roles of humor, dreams, and fantasy. Because psychoanalytic theory is complex, most of these experiments use elaborate operationalizations and complicated designs.

In the rest of this chapter, I will describe investigations of psychoanalytic theory that use correlational and experimental research strategies. In choosing studies, I have relied on the thorough surveys by Kline (1972, 1984) and Fisher and Greenberg (1977), as well as others (for example, Eysenck & Wilson, 1973; Farrel, 1981; Sears, 1943). These various authors differ markedly in their enthusiasm for psychoanalytic research, but they agree on which investigations are the most pertinent.

PARTICULAR LINES OF RESEARCH

Instincts and Drives

The most basic premise of psychoanalytic theory is that people are energy systems. The life and death instincts provide this energy and are regarded as innate characteristics of all human beings. However, contemporary opinion within the social sciences does not accept human instincts. What brought about this skepticism?

An **instinct** is defined as *an innate pattern of behavior, arising from biological inheritance, not learning, and characterizing a species as a whole.* A good example of an instinct is the song of the cowbird. All cowbirds sing as adults, whether or not they heard the song when they were young.

Studies with animals make use of isolation experiments to investigate instincts. Quite literally, the animal is isolated from environmental events that might confound the interpretation of some behavior as instinctive. Such experiments are impossible to conduct with people, and so we cannot use these tests to say with certainty that there are human instincts. Further,

"And now, Randy, by use of song, the male sparrow will stake out his territory... an instinct common in the lower animals."

SOURCE: "The Far Side" cartoon by Gary Larson is reproduced by permission of Chronicle Features, San Francisco.

anthropological observations challenge the idea that there are universal behaviors, while experimental investigations demonstrate the *responsivity* of people to the world.

The contemporary psychologist therefore dismisses the possibility of human instincts. The closest that most researchers get to instincts is to speak of biological **drives**. Like an instinct, *a biological drive is innate and universal; it motivates behavior*. Unlike an instinct, a drive is expressed in a variety of ways sensitive to the environment. All people have a hunger drive, for instance, but it gives rise to all sorts of different activities to satisfy it. Some folks drive to Wendy's; others raid the refrigerator; still others shake their neighbor's mango tree.

In all fairness to psychoanalytic theory, then, Freud's life and death instincts should better be regarded as (potential) drives. And what is the evidence that these drives exist and work in the ways implied by Freud? Let us start by considering Eros: *the twin urge for self-preservation and sexual satisfaction.* We can regard the drive for self-preservation as obvious, and all of the mechanisms for seeking pleasure and avoiding pain serve this drive.

The evidence for the other half of Eros is less obvious. As adolescents and adults, we have a sex drive. We are motivated to satisfy this drive in one or more of the ways catalogued by Kinsey and his colleagues (Kinsey, Pomeroy, & Martin, 1948; Kinsey, Pomeroy, Martin, & Gebhard, 1953) or chronicled on restroom walls. However, psychoanalytic theory additionally concerns itself with infant and childhood sexuality. Here there is considerable disagreement over what to make of the available evidence.

Following Freud's original hypotheses, a number of researchers tested claims about infant sexuality through observations and interviews. They talked to parents and teachers about the practices of children. They sat in the corners of nurseries and playgrounds making notes. They interviewed adults about what they remembered from childhood. Sears (1943) provides an overview of this early research, which is unaltered by more recent findings (see, for example, Farrell, 1981; Fisher & Greenberg, 1977; Kline, 1972).

First, the genitals of infants are susceptible to stimulation. Penis erection occurs even among the youngest boys. Both infant boys and girls manipulate their own genitals.

Second, when slightly older, children show oral, anal, and phallic concerns. However, these do not fall into the simple progression hypothesized by Freud: oral to anal to genital.

Third, children evidence curiosity about sexual matters. As Freud proposed, children are quite interested in the origin of babies. They are also interested in sex differences, but there are few signs that children are confused about the difference between male and female genitals.

Fourth, at least in our society, children come to regard their sexual curiosity with shame. They hide their interest and any related activities from adults. And contrary to Freud's ideas of repression, the majority of adults recall such childhood secrets, even though they were associated with guilt.

If continuity between infant and child and adult sexuality is to be demonstrated, then one must show that pleasure is obtained through "sexual" activities across the lifespan. However, we don't know if infants and young children engage in the behaviors of concern because they are pleasurable or for some other reason (Farrell, 1981). For instance, erections among infant boys occur at times of distress. This argues against the idea that

Although Freud theorizes extensively about childhood sexuality, research evidence fails to support his central hypotheses.

infant erections are sexual (that is, pleasure-driven) in origin and function. What looks like sexuality in the young child may not be sexuality in Freud's sense.

Let us turn our attention to Thanatos. Again, strict interpretation of Thanatos as an instinct is unreasonable. Even the most loyal of Freud's followers kept politely silent about the death instinct. How could it have evolved? If it did evolve, what prevents children from killing themselves? Suicide among the very young has been reported, but it is extremely rare when compared to suicide rates among adolescents and adults.

Most researchers have therefore interpreted Thanatos as *a drive for aggression, usually directed against others.* Konrad Lorenz (1966) and Robert Ardrey (1966), for instance, use animal evidence to argue that human aggression is innate—inherited from an animal past. Sociobiologists make the same point. Such arguments proceed first by showing that aggression in animals has a biological basis, then by invoking the similarity of human beings and animals, and finally by concluding that human aggression is the result of a biological drive (Mazur & Robertson, 1972).

In contrast, psychologists like Albert Bandura (1973) and Leonard Berkowitz (1974) have mustered a great deal of support for the notion that human aggression is learned behavior. I mentioned in Chapter 1 Bandura's studies in which children watch someone else beat up a Bobo doll. When given their own opportunity to attack the doll, the kids often have at it as well. But, if the first child suffers some indignity or punishment as a result of his attack on the Bobo doll, then the observing children do not follow his example.

Bandura calls this process **modelling** and sees it as the most important determinant of violence (or nonviolence). This research is cited by those who want violent television shows like the "A-Team" pulled off the air: no exposure to violence, no violence; so goes the reasoning. The point here is not whether this argument is justified or not. Rather, this social psychological research suggests that human aggression is not a drive. It is too responsive to the social context to result from an innate drive.

SOURCE: "The Far Side" cartoon by Gary Larson is reproduced by permission of Chronicle Features, San Francisco.

Berkowitz investigated another aspect of human aggression pertinent to Freudian theory: are violent acts cathartic? If aggression is a drive, then it can be satisfied like hunger, thirst, or sex. And after satisfaction, the individual should be less likely to act in an aggressive way.

Examine your own beliefs about this possibility. Everyday language is filled with expressions that assume that one's appetite for violence can be sated:

"Go ahead, get it out of your system."

"I got it off my chest."

"Make my day."

"Saturday night's all right for fighting."

I think you can imagine how this notion can be tested. Researchers would assign their subjects to one of two experimental conditions: one in which violence was perpetrated or observed, the other in which there was no violence. All subjects would then be given the opportunity to act violently. In repeated experiments by Berkowitz and others, subjects exposed to violence act *more* violently. Turning the other cheek is not only moral but also practical. And Freud is wrong that aggression is a drive.

So, the research argues against Eros and Thanatos. Does this mean that the essence of psychoanalytic theory must be discarded? Not necessarily. For instance, we can draw the same conclusion as the neoFreudians in light of similar research evidence. A strictly biological interpretation of libido is untenable. However, people can still be described in energy terms. People have a variety of motives, chief among them those described by Freud and other psychoanalytic theorists. But it is unreasonable to elevate any of these to the status of primary motive for all people, and it is even more unreasonable to argue that any are innate.

Unconscious Motivation

For decades, experimental psychologists have tried to demonstrate the existence of the *motivated unconscious*. Unambiguous demonstrations have been somewhat elusive, but so many different lines of evidence point to the reality of the motivated unconscious that it seems a good bet. Let me describe some of the studies, and you can form your own opinion.

Perceptual Defense   Some of the earliest experimental investigations of the motivated unconscious were part of a psychology movement which argued that *a person's literal perception of the world is influenced by his needs and drives.* An interstate highway traveler in dire need of stopping "sees" every miscellaneous roadsign as an announcement of a rest area with comfort facilities. Further, the influence of needs and drives on perception can occur without an individual's awareness. This is most apt to occur when the stimuli are seen as threatening or upsetting.

Consider this experiment by McGinnies (1949). College students were shown words on a *tachistoscope,* a device that presents visual stimuli for extremely brief periods of time. As soon as they recognized the word, they were to push a button, and the time between initial presentation and recognition was recorded. During the experiment, their *galvanic skin response* (GSR), a measure of emotional arousal, was monitored.

Some words were innocuous, like child, glass, and river, whereas other words were somewhat "less than polite," like whore, bitch, and Kotex. Subjects took longer to recognize the risque words than the innocuous words, and their GSR was higher while viewing them. These results are of course consistent with the notion of **perceptual defense**, and therefore with the notion of a motivated unconscious.

Or are they? If you think for a moment, you may have several objections (see, for example, Howes & Solomon, 1950). Perhaps the subjects recognized the taboo words as readily as the innocent words, but were too shy to call them out until they were sure. This would also account for the results.

Perhaps the subjects were less familiar with the taboo words than with the innocent words. Although subjects may indeed have taken longer to recognize them, the reason for the delay may well have been lack of familiarity, not perceptual defense. This objection has some trouble accommodating the GSR data, but perhaps the delay led to frustration and therefore to elevated GSR.

However, subsequent investigations vindicated the notion of perceptual defense against such charges (Maddi, 1980). Indeed, Matthew Erdelyi (1974, 1985) observes that current theorizing in cognitive psychology is quite amenable to phenomena like perceptual defense. Older theories tended to regard perception as unitary, an event that does or does not occur. At the present, perception is seen as a process characterized by selectivity at every stage. We are aware of only some of this selectivity.

I'll add one more idea here about perceptual defense. Although many experiments show that it exists, as psychoanalytic theory predicts, most of these experiments also show an opposite effect for some subjects. These folks perceive threatening stimuli more readily than neutral stimuli. This is called **perceptual vigilance**.

Does perceptual vigilance call into doubt psychoanalytic theory? Yes and no. Freud described defense mechanisms that have the effect of attuning individuals to aversive occurrences, for example, *reaction formation* and *intellectualization* (Maddi, 1980). From this point of view, perceptual vigilance is another form of defense. Nevertheless, repression is thought to be the foundation of all defense mechanisms, even those defense mechanisms that attune the individual to threat. Reaction formation and intellectualization, for instance, obscure what is really threatening to the individual. From this point of view, perceptual vigilance is something other than just a defense, and it is thus difficult to accommodate with orthodox psychoanalytic theory.

Subliminal Stimulation   Psychologist Lloyd Silverman (1971, 1976; Silverman & Fishel, 1981) has conducted an extensive line of research investigating the motivated unconscious. Silverman is particularly concerned with the psychoanalytic hypothesis that *psychopathology expresses unconscious conflict.* You have seen this idea in Freud's case histories. A patient's unconscious conflict showed itself in overt behavior.

Silverman's approach is experimental, making use of the tachistoscope. Stimuli thought to produce conflict, because they pertain to sexual or aggressive drives, are presented to subjects at **subliminal** levels, that is, for *durations so brief that a person cannot consciously recognize the stimuli.* Does this **subliminal stimulation** affect subsequent behavior? In particular, does it support the psychoanalytic prediction that behavior will be disrupted by the activation of unconscious conflict?

Here is a representative experiment conducted by Silverman, Bronstein, and Mendelsohn (1976). Male college students participated in a competitive dart-throwing tournament. During a baseline period, they were exposed to one of three different subliminal messages: BEATING DAD IS WRONG, BEATING DAD IS OKAY, and PEOPLE ARE WALKING. The first message is thought to increase Oedipal guilt, the second to decrease it, and the third to be neutral. The dependent measure was the dart-throwing score obtained by the subjects after subliminal stimulation. Silverman and his colleagues predicted that guilt would impair dart-throwing. In keeping with this prediction, the subjects seeing the message BEATING DAD IS WRONG scored the lowest, while the subjects seeing BEATING DAD IS OKAY scored the highest. Subjects seeing the neutral message scored intermediate.

Silverman's research is extensive and intriguing. It is also controversial. Critics point out that other research groups have failed to replicate it. Also, the studies are examples of what is known as *analogue research.* The "psychopathology" produced by Silverman's manipulations is only *analogous* to the psychopathology that brings people to the attention of mental health practitioners.

But the most fundamental criticism of the subliminal stimulation research, at least in the present context, questions the very notion of subliminal stimulation, a phenomenon with a controversial history (Bevan, 1964). How does Silverman ascertain that subjects are not aware of the stimuli presented by the tachistoscope? He chooses a tachistoscopic exposure level where "over 90% of the subjects cannot distinguish, at better than a chance level, one stimulus from another in a 'discrimination task' . . . even when they are offered a monetary incentive" (Silverman & Fishel, 1981, p. 63).

You can see how this operationalization might be questioned. What about the other 10 percent? If they are perceptually vigilant, then they are *not* being stimulated subliminally. Might subjects who are aware of the stimuli respond to demand characteristics, giving Silverman the results that his stimulus material seems to request? Counting against this latter possibility is the finding that none of the effects described are obtained when stimulus messages are presented at more lengthy intervals, when all subjects are conscious of their content.

Self-deception   Ruben Gur and Harold Sackeim (1979) reported two intriguing studies pertinent to the motivated unconscious. Their concern was with **self-deception**: people lying to themselves. In everyday life, we presumably see frequent examples of self-deception by others: "My roommate actually thinks he'll get into medical school with a 2.33 grade-point average!" "Uncle Bartholomew acts like his wife is going to return to him, but she left him seventeen years ago and moved to Rio!"

Casual gossip is not the same thing as hard evidence. Are we really sure that Uncle Bartholomew expects his wife to return? Maybe he knows full well that she won't, and he's just putting up a front for any of a number of reasons. We can't tell. On the other hand, if Uncle Bart is lying to himself, then this act is an example of the motivated unconscious. One aspect of his mind (the unconscious) is deceiving another aspect (the conscious). Gur and Sackeim (1979, p. 149) took as their goal the creation of a laboratory phenomenon satisfying the definition of self-deception.

From the earlier discussion of perceptual defense, you know that the unambiguous demonstration of such behavior requires a complex method. Gur and Sackeim used the following procedure. Research subjects were played audiotapes and asked to identify whether each of a series of voices they heard was their own or not. At the same time, GSR was recorded. Previous research has shown that when a person hears his own voice on a tape, GSR goes up, whether or not correct identification is made. (By the way, this is the principle behind the use of GSR in lie detection.) So, if a person incorrectly identifies a voice as *not* his own, and his GSR is elevated, then he is simultaneously holding contradictory beliefs.

What about the criterion of nonawareness? Again, Gur and Sackeim made use of information from previous research. When a research subject has identified a voice as his own, subsequent identification of a different voice as *not* his own is easier to make. This happens whether or not the initial identification is correct. Thus, by comparing the speed of identification following different types of responses, Gur and Sackeim could ascertain whether subjects were unaware that their own voices had been falsely identified. In other words, if someone falsely identifies a voice as his own and then shows rapid and correct identification of a different voice, it can be concluded that the person is unaware of the false identification.

Finally, how did the researchers show that self-deception is motivated? This was done in two different ways, in two different experiments. In the first, subjects had earlier completed a measure of self-esteem. Subjects with poor self-esteem were assumed to have more of a motive to avoid self-confrontation than those with good self-esteem: accordingly, if self-deception is to be demonstrated, results should be more pronounced for subjects with poor self-esteem than for the others. In the second experiment, self-esteem was manipulated by the researchers just prior to the voice-identification task. Half of the subjects were given difficult verbal problems to solve, leading to failure and poor self-esteem, while the other subjects were given easy problems, leading to success and good self-esteem. Again, if self-deception exists, results should hold more strongly for subjects experiencing failure than for those experiencing success.

The results demonstrate the phenomenon of self-deception. GSR response to one's own voice was high, whether or not the voice was correctly identified. Following the incorrect identification of a stranger's voice as their own, subjects more quickly identified a different voice correctly. Finally, errors in identifying one's own voice were more likely for subjects with low self-esteem.

This research is important because it experimentally demonstrates the motivated unconscious. Is it definitive? No, because it is always possible to raise questions about research. For instance, some argue that GSR is not the same thing as an unconscious belief; it is merely an instance of physiological functioning, like the growth of hair or the secretion of hormones. A counterargument states that GSR is a measure of an unconscious belief— not the belief itself. But the demonstration is one of the best yet conducted, and it should give you a flavor of the challenge that psychoanalytic theory poses to the psychological researcher, and of the way sophisticated investigators have risen to the challenge. This research, in conjunction with the other studies mentioned in this section, convince me that there is a motivated unconscious.

Evaluation   I've described several experimental studies that have investigated the motivated unconscious. They converge in their support for this basic psychoanalytic idea. Other investigations not surveyed here, like those of hypnosis (for example, Stross & Shevrin, 1969), also suggest that the motivated unconscious exists. At the same time, the notion of perceptual vigilance arises from this research, and it is difficult to accommodate within psychoanalytic theory.

Case histories and experiments have different strengths and weaknesses. They are most sensibly employed for different purposes. The experimental studies described here, despite the circumscribed and qualified conclusion to which they lead, accomplish what Freud's case histories cannot. They allow the researcher to get a handle on the motivated unconscious. Their demonstrations are repeatable, and the operative causes are identifiable.

Oedipus Complex

According to psychoanalytic theory, the crucial determinants of adult personality reside in childhood. In particular, the way in which a child experiences the Oedipus complex is thought to determine the adult he or she becomes. What is the evidence that the Oedipal complex exists and is played out according to Freud's scenario?

Fisher and Greenberg (1977) classify investigations of the Oedipus complex in terms of the specific question addressed. Does the newborn child show closeness to the mother? Do people show different attitudes toward the same-sex versus opposite-sex parent? Does the developing child come to identify with the same-sex parent? Is this identification brought about by anxiety? Do young boys experience castration anxiety? Do young girls experience penis envy? Does a person's moral sense develop from resolution of the Oedipal conflict?

Research provides affirmative answers to some of these questions, negative answers to others, and equivocal answers to the remaining. On the whole, support is lent to those early critics who questioned the Oedipus complex. But, like his assertions of infant sexuality, Freud's claims about Oedipal dynamics are not completely wrong. However, they are sufficiently off-center to warrant considerable doubt about this important aspect of psychoanalytic theory.

Let me borrow from Fisher and Greenberg (1977) to explain where Freud's claims are supported by research and where they are not. On the positive side, young children of both sexes indeed show stronger attachment to mother than father. For instance, Schaffer and Emerson (1964) showed that infants reacted more negatively if separated from mother than from father. Of course, psychoanalytic theory is not the only theory that predicts this finding.

Also on the positive side, developing children come to identify with the opposite-sex parent. In a variety of studies, children are first asked to describe themselves in response to a variety of questions about their beliefs, attitudes, and behaviors, and then to respond to the same questions from the perspective of their father and from the perspective of their mother. Usually, after age five or six, a child's responses resemble those of the opposite-sex parent more than the same-sex parent.

On the equivocal side, individuals often show different attitudes toward the same-sex versus opposite-sex parent. The differences themselves correspond to the Oedipal model: positive toward the opposite-sex parent, negative toward the same-sex parent. However, studies that have investigated the process by which these attitudes are formed yield results that do not exactly follow the Oedipal script.

Let me describe two studies with adult subjects that support Oedipal predictions. Schill (1966) showed male and female college students a cartoon picture of a dog about to have its tail cut off by a knife. Research subjects were asked to speculate about which member of the dog's family was responsible for this impending doom (which you should recognize as symbolic castration). As Freud would expect, males saw the dog's father as the perpetrator of castration, while females saw the dog's mother as responsible.

Calvin Hall (1963) investigated Oedipal predictions through the content analysis of dreams. He operationalized father's hostility as the presence of a male stranger in one's dream. If this operationalization is plausible, then the validity of the Oedipal model would be supported if males dreamed more than females about male strangers. This is exactly what Hall finds.

Such adult studies do not, however, get at the process by which attitudes toward mother and father are formed. A study is needed that looks at children across the age span when Oedipal feelings are presumably aroused and resolved. Friedman (1952) conducted one such study by asking children of different ages to tell stories in response to two different picture cues: one depicting a child with an adult male, the other depicting a child with an adult female. Boys told more stories containing conflict when the figure represented father than when it represented mother, while girls showed the opposite pattern. In these broad terms, then, the research once again confirms psychoanalytic predictions. However, the details of Friedman's findings do not. Taking age into account fails to reveal the trends Freud proposed. Indeed, some of the age changes predicted by the Oedipal hypothesis occur exactly backwards! From ages five to sixteen, girls showed conflict with mother that increased, not decreased.

On the negative side, research strongly disagrees with Freud's assertion that identification with the opposite-sex parent is brought about by anxiety. Several studies show that little boys are most likely to adopt a masculine role if their father is warm, affectionate, and nurturant (see, for example, Sears, 1953). More generally, Bandura's investigations of modelling suggest that adult models will be followed to the degree that they are friendly instead of

In contradiction to Freud's theories about Oedipal conflicts, research shows that a child who is given an accepting, friendly model shows no anxiety in his identification with the same-sex parent.

threatening. So, in personality development, as in other spheres of life, one gets further with honey than vinegar.

Also on the negative side, research somewhat disagrees with the idea of castration anxiety and altogether disagrees with the idea of penis envy. Studies show that males are more afraid of bodily damage than are females, but they have not shown that this fear particularly centers around loss of the genitals. Further, as Eysenck and Wilson (1973) have observed, the typical investigation of castration anxiety compares responses of males and females, and this is silly. Of course, boys are more likely to fear the loss of a penis than are girls: "If you ain't got nothing, you got nothing to lose!" Such investigations presuppose the Oedipal model they are trying to test.

How about the prediction that a person's moral sense develops from the resolution of the Oedipal conflict? By Freud's reasoning, father's strictness accelerates identification and superego formation. "Conscience" among boys should correlate positively with strictness of father. Many of you are no doubt rolling your eyes over this prediction, because you're thinking of the local juvenile delinquent whose father raised him like a drill sergeant. Good for you: your skepticism corresponds with a number of studies. Punitive fathers raise sons with weak moral standards. The development of conscience seems to be facilitated by nurturance and friendliness, not by punishment (Hoffman, 1963; Kohlberg, 1963, 1966).

Moral Development: Gilligan and Kohlberg

A related line of research compares the moral standards of males and females. As you recall, Freud argues that girls do not resolve the Oedipal conflict as neatly as do boys. So, their moral standards should not be as strong as boys' are. Freud is supported by some studies which show that males have a superior moral sense to females, but other studies show that females are superior to males, and yet other studies show no difference. Probably critical in deciphering these contradictory results is the particular operationalization of morality that the researcher chose (Sears, Rau, & Alpert, 1965). Is conscience regarded as harsh and aggressive? Is it regarded as timid and acquiescent?

Rather than describe a number of studies and end up concluding that matters are confusing, let me instead discuss in detail the arguments of Carol Gilligan, whose 1982 book *In a Different Voice* points the researcher in a new direction for understanding sex differences in morality. Gilligan does not join the debate over which sex shows higher moral sense. Instead, she suggests that in our society males and females tend to have different moral standards. In attempting to compare them, one overlooks what is most interesting and most important.

Gilligan suggests that women's morality centers on not hurting others. In contrast, men's morality emphasizes rights. She describes the responses of two eleven-year-old children faced with moral dilemma: should a man steal a drug he cannot afford to save his dying wife? Jake, a young boy, argues that the man should steal the drug:

> A human life is worth more than money. . . . the druggist can get a thousand dollars later from rich people with cancer, but Heinz can't get his wife again. (p. 26)

Amy, a young girl, says the man shouldn't steal the drug:

> I think there might be other ways besides stealing it, like if he could borrow the money. . . . if he stole the drug, he might save his wife then, but if he did, he might have to go to jail, and then his wife might get sicker. (p. 28)

The critical contrast here is not that they recommend different courses of action, but that they justify them in different ways. Indeed, they see different moral problems. As Gilligan observes, "Jake [sees] a conflict between life and property that can be resolved by logical deduction, Amy [sees] a fracture of human relationship that must be mended with its own thread" (p. 31).

For a more personal example, let me describe what happens when my friend Lisa and I watch a sports event together. I always want "my" team to win. In contrast, before the game, Lisa roots for whatever team is the underdog. In the course of the game, she roots for the team that is behind. In contrast to my masculine vision of a 98–0 shutout by my team, Lisa wants frequent lead changes ending in a 98–98 tie.

Gilligan's ideas take issue not only with those of Freud but also with those of developmental psychologist Lawrence Kohlberg (1981). Like Freud, Kohlberg describes development in terms of stages. Moral reasoning develops from an egocentric stage, where moral decisions are based on one's own self-interest, to a principled stage, where moral decisions are based on considerations of justice. Gilligan criticizes Kohlberg's scheme of development because it embodies a masculine bias; Kohlberg (1981) seems to regard concern with rules as a more advanced moral stance than concern with the well-being of others.

Kohlberg (1984) has recently responded to Gilligan's criticisms, acknowledging that morality involves not just abstract principles but also care and concern for other people. His approach in the past has perhaps placed too much emphasis on justice. So, he agrees with some of Gilligan's arguments.

But he does not agree with all of her points. Most basically, he disagrees with her dichotomy of justice on the one hand and social concern on the other hand. Someone with a highly developed moral sense will consider both. Further, Kohlberg disagrees that men and women differ in the moral reasoning they employ. He faults researchers who seem to show a sex difference for not taking into account potential confounds like education, employment status, and so on.

At any rate, Gilligan's work remains important for challenging the way that theorists and researchers have conceived morality. Attempts to measure all superegos against the psychoanalytic standard and its masculine bias obscure the whole of moral reasoning. Gilligan recommends that each type of morality be studied in its own right. And Kohlberg in effect agrees with her in recommending that the two be studied in conjunction with each other. In the present context, I second these recommendations. The Oedipal hypothesis has put blinders on researchers investigating morality for far too long.

In sum, Freud was correct in attributing lasting importance to family dynamics. Who we are reflects how we have interacted with mother and father. However, he was incorrect in choosing the myth of Oedipus as the prototype of personality development. "Leave It to Beaver" seems a better model of what actually happens. Friendly and supportive parents who provide good examples of how to behave result in a child's healthy development.

Birth Order

Now let me turn from Freud's account of personality development with its emphasis on Oedipal dynamics to Adler's account with its emphasis on birth order. As you recall, Adler thinks that a child's ordinal position within the

The Cleaver family may offer us more insight into personality development than the myth of Oedipus.

family creates different social realities to which the child reacts. First-born children are overly mature, second-born children are particularly insecure, and so on. Researchers have been intrigued by these predictions, and have conducted a variety of investigations testing them.

Achievement   One line of birth order research has looked at achievement, expecting first-borns to be particularly eminent. In a number of studies, this is the case. For example, among United States presidents, first-born sons are overrepresented (Wagner & Schubert, 1977). George Washington, Harry Truman, and Gerald Ford are examples. Interestingly, a preponderance of first-born sons does not appear among defeated candidates for the presidency.

Intelligence   A related line of research has investigated intellectual development, again with the expectation that first-born children will distinguish themselves, since they have had the opportunity to tutor others. In a massive investigation of some 400,000 males from the Netherlands, Belmont and Marolla (1973) found that birth order was positively correlated with performance on the Raven Progressive Matrices, a nonverbal test of intelligence. However, you may be skeptical that family dynamics are responsible for this intriguing relationship. Aren't there other variables that might explain it? How about family income during one's childhood? How about mother's age? In a study of how American students performed on the National Merit Test, Breland (1974) ruled out these and other confounds, showing that the relationship between birth order and intelligence occurred even when these factors were controlled.

Psychologists Robert Zajonc and Gregory Markus (1975) took an even closer look at the relationship between birth order and intellectual attainment. They reanalyzed the data of Belmont and Marolla (1973) and found that in addition to birth order, the spacing of children in a family affected intelligence. The more closely in time that brothers and sisters are born, the lower their intelligence. This effect is particularly pronounced among the youngest children.

To account for these findings, Zajonc and Markus proposed what they call a **confluence model**. This model makes three reasonable assumptions. First, *people attain a given level of intelligence according to the amount of intellectual stimulation they receive from their family.* Second, *the amount of stimulation is determined by the average intelligence of the family members.* Third, *older children are more intelligent than younger children.*

Do you see how these assumptions explain the patterns in the Belmont-Marolla data? The more young children present in a family, the less intellectual stimulation the family provides to each. First-born children escape this handicap for at least their early years, while latter-born children are born into this situation. Particularly at a disadvantage, according to the confluence model, should be twins and triplets. And this is exactly what the data show. (I'm a twin, so I probably don't understand the confluence model as well as if I were not, but the point seems to be that "spaced-out" siblings are advantageous.)

The confluence model provides a possible explanation for why SAT scores declined through the sixties and seventies: high school students taking the SAT tended to come from increasingly large families. Zajonc and Bargh (1980) tested this explanation and concluded that birth order and family size indeed account for some of this decline, but by no means all of it. Still, they predicted that SAT scores would start to rise again in the eighties and nineties, as the family composition of high school students again changed. And their prediction appears to be correct!

Although the confluence model points to a process linking birth order to intellectual attainment that is somewhat different than what Adler proposes, it is still in the spirit of his theorizing. A child's place in the family determines his environment, which in turn determines the sort of adult he will become.

Psychopathology   Another line of research has studied the relation of birth order to different psychological disorders, again supporting the gist of Adler's theories. Barry and Blane (1977), for instance, reviewed a number of studies that assessed incidence of alcoholism among individuals of various birth orders. The majority of these investigations found that last-borns were over-represented among alcoholics. Do you see how this finding is consistent with Adler's claim that the youngest in a family is particularly insecure?

Affiliation   A final line of work has looked at patterns of affiliation as a function of birth order. Psychologist Stanley Schacter (1959) reported several intriguing investigations that support Adler's conjecture that first-borns are marked for life by the birth of a younger sibling, displacing them from the center of attention. First-borns should therefore be made more anxious by threat than latter-borns, and they should be more likely to reach out to others (as parental figures) when they experience anxiety.

Schacter recruited female subjects for an experiment and told them that it would involve painful electric shock. While the experimenter was supposedly preparing the equipment, he gave them the option of waiting alone or with other women. Consistent with Adler's ideas, first-born women reported more anxiety than latter-born women, and were also more likely to prefer to wait in the presence of others.

Other studies similarly show that first-born children are unlikely to pursue solitary and dangerous professions like being a fighter pilot or a skydiver; at the same time, they are more likely to seek help from a psychotherapist when experiencing problems (Freedman, 1982, p. 493). When an earthquake struck Los Angeles in 1971, first-borns reported that they spoke to more people immediately following the quake than did latter-borns, implying again the link among birth order, anxiety, and affiliation (Hoyt & Raven, 1973).

A few years ago, I conducted an informal study and asked students how they procrastinated during final exams. I also asked them their birth position. Two findings were interesting. First, almost everyone procrastinated when it came time for finals. The entire campus seethed with procrastination. But second, as a function of their birth order, students did different things while procrastinating. First-borns wasted time socially, by going out to drink with others or by writing letters. Latter-borns wasted time alone, by playing video games or by alphabetizing their spice racks. Again, these results are consistent with Adler's ideas about birth order.

Evaluation   Not all studies of birth order yield positive results (Ernst & Angst, 1983; Jones, 1931; Schooler, 1972). I've selected some of the investigations consistent with Adler's position to show its merit. Keep in mind all of the possible influences on the behaviors of concern in these studies. The fact that birth order has any effect at all is impressive; that these effects are consistent with Adler's ideas argues that we should take into account the child's position within the family in order to understand adult personality.

Character Types

I want to conclude this section by describing research that supports the psychoanalytic character types. These concepts have the most obvious relationship to personality as we usually think of it. What does the evidence say about the types of people proposed by the psychoanalytic theorists? Actually, two hypotheses are embedded here. The first is a descriptive one, asking whether the characteristics of people cohere in the ways suggested by theory. For instance, is there an identifiable constellation of anal traits? Do the same people tend to be stingy, neat, and stubborn? The second hypothesis is a developmental one, asking whether a particular character type is brought about by unusual events during the corresponding stage of psychosexual development.

In light of the research already described regarding the theory of psychosexual development, you can probably guess that there is little support for the developmental hypothesis. On the other hand, the descriptive hypothesis has been mostly supported by research (Fisher & Greenberg, 1977; Kline, 1972). People's characteristics do indeed cohere in ways predicted by the character types.

Before I go over the pertinent investigations, let me remind you of the *consistency of personality* issue. How the researcher goes about identifying a character type requires assumptions about consistency and how it should be regarded. Character-type identification might seem the easiest task of the personality psychologist, a matter of going out and finding them, like a coin collector locating a 1955-S penny. But it's not that easy.

Although types are pigeonholes, discrete categories, they exist in the realm of theory, not in the realm of actual instances. Most of us do not neatly fit into only one character type. We may be more similar to the ideal of one type than another, but we are not—simply—of that type and no other. The personality psychologist in search of character types must realize that these types are idealizations. The psychoanalytic character types are modelled on biological types, and these are among the best instances of a small gap between examples and theory. But the personality psychologist must speak of ideal types, prototypes that allow us to understand what actually exists in the world.

In research, the personality psychologist uses correlation coefficients to investigate claims about character types. As I explained in Chapter 2, these statistics assess the degree of association between two variables. They do not show that people fall into or out of discrete categories. This seeming inconsistency is resolved if you keep in mind what I've been saying: personality types reside in theories, not in actual people.

Oral and Anal Character Types   A great deal of research has looked at the character types supposedly resulting from fixation at the oral or anal stages of psychosexual development. As you'll recall from Chapter 5, the oral character is thought to show a variety of characteristics:

- preoccupation with issues of giving-taking
- concern about dependence-independence and passivity-activity
- special attitudes about closeness and distance to others—being alone versus attachment to the group
- extremes of optimism-pessimism
- unusual ambivalence
- openness to novel experience and ideas, which involves enhanced curiosity and interest in investigating nature
- a hasty, restless, impatient orientation—wanting to be "fed" with events and things
- continued unusual use of oral channels for gratification or compensatory denial of oral needs; for example, overeating, not eating enough, smoking, excessive talking (from Fisher & Greenberg, 1977, p. 88)

If the idea of an oral character is to make sense, these characteristics should be correlated. Similarly, the anal character is also thought to show a constellation of characteristics: the traits of obstinacy, parsimony, and orderliness. Borrowing from Abraham (1927) and Jones (1923), Kline (1972, pp. 10–11) elaborated this set of anal characteristics to include:

- procrastination followed by intense concentration
- a belief that nobody can do anything as well as oneself
- minute attention to detail
- strong drive to clean things
- profound interest in handwriting
- opposition of any attempt to guide one's conduct
- dislike of time being used up against one's will
- pleasure spoiled by small things out of place
- love of self-control
- interest in the backs of things

- love of exactitude, delight in organizing
- reliability
- hatred of waste
- pleasure in possessing something rare or unusual
- pleasure in statistics or tables
- dislike of spending money on perishable things

Researchers have tested these claims in dozens of studies. Most frequently, research subjects answer questions about various oral and/or anal characteristics. Responses are correlated with each other, and oral characteristics go together more frequently than one would expect by mere chance, as do anal characteristics (Fisher & Greenberg, 1977; Kline, 1972).

Some of the most intriguing of these studies use the **Blacky Test** developed by psychologist Gerald Blum (1949, 1962; Blum & Hunt, 1952). This is a projective test specifically designed to investigate psychoanalytic character types. The name of the test refers to a dog, Blacky, who figures with its family in twelve cartoons depicting situations of psychosexual relevance. So, in one picture, Blacky is nursing. In another, Blacky is defecating. Earlier in this chapter, I described the Blacky picture used in Schill's (1966) investigation of castration responsibility: Blacky watches its sibling Tippy, who has a knife poised over its tail.

Blacky's sex is identified to the research subject as the same as that of the subject. The subject then tells a story about each picture. What's going on? How do the characters feel? Stories are scored for the presence or absence of oral concern, anal concern, and so on. In the present context, we are interested in the designation of research subjects as oral (or not) and as anal (or not). Once subjects are so designated, do they act in ways consistent with their putative character type?

Various studies show that they do. Although inconsistencies exist, researchers have shown that oral subjects, as identified by the Blacky Test, are prone to suggestion and influence (Tribich & Messer, 1974), ambivalence regarding autonomy (Blatt, 1964), obesity (Friedman, 1959), excessive cigarette smoking (Kimeldorf & Geiwitz, 1966), and overindulgence in ice cream (Blum & Hunt, 1952). Anal subjects, as identified by the Blacky Test, show good memory for details (Adelson & Redmond, 1958), concern with order (Blatt, 1964), resistance to influence and suggestion (Tribich & Messer, 1974), and obsessive symptoms (Kline, 1968).

Psychologist Charles Noblin and his colleagues conducted an impressive series of studies comparing oral and anal subjects as the Blacky Test identifies them. They were concerned with the way these types of individuals respond to different forms of reinforcement. All studies used a similar procedure.

Subjects were given a series of cards with incomplete sentences preceded either by a first-person pronoun or a third-person pronoun. They were asked to complete the sentences any way they wished, and it was noted whether they chose first-person or third-person pronouns. Then the experimenter instituted different forms of reward for the choice of one over the other type of pronoun. The subjects' responses to the rewards were then ascertained.

In one study, Noblin, Timmons, and Kael (1966) compared the effects of reward versus punishment on the response of subjects in the sentence completion procedure. In this investigation, half of the subjects (both oral and anal) were verbally praised for their choice of the target pronoun. The other half were verbally criticized for their choice of the other type of pronoun ("You can do better"). The obtained results nicely supported predictions. Oral subjects increased use of the target pronoun in response to praise but not to criticism, while anal subjects did the same following criticism but not praise.

In a second study, Noblin (1962) chose psychiatric patients who represented either an oral or anal orientation. The reward for the choice of pronouns was either gumballs (as food requiring a great deal of chewing, an oral reward) or pennies (as symbolic feces to be hoarded, an anal reward). Consistent with predictions, oral subjects responded more to the gumballs than to the pennies, while anal subjects showed the exact opposite pattern. Cyndi Lauper notwithstanding, money does not change everything . . . only for anal character types!

I'm going to move from these studies, which show that oral and anal characteristics tend to cohere, to studies investigating the developmental hypothesis about character types. Does excessive frustration or indulgence at a particular stage of psychosexual development show up later as the respective character type? Researchers have correlated adult characteristics with methods of child-rearing, especially stringency or leniency in weaning and toilet training. If the developmental hypothesis is correct, the child who nursed too short or too long a time will show oral traits as an adult. Likewise, the child who was potty-trained in an extreme fashion will show anal traits as an adult.

There are several types of these studies. Retrospective studies assess child-rearing practices after-the-fact, from the reports of the individual or the parents. These assessments are correlated with oral or anal personality measures (see, for example, Thurston & Mussen, 1951). But, prospective studies are methodologically preferable, since they assess child-rearing practices at the time they are occurring. The children are followed for a period of time, hopefully post-puberty where fixations show up, and then their character traits are measured and correlated with the child-rearing variables (see, for example, Heinstein, 1963). Yet another type of study characterizes the weaning or toilet-training typical of an entire culture, and attempts to draw connections between these practices and the model personality of adults in that culture (for example, Whiting & Child, 1953).

Regardless of how the studies are conducted, there is scant support for the developmental hypothesis (Fisher & Greenberg, 1977; Kline, 1972). Although some investigations have found relationships among child-rearing and personality, the links are not those specifically proposed by Freud's psychoanalytic theory.

Phallic Character Type   In contrast to the large research literature investigating Freud's oral and anal characters, few studies have looked at the phallic character, which is presumably produced by unusual events at the phallic stage of psychosexual development, showing itself in the form of exaggerated sexuality and preoccupation with the self. However, a recent study by psychologists Donald Mosher and Mark Sirkin (1984) is relevant. These researchers were concerned with what they call the **macho personality constellation**, defined as *hypermasculinity* and measured by a questionnaire that asks subjects to endorse one statement from each of a number of pairs of statements like:

1.   I like wild, uninhibited parties.
2.   I like quiet parties with good conversations.

1.   I like fast cars and fast women.
2.   I like dependable cars and faithful women.

1.   So-called prick teasers should be forgiven.
2.   Prick teasers should be raped.

1.   I like to drive safely, avoiding all risks.
2.   I like to drive fast, right on the edge of danger.

1.   Lesbians have chosen a particular lifestyle, and should be respected for it.
2.   The only thing a lesbian needs is a good, stiff cock.

Although Mosher and Sirkin do not explicitly link their research to the phallic character type, there is considerable overlap between this character type and the macho orientation as they have measured it. In a study of 135 male college students, Mosher and Sirkin found good evidence for the coherence of the macho personality constellation. Subjects who choose the macho (phallic) alternative in one pair of statements from the questionnaire tend to choose the macho alternative in other pairs. Further, those who score high on the macho scale are apt to use drugs and alcohol excessively, to have physical fights, to get in automobile accidents, and to be sexually promiscuous.

Missing from this research is any evidence of development. Mosher and Sirkin speculate that the macho orientation is rooted in parental use of contempt and humiliation, while psychoanalytic theory predicts that this character type results specifically from too much or too little genital stimulation during the phallic stage of psychosexual development. In light of the developmental evidence concerning oral and anal character types, Mosher and Sirkin's speculations seem more likely to be supported by longitudinal investigations than the psychoanalytic hypothesis.

Fromm's Character Types   Descriptively, some of the character types suggested by Erich Fromm are quite similar to Freudian character types. *Receptive characters* sound like oral characters, *hoarding characters* like anal characters, and *exploitative characters* like phallic characters. Since research tends to support the coherence of these Freudian character types, we can conclude that Fromm's descriptions are valid as well.

The most extensive investigation that explicitly looked at Fromm's typology is Fromm and Maccoby's (1970) investigation of social character in a Mexican village. Remember Fromm's emphasis on the social determinants of personality? Social character is the personality "common to most members of groups or classes within a given society. . . . a syndrome . . . which has developed as an adaptation to the economic, social, and cultural conditions of that group" (p. 16).

These investigators administered what they call an *interpretive questionnaire* to 406 peasants in an isolated Mexican village. Subjects were asked a variety of open-ended questions such as:

- Give a brief description of your mother as you see her.
- What do you do with your free time?
- What experience in your life has been the happiest?
- What do you consider the worst crime a person can commit? Why?
- A young man marries a woman of whom his mother disapproves, and he must go to live far away from the village where his mother lives. His mother becomes sick because of the separation and finally dies. What do you think of the young man? What did he feel? And the wife? (from Fromm & Maccoby, 1970, pp. 240–243)

Responses are interpreted as a whole, and are used to assign subjects to one of Fromm's character types. Although this procedure involves unknown bias, Fromm and Maccoby argue that interpreting what their subjects say is necessary for classification.

Consistent with expectation, two character types predominated. Lower-class individuals tended to be receptive, while upper-class individuals tended to be hoarding. Further, within classes, a hoarding orientation was positively associated with economic success. Hoarders tended not to plant sugar cane, a crop requiring little work but yielding few profits, while among receptive individuals sugar cane was the favorite crop.

Fromm and Maccoby interpreted their findings in terms of social and economic characteristics of the village:

> The hoarding orientation has been the one best adapted to the economic demands of farming in the village. . . . because his character and work fit together, the hoarding peasant is likely to be more productive and energetic, indeed more confident and hopeful, than the receptive peasant who finds himself increasingly out of tune with his work. (p. 142)

This investigation impressively supports Fromm's social version of psychoanalytic theory. However, the research is more of an extended case study than anything else. Although a large number of individuals were studied, the real focus was the village itself. Generality to other groups, with different social and economic demands, is unknown.

Jung's Character Types   A number of investigations of Jung's typology have used the **Myers-Briggs Type Indicator** (Myers, 1962) to classify individuals. This is a self-report questionnaire that presents subjects with a number of forced choices between alternatives. For instance:

1. When you are with a group of people, would you usually rather
    (a) join in the talk of the group, or
    (b) talk with one person at a time?

2. In reading for pleasure, do you
    (a) enjoy odd or original ways of saying things, or
    (b) like writers to say exactly what they mean?

3. Is it a higher compliment to be called
    (a) a person of real feeling, or
    (b) a consistently reasonable person?

4. Does following a schedule
    (a) appeal to you, or
    (b) cramp you?

The alternatives to each item capture the ends of one of the dimensions described by Jung: introversion versus extroversion (Item A), sensation versus intuition (Item B), or thinking versus feeling (Item C). Myers and Briggs also include items to measure a dimension not explicitly described by Jung: preference for judging versus perceiving the outside world (Item D). For each of the dimensions, the preponderance of endorsed alternatives is used to classify a research subject. The Myers-Briggs Type Indicator seems to be internally consistent and stable over time (Carlyn, 1977).

To date, much of the research that has used this questionnaire has looked at the influence of type on college students' choice of major, and academic performance on workers' choice of occupation and vocational performance. Most of the positive findings make sense within a Jungian perspective: introverted types are attracted to technical and scientific fields; sensation types to practical fields; feeling types to helping professions; and so on (Stricker & Ross, 1964).

Although the Myers-Briggs manual recommends that scores be used to lump people into two groups (for instance, introverts and extraverts), studies fail to show that this improves the researcher's ability to predict behavior better than using the scores to define a continuous dimension. Also, studies do not conclusively show that anything is gained by simultaneously classifying subjects on all four dimensions. In other words, results for thinking versus feeling types are not qualified by taking into account their introversion versus extraversion. These latter results are at odds with Jung's emphasis on the integration between a person's attitudes and functions, since one would not expect them to operate as independently as they seem to.

The use of the Myers-Briggs inventory appears to be growing among personality researchers. Future research might do well to test some of Jung's more intriguing predictions about types. How do people change across the lifespan? Do the functions become balanced? What about Jung's idea that there is a dominant function in the unconscious; might this be apparent under conditions of subliminal stimulation or hypnosis?

CONCLUSIONS: PSYCHOANALYTIC THEORIES IN LIGHT OF THE RESEARCH

The research shows that Freud was right about most things except sex. There is considerable irony in this conclusion, since Freud's name is inextricably linked to the role of sexuality in personality. What do we do with psychoanalytic theory if its libidinal core is removed? Is the bathwater of any interest after the baby is thrown out? I think so. Remember what is left when we use research evidence to strip away incorrect claims: unconscious motivation, transference, defense mechanisms, character types, and the importance of early experiences, especially the nuances of family dynamics. These are important ideas. Taken together, they make a coherent statement about personality.

To say it another way, Freud's hypotheses about the processes underlying personality development and expression are often correct, while his claims about sexual and aggressive contents are often wrong. He may have been overly influenced by Victorian Europe and its strict prohibitions against overt sexuality, elevating this striking aspect of his culture to the status of universal human nature. The patients in his case histories clearly experienced conflicts with sexuality. However, not all times and places have been so uptight about sex. Nevertheless, Freud's observations about the way that people deal with these particular prohibitions lead to considerably general conclusions.

How is the composite psychoanalytic theory presented at the end of the last chapter altered by these conclusions? Most of the points of view are vindicated: the empirical, the gestalt, the organismic, the genetic, the topographic, the adaptive, and the psychosocial. The dynamic and economic points of view are deleted. The structural point of view is supported insofar as the ego and superego are on focus; it is not supported with respect to the id.

This revised composite psychoanalytic theory sounds a neoFreudian one. However, this research-informed revision of psychoanalysis does not agree with the theory of any particular neoFreudian. Research fails to support claims that people are driven by a single dominant motive, be it sex, superiority, affection, approval, identity, integration, or whatever. The human family does not march to a single drummer. There are lots of beats in the air, and most of us listen to several.

What should you take with you after reading this chapter? First, appreciate that the common assertion that psychoanalytic theory is impossible to test is wrong. The theory can be tested, and it has been tested. Second, appreciate that Freud and the other psychoanalytic theorists were correct about a number of matters concerning personality. Their influence is felt throughout the entire field of personality psychology. The evidence suggests that this influence is warranted. Third, appreciate that research shows that Freud's emphasis on sexuality was incorrect.

SUMMARY

In this chapter, I described psychoanalytic research. I started by considering the criticism that psychoanalytic theory is impossible to test because its concepts are ambiguous and its predictions are muddled. I disagreed. Psychoanalytic concepts can be operationalized if the researcher is willing to gather enough information to make a good inference about their presence or absence. Clear psychoanalytic predictions can be made if the researcher distinguishes between clinical predictions (aspects of theory amenable to test) and metapsychological assumptions (bedrock aspects of a paradigm that underlie testable predictions).

I described several of Freud's well-known case studies. Despite their importance in providing the raw material for psychoanalytic theory, these studies are only borderline instances of satisfactory research. Three contemporary refinements of the case history research strategy are much more rigorous: the **symptom-context method**, the **core conflictual relationship theme method**, and the **natural history method**. Research that uses these approaches supports psychoanalytic predictions regarding symptom formation, transference, and defense mechanisms.

Finally, I described a variety of correlational and experimental studies investigating specific topics pertinent to the psychoanalytic account of personality: **instincts** and **drives**, **unconscious motivation**, the Oedipal complex, birth order, and character types. Research support for psychoanalytic predictions is mixed; most claims are supported except when they specifically address sexuality. In other words, research bears out the neoFreudian criticism of a sexual libido.

7

PSYCHOANALYTIC PARADIGM: APPLICATIONS

Freud's ideas about human nature reverberate not just through personality psychology but throughout all of contemporary culture. His ideas and terminology have been thoroughly assimilated by the Western World, as have those of the other psychoanalytic theorists. We sprinkle our conversations with mention of defense mechanisms ("Now don't be defensive— you know that you do that"), with reference to one sort of complex or another ("Short men act that way"), with speculation about archetypes ("You've always been attracted to the earth mother type"). And we blame mother and father for how we turned out, sometimes to the point of suing them for incompetence.

But the influence of psychoanalytic thought on contemporary life has been even more profound. Psychoanalytic ideas, by virtue of their general acceptance, have literally changed the world and thereby changed who we are. Like Adam and Eve, we have tasted the fruit of our knowledge, and we are not the same. Once we accept the possibilities that our motives are hidden from us, that our sexuality is paramount, that behavior is over-determined, then we think, feel, and act differently, even if these possibilities are not strictly true.

Dissemination of ideas in the social sciences may have opposite consequences. On the one hand, through self-fulfilling prophecies, a theory's popularity sometimes leads to the appearance of an even greater validity, as people act in expected ways. For instance, some managerial theories regard workers as lazy, disinterested sweathogs; workplaces that embody this assumption produce the very slackers assumed in the first place.

On the other hand, a theory's popularity sometimes leads to its own invalidation. Kenneth Gergen (1973) calls this an **enlightenment effect**. People may use their knowledge of the theory to act in ways that are not quite consistent with it. Slowly, the theory becomes wrong, as people find the psychological equivalent of income tax loopholes.

As an example, consider the *unresponsive bystander effect* documented by social psychologists John Darley and Bibb Latané (1968). The more people witnessing an accident, the less likely anyone is to help. If someone drops a handful of change on a crowded sidewalk, he is less likely to receive help than if he drops it on a secluded side street. This phenomenon is attributed in part to the **diffusion of responsibility** among the bystanders. Everyone assumes that the other fellow will help.

Diffusion of responsibility is an intriguing theory that explains what is otherwise puzzling: bystander apathy in cases of dire emergency. It is so intriguing, in fact, that it is taught to tens of thousands of students each year

The unresponsive bystander effect—is it a thing of the past?

in social psychology courses. And what is the result? At least some of these students may do what I do when I see a stranger in distress: look to see how many bystanders are present. The *more* people around, the more likely I am to help. Bye-bye bystander effect!

Let's return to psychoanalytic ideas. How about hysteria? Cases are much more rare today than during Freud's time. This may be an enlightenment effect: the result of widespread knowledge of psychoanalytic ideas. People know that sensory systems don't stop working all of a sudden. If sudden blindness or deafness does occur, people know that this may be a cop-out, a response to stress. People know that they have conflicts that may be outside their awareness. Such insights may preclude the bizarre hysteria cases that Freud and Breuer and others of their era treated.

How about sex? By all estimates, sexual frequency and variety are up, so to speak, from the turn of the century. Of course numerous factors are responsible, not least of which is the improved technology of contraception. Psychoanalytic theory is another factor responsible for the sexual revolution. Freud is the father of the sexual revolution because his ideas have changed the way that sex is regarded. He may not have agreed with the way that sexual activities have evolved, but he certainly started the ball rolling.

And not only are sexual activities more common, but our attitude toward them is different as well. It's okay and healthy to have a sex drive. We feel guilty when we say no. We seek psychotherapy because we are virgins. We expect young children to be interested in sex, and we expect the same of senior citizens. Masturbation is harmless. There is no clear line between normal and abnormal sexual practices. Our bodies contain many erogenous zones. Thanks Sigmund, we needed that. Or maybe we didn't. Regardless, the times have changed with regard to sex, and so have we.

How about primary process? Freud's description of another way of thinking, one in which all wishes come true, has beckoned people to indulge themselves in it. I remember talking to a fifty-year-old psychiatrist a while ago. He was puzzled why so many young people use drugs excessively. "In my day," he said, "we used to be afraid of losing control. Now, people pay lots of money for exactly that to happen."

The two of us speculated that children who grew up believing that *altered states* were just as much "them" as their normal consciousness regard primary process in a different way than people unenlightened by Freud's ideas. When earlier generations caught glimpses of the unconscious, they were

Altered states of consciousness providing access to primary process have become "normal" states for an entire generation

frightened. But some members of the new generation recognize themselves in the unconscious, and find access to primary process a hard-to-resist temptation.

Against the context of Freud's profound influence on our times, there are also discrete instances where psychoanalytic ideas have been applied. I've selected several topics in which people have taken psychoanalytic ideas and done something with them. Although I'll comment on the general success or failure of these applications, let me remind you that application is not the same thing as research. Theories are not explicitly tested by applications. Reasonableness of a theory is assumed—not evaluated.

So, it is interesting that many of the applications I'll be discussing are concerned with psychoanalytic notions of sexuality. This is the precise area of psychoanalytic theory that the research evidence finds most contradictory. But undaunted by these facts, practitioners have gone ahead with libido-based applications. These applications have sometimes proven satisfactory, so perhaps they are produced by self-fulfilling prophecies.

PSYCHOPATHOLOGY: PRODUCED BY UNCONSCIOUS CONFLICTS

Hardly surprising is the widespread application of psychoanalytic ideas to help understand psychological abnormality. After all, the important psychoanalytic theorists have mostly been psychotherapists. The raw material of psychoanalysis was clinical material: facts about distressed people. In this section of the chapter, I will sketch the general psychoanalytic formula for conceiving abnormality, and then illustrate it by a number of examples.

Conception of Abnormality   The psychoanalyst sees psychopathology as a developmental problem, as an inevitable hazard of passing through the psychosexual stages to reach a compromise between instinctive drives and societal prohibitions. Because personality development is seen as cumulative, early events can be particularly traumatic, and, if adult personality is built on a flawed foundation, psychopathology results.

A person experiencing difficulties with thoughts, feelings, or actions is regarded as poorly handling her needs and drives. She holds them too much in check, or not enough. As we used to say on the psychiatric ward where I worked: check the lid on the id. Too tight, too loose, or missing altogether? Problems result from childhood events, from constitutional weaknesses, or from an interplay between the two.

Regardless, the symptoms a person experiences are viewed by psychoanalysts in two ways. First, they represent a literal tying-up of libidinal energy that would be better employed elsewhere. What is mental health if not the abilities to love with joy and to work with joy (Vaillant, 1977)? Both take energy. Second, symptoms symbolize the particular conflict that underlies them. The woman who is hysterically mute, for instance, is thought to have a problem with something she might say, and wishes that she won't.

Hysteria   Hysteria is called **conversion disorder** (American Psychiatric Association, 1980). Conversion refers to the psychoanalytic notion that *the particular symptom results from the transformation of psychic conflict into physical malfunction.* Before Breuer and Freud implicated the role of conflict in hysterical symptoms, the disorder was thought to be purely physical in nature.

Through the use of hypnosis and, later, free association, Freud showed that hysteria was a psychological disorder involving sexual conflicts that the patient was unable to acknowledge or resolve. Her paralysis represented a solution to her dilemma, albeit a poor one. The psychoanalytic account of conversion disorders is still widely accepted (see, for example, Sackeim, Nordlie, & Gur, 1979), but the precipitating conflict is no longer seen as only sexual. A variety of conflicts give rise to hysterical symptoms. Further, contemporary views emphasize the role of reinforcement in maintaining hysterical symptoms once they appear (Nemiah, 1980c).

Conversion disorders are not nearly as common today as they once were. In my personal experience, I have encountered only two individuals with clear conversion symptoms. Both fit the psychoanalytic formula. One was a young woman who was hysterically deaf. She had grown up in a highly critical family, and eventually turned off the criticism—literally. The other was a middle-aged man who was hysterically blind. He was married to a woman who in recent years had become obese, and he dealt with his anger at her grotesque appearance by blinding himself to it—again, literally.

Phobia   Excessive and inappropriate fears have been described throughout history. Hippocrates described phobias like that of Nicanor, who was deathly afraid of the sound of flutes, and that of Damocles, who was afraid to walk near cliffs or over bridges. In *The Merchant of Venice*, Shakespeare mentioned "some, that are mad if they behold a cat." Among famous people suffering from phobias were Augustus Caesar, Pascal, King James I of England, Samuel Johnson, and Sigmund Freud himself. The fact that John Madden and Mr. T's character on the "A-Team" are afraid of flying is part of contemporary lore.

Before Freud, phobias did not receive much theoretical attention in their own right. They were regarded as just another manifestation of neurological disorder. Freud proposed a theoretical account of phobias per se, which we've already seen in the case of Little Hans (Chapter 4). A phobia is thought to result from displaced anxiety. Unlike hysterics, who blot anxiety from awareness, phobics still experience it. However, they attach it to an object or event that is not the original source of conflict.

Phobic objects are not chosen capriciously. They symbolize the real source of anxiety. Little Hans feared horses because they represented his father, in all of his sexual prowess and wrath. Or consider this case history:

> A young woman suffered from a fear of insects, particularly cockroaches. She was so frightened that she might encounter a roach that she avoided all places where one might cross her path: restaurants, stores, even the homes of friends and family members. She removed almost all the furniture from her own apartment, fearful that an insect might be hiding underneath them. And, because roaches rarely venture forth in bright light, she equipped all of her lamps with high wattage bulbs that burned continually. In the course of therapy, it was discovered that the woman's symptoms had started during adolescence, when she had a brief sexual encounter with a neighborhood boy. Her experience left her confused and frightened. She was attracted to the boy, but believed her parents would be greatly disappointed in her because of her sexual feelings. Not long afterwards, her fear of insects appeared: a symbol of sexuality best kept out of sight.

This particular phobia conforms well to psychoanalytic theory.

Today, the psychoanalytic account of phobias is not as widely accepted as it once was. While most clinicians acknowledge that some phobias represent displaced anxiety, even contemporary psychoanalysts look beyond sexual conflicts in explaining phobias (Nemiah, 1980b). As in hysteria, practitioners increasingly look to the environment to explain how phobias originate. Traumatic experience with the phobic object is now a popular etiological account (Marks, 1969). You can see how such explanations—based on mundane principles of classical conditioning—are diametrically opposed to the symbolic explanation of psychoanalysis. That the phobic individual may avoid unpleasantries by her fear is also a popular contemporary explanation. In the case of the woman who was afraid of boats, one might imagine how this fear serves to extricate her from difficult situations, like other dates where her sexual ambivalence would again become an issue.

Obsession and Compulsion   As noted in the Rat Man case described in the last chapter, Freud regards obsessions and compulsions as symbolic struggles. Underlying these problems is a conflict regarding sex or aggression. He proposes that people suffering from what is now called obsessive-compulsive disorder have displaced anxiety from one psychic realm to another. Along the way, a reaction formation occurs, so that the patient is consciously repulsed by what is unconsciously desired. Once again, Freud proposes that this process is not arbitrary. The obsessive idea or the compulsive behavior symbolizes the real conflict.

Consistent with this interpretation, the content of obsessions and compulsions tends to be limited to several themes: worry about dirt or disease; violence or loss of control; and religious blasphemy. All of these make sense within psychoanalytic theory (Nemiah, 1980a). Obsessions involving cleanliness versus contamination reflect concerns of the anal stage, as do those about violence or loss of control. Blasphemy symbolizes anger against Dad and Mom, for all their offenses, real and imagined.

Here is a case I once encountered:

> A 35-year old woman with two young children was obsessed with the idea that she would take a large knife and plunge it first into the heart of one child and then into the heart of the other. The thought repulsed her, since she loved her children, and it also frightened her, since she experienced the impulse as a very real one. When she found herself repeatedly opening the kitchen drawer containing knives, she started to hide the knives in unlikely places around the house. Then she feared that the hiding places were not all that secure after all, so she started to check them to make sure the knives were still there. The more she checked, the more accessible the knives seemed, and the more obsessive she became.

I talked with this woman on several occasions, eventually learning that she greatly resented the responsibility of raising two children with minimal help from her husband, who travelled for his employer. And while still a child, the woman had been assigned primary responsibility for raising her younger brother. From the viewpoint of psychoanalytic theory, all of the facts of this case fit together. The one thing the woman does not want is to be responsible for others: her children, her husband, her brother, her parents, even herself. Her obsessive-compulsive disorder expresses her unconscious belief that others have robbed her of her freedom, since she has never been able to follow her own heart.

The psychoanalytic explanation of obsessive-compulsive disorders is challenged by behavioral theories that emphasize the consequences of the repetitive thought or act (Rachman, 1978). Such preoccupations can be highly reinforcing since they distract the individual from considering the real sources of anxiety. Missing from behavioral theories is an explanation of the particular content of obsessions and compulsions, so perhaps the two rival accounts are better viewed as complementary. Psychoanalytic theory may explain why obsessive-compulsive disorder arrives on the scene, while learning theory may explain why it lingers so long (Rosenhan & Seligman, 1984).

Depression   Freud grapples with the problem of depression in his 1917 paper, "Mourning and Melancholia." Sadness occurs in both grief (mourning) and depression (melancholia), but only in the latter is it accompanied by loss of self-esteem. The depressed individual, unlike the merely sad person, reviles herself as worthless and incompetent, responsible for all sorts of bad events.

To Freud, the depressed person seems angry, and so Freud proposes that she is: angry at herself. How does this come about? Remember, personality develops when we incorporate the characteristics of significant others, usually our parents. If these significant others disappoint us in some way— if we lose their love—then the anger that wells up within us in response to this loss of love seeks a target. According to Freud, we turn our anger inward, punishing that part of us which is them.

Psychoanalysis thus explains why suicide often accompanies severe depression. *Suicide is symbolic murder.* Psychoanalysis also explains why losses are common in the childhood of some depressives (Wolpert, 1980). Consider this case:

> A 45 year-old man had been depressed ever since his early twenties. His history revealed an austere childhood in an extremely poor family. He grew up without new clothes, toys, or vacations. He had few friends during his school years, although as a young man he had both a best friend and a fiancée. But then he was drafted into the Army, and after several months received a terse letter from his fiancée stating that she planned to marry his best friend. The man eventually married someone else, but his wife refused to have children, much to his disappointment.

This man felt cheated by his parents, by his country, by his best friend, by his fiancée, and by his wife. A psychoanalyst would focus on his presumed anger at all these people, anger he never expressed but instead turned against himself.

Contemporary opinion holds that depression has numerous causes, including biological and sociological determinants (see, for example, Akiskal & McKinney, 1975). Some accounts emphasize the role of conscious thoughts in bringing about depressive disorders (for example, Beck, 1967; Peterson & Seligman, 1984). Nevertheless, the psychoanalytic idea of unexpressed hostility is still widely accepted as one of the determining factors (Lewis, 1981).

Paranoia and Homosexuality   We encountered the psychoanalytic equation of paranoia and latent homosexuality in the case of Schreber. This case history has given rise to a number of related proposals. First, paranoia is a defense against unconscious homosexual impulses. Second, overt homosexuality results from a poorly resolved Oedipal conflict. Third, male homosexuality is associated with excessive castration anxiety, while female homosexuality is associated with excessive penis envy.

The proposals pertaining to overt homosexuality have been tested, and results have been largely equivocal for males and decidedly negative for females

(Fisher & Greenberg, 1977). Homosexual orientation may indeed result from childhood experiences, but the Oedipal script does not tell the whole story.

What about paranoia? By definition, this disorder involves an unshakeable delusion of persecution. According to the psychoanalytic model, paranoia is a defense against homosexual impulses, the projection of one's own unacceptable wishes onto another. So, male paranoids fret about other males, while female paranoids worry about the advances of other women. Actually, both male and female paranoids fear males—not an unreasonable belief granted the more violent nature of men in our society (Lewis, 1981).

The content of paranoid delusions may include hints of homosexuality. For instance, Lehmann (1980) describes a letter written to a doctor by a paranoid patient. The patient scolds the medical staff for invading his bodily orifices, particularly his anus. They use secret machines that interfere with all of his organs: "I am at a loss to understand why those who are responsible are permitted to indulge in this peculiar pastime" (p. 1169). Along these same lines, I once worked with a paranoid patient who would walk up to me several times a day on the hospital ward, fix me with a stare, and announce in a loud voice, "I am *not* a faggot," as if I had made this accusation, which of course I had not. But, the content of persecutory delusions is not limited to homosexual wishes; it encompasses the entire gamut of unacceptable impulses.

The causal role of repressed homosexuality in paranoia is no longer widely believed. However, more general psychoanalytic ideas are still invoked to explain paranoid disorders. In particular, contemporary theories stress childhood events that lead to the use of the defense mechanism of projection (Walker & Brodie, 1980). Sullivan's attention to the role of disturbed family relationships has also influenced contemporary thinking about how paranoia develops.

Drug Use and Abuse   In *Civilization and Its Discontents*, Freud (1930) describes alcoholism and drug addiction as slow suicide: manifestations of the death instinct. At a descriptive level, Freud is right. The toll that drug abuse—particularly alcoholism—takes on physical health is almost incalculable (Vaillant, 1983). But, as a statement about the cause of drug abuse, Freud's hypothesis is unreasonable. A person starts to drink or use drugs as the result of social and cultural factors. He continues to use drugs because of the biological phenomenon of addiction. A death instinct is superfluous to all of this. The person may end up dead whether he wishes to return to nothingness or not.

Among the consequences of drug use is an alteration in consciousness that some find enjoyable, though most explanations of drug use overlook this fact (Becker, 1953). Psychoanalytic theory explains why drug use is sometimes enjoyable. It puts secondary process on hold, gives the superego the night off, and opens a door—if only briefly—into a world where experiences and wishes seem to meld together.

Two other psychoanalytic ideas about drug abuse warrant mention. First, theory links the potential to abuse drugs to childhood events, in particular, to disturbances in the oral stage of development. For instance, alcoholics turn to the bottle as a substitute for mother's breast. In keeping with their oral character type, they are passive and dependent. But research support for these possibilities is mostly negative (Fisher & Greenberg, 1977; Kline, 1972, Vaillant, 1983). If anything, dependency and passivity follow alcohol abuse rather than precede it.

Second, theory interprets the choice of a particular drug to abuse in symbolic terms: a representation of the underlying conflict giving rise to the abuse (Kernberg, 1975). As already seen, psychoanalytic theory says that alcohol users react to dependency needs. Similarly, heroin users attempt to control an otherwise overwhelming environment. But there is little support for this neat explanation, and it cannot explain why many drug users are quite ecumenical in their chosen substances.

Does the psychoanalytic interpretation of drug use contain anything useful? On a general level, the psychoanalytic view is reasonable, since one must consider the significance of a drug to the person who abuses it. But while the causes of drug abuse are not found solely in physiology (Vaillant, 1983), the particular meanings assigned by psychoanalytic theory are not generally accepted.

Evaluation   The influence of psychoanalytic thought on our understanding of abnormal behavior cannot be overestimated. Almost all mental health professionals accept certain psychoanalytic notions as truisms: the role of unconscious conflicts, the use of defense mechanisms, the importance of childhood events, the coherence of symptoms and lifestyle. With respect to given types of abnormality, specific psychoanalytic interpretations may or may not be popular today.

Let me raise a question about the way psychoanalytic theory views psychopathology. You may have raised a similar one while reading this section. Granted that similar conflicts precede a variety of different problems, what determines the exact symptoms that a person develops? In response to the Oedipal complex, why did Schreber become psychotic, but Dora hysteric? Psychoanalysts answer this question partly by positing constitutional weaknesses that predispose particular symptoms. But this is post hoc and circular, since we can know the weakness only by seeing the symptoms.

Psychoanalysts also answer this question by linking personality makeup to psychopathology. People with certain personality characteristics are at risk for analogous psychopathologies. For instance, obsessive characters develop

"So, Mr. Fenton . . . Let's begin with your mother."

SOURCE: "The Far Side" cartoon by Gary Larson is reproduced by permission of Chronicle Features, San Francisco

obsessive-compulsive disorders. This is a compelling hypothesis, but research support is decidedly negative (Rosenhan & Seligman, 1984). So the question of symptom-choice remains an important issue.

PSYCHOTHERAPY: RESOLVING UNCONSCIOUS CONFLICTS

In recent years, psychoanalytic therapy has become the favorite whipping boy of just about everybody. Close examination of its effectiveness has not been able to show that it works in the sense, say, that penicillin works or that relaxation training works. This criticism is important, and I will return to it later. However, concern with the effectiveness of psychoanalysis obscures some important ideas about this approach to alleviating human suffering.

First, psychoanalysis was regarded by Freud as a research technique, a way to investigate the unconscious. Freud and his followers sometimes claimed that it cured neuroses, but the fact remains that *psychoanalysis did not originate as a way of doing psychotherapy*.

Second, Freud himself was pessimistic that psychopathology could be changed much, that people could be liberated from unhappy lifestyles that originated in early childhood. Is it fair, then, to criticize psychoanalytic therapy for failing to do what it regards as all but impossible?

Third, regardless of these disclaimers, and regardless of the evidence about its effectiveness, psychoanalytic therapy has shaped the format of almost all contemporary psychotherapies, including those of demonstrated success. Other systems of therapy borrow psychoanalytic techniques and concepts extensively. In particular, consideration of the relationship between client and therapist occurs in all types of therapy, even behavior modification, and ranks as the outstanding contribution of psychoanalysis to clinical practice (Luborsky, Crits-Christoph, & Mellon, 1986).

Conception of Cure   My intention is not to evaluate psychoanalytic therapy so much as to document its impact on how contemporary mental health practitioners go about their business. One such impact is on how *cure* is regarded. Psychoanalysts move beyond circular definitions of health and illness that point to the absence of one to define the other, and vice versa.

Instead, psychoanalysis regards cure as *the freeing of psychic energy from symptoms for use in working and raising a family*. It is obvious that this embodies a value judgment, but attempts at value-free conceptions of health have always failed (Vaillant, 1977). Psychoanalytic theory takes the stance that it is better to do some things than others, and psychological abnormality can be recognized by the impairment of the things worth doing. Cure resides in their facilitation.

At the same time, psychoanalysis does not regard cure as simply the alleviation of symptoms or the creation of occupational and social success. A businesswoman may gain continual promotions, and even be loved by her husband, but this need not mean that her ego has struck a healthy balance between the demands of the id and the superego. If she works at her profession twenty-four hours a day, if she drives people under her without mercy, if she regards success as the only possible outcome, then she is not healthy.

Instead, the healthy individual is one who solves her unconscious conflicts. Symptoms will thereby be relieved, and problems in living will dissipate. Attention to underlying conflicts is the hallmark of the psychoanalytic conception of cure. This has become popular among therapists of almost all theoretical persuasions.

Psychoanalytic Techniques In *Principles of Psychoanalytic Psychother-apy*, Lester Luborsky (1984) describes three active ingredients in psycho-analysis. The first is self-understanding: the patient reaches insight regarding unconscious conflicts and their nature. A variety of expressive techniques are used to bring about self-understanding: free association, dream interpreta-tion, and analysis of transference, for example. These techniques provide insights into the patient's unconscious and require the psychoanalyst to be a skillful listener.

Accompanying each step toward insight is **resistance** on the part of the patient. Regardless of the patient's sincere intentions to solve his problems, considerable inertia exists:

> The patient pauses abruptly, corrects himself, makes a slip of the tongue, stam-mers, remains silent, fidgets with some part of his clothing, asks irrelevant questions, intellectualizes, arrives late for appointments, finds excuses for not keeping them, offers critical evaluations of the rationale underlying the treat-ment method, simply cannot think of anything to say, or censors thoughts that do occur to him and decides that they are banal, uninteresting, or irrelevant and not worth mentioning. (Meissner, 1980, p. 722)

Patients do not relinquish their neuroses easily, and resistance is an excellent defense against health. In my role as a teacher, I have sometimes seen an analogous resistance to learning. Change does not come easily, in the clinic or the classroom.

The second important factor in psychoanalysis is the creation of a **help-ing alliance:** the patient's experience of the therapist and the therapy as useful. Ego psychology has contributed this idea to psychoanalysis, a reminder that therapy is the collaboration between two real people with real personal-ities that go beyond projected and imagined characteristics (Meissner, 1980). The patient and the therapist rely on the therapeutic alliance to weather the difficulties encountered in the course of therapy.

A good therapeutic relationship is determined in part by the personality characteristics that the patient and the therapist bring to therapy. Additionally, the therapist can make use of various supportive techniques. She allows the patient to set his own goals in therapy. She conveys understanding and accep-tance of him. She is realistically hopeful. And so on. Luborsky (1984) regards the helping alliance as the most critical component of psychoanalytic therapy, even though self-understanding has received more attention over the years.

The third curative factor in psychoanalysis is the incorporation of gains occurring in the course of therapy. Backsliding is common in all forms of therapy. "Revolving door psychiatry" expresses the typical difficulty in helping patients maintain improvements brought about in therapy. How do you keep them out of therapy once it has finished? Luborsky (1984) suggests that the patient and therapist explicitly address the meaning of therapy termination.

Patients may be anxious at the prospect of severing the therapeutic alliance and may react with a resurgence of symptoms.

Again, specific psychoanalytic techniques are deployed to handle this problem. Termination is treated as the accomplishment of a goal—not as a rejection. Previous separations in the patient's life should be discussed. Contact between patient and therapist after termination is allowed, and a follow-up appointment, six months or so after treatment, is encouraged for the typical patient.

Luborsky's (1984) depiction of psychoanalytic therapy moves beyond the stereotypes held by most of us: a bearded therapist tossing out obscure interpretations which have miraculous effects on the patient is a caricature of psychoanalysis. If only cures were so easy! Psychotherapy is not a one-liner, and no practicing analyst ever claimed that it was. Insight is only one ingredient, and it is established slowly. Without a therapeutic alliance to overcome resistance and incorporate gains, insight is useless.

The therapy techniques I've described have also been assimilated by other schools of clinical psychology. Even therapists who have no use for the larger picture of psychoanalytic theory speak of insight, transference, the helping alliance, resistance, and termination anxiety. The impact of psychoanalysis on psychotherapy in general has indeed been profound.

Therapy Effectiveness   After reading this glowing account of psychoanalytic therapy, you might expect the typical patient to come bounding off the couch, a fully functioning human being, ready for the challenge of the world. Well, sometimes it works that way. But sometimes it does not.

In fact, I've already mentioned the belief among many that psychoanalytic therapy is not effective. In 1952, Hans Eysenck leveled one of the most serious criticisms against psychoanalysis. He claimed that 70 percent of individuals suffering from the sorts of problems that psychoanalysts treat get better without treatment. They show what is called **spontaneous remission**, as when your sore throat goes away without you doing anything about it. Eysenck further claimed that the effectiveness rate of psychoanalytic therapy was less than 70 percent.

According to Eysenck (1952a), we now know what is worse than nothing: psychoanalytic treatment. Needless to say, this conclusion was not accepted in the psychoanalytic community without protest (see, for example, Rosenzweig, 1954). Eysenck's figures have been challenged, along with his operationalization of therapeutic cure. Apparently, Eysenck failed to use the same criteria in judging spontaneous remission versus psychoanalytic cure.

Nevertheless, the fact that Eysenck overstated his criticism does not mean that psychoanalytic therapy is effective. In a recent review of the research literature, Kline (1984) reports that he was unable to find a single investigation of the effectiveness of psychoanalytic therapy that was methodologically sound. And so we are left without a firm answer to the question about the effectiveness of psychoanalysis.

Recent Developments in Psychoanalytic Therapy   Some psychoanalysts prefer to practice therapy the way that Freud did. (It is somewhat difficult to pin down exactly what Freud did; some reports reveal him as a highly unorthodox "psychoanalytic" therapist, at least as we have come to understand the term; Roazen, 1975). But other analysts have followed the spirit of Freud's example and changed psychoanalysis in response to the times.

Luborsky (1984) describes three contemporary variants of psychoanalytic therapy. The first sets a time limit on the duration of therapy. Traditional analysis is open-ended. It has no time limit, and it may go on for years. In contrast, **time-limited psychoanalysis** sets an upper limit, usually twenty-five sessions. As a result, it is more organized and focused than open-ended therapy.

A second variant is family or group therapy conducted from a psychoanalytic perspective. Here the therapist has a great deal of information available about how patients deal with each other. The therapeutic alliance is established not just between the patient and the therapist, but also between the patient and the group.

Family therapy moves the therapeutic alliance from the patient and therapist to the patient and group.

Finally, some analysts use medication in conjunction with conventional therapy techniques. In recent years, there have been breakthroughs in the pharmacological treatment of anxiety and depression. However, Luborsky (1984) cautions against the over-reliance on medication, which may mask symptoms, work against insight, and substitute for the therapeutic alliance. If medication is used, the patient and therapist should discuss its meaning in the context of therapy. What does it do? What does it not do? Some evidence suggests that medication plus psychotherapy is more effective than either alone, so I suspect this variant will become even more popular in the future.

PSYCHOSOMATIC MEDICINE: ILLNESS AS CONFLICT

Early in his career, Freud turned from treatment of individuals with neurological disorders to treatment of hysterics. However, one of the important applications of psychoanalysis goes back to the domain of physical disease and illness. It has been recognized for centuries that the mind can effect the functioning of the body, but psychoanalysis provides a specific account of how this might take place.

A **psychosomatic disorder** is defined as an organic pathology (that is, a physical problem) preceded by meaningful environmental stimuli (that is, mental representation). **Psychosomatic medicine** is the field that explains and treats these disorders. Freud's insight that hysteria involves unconscious conflict marked the beginning of the modern era in psychosomatic medicine. Although his work led to the conclusion that the hysterical symptoms did not represent actual physical dysfunction, it legitimized the attempts of subsequent workers to examine the possible relationship between psychological factors and physical illness.

The most famous of the psychosomatic pioneers is Franz Alexander (1939, 1950), who uses psychoanalytic terms to explain susceptibility to illness. He distinguishes between conversion disorders like hysteria and psychosomatic disorders like peptic ulcers. Although both are responses to psychological events, conversion disorders are the symbolic expression of an emotion, while psychosomatic disorders are the physiological response to an emotion. In and of themselves, they convey no meaning and serve no purpose. To say it another way, Alexander distinguishes conversion disorders from psychosomatic disorders by proposing the role of the voluntary nervous system in the former versus the involuntary nervous system in the latter.

The involuntary nervous system is involved in turning on and off the flight-or-fight response we have to danger. Our body's resources mobilize in response to an emergency: our skin turns pale; our heart beats faster; our breathing becomes more rapid; our digestive process slows. When danger passes, these changes are reversed. According to Alexander, some people show chronic excitation of the emergency response. They are at risk for such illnesses as hypertension. Other people show chronic inhibition of the emergency response, and they are at risk for disorders like peptic ulcer.

Psychological factors enter into this process by dictating a person's chronic emotional state. A person who is hostile and competitive is always expecting combat. She may develop hypertension. A person who is passive and dependent is always ready to be fed. He may develop an ulcer.

Alexander theorizes about seven psychosomatic disorders. Two of these have just been mentioned: hypertension and peptic ulcer. The other illnesses he discusses are asthma (linked to fear of being separated from mother), arthritis (attributed to inhibition of hostility), colitis (produced by the inability to fulfill obligations), acne (traced to guilt over exhibitionism), and hyperthyroidism (linked to psychic trauma, like the loss of mother during childhood).

What is Alexander's evidence for linking these illnesses to the chronic experience of particular emotions, and hence to particular personality types? Some case histories provide startling confirmation. Here is one he describes in which a woman experiencing recurrent diarrhea responds to the pressure of having a financial obligation:

> A young woman married for six months began suffering from early ulcerative colitis. Under medical management . . . the bowel had become entirely quiescent. . . . After three months of medical management she complained of a precipitous recurrence of her diarrhea on the preceding Sunday morning. Careful interrogation revealed that she had no undue excitement on the previous Saturday evening. She had eaten at home on Saturday and Sunday, followed her diet religiously and taken her medicine as directed. About one hour after breakfast, while she was working around the house, diarrhea appeared. When further questioned on the situations of that Sunday morning when she was at home with her husband, at first she denied any unusual happening, but further prying revealed that her husband asked her, facetiously or otherwise, "What about the $400 I loaned you when we first got married to buy your trousseau? When am I going to get it back?" She didn't have the $400. She felt distinctly disturbed, regressed into a childhood pattern and got diarrhea. When the analyst pointed out to her the association with the money and her inability to give it back except with bowel movements, the condition immediately cleared up—mind you, with no change in diet or medical management. (1950, pp. 124–125; quoting from Portis, 1949)

Remember the psychoanalytic equation of feces and money? One suspects that this young woman suffered from the runs in exact proportion to the $400 debt she had incurred. One can only speculate how our President responds to the national debt.

Alexander made an interesting observation about the preponderance of high blood pressure among black Americans. He attributes this finding to the inferior position relegated to blacks in our society. Blacks consequently need to maintain extraordinary self-control in the face of the associated indignities. Self-control is not achieved without a cost, and hypertension may represent the debit.

Grace and Graham (1952) investigated a more modest version of Alexander's psychosomatic theory. Rather than look for predispositions to illness within general personality characteristics established early in life, they ascertained the specific attitudes held at the time that a given symptom appeared. They interviewed patients about how they felt and what they wanted to do at the time they experienced a particular symptom. Interviews with 128 patients suffering from twelve different symptoms/illnesses revealed striking similarities within symptom classes.

Here is a summary of the attitudes Grace and Graham identified. I've paraphrased a typical statement for each symptom from among the several quoted by these researchers.

1. **Urticaria:** Patients suffering from this allergic reaction of the skin felt mistreated yet did not retaliate. A typical statement was "they walked all over me, and I took it."

2. **Eczema:** In this case, patients felt that other people were interfering with their activities. They felt frustrated. "My mother will not let me lead my own life."

3. **Cold Hands:** Patients with cold hands did not have warm hearts so much as an attitude that they should undertake some course of action without knowing quite what it was. "Somebody really should have done something."

4. **Vasomotor Rhinitis:** Nasal irritation was suffered by patients who wished to throw off responsibility for what was occurring. A typical statement was "I wish they'd go away."

5. **Asthma:** Grace and Graham reported that patients with asthma reported the same attitude as those with rhinitis, presumably to a much greater degree. "I really wish they'd go away."

6. **Diarrhea:** Patients with diarrhea wanted to be done with some situation, to get it over with. "I wish the economy would improve."

7. **Constipation:** This symptom was associated with an attitude of grim determination to carry on in the face of insurmountable odds. "I'll do it even though it won't work."

8. **Nausea and Vomiting:** These patients reported thinking of an event which they regretted. "I wish that had never happened" was a typical statement.

9. **Duodenal Ulcer:** Attacks of pain occurred with thoughts of revenge. "I'm going to get even with that son of a bitch if it kills me!"

10. **Migraine Headache:** Migraines followed the cessation of intense effort, whether or not it resulted in a successful outcome. "I had to get it there overnight."

11. **Arterial Hypertension:** Patients with this symptom felt under pressure from all sides. "Everyone depends on me; this place would fall apart if I were to leave."

12. **Low Back Pain:** Such backaches occurred when patients wanted to carry out some activity involving the entire body, like walking or running away. "I wanted to walk out of the office and never go back."

What are we to make of these findings? On the one hand, they support the psychosomatic premise that psychological states can lead to particular symptoms. On the other hand, they have the typical weaknesses of case histories. The role of interviewer bias is highly possible. Grace and Graham (1952) claimed that the correlations they obtained between symptoms and attitudes were perfect. This is so high that it is suspicious.

Further, the direction of causality is unclear. Diarrhea might result in the desire to be done with something (the attack of diarrhea), constipation in the determination to continue with something (attempts to move one's bowels), nausea with regret (about the retching), and so on. A better demonstration of the point would have been to show that attitudes precede symptoms.

On the whole, research has not supported the details of Alexander's theories. His formula linking specific diseases to specific conflicts has been abandoned by contemporary workers (Weiner, 1977). So, while Alexander is honored as the first to link conflict to disease, current thinking sees this association as nonspecific. Instead, general states of helplessness and hopelessness are emphasized as bringing about a variety of illnesses (Engel, 1971). Also, conflicts are no longer located solely within the person, but are seen as involving stressful events in the immediate environment (Holmes & Rahe, 1967).

The question of which disease develops in response to stress remains pertinent, and explains the renewed interest in recent years to link specific diseases to specific personalities. The **Type A coronary-prone behavior pattern** is the best known of these contemporary formulations (Jenkins, Rosenman, & Zyzanski, 1974). The Type A individual is time-urgent (living from deadline to deadline), competitive, ambitious, aggressive, and hostile.

The Type A individual is also at risk for heart disease. Some research suggests that this personality style predicts recurrent heart disease better than cholesterol and cigarette smoking (see, for example, Jenkins, Zyzanski, & Rosenman, 1976)!

Psychosomatic medicine originated in the application of psychoanalytic ideas to physical illness. Modern medicine has incorporated the general formula of theorists like Alexander linking conflict to susceptibility to disease. However, specific psychoanalytic hypotheses are no longer taken seriously. Health psychology and behavioral medicine thrive in contemporary psychology. Although they often apply the theories of other paradigms, appreciate that their roots lie in the psychoanalytic paradigm.

CHILD-REARING

Because of its emphasis on early childhood, psychoanalytic theory has greatly influenced the way we treat children in our society. Once psychoanalysis became generally known, parents and teachers grew determined not to raise up contemporary versions of Anna O., the Rat Man, or Schreber. Their intentions led to changes in both child-rearing and educational practice.

Paramount among these changes was the desire to avoid frustrating the child. No frustration—no conflict . . . no conflict—no pathology. This formula oversimplifies psychoanalysis almost to the point of contradicting it. Remember that overindulgence is just as damaging to personality development as is harsh discipline, but this was overlooked by many individuals who thought they were applying the "scientific" ideas of psychoanalysis to cultivate happy children.

At the present time, we are seeing a societal backlash against parental and educational permissiveness. Back to the basics. The generation of kids raised permissively is now raising you, and they're not doing it like Grandmother and Grandfather did. Maybe conversion disorders will come back in vogue. Any young person who is suddenly struck blind as he reads this paragraph is encouraged to contact me.

Do not hear me say that this point-counterpoint revolves exclusively around the acceptance versus rejection of psychoanalytic pronouncements about personality development. Other factors play critical roles. However, psychoanalysis is certainly pertinent. And in this section, I'll describe the ideas of two individuals who explicitly acknowledge the influence of psychoanalysis: Benjamin Spock, author of *Baby and Child Care*, next to the Bible the best-selling book ever, and A. S. Neill, founder of Summerhill, the prototype of experimental education.

In Search of Dr. Spock

To appreciate the impact of the baby doctor, you have to understand that methods of child-rearing have changed dramatically over the last one hundred years. His message fell on ears accustomed to quite different advice about how to treat children. Let me describe some of the earlier approaches to raising kids.

For an extreme example, consider this excerpt from the 1839 *Book of Health* written by the father of Daniel Paul Schreber, whom we met in Chapter 5:

> Crying and whimpering without reason express nothing but a whim, a mood, and the first emergence of stubborness; they must be dealt with positively, through quick distraction of attention, serious words . . . or if all this be to no avail, through the administration of comparatively mild, intermittently repeated, corporeal punishments. . . . From then on one glance, one word, one single menacing gesture are sufficient to rule the child.
>
> This is also the best time to train the child in the art of renouncing. The mode of training here recommended is simple and effective: While the child sits in the lap of its nurse or nanny, the latter eats and drinks whatever she desires: however intense the child's oral needs may become under such circumstances, they must never be gratified. Not a morsel of food must be given the child besides its regular three meals a day. (Niederland, 1959, pp. 387–388)

Can you apply the theory of psychosexual development to the child raised in this way? Do you see why personality fixation is apt to result?

In the United States during the early part of the twentieth century, discipline was stressed. Parents were advised not to handle their babies under the assumption that handling would deprive the babies of their strength! Toilet training was to be initiated by the third month or earlier. (Maybe the lack of Pampers had something to do with this advice. If you're not a parent, realize that modern kids are toilet trained at fourteen months or later.) Behaviorist John Watson echoed such advice in his influential books on child-rearing: children should not be coddled or cuddled by their parents.

Against this trend of advice, Freud's ideas were revolutionary indeed. Freud held that harshness, restriction, and coercion harmed the emotional growth of the child, and would show up later in severe disturbances in personality. In his *Baby and Child Care*, first published in 1946, Dr. Spock drew liberally on psychoanalytic ideas as well as those of the philosopher and educator John Dewey.

> "Freud was much too smart to get involved with child-rearing himself," Spock laughed. "Freud's philosophy was embodied in the idea that too much repression of sex and hostility created neuroses later in life. It was important to be loved by parents, rather than taught to fear." (*Newsweek*, 1968, p. 71)

Spock preached a message of flexibility and relaxation. In his own words, he attempted to take the "Thou Shalt Nots" out of raising children. He reassured new parents that they knew more than they thought.

Did Spock advocate permissiveness? Yes and no. On the one hand, his advice was permissive in comparison to immediately preceding dictates on child-rearing. Kids need not be fed on a rigid schedule, but only when they are hungry. Toilet training should not start until the child is ready. Learning occurs through exploration—not punishment. Above all, parents must express their love for the child. On the other hand, some parents followed Spock's relaxed advice to an extreme, becoming submissive to their children's demands at every juncture.

In the 1960s and 1970s, during the era of campus revolts and radical activities among young adults, Dr. Spock and his advice were blamed for producing an entire generation with no respect for authority. This perception was aided by the fact that Spock was an outspoken opponent of the Vietnam War, and an unsuccessful presidential candidate in 1972 on the ticket of the radical People's Party (Viorst, 1972).

By the logic of this chapter, the thread of responsibility might thus extend to the turn-of-the-century and the psychoanalytic ideas of Sigmund Freud. Definitive support for such a link is of course impossible, and the idea of Zeitgeist cautions us not to overattribute responsibility for society-wide change to the activities of particular individuals. But it is intriguing to speculate about Spock's role in the unrest of the recent past. Let Dr. Spock do some of his own speculating:

> I would be proud if I thought I was largely responsible for the idealism and courage shown by the young. . . . The first person to hold me responsible for the rebelliousness of youth was the Rev. Norman Vincent Peale, author of *The Power of Positive Thinking* and President Nixon's New York pastor. It was Dr. Peale's view that I advised parents of small children: "Feed 'em whenever they want, never let them cry, satisfy their every desire." With his piety about him, Peale painted a picture of me "out in the streets with these babies raised according to his books, demonstrating with them for things they claim we should not deny them." . . . But I don't think I had anything like the amount of influence ascribed to me. . . . *Baby and Child Care* . . . is popular because it is cheap, complete, and friendly. (1971, pp. 37–38)

If psychoanalytic ideas about child-rearing did not directly bring about these social changes, they certainly accompanied the factors that did.

Through the many editions of his book, Spock has followed social change as much as he has created it (Kellogg, 1976). In recent versions of *Baby and Child Care*, he has banished sexist pronouns and advises that the father should share equally in the mundane tasks of raising kids. Pictures of black parents and black children have been added. New chapters address working mothers, day-care, drug use, hyperactivity, natural childbirth, and other topics of contemporary concern. And, Spock belatedly acknowledges the collaboration of his wife in creating the original book during the 1940s.

But regardless of these changes, two themes remain constant in Spock's advice. Coercion and harsh discipline have no place in the raising of children. Love and support must be abundant. Both themes spring from the psychoanalytic root metaphor of organicism. In the course of development, children reveal their inherent nature. The environment can thwart or facilitate this process, but the motivating force lies within the developing child.

In a recent article on education, Spock (1984) once again stresses these themes. Responding to the National Commission on Excellence in Education report calling for more homework, longer school days, and longer school years, he sarcastically labels it "A Plea for More Coercion in the Schools." He goes on to say that schools are ineffective to the degree that they already coerce students. More of the same will not bring about excellent education.

Here's what Spock says about grading. Please don't throw these ideas in your teacher's face! Spock refers to the entire system of grading, not simply Personality Psychology grades assigned at the end of this particular school term. However, it might be productive to discuss in class the underlying model of human nature assumed by different strategies of assigning grades.

> I believe that grading is an abomination, misdirecting student efforts into memorizing for recitations and tests, and misleading teachers into thinking that the grades they give represent something gained from the course. What grades do measure, I would say, is the ability to memorize, freedom from learning disabilities, and conformity in thinking, which is not a valuable trait, to my mind. (1984, p. 29)

You can see that Spock assumes that students are inherently motivated to learn, that excessive discipline can thwart this tendency toward growth.

Spock recommends that schools cultivate such personality traits as creativity, originality, initiative, and responsibility. Several ingredients are needed for this to occur. First, children must identify with teachers worthy of love and respect. Second, children must make school lessons part of their everyday activities, through learning by doing and through encouragement by teachers. It is no coincidence that these ingredients are similar to those identified by Luborsky as crucial for effective psychoanalytic therapy. Both education and therapy involve behavior change; the application of psychoanalysis to both of them ties this behavior change to underlying feelings and emotions.

In Search of Freedom

Over the decades, psychoanalytic ideas have made their way directly into education. One notable avenue has been through Summerhill, the radical school founded in 1921 in England by A. S. Neill. Students at Summerhill were allowed total freedom of choice—in work and in behavior. The school's approach was derived in large part from the explicit application of psychoanalytic ideas about child-rearing.

The most important premise of Summerhill is that children can be thwarted and perverted by harsh discipline and coercion. If they are unhappy, then they will not develop in a healthy way. They will not be able to learn. As Neill (1960) explains:

> In psychology, no man knows very much. The inner forces of human life are still largely hidden from us.
>
> Since Freud's genius made it alive, psychology has gone far; but it is still a new science. . . . Years of intensive work in child training has convinced me that I know comparatively little of the forces that motivate life. I am convinced, however, that parents who have had to deal with only their own children know much less than I do.
>
> It is because I believe that a difficult child is nearly always made difficult by wrong treatment at home that I dare address parents. . . . The difficult child is the child who is unhappy. He is at war with himself; and in consequence, he is at war with the world.
>
> The difficult adult is in the same boat. No happy man ever disturbed a meeting, or preached a war, or lynched a Negro. No happy woman ever nagged her husband or her children. No happy man ever committed a murder or a theft. No happy employer ever frightened his employees.
>
> All crimes, all hatreds, all wars can be reduced to unhappiness. . . . Summerhill [is a place] where children's unhappiness is cured and, more important, where children are reared in happiness. (pp. xxiii–xxiv)

Summerhill began by renouncing discipline, direction, suggestion, moral training, and religious instruction. What took their place was what the child brought to the school: a nature that would develop to its potential if left alone. Courses were offered, but children were not required to attend. Examinations were given, but only as fun. Rigid distinctions between teachers and students were never defined.

Neill was greatly influenced by Wilhelm Reich, a one-time Freudian who melded psychoanalytic ideas with Marxist politics. Among Reich's most important contributions to psychoanalytic thought is the concept of **character armor:** the manifestation of conflict in a person's posture. The person may wear his problems like armor. A rigid and inflexible character shows in rigid and inflexible movements.

Reich is also known for his radical ideas about sex. Years before Masters and Johnson became famous, Wilhelm Reich conducted sex therapy, under the assumption that people's sexuality had become so repressed by society that they no longer knew how to have pleasure. And so he taught them. He dubbed his version of libido **orgone**, the energy of the orgasm, and regarded it as a tangible reality. Reich built a device to retrieve orgone from the sky, and was eventually imprisoned in New York for claiming that his orgone accumulator could regulate weather and cure cancer. Despite the bizarre nature of Reich's later theories, he was a profound thinker. His notions about emotional expression and freedom directly foreshadowed the human potential movement and provided an impetus for the sexual revolution.

At any rate, Reich and Neill were friends, and they frequently discussed Summerhill. Neill was so impressed with Reich's warnings of the dire consequences of sexual repression that he came to advocate total honesty in sexual matters.

> The Summerhill pupils . . . appeared to have none of the normal inhibitions; they shared the same bathrooms, they would occasionally bathe in the nude, they used sexual swear-words freely, there was no censorship of their reading. They would fall in love. . . . There was no supervision of the students to keep them out of each other's beds. (Hemmings, 1972, pp. 122–123)

At the same time, Neill did not go out of his way to facilitate sex among his students, despite Reich's urgings that he do so. Contraceptives were not made available to Summerhill students. Neill feared—no doubt correctly—that his school would be closed down if he took such steps. Interestingly, not a single pregnancy occurred among Summerhill students in the thirty-some years that the school existed (Hemmings, 1972).

Neill was aware that his school existed within a larger society that was at odds with its principles of freedom. Children who came to Summerhill were inevitably products of repressive child-rearing, and despite the freedom of Summerhill, their early experiences left a residue. At best, the child with such a beginning could become semi-free. In contrast, a child reared with freedom from the beginning could become truly free.

Neill and his wife raised their only child, Zoe, with this goal. The only restriction placed upon her was that she wear clothes when it was bitterly cold. Otherwise, she made her own decisions. She ate when and what she wanted. She acquired sphincter and bladder control on her own (much later than "normal" children). By reports, Zoe was happy and healthy, intelligent and friendly.

Zoe may be a special case. We know that we cannot generalize too far from single instances, no matter how compelling. Did the approach of Summerhill work for other children? This of course is a loaded question, since the criterion of working varies with one's value system. Neill regards Summerhill as a success because it allowed the child to live his or her own life. Did it prepare children for the best universities? Did they win admission to law school or medical school? Did they make a lot of money? Neill dismisses these criteria as irrelevant if they aren't goals freely chosen by the individual:

> You cannot *make* children learn music or anything else without to some degree converting them . . . into accepters of the *status quo*—a good thing for a society

that needs obedient sitters at dreary desks, standers in shops, mechanical catch-
ers of the 8:30 suburban train—a society, in short, that is carried on the shabby
shoulders of the scared little man—the scared-to-death conformist. (Neill, 1960,
p. 12)

In the battle between the individual and society, Summerhill champions the
individual.

Do you think this is all pretty far-fetched? Maybe it is, in the sense that
few of you attend a school as permissive as Summerhill. On the other hand,
consider pass-fail courses, independent studies, self-designed majors, and
field placements. These are now standard curriculum components at most
schools. Do you see how they reflect the Summerhill philosophy? Do you see
how they stem from the application of psychoanalytic theory to education?
Maybe Neill's ideas are not so far-fetched after all.

Evaluation

Other applications of psychoanalytic ideas to child-rearing and to education
could be described, but the work of Spock and Neill illustrate the nature of
this influence. In general terms, psychoanalysis has changed the way that
children are regarded. They have emotional needs. Conflicts can interfere
with their development and with their learning. Contemporary child-rearing
has become child centered, and contemporary education has become more
student centered. Both now stress feeling and experience. In no small way,
this is the legacy of psychoanalysis.

PSYCHOHISTORY: PSYCHOANALYZING HISTORICAL FIGURES

Psychohistory is sometimes defined as the application of psychoanalytic
ideas to the understanding of historical figures and events (Friedlander, 1978).
Although contemporary psychohistorians partake of additional psychological
perspectives, the psychoanalytic roots of the field are unmistakeable. Psychoanalysis is well-suited to the analysis of historical material, particularly
the roles played by individuals.

Psychohistories have been written from a psychoanalytic view about
Napoleon, Abraham Lincoln, Houdini, Socrates, Margaret Fuller, Isaac Newton, Emily Dickinson, Beethoven, Trotsky, Benjamin Franklin, Bertrand Russell, Anne Hutchinson, Henry Kissinger, and—of course—Sigmund Freud
himself (Anderson, 1978; Crosby & Crosby, 1981; Runyan, 1982). As previously noted, Freud pioneered this application of psychoanalysis in his

examinations of Leonardo da Vinci, Moses, and Dostoevsky. Erik Erikson contributed to the development of the field by his psychohistorical studies of such individuals as Martin Luther, Thomas Jefferson, and Mahatma Gandhi.

Psychohistory remains a controversial endeavor. Terry Anderson (1978) describes the three major reactions to psychohistories as praise, neglect, or disdain, and concludes that until quite recently, the latter two reactions were by far the most common. When Erik Erikson (1958) first published *Young Man Luther*, it was not even reviewed in history journals. Still, psychohistory shows no sign of going away, and scholars in and out of the field are taking increased note of it.

Although no overall agreement regarding the worth of psychohistory has emerged, there is consensus about its strengths and weaknesses. Let me summarize these for you. What are the advantages of psychohistory? To begin with, all historical analysis makes use of psychological assumptions at least implicitly; psychohistory makes these assumptions clear. History is not simply a chronicle of facts. The historian attempts to tie these facts together into a coherent whole. Psychoanalytic theory may help do so by suggesting the motives of historical figures and linking them to prior events.

Since historical material is analogous to clinical material, psychoanalysis allows it to be sifted for significance. It helps the historian choose exactly where to look for motives. Attention is forced to childhood events and relationships with parents, and, consequently, most psychohistories place great emphasis on Oedipal dynamics.

Further, psychoanalysis is one of the few approaches to history that recognizes and explains the historian's emotional reaction to the historical figure about whom he or she writes. This reaction is akin to counter-transference from the therapist onto the patient. In historical analysis as well as psychotherapy, these reactions must be worked through for an unfettered interpretation.

Finally, from its beginning psychoanalysis has grappled with the analysis of the single case. What can be concluded from the investigation of one life? What are the limitations of this approach? The strengths and weaknesses of case histories are well-recognized within psychoanalysis, and the psychohistorian brings this sensitivity to a historical study.

Despite these reasons for expecting psychohistory to be viable, there are all sorts of problems with the approach. Some of these are inherent difficulties. Others involve the way that psychohistories have sometimes been conducted. As with our examination of case studies, we must distinguish the in-principle flaws of psychohistory from those brought about by sloppy execution.

What are the difficulties that go with the territory, regardless of the care taken by the psychohistorian? First, the available material is usually not of great interest to psychoanalytic theory. Access to dreams is usually lacking, and there is often little evidence about a historical figure's childhood. Who would know that Junior will grow up to be a mover and a shaker of world history? Three of the most important people in the twentieth century—Hitler, Nixon, and Mao—led childhoods that we know almost nothing about (Crosby & Crosby, 1981). Relatedly, a psychohistorian hardly ever interviews a subject face-to-face. Usually these subjects are dead, or if living, they do not submit to such an examination.

Second, the psychohistorian often studies an individual from another time and place. If that individual's behaviors are pulled from their cultural context, unwitting misinterpretation occurs. I've read about a psychohistorical analysis of Gandhi that placed great emphasis on his supposedly feminine characteristics, in particular, his weaving. This "fact" is not at all striking if Gandhi's life is placed in the culture of India, where it of course belongs. In that context, weaving is not feminine in the same sense that knitting might be in contemporary America. Psychohistory proceeds best when the psychohistorian has a full appreciation of the subject's social world. When Erik Erikson discussed Hitler in *Childhood and Society*, he drew on his own experiences growing up in Germany in the first third of this century (Loewenberg, 1983).

Third, because of its focus on the individual historical figure, the typical psychohistorian is often accused of reductionism. Attention to the roles of particular people with particular motives precludes the examination of the social and economic causes of historical events. Remember the ideas of Zeitgeist and Ortgeist? They pertain to historical change as well as to scientific change. Indeed, social psychologists argue persuasively against what is known as the great man (or woman) theory of leadership, the notion that a leader's influence resides in particular personality characteristics. Social factors are emphasized instead, which have nothing to do with an individual personality.

By extrapolation, this argument cautions the psychohistorian against reducing the course of history to the personalities of its players. Psychohistorical examinations of Hitler often emphasize the fact that his beloved mother Klara died of breast cancer despite the efforts of the family doctor, Eduard Bloch—a Jew (Crosby & Crosby, 1981). Although this incident was no doubt important to the young Adolph Hitler, to regard it as a primary determinant of his later anti-Semitism is to overlook the centuries-old reality of German prejudice.

Fourth, in keeping with the basic premise of psychoanalytic theory, psychohistorians emphasize unconscious determinants of behavior. However, as I've already described, this is exactly the area where the historian has the least information. Accordingly, explanations via unconscious motivation strike many people as forced. For example, the Third Reich's military defeats have been attributed by some to Hitler's unconscious desires for self-punishment, but this is to ignore a host of more observable factors, like the bitterly cold winters in Russia (Crosby & Crosby, 1981).

Fifth, psychohistory based on psychoanalysis is only as plausible as its foundation. As you saw in Chapter 6, psychoanalytic theory cannot be regarded as simply right or wrong. Parts of it are reasonable, and other parts are not. Psychohistory applies all of psychoanalytic theory—a risky approach. In particular, it is dubious to transpose the psychoanalytic emphasis on repressed sexuality to other times and places.

So much for the inherent difficulties of psychohistory. They are serious problems, and they have been widely recognized by those who conduct psychohistories. However, what about the other difficulties, those resulting from sloppy scholarship? It seems that there is a long list of such problems as well, and they apparently have not been as widely recognized. The psychohistory reviews I have read are highly critical of most studies.

One difficulty is that psychohistorians sometimes fill in factual blanks with what psychoanalytic theory expects to be there. Childhoods are reconstructed from the wispiest of facts, and not surprisingly, Oedipal conflicts result. Motives and feelings are attributed to historical figures because it seems plausible to posit their existence. For example, Richard Nixon's mother is said to show "repressed anger" in photographs (Abrahamsen, 1978), quite a conclusion granted the meaning of repression! Psychohistorians would be better off if they just admitted gaps in their knowledge.

Another difficulty in the way that psychohistorical studies have been conducted is an illness bias. Psychohistorians frequently diagnose historical figures as suffering from one neurosis or another, relegating important events to mere symptoms. When diagnosis from afar is done with living individuals, psychohistory becomes not just unreasonable but insidious. Kissinger has been called depressive, Nixon obsessive-compulsive, and so on. When these labels are assigned by "scientific" psychohistorians, the general public will see them as formal diagnoses rather than value-laden adjectives. Contemporary psychodiagnosticians regard it as unethical to diagnose a living figure on the basis of his or her public actions.

This attitude stems in part from a 1960s flap when a survey of the American Psychiatric Association's members found 1,846 psychiatrists (of 12,356 polled) willing to take a stand on Barry Goldwater's psychological fitness for the presidency. Many were further willing to give him such diagnoses as megalomaniac, paranoid, narcissistic, psychotic, anal-compulsive, and/or schizophrenic. Goodness! Most of us have to wait in line to have a doctor tell us what is wrong with us. Needless to say, this survey has been blasted from numerous quarters, and it is a good bet that mental health professionals will not participate in a similar poll in the near future.

A final difficulty in the way psychohistories are conducted is that the investigator may not be sophisticated at historical research. Crosby and Crosby (1981) describe numerous psychohistory examples that violate fundamental tenets of historical inquiry. Psychohistorians may rely on biased sources, consult too few sources, or select only those facts that fit the argument they are mounting.

Good versus Bad Explanation in Psychohistory

Although what I've said so far has been largely critical of psychohistory, I'll conclude this section in the same way as I did the discussion of case histories in Chapter 6. Collectively, psychohistorical studies can be neither dismissed nor embraced. Psychohistory has a role to play in the larger field of history if its avoidable difficulties can be handled and its unavoidable difficulties acknowledged. Psychohistorical explanation on a case-by-case basis can be evaluated as good or bad, using much the same criteria by which we evaluate a case history (Runyan, 1982).

Is it logically sound? Is it comprehensible? Does it survive attempts to prove it wrong? Is it consistent with available evidence? Is it superior to alternative explanations?

In an intriguing article, William Runyan (1981) poses the question, "Why did Van Gogh cut off his ear?" This well-known historical event might seem inexplicable, because it is singular and bizarre. Nevertheless, it has stimulated considerable speculation in the historical literature. Indeed, Runyan describes thirteen different explanations for why it happened. All embody a psychoanalytic flavor. For instance, some psychohistorians have suggested that Van Gogh was frustrated because his brother Theo became engaged. Others have suggested that he was struggling with homosexual impulses toward the artist Paul Gaugin. Perhaps he was inspired by bullfights, since the matador gives the ear of a vanquished bull to his favorite lady. Perhaps he followed newspaper stories of the then-contemporary Jack the Ripper, who sometimes cut off the ears of his victims. And so on.

(Woody Allen, 1975, even takes a "stab" at explanation in his book *Without Feathers*. First, he decides that we can better understand the impressionist painters if we assume they were dentists. Second, he concludes that Van Gogh's severed ear was intended as a birthday present. Why didn't he simply buy a conventional gift? Well, he worked six days a week, and the stores were closed on Sunday.)

At any rate, Runyan sifts through a number of explanations to brand some of them good and others bad. For instance, there is no evidence that Van Gogh knew anything about Jack the Ripper. The "fact" of Van Gogh reading newspaper stories about the Ripper is merely assumed by psychohistorians favoring this possibility. On the other hand, Van Gogh's self-punitive reaction to frustration is well-documented. Explanations that point to frustration are therefore reasonable.

Runyan gives us no single answer to his question, but that is the point he is trying to make. Sometimes the best that psychohistory can do is to winnow numerous possibilities to a few, and then acknowledge that further choices cannot be made. Psychohistory thus becomes more eclectic and more tentative. Perhaps it is also less sensational, but that is the price to be paid.

ADVERTISING: UNCONSCIOUS MOTIVES FOR BUYING

Sex sells products, or so we must assume from the ads where an outlandishly gorgeous man or woman tells us to buy oil filters, drain cleaners, exercise machines, laundry detergent, beer, cigarettes, used cars, hemorrhoid cream, and all sorts of other things that aren't sexy at all. Of course, this blatant appeal to sex is not uniquely suggested by psychoanalysis. Common sense as well as other psychological theories tells us that the more attractive a product, the more likely we are to want it (or nothing at all). One way to make a product attractive is to show that its users are attractive. I've yet to walk into a tavern and see a racially mixed group of good-looking men and women toasting the winners of their recently completed volleyball game, sharing a table with several laborers in designer jeans. But I'll keep trying. I see this scene frequently on TV. How wonderful it all seems.

Where psychoanalysis has made its own mark is in the subtle use of sex to sell products, by appealing to unconscious processes. I'll describe some of the possible ways that this is done. I draw here from examples presented by Vance Packard in *The Hidden Persuaders* (1957) and Wilson Key in *Subliminal Seduction* (1973) and *Media Sexploitation* (1976). All three books are highly critical of the advertising industry, which is accused of using psychoanalytic ideas to manipulate the buying preferences of an unknowing public. Their case is probably overstated in a number of instances, but if it is at all plausible, we have an intriguing and frightening example of applied psychoanalysis.

The basic premise comes directly from psychoanalytic theory: people's motives are often hidden to them, including motives for buying one product over another. Most of us no doubt believe that we buy a product because of its inherent qualities, but research has repeatedly shown that consumers are unable to distinguish among different beers, different cigarettes, and different gasolines when clues about their identity are removed. Nevertheless, we would rather fight than switch from (or to) Michelob, Camels, or Shell.

What's going on? Our preference extends beyond the product itself and embraces the image that is used to advertise it. According to Packard and Key, the real attraction of this image is below the level of awareness. Subliminal messages and symbols arouse our sexual interest, promising pleasure if only we buy the product. We don't get up from the couch in front of the tube and walk like a hypnotized zombie to the nearest convenience store and buy Screaming Yellow Zonkers. However, some of us some of the time are subtly persuaded to grab one brand of munchies instead of another when we are in a store. That's all it takes for advertising to be successful.

In the 1950s, advertising researchers determined that buying preferences were hardly rational. In fact, ad campaigns based on "logical" assumptions were highly unsuccessful. For instance, the Chrysler Corporation surveyed consumers in the early fifties and found that people voiced strong opinions about the need for sensible and simple cars. So, that's what Chrysler made available, and promptly saw its share of the auto market drop from 26 percent in 1952 to 13 percent in 1954. Chrysler rebounded by producing the most extravagant cars possible (Packard, 1957). And the rest is history.

In searching for a way to understand consumer irrationality, advertising executives discovered the psychology of motivation. Psychoanalysis was recognized as a good source of ideas about people's motives to buy. The so-called **depth interview** was developed to ascertain unconscious needs and desires. Hypnosis, free association, and projective techniques were borrowed from psychoanalytic practice to identify desires that could be met by particular products. Ads were geared to satisfy these desires.

It was determined, for instance, that young people smoke cigarettes to appear old, while old people smoke cigarettes to appear young. So, everyone who appears in a cigarette ad should be youthfully mature, or maturely youthful, as the case may be. The Marlboro Man with his craggy face and full head of hair is a marvelous creation, a human Rorschach onto which young and old alike can project their ideal self. How old is he? You can't really tell, and that is the point. (You might also consider Ronald Reagan and Dan Rather as cases in point.)

It was also determined that people buy soaps and detergents because of a host of subtle fears and worries surrounding filth and odor, that is, concerns that originated in the anal stage. What better way to soothe these anxieties than by associating a cleaning product with mother's approval? Ivory Soap has taken this approach to an extreme. Perhaps their inadvertent casting of X-rated film star Marilyn Chambers as the maternal symbol is not so far-removed from the Oedipal premise on which Ivory tries to capitalize.

One of the most insidious uses of psychoanalytic ideas in advertising is a subliminal stimulation technique where messages urging the viewer to buy a particular product are flashed on television or movie screens below the level of conscious awareness. In 1956, an experiment was reported in which a movie theater briefly flashed such messages as EAT POPCORN and DRINK COCA-COLA on the screen. Although these messages could not be consciously perceived, in a six-week period, popcorn sales in the theater increased 58 percent and Coke sales 18 percent!

The actual details of this experiment are elusive, since it apparently was reported only in the popular press, attributed to sources who wished to remain anonymous (Key, 1973; Packard, 1957). We know from the research reviewed in Chapter 6 that subliminal suggestion might sell products, but we also know that its influence is probably small. Whether or not invisible commercials are common or effective is a matter of speculation. They are not illegal, and advertising firms do indeed offer such services (Key, 1973).

Sexual symbols that work at an unconscious level are often used to sell products. And, since there are innumerable ways to package perfumes, creams, and lotions, isn't it interesting how frequently a phallic shape is chosen?

One of the best-known magazines in the United States is *Playboy*. It has a large newsstand sale, which means that the typical reader does not subscribe to *Playboy* but rather buys it on the spur of the moment. Critical in such sales is the cover. It has to attract the attention of the would-be purchaser and promise something attractive enough for him to part with a few dollars.

According to Wilson Key, *Playboy*'s cover picture is its most carefully crafted aspect. So, who is pictured there? The typical *Playboy* cover suggests a clue about the identity of its cover girl: the woman pictured is invariably holding something, often against her chest (see Figure 7-1). Key argues that it is dear old Mom on the cover, symbolically nursing dear old us and approving of our naughty purchase. Contrary to the manufactured image of the *Playboy* man as a sophisticated swinger, the actual reader is a self-conscious post-adolescent who feels embarrassed that he is looking at pictures of naked women. The cover picture tells him that it is alright to do so. After all, the centerfold is invariably a boring person, someone Mom would like.

Key (1973, 1976) describes two other subliminal advertising techniques. The first he calls **embedding**, a procedure of superimposing words over pictures. Their presence is not consciously perceived, but they supposedly attract our unconscious attention. He claims that the most frequently embedded word is SEX, which often shows up in ice cubes, in the folds of clothing, and in the creases on faces (see Figure 7-2). We are more likely to buy a product advertised with sexual embeds.

The second technique is even more clever, if it is intentionally employed by advertisers. What Key calls **see-through illusions** occur in magazines on

Figure 7-1
Playboy Cover, February 1970

SOURCE: Reproduced by special permission of PLAYBOY Magazine: Copyright © 1970 by PLAYBOY.

back-to-back pages. An innocuous ad becomes sexually provocative when light shines through the page to show the picture on the opposite side; the superimposed images enhance the mundane message of the advertisement. Key (1976) presents an example from *Penthouse* magazine in which a cigarette ad is backed with a picture of a woman's naked crotch. When the ad is held up to light, we see a burning cigarette protruding exactly from her vagina. Cigarettes are thereby associated with sex, and our conscious belief that smoking is bad for our health is unconsciously undermined.

Does advertising make use of psychoanalytic ideas to sell products? The answer is clearly yes. Are such techniques successful? The answer is probably yes, but the technique per se is only one of many factors that determine product preference. Are such techniques as widespread and outlandish as Wilson Key argues? The answer is probably no . . . at least, I hope that's the answer. When one considers the amount of money spent each year on advertising, one comes to the conclusion that few stones have been left unturned (or unembedded, as the case may be). If nothing else, the possible application of psychoanalytic theory by Madison Avenue professionals is a topic for

Figure 7-2
Embedded Words

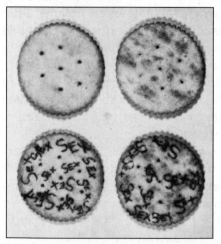

SOURCE: Figure 4 in W. B. Key. (1976). *Media sexploitation.* Englewood Cliffs, NJ: Prentice-Hall.

serious consideration. Suppose the same techniques were used to sell candidates for political office. Have you checked the back of your favorite bumper sticker lately?

CREATIVITY

Creativity has intrigued psychoanalytic theorists since Freud (1900) analyzed plays by Sophocles and Shakespeare for Oedipal themes in *The Interpretation of Dreams*. Because of its emphasis on symbols and its assumption of over-determined behavior, psychoanalysis is unique among psychological theories in its ability to speak to the complexity of art and literature. Accordingly, psychoanalytic pronouncements on these subjects have been widely noted.

Psychoanalysis provides a cluster of related hypotheses about creative works, the act which gives rise to them, the personality of the creative individual, and the reaction of their audience. One important psychoanalytic application is by critics who use it as a vantage point to aid our understanding of art and literature. Another important application is by artists and writers who use it intentionally as a source of techniques. You can see how this second application confounds the first, since the psychoanalytic criticism of a work produced in explicit accordance with psychoanalytic ideas is hopelessly complex. This epitomizes both the self-fulfilling prophecies *and* the enlightenment effects discussed at the beginning of the chapter. What does it mean when an artist consciously uses the language of the unconscious?

At any rate, Freud's (1908b) essay "Creative Writers and Day-Dreaming" proposes that some literary works are strictly analogous to dreams, little more than the disguised fulfillment of unsatisfied wishes. He argues that this is particularly the case for popular literature, what we call romances or pulps. Is there anyone in America who doesn't want to wear an Indiana Jones hat? Nevertheless, the basic psychoanalytic formula for all art and literature is introduced here. Creative products satisfy unconscious wishes. These wishes are usually unacceptable, and so they must be disguised. Artistic and literary techniques are deployed for this purpose.

In *Leonardo da Vinci and a Memory of His Childhood*, Freud (1910) elaborates on these ideas. He proposes that the famous artist and scientist suffered from an extreme inhibition of his sexual drive brought about by castration anxiety. His libidinal energy was then channeled into the well-known works of art and scientific discoveries. The Mona Lisa's mysterious smile is no mystery to Freud. It is the smile of Leonardo's mother, rediscovered on the model and committed to canvas.

Freud's interpretation of Leonardo has been challenged on factual grounds (for example, Schapiro, 1956), but the general equation of creativity and Oedipal conflict has transcended this debate. It often translates itself into an examination of what creativity and madness have in common. The person in the street often believes that genius and insanity are separated by the finest of lines, an opinion bolstered by statements of artists themselves. Salvador Dali is reputed to have said, "The only difference between myself and a mad man is that I am not mad" (Ades, 1978). Certainly, creative individuals may strike the rest of us as strange.

However, research does not support the hypothesis that the creative artist or writer is neurotic. If anything, creative individuals are particularly stable (Trilling, 1977). They may seem different because they tolerate ambiguity, show independent judgment, and are frequently curious (Singer, 1984). But these are strengths, not weaknesses.

According to Freud, the creation of art and literature and their appreciation reflect the same underlying process. What distinguishes the creative individual from others is an ability to represent fantasy in such a way that others can partake of it. Ernest Kris (1952) extends this idea and assigns the ego a more important role in the creative act than does Freud. In a process called **regression in the service of the ego**, the creative individual retreats into primary process thinking for artistic insights and discoveries (Suler, 1980). Once the artist reaches an insight, she employs secondary process thinking to turn the inspiration into a socially valued product. Creative individuals are skilled at this process; they are active masters of their unconscious rather than passive recipients of its impulses.

When LSD first became popular as a recreational drug, advocates touted it as an aid to creativity. No one makes this claim anymore, and the notion of regression in the service of the ego explains why. LSD facilitates primary process thinking, providing all sorts of sparks and tickles, but it does not give an individual the technical skills to turn insight into creative products. That takes training, practice, and hard work . . . the result of ego functioning.

Literary Criticism

Literary critics have made extensive use of psychoanalysis to understand particular works and particular writers (Mollinger, 1981). Shortcomings of this approach parallel those already detailed for psychohistory. The psychoanalytic critic may focus too narrowly on the psychoanalytic formula, sometimes losing the work itself in the process. And when psychoanalytic theory is applied to literary characters themselves, credibility is stretched. So, in his interpretation of Shakespeare's Hamlet, Jones (1910) speculates about Hamlet's childhood experiences!

Psychoanalytic criticism is more reasonable when integrated with standard approaches to literary criticism. As C. S. Lewis (1941, p. 7) notes, the purpose of criticism is to answer the question, "Why, and how, should we read this?" Overly zealous psychoanalytic critics brush aside this question in favor of a different one: "Why did he write it?" What results is no longer literary criticism.

In recent years, literary critics have turned from Freud's version of psychoanalysis to that of Jung. This is not surprising. To Freud, symbols were ultimately personal. To Jung, symbols transcended the individual. Universal meanings could be sought. And, since literature often seeks to cross the boundary between the personal and the universal, Jungian theory is a more popular source of interpretations for symbols.

Dadaism and Surrealism

One of the intriguing chapters in the intellectual history of the twentieth century is the relationship between psychoanalysis and the movements of Dadaism and Surrealism. The links are complex. Most agree, however, that the important Dadaists and Surrealists were influenced by Freud. A number of these artists and writers explicitly acknowledged psychoanalytic theory as the source of techniques and themes.

What is Dadaism? It was a creative movement within Europe toward the end of World War I. Painters and poets profoundly disenchanted with a world that produced the horrors of the first "modern" war criticized society on numerous grounds. Their criticism included art itself, which they saw as the product and prop of a decadent society (Ades, 1978). Mere convention dictated who was considered creative and who was not, and convention was a habit shaped by the bourgeois world (see, for example, Becker, 1982).

But the Dadaists were still artists and writers, produced by the world that had deserted them. Their paradoxical position sometimes resulted in anger and frustration, and sometimes in whimsical works that were deliberately made difficult to regard as art. In 1913, Marcel Duchamp pioneered the use of **ready-mades**, everyday objects exhibited as if they were classic paintings or sculptures. This is now a standard artistic technique, but at the time, it attempted to show that art is produced merely by men and women, not by "artists" of special status.

If artistic conventions are distrusted and dismissed, what is left? In the early 1920s, André Breton seized upon psychoanalytic ideas to answer this question. In particular, Freud's notion of the unconscious provided a means

Marcel Duchamp, *Bicycle Wheel,* 1951 (third version, after lost original of 1913).

to rail against coercive logic and rationality. Unfettered creativity was to be found only in the unconscious. And so Surrealism was born from the attempt of artists and writers to reach that place. Breton proclaimed the First Manifesto of Surrealism in 1924, defining the movement as:

> SURREALISM, noun. Pure psychic automatism by which it is intended to express . . . the true function of thought. Thought dictated in the absence of all control exerted by reason, and outside all aesthetic and moral preoccupations. (Ades, 1978, p. 33)

Surrealist writers and artists developed a variety of techniques with which to tap the unconscious: dream analysis, automatic writing and drawing, and hypnosis. They threw paint onto canvas and words onto paper at random. They imitated primitive art. They substituted rags for brushes. They dictated their poems and refused to edit them.

Two of the best known Surrealists are the painters René Magritte and Salvador Dali. Magritte painted memories of his dreams, and he is famous for the distortion of perspective in his works. Dali used Freudian symbols to depict explicit sexual themes: guilt, sex, incest, and masturbation.

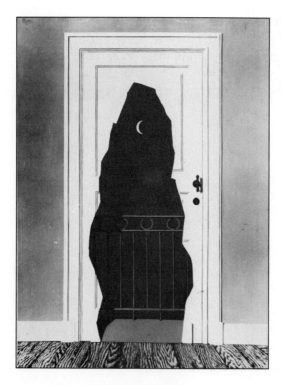

René Magritte, "L'Acte de Foie."

Salvaldor Dali, *Illumined Pleasures,* 1929.

Dali and Freud met in London shortly before Freud's death. They enjoyed their brief interaction and were impressed with each other. Dali sketched Freud, but it is much more difficult for psychoanalysts to capture what Dali and the other Surrealists were about. Do their works validate the psychoanalytic account of creativity, or not? The entire movement defies such a question.

Salvador Dali's sketch of Freud.

SUMMARY

By far the most generally influential approach to personality psychology is the psychoanalytic paradigm. In this chapter, I described the application of psychoanalytic ideas within the fields of psychopathology, psychotherapy, **psychosomatic medicine**, child-rearing and education, **psychohistory**, advertising, and creativity. What do these applications have in common? Most basically, the workers within these fields are attracted to psychoanalysis because it is a theory that does justice to complex phenomena. The motivated unconscious is particularly attractive. Each application takes its particular formula more-or-less directly from Freud and uses it to predict, control, and/or understand a domain of human activity.

At the same time, the psychoanalytic applications described here are controversial. Within each field, there are advocates and critics of equal fervor. Their debate is usually not over the pertinence of psychoanalysis but instead over the exclusive reliance on this perspective. Is psychoanalysis the best way to look at psychopathology, at history, at advertising, at literature? The answer is not found in any particular application. It resides in the judgment of the individual practitioner, shaped by the paradigm he or she accepts.

8

TRAIT PARADIGM:
THEORY

*T*he trait paradigm is a commonsense approach to the description and explanation of personality. Embracing the root metaphor of formism, its key assumption is that people fall into categories defined by stable and pervasive characteristics, often of a biological nature. Researchers use various procedures to describe individuals with respect to these characteristics, but most often they gather information through questionnaires. The trait paradigm originated in the tradition of psychological testing, and so its important role model—for better or for worse—has been the IQ test. The trait paradigm more generally reflects Darwinian thought applied to personality.

The importance of Darwin's (1859) theory of evolution to psychology in general and to the trait paradigm in particular cannot be overestimated. First, it focuses attention on biological characteristics, explicitly stating that they vary across individuals. Although genes as the mechanism of evolution were not recognized at the time of Darwin, subsequent elaborations of evolutionary theory were phrased in genetic terms. A topic of great interest to the trait paradigm is whether personality characteristics are inherited.

Second, the theory of evolution explains by pointing to the consequences of something, for example, an opposable thumb, an upright posture, or a large brain. These are known as **functional explanations.** Trait theories of personality have been functional as well, inspired by the success of evolutionary theory. But how are traits related to a person's adaptation to the world?

There are literally hundreds of personality characteristics that have attracted the attention of psychologists working within the trait paradigm. In each instance, a specific theory is proposed to explain the particular characteristic. I won't catalogue these circumscribed theories, but rather I'll talk about general trait theories because they address traits as a whole.

Some of the common questions posed by these theories include:

1. What are the fundamental ways in which people differ? What is the best way to ascertain these differences?

2. How do individual differences predispose good or bad functioning?

3. What is the origin of a particular individual difference? Can the relative contributions of nature versus nurture be determined?

Perhaps the most important question is how trait theorists discover individual differences. There is no single way. Sometimes a theorist takes a simple observation and turns it into a full-blown trait theory. Cesare Lombroso did this in the 1800s when he noticed (incorrectly) that criminals seemed to bear a physical resemblance to apes (Gould, 1981). So, criminals were thought to be evolutionary throwbacks, which in turn inspired an entire theory of moral behavior.

Sometimes a theorist deduces pertinent individual differences from an already-existing account of personality. Psychoanalytic theorists have identified numerous traits in this manner. Donn Byrne (1961), for instance, started with the Freudian notion of repression and regarded it as a characteristic that people possess to varying degrees. At one extreme is **repression,** while at the other is **sensitization** (akin to perceptual vigilance).

And sometimes a theorist takes a striking behavior and turns it into a personality trait by finding out if people differ in terms of how frequently they show it. Christie and Geis (1970) fashioned the personality characteristic of **Machiavellianism** in this manner. Machiavelli was the fifteenth century figure known for his advice to rulers that the end always justifies the means. Machiavellianism as a trait is the degree to which someone acts on this advice.

Regardless of the source of each personality characteristic, each is assimilated to the trait paradigm by the same process. Developing a way to measure individual differences in the characteristics is critical. This measure usually is a questionnaire completed by the person. Once a questionnaire is devised, and reliability and validity are ascertained, researchers investigate the relationship of the trait to function and dysfunction. Further, they explore the origins of the trait, looking for places where biology and environment contribute.

Against this common background are several different approaches to the trait paradigm. I'll describe these in this chapter. The first approach concerns itself with the very notion of a personality trait. The giant figure here is Gordon Allport, noteworthy because he set the agenda for the trait paradigm. He phrased the key issues that still define this approach to personality.

Next I'll discuss a concern with the biological basis of personality: the constitutional approach. Although most trait theorists are interested in the biological underpinnings of personality characteristics, constitution theorists *start* with biology and proceed to personality. I'll discuss the early ancestors of this approach—humoral theory and phrenology. I'll then explain the theories of Kretschmer and Sheldon, who locate personality within the physique. (How should steroids be regarded if this is a reasonable idea?) Finally, I'll cover theories of temperament: inborn styles of behaving.

The next area within the trait paradigm has been influenced by psychoanalysis. It concerns itself with individual differences in needs, drives, and motives. Here, I'll discuss the theories of Henry Murray and Abraham Maslow.

The final approach I'll describe uses the statistical technique of factor analysis in an attempt to identify the basic dimensions along which people differ. I'll close by describing the work of the two most important factor analytic personality theorists: Hans Eysenck and Raymond Cattell.

GORDON ALLPORT: SETTING THE AGENDA

What Sigmund Freud is to the psychoanalytic paradigm, Gordon Allport is to the trait paradigm. Whether or not they agree with Allport, all subsequent trait theorists use his terminology and take positions on his issues. Let me therefore tell you about Allport the man before I describe Allport the theorist.

Allport's Life   Allport was born in 1897 in Montezuma, Indiana. His father was a country doctor, and his mother taught school. In Allport's (1968b) own words, his "home life was marked by plain Protestant piety and hard work (p. 379)." Allport was a dutiful but uninspired student until he followed his older brother Floyd to college at Harvard. There his eyes were opened to intellectual matters.

He studied psychology and social ethics, and he spent his time helping his brother with psychological research and doing social service work: running a boys' club, working as a probation officer, helping foreign students, registering homes for war workers, and so on. Allport's later career can be seen as a sustained attempt to bridge science and social service. His concern with personality arose from this goal, since he felt that service programs must be grounded in an adequate conception of personality to be truly useful.

Before going to graduate school at Harvard, Allport lived abroad for a year, where he taught English and sociology in Constantinople. It was at this time that an intriguing event occurred: Allport met Freud for the first and only time. The meeting achieves significance in light of Allport's later theorizing, which starkly contrasts with the psychoanalytic approach to personality.

> With a callow forwardness characteristic of age twenty-two, I wrote to Freud announcing that I was in Vienna and implied that no doubt he would be glad to make my acquaintance. I received a kind reply in his own handwriting inviting me to come to his office at a certain time. Soon after I entered the . . . room with pictures of dreams on the wall, he summoned me to his inner office. He did not speak to me but sat in expectant silence, for me to state my mission. I was not prepared for silence and had to think fast to find a suitable conversational gambit. I told him of an episode on the tram car on my way to his office. A small boy about four years of age had displayed a conspicuous dirt phobia. He kept saying to his mother, "I don't want to sit there . . . don't let that dirty man sit beside me." . . . His mother was a well-starched *Hausfrau,* so dominant and purposive looking that I thought the cause and effect apparent.
>
> When I finished my story, Freud fixed his kindly therapeutic eyes upon me and said, "And was that little boy you?" Flabbergasted and feeling a bit guilty, I contrived to change the subject. While Freud's misunderstanding of my motivation was amusing, it started a deep train of thought. I realized that he was accustomed to neurotic defenses and that my manifest motivation (a sort of rude curiosity and youthful ambition) escaped him. For therapeutic progress he

would have to cut through my defenses, but it so happened that therapeutic progress was not here an issue.

This experience taught me that depth psychology, for all its merits, may plunge too deep, and that psychologists would do well to give full recognition to manifest motives before probing the unconscious. (Allport, 1968b, pp. 383–384)

This embarrassing incident at least allows a useful perspective on Allport's approach to personality. In a number of important ways, it breaks with the psychoanalytic approach. While acknowledging the usefulness of psychoanalysis for understanding neurotics, Allport regards his theory as one for normal individuals. He emphasizes consciousness and rationality. It is a teleological theory with little to say about the influence of early traumatic events.

Once in graduate school, Allport suffered some misgivings. As described in Chapter 3, American psychology in the 1920s was a laboratory science of experiments concerned with molecular phenomena: sensation, perception, and learning. Comparing himself to his fellow students, Allport found himself without "giftedness in natural science, mathematics, mechanics (laboratory manipulations), nor in biological or medical specialties" (1968b, p. 384). Allport wanted to study such topics as social values and personality, but he had no role models.

So, with encouragement to pursue his own interests, he began to create what we now can see as personality psychology. His dissertation was the first investigation in the United States of the components of personality. In 1921, he published a paper (with brother Floyd) on the classification and measurement of personality traits, and in 1924, he taught the first personality course ever offered in the United States.

Except for four years at Dartmouth, Allport spent his entire professional career at Harvard, where he made important contributions to the development of psychology. Among his academic pursuits, he investigated such social psychological topics as rumors, prejudice, and attitudes. And of course, Allport continued his investigation of personality. In 1937, he published *Personality: A Psychological Interpretation*, detailing his perspective on personality. In 1961, he revised this influential book under the title *Pattern and Growth in Personality*.

Unlike the other major personality theorists, Allport never developed a school of followers. This is mainly because his theoretical stance was eclectic and open-ended. He gave would-be disciples little dogma to embrace. Nevertheless, his particular ideas have been widely influential. Against the dominant trends of psychoanalysis and behaviorism, he forced attention on consciousness and intentionality. Allport was one of the few theorists conversant with all of the disparate strands of personality psychology, arguing persuasively that the field must pertain to the specific individual. "His work stands as a monument to a wise and sensitive scholar who was committed to the positive aspects of human behavior in terms that respected the uniqueness of every living organism" (Hall & Lindzey, 1978, p. 295). Gordon Allport died in 1967.

Allport's Ideas   Here is Allport's (1937) definition of personality:

> Personality is the dynamic organization within the person of those psychophysical systems that determine his unique adjustments to his environment. (p. 48)

Let's focus on this definition, since Allport carefully chose each word.

Personality is *dynamic*—always changing. Personality is an *organization;* its components are coherently related to each other. Personality is *psychophysical,* neither just mind nor just body. To Allport, a person's mind and body work in concert. Personality is made up of *systems,* which means that its building blocks can be identified. The most important of these are an individual's traits. Personality *determines* behavior. It lies behind what a person does and has causal status. Finally, personality results in someone's *unique adjustment* to the world. Each person is unlike all others in how he lives his life. According to Allport, personality psychology must recognize and explain this uniqueness or be doomed to misleading generalizations.

Aspects of this definition may remind you of some of Rapaport's (1959) psychoanalytic points of view that I described in Chapter 5. In particular, Allport's definition of personality embraces the empirical, gestalt, organismic, and adaptive points of view. However, his emphasis on uniqueness stamps it as markedly different from psychoanalytic theory, not only in its detail but in its general thrust as well. Where psychoanalysis attempts to explain all people in the same way, Allport feels that each person merits his or her own sort of explanation.

People's unique personalities can be captured by specifying their particular personality traits. Of the various terms available to describe personality, Allport opts for traits, defining a **trait** as a

> neuropsychic structure having the capacity to render many stimuli functionally equivalent, and to initiate and guide equivalent (meaningfully consistent) forms of adaptive and expressive behavior. (1961, p. 347)

Again, Allport explicitly states that traits are real, that they underlie a variety of thoughts, feelings, and actions, and that they determine adaptation to the world.

Traits filter the way we experience the world, and then they channel the way we respond to our experience. We all know people who treat every chance comment as a challenge, turning polite conversation into an argument. "Nice day." "What's right with it?" Other people—with different traits—bring calm to themselves and others.

Where do traits come from? According to Allport, we have no personality at birth. Through learning, maturation, and socialization, traits emerge. However, Allport does not dwell on an individual's history. He feels that behavior occurs because of contemporary factors—not past ones. He introduces the concept of **functional autonomy of motives** to make his point explicit. According to this idea, behaviors originally undertaken to satisfy some extrinsic goal may become self-sufficient, continued because they are now intrinsically satisfying. A child may begin piano lessons under parental threat, but as an adult, she continues to play the piano because she loves it. The adult motive is autonomous. Unlike psychoanalytic theorists, *Allport liberates personality from its past.*

Allport also anticipated the *consistency controversy.* To him, consistency does not mean that someone does the exact same thing in different situations. Someone who is chronically bored, for instance, may fall asleep during a movie, doodle during a lecture, and read the newspaper during a poker game. If we look only at the surface of what this man does, we wouldn't understand why his friends dub him Bored Boris. On the other hand, if we take a look at the meaning of his activities, we see consistency. In each setting, he is underwhelmed by the ongoing activity and does something else. His behavior is meaningfully consistent, if not literally so.

Why are people consistent? This question led Allport to consider the notion of the self. The integration of personality seemed to demand something beyond behavior. What is responsible for self-identity and self-esteem? What strives for distant goals? Psychoanalysis holds the ego responsible, but Allport was reluctant to posit such a copilot. Instead, he calls the functions themselves the **proprium.** The proprium is not a thing but a set of processes. It does not exist apart from personality.

The proprium is all the ways that people project themselves into the future. According to Allport, we must understand an individual's hopes and fears, wishes and dreads. To understand personality, we must look to the individual's future intentions, and the person is usually aware of these intentions.

Allport distinguishes two types of traits: **common traits** and **personal traits.** A common trait is used to characterize a group of individuals. Everyone is described with respect to the characteristic. So far in this book, I have described only common traits. Consider the strength of oral needs, as measured by the Blacky Test. We can array all people along this dimension, from not at all oral through somewhat oral to absolutely oral.

A personal trait is sometimes called an **individual disposition,** and it is specific to the individual. It need apply to no one else. So, I know someone

SOURCE: © 1971 S. Gross.

who loves small animals. This characteristic organizes her entire personality. She is the best friend that a dog or cat ever had. She won't eat veal marsala. Pictures of wide-eyed lion cubs hang inside her house, and bird feeders hang outside. She is a volunteer guide at the Children's Zoo. Any description of her personality has to start with this trait of loving small animals.

Can we place all people along a continuum called "loving small animals"? Not if we expect them to stay where we put them. Some people are as consistently hateful toward small critters as other people are loving, but most of us show no particular consistency one way or another. We love some small animals some of the time in some situations, while we hate other small animals at other times in other situations. There is no general trait that organizes the way we behave. The degree to which we love small animals does not characterize our personality. Thus, "loving small animals" is a personal disposition.

Allport further distinguishes among three types of personal traits, according to their centrality to someone's personality. Someone who is stamped with a single personal trait has a **cardinal disposition.** It determines *everything* that they do. Famous historical and literary individuals are remembered for the personality characteristics they so perfectly exemplify: Don Juan, Pollyanna, the Marquis de Sade, Don Quixote, Uncle Tom, Mata Hari, Puck, Sad

Sack, and so on. I believe contemporary characters such as Richard Nixon, the Ayatollah Khomeini, George Steinbrenner, and Margaret Thatcher will also be remembered for their cardinal traits. (I don't think John Travolta or Madonna will catch on, if you want some counterexamples.)

Most of us do not have a cardinal trait. Instead, we are characterized by five to ten **central dispositions:** highly characteristic and frequently evidenced traits. Stop and think about the five to ten traits you would use to describe your own personality. These are your central dispositions.

The third type of personal trait is a **secondary disposition,** which is more circumscribed than central dispositions. It does not appear in a variety of situations or give rise to a variety of behaviors. For example, I often sing in the shower and whistle when I drive on I–94, but that's the extent of me and music.

Allport distinguishes between **nomothetic research,** which is concerned with establishing generalizations about all people, and **idiographic research,** which is concerned with the particular individual. Common traits fall within nomothetic research, whereas personal traits are the subject of idiographic investigation. Unlike other psychologists, who justifiably conduct nomothetic studies, the personality psychologist must do idiographic research.

The distinction between common traits and personal traits is therefore more profound than it first seems. All theorists within the trait paradigm accept common traits. Individual differences are investigated by using personality tests to place all people along the same basic continuums. But to accept personal traits is to step out of this research tradition. Personal traits are applied only to specific individuals, and so they are antithetical to the typical use of personality tests. The relative placement of the individual with respect to others is at best irrelevant and at worst misleading.

Consider the danger of regarding the personal disposition of loving small animals as a common trait. How do we interpret people placed at the midpoint of the continuum ranging from extreme love at one end to extreme hate at the other? A person with "some" of this trait may indeed be consistent, showing moderately positive feelings toward small animals. But another person designated as having "some" of this trait may have extreme feelings from situation to situation. Or a person with "some" of the trait of loving small animals may live in a fancy apartment that has eradicated rats, roaches, and poodles; he has never had any personal contact with small animals but in the abstract thinks they are cute. You can see from examples like these why Allport argues for the necessity of personal traits to describe personality.

Although Allport's points are sensible, researchers have come up short in devising measures for personal traits. Allport himself didn't have any concrete suggestions. In fact, his own research was concerned with common traits.

Two of his well-known projects are the Allport-Vernon-Lindzey Study of Values (1960) and the Allport-Vernon study of Expressive Movement (1933). Both are instances of nomothetic research. In his study of values, Allport scores subjects from their endorsement of items reflecting one of six different values: theoretical; economic; aesthetic; social; political; and religious. Counselling psychologists widely use these scales to help people choose among different vocations. The study of expressive movement looks at the style in which people do what they do. In a series of studies, Allport and Vernon asked research subjects to do a variety of things: tap their finger; draw a circle; count; shake hands; and so on. Results showed that across diverse acts, people have a consistent style of expression. Can you see that these investigations treat people's characteristics as common traits, not as personal dispositions?

The closest that Allport (1965) got to idiographic research was his analysis of 301 letters written by a woman over a number of years. These *Letters from Jenny,* as they have come to be known, provide what Allport regards as the acid test for the personality psychologist. Can the researcher explain an individual life? By reading the letters, Allport identified eight personal traits: quarrelsome-suspicious; self-centered; independent-autonomous; dramatic-intense; aesthetic-artistic; aggressive; cynical-morbid; and sentimental.

So what? From the perspective of the trait paradigm, the explanation of Jenny is complete, since she has been categorized (as quarrelsome, self-centered, and so on). But is this really idiographic research? Those reading Jenny's letters can only arrive at their conclusions by comparing Jenny to other individuals, as relatively aggressive, as relatively sentimental, and so forth. If pushed to the extreme, idiographic research implies that each individual merits unique theoretical language. And that is impossible.

Perhaps the best way to regard idiographic versus nomothetic research is in terms of relative emphasis. Does the researcher make conclusions about people in general or one person in particular? A given investigation may emphasize one goal more than the other. The thing to remember here is Allport's important statement that personality psychologists should attempt idiographic research.

Evaluation   Allport's contribution to the trait paradigm is that he set the agenda. He distinguished the trait approach from the psychoanalytic approach. He made an articulate plea that personality psychology should study what is unique about individuals. He introduced concepts still employed today: functional autonomy of motives, proprium, common trait, personal trait, and idiographic versus nomothetic research.

On the negative side, Allport's theory failed to stimulate research, in part because particular techniques for achieving idiographic goals are lacking and in part because it makes few predictions. His theory is difficult to prove wrong, since uniqueness and functional autonomy serve as convenient escape clauses. Nevertheless, subsequent researchers have kept what is valuable about Allport's approach while discarding what is unwieldy to make the trait paradigm a viable approach within personality psychology.

The remaining sections in this chapter can be viewed in terms of how they elaborate a particular aspect of Allport's vision of personality psychology. Where Allport sketchily discussed the biological basis of traits, constitution theorists specifically explain how personality is grounded in biology. Where Allport failed to make clear just how traits were causes of behavior, needs theorists do so by stressing individual differences in motives and drives. And where Allport took only preliminary steps toward identifying the range of traits, factor analytic theorists specify the primary dimensions along which people differ.

THE BIOLOGICAL BASIS OF PERSONALITY

Theorizing about personality is probably as old as humanity itself. The early personality theories are **typologies:** mutually exclusive and exhaustive categories of types of people (Jastrow, 1915). Some of the pigeon-holes of early typologies were based on a moral or religious view of the world. Types were characterized by a predominant virtue or vice, which catalyzed everything that a person thought, did, or felt. Taken together, these virtues or vices made up an all-encompassing perspective on the universe and people's place within it.

Such characterization can be traced as far back as Theophrastus (372 BC–287 BC), who described a variety of undesirable folks, each with an overriding way of being offensive. Among the types sketched by Theophrastus were the gossip, the miser, the fool, and the bore. If you spend your Saturday mornings as I usually do, perhaps you've wondered why the Smurf cartoons fail to credit Theophrastus. Surely, Clumsy Smurf, Brainy Smurf, Hefty Smurf, and the others stepped off the pages of Theophrastus.

Similarly, we can look at the Seven Deadly Sins as a personality typology based on character flaws, since any given sinner usually overdoes one particular vice. So, pride, covetousness, lust, envy, gluttony, anger, and sloth are labels for categories where we can more or less place our friends and enemies. Or we can read the *National Enquirer* and find lusting and coveting characters on the first few pages, followed by stories about gluttonous, angry, and proud people. As readers, we are either envious or slothful, but using the logic of a personality typology, we can't occupy both categories at the same time.

Other early typologies were based on differences in biology. Unlike moral typologies, variants of these are still a part of personality psychology. Biological typologies assume that people differ in personality because they differ physically—in terms of bodily fluids, bumps on the skull, physique, or the nervous system. These physical differences are regarded as fixed and pervasive characteristics inherited from one's ancestors. Taken together, biologically based personality theories comprise the *constitutional approach,* an important line of theorizing within the trait paradigm. I'll describe the most popular constitutional theories in this section.

Humours

The ancient Greeks proposed a personality typology based on the relative preponderance of different **humours** (fluids) in the body. Four humours were specified: blood, phlegm, yellow bile, and black bile. The healthy individual is one whose fluids are in balance. In fact, the expression "to be in good humor" can be traced back to this early personality theory.

Each humour was associated with a personality type. A preponderance of blood characterizes the **sanguine type,** a person who is "warm, jovial, outgoing, and emotionally expressive" (Metzner, 1979, p. 42). The **phlegmatic type,** calm and steady, results from an imbalance of phlegm. Next, the **choleric type** has a preponderance of yellow bile and is "ardent and excitable . . . passionate, electric, impulsive, sparkling, and enthusiastic" (p. 43). And too much black bile characterizes the **melancholic type,** who is pessimistic and prone to attacks of depression.

If you squint your eyes a bit, you can see that the four members of the A-team exemplify these humoral types. Hannibal Smith is sanguine, the Face Man is phlegmatic, B. A. Barracus is choleric, while Mad Dog Murdock is—among other things—melancholic. Well, maybe you have to squint your eyes a lot.

Phrenology

A more recent personality typology that also accords importance to biological factors is **phrenology,** a popular approach in the 1800s (Boring, 1950). As developed by Franz Joseph Gall and Johan Caspar Spurzheim, phrenology proposed that protrusions of the skull (bumps) revealed dominant traits of the individual, such as self-esteem, conscientiousness, hope, and so on. These bumps were believed to reflect protrusions of the brain. Phrenologists felt that the brain was the organ of the mind, and that the faculties or powers of the mind were localized in different areas of the brain. The more developed the area, the more pronounced the faculty.

Phrenology was at odds with what has long been a dominant opinion within physiological psychology: that the brain acts as a whole (Lashley, 1929).

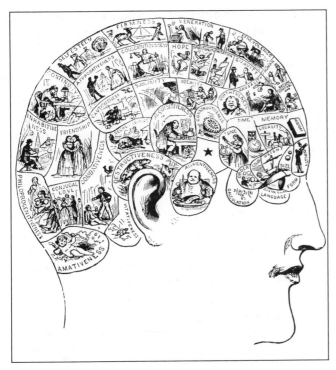

This nineteenth century phrenology chart shows the locations of
various mental functions, as they were thought to exist.

In contrast, the premise of phrenology is that brain functions are localized.
Even though phrenology was wrong in almost all of its particulars, it played
an important role in the history of personality, legitimizing the search for
individual differences within physiological functions.

The contribution of the early ancestors of personality psychology to the
later development of the field lies not in their details, but rather in their attempt
to describe and explain what is general, characteristic, enduring, and functional about individual people. As such, they foreshadowed contemporary
personality psychology, even if they were not successful. But stay tuned.
Contemporary opinion is swinging somewhat back toward the assumption of
localization of function. The general strategy of phrenology may yet be
vindicated.

Physique

One of the most enduring beliefs is that personality differences reside in the
physique. Hence, typologies based on **body build** have been proposed since
the time of the early Greeks. In reviewing these early theories, Hans Eysenck
(1967) found considerable agreement that there are three basic body types:

round, muscular, and thin. Picture Jonathan Winters, Herschel Walker, and Ralph Sampson, and you have good examples of each physique.

In 1921, the German psychiatrist Ernst Kretschmer proposed a theory that linked physique to mental illness. This marked the beginning of modern constitutional psychology (Hall & Lindzey, 1978). He observed that those individuals suffering from the two dominant forms of psychosis—schizophrenia and manic-depression—tended to have different body builds. Schizophrenics were thin and frail, while manic-depressives were plump and round.

To test this informal observation, Kretschmer studied the differences in people's bodies. Consistent with previous theorists, he identified three major types of body build. The linear physique he called **asthenic,** the muscular he called **athletic,** and the roly-poly he called **pyknic.** (A fourth type, the **dysplastic,** was comprised of those rare individuals with inconsistent body builds that struck the observer as "ugly.")

Kretschmer then found support for his speculations. He classified psychiatric patients by their body build and by their diagnosis, and found that schizophrenics were apt to be asthenic, while manic-depressives tended to be pyknic. However, he didn't control for the age of his patients. With age, we all tend toward a pyknic physique (too many picnics?), as well as an increased risk for bipolar depression (Hall & Lindzey, 1978).

Kretschmer believed that his theory could be extended to normal individuals as well, although he presented no evidence to support this. It remained for the American William Sheldon (1940, 1942) to build on the earlier ideas of Kretschmer and extend constitutional psychology to the normal individual.

Sheldon was a psychologist and physician who worked mainly at Harvard and Columbia. In the course of his career, he published a number of books on the human physique, on human temperament, and on the relationship between the two. His major contributions to constitutional theories of personality are twofold. First, he suggested that physique be described along continuous dimensions, not in terms of discrete types. Second, he described in great detail how one should characterize physique.

So, Sheldon proposed that each physique held three components: **endomorphy** (round), **mesomorphy** (muscular), and **ectomorphy** (linear). Bodies are rated on 7-point scales in accordance with each of these components. These ratings yield a person's **somatotype:** his or her profile of the three components of physique. Ralph Sampson, for instance, might be rated 117, since he is high on ectomorphy, but low on endomorphy and mesomorphy. Herschel Walker would probably be rated 171. You and I, on the average, are 444.

According to Sheldon, each component of physique is associated with a particular personality style. Endomorphic individuals conform to our stereotype of the jolly fat man: "calm, easygoing, affable, sympathetic, affectionate

. . . amiable, jovial" (Metzner, 1979, p. 23). Mesomorphy is associated with the action-oriented. These people "are the actors, the athletes, the executives, the achievers, the fighters" (p. 25). Finally, ectomorphic individuals are overly sensitive, erratic, and inhibited: "critical, superior, judgmental, and suspicious . . . guarded and cautious" (p. 28).

What is the evidence that people of different physiques indeed have different personality characteristics? There is some, although Sheldon has been criticized for overestimating the strength of the correlation. Still, it does seem that mesomorphic individuals tend toward active and outgoing behaviors like pursuing sports and/or members of the opposite sex (for example, Hendry & Gillies, 1978). The consistency of such behaviors exceeds what one would expect by chance.

But such correlations between physique and personality do not address a fundamental premise of constitutional psychology, that physique directly brings about characteristic thoughts, actions, and feelings. Notice that the personality traits thought to be associated with ectomorphy, mesomorphy, and endomorphy correspond well to society's stereotypes about fat people, muscular people, and thin people. Perhaps young people with a given body build incorporate the "appropriate" stereotype and act it out. This would produce correlations between physique and personality, although not because physique has a simple causal role. Or a muscular youth might find success at sports to come easily, and thereby develop competitiveness.

Regardless of the causal links, it would be a mistake to dismiss physique from our explanation of personality. As Brian Wells (1983) observes, "the physical self is always an important element in our previous history, present self-perception, and future expectations" (p. vii). But the effects of physique on personality are likely to be subtle and complex, and in many cases mediated by our own beliefs as well as those of others.

Temperament

Yet another approach to the biological basis of personality is concerned with **temperament**, usually defined as a genetic predisposition that encourages a person to respond to events in some ways but not others. Temperament refers to a person's way of interacting with the world, particularly his or her emotional style. (By the way, the word "temper" is derived from temperament.) Many theorists distinguish between temperament and personality, viewing the former as one of the raw ingredients of the latter. This may be too fine a distinction, but it underscores the notion that temperament is a biologically based style of behaving and not the whole of personality.

Temperament theories have been proposed throughout the century (for example, Diamond, 1957; Eysenck, 1947; Thomas, Chess, Birch, Hertzig, &

Korn, 1963) and are currently enjoying new popularity in research programs that use techniques of behavior genetics to investigate how personality styles are inherited.

The young of many species show wide variation in behavior almost from birth, suggesting a biological basis (Scott & Fuller, 1965; Yerkes, 1943). Perhaps the most striking variation is that observed among human infants. Thomas and Chess (1977) describe the original impetus for their study of temperament:

> Like innumerable other parents, we were struck by the clearly evident individual differences in our children, even in the first few weeks of life. There were differences in the regularity of biological functions such as sleep and hunger, in levels of motor activity, in the intensity of laughter or crying, in the initial reactions to new stimuli, in the ease with which the baby's reactions could be modified. . . . In many, though not all . . . children, there appeared to be a remarkable persistence of at least some of these characteristics of individuality as they grew older. (pp. 3–4)

Of course, this example does not prove a strictly genetic basis for individual differences.

Prenatal occurrences and birth itself affect subsequent behavior. Dangers of maternal malnutrition, drug use, and/or illness during pregnancy are well-known examples. In some cities, there are signs in bars warning pregnant women not to drink. (Maybe the nonpregnant should be warned about drinking as well.) Compared to infants of nondrinking women, those born to drinking women show not only physical differences but also behavioral differences. These newborns are likely to be tremulous and irregular in their sleep. They tend to cry in a way that is aversive to listeners, and to dramatically swing from drowsiness to excitation and vice versa. These ways of behaving—although present at birth—are not genetic.

Similarly, the way in which parents react to children affects the way their kids behave. This process occurs very early in life. Again, we are tempted to identify those differences as genetic, but they may really be the result of the environment. How many differences between little boys and girls are due more to the way their parents react to them than to the difference between an X and a Y chromosome? Or remember Adler's ideas about birth order. Infants may behave quite differently because they are born into different social environments.

It is a mistake to try and classify complex behaviors into two neat piles of those determined by nature and those determined by nurture. Temperament theorists agree and try to show that *aspects* of behavior—not behaviors as a whole—are influenced by hereditary factors. This is why they call temperament a style, a way of engaging in activities that themselves have numerous determinants.

Hereditary explanation within personality psychology has always been controversial. Much of this controversy stems from the political and social implications of the argument that racial differences in intelligence are genetically based (see Chapter 3). Hitler's pronouncements about pure and impure human races did nothing to win acceptance of the notion that aspects of personality are inherited. Finally, American ideology about all men (and women) being created equal is often at odds with the intent of temperament theorists.

Nevertheless, there is equal reason to distrust an extreme environmentalism which dismisses biology and particularly genetics as irrelevant in understanding what people are about. Thomas and Chess discuss one of the dangers of this position:

> As mental health professionals we became increasingly concerned at the dominant professional ideology . . . in which the causation of all child psychopathology, from simple behavior problems to juvenile delinquency to schizophrenia itself, was laid at the doorstep of the mother. . . . The guilt and anxiety created in mothers whose children had even minor behavioral deviations were enormous. (1977, p. 5)

Thomas and Chess dub this ideology the *Mal de Mere* syndrome, literally the "sickness of the mother," arguing that excessive guilt on the part of the mother could indeed screw up her kids, completing a self-fulfilling prophecy.

What are the basic temperaments? Early attempts to catalogue temperaments were hampered by the aforementioned difficulties in determining whether or not a genetic influence was present. Recent attempts have been more successful because they use Galton's **twin method** for disentangling nature and nurture (see Chapter 3). The behavior of identical and fraternal twins is ascertained and then compared. Do identical twins resemble each other more than fraternal twins? If so, a case is made for a genetic influence on the behavior being studied. Notice that this is not foolproof. As a correlational research strategy, the twin method is subject to various confounds, and one can draw the wrong conclusion. Stop and think of reasons other than heredity why identical twins might behave more similarly than fraternal twins.

In some domains of investigation, like intelligence and schizophrenia, the twin method is refined to include comparisons not only of identical and fraternal twins, but also of twins raised together and twins raised apart. The assumption here is that twins in the same family are exposed to the same environmental determinants, while twins in different families are not. With this approach, the effects of similar versus dissimilar "nature" and similar versus dissimilar "nurture" can be examined simultaneously.

Again, this is not a foolproof strategy. How many twins are reared in different families? And of those who are, how dissimilar can we assume the families to be? *The Prince and the Pauper* is a compelling story, but it is implausible. At any rate, this refinement of the twin method has not been used extensively to study temperament.

Since it is impossible to use an experimental approach to remove these inherent confounds in the twin method, researchers have supplemented it with other research strategies (Plomin, Defries, & McClearn, 1980). One intriguing method is to compare the similarity of identical twins with respect to some characteristic to the similarity of fraternal twins mistakenly regarded by their families as identical (Scarr, 1968). (Appreciate that researchers ascertain whether twins are identical or not by comparing blood proteins, while parents do so just by looking at their children.) This method presumably holds "nurture" much more constant than in typical twin studies. A related strategy is to explicitly assess the degree to which twins are treated alike or differently as they grew up, and to take this into account in making inferences about heredity (Loehlin & Nichols, 1976). Researchers also employ **family studies**—comparing the similarity of family members according to the distance of their relatedness (the more distant a relative, the less genetic similarity)—and **adoption studies**—comparing the resemblance of children to their biological versus adoptive parents.

Arnold Buss and Robert Plomin (1975, 1984) have identified three temperaments that have good evidence for a genetic basis: emotionality, activity, and sociability. As styles of behavior, each temperament is inferred from actual behavior by quantifying responses in terms of frequency (how many responses per unit of time), duration (how long each response lasts), and amplitude (how intense each response is).

Buss and Plomin suggest these ways to measure the three temperaments:

Emotionality

1. frequency: of crying, shrinking back, hiding, temper tantrums, and so on;
2. duration: soothability, or how long it takes for a return to placidity;
3. amplitude/intensity: changes in pulse, breathing, blood pressure, and GSR; or intensity of crying, panicky expression, temper tantrums, or pouting;

Activity

1. frequency per unit time (rate): walking speed, talking speed, observed tendency to hurry;
2. duration: time spent in high-energy activities, persistence in energetic activity after most people have stopped;
3. amplitude: tendency to jump or bounce up and down when others are more still;

Sociability

1. frequency: number of attempts to initiate contact;
2. duration: the amount of time spent with others or in shared activities with others;
3. amplitude: degree of social responsiveness. (Buss & Plomin, 1984, pp. 93–94)

Note that these measures can be adapted for infants, children, and adults. Individuals are arrayed along each of these quantitative dimensions according to "how much" (frequency, duration, and/or amplitude) of the temperament they show in their behavior. It's easy to find the extreme of each temperament: haven't you noticed that emotional, active, and sociable people usually sit in front of you at the movies?

Research converges to support Buss and Plomin's contention that these three styles of behaving are influenced by heredity. With respect to these temperaments, identical twins resemble each other much more than do fraternal twins. In fact, there is a tendency for fraternal twins to show a slightly negative correlation. So, if Twin A is high on emotionality, Twin B is likely to be somewhat low. Buss and Plomin term this a **contrast effect,** and suggest that it's due to labeling on the part of the parents:

> Parents might contrast their fraternal twins, labeling one as active and the other as inactive. The twins might contrast themselves and become more differentiated behaviorally. One twin partner, who might be slightly more active than the other, converts this slight edge into a consistent advantage in initiating activities, and the other twin relinquishes the initiative to his partner. (1984, p. 119)

This might not happen with identical twins because parents are always stressing their similarities. At any rate, remember my earlier point that temperament studies do not necessarily ignore the role of the environment in determining personality. The contrast effect, although emerging from heredity investigations, leads to an insight about the special social environment of twins.

Some recent research compared personality traits of identical and fraternal twins, including pairs of twins raised separately (Goleman, 1986). On a variety of traits, pairs of identical twins resembled each other much more than pairs of fraternal twins—even if Twin A and Twin B grew up in different families. If these results hold up, they argue for a strong influence of genetics on personality. At the same time, the hardest work of the trait theorist will then begin: explaining how this influence occurs.

Granted a particular set of behavioral styles, how does a person's temperament interact with the other determinants of personality to bring about a behavior? Temperament theorists stress that the answer is a complex one. Thomas and Chess (1977) cite the example of a child who is highly active. In an urban environment, she "is more apt to get burned and bruised, to break things, to dart out into the street in front of an oncoming car and to interfere unintentionally with the activities and comforts of others than is the child with a moderate or low activity level" (p. 73). She will bring down on herself a whole host of prohibitions and punishments, which will have profound effects on her entire personality.

Current studies of twins suggest that genetics may play an even larger role in personality development than was previously believed.

But suppose this same child was in a rural environment. Her high activity style would not put her at risk for so many dangers, and would not bring about parental restriction. Being in a different environment, she would grow into quite a different person than her urban counterpart. We can think of many other environmental factors that would interact with particular temperaments to influence the course of personality development.

I've sketched the larger context in which temperament theorizing and research occurs. I believe there is good evidence for genetic influences on personality, as long as it is not misunderstood to mean that complex behaviors are caused by one's heredity. Instead, genetics predispose certain styles of behaving, which interweave with environmental characteristics to determine who and what we are.

NEEDS APPROACHES

Another influential approach within the trait paradigm describes people according to their dominant needs, borrowing from psychoanalytic theory, since needs are motivating forces within the person that impel him to try and satisfy them. So, the needs approach explains how traits are related to behavior.

Unlike psychoanalysis, though, this approach does not limit itself to sexual and aggressive needs. Instead, different needs theorists have proposed rather extensive lists of needs. These theorists are also much more concerned with how people differ with regard to particular needs. In this section, I will describe the theories of Henry Murray and Abraham Maslow, two of the most important figures in this tradition.

Henry Murray: Personology

Henry Murray was not a psychologist by original training. Born in 1893 in New York City, he was a physician, biologist, and chemist who turned to psychology at about the age of thirty. He changed his interests upon reading Jung's (1924) *Psychological Types.* Intrigued by the book, he used the opportunity of a visit to Zurich in 1925 to meet with the author. The two talked for hours, and Murray came away from the meeting dazzled by Jung's intelligence and by the notion of the unconscious. He was subsequently trained in psychoanalysis by Franz Alexander, the founder of modern psychosomatic medicine (see Chapter 7), and was influenced by psychoanalytic theory throughout his career. Although some classify Murray with the Freudians and neoFreudians, I've placed him within the trait paradigm because he is best known for his catalogue of individual differences in needs and for his methods of assessing them.

Upon Murray's return to the United States in 1928 he was appointed director of the newly created Harvard Psychological Clinic. It was there that he developed his own theory of personality and broadly addressed the purpose and procedure of the field as a whole. He coined the term **personology** to stress that personality psychology should concentrate on the individual case: the person. He advocated the intensive study of a small number of individuals, rather than the cursory examination of large numbers, as is often the case within the trait paradigm.

To fashion his theories, he drew upon biology, cultural anthropology, psychoanalysis, literature, and mythology. His fellow workers at the Harvard Psychological Clinic came from a variety of backgrounds, so his approach was interdisciplinary long before this was fashionable. Of the many men and women who worked with Murray, I cite Erik Homburger Erikson, since you have encountered him in Chapter 5. Murray importantly influenced the then-young Erikson, and Erikson's psychosocial theory can be seen as an instance of Murray's personology.

Nowhere was the eclectic and interdisciplinary character of Murray's approach better represented than in his assessment strategy. He developed the **diagnostic council** to best describe the individual's thoughts, feelings, and actions. Different researchers from different backgrounds observe the same subject in a variety of settings. Each researcher employs the specialized techniques at his or her disposal to make these observations. So, *Explorations in Personality* (Murray, 1938), a study of several dozen young men, employed questionnaires, interviews, projective tests, experiments, and so on, each administered by an expert. Then all of the experts would bring their findings to a conference where the information was synthesized to characterize the personality of the individual.

Murray's aim was to observe the individual as a whole, in his natural setting. To this end, he developed a number of assessment techniques that allowed people to be themselves, providing rich information about their personalities. The best-known of these techniques is the **Thematic Apperception Test** (or **TAT**), a projective test developed with Christina Morgan. The subject is shown an ambiguous picture and then asked to tell a story about what she sees. The subject's responses are not constrained, so the ensuing story reveals the personality of the storyteller. In particular, the TAT is thought to reveal the needs of the person, since they are projected onto the characters in the picture (Morgan & Murray, 1935).

What is a **need**? In general terms, Murray calls it "a push from the rear . . . an impulse which does not as a rule completely subside until a situation of a certain kind has been arrived at" (1938, p. 68). Needs arise from internal or external stimuli, and directly catalyze action to appease or satisfy them. Each need is accompanied by a particular emotion.

Needs are identified by observing behavior. A number of criteria point to the operation of a need:

- Attention to certain aspects of the environment, and not others.
- Reports of particular feelings.
- Repeated patterns of behavior.
- Typical consequences of these behaviors.
- Satisfaction with attainment of these consequences (and dissatisfaction with failure to achieve).

As an example, let's consider how one of the needs Murray describes—the need for play—can be identified. Some people have a higher need for play than others. They know where video games are set up, where tennis courts are located, and where movies can be rented (selective attention). Merely hanging out, fooling around, cruising, or killing time is pleasurable (particular feeling). As they pursue everyday activities, they laugh and joke and tease (characteristic behavior). Amusement is the result of this approach to life (typical consequence). And people with a high need for play are pleased when the world lets them be light-hearted, and they are displeased when told to "get serious" (satisfaction versus dissatisfaction).

Do you have a high need for play? Look back through the book and see what you have highlighted or underlined. If you regard those paragraphs that contain jokes or anecdotes as memorable, you probably need to play more than others. Murray suggests that you would also agree with these statements:

I feel that if I were free from the necessity of making a living, I should devote a good deal of time to the pursuit of unmixed pleasure.

I spend a fair amount of my time amusing myself—parties, dances, shows, card-games, or drinking bouts.

I seek, at the cost of some distant goal, whatever makes me feel most cheerful here and now.

I seek amusement as an antidote for worry. (1938, p. 173)

The rest of you may be interested to know that Murray (1938) identified approximately twenty needs (see Table 8-1 for brief definitions). Some of these have attracted more research attention than others, notably the need for achievement. We'll consider some of the research findings in the next chapter.

The important point here is that a variety of human needs exists. They encompass a variety of distinctions: between more versus less biological involvement, between direct versus indirect expression, between more versus less reliance on particular environmental circumstances, and so on. The strength of peoples' needs differ, and personality is characterized by the particular mix of these needs.

Two other concepts of Murray's are important. First is that of the **press.** Unlike many personality theorists, Murray explicitly recognized the environment's role in facilitating or thwarting behavior. A press is *an environmental property that determines whether or not a person reaches a given goal.* What a person does is not simply a function of his or her needs, but also of the existing environmental press. An important distinction here is between the individual's perception of the environment (**beta press**) and the reality of the environment (**alpha press**). Murray suggests that behavior occurs in response to the beta press. The local tavern is just a shabby building (alpha press), but it may also be the only place where a man feels accepted (beta press). The latter is more important in understanding his behavior at the tavern than the former.

The second concept is Murray's notion of the **thema,** which is *the fundamental unit of behavior and the building block of personality.* Quite simply, a thema is the combination of an operative need and a prevailing press. Themas range from a single episode (you feel hungry in the presence of a bag of M & M's) to a series of episodes (you bring a high need for understanding to a challenging university) to an overarching style of life (you have a high

Table 8-1
Murray's Needs

Need	Characterization
Abasement	Need to submit to external forces
Achievement	Need to accomplish
Affiliation	Need to form and maintain a friendship
Aggression	Need to overcome opposition
Autonomy	Need to be free of restraint
Counteraction	Need to make up for failure
Defendance	Need to defend self against criticism
Deference	Need to admire a superior
Dominance	Need to control one's environment
Exhibition	Need to make an impression
Harmavoidance	Need to avoid physical harm
Infavoidance	Need to avoid humiliation
Nurturance	Need to assist the helpless
Order	Need to put things in order
Play	Need to have fun
Rejection	Need to snub
Senitence	Need to enjoy sensuous feelings
Sex	Need to have sexual intercourse
Succorance	Need to have one's need gratified by another
Understanding	Need to ask and answer questions

SOURCE: Murray, 1938.

need for nurturance, and thus you become a veterinarian). The full description of personality places the person in context—physical, social, and cultural.

Murray's personology is important because it argues that a variety of motives are crucial, while at the same time suggesting procedures for identifying and measuring these motives (Hall & Lindzey, 1978). Murray influenced an entire generation of personality psychologists by directing their attention to the whole person, to the importance of the environment, and to the need for sophisticated assessment. His influence may have waned through the 1960s and 1970s, but in the 1980s there is renewed interest in his approach to personality (see, for example, Runyan, 1982).

Abraham Maslow: Hierarchy of Needs

Another important figure who stressed the role of needs in personality is Abraham Maslow (1908–1970). Maslow was born in Brooklyn, the son of Russian immigrants. He first attended City College and Cornell University, and then the University of Wisconsin, where he was trained as an animal learning psychologist.

Maslow's first allegiance within psychology was to John Watson's behaviorism, but he turned away from this vision of human nature in response to several important life events. The birth of his first child and the outbreak of World War II were impossible for him to accommodate within behavioristic psychology (Hall, 1968). Further, Maslow felt that the other dominant force within psychology—psychoanalytic theory—also fell short of explaining them. Approaches to psychology based on animals or neurotics had little to say about the wonder of human development or the possibility of ending hatred and warfare.

To Maslow, behaviorism and psychoanalysis were psychologies of deficiency. People were viewed as victims of the pushes and pulls of their environment or their hormones. These approaches were pessimistic because they made no mention of the good and noble things which people can accomplish.

So, Maslow (1970) self-consciously proposed "a positive theory of motivation" to encompass both "the highest capacities of the healthy and strong man as well as . . . the defensive maneuvers of crippled spirits" (pp. 35–36). He acknowledged the influence of William James, John Dewey, Max Wertheimer, Kurt Goldstein, Alfred Adler, and the neoFreudians. Maslow elaborated on their suggestions that people strive toward higher goals than the satisfaction of physical drives, stressing that people are inherently good and always moving toward health and wholeness.

Maslow is a central individual in **humanistic psychology,** a movement that takes issue with the dehumanizing aspects of many psychological theories. Humanistic psychology is sometimes called the Third Force, to distinguish it from psychoanalytic approaches on the one hand and behaviorist approaches on the other. Maslow and other humanistic psychologists believe that psychology should concentrate on what is good and healthy about people. (Another important humanistic psychologist is Carl Rogers, and his ideas will be described in Chapter 11.)

Central to Maslow's humanistic approach is the notion that people have a variety of needs arrayed in a hierarchy. This **hierarchy of needs** ranges from *basic* or **deficiency needs** that provide something lacking within the person—like food or air—to *growth* or **metaneeds** that reflect uniquely human values—like truth and beauty (see Figure 8-1). People must satisfy lower needs before they can satisfy higher needs. However, it is only in satisfying the higher needs that people can become truly fulfilled.

Figure 8-1

Maslow's Hierarchy of Needs

Self-actualization

Esteem

Love

Safety

Physiological

SOURCE: Maslow, 1970.

Maslow's hierarchy is an intriguing idea, capturing something important about the interrelation of human motives. When basic needs are salient, many higher needs are irrelevant. Who hasn't felt sexual desire crowd out other considerations, like honesty and love? And what about the truism among revolutionaries that radical ideology is well-received when it's accompanied by food and safety?

My parents were teenagers during the depression, and so their attitude toward employment is quite different than mine. This has made for a genuine gap in understanding over the years. I've sometimes complained to my parents that my job isn't always as fulfilling as I would like it to be. They always ask, "But aren't you getting paid?" For them, growing up in a time of massive unemployment, jobs are regarded as vehicles for basic needs. For me, growing up in a time of opportunity and affluence, jobs are the means to satisfy higher needs. But perhaps things are changing yet again as the job domain becomes increasingly uncertain. Maybe my children won't understand me either, but they'll see eye-to-eye with their grandparents about employment.

Here is a series of postulates that presents Maslow's theory more formally:

1. The higher need appears later in evolutionary development.
2. The higher need appears later in personality development.
3. The higher the need, the less imperative it is for sheer survival, the longer gratification can be postponed, and the easier it is for the need to disappear permanently.
4. Living at the higher need level means greater biological efficiency, greater longevity, less disease, better sleep, appetite, etc.
5. Higher needs are less urgent subjectively.
6. Higher need gratifications produce more desirable subjective results, i.e., more profound happiness, serenity, and richness of the inner life.
7. Pursuit and gratification of higher needs represent a general healthward trend, a trend away from psychopathology.
8. The higher need has more preconditions (i.e., satisfaction of lower needs).
9. Higher needs require better outside conditions to make them possible.
10. A greater value is placed upon the higher need than upon the lower by those who have been gratified in both.
11. The higher the need level, the wider is the circle of people loved.
12. The pursuit and gratification of the higher needs have desirable civic and social consequences.
13. Satisfaction of higher needs is closer to self-actualization than is lower need satisfaction.
14. The pursuit and gratification of the higher needs leads to greater, stronger, and truer individualism.
15. The higher the need level the easier and more effective psychotherapy can be: at the lowest need levels it is of hardly any avail.
16. The lower needs are far more localized, more tangible, and more limited than are the higher needs. (from Maslow, 1970, pp. 98–100)

The problem with behaviorism and psychoanalysis is not in what they study, but in what they do not. These approaches have limited their view of human nature by exclusively focusing on basic needs. Maslow inquires about higher matters.

Chief among these higher matters is **self-actualization,** "loosely defined as the full use and exploitation of talents, capacities, potentialities, etc."

(Maslow, 1970, p. 150). Maslow explored self-actualization by studying such individuals as Thomas Jefferson, Abraham Lincoln, Eleanor Roosevelt, Albert Schweitzer, and Jane Addams. According to Maslow's findings, these people were all self-actualized. They shared certain characteristics, like acceptance of self and others, spontaneity, autonomy, sense of humor, and deep interpersonal relations.

Self-actualized individuals are also likely to have **peak experiences,** feelings of intense enjoyment where the sense of self is lost. Other writers have called this the mystic experience:

> Feelings of limitless horizons opening up to the vision, the feeling of being simultaneously more powerful and also more helpless than one ever was before, the feeling of great ecstasy and wonder and awe, the loss of placing in time and space with, finally, the conviction that something extremely important and valuable has happened, so that the subject is to some extent transformed and strengthened even in his daily life by such experiences. (Maslow, 1970, p. 164)

But where other writers interpreted this experience in religious terms and regarded it in an all-or-nothing fashion, Maslow described it as a psychological phenomenon that exists in varying degrees and intensity in all people.

The frequency with which someone has peak experiences and the overall degree of self-actualization are critical dimensions of personality. More generally, Maslow's hierarchy of needs suggests that each of us can be characterized by the level of needs that are currently salient. Although self-actualization and peak experiences are inborn potentials for us all, most people remain at the level of deficiency needs.

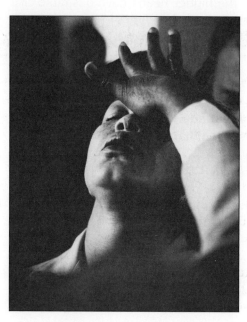

During a peak experience, the sense of self is lost.

Reminiscent of psychoanalytic theory, the environment is once again the culprit that thwarts natural development. Conflict, frustration, and threat make it difficult to satisfy basic needs. In the absence of such satisfaction, the individual never proceeds to higher needs. Much of Maslow's writings are recommendations to society about how to encourage self-actualization among its members.

Maslow's ideas have greatly influenced psychology by focusing on the positive aspects of the human enterprise. Also, his attempt to specify relationships among needs is compelling. Nevertheless, there are problems with his approach to personality. Maslow did not conduct conventional research; indeed, there is more than a hint of distaste for "science" in his books (see, for example, Maslow, 1966). Furthermore, how is one to assess where an individual is located in the hierarchy of needs? It seems implausible to ask them.

Above and beyond the issue of assessment, counter-examples seem to exist with respect to the hierarchy. A mother may run into a burning building—ignoring safety needs—to save her children. A hungry man may give all of his money to another man who is starving. A highly religious woman may forego the satisfaction of basic needs because they conflict with her principles of faith. These instances all capture something good and noble about people, and are therefore consistent with Maslow's overall vision. But they also contradict the details of his theory. The hierarchy of needs is a good approximation of the order in which most people attend to needs, but it fails to describe matters for all of us.

FACTOR ANALYTIC APPROACHES

Workers within the trait paradigm are more concerned with measurement and statistics than those who prefer other personality approaches. Nowhere is this better seen than in the research of those who rely on **factor analysis** to discover the basic dimensions of personality. You may recall that I briefly described factor analysis in Chapter 2. It is a procedure for analyzing a set of correlations among various measures into what one hopes is a simpler underlying pattern. This basic pattern is called the **factor structure** of the set of correlations, and is inferred from the sets of measures that correlate highly with each other (Child, 1970; Gorsuch, 1974).

Many researchers are not content to use factor analysis merely as a tool to describe their data in simpler terms. Instead, they go further and interpret the factors they find as the basic structure of personality itself. The distinction between the description and interpretation of factors is important. Consider the typical application of factor analysis to questionnaire measures of personality traits. Let's assume that three hundred individuals complete ten questionnaires, each of which yields a score that places the person along some personality dimension. A factor analysis of these scores shows that there are two factors that mainly account for the correlations among the questionnaires.

Factor One reflects scores from questionnaires 1, 3, 5, 7, and 9, while Factor Two reflects scores from questionnaires 2, 4, 6, 8, and 10. From the descriptive point of view, we are done. We know that individuals who scored high on questionnaire 3 also tended to score high on questionnaires 1, 5, 7, and 9. We know that individuals who scored low on questionnaire 8 also tended to score low on questionnaires 2, 4, 6, and 10. We also know that how individuals scored on the odd-numbered questionnaires tells us little about how they scored on the even-numbered questionnaires, and vice versa.

Suppose that questionnaires 1, 3, 5, 7, and 9 reflect the traits of thrifty, reverent, courteous, prepared, and brave. We feel justified in calling Factor One the "boy scout" factor and concluding that the degree to which someone is or is not like a prototypic scout is a basic dimension of personality. Factor Two is similarly interpreted by abstracting the gist of the meanings assigned to questionnaires 2, 4, 6, 8, and 10.

So far so good, except that the interpretation of factors is a lot more difficult than this example suggests. Stephen Gould describes the biggest pitfall in the interpretation of factors:

> Factorists have often fallen prey to a temptation for *reification*—for awarding *physical meaning* to all strong [factors]. . . . Sometimes this is justified . . . but such a claim can never arise from the mathematics alone, only from additional knowledge . . . of the measures themselves. (1981, p. 250)

Factors cannot reflect reality unless the component scores themselves do. And even then, interpretation may run afoul. Here is Gould again:

> Nonsensical systems of correlation have [factors] . . . as well. . . . A factor analysis for a five-by-five correlation matrix of my age, the population of Mexico, the price of Swiss cheese, my pet turtle's weight, and the average distance between galaxies during the past ten years will yield a strong [factor] . . . since all the correlations are so strongly positive. . . . It will also have no enlightening physical meaning whatever. (1981, p. 250)

In other words, the passage of time confounds all the correlations here, and the single "factor" revealed by factor analysis reflects merely this confound. My point is to suggest that this statistical tool cannot be used blindly. It does not create theory out of data by an automatic process.

Personality psychologists are understandably reluctant to use factor analysis only as a descriptive tool. After all, they are not really interested in the questionnaire scores of particular people at a particular time under a particular circumstance. They want to go beyond these particular data. They especially want to assume that questionnaire scores reflect personality traits and that factors reflect the underlying structure of personality. So they interpret the factors they discover by assigning substantive meaning to the questionnaire scores and then looking for common meanings that are reflected in a given factor.

In the hands of skillful theorists, factor analysis can be an extremely useful way to process an overwhelming amount of information about people. The two most famous theorists are Raymond Cattell and Hans Eysenck, and it is to their research programs and resulting theories that we now turn.

Raymond Cattell

Raymond Cattell was born in England in 1905, the son of middle-class parents. He attended the University of London as a chemistry major, but then changed his mind. Here is how Cattell describes his switch into psychology:

> On a cold and foggy London morning in 1924 I turned my back on the shining flasks and tubes of my well-equipped chemistry bench and walked over to Charles Spearman's laboratory to explore the promise of psychology. . . . This seemingly quixotic act . . . sprang from my broader reading having led me to see that psychology was the really new, challenging frontier of science, and the source of rational hopes for human progress. (1981, p. 121)

(You may recall from Chapter 3 that Spearman was one of those who invented the statistical technique of factor analysis.)

After receiving his doctorate in psychology, Cattell worked for five years as a clinician. He came away unimpressed with the merits of psychotherapy, concluding that psychology's biggest need was for basic research on learning and personality. In 1937, he was able to follow through on this belief when E. L. Thorndike of Columbia University invited him to come to the States and be his research assistant. Cattell said yes, and has stayed in the United States ever since. He has held appointments at several universities, most notably at Harvard (where he associated with many of the other subjects of this chapter: Allport, Sheldon, and Murray) and at the University of Illinois (where he stayed for almost three decades: 1946–1973).

Cattell's basic scientific premise is that the scientist's topics should dictate the methods used to investigate them. Personality demands a method that can simultaneously take into account its numerous facets. Experimentation has little value. Instead, multivariate statistics in general and factor analysis in particular are the preferred methods for personality psychology:

> Whereas the physicist or the bivariate brass instrument experimenter [that is, experimental psychologist] can hope to reach a law with a few bits of wire and glass and a couple of checking experiments the [personality] psychologist in his

multidetermined uncontrollable world needs say 200 subjects, 30 variables in five hours of measurement, and some repetitions of it all. This prospect turns off the less dedicated Ph.D. and many others toward easier—if more trivial problems. (Cattell, 1984, p. 172)

Throughout his long career, Cattell has used factor analysis to identify the underlying structure of the various aspects of personality.

What are these aspects? Among the more important are traits, attitudes, sentiments, drives, moods, roles, and environments. Personality is the combination of all these into what Cattell calls a **specification equation,** the goal of which is to predict exactly what a person will do in a given situation. So, Cattell regards personality as an equation that predicts behavior.

Cattell has investigated traits most thoroughly, defining them as *relatively permanent and pervasive tendencies to respond.* There is an important distinction between surface traits and source traits. **Surface traits** are the innumerable differences we see among people. Language gives us the total domain of surface traits. Remember the list of trait names compiled by Allport and Odbert (1936)? Cattell began his personality research with the same list. He eliminated synonyms and obscure traits, leaving 171 surface traits. He then asked observers to rate people they knew with respect to these traits. Factor analysis revealed the underlying structure of these surface traits: what Cattell calls **source traits.**

The **Sixteen Personality Factor Test** (or **16PF**) is a questionnaire that measures the most important source traits. Table 8-2 gives brief descriptions of these traits in terms of their endpoints. Appreciate that each of these traits represents a dimension along which people vary. In Allport's terms, they are common traits.

Table 8-2
Source Traits (as Measured by the Sixteen Personality Factor Test)

Casual versus Controlled	Placid versus Apprehensive
Conservative versus Experimenting	Practical versus Imaginative
Emotional versus Stable	Relaxed versus Tense
Expedient versus Conscientious	Reserved versus Outgoing
Forthright versus Shrewd	Shy versus Venturesome
Group-tied versus Self-sufficient	Sober versus Happy-go-lucky
Humble versus Assertive	Tough- versus Tender-minded
Less- versus More-intelligent	Trusting versus Suspicious

SOURCE: From Cattell, 1984.

Cattell has no place for personal dispositions, but his sixteen source traits allow a dazzling variety among people. Suppose that each trait has just three levels: high, medium, and low. How many unique combinations are there? Three to the sixteenth power, which is in excess of 43 million "types" of people! Some of these people like John McEnroe, and some of them don't. Multivariate research is certainly able to accommodate the complexity of personality.

Although many personality psychologists assess traits only with a questionnaire, like the 16PF, Cattell recognizes that one should not rely on a single source of data. So, he gathers and analyzes not only responses to questionnaires, which he calls **Q-data,** but also information from the individual's life (**L-data**), such as whether or not she is married, and information from objective psychological tests as well (**T-data**), such as how many anagrams she can solve in five minutes.

Cattell looks for convergence among the source traits found in the three types of data. So far, these efforts have not been entirely successful. Some traits "appear" only in one or two types of data. Thus, the exact number of source traits deemed critical by Cattell is uncertain.

The factors themselves have been subjected to factor analysis. Let's stop for a minute and look at what this procedure provides: a simpler (and even more abstract) structure of underlying personality. Two of these **second-order factors** are noteworthy. The first is identified as *introversion-extraversion* (after Jung's dimension), and the second as *anxiety* (Maddi, 1980). Taken together, these suggest four basic types of people: introverted-anxious, introverted-nonanxious, extraverted-anxious, and extraverted-nonanxious. (Again I think of the A-team.)

There is more of Cattell's work that deserves mention. Influenced by his English mentors, Cattell has investigated the heritability of personality characteristics (Cattell et al., 1955, 1957). He developed a statistical technique for this purpose—**multiple abstract variance analysis (MAVA)**—that estimates not only the presence or absence of genetic influence, but also the degree to which a trait has a genetic basis. Results from the MAVA technique suggest that traits such as intelligence and assertiveness have a relatively strong genetic underpinning, while traits like conscientiousness and control do not (Loehlin, 1984).

Cattell has also been interested in psychopathology. He's investigated the structure of the "abnormal" personality (Cattell & Scheier, 1961). Additional factors are used to explain emotional disorders, and Cattell draws on psychoanalytic notions to interpret them. People with problems tend to be highly anxious, and the source of this anxiety is two-fold: a genetic predisposition to be sensitive to threats and a family environment where conflict and inconsistency dominate.

In recent years, Cattell (1979) has recognized the importance of the situation in determining what a person does. Following his research program of identifying source traits, he has attempted to discern the underlying structure of the environment. He calls this attempt **econetics** (the study of ecology), which involves sampling encyclopedia entries for the kinds of situations commonly encountered in a given culture. Eventually, the psychological significance of each situation will be ascertained, and factor analysis will reveal the underlying structure of the setting in which behavior occurs.

A final interest of Cattell's is sketched in his 1972 book *A New Morality from Science: Beyondism*. This book is a bold attempt to use the techniques of science—that is, multivariate statistics—to decide which system of morality is the best! Cattell proposes that societies throughout the world be characterized first by their differing religions, social systems, and political organizations and then by the degree to which they achieve "the greatest good for the greatest number" of their citizens. It is then a simple matter to see which morality is most highly correlated with this measure. Needless to say, this is controversial and unlikely to be taken seriously by world leaders. This may be just as well, but Cattell's *Beyondism* epitomizes the only person who rivals and perhaps surpasses Freud as a personality theorist of scope and audacity.

Hans Eysenck

The other major figure in factor analytic studies of personality is Hans Eysenck. Comparisons and contrasts between Cattell and Eysenck are inevitable and intriguing. Here is what they have in common. Both are immigrants: Cattell from England to the United States, Eysenck from Germany to England. Both studied at the University of London where they were influenced by psychologists and statisticians who can trace their intellectual ancestry to Francis Galton. Both believe measurement is fundamental to personality psychology. Both employ factor analysis to identify the underlying structure of personality. Both believe that important aspects of personality are inherited. And both have been extremely prolific throughout their careers.

At the same time, there are important differences between them. Cattell is influenced by psychoanalytic ideas and speaks approvingly of Freud's intuitive insights into personality, while Eysenck is vehemently opposed to psychoanalysis. Also unlike Cattell, Eysenck has always been interested in therapy and has been a proponent of behavior modification. Finally, through their respective versions of factor analysis, Cattell and Eysenck arrive at different underlying structures of personality. Where Cattell points to at least sixteen factors of personality, Eysenck believes that no more than four are necessary.

Eysenck was born in Germany in 1916 to parents who were traveling actors, so he was raised by his grandmother. He was a teenager in the 1930s, a time when Hitler was solidifying his grasp on the country. Opposed to the

Nazi regime, he left Germany for good when he turned eighteen and was up for military service.

He went to England, where he studied psychology at the University of London, receiving his doctorate in 1940. During the war he worked as a psychologist at a psychiatric institution. During the war, he took positions which he still holds: in the Institute of Psychiatry at Maudsley Hospital and in the Department of Psychology at the University of London.

Eysenck is a controversial figure within psychology. Part of this controversy is inevitable, since he advocates the politically unpopular idea that personality and intelligence are inherited. But part of the controversy is also due to Eysenck's style of writing and speaking (Gibson, 1981). He is critical of other psychologists to the point of sarcasm. He has written a number of books calling things as he sees them. To give you a flavor of this, the titles of two of his better-known books are *Sense and Nonsense in Psychology* (Eysenck, 1953) and *The Inequality of Man* (Eysenck, 1973).

Eysenck has used a variety of procedures for gathering data about research subjects: questionnaires, ratings by others, assessments of physique and physiology, objective psychological tests, and biographical information (Hall, Lindzey, Loehlin, & Manosevitz, 1985). These data are factor analyzed to find the basic structure that underlies personality. In his early research, Eysenck found two factors: **introversion-extraversion** and **normality-neuroticism.**

> Extraversion is defined in behavioural terms by the various traits that are correlated together to define this factor, traits such as sociability, impulsiveness, activity, carelessness, liveliness, jocularity, and so forth. (Eysenck, 1976, p. 11)

> Neuroticism is conceived of as strong, labile emotionality, predisposing a person to develop neurotic symptoms in case of excessive stress. Traits correlating to define this 'type' are moodiness, sleeplessness, nervousness, inferiority feelings, irritability. (pp. 15–16)

Notice that these are the two second-order factors of Cattell's sixteen source traits, so perhaps the findings of Eysenck and Cattell are not as discrepant as they first seem.

More recently, Eysenck has found a third factor: **psychoticism.** He is still describing this dimension but provides a sketch of the individual high in psychoticism

> as being solitary, not caring for people . . . often troublesome, not fitting in anywhere. He may be cruel and inhumane, lacking in feeling and empathy, and altogether insensitive. He is hostile to others, even his own kith and kin, and aggressive, even to loved ones. He has a liking for odd and unusual things, and a disregard for danger. (Eysenck, 1976, p. 19)

Psychoticism can characterize the extremely disturbed individual, but Eysenck conceives it as a personality dimension along which all people can be arrayed.

Finally, in some of his writings, Eysenck regards intelligence as a fourth basic dimension of personality. If you recall our discussion in Chapter 1, intelligence is a fuzzy example of personality, as most people use the term. You thus can understand Eysenck's ambivalence about including intelligence.

An intriguing aspect of Eysenck's approach to personality is his attempt to specify a physiological basis for each of his personality dimensions. Introversion-extraversion is linked to chronic levels of excitation in the cortex. Introverts are over-aroused and hence easy to stimulate; for this reason, they avoid situations that are apt to overwhelm them. In contrast, extraverts are under-aroused and thus difficult to stimulate; accordingly, they seek out exciting situations. Neuroticism is thought to reflect the degree to which the autonomic nervous system reacts to stimuli. The more reactive a person, the more neurotic he is. Finally, Eysenck tentatively links psychoticism to one's level of male sex hormone. (It's bad enough that excess testosterone makes us bald; does it have to make us peculiar as well?)

A theory of psychopathology emerges from this physiological interpretation of the dimensions of personality. The person who is high on neuroticism and introversion is at risk for anxiety disorders: fears, phobias, obsessions, and compulsions. The person who is high on neuroticism and extraversion is a candidate for psychopathy (antisocial personality).

Disorders do not occur automatically. They befall a person with the appropriate predisposition and environmental circumstances. People *learn* their problems. Because of one's particular personality, one tends to learn some things more easily than others, and so different personalities are associated with different problems. For example, the introverted neurotic will easily associate fear with objects in the environment. A phobia may result.

Traits and therapy are usually strange bedfellows. A trait is a fixed characteristic of an individual, and if one believes traits to be the basic units of personality, then one usually believes personality to be fixed as well—resistant to change, including therapy. But Eysenck's interest in behavior modification follows naturally from his theory of emotional disorders. What has been learned can be unlearned. The physiological account of traits explains how therapy can work. Traits represent *predispositions to learn.* As people learn and unlearn particular behaviors, their traits do not change, although their behavior does. To Eysenck, a trait is thus a vehicle for change.

Similarly, Eysenck's physiological theory allows him to combine interests in heredity and learning: the traditionally opposed nature versus nurture. What is inherited is the biological apparatus that makes learning possible. So, the physiological underpinnings of personality make Eysenck's approach to personality extremely powerful. At the present time, though, there is not enough research to support his hypothesized processes of the brain and nervous system.

Conclusion: Factor Analysis and Personality

Factor analytic approaches to personality have probably not received the attention and acclaim they deserve. The theories of Cattell and Eysenck are complex enough to capture the richness of personality, and at the same time they are grounded in empirical research of a type acceptable to most psychologists. More than any other approach described in this chapter, these theories bring Allport's original vision of personality psychology into reality.

What's the problem then? I think the technique of factor analysis is largely to blame. The statistics involved are difficult to understand, since they require mathematical sophistication that many personality psychologists do not want to acquire. Further, the pitfalls of factor analysis are easier to understand than its potential contributions. Cattell and Eysenck have painstakingly tried to show that their factors are more than just statistical abstractions. In large part they have succeeded, but this success has gone unnoticed.

The theorists themselves often fail to make their techniques more comprehensible to a larger audience. Both Cattell and Eysenck fill their articles with technical quibbles about the theoretical and procedural shortcomings of the other theorist. I suspect that readers are turned off by what appears as massive disagreement between the major proponents of factor analysis. If Cattell and Eysenck think each other to be idiots, why should the rest of us take them seriously? When factor analysts emphasize what is common to the different approaches, this strategy will be more accepted.

SUMMARY

This chapter described the major theories of those who work within the trait paradigm. All share the assumption that personality can be described by using the ways that people differ from each other. These differences—or **traits**—are stable and pervasive characteristics, often with a biological basis that can be measured with questionnaires.

Gordon Allport is the father of modern trait theory, and I described his approach to personality in some detail. Allport set the agenda for later trait theorists. In much of the chapter, I covered the theories of those who filled in the details of his agenda. First are biological theorists like Sheldon, Kretschmer, and Buss and Plomin who study the physical basis of personality. Next are needs theorists like Murray and Maslow who focus on individual differences in needs that motivate behavior to try and satisfy them. Third are factor analytic theorists like Cattell and Eysenck who use sophisticated assessment and statistical techniques to discover the basic traits that underlie personality.

9

TRAIT PARADIGM:
RESEARCH

Because the trait paradigm is concerned with the classification of personality, its research goals are straightforward. As you saw in Chapter 8, theories are phrased in terms of individual differences, and investigations test predictions by calculating correlation coefficients between measures of these variables. Which individual differences correlate with each other? Are correlations more likely under certain circumstances than others? Can confounds be ruled out?

Recall Maslow's hierarchy of needs theory. It predicts that "the higher the need . . . the longer gratification can be postponed" with respect to that need. Someone can postpone satisfaction of an aesthetic need longer than satisfaction of a hunger need. Further, "the higher need has more preconditions," which means that the correlation between high-level needs and delay of gratification is more likely to occur when lower needs are satisfied (1970, pp. 98–100). Maslow's theory gives rise to this prediction: people are willing to stand in line longer to hear a concert (aesthetic need) than to eat a meal (hunger need). One could therefore test Maslow's theory by observing what people do in theater and restaurant lobbies.

By now you're probably shaking your head and saying: "Wait a minute. That's not a good test of the theory. All sorts of other things have to be taken into consideration." These "other things" are the confounds that continually threaten correlational research. Suppose it's a lousy concert and a great meal. Is this different than a great concert and a lousy meal? Is Bruce Springsteen more or less appealing than a lobster dinner? I know folks who drool over both.

One cannot test Maslow's theory by simply comparing what people do in restaurants and theater lobbies. It would be better to examine people's behavior with respect to a large variety of needs in a large variety of situations, to ask, "On the average, are people willing to wait longer to perform activities that satisfy higher needs?" If so, then Maslow is right. If not, then he is wrong.

Now we face a logistical problem. With infinite time and energy, we could follow all sorts of people around to observe what they do, keep track of how long people wait between satisfying different needs, and see how these times are influenced by the satisfaction (or not) of lower-level needs. Most researchers agree that this is a good way to test the predictions, but many would also say that it is impractical.

So, researchers often use questionnaires to test predictions because they are efficient. A researcher might draw up a list of one hundred activities that satisfy a range of needs: going to a Bruce Springsteen concert; attending a lecture on statistics; playing pinball; watching "Dynasty" reruns; and so on. Then research subjects are given brief descriptions of Maslow's different needs and asked to rate the degree to which each activity would satisfy each need. Statistics lectures would receive a high "intellectual" rating, while "Dynasty" reruns would not. Other research subjects estimate how long they would wait in line to do these different activities. Ratings of the degree to which different activities satisfy needs (made by the first group of subjects) could be correlated with estimates of tolerated delay in performing these activities (made by the second group of subjects). The resulting correlation tests Maslow's prediction.

I've provided this example in detail because it leads you through the mentality underlying the widespread use of questionnaires to test trait theories. The most compelling rationale for questionnaires is their efficiency. All personality researchers use questionnaires, but the trait paradigm in particular leads to their use. Besides underlying a variety of thoughts, feelings, and actions, a trait should also underlie responses to personality questionnaires. To the degree that someone is anxious, for instance, she'll answer questions in an anxious fashion. To the degree that someone has a high need for achievement, she'll show it in her response to questions. Why bother to study the particulars of a person's life if responses to a questionnaire can provide the same information, saving lots of time and energy?

Unfortunately, responses to personality questionnaires do not always provide the same information. Some critics go so far as to claim that questionnaires give no useful information whatsoever. Others are more lenient. However, all agree that questionnaires should be used with caution.

Unlike intelligence tests, which usually present research subjects with actual problems to be solved and thus sample some aspect of "intelligent" behavior, personality questionnaires simply ask subjects to report on behaviors that reflect different traits. For instance, here are some questions about introverted or extraverted behaviors:

1. Do you often long for excitement?
2. Do you stop and think things over before doing anything?
3. If there is something you want to know about, would you rather look it up in a book than talk to someone about it?
4. Are you slow and unhurried in the way you move?
5. Would you be unhappy if you could not see lots of people most of the time? (Wilson, 1978, p. 219)

On the face of it, responses to these questions indicate how introverted or extraverted a person is. However, one must assume that the responses accurately describe what the person actually does.

What should the cautious researcher consider when evaluating the adequacy of a personality questionnaire? Here are some common pitfalls. First, people may not answer questions truthfully if the accurate answer puts them in an undesirable light. Psychologist Donald Fiske (1971) studied the way research subjects regard personality questionnaires. (By the way, he interviewed and observed people; he did *not* ask them to fill out questionnaires about filling out questionnaires.) He concludes:

> To test a person is to try him, and a person on trial is threatened by the possibility of being found wanting. When we give a subject a test, we must recognize that he perceives the possibility of the test's indicating that he is inadequate in some way, that he does not meet the standards set by himself and others. (pp. 205–206)

Since personality traits often relate to adaptation, they have "good" and "bad" endpoints. None of us want to function at the level of deficiency needs, and high levels of neuroticism or psychoticism are clearly not attractive. So, if personality questionnaires let a subject present a desirable view, then he will do it. This problem is referred to as contamination by **social desirability** (Edwards, 1957). The opposite confound may also occur if there is some payoff—like access to psychotherapy, educational programs, or disability pensions—for being scored as sick, helpless, or feeble.

There are several popular strategies that minimize the role of social desirability. Some questionnaires are rewritten so that different responses to the same question are equally desirable. And researchers can use a questionnaire specifically designed to measure the degree that someone gives self-enhancing responses. Scores of these questionnaires are then compared to scores of other questionnaires to see how strongly they correspond. If the correlations are high, then social desirability is probably playing a role. Also, theorists reinterpret certain personality traits to incorporate their social value. By this view, traits are interpersonal strategies, and social desirability stops being a confound and becomes an important component of what is being measured. Coyne (1976) reinterprets depression in this way by looking at depressive symptoms as a way of relating (poorly) to others and not as a property of the person per se.

A second common pitfall occurs when people do not answer questions accurately because they simply don't know the answers! A person cannot convey every matter relevant to personality. Remember the psychoanalytic concepts that pertain to the unconscious? Asking people about their unconscious makes absolutely no sense because responses will be inaccurate (see, for example, Nisbett & Wilson, 1977). The researcher can avoid this problem if she has a good handle on the meaning of the trait she's measuring. Theory dictates method, and sometimes questionnaires are precluded.

A third pitfall is that people might answer questions according to idio-syncratic styles that have nothing to do with the content of the questions. These styles are called **response sets** (Cronbach, 1946). They can be iden-tified by correlations between tests with similar formats (like 7-point rating scales or yes-no answers) that appear too high granted the meanings of the traits being measured. Fiske catalogued some of the styles that have been identified in this way:

Acquiescence: agreeing with . . . statement; marking the "yes" alternatives;

Extremity: marking the more extreme alternatives on a graded list, as in a mul-tistep rating scale;

Evasiveness or cautiousness: unwillingness to commit oneself; marking the "?" or "can't say" alternatives;

Carelessness: making inconsistent judgments;

Deviance: marking many unusual responses;

Position set: tendency to mark an item, especially on a multistep rating scale, in the same general position as the mark for the preceding item. (1971, p. 214)

Response sets are a particular problem when subjects complete a number of questionnaires with common formats. Suppose positive correlations are found. Do these reflect associations among traits—a finding with consequences for trait theory? Or do these merely reflect one or more response sets—a finding with no consequences for trait theory?

One can minimize response sets by varying the format of questions used within a particular test or across tests. To control for acquiescence, for instance, the researcher makes sure that "yes" answers do not always count toward the presence of a trait and that "no" answers do not always count toward its absence.

It is not my intention to build a case against using questionnaires to assess traits. In some cases, questionnaires pose questions about behavior that people can and do answer accurately. In other cases, questionnaires are calibrated against what people actually do, just as IQ scores are calibrated against actual academic performance. Questionnaires may even sample the behaviors being studied. Any personality questionnaire demands scrutiny. The reliability and validity of scientific procedures are constantly threatened, and personality questionnaires are hardly exempt. There are instances when a researcher decides that a particular trait should *not* be measured with a questionnaire.

Some critics add to this list of problems by suggesting that there are no such things as traits (for example, Fiske, 1973; Mischel, 1968; Peterson, 1968; Vernon, 1964). If there is nothing general and stable about personality, then a questionnaire can hardly measure it. This criticism is more profound than the other problems I've sketched because it doubts the basis of the entire trait paradigm.

INVESTIGATIONS OF PARTICULAR TRAITS

Most of the research within the trait paradigm is concerned with particular dimensions of personality. Literally hundreds of traits have been proposed and studied, but I'll focus only on ten of the most important ones.

Achievement Motivation

For two reasons, research in **achievement motivation** is traced to Henry Murray (1938). First, he included the need for achievement among his list of human motives, defining it as the drive

> to accomplish something difficult. To master, manipulate, or organize physical objects, human beings, or ideas. To do this as rapidly and independently as possible. To overcome obstacles and attain a high standard. (p. 164)

Second, using Murray's TAT, one could measure the need to achieve. Researchers prefer the TAT as a measure of the need for achievement over standard questionnaires because motives seem more likely to "appear" in people's fantasies than in questionnaire responses (McClelland, 1980). So, our needs influence the themes of stories we create in response to the TAT's ambiguous pictures.

Psychologist David McClelland (1961) provides these two stories told about a boy sitting at a desk with a book in front of him:

> A boy in a classroom who is daydreaming about something. He is recalling a previously experienced incident that struck his mind to be more appealing than being in the classroom. He is thinking about the experience and is now imagining himself in the situation. He hopes to be there. He will probably get called on by the instructor to recite and will be embarrassed. . . .

> The boy is taking an hour written. He and others are high-school students. The test is about two-thirds over and he is doing his best to think it through. He was supposed to study for the test and did so. But because it is factual, there were items he saw but did not learn. He knows he has studied the answers he can't remember and is trying to summon up the images and related ideas to remind him of them. (p. 41)

The second story clearly reflects a high need to achieve, while the first one does not. McClelland scores the TAT by counting the number of achievement-related ideas per story. The higher the count, the higher the motive to achieve.

High need to achieve predicts good performance in situations where a standard of excellence is present (McClelland, Atkinson, Clark, & Lowell, 1953). For instance, students high in need for achievement get better grades than other students, if the grades are in courses relevant to their long-term goals (Raynor, 1970). Otherwise, achievement motivation is unrelated to performance.

How does achievement motivation originate? Some researchers trace it back to our early socialization, perhaps to when our parents encouraged us to be independent and to succeed (Weiner, 1978). No one argues that achievement motivation has a genetic basis. Instead, McClelland and others emphasize that achievement motivation can be changed by life experiences, whenever they may occur.

One of the most intriguing lines of research in achievement motivation (as well as of personality psychology in general) is McClelland's study of the economic development of nations and how it might be fostered. There have been two stages in his research program. First, in *The Achieving Society*, McClelland (1961) argues that societies with large proportions of people who have a strong need for achievement show impressive economic development. One finding that supports this argument is the positive correlation between

For many Americans, Lee Iacocca represents the achievement motivation in its most positive form.

the number of achievement-related ideas in a particular country's grade-school readers in 1925 and the economic growth of that country in 1950! Second, in *Motivating Economic Achievement,* McClelland and Winter (1969) describe training programs for businessmen in different countries that foster their need for achievement by stressing the importance of self-responsibility. These programs appear to be effective, but the final results are not in yet (Weiner, 1978).

In his most recent research, McClelland (1975) investigates **power motivation** and its relationship to physical health. Power is defined as the need to have an impact on others, and it is measured with the TAT by counting references to social impact. McClelland finds that a particular pattern of motives involving the need for power is a risk factor for a variety of physical ills. More specifically, individuals with a relatively high need for power and a relatively low need for affiliation, who exercise a high degree of self-restraint, are vulnerable to high blood pressure, respiratory illness, and immunological dysfunction (Jemmott & Locke, 1984)! McClelland must be numbered among the boldest and most creative researchers in all of personality psychology.

Androgyny

In the 1960s, we questioned everything basic in our society: politics, religion, and morality. Sex and gender were scrutinized as well, leaving us with a richer vocabulary to describe what it means to be a man or woman. Where previous generations used terms like masculine and feminine interchangeably with biological maleness and femaleness, we now use masculinity and femininity to describe dimensions of personality that may apply to both biological males and biological females.

Psychologist Sandra Bem (1974) extends this trend by suggesting that some males and females can be described as both masculine and feminine: as psychologically androgynous. **Androgyny** reflects the degree to which an individual shows both traditionally "masculine" and traditionally "feminine" traits. Bem uses 7-point rating scales to measure androgyny by asking subjects to indicate how well different personality characteristics describe themselves. Some of these traits are masculine: aggressive, ambitious, and independent. Others are feminine: affectionate, gentle, and yielding.

Ratings are used to classify subjects as masculine (high on masculine traits, low on feminine traits), feminine (high on feminine traits, low on masculine traits), androgynous (high on both), or undifferentiated (low on both). Bem's (1974) approach to combining masculine and feminine ratings has been criticized (for example, Pedhazur & Tetenbaum, 1979), and alternative scoring rules have been suggested (for example, Bobko & Schwartz, 1984; Hall & Taylor, 1985). Still, all preserve Bem's idea that the androgynous individual shows characteristics traditionally regarded as masculine and feminine.

Androgyny is thought to be most likely fostered among children whose parents are warm and encouraging (Kelly & Worrell, 1976), but androgyny is still a recently described trait, so no prospective studies have yet been conducted. Common sense suggests that parents' gender stereotypes are an important factor in producing androgynous children or not. I have friends who intentionally dress their little boys in pink and their little girls in blue, and other friends who just as intentionally do the opposite.

Bem (1975) proposes that androgyny has advantages in a society like our own which puts complex demands on its members. The individual who is tough and tender, logical and emotional, aggressive and tactful—as the situation requires—has an advantage over the individual who isn't so flexible. In two experiments, Bem found that "androgynous subjects of both sexes display 'masculine' independence under pressure to conform, and 'feminine' playfulness when given the opportunity to interact with a tiny kitten. In contrast, all of the nonandrogynous subjects were found to display behavioral deficits of one sort or another" (1975, p. 634). Several studies find androgyny to be correlated with happiness and psychological well-being, further supporting Bem's research (for example, Flaherty & Dusek, 1980; Shaw, 1982).

On the other hand, the relation of androgyny to individual adjustment has important qualifications (Taylor & Hall, 1982). First, the correlation is stronger for women than it is for men. Alan Alda and Phil Donahue notwithstanding, society accepts the androgynous female more than the androgynous male. Second, the reason that "androgynous" women fare better in the

Androgyny may be the successful blending of diverse psychological traits.

world may be due to their masculine traits—not the blend of these characteristics with feminine traits. Perhaps research on androgyny is simply rediscovering the societal truism that men and the things of men, including their traits, are more valued (Broverman, Vogel, Broverman, Clarkson, & Rosenkrantz, 1972).

Definitive answers about androgyny and its relationship to individual adjustment are not yet fully known. Like other personality psychologists working within the trait paradigm, Bem is criticized for neglecting the situation in which a particular behavior occurs. In some settings, androgyny is advantageous, while in others, it creates profound difficulties (Porter, Geis, Cooper, & Newman, 1985). So, imagine androgynous behavior in San Francisco, California, and Smalltown, U.S.A. Society is still undergoing change with regard to sex roles and how they are received, with some areas of the country changing more rapidly than others. What is true of androgyny in the 1980s may not be true in the decades to come.

Anxiety

A key concept in personality psychology is anxiety. Freud and other clinically oriented theorists treat anxiety as an emotional state that defines psychopathology. Other theorists, like Cattell and Eysenck, expand its conception to include a personality dimension along which all individuals can be placed. Charles Spielberger (1966) terms this **trait anxiety** and has developed a questionnaire which measures the degree to which a person responds to situations with apprehension and uneasiness. Here are some sample questions:

Read each statement and choose the appropriate answer to indicate how you *generally* feel: almost never; sometimes; often; almost always.

1. I feel that difficulties are piling up so that I cannot overcome them.
2. I lack self-confidence.
3. Some unimportant thought runs through my mind and bothers me.
4. I take disappointments so keenly that I can't put them out of my mind.

Spielberger's Trait Anxiety measure correlates well with other measures of anxiety, including the questionnaires used by Cattell and Eysenck (Lamb, 1978).

Where does trait anxiety come from? Remember from the last chapter that Eysenck (1967) argues that anxiety has a genetic basis. Twin studies and family studies support this contention (for example, Roubertoux, 1985). At the same time, early socialization and later life experiences are also critical in determining trait anxiety (Phillips, Martin, & Meyers, 1972). If children experience frequent bad events—like failure in school or parental disapproval,

Although anxiety can be dysfunctional in the extreme, it can also serve to enhance performance.

they will grow up anxious. Studies with animals also show that unpredictable and uncontrollable situations produce chronic fear and anxiety (Mineka & Kihlstrom, 1978).

At its extreme, trait anxiety is dysfunctional. Excessive apprehension accompanies neuroses like phobias, panic attacks, and obsessions, as well as disorders like depression, schizophrenia, anorexia, and bulimia. Does this mean trait anxiety is always maladaptive? Not exactly, since research shows that moderate levels of anxiety may facilitate both classical and instrumental conditioning (for example, Spence, 1960; Spielberger, 1966). Moderate anxiety may thus facilitate learning and performance and bring about good adjustment to the world.

Before you work yourself into a tizzy over your next class exam, consider these further qualifications of the relationship between anxiety and performance:

1. On a simple task, subjects high in anxiety perform better than subjects low in anxiety. . . .

2. On more difficult or complex tasks, subjects high in anxiety perform more poorly than subjects low in anxiety—particularly in the early stages of the task. As learning proceeds, the performance of . . . anxious subjects will improve and often surpass that of subjects low in anxiety. (Phares, 1984, p. 463)

A good illustration of this complexity is found in studies of test anxiety (Sarason, 1980). As most of you well know, if you have mastered the material for a course, some arousal (anxiety) helps you to zip through a test and do well. But if you are not on top of the course material, your arousal during the test works against you.

Authoritarianism

In 1950, Theodore Adorno, Else Frenkel-Brunswik, Daniel Levinson, and Nevitt Sanford published *The Authoritarian Personality*, an explanation of the fascism that swept through Europe in the 1920s and 1930s, culminating in Nazism, the Holocaust, and World War II. Remember Erich Fromm's (1941) argument that totalitarian ideologies appeal to people who fear freedom? Fromm described the character type that finds fascism attractive as **authoritarian,** and Adorno et al. (1950) picked up this term to describe the personality syndrome that underlies prejudice. According to the authors of *The Authoritarian Personality*, the authoritarian rigidly adheres to conventionality, gladly submits to authority, and bitterly degrades minority groups. He or she is preoccupied with power, toughness, and the sexual activity of others.

Authoritarianism is measured with the *F*-Scale. (The *F* stands for fascism.) Here are some sample questions:

Indicate your agreement or disagreement with each statement by using one of these: strong agreement; moderate agreement; slight agreement; moderate disagreement; strong disagreement.

1. Obedience and respect for authority are the most important virtues children should learn.
2. Nobody ever learned anything important except through suffering.
3. Sex crimes, such as rape and attacks on children, deserve more than mere imprisonment; such criminals ought to be publicly whipped, or worse.
4. The true American way of life is disappearing so fast that force may be necessary to preserve it.

Authoritarianism is scored as the degree of agreement with these statements. Researchers have argued that the *F*-Scale confounds authoritarianism with a response set of acquiescence. From one point of view, acquiescence is indeed a part of the authoritarian syndrome, but most agree that this is a flaw in the original *F*-Scale. Newer versions of the scale phrase questions so that both "agree" and "disagree" responses count toward a high authoritarianism score (Goldstein & Blackman, 1978).

The *F*-Scale and its variants have been used in a number of studies, and results support Adorno et al.'s original conception. We probably don't want to live next door to an authoritarian, since this trait is positively correlated with prejudiced attitudes toward a variety of people, with membership in restrictive groups, and with susceptibility to propaganda (Dillehay, 1978). Authoritarianism might even be associated with destructive obedience to authority like that studied by Stanley Milgram (see, for example, Elms & Milgram, 1966; Epstein, 1966).

The origin of authoritarianism has usually been explained in psychoanalytic terms, so you should be able to anticipate the hypotheses. Adorno et al. suggest that the critical determinant of authoritarianism is the child's failure to control id impulses in a constructive way, presumably because parents are excessively harsh. The child becomes hostile and rigid, using the defense mechanism of projection. And so an authoritarian is made. Research supports the general link between parental punitiveness and authoritarianism among children (for example, Lyle and Levitt, 1955), but the details of the Oedipal dynamics are not confirmed.

According to the psychoanalytic interpretation of authoritarianism, a strong sexual drive might also be an antecedent. Indeed, Byrne, Cherry, Lamberth, and Mitchell (1973) report that authoritarianism is positively correlated with arousal to pornography but negatively correlated with beliefs that pornography should be allowed. However, their study does not show whether strong sexual drive precedes authoritarianism, or follows from it. Whether or not

Adolf Hitler is perhaps the single most glaring example of authoritarianism in our time.

there is any genetic basis for authoritarianism (perhaps through an influence on sex drive) has not been investigated.

Is authoritarianism adaptive or maladaptive? In the short run, high authoritarianism helps a person get along in a rigid society. In the long run, however, high authoritarianism may bring an entire society to ruin. Adorno et al. thus regard authoritarianism as unequivocally bad, despite the occasional advantage it may confer to the individual.

Field Dependence

The personality dimension of **field dependence/independence** is "the degree to which people function autonomously of the world around them" (Goodenough, 1978, p. 165). At one end of the dimension is the field independent person, who uses internal frames of reference to interpret incoming information. At the other end is the field dependent person, who uses external frames of reference to interpret the world.

Field dependence and independence are conceived in extremely broad terms, and are thought to affect not only perception, but also intellectual, social, and cultural matters. This dimension does not, however, lend itself easily to a bad versus good interpretation; depending on the situation, both field dependence and field independence have assets and drawbacks.

Interest in field dependence arose from studies by Herman Witkin (1949) of how people use cues to perceive what is upright in space. He investigated situations where different types of cues conflicted. Usually, we rely on some combination of visual cues (horizontal or vertical lines) and bodily cues (the pull of gravity) to tell us which way is up, and it doesn't matter which cues we use since they agree. But what happens when they disagree, when what we see doesn't jibe with what we feel?

Researchers use an apparatus which may be familiar to you if you have taken a course in the experimental psychology of perception. The Tilting-Room–Tilting-Chair Test is a device well-explained by its name. A subject sits in a chair which tilts from a horizontal position; the chair is in a room which also tilts from a horizontal position. The subject is asked to move the chair so that it is upright. Does she use an external frame of reference (position of the room) or an internal frame of reference (bodily sensations)?

Witkin and his colleagues (1954) discovered that subjects differed with respect to the cues they habitually employed. The individual difference of field dependence/independence was thus defined, and simpler ways of measuring the trait were developed. Today one of the simplest is the Embedded Figures Test, a puzzle where "hidden" designs must be located (see Figure 9-1). The quicker and more accurately someone can find the designs, the more field independent she is.

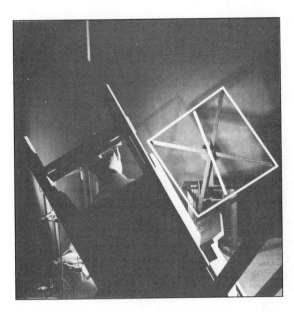

Field dependence/independence can be measured with the Tilting-Room–Tilting-Chair Test.

Studies find that field dependence/independence relates to social inter-action. The field dependent person, for instance, is more likely to rely on others for guidance in ambiguous situations (Culver, Cohen, Silverman, & Shmavonian, 1964), to base judgments on the opinions of others (Oltman, Goodenough, Witkin, Freedman, & Friedman, 1975), to attend to social stim-uli (Nevill, 1974), to disclose personal information (Berry & Annis, 1974), and to be popular (Oltman et al., 1975).

Goodenough points to child-rearing practices for the origins of this trait:

> The evidence supports the common sense hypothesis that when socialization practices encourage separation from parental control, then development pro-ceeds toward great field independence. However, when the course of develop-ment is either governed by a tightly organized, strictly enforced set of rules and prescriptions for behavior, or when parental nurturing and protective functions inhibit separation, then greater field dependence ensues. (1978, p. 195)

His comments are consistent with the finding that men in our society tend to be more field independent than women, perhaps because boys are more frequently encouraged to separate from their families than are girls. Field dependence/independence may also have a genetic basis (Vandenberg, 1962), but this has not been well-documented.

Researchers have also compared the field dependence/independence of people in different cultures (Goodenough, 1978). Societies like the Eskimo of Baffin Island tend to have members who are field independent, while those like the Temne of Sierra Leone tend to have members who are field dependent

Figure 9-1

Embedded Figures Test

An Embedded Square.
Find the square (a) that is camouflaged in the coffeepot (b). The solution is shaded in (c).

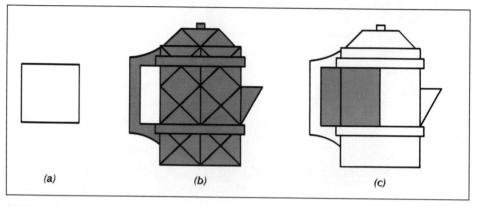

(a)   (b)   (c)

SOURCE: page 175 in D. R. Goodenough. Field dependence. In H. London & J. E. Exner (Eds.), *Dimensions of personality.* Copyright © 1978. Reprinted by permission of John Wiley & Sons, Inc. New York.

(Berry, 1966). This difference maps neatly into the characters of the two societies. The Eskimo are migratory, with little social organization or political authority, and the Temne are sedentary, with intricate social and political stratification. Clearly, field dependence and field independence are useful traits for members of these respective cultures.

Introversion-Extraversion

This personality dimension plays a role in many formulations. The *introvert* is quiet, retiring, and reflective, while the *extravert* is sociable, outgoing, and impulsive. **Introversion-extraversion** is usually measured with questions like those described earlier in this chapter, although Wilson (1978) reports an alternative measure of dropping lemon juice on a subject's tongue and measuring how much saliva is produced! Saliva increase is substantially correlated with introversion as measured by questionnaire ($r = .70$), a finding that supports Eysenck's physiological interpretation of introverts as over-aroused and easily stimulated.

Since introversion-extraversion reflects general levels of arousal, this trait pertains to adaptation in a number of ways. For instance, introverts have a lower pain threshold than extraverts (Eysenck, 1971), which means that aversive stimuli have a greater impact on them. Imagine the innumerable situations that people will seek out (or avoid) granted a particular pain threshold

(Geen, 1984). If people can match their chronic arousal to the demands of a particular setting, they'll adapt quite well. Otherwise, they'll be in trouble. Following this line of reasoning, researchers find that extraverts outperform introverts as salesmen and personnel directors, while introverts outperform extraverts in more solitary professions. Furthermore, extraverts are more likely to wind up in prison, to get venereal disease, and to change jobs frequently (Wilson, 1978).

According to researchers, introversion-extraversion reflects more of a hereditary influence than most personality characteristics studied to date (Wilson, 1978). This should not be surprising, since this personality dimension includes the genetically based temperaments—excitability, activity, and sociability—studied by Buss and Plomin (1975, 1984).

Interestingly, there is a hint that identical twins raised apart are even *more* similar with respect to introversion-extraversion than those raised together (Shields, 1976). Stop for a minute and think about this. It implies both genetic influence (to account for the overall similarity between twins) and environmental influence (to account for the difference between those raised together and those raised apart).

Both introverts and extraverts are capable of success in our society—witness the varied (but also similar) careers of Michael Jackson and David Lee Roth.

Repression-Sensitization

As I discussed in Chapter 5, defense mechanisms are the strategies people deploy against psychological threats. We can distinguish between two general types of strategies. Defenses like denial let the individual escape anxiety by burying his head in the sand and not consciously acknowledging the threat. In contrast, defenses like intellectualization let the individual avoid anxiety by acknowledging threat and "thinking away" its danger. Do these two types of defense mechanisms represent the extremes of a personality dimension?

Theorists speculated that individuals habitually use repressing versus sensitizing strategies in response to anxiety. And so the trait of **repression-sensitization** was created. Byrne (1961) developed a questionnaire measure of this dimension by choosing items from the Minnesota Multiphasic Personality Inventory (MMPI; Hathaway & McKinley, 1943) that reflected repressing versus sensitizing defenses. Some of the items from Byrne's scale are:

Read each statement and decide whether it is true as applied to you or false as applied to you.

1. I wake up fresh and rested most mornings.
2. Most of the time I feel blue.
3. When I leave home I do not worry about whether the door is locked and the windows closed.
4. Bad words, often terrible words, come into my mind and I cannot get rid of them.

The repression-sensitization scale is read so that high scores indicate sensitization. So, agreement with statements 2 and 4 count toward a high score, as does disagreement with statements 1 and 3.

Byrne (1961, 1964, Bell & Byrne, 1978) describes validity evidence for the repression-sensitization scale. For instance, in studies like those described in Chapter 5 investigating the role of the unconscious, repressors are more likely to show perceptual defense, while sensitizers are more likely to show perceptual vigilance. When repressors and sensitizers are put in stressful situations, repressors show greater physiological arousal than sensitizers, presumably because the anxiety repressed from their consciousness shows itself physiologically. And repressors apparently dream more than sensitizers (since they have more repressed material to surface in their dreams). Repressors fail to acknowledge hostility and aggression on the part of themselves and others, and the same is true when it comes to sexual impulses. And they are less likely to get the point of a dirty joke.

These findings make it sound like sensitization is more desirable than repression. This is not always so. Contrary to psychoanalytic theory's position that repression is immature, under some circumstances, the healthiest reaction to threat is *not* to face reality, to engage in **positive denial** (Lazarus, 1979). To expect things to work out well, even in the face of evidence that they may not, sets into motion processses that work against the odds. For instance, studies of how patients respond to serious illness show that immediate denial is healthy, since the patients can then face their crisis slowly. Hackett and Cassem (1974) find that early denial after a heart attack decreases the risk of death.

Byrne believes that people attain their habitual degree of repression-sensitization by virtue of how they were raised. Repressors and their parents report that child-rearing occurred in an affectionate, accepting, and warm atmosphere, while sensitizers and their families report abundant stress, unhappiness, and criticism. What do we make of these findings? On the one hand, since most of these studies rely on subject report, it isn't surprising that repressors paint a rosy picture, while sensitizers highlight what is wrong. This is the very essence of the trait.

On the other hand, if these results are valid, psychoanalytic theorists must drastically reinterpret psychological health and illness. If we assume that affectionate and warm families produce psychologically healthy kids, and that repression is one of the personality characteristics of these kids, then perhaps we should stop thinking of repression as something undesirable. Why not relabel it as optimism (see, for example, Scheier & Carver, 1985)?

Self-esteem

Another personality dimension that has attracted a great deal of attention is **self-esteem:** the degree to which a person has high regard for himself. Self-esteem is associated with a host of desirable outcomes. It is measured with questionnaires like the Coopersmith (1967) Self-Esteem Inventory. Here are some sample questions:

> For each of the following items, please indicate whether it is generally true for you ("like me") or generally false for you ("unlike me").
>
> like me   unlike me   1. I often wish I were someone else.
> like me   unlike me   2. I'm a lot of fun to be with.
> like me   unlike me   3. I get easily upset at home.
> like me   unlike me   4. I'm popular with people my own age.

High self-esteem is indicated by "like me" responses to questions 2 and 4 and by "unlike me" responses to questions 1 and 3.

Here is how Singer (1984) summarizes the results of research with elementary school children:

> Children characterized as high in self-esteem are more active, more expressive, and more confident than children scoring at either low or moderate levels. They

are better at assessing their own or others' abilities, more successful in school-work, social, and athletic activities; more creative and less willing to be influenced in their judgments by pressure from authorities. They also show more curiosity and exploratory behavior. By contrast, children who score low on a measure of self-esteem are more socially isolated, physically weaker and incapable of defending themselves, more fearful in interpersonal encounters and more preoccupied with "inner" problems. (pp. 266–267)

No wonder books urging you to be your own best friend are best sellers. A person benefits from high self-regard. These benefits then heighten self-esteem even further. On the dark side, low self-esteem can also become a self-fulfilling prophecy. A person with a poor opinion of himself eventually gets others to agree with him (for example, Coates & Wortman, 1980). Most theorists believe that self-esteem results from our actual successes and failures, as well as from the way friends and family treat us (Sears, 1970). Also important are a person's accomplishments relative to his or her peers (Marsh & Parker, 1984).

Sensation Seeking

This personality dimension grew out of research looking at the effects of **sensory deprivation** (Zuckerman, 1974, 1978, 1985). What happens when people are placed for some period of time in situations with minimal stimulation? This question has practical implications (for example, anticipating the consequences of prolonged spaceflight) as well as theoretical importance. Psychoanalysis and certain versions of learning theory propose that people seek out quiescence; however, results from sensory deprivation experiments show that "quiescence" can be extremely disconcerting. It produces anxiety, hallucinations, and delusions.

Theorists have therefore suggested that people have optimal levels of arousal and stimulation. Sensory deprivation is unpleasant because it brings people below these optimal levels. Marvin Zuckerman (1969a, 1969b) further suggests that these levels are stable and general individual differences. Since some people have higher optimal levels than others, they are more likely to seek out stimulation from the environment. These people are high on the trait with Zuckerman (1978) calls **sensation seeking**, measured with questions like these:

Each of the items below contains two choices, A and B. Please indicate which of the choices most describes your likes or the way you feel.

1. A. I dislike the sensations one gets when flying.
    B. I enjoy many of the rides in amusement parks.
2. A. I can't wait to get into the indoors on a cold day.
    B. I am invigorated by a brisk, cold day.

3. A.   I often wish I could be a mountain climber.
   B.   I can't understand people who risk their necks climbing mountains.
4. A.   I dislike all body odors.
   B.   I like some of the earthy body smells.

In each case, it is obvious which response alternative counts toward a high sensation-seeking score.

Considerable evidence has been gathered in support of Zuckerman's original notion that sensation seeking is a general trait. Here are some of the behaviors with which sensation-seeking scores are correlated: quantity and variety of sexual activity; drug use; cigarette smoking; preference for spicy, sour, and/or crunchy foods; gambling; skydiving; volunteering for unusual psychology experiments (like studies of hypnosis); preference for complex designs; and tolerance for primary process thinking (Zuckerman, 1978).

How does sensation seeking relate to adjustment? Again, the particular setting must be taken into account. People low in sensation seeking are fearful in novel or dangerous settings (Mellstrom, Cicala, & Zuckerman, 1976), while those high in sensation seeking are bored and restless in bland or confining situations (Zuckerman, 1974). At either extreme, sensation seeking is associated with psychopathology. Some evidence exists showing that psychopaths are particularly high sensation seekers, while schizophrenics are particularly low (Zuckerman, 1978).

The sensation seeking individual is always on the look-out for a new challenge.

Zuckerman believes that sensation seeking has a substantial genetic basis. Twin studies support this notion (for example, Fulker, Eysenck, & Zuckerman, 1980). In his most recent investigations of the origin of sensation seeking, Zuckerman (1985) looks at biological correlates of the trait to discover just how genetic determination of sensation seeking occurs. Studies point to the involvement of the neural enzyme monoamine oxidase (MAO). Sensation seeking is negatively correlated with MAO levels (Schooler, Zahn, Murphy, & Buchsbaum, 1978). What does this mean? The function of MAO is to reduce the level of such neurotransmitters as norepinephrine, dopamine, and serotonin. High levels of these neurotransmitters in turn are associated with reduced activity and arousal. So, the sensation-seeking individual may be biologically predisposed to activity and arousal. Note the similarity between Zuckerman's notion of sensation seeking and Eysenck's notion of extraversion.

Type A Behavior Pattern

The final personality dimension I'll describe is not yet regarded as a personality trait, although research findings are nudging it in that direction. The **Type A behavior pattern** arose from epidemiological findings linking certain ways of behaving to increased risk of cardiac disease (Friedman & Rosenman, 1974). As originally formulated, the Type A individual is "aggressively involved in a chronic, incessant struggle to achieve more and more in less and less time, and if required to do so, against the opposing efforts of other things or other persons" (p. 67). Someone without these characteristics is termed a Type B.

These contrasting ways of behaving have attracted the attention of medical and psychological researchers. In the last decade, two interesting trends have come about (Matthews, 1982). First, the correlation between Type A behaviors and heart disease—although still positive—is becoming smaller in magnitude. Second, the characterization of Type A's in psychological terms is becoming richer in detail.

The first trend may reflect an enlightenment effect; individuals at risk for heart problems because of their behavior are taking compensatory steps (more frequent visits to physicians, exercise, and so on.) Particularly in view of the first, the second trend means that the Type A behavior pattern will become the province not of the physician but of the personality psychologist. The effect of this change in ownership will be a move from the mere description of Type A as a complex of behaviors to the explanation of these behaviors in terms of an underlying trait.

In the original epidemiological research, Type A or Type B was ascertained by a structured interview. But current researchers use one of several self-report questionnaires like the Jenkins Activity Schedule (JAS; Jenkins, Rosenman, & Zyzanski, 1974). Here are some representative items:

For each question, choose the answer that is true for you.

1. Do you ever have trouble finding time to get your hair cut or styled?
   a. never
   b. occasionally
   c. almost always

2. Has your spouse or a friend ever told you that you eat too fast?
   a. yes, often
   b. yes, once or twice
   c. no, never

3. When you listen to someone talking, and this person takes too long to come to the point, how often do you feel like hurrying the person along?
   a. frequently
   b. occasionally
   c. almost never

4. How is your temper nowadays?
   a. fiery and hard to control
   b. strong but controllable
   c. no problem
   d. I almost never get angry

The JAS is scored so that high scores indicate Type A behaviors. Scores are used to assign subjects to categories: Type A or Type B or an in-between category called Type X. If the coronary-prone behavior pattern becomes a full-blown personality trait, we can expect future researchers to use JAS scores to define a dimension, not just discrete types.

Matthews (1982) has summarized what we know about individuals who score high on the JAS. They are

vigorous achievement strivers, who can be aggressive and competitive; they also show some indication of cardiovascular changes during difficult and moderately competitive events. (p. 304)

In other words, the Type A individual creates for herself both good and bad outcomes. The good outcomes result from perseverance in the face of fatigue and frustration: academic and athletic honors, career advancement, high salary (Glass, 1977). The bad outcomes include increased risk for disease as well as strained relationships with others, who are apt to be put off by the incessant striving of the Type A individual (Van Egeren, 1979).

The origin of Type A behavior has been conceived in psychological terms. Individuals encouraged to excel at activities with no clear standard of evaluation come to show Type A behavior (Matthews, 1982). Suppose a child is encouraged to "work harder than anyone else." She will never know for sure

Type A individuals are time-urgent, competitive, and often aggressive in the face of
frustration.

whether she has achieved this goal, so she constantly redoubles her efforts.
See how this becomes a vicious circle, like a puppy chasing its own tail?

Future research will explore the possibility that Type A behavior has not
only biological consequences but also biological antecedents. Also, a better
picture of Type B individuals is needed. Researchers regard these people as
those who do not show Type A behaviors, but there is more to their personalities than what they do not do. Ordinary language gives us terms like mellow
and laid-back. But what behaviors do these terms describe?

Evaluation

I've reviewed research approaches and findings for ten personality traits. I
might have considered additional dimensions of personality (indeed, see
Chapter 12), but these ten are certainly among the most interesting and best
investigated. And conclusions and criticisms concerning these traits apply to
research for other traits as well.

On the positive side, research findings leave me convinced that individual
differences in personality can be defined and measured. Many of these differences are associated with good and bad adjustment in the world. We know
something about their origins. In general terms, then, at least part of the
vision of Gordon Allport has been achieved. On the negative side, research

findings leave me convinced that we are nowhere near a fully satisfactory trait approach to personality. A number of important questions remain unanswered.

First, one more time—what are the basic ways in which people differ? Personality inventories like Cattell's 16PF, Eysenck's Personality Inventory, or the MMPI purport to encompass the basic individual differences, but I remain skeptical. As I noted in the last chapter, theorists like Cattell and Eysenck disagree about the basic factors of personality. Further, as this section shows, different dimensions of personality require different strategies of assessment. Personality inventories measure all traits with the same questionnaire format, and so they preclude important dimensions. The trait paradigm awaits consensus on the range of basic individual differences (Guilford, 1975).

Second, how are the dimensions which have been identified related to each other? Some of the ten traits I have described overlap. What is the significance of correlations between—let us say—achievement motivation and extraversion? Is one characteristic derived from the other? Do both reflect a more basic trait? Research doesn't tell us, because most investigations which correlate one trait measure with another do so to establish *disciminant* validity. The focus has been on what is different rather than on what is the same.

Third, in their concern with function and dysfunction, have trait researchers neglected neutral traits in favor of those with value-laden end points? Further, is it any coincidence that the "desirable" ends of these personality dimensions describe the personalities of upper-middle-class university professors? Subtle bias is introduced when characteristics are termed authoritarianism, field independence, androgyny, introversion, and self-esteem rather than firmness, autism, sex-role inconsistency, social withdrawal, and conceit (respectively).

Fourth, what is the exact process by which a given individual difference originates and develops? It is important to know that a personality trait does or does not show a genetic influence, and that certain family practices are more apt to produce certain characteristics than others, but research has been rough-grained. Can it really be that low authoritarianism, high androgyny, low anxiety, high repression, and high self-esteem are all produced by the Cleaver family? Prospective studies are needed to see exactly what occurs within families to produce individual differences. We also need more thinking along the lines of Eysenck to specify the physiological mechanisms responsible for the heritability of personality characteristics.

Fifth, in assuming that traits are biologically based, have researchers looked past the contribution of cultural factors? Personality psychologists do not analyze individual differences as a function of group membership other than gender. But surely our social class, occupation, ethnic group, and religious affiliation have some effect on who we are. But these classifications do not map into biological factors, and they have therefore been neglected. A mature trait theory would ground individual differences in a particular culture and historical period. If nothing else, this allows for a better perspective on the adaptive value of particular traits. More profoundly, it might allow the discovery that some individual differences are universal (field dependence/independence for example) and others culturally bound (androgyny for example).

Sixth, are traits the best way to conceive individual differences? Most of the research I've described focuses on the individual to the exclusion of the setting. Perhaps individual differences reflect consistencies in a person's environment more than the manifestation of inherent personality traits. This of course is the essence of Mischel's (1968) criticism of the trait paradigm and his reconceptualization of personality. The next section considers his arguments in detail.

MISCHEL'S CRITIQUE: BEHAVIOR IS NOT CONSISTENT

So far I've been describing typical trait research, and the results suggest the utility of this approach to personality psychology. But as I have emphasized, important questions remain. The most basic is whether or not traits exist. To a large degree, this question is not asked within the trait paradigm, since the existence of traits is a bedrock assumption of the paradigm.

However, the question can be phrased in such a way that the results of trait research bear on its answer. This is what Walter Mischel (1968) does in his book *Personality and Assessment.* Here is his argument: *if traits exist, then the thoughts, feelings, and actions which reflect a given trait should be highly correlated across different situations.*

This question is not exactly the one asked by researchers whose studies I described in the previous section. These investigators looked at the antecedents and consequences of a particular trait, or—more exactly—of a measure of a particular trait (usually a self-report questionnaire). They are interested in whether or not relationships exist. Mischel asks instead about the size of these relationships. You should recognize the debate here as disagreement about how to evaluate correlation coefficients: in terms of their statistical significance or in terms of their absolute magnitude (see Chapter 2). Needless to say, if behaviors supposedly reflecting a particular trait are not consistent, then the entire trait paradigm is called into question.

Although trait consistency per se has not been a major focus of trait research, over the years a number of studies have investigated the topic, and

Mischel surveyed these studies in his book. Let's consider the investigation by Hartshorne and May (1928) of cross-situation consistency in children's moral conduct. In different situations where one could lie, cheat, or steal, is there evidence of a general trait of honesty versus dishonesty? Would one group of kids transgress at every opportunity, and another group of kids hold themselves in check? Or would the conduct of the kids in one situation be unrelated to their conduct in another?

Using common sense as well as prominent personality theories (like Freud's or Maslow's or Cattell's), we would expect substantial consistency: evidence for the presumed trait of honesty. However, this is not what Hartshorne and May found. They observed thousands of kids when at home, the classroom, parties, sports events, and so on. Moral conduct was not highly consistent. What children did in one situation correlated no higher than $r = .30$ with what they did in another situation. These correlations exceed what would be expected by chance, but Mischel claims that they are surprisingly small granted the pronouncements of common sense and personality theory.

Further, as situations became more dissimilar, correlations decreased. For instance, measures of deceit within the classroom correlated on the average $r = .26$ with each other, but only $r = .17$ with measures of deceit outside the classroom. Mischel uses these findings to argue that the situation is of paramount importance in explaining moral conduct. The "trait" of honesty is superfluous to the explanation of actual behavior.

What other "traits" does Mischel include in his indictment? According to the investigations he reviewed, *any trait that pertains to attitudes toward others, sexual identification, dependency, aggression, rigidity, avoidance, and conditionability is suspect* since there is little evidence that behaviors reflecting these individual differences are consistent. Appreciate that this list is not an arbitrary set of human characteristics; it includes notions that reside at the core of the major psychoanalytic and trait theories.

Mischel makes some exceptions. *Behaviors reflecting "intelligence"* are relatively general across situations and stable across time; *achievement strivings* show consistency as well; and diverse behaviors reflecting *field dependence/independence* correlate as highly as $r = .50$. But according to Mischel, these are the exceptions rather than the rule. Further, unlike other individual differences, these traits are explicitly defined with respect to the setting. Their consistency therefore results from the similarity of these situations.

Mischel addresses the results of trait research programs:

> Some research programs have carefully investigated particular theoretical constructs, like anxiety . . . conditionability . . . extraversion-introversion . . . or achievement motivation. . . . The results provide some evidence for the research value of the construct. These construct validity studies often have theoretical interest. . . . [However] definitive interpretations are complicated by the fact that generally the intercorrelations among variables depend on numerous other

moderating considerations. . . . Moreover, impressive external correlates usually are not found. (1968, pp. 99–100)

Mischel concludes that these traits are not useful to the psychologist who
wishes to describe or change the individual. (You might recognize that this
criticism of nomothetic traits echoes that of Allport.)

If one is to question the utility of traits to personality psychology, one
must answer two important counterarguments. First, *if traits are useless concepts, then what is it that trait research has been looking at for the last fifty
years?* Second, *if traits have no basis in people's behavior, then why do so
many personality psychologists and ordinary people believe they exist?*

In the remainder of *Personality and Assessment,* Mischel (1968) answers
these questions. To explain what trait research has actually investigated over
the years, he makes the valid point that much of this research employs self-
report questionnaires. This procedure is open to confounds (see, for example, Nicholls, Licht, & Pearl, 1982). Mischel argues that many of these confounds have not been ruled out, and that "trait" research may be questionnaire research in the most trivial sense:

> Typical of the fate of . . . personality measures is the fact that . . . [they are]
> most strongly correlated with other paper-and-pencil measures, but much less
> systematically associated with nonquestionnaire measures. . . . Indeed, the phrase
> "personality coefficient" might be coined to describe the correlation between
> .20 and .30 which is found persistently when virtually any personality dimension
> inferred from a questionnaire is related to almost any conceivable external cri-
> terion involving responses sampled in a *different* medium—that is, not by another
> questionnaire. (1968, p. 77)

So, Mischel states that typical trait research is based on a flimsy foundation
of response sets, low correlations, and confounds.

Turning to why so many mistakenly believe that traits exist, Mischel argues
that "consistency" exists largely in the eye of the beholder. In other words,
*our preconception that people have traits encourages us to see their behavior
as more consistent than it really is.* We may bring to bear on our observations
all sorts of biases that lead to the "construction" of consistency and the mistaken conclusion that people have traits.

A study by Chapman and Chapman (1969) is illustrative. These researchers showed subjects a series of responses to different Rorschach cards supposedly made by psychiatric patients. The subjects also saw the diagnosis of
each patient. The responses and diagnoses were arranged so that they showed
no relationship to each other: they were uncorrelated. However, when subjects
were asked to report on relationships present in the series of cards, most
affirmed that they saw strong correlations. So, a diagnosis of homosexuality
was seen as associated with Rorschach responses mentioning rear ends. What's

going on here? Chapman and Chapman (1969) term the phenomenon of "seeing" nonexistent relationships consistent with stereotypes **illusory correlation.** Mischel argues that illusory correlation and similar biases are responsible for the widespread belief in traits.

If you believe your best friend is competitive, you *interpret* many of her behaviors to reflect this trait, even though another person assigns quite different meanings to what she does. You *notice* her competitive acts more than her cooperative ones: "There she goes again." You *remember* instances of her competitiveness better than her other behaviors.

Mischel closes *Personality and Assessment* with a call for personality psychology to throw out the outmoded approach of the trait paradigm: "This conceptualization of man, besides being philosophically unappetizing, is contradicted by massive experimental data" (p. 301). In its place, he calls for a psychology of personality based on learning theory, one that reflects the sensitivity of behavior to the situation.

Mischel's arguments stimulated so many reactions within the trait paradigm that he is today regarded as responsible for a renaissance in personality research (West, 1983). Before I describe these research reactions, let me make some general points that blunt Mischel's criticisms.

First, in his 1968 book, he is careful to say that some traits—like field dependence/independence—are supported by the evidence. Many who read Mischel hear stronger claims than he actually makes.

Second, he does not deny that behavior is consistent across situations, or that personality questionnaires predict what people do. In both cases, correlations of $r = .30$ are found, and these exceed what we would expect by chance. So, Burton (1963) did a factor analysis of Hartshorne and May's (1928) original data and found evidence for one general factor: honesty versus dishonesty.

Mischel's argument is that the typical correlations are too small to be of any practical value. However, far smaller correlations are taken seriously in medical research, meteorology, economic planning, election forecasting, genetic counselling, parole decisions, and so on. The absolute magnitude of a correlation coefficient is tricky to evaluate in cases where it is not .00 or 1.00. Mischel dismisses the $r = .30$ typical of trait research much too glibly.

The issue of "how big" a correlation coefficient must be before one takes it seriously has been addressed by several researchers. Robert Rosenthal and Donald Rubin (1982) observe that correlation coefficients are difficult to interpret because their values are not intuitive. What does a correlation coefficient of $r = .30$ mean in everyday life? Here's an interesting answer that Rosenthal and Rubin provide. Suppose you are seriously ill and have a 65 percent chance of dying. A medical treatment is available that will reduce your chance of dying to 35 percent. Would you be interested in receiving the treatment? Of course you would, so appreciate that if the relationship here between treatment (or no treatment) and your chances of living (or dying) were expressed as a correlation coefficient instead of percentages, the absolute magnitude would be exactly $r = .30$! Is this too small to take seriously?

Another perspective on interpreting the absolute magnitude of correlation coefficients is provided by David Funder and Daniel Ozer (1983). They start with Mischel's assertion that situations have a greater impact on behavior than do personality traits. What is the evidence for this claim? Usually it is not specifically tested. Instead, a researcher shows that a trait measure correlates .30 with some behavior; then she observes that this doesn't seem like a strong relationship; and finally she concludes that situations are overwhelmingly important. On the face of it, this seems like okay logic, since what is not due to traits must be due to situations.

Right? Wrong—there is also random variation in behavior associated with neither traits nor situations. Maybe the research subjects have the flu. Maybe the measures are unreliable. Regardless, if one wishes to say that situations are more important than traits, one must explicitly look at how strongly each is related to behavior.

We already know that the correlation between traits and behaviors is $r = .30$. So how strongly are situations correlated with behaviors? This statistic is usually not calculated by experimental psychologists, the researchers who study the impact of situations on behaviors. Instead, experimentalists are interested in the statistical significance of their findings.

It is an easy matter, though, to express the strength of situational effects in terms of correlation coefficients. This is exactly what Funder and Ozer (1983) do, computing the correlations between situational factors and behaviors for such well-known experiments as the investigation of destructive obedience by Milgram (see Chapter 1) and the study of bystander apathy by Darley and Latané (see Chapter 7). Guess what? These barely exceed .30, essentially the same as the typical correlation between traits and behaviors!

A third point I wish to make about Mischel's argument is that it is unclear which trait theory or theories Mischel attacks in his book (see, for example, Eysenck, 1982; Hogan, deSoto, & Solano, 1977; Pervin, 1985). With the possible exception of early personality typologies like the humoral theory, none of the trait theories reviewed in Chapter 8 make the bold claim that people will act the same regardless of the situation. Yet this is the hypothesis Mischel evaluates in *Personality and Assessment*.

Fourth, Mischel by and large ignores research bearing on the biological and genetic basis of personality, an important aspect of the trait paradigm. It is difficult to dismiss the results of twin studies like those conducted by Buss and Plomin (1984) as due to response sets or illusory correlations. Interestingly, Hartshorne and May (1928) report that measures of dishonesty correlate between siblings, even if they are orphans. From the same data used by Mischel to argue against traits, Hartshorne and May conclude that a hereditary factor is present!

REACTIONS TO MISCHEL'S CRITIQUE

Despite these qualifications of Mischel's conclusions, his criticisms had great impact. Personality psychologists at first ignored *Personality and Assessment,* but other psychologists read the book and took seriously its criticisms of the trait paradigm. So, in response to the growing belief (among these other psychologists) that personality was a dying field, trait researchers undertook various lines of research designed to show that personality concepts were indeed sensible.

Trait Stability

One of the first reactions to the charges against traits was the mustering of evidence showing that measures of traits are highly stable over time. Personality characteristics we show when young are those we show when old. Consider this well-known description of personality stability from a lecture by William James:

> Already at the age of twenty-five you see the professional mannerism settling down on the young commercial traveller, on the young doctor, or the young minister, on the young counsellor-at-law. You see the little lines of cleavage running through the character, the tricks of thought, the prejudices, the ways of the "shop" . . . from which the man can by-and-by no more escape than his coat-sleeve can suddenly fall into a new set of folds. On the whole, it is best that he should not escape. It is well for the world that in most of us, by the age of thirty, the character has set like plaster, and will never soften again. (1890, p. 121)

Research reviewed by Hogan et al. (1977), Conley (1984a), Pervin (1985), and others show that a variety of individual differences stay much the same over decades: temperament, vocational interests, achievement, neuroticism, psychopathology, anti-social behavior, sex-role adherence, expressiveness, moral conduct, introversion-extraversion, aggression, altruism, and so on.

One of the most impressive demonstrations of personality consistency across the life-span is by Jack Block (1971). In his research, Block surmounted a procedural problem that plagues longitudinal research: personality measures valid for one age group are inappropriate for another age group. There are aggressive children and aggressive adults, for instance, but the behaviors reflecting aggressiveness differ. If this is the case, how can we ascertain correlations over time? Giving subjects the identical tests or questionnaires is silly. Small correlations will perhaps reflect lack of trait consistency, but they could also result from noncomparable measures.

Block's solution is ingenious. Approximately 170 individuals were studied as early adolescents, late adolescents, and adults: a period spanning almost thirty years. At each stage in life, extensive information about each subject was gathered: from interviews, objective tests, reports of others, school and work records, and so on. (Note the similarity between this procedure and George Vaillant's natural history approach described in Chapter 5). Clinical psychologists then read through each subject's material at each stage in life. They judged the relative importance or unimportance to the subject's personality of a standard set of trait descriptions: for example, is a talkative individual; tends to be self-defensive; is calm, relaxed in manner. So, the raw data available at different points in life differed, but they were used to make ratings with respect to the same personality characteristics.

This procedure is called a **Q-Sort,** and it is a compromise between nomothetic and idiographic personality assessment. The same set of traits is used for all subjects (nomothetic procedure), but the salience of traits for a given subject is ascertained by comparing it to his or her other traits (idiographic procedure). In Block's research, different judges rated a subject's personality at different points in time, thus precluding illusory correlation.

Personality consistency is ascertained by seeing if traits salient (or nonsalient) for an individual at Time One remain salient (or nonsalient) at Time Two. Although his findings are complex, Block reports that a number of traits are stable over years:

> The unity or consistency of personality is compellingly apparent in these data and is manifest in so many and diverse ways as perhaps to establish the unity principle once and for all. Personality coherency has always been assumed by personologists because it *must* be assumed. But the empirical support for this proposition has appeared to be weak or contrary . . . vigorous arguments against the very *idea* of personality consistency have been mounted.
>
> I view the sets of empirical relationships . . . as sufficient proof for the principle of personality consistency. (1971, p. 268)

For instance, among the traits studied by Block are **ego-control** and **ego-resiliency.** The former trait is the degree to which people can control their impulses. Someone high in this trait can eat just one potato chip. The latter trait is the degree to which people are flexible in response to environmental demands. Someone high in this trait can eat one million potato chips if no other food is available, while refraining altogether under other circumstances. These traits show impressive stability throughout childhood and into adult life (see, for example, Funder, Block, & Block, 1983). They relate to a variety of behaviors and characteristics, like delay of gratification, irritability, attentiveness, and aggression.

Do you see how Mischel could answer these findings? He does not deny the reality of individual differences—he takes issue with their interpretation in terms of traits. According to Mischel, people are consistent to the degree that the situations where they find themselves are consistent. I bet that the subjects studied by Block and other longitudinal researchers stayed within characteristic settings across the life-span. The stability of their "personality" may reflect the stability of the context in which their behavior occurred. Angry young men become angry old men not because they have a trait of anger but because they hang out in places that elicit and reward expressions of anger.

The Act-Frequency Approach

One of the problems with the studies reviewed in *Personality and Assessment* is that many arrived at the specific behaviors assumed to reflect particular traits in an unsystematic fashion. It simply seemed to the researcher that these sorts of behaviors reflect this sort of trait. But says who? There should be a less arbitrary way of deciding which behaviors reflect which traits. Psychologists David Buss and Kenneth Craik (1984) give us this procedure in their **act-frequency approach.**

Buss and Craik start by assuming that personality dispositions summarize the general thrust of a person's thoughts, feelings, and actions. Stanley is bold to the degree that he thinks bold thoughts, experiences bold feelings, and performs bold deeds. Although Stanley occasionally acts like a wimp, bold is a reasonable summary of his behavior. Dispositions are ascertained by counting the number of pertinent acts occurring within a certain time limit.

The first task of the personality psychologist is therefore to ascertain which acts map into which dispositions. Following this, several other questions can be answered. Among the most important is which acts are central to a trait and which are more peripheral? Or, using the terms of Chapter 1, which acts are good examples of a trait and which are poor examples?

Here is an example of how Buss and Craik proceed in characterizing a disposition. They solicit nominations of acts that exemplify a particular trait by asking a large number of individuals to

> think of the three most extraverted males (or females) you know. With these individuals in mind, write down five acts or behaviors they have performed that reflect or exemplify their extraversion.

Nominated acts are combined until they have a list of approximately one hundred acts for the disposition of extraversion. Other individuals judge each of these acts in terms of how good or poor an example it is of the trait in question. Table 9-1 presents some examples.

Table 9-1

Extraverted Acts

I told several jokes in a row.

I got people together to play a sport.

I addressed a group of people.

I went to a bar to socialize.

I threw a big party.

I sang loudly in the street.

I organized a group gathering.

SOURCE: From Buss & Craik, 1984.

A particular person is assigned an extraversion score according to how many of the extraverted acts he or she performs in a given time period: two weeks, four weeks, and so on. Ideally, scoring constantly monitors what a person does, but Buss and Craik have so far been unable to surmount the technical difficulties involved. Instead, research subjects are asked to rate the frequency of their acts retrospectively. These ratings are then checked against comparable ratings by friends and relatives, and agreement has been substantial.

Buss and Craik have investigated such dispositions as extraversion, introversion, dominance, submission, quarrelsomeness, agreeableness, gregariousness, and aloofness. They have established that these dispositions are composed differently. Some dispositions (like agreeableness) have highly prototypical acts, while others (like aloofness) do not.

What is the relevance of this approach to Mischel's critique of personality traits? Buss and Craik (1984) find that prototypic acts (with respect to a particular trait) are more consistent than other acts. Further, prototypic acts correlate more highly with personality questionnaires. In these cases, the $r = .30$ "limit" is exceeded. Perhaps the studies reviewed by Mischel (1968) were unfair tests of personality consistency because they only assessed peripheral acts.

Of course, the act-frequency approach is not foolproof. The frequency of acts exemplifying dispositions is not the only parameter. Indeed, frequency of acts may be irrelevant in attributing certain dispositions. How many people must someone kill to be considered murderous? Is Charley Manson eight times as murderous as Sirhan Sirhan? Is John Gacy five times as murderous as Charley Manson?

Also, some dispositions are defined by things that a person does not do. Buss and Craik acknowledge that their approach is biased towards acts of commission rather than omission. Judges had difficulty nominating representative acts for aloofness, since an aloof person is mostly refraining from acts that a non-aloof person performs. The act-frequency approach seems incapable of studying many of the dispositions of concern to psychoanalytic theory, an account of personality based in large part on what people do not do.

Finally, there are practical problems with the act-frequency approach. It is only as useful as the assessment of act frequency. Retrospective measurement is subject to bias and distortion. And a given act reflects more than one disposition. Suppose you punch out your boss and walk off your job. How are these acts to be apportioned among the various personality traits they reflect?

Buss and Craik are aware of the difficulties in implementing the act-frequency approach to personality dispositions, and, for the moment at least, we should regard their strategy as preliminary but promising. The approach offers a sophisticated way to think about traits and their relationship to behavior, improving upon previous approaches because it tells the researcher which behaviors reflect which traits. Such information is obviously an important prerequisite for investigation of trait consistency.

The Modified Idiographic Approach

Gordon Allport anticipated the possibility that individuals don't act consistently across situations. It was for this reason that he did not regard common traits as the main units of personality. In contrast, the research reviewed by Walter Mischel (1968) was exclusively concerned with common traits—personality dimensions along which all subjects can be placed. Allport would not be surprised at the results of Mischel's review; in fact, some of the studies which figured prominently in Mischel's negative view were cited by Allport (1937, 1961) in his own books.

But as you recall, Allport did not discard traits in light of these studies. Instead, he proposed that different traits apply to different people: people are consistent across situations only with respect to their personal dispositions, which are different than those of someone else. But Allport's call for an idiographic approach to personality went unanswered because research procedures for idiographic assessment were not available.

In 1974, Daryl Bem and Andrea Allen resurrected Allport's ideas to champion the commonsense belief in behavior consistency. Bem and Allen suggested that for any given trait, some people are more consistent with respect to it than other people. In other words, the degree that a trait is relevant to behavior is an individual difference. They argued that "one simply cannot, in principle, ever do any better than predicting some of the people some of the time" (p. 512). But this ain't bad relative to Mischel's view of the matter.

How do you identify those people who are consistent or inconsistent with respect to a given trait? Here is what Bem and Allen do: they ask their research subjects how consistent versus inconsistent they are. This approach seems simple, but it is an important approximation to Allport's goal of idiographic assessment, a step taken some four decades after Allport's (1937) call for the study of personal traits.

Bem and Allen describe the hypotheses of their research in the following way:

> Individuals who identify themselves as consistent on a particular trait dimension will in fact be more consistent cross-situationally than those who identify themselves as highly variable. . . . The cross-situational correlation coefficient of the self-identified low-variability group should be significantly higher than the coefficients of the high-variability group. . . . We tested this hypothesis twice on the same population of subjects, using two orthogonal personality traits, friendliness and conscientiousness. (1974, p. 512)

The same sixty-four college students were asked to rate "How much do you vary from one situation to another in how friendly and outgoing you are?" The same rating was made with respect to conscientiousness.

Friendly (or unfriendly) behavior was assessed in six different ways, including reports by self and others and observations. Conscientious (or non-conscientious) behavior was assessed in seven different ways. To test their predictions, Bem and Allen divided their sample in two at the midpoint of self-rated consistency with respect to friendliness, and then calculated correlations between measures of friendly behavior for the two groups. In the consistent group, correlations averaged $r = .57$, while in the inconsistent group, they averaged $r = .27$. So, Mischel's .30 personality coefficient can be exceeded if the researcher limits her attention to subjects for whom the trait in question is more of a personal disposition.

The results for conscientiousness were not so straightforward, but they are informative. When subjects were divided into two groups on the basis of self-rated consistency or inconsistency, and intercorrelations computed among measures of conscientiousness within these two groups, the findings for friendliness were *not* replicated. However, further information available to Bem and Allen revealed that the subjects did not agree with them regarding the behaviors reflecting conscientiousness. For instance, Bem and Allen used neatness and cleanliness of one's hair as an index of conscientiousness, an interpretation at odds with the subjects. Failure to replicate the friendliness findings is not so surprising. More generally, personality researchers need to check *their* assumptions that behaviors reflecting particular traits have the same meaning for their research subjects.

Kenrick and Stringfield (1980) used the approach of Bem and Allen to investigate consistency of Cattell's sixteen source traits. Research subjects used 7-point scales to describe themselves with respect to each of these traits (see Chapter 8). For each of the subjects, one of their parents and one of their friends used the same scales to describe the subject. Subjects also rated how consistent or inconsistent they were with respect to each trait, and were asked to nominate their single most consistent trait. Finally, Kenrick and Stringfield further refined Bem and Allen's approach by asking subjects to rate the degree that their behavior with respect to each trait was publicly observable. The thinking here is that some people might be consistently anxious, for instance, but hold this in check, preventing the observer from seeing the "true" consistency.

Results strongly confirmed the findings of Bem and Allen. When self-, parent-, and peer-ratings were intercorrelated, they averaged only $r = .25$. (There's that limit again.) But when analyses were limited to the most consistent trait, average intercorrelations increased to $r = .61$. And when analyses were further limited to the most consistent traits that were also high in observability, correlations entered the $r = .7$ to $.9$ range.

The **modified idiographic approach** pioneered by Bem and Allen (1974) is noteworthy. However, criticism is not lacking (see, for example, Chaplin & Goldberg, 1984). Mischel and Peake (1982), for instance, repeated the original study with another group of subjects, assessing conscientiousness in the same way as Bem and Allen. They also extended the original study by including additional measures of conscientiousness. Results were confusing. If you recall, a number of Bem and Allen's measures were based on observer ratings. When Mischel and Peake looked at agreement among raters for consistent versus inconsistent subjects, correlations were much higher for consistent subjects than for inconsistent subjects. But when they looked at consistency among behaviors, correlations were uniformly low regardless of the subject's consistency or inconsistency.

Mischel and Peake (1982) explain these results by suggesting that global ratings are distorted. Suppose Joey regards himself as consistently belligerent. His friends and family are aware of this self-definition and come to accept it. So, all parties involved agree when asked to rate how belligerent Joey is. But this is not the same thing as showing that Joey actually behaves in a belligerent fashion. Mischel and Peake argue that he probably does not. Bem and Allen's (1974) research is thus dismissed.

Or is it? Bem (1983) rebutted the Mischel and Peake (1982) article (see also Conley, 1984b; Epstein, 1983b; Funder, 1983; Jackson & Paunonen, 1985). Perhaps Mischel and Peake chose inappropriate behaviors. Remember that Bem and Allen (1974) also ran into trouble when they studied conscientiousness. Subjects' beliefs about what constitutes conscientious behavior differs not just from those of the experimenter but also from each other. Perhaps conscientiousness fails to be a personal disposition for anyone.

A study by Amabile and Kabat (1982) bears directly on the argument by Mischel and Peake that global ratings are distorted by self-definition, and it suggests that their argument is wrong. In this experiment, subjects saw a videotape of another person. Manipulated in the videotape were both self-definition (as an introvert or extravert) and actual behaviors (reflecting introversion or extraversion). Although both self-definition and behavior influenced the subjects' global ratings, when these conflicted, subjects paid more attention to the behaviors. In other words, "actions speak louder than words" because global ratings reflect actual behavior more than self-definition.

The Aggregation Approach

Seymour Epstein (1979) also takes issue with Mischel, proposing that we can predict "most of the people much of the time" if we take the simple but painstaking step of improving the reliability of the way we measure behaviors reflecting traits. Epstein observes that many studies assess single behaviors in several settings and then look at their correlation. The correlation will often be low.

What would happen if a researcher asked students in a math class to work one long division problem, and then followed them into an English class and asked them to conjugate one verb. If students were scored as right versus wrong at each of these tasks, would these scores correlate highly? Would they correlate highly with an intelligence test?

Of course not, since any given behavior—even if it reflects the individual difference of interest, be it intelligence, conscientiousness, or friendliness—has innumerable determinants. It is only when we look across a variety of behaviors that we see convergence. Level of mathematical ability becomes evident when students work many long division problems over many days in many courses. Verbal competence similarly shows its characteristic level only in repeated instances. Summary measures of the two correlate appreciably, and both in turn correlate with intelligence tests.

Can the personality researcher apply the same mentality to the issue of personality consistency? They do so routinely when they create questionnaires; all have multiple items. They do not do so when they study actual behavior. In his research program, Epstein demonstrates the benefits of multiple assessment of behavior. He calls his strategy one of **aggregation.** Epstein obtains repeated measures of behavior across different days. Scores on any two days may not be appreciably correlated, but scores over seven days or fourteen days or longer cohere. Averages computed across the days correlate highly with questionnaire measures of the traits these behaviors presumably reflect (Epstein, 1979). The $r = .30$ limit is often exceeded.

For instance, Epstein (1979) asked subjects to make daily ratings of their spontaneity, outgoing feelings, and number of social contacts they initiated.

Averages across fourteen days correlated $r = .45$, $r = .47$, and $r = .52$ with Eysenck's questionnaire measure of extraversion, respectively. Since one expects an extravert to be spontaneous, outgoing, and social, these findings make a strong case for the utility of trait concepts.

Is there anything about Epstein's aggregation approach we can criticize? In his original demonstrations, two considerations got in the way of the strongest possible answer to Mischel. First, as the last example illustrated, Epstein relied a great deal on ratings by subjects; as you well know, these ratings are not the same thing as the behaviors they attempt to summarize. Second, Epstein used data regarding stability over time to make conclusions about generality across situations (Mischel & Peake, 1982).

However, Epstein's (1984) more recent studies correct these flaws. Objectively measured behavior shows substantial coherence if aggregated over a sufficient number of instances and a sufficient number of situations. And psychologists are increasingly aware that aggregation improves their ability to predict behavior (Rushton, Brainerd, & Pressley, 1983). Aggregation is now a standard tool of the personality researcher (see, for example, Woodruffe, 1984). However, as Epstein (1984) notes, all of this attention is welcome but somewhat ironic since the approach began with Henry Murray's (1938) *Explorations in Personality*. What was the diagnostic council if not a procedure for aggregating vast amounts of information about people's behavior?

The Interactionist Approach

A final reaction to Mischel's criticism of traits is one which integrates both trait approaches and situation approaches to personality. This position proposes that both the person and the situation are critical in determining behavior. One popular version of this position holds that it is the **interaction** between a person and his environment that is important to understanding what he does.

Interaction here is used in a particular sense. Suppose we have two people: a prototypic extravert and a prototypic introvert. Suppose we have two situations: a crowded party and a quiet library. And suppose we are interested in studying happiness. Can we say who is happier: the extravert or the introvert? Not unless we know the setting they are in. Can we say which setting is more likely to lead to happiness? Not unless we know which person is in the particular setting. This is what is meant by an interaction between person and situation. The effect of an individual difference depends on the setting; the effect of the setting depends on the individual difference (see Figure 9-2).

The call for personality psychologists to study interactions of this type was raised by several people following the appearance of Mischel's *Personality and Assessment*, most notably by Kenneth Bowers (1973), Bo Ekehammar (1974), and Norman Endler and David Magnusson (1976a, 1976b). There is

Figure 9-2

Person-Situation Interaction

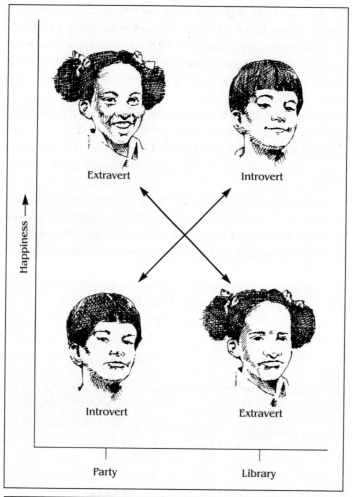

nothing new in suggesting that personality psychology should study the person in the situation. In the 1930s, Kurt Lewin stressed that the field can go awry in two ways: by making statements about types of people without reference to settings and by making statements about types of settings without reference to people. Allport, Murray, Maslow, Cattell, and others had similar views, despite their interest in individual differences. All said that the relevance of any particular personality characteristic depends on the situation.

But like many theoretical insights, the importance of interactions was not translated into actual research practice until years later (Magnusson & Endler,

1977). Then an explosion of studies appeared demonstrating that such interactions were indeed important. Most had a similar research design. Subjects
were recruited and given a personality test. On the basis of their test scores,
they were divided into two groups: high and low with respect to some trait
(achievement motivation, androgyny, anxiety, and so on). They were then
randomly assigned to one of two experimental treatments, chosen because
the researcher believed the factor distinguishing the two treatments would
interact with the personality trait under study. An appropriate behavior was
assessed for all subjects.

Bowers (1973) summarized a number of such studies, the consistent
finding being that interactions were important in explaining the observed
behavior. Consideration of just the personality trait or just the experimental
manipulation didn't account for behavior, since the results of these studies
took the form depicted in Figure 9-2.

So what? According to the interactionist approach, people are consistent,
although consistency isn't in their literal behavior. Rather, it resides in the
process of how they respond to situations. Traits are important inasmuch as
they determine this process. But they are not useful for predicting behavior
in the absence of information about situations.

When the modern interactionist approach took shape in the 1970s, there
was a tendency to regard the person-situation interaction in monolithic terms:
all interactions were regarded as equally important and powerful in determining behavior. But recent extensions regard interactions with increasing
sophistication. So, one line of research finds that some settings are more apt
to interact with personality dimensions than are others. A highly constrained
environment, one with strong pressures to behave in certain ways, does not
allow a trait to manifest itself (see, for example, Monson, Hesley, & Chernick,
1982; Price & Bouffard, 1974; Schutte, Kenrick, & Sadalla, 1985). One of the
things that funerals and final examinations have in common is highly uniform
behavior on the part of the people present. The trait researchers would have
little to study at such events. However, other settings allow more variability
in behavior, and consistent individual differences are evident.

For instance, Epstein (1983a) studies the relationship between personality traits and the behavior of people in a threatening situation: their first
parachute jump. Correlation coefficients go sky-high, so to speak. But when
the analogous study is conducted in a laboratory using a different threatening
circumstance (an anticipated electric shock), the link between traits and
behaviors is not nearly so robust.

Another line of research finds that some types of people are more apt to
be influenced by situations than are others. Whether or not someone is well-
described by simple trait notions, by simple situationalist notions, or by interactions may be an individual difference! Mark Snyder (1983), for example, studies a personality characteristic called **self-monitoring.** High self-monitors

Sid has less need than most to know exactly
where he's going.

SOURCE: "The Neighborhood" cartoon by Jerry Van Amerongen is reproduced with special permission of King Features Syndicate, Inc.

guide their behavior by attending to situational feedback about how appropriate that behavior is, and then modifying how they act. Low self-monitors
guide their behavior by attending to inner states and feelings. I suspect Miss
Manners and Billy Carter live at opposite ends of this dimension. At any rate,
Snyder finds that high self-monitors do not act consistently across situations
(since they are responsive to particular demands within each), while low self-
monitors act consistently (since they are oblivious to situational demands).

Yet another spin-off of the interactionist perspective is that of Daryl Bem
and David Funder (1978), who chide researchers for neglecting the "personality" of situations. What? A given setting can be described in terms of the
characteristic behaviors shown by people within it. If these characteristic
behaviors are phrased in trait language, then it is possible to assess the fit
between actual people and actual situations. When the fit is good (that is,
when the personality of the person is similar to the personality of the situation), then the person behaves in typical fashion there—consistently with her
traits. When the fit is poor, she will act inconsistently with her traits. However,
this does not mean that traits do not exist, only that the setting in question

is a poor one in which to look for trait-relevant behavior of that person. A favorite theme in books and movies places a good old boy in the company of stuffed-shirts amid grand surroundings. In the story, the protagonist triumphs by remaining himself. In real life, he probably does not behave like he used to down on the farm.

Bem and Funder (1978) demonstrate these arguments in several studies using Q-sort procedures to describe both people and situations in the same trait terms. Prediction of behavior was greatly enhanced when people were matched to situations instead of mismatched.

A corollary of this matching notion is that behavior will be consistent across two situations to the degree that the situations are perceived to be similar. Lord (1982) demonstrates this for behaviors reflecting the trait of conscientiousness. The more similar a person regarded two situations (via a Q-Sort), the more likely he is to behave consistently in them.

Finally, one more version of the interactionist approach investigates the degree that people select and create their own environments (for example, Buss, 1984; Snyder & Gangestad, 1982). Decades ago, Gordon Allport proposed that people consistently seek out some settings rather than others (see Wachtel, 1973). Once they are in these settings, the pattern of rewards and punishments determines exactly what they do. These behaviors in turn affect future choices of settings. And so on.

For instance, one of my central dispositions is my sweet tooth. If cookies (Rich'n'Chips) or candy (Peanut M & M's) are in my apartment, I cannot resist eating them. But I am not obese (yet). Why is this? Because I have learned not to take enough money to the grocery store to buy cookies and candy. Temptation seems easier to avoid than to resist.

Is my behavior better described in terms of traits or situations? Both person-oriented and situation-oriented approaches to personality are relevant, depending on the aspect of the process under scrutiny. In fact, Walter Mischel's (1973, 1977, 1979, 1984, 1986) more recent statements about personality endorse the bidirectional influence of person and situation (see Chapter 11). As you can see, the interactionist approach strikes many as a compelling perspective.

CONCLUSIONS: TRAIT THEORIES IN LIGHT OF THE RESEARCH

As the Grateful Dead said, "What a long, strange trip it's been"—from the theories covered in Chapter 8 through the research described here in Chapter 9. Sophisticated accounts of personality stressing individual differences gave rise to simplistic research which gave rise to criticisms which gave rise to conclusions that we need sophisticated accounts of personality stressing individual differences! Maddi (1984) notes the wry fact that "despite Allport's (1937, 1961) outspoken criticism of common trait theorizing . . . in many textbooks . . . [he is] ironically criticized with his own criticisms" (p. 12). With any luck you won't leave this chapter with this mistaken view of Allport and the other theorists who work within the trait paradigm.

Allport stresses the importance of the situation by defining personal dispositions in terms of their ability to render different settings the same. (Doesn't this sound like Bem and Funder's matching approach?) Murray and Maslow approach personality in terms of needs, so of course the situation is important to behavior. The situation determines whether a given need is satisfied or not. Hungry people eventually stop eating. High-achievers eventually take a break from the rat race (or die trying).

Mischel's (1968) critique applies to typical trait research, not typical trait theory. Even staunch defenders of the trait paradigm admit that much research is "mindless" (Hogan, deSoto, & Solano, 1977). The culprit is the ubiquitous questionnaire, which lets the researcher study "personality" and "behavior" without seeing research subjects do anything more than fill out computer-scored answer sheets.

Here are some of my conclusions about trait theories in light of the research—both good and bad. First, results underscore the importance of individual differences. These differences are often stable, often consistent, and often related to adaptation. Second, results also underscore the importance of the setting where behavior occurs. In particular, the consistency (or inconsistency) of individual differences cannot be understood unless situational factors are simultaneously on focus. Current researchers have developed a variety of procedures for accomplishing this. Third, the general thrust of trait theories is supported by research (although no particular theory is supported over any other). In a recent comment, Walter Mischel draws similar conclusions:

> What is *not* at issue? No one questions that psychology journals are full of significant correlations among personality measures. No one suggests that behavior is entirely situation-specific. . . . Obviously people have characteristics, and overall "average" differences in behavior between individuals can be abstracted on many dimensions and used to discriminate among persons for many purposes. Obviously, knowing how a person behaved before can and does help predict how he or she will behave again. Obviously, the impact of any event depends on the organism that experiences it. . . . There is now abundant evidence that threads of coherence and continuity characterize human development even over long periods of time. (1984, p. 278)

Still, I suspect the most important research within the trait paradigm has yet to be conducted.

Here are my ideas about a future research agenda for the trait paradigm. Researchers should start by burning all but a few of the questionnaires typically used to measure "traits" of personality. They should go out into the world and observe what people do and the circumstances in which they do them. Additionally, researchers can ask friends and family members to report what people are all about. Observer ratings fell out of favor in the wake of Mischel's (1968) criticisms, but recent studies suggest that procedures relying on knowledgeable informants are both reliable and valid (Funder, 1983; Moskowitz & Schwarz, 1982). Following Cattell and Eysenck's earlier example, these researchers should then look for the range and structure of individual differences in behavior (instead of questionnaire responses). Using some variant of the act-frequency approach, they should map traits and behaviors into each other. (The exact equation will probably vary with the setting.)

Then, trait research should begin in earnest. Issues of stability, change, consistency, and person-environment fit can be studied much more definitively with respect to behavior than with respect to questionnaire responses. Contributions of biology and socialization can be specified more exactly. Understanding of adaptation can be advanced more certainly.

Actually, researchers already know how to do all this. The best research within the trait paradigm (that on achievement motivation, androgyny, anxiety, and so on) has always supplemented questionnaires with other assessment procedures, has always studied behavior in settings where the individual difference of concern is highly pertinent, and has always acknowledged the complexity of the subject matter. When mindless research is eradicated, the trait paradigm will remain, more viable than ever.

SUMMARY

I described trait research in this chapter, beginning with a discussion of the rationale behind the use of questionnaires to study individual differences and the problems inherent in this strategy. I then described research concerning ten individual differences: **achievement motivation, androgyny, anxiety, authoritarianism, field dependence/independence, introversion-extraversion, repression-sensitization, self-esteem, sensation seeking,** and **Type A behavior pattern.** In each case I asked how is the trait measured, how is it related to adaptation, how does it originate?

The next section shifted gears, looking in detail at Walter Mischel's 1968 book *Personality and Assessment* and his conclusion that trait conceptions of personality are of little use since people do not behave consistently across situations. This criticism stimulated studies of trait stability over time as well as a great deal of research into issues of behavioral consistency: the **act-frequency approach,** the **modified idiographic approach,** the **aggregation approach,** and the **interactionist approach.** I concluded that consistency indeed exists, but it is complicated and affected by a variety of factors, the most important of which is the nature of the situations where behaviors occur.

This conclusion is ironic, since it was the starting point of Gordon Allport and other early theorists within the trait paradigm. Trait research has gone the long way around the barn, but perhaps this was necessary. Research sophistication now matches theory sophistication, and, I predict, the most intriguing trait research still lies ahead.

10

TRAIT PARADIGM: APPLICATIONS

*D*o you have a number two pencil?

We all know what follows this question: more questions, to be answered by filling in little circles on a computer-scored answer sheet. Right now, you run across such tests mainly in the classroom, but you won't leave them behind when you finish school. You'll be asked about that number two pencil for the rest of your life.

Many of the questionnaires you'll complete will be measures of individual differences: abilities, opinions, interests, values, needs, and so on. These individual differences are examples of personality as viewed from the trait paradigm. Not surprisingly, then, the purpose of questionnaire measures is to decide about your fitness relative to that of others.

We can recognize applications within the trait paradigm by their concern with individual differences, with assessment, and with function or dysfunction. Many such applications exist within our contemporary world, and I'll survey some of the more intriguing ones in this chapter. First, though, let me make some general comments.

In Chapter 7, I described applications within the psychoanalytic paradigm, pointing out that most focused on the sexual aspect of psychoanalytic theory and were thus out-of-touch with research findings. Applications within the trait paradigm are different. In one important way, these applications converge with contemporary research results: they usually recognize that behavior is not highly consistent across situations. If a measure of an individual difference is to be useful in predicting success or failure, then the measure needs to be specific. To the degree that an application stays within a specific domain of behavior, it is likely to be sensible: predicting typing performance from a typing test for example. To the degree that it generalizes wildly across situations, it is likely to be silly: predicting managerial skill from a golf score. (Don't think this isn't done by some people with the utmost of sincerity!)

Here's another general point. As you are well aware, the ethics of psychological tests are often questioned. Since important decisions are based upon test results, it is not uncommon to scrutinize the whole endeavor. Tests and the use of tests are obviously unethical when the measures are invalid. But, the deeper issue involves measures that are only somewhat valid.

Validity is not an all-or-none thing, since it is usually judged by patterns of correlation coefficients. Values other than the extremes, or absolute zero, are difficult to interpret. After reading Chapter 9, you can imagine that most applied measures of individual differences "work" after a fashion. Mischel's (1968) personality coefficient of $r = .30$ shows up in applied domains as well.

So what? Well, these measures are valid for nomothetic purposes: for making generalizations about people. But they are not as valid for idiographic purposes: for making specific statements about Peter, Paul, or Mary. Because no test correlates 1.00 with what it is predicting, mistakes are inevitable. While society as a whole may be satisfied that medical school admissions tests see to it that doctors tend to be pretty smart, you or I would not be satisfied if the test results said no to the application of a good friend, whom we *know* to be more intelligent than many doctors.

Another problem is that tests can become self-fulfilling prophecies. Suppose we want to use a personality test to determine if someone should be allowed to drive an automobile. The ideal way to do this would be to gather hundreds of sixteen-year-olds who don't know how to drive a car and administer all sorts of questionnaires to them. Then we would give them cars and let them drive for a few years. At the end of this period, if they (and we) are still alive, we would see who had good or bad driving records. Then we would look at the questionnaires and see if any of their answers discriminate the good from the bad drivers. If so, we have a valid test.

But this isn't how it's done. Society can't allow all potential drivers behind the wheel in order to develop a procedure that determines who should not be allowed there in the first place. And the same holds for would-be doctors, lawyers, policemen, and soldiers. What happens in actuality is that psychologists work backwards: how do people who are already driving, doctoring, or lawyering respond to questionnaires? Their answers are used to choose future drivers, doctors, and lawyers.

This strategy differs from the first. It perpetuates the status quo. It has to, since the past determines the future. The potential harm is that the measures may not have as much to do with their stated purpose as they should.

Consequently, a refinement of this strategy is often followed. See what responses determine great drivers from good drivers, great doctors from good doctors, and so on. Then compare these responses with those of people to be screened. This strategy has its merits, but it is based on the fine distinction between what it means to be great versus what it means to be good. The finer the distinction, the more difficult is it for a test to be reliable and valid in making it.

Think about cooking. Good cooks are different from bad cooks because they know how to follow a recipe. But a great cook departs from a recipe. If we studied just good cooks and great cooks, we would see if a potential cook departs from a recipe. Then we would hire a lot of cooks who do not follow recipes to work in our restaurant chain. And we would go broke.

The trait paradigm encourages us to think in terms of single dimensions. We rank order everything, and believe our rank reflects a pervasive and eternal dimension. No wonder we are so perplexed when rankings fall apart. Why can't a sports team win year after year? Why isn't this beautiful person a brilliant worker?

Some critics argue that psychological tests should be abandoned. Tests work for individuals and the society only by perpetuating the status quo. But we are not likely to see an end to testing. People will, however, be more cautious in using them. In some professional schools, tests are *not* required anymore, and "truth in testing" laws have been passed requiring the details of tests used to screen individuals for work and school to be made public (Bersoff, 1981).

Within psychology, principles for the ethical use of tests are widely available (London & Bray, 1980). Here, for example, is Principle 8 of the American Psychological Association's (1981) "Ethical Principles of Psychologists":

Assessment Techniques. In the development, publication, and utilization of psychological assessment techniques, psychologists make every effort to promote the welfare and best interests of the client. They guard against the misuse of assessment results. They respect the client's right to know the results, the interpretations made, and the bases for their conclusions and recommendations.

Principle 8 goes on to say

Psychologists respect the right of clients to have a full explanation of the nature and purpose of the techniques in language that the client can understand, unless an explicit exception to this right has been agreed upon in advance. . . .

In reporting assessment results, psychologists indicate any reservations regarding validity or reliability because of the circumstances of the assessment or the inappropriateness of the norms for the person tested. . . .

Psychologists recognize that assessment results may become obsolete. They make every effort to avoid and prevent the misuse of obsolete measures.

These principles reflect the opinion that tests are neither fair nor unfair. How people use them makes tests reasonable or unreasonable.

Another point is that employers, teachers, and others charged with making decisions about people indeed make judgments about personality. The issue is not whether they will do this, but rather how. Should they rely on their intuitions or on psychological tests? I think you can see that the alternative to psychological testing has its own problems.

In the following sections, keep these ethical issues in mind. How many applications within the trait paradigm adhere to Principle 8? Also keep in mind the relationship of application to theory and research. Applications are based on acceptance of a paradigm; they do not question its key assumptions. As a result, applications may not be scrutinized as Principle 8 mandates.

PSYCHODIAGNOSIS: IDENTIFYING PEOPLE'S PROBLEMS

Intelligence testing is the most popular application of the individual differences approach. I've scattered so many ideas about intelligence testing throughout the book that I won't give it a separate section here. Rather, I'll describe the second most popular application within the trait paradigm: the use of psychological tests to diagnose abnormality.

The first clinical psychologists did not do psychotherapy. Instead, they gathered information to help psychiatrists identify a patient's particular problem and plan the best way to treat it. They observed, interviewed, and gave psychological tests. In fact, one of the first questionnaires ever developed— the Personal Data Sheet of Woodworth (1919)—was devised to screen neurotic men from military service during World War I. Although the role of the modern clinical psychologist is much more varied, **psychodiagnosis** in general and psychological testing in particular remain central activities.

Korchin and Schuldberg (1981) distinguish two general approaches to psychodiagnosis. The first they call **personological assessment;** its "primary purpose is to describe the particular individual in as full, multifaceted, and multilevel a way as possible" (p. 1147). The second approach is **psychometric assessment** which emphasizes carefully developed questionnaires that place people along a well-defined continuum. "Objectivity is sought both in the acts required of the client and the examiner; judgment and inference are minimized. . . . Test reliability and validity . . . are of central importance" (p. 1148). (You may recognize that this contrast reflects the more general debate of idiographic versus nomothetic goals.)

As examples of these respective approaches, consider the Rorschach and the MMPI. Some clinical psychologists prefer the Rorschach because it reveals rich information about the person responding to it. I once administered the ten inkblots of this test to a young man who carefully looked at not just the front of each card, where the inkblot is printed, but also at the back of the card (blank except for a copyright in the corner). He also inspected the edges! I trust you'll agree that my characterization of him as suspicious seems reasonable.

At the same time, the Rorschach is easy to criticize on the grounds of poor reliability and validity (Anastasi, 1982). Different psychologists arrive at highly discrepant diagnoses of the same individual. And the diagnoses suggested by the Rorschach don't always relate to other information about the individual. Remember the "illusory correlation" study described in the last chapter? Chapman and Chapman (1969) did not arbitrarily choose the Rorschach for this research. They wanted to make a point about the invalidity of this projective test.

Other clinical psychologists prefer the MMPI because of its objectivity. The MMPI was developed through a procedure of criterion validation. It includes only questions that have in the past distinguished groups of individuals with a given psychiatric diagnosis (for example, depression, schizophrenia, hysteria) from "normal" individuals not under a doctor's care. Depending on the way the MMPI is scored, there are about a dozen different scales (Butcher & Keller, 1984). A person who responds to the MMPI receives a profile of scores along these scales.

The MMPI has been administered to hundreds of thousands of individuals, in over ninety foreign language translations, and there is extensive information about the range of scores and the behaviors that correlate with them. The MMPI is frequently scored in a mechanical fashion, using what is known as a **cookbook approach.** If a person has a certain profile (scores above cutoffs on particular scales, and below cutoffs on other scales), then a given diagnosis and treatment recommendation can be found in a book. (And since we live in the 1980s, we can now read them directly off a computer printout.)

Critics of the MMPI acknowledge its objectivity and usefulness in making broad generalizations about people, but they point to its inability to speak to the concrete individual. After all, the patient involved is a single person. Thus, an idiographic approach is needed.

The personological and psychometric traditions came into sharp conflict when psychologist Paul Meehl (1954) produced strong evidence that clinical intuition was less accurate in predicting individual behavior than cookbook formulas. Granted certain information about a patient, how best to combine it in order to predict his future behavior? If we have Rorschach responses and/ or MMPI profiles, what is the best way to use this information to predict that patient Jones will profit from group therapy, will have a fist-fight with an orderly, or will pay his bills on time?

Meehl argues that the clinician who mulls over the available information and makes his best prediction will consistently do worse than someone who mechanically predicts that patient Jones will act the same as other people with similar Rorschach responses and/or MMPI profiles have acted in the past. Knowing this patient as a "person" is not as helpful as knowing about patients in general.

Needless to say, Meehl's argument in favor of statistical prediction raised controversy (see, for example, Holt, 1970). Was he saying that clinical psychologists were useless? Not exactly, since clinicians have to decide what information to gather in the first place (Meehl, 1957). But he was saying that the personological approach to psychodiagnosis failed by its own test: making predictions about the individual.

I wonder if idiographic approaches to psychodiagnosis would be resurrected if Bem and Allen's (1974) strategy of dividing subjects into consistent versus inconsistent groups was extended to clinical assessment. By this logic, we would make predictions based on information only about consistent individual differences. While we might still use a cookbook in making treatment recommendations, different patients would warrant different recipes.

Finally, let's look at two future trends in psychodiagnosis. First, clinical psychologists are turning from personality-like tests to actual observations of behavior (Korchin & Schuldberg, 1981). **Behavioral assessment,** as this strategy is known, is a reaction to the same misgivings with trait conceptions of personality that Walter Mischel (1968) expressed.

In behavioral assessment, the clinician describes what a person actually does and the circumstances where he behaves in that particular way (Goldfried & Kent, 1972). Treatment recommendations are presumably based less on inference than with traditional assessment. So, one strength of behavioral assessment is its recognition of the situation in which behavior occurs.

A second trend in psychodiagnosis was set into operation by the American Psychiatric Association's (1980) third revision of their diagnostic manual: DSM-III. If you have taken a course in abnormal psychology, you know that previous versions of this widely used catalog of disorders embody psychoanalytic notions of abnormality and describe problems in terms of underlying mental processes and states. These processes and states were inferred from what the patient did. A reasonable way to accomplish this goal was with psychological tests.

However, DSM-III is not strongly committed to Freudian dynamics. Problems are more often defined in behavioral terms. A depressed person is not someone who has turned anger inward, but rather someone who shows sadness, appetite disturbance, and low self-esteem. Diagnosis using DSM-III categories requires less inference and more observation. This means that the traditional tests of clinical psychologists are less relevant to the contemporary needs of the mental health profession.

PERSONALITY DISORDERS

Nowadays typologies reside mainly in casual gossip ("people like that can't be trusted") or in the history of personality psychology ("the four humours"). But typologies are also alive and well in the psychiatric notion of a personality disorder. **Personality disorders** are based on these assumptions:

1. There exist types of people.

2. Some types are inherently dysfunctional. That is, these individuals experience chronic distress and consistently show impairment in their work and relations with other fellows.

3. Each type predisposes a more severe psychopathology; under stress, a person with a personality disorder breaks in a particular way.

4. These types of people are set in their ways early in life through some interplay of biological and environmental factors. However, the biological factors are emphasized.

5. Mental health professionals regard these people as poor clients, because they resist change.

You can see how personality disorders are particularly good examples of the trait paradigm.

Personality disorders also exemplify what is wrong with the trait paradigm. Not all mental health professionals recognize the existence of personality disorders, pointing to problems with the concept. First, the entire notion ignores the social and cultural context in which people live. Second, psychiatry rarely agrees about the basic types of people. Throughout the years, drastic revisions in the catalog of personality disorders have been the rule, not the exception. Third, the evidence that personality disorders lead to particular psychopathologies is mostly negative. Fourth, the belief that someone with a personality disorder resists therapeutic change may be a self-fulfilling prophecy. (The label may reflect the therapist's frustration and inadvertently be used to rationalize half-hearted attempts at future therapy).

DSM-III describes eleven personality disorders. Where did the ideas for these particular origins come from? Their sources are varied, echoing the diversity of the origins of personality traits themselves. One source of particular personality disorders is—quite bluntly—confusion. The *borderline personality disorder* arose from the observation that some patients appeared psychotic (out of touch with reality) part of the time and neurotic (too much in touch with reality) at other times (Gunderson & Singer, 1975). How do you classify people who fall at the metaphorical border between psychosis and neurosis? Call them borderline personality disorders.

A second inspiration for particular personality disorders has been clinical experience. If therapists stumble across certain types of people frequently enough, they assume something basic is going on. The notion of *antisocial personality disorder* originated this way. Some people are just no damn good. (As you will see, the antisocial personality disorder is the best-supported "type" among all those described by DSM-III.)

A third suggestion for disorders, and the most popular, is some theory used to deduce basic types of deficient personalities. So, Hirt (1902) used the typology of humours to explain why different people are more likely to have one form of psychopathology than another; humoral imbalance predisposes particular problems:

Phlegmatic	→ Morbid Apathy	→ Process Schizophrenia
Sanguine	→ Excitability	→ Hysteria
Choleric	→ Suspicion	→ Paranoid Schizophrenia
Melancholic	→ Pessimism	→ Depression

With such a variety of sources of personality disorders, no wonder the endeavor is chaotic.

Psychologist Theodore Millon (1981) brings some order to the personality disorders described in DSM-III by classifying them into three clusters. Cluster One is made up of people who are dramatic, emotional, and erratic: soap opera characters.

The **histrionic personality disorder** applies to a person who is melodramatic and intense. "You won't believe what just happened to me!" This person incessantly draws attention to himself, craves excitement, overreacts to minor events, and throws tantrums.

The **narcissistic personality disorder** takes its name from the mythological character who fell in love with his own reflection. "I've talked enough about myself. Why don't you talk about me now?" A person with this disorder has an overblown sense of self-worth.

The **antisocial personality disorder** describes people who can't get along with others. In adolescence, it shows itself as truancy, delinquency, persistent lying, vandalism, promiscuity, and fighting. "Smoking in the boys room," plus a whole lot more. As adults, these people fail to meet obligations as workers, spouses, parents, or citizens. They get themselves (and others) into trouble.

The final personality disorder in the soap opera cluster is the **borderline personality disorder,** which has already been mentioned. Borderline individuals are unpredictable, unstable, and intense. They act in self-dam-aging ways—overdoing sex, gambling, and shopping. They cannot tolerate being alone, but their relationships with others are volatile and ambivalent. Once I was the therapist of a man who fit this characterization. In our first few meetings, he praised me to my face and behind my back (so I heard). Then one day I told him about a clinic procedure that he didn't like; all of a sudden I was the world's worst therapist and prototypic scum (so he said).

Millon (1981) identifies Cluster Two of personality disorders as those people who are chronically anxious and fearful: cartoon characters, shy wood-land creatures who lurk in the corners hoping no one will notice them.

People with an **avoidant personality disorder** are so sensitive to rejec-tion that they beat others to the punch. They refuse to enter relationships without guarantees. Before a first date, they want to know about a second date; they may even want to choose names for the children. Avoidant person-alities want acceptance but tend not to find it. As you might imagine, their self-esteem is low.

A **dependent personality disorder** refers to people who let others run their lives for them. Other people make their decisions. They subordinate their own needs: "No that's okay. I don't mind going to a restaurant that specializes in prime rib. Sure, I'm a vegetarian, but I can eat the crackers."

Compulsive personality disorders are perfectionists who insist that others submit to them. I work with some people like this. I let them do every-thing from the start, since they always end up doing everything anyway. According to DSM-III, to warrant this label, a person must additionally show an inability to express feelings and have an excessive devotion to work. "Oh you know Mabel, she's married to the job."

The final personality disorder in this cluster is the **passive-aggressive individual,** who resists the social and occupational demands in a variety of indirect ways. He procrastinates, dawdles, and forgets. He is intentionally inefficient. "But you told me to call you if the hot water line broke. This is the *cold* water line! I just did what you told me to do." Hostility is at the root of this person's ineffective passivity.

Cluster Three describes personality disorders characterized by oddness and eccentricity. These people are weird, and others feel uncomfortable around them.

Someone with a **paranoid personality disorder** lives a life of suspicion and mistrust. He is always looking for trickery on the part of others, and he continually questions the loyalty of friends and family members. He is secre-tive, overly jealous, and quick to take offense.

The **schizoid personality disorder** describes someone who is cold and aloof. She is indifferent to praise, criticism, or the feelings of others. This type of person has only one or two friends, at the most.

Finally, the **schizotypal personality disorder** is a person who combines undue social anxiety with peculiar ideas and habits. This person has problems with reference: reporters on the evening news, bumper stickers, and subway advertisements are directed specifically at him. He says things that don't fit into the ongoing conversation. "Speaking of the price of tea in China, have you noticed how Mrs. Green has painted her shutters chartreuse? I wonder who will be elected President in the year 2000?" The schizotypal individual establishes poor rapport with others (are you surprised?) and tends to live an isolated life.

Okay, I've described the eleven personality disorders currently recognized by the American Psychiatric Association (1980). On the face of it, this typology has a ring of truth, since we can easily recognize one or two people in our immediate vicinity who fit nicely into each of the categories. But this is a superficial test of the typology's validity.

Let's return to the original assumptions about personality disorder. Many of them are not supported by available evidence. Although some individuals are more dramatic, more timid, and/or more bizarre than others, they don't exist in discrete clumps like four-leaf clovers or condominiums. These "types" are much more fuzzy than DSM-III assumes. So, the reliability with which mental health professionals can diagnose personality disorders is notoriously low.

The assumption that personality disorders have a biological basis has also not been sustained by research, with one striking exception. The antisocial personality disorder has a physiological underpinning. People who lack a conscience also lack the ability to learn to avoid punishment, perhaps because they experience little anticipatory fear (Lykken, 1957). Most of us lead reasonably ordered lives because we learn early on that certain transgressions lead to punishment. If we want to take a walk on the wild side, the anticipation of punishment makes us fearful, so we stay on the boring side.

But suppose we did not experience a welling-up of fear? Suppose our nervous system was such that this fear simply did not occur? Then we would be predisposed to a reckless existence. This may be the case for people with an antisocial personality disorder (Hare, 1970). Notice that this argument does not point to physiology as a necessary and sufficient cause of antisocial behavior—it is a predisposition that interacts with other characteristics of the person and the environment to eventually lead to this dysfunctional style.

Only one of the eleven DSM-III personality disorders has anything to do with biology. And yet another reason to be skeptical of these personality disorders is that they don't predispose severe problems. As you read my descriptions of these disorders, I'm sure you saw the seeds of later psychopathology within each. The histrionic personality disorder encourages hysteria. The avoidant personality disorder makes fears and phobias more likely.

The compulsive personality disorder is the training school for obsessions and compulsions. And the schizotypal individual is a schizophrenic waiting in the wings. So goes the logic, but none of this works in actuality (Rosenhan & Seligman, 1984). People diagnosed with a given personality disorder are not particularly likely to develop the corresponding psychopathology.

This topic seems a mess. Is there any way to bring order to it? Well, it's reasonable to say that some people have trouble making it in the world. We just have to read the newspaper or walk down the sidewalk to know this is true. Where the assumption goes astray is in attempting to separate "them" from "us" with a typology grounded in biology. Function and dysfunction must refer to particular environments, and for people this means the social and cultural context of their behavior. As noted earlier, personality disorders are described without reference to this context.

If we acknowledge that disordered personalities exist in particular settings, we have a more sophisticated perspective on dysfunction, one compatible with recent research in the trait paradigm (Chapter 9). First, the basic types of dysfunction do not transcend time and place. Second, any biological basis of dysfunction is relegated to a predisposing, not determining, role. Third, the social nature of dysfunction is explicit: difficulties with friends, family, and work are not consequences of a personality disorder—they *are* the disorder. Fourth, personality disorders are exaggerations of roles that a particular society provides.

Of late, a great hue and cry has been made about sex differences in the prevalence of personality disorders (for example, Kaplan, 1983). Some disorders apply mainly to women, and others mainly to men. Does this represent a bias in DSM-III or not? Not from my view. Of course women are more apt to be dependent, and of course men are more apt to be antisocial. Traditional sex roles pushed to their respective extremes and acted out in an inordinately rigid way bring about such personality disorders.

"New" personality disorders will therefore always appear. What happens when an androgynous individual raises his or her androgynous role to the nth power? I don't know, but I bet that a disorder will result, just as the exaggeration of any social role leads to difficulties.

To help the American Psychiatric Association formulate a contemporary list of disordered personalities, one that mirrors the social realities of the 1980s, I nominate these types for inclusion:

- *Mr. Spock Personality Disorder*—characterized by excessive rationality and objectivity, even in situations demanding passion; biological basis suggested by peculiar cartilage structure of the ears.

- *Mr. Wizard Personality Disorder*—sometimes called Hacker Mentality; marked by the habitual attitude that objects of the world (including other people) comprise a mechanical playground, to be manipulated, sabotaged, and/ or boobytrapped.

- *Lombardi Personality Disorder*—all thoughts, actions, and feelings crystalize around occupying first place; biological basis indicated by elongated index finger frequently waved in the air.

- *Young Professional Personality Disorder*—a lifestyle characterized by affluence accompanied by a systematic delusion that a BMW equipped with a telephone ranks with food and water as a basic life necessity.

- *Dead Head Personality Disorder*—a group phenomenon; people with this problem mass together and follow middle-aged drug users around the United States, stopping every few hours to buy a t-shirt.

- *Jock Personality Disorder*—an alternative to the life of the mind or the spirit, this disorder is marked by heightened kinesthetic sensitivity; people with this problem frequently touch their private parts in public places.

- *Preppie Personality Disorder*—marked by the inability to distinguish bland from blonde; there are several reasons to suspect biological involvement: obvious color-blindness by women suffering from this problem, chronically hoarse voice, and frequent layering of clothes, suggesting hypothermia.

By the way, these new disorders illustrate the appeal of personality typologies. Despite any evidence showing these to be well-defined categories, these pigeon-holes strike us as at least plausible!

CRIMINALITY: A BIOLOGICAL PREDISPOSITION?

In Chapter 8, I mentioned the work of Cesare Lombroso. This nineteenth century criminologist proposed that some criminals were evolutionary throwbacks, marked by their ape-like characteristics. Research did not support his speculations, and Lombroso's theory faded away. As criminology became part of the larger discipline of sociology, explanation of crime in terms of personality characteristics also faded away.

But recent years have seen a resurgence of interest in possible personality predispositions to crime. This is an aspect of the Zeitgeist: concern with law and order accompanies the belief that crime originates within the individual and not social conditions. At any rate, in *Crime and Human Nature*, James Q. Wilson and Richard J. Herrnstein (1985) argue that individual differences determine criminality. The factors they identify are mainstay constructs of the trait paradigm, in particular, those personality characteristics with a genetic basis.

Wilson and Herrnstein's book is controversial, since in some ways it is a modern version of Lombroso's thesis (Leo, 1985). However, their thesis is more sophisticated; they argue that individual differences interact with environmental conditions to produce criminals. No gene produces crime; rather, genes determine individual differences which make crime more or less likely granted certain situations.

Who do Wilson and Herrnstein identify as the potential criminal? Here is their description:

> People who break the law are often psychologically atypical. . . . Offenders are, for example, disproportionately young, male, mesomorphic . . . and from the low normal or borderline region of the distribution of intelligence test scores. (p. 173)

> [They are] emotionally unstable, impulsive, suspicious, hostile . . . egocentric . . . unhappy, worried, and dissatisfied. (p. 179)

Note that these are individual differences in physique, intelligence, and constitution—characteristics that are genetically influenced.

According to Wilson and Herrnstein, criminals tend to be young, male, and mesomorphic.

Wilson and Herrnstein describe studies showing that chronic violation of the law runs in families even when criminal parents give up their children for adoption to noncriminal parents. For instance, Mednick, Gabrielli, and Hutchings (1984) investigated almost 15,000 adoptions in Denmark between 1924 and 1947. Adoptive parents and biological parents were classified as "criminal" if either parent of a pair had an on-record conviction. Children were similarly classified. (Too few daughters were ever convicted of a crime to include in the analyses, so results are limited to the sons.) Table 10-1 summarizes the findings of this study. As you can see, the criminality of biological parents affects the criminality of their sons more than the criminality of adoptive parents does. Shades of the movie *Bad Seed*!

Wilson and Herrnstein summarize further details of this study, all of which point to the role of heredity in predisposing crime:

> Adoptee crime was predicted by biological-parent crime no matter what the crime category. . . . The genetic predisposition is toward crime in general, not toward specific offenses. Over the period covered by the study (adoption from 1924 to 1947) no change in the major findings could be detected, despite the upheavals of a deep economic depression, a world war, and occupation by a foreign power, suggesting that the biological links in the chain of causation are strong. . . . The age of placement exerted no effect on the relationship between biological-parent–male-adoptee criminality. Finally, the transmission of criminality . . . was unaffected by whether the biological parents committed their crimes before or after the children were placed in foster homes, or by whether the adoptive parents knew the biological parents' criminal records. (1985, p. 99).

Further evidence that criminality can be attributed to personality traits comes from studies showing that the predispositions that Wilson and Herrnstein identify are consistent across situations and stable across time. Consider *impulsiveness*, which is plausibly linked to criminality in several ways—for

Table 10-1
Proportion of Sons Convicted of Crime

Biological Parents Convicted	
Adoptive Parents Convicted	24.5%
Adoptive Parents Not Convicted	20.0%
Biological Parents Not Convicted	
Adoptive Parents Convicted	14.7%
Adoptive Parents Not Convicted	13.5%

SOURCE: Mednick et al., 1984.

instance, by making immediate rewards (of crime) seem attractive and distant punishments unlikely. Impulsiveness is measured with a simple paper-and-pencil task: the Porteus Maze Tests, where subjects trace their way through different mazes. Impulsiveness is shown by lifting one's pencil, cutting corners, straying from the path, and so on, and these behaviors distinguish criminals from noncriminals (Riddle & Roberts, 1977).

Similarly, *misconduct* is highly stable across time. In a longitudinal study started in the 1930s, Glueck and Glueck (1950, 1968) followed 500 delinquent boys and 500 nondelinquent boys into adulthood. (By the way, the nondelinquent sample is the one also studied by George Vaillant, 1983, as described in Chapter 6.) Of the delinquents, originally chosen at fourteen years of age, 354 were arrested between the ages of seventeen and twenty-five, and 263 were arrested between twenty-five and thirty-one. In contrast, only 62 of the nondelinquents were arrested before the age of thirty-one. So, breaking the law (or not) is a stable individual difference.

Where does this leave us, as individuals and as a society? Let's first consider some criticisms of the approach of these authors. The studies they review are correlational and therefore subject to various confounds. As Wilson and Herrnstein point out, not all available data lead to the same conclusion about the causes of crime. For instance, national differences in crime point to explanations transcending personality characteristics. Here are some intriguing facts pulled from *Crime and Human Nature.* In Japan, total crime fell 20 percent between 1962 and 1972, while it almost tripled in New York City. In 1976, the risk of being robbed in Japan was about 1/200th of the risk of being robbed in the United States!

Clearly, culture has something to do with criminality. Wilson and Herrnstein counter this by saying that whatever this something might be, it doesn't explain differences within a culture. Yes and no. Cultural factors that distinguish Japan and the United States with respect to crime rates may not vary appreciably within a particular culture, but then again they may. We simply don't know. Perhaps Japanese are more law-abiding than Americans because they wish not to bring shame to their families. But perhaps some Americans are more law-abiding than other Americans for the exact same reason: they want to protect their families from what the neighbors would think.

One of the things that is bothersome about the research reviewed in *Crime and Human Nature* is that most studies operationalized criminality in terms of conviction by the authorities. This is far from a perfect measure of criminality. Is it implausible to argue that young, unintelligent males with mesomorphic builds and an inability to take the future into account are more likely to be accused and convicted of crimes than other types of people, even if these other types do the same sorts of criminal things? Think of Eddie Haskell.

Studies using self-report of criminal activity give the same results as those using conviction to operationalize criminality, but this need not mean that the two measures are valid. I wouldn't admit on a questionnaire that I'd broken the law. Maybe the person who would admit this is the same sort of person who would admit it to casual acquaintances, some of whom tip off the police.

Still, I'm not fully convinced by my own arguments that Wilson and Herrnstein are wrong. At the same time, I'm not fully convinced they are right. Regardless, in the years to come, the application of trait ideas to criminality will become more popular, so let's consider what this means.

Suppose society accepts the argument that criminality can be explained by individual differences in personality, and that personality can be explained by genetic predispositions. Personal responsibility is the cornerstone of the legal system. Does this argument excuse criminals from responsibility for their misdeeds? "Hey, it's the fault of my ancestors. I just live with it."

Wilson and Herrnstein address this idea, noting that "if society should not punish acts that science has shown to have been caused by antecedent conditions, then every advance in knowledge about why people behave as they do may shrink the scope of criminal law" (1985, p. 504). This is true whether crime is explained in terms of social conditions or in terms of personality traits. However, Wilson and Herrnstein further argue that punishment would still be necessary. Indeed, they believe that individual differences affect the likelihood of crime in large part because of the way they lead people to choose courses of action with different payoffs. To the degree that a given crime is punished swiftly and surely, all people—regardless of their personality—will be less likely to choose it.

I have another point of view. The debate between the personal responsibility of the criminal versus the scientific explanation of his crime is an echo of the idiographic-nomothetic debate within personality psychology. The legal system takes an idiographic approach to the criminal, who is after all an individual. This approach assumes free will (that is, personal responsibility) unless there is a good reason not to assume it. This is the way society attempts to understand the individual.

The scientific research of Wilson and Herrnstein (1985) and other criminologists takes a nomothetic approach to crime, generalizing across individual criminals and the circumstances of their behavior. This approach assumes no free will. This is the way psychology attempts to understand the individual.

As you know from Chapters 8 and 9, the idiographic and nomothetic approaches are never fully compatible. They are appropriate for different purposes. The idiographic approach may not be appropriate for the purpose of science, except as an ideal goal for personality psychologists, yet it is indispensable for a legal system like our own that recognizes individual rights.

To throw personal responsibility out of the courts is to invite the use of Meehl's cookbook—not to make predictions but to make justice. It won't work.

Let me raise one more point about applying the trait paradigm to criminality. Is it ethical to conduct and report research of the kind surveyed by Wilson and Herrnstein? These authors do their best to call the data as they see them. They try to be cautious and fair. But what will the public do with this book? Will the qualifications be overlooked, but the juicier "facts" remembered?

I became aware of *Crime and Human Nature* through a *Time* magazine review, under the title "Are Criminals Born, Not Made?" (Leo, 1985). This question is *not* the thesis of Wilson and Herrnstein. They believe that criminals are made—with physique, intelligence, gender, and constitution being among the ingredients. A great deal of their book is devoted to examining how these individual differences interact with particular situations to produce criminality (or lack of criminality). So, they are in keeping with contemporary interactionists. I doubt that John and Jane Public will be as sophisticated in their consumption of the book, as shown by the title of the *Time* review. I doubt that all of our nation's lawmakers and judges will consider the possible distinction between idiographic and nomothetic understanding.

Should we fault Wilson and Herrnstein for publishing a book that may be used in a bad way, like similar books on race differences in intelligence have been used? Should we fault physicists and engineers for providing the ideas that have been used to build nuclear arsenals? What do you think?

CAREER COUNSELLING: MATCHING PEOPLE TO CAREERS

Sorry, Charlie, but you're just not cut out for a career in crime. But the trait paradigm can still help you choose another career. One of the more popular applications of this approach to personality is the use of **interest inventories** by vocational counselors. As Zytowski (1973) describes these questionnaires, they fit round pegs into round holes by matching one's interests with those apt to be satisfied by a particular profession.

The **Strong Vocational Interest Blank** (SVIB) is the best-known of these interest inventories. You may have completed this questionnaire at some point in your life—it's been around since 1927. (Because David Campbell has taken over the SVIB since Edward Strong's death in 1963, it is often called the Strong–Campbell Inventory.) The format and underlying logic of the SVIB are simple. A person is given a list of hundreds of activities. He indicates his reaction to each as "like," "indifferent," or "dislike." Here are some sample items (Campbell, 1971, p. 3):

1. Actor
2. Advertising Man
3. Architect
4. Military Officer
5. Artist
6. Astronomer
7. Athletic Director
8. Auctioneer
9. Author of novel
10. Author of technical book
11. Auto Salesman
12. Auto Racer
13. Auto Mechanic
14. Auto Pilot
15. Bank Teller
16. Designer, Electronic Equipment
17. Building Contractor
18. Buyer of Merchandise
19. Carpenter
20. Cartoonist

The person's profile of responses is then compared to the average responses of individuals working successfully in different occupations. The greater the match, the more seriously he should consider choosing that occupation.

This is a cookbook procedure. Administration, scoring, and interpretation of the SVIB are now fully automated via a computer program. Results of the SVIB are useful in matching people to occupations they are interested in, and in steering them away from others. If one is interested in a profession, one is more likely to stay with it and do well (Reeves & Booth, 1979). But the SVIB does *not* measure ability. If I'm interested in being an auctioneer, but I stutter, I'd be better off not pursuing this career.

As a self-report measure of individual differences, the SVIB fares well. Scores are highly stable over time (Johansson & Campbell, 1971) and predict which professions people actually enter (Hansen, 1984). Further, the interest profiles associated with different professions have stayed the same over the decades. Despite incredible social changes during the past fifty years, chemists in the 1980s express the same likes and dislikes as did chemists in the 1930s. The same is true for workers in other occupations (Hansen, 1984).

The biggest problem with the SVIB and related interest inventories is that they use already-existing groups to provide the bottom line. So, they are tied to the status quo. Still, those who use interest inventories are sensitive to the possibility of bias on the basis of race or gender. If most chemists are white males, is it reasonable to use the SVIB procedure to counsel a black female if she is considering chemistry as a career? Traditionally, separate questionnaires for men and women respondents have been used to solve this problem, but this falls short if an insufficient number of women (or men) work at a particular profession.

At one time, the SVIB was printed on blue paper for men and pink paper for women! David Campbell has himself labelled this a blunder, and I mention it to show how insidious bias can be. But the problem lies not in the tests themselves. Our society encourages men and women to consider different vocations, and the majority follow this advice. The SVIB is not to be faulted for reflecting this social reality.

The more general shortcoming of interest inventories is that jobs themselves change. In particular, someone taking the SVIB today may be ideally

Interest inventories are of little use in counselling a woman who is considering a career typically reserved for men.

suited for an occupation that does not yet exist. If the interests associated with future jobs overlap with those of past jobs, then interest inventories will help steer people toward them. But if future jobs combine interests in novel ways, then these questionnaires will not help respondents choose them.

Interest inventories have also been criticized because they lack a theoretical basis. To some degrees, this is untrue, since they apply the basic tenets of the trait paradigm (if not the particulars of a given theory). Regardless, a notable exception is John Holland's (1966, 1985) theory of vocational personalities.

Holland assumes that "the choice of a vocation is an expression of personality" (1985, p. 7). This is fully compatible with the perspective on personality I presented to you in Chapter 1. And Holland corrects a serious shortcoming of many personality theories: they ignore what most people do forty hours a week, fifty weeks a year, from age eighteen to age seventy.

From Holland's assumption, we can conclude that interest inventories are personality inventories. Factor analysis of interest inventories reveals six clusters of interests, and therefore six basic types of people:

- *Realistic Type*—prefers "the explicit, ordered, or systematic manipulation of objects, tools, machines, and animals."

- *Investigative Type*—prefers "the observational, symbolic, systematic, and creative investigation of physical, biological, and cultural phenomena."

- *Artistic Type*—prefers "ambiguous, free, unsystematized activities . . . to create art forms or products."

- *Social Type*—prefers "activities . . . to inform, train, develop, cure or "enlighten" other people.

- *Enterprising Type*—prefers "activities that entail the manipulation of others to attain organizational goals or economic gain."

- *Conventional Type*—prefers "the explicit, ordered, systematic manipulation of data, such as keeping records." (Holland, 1985, pp. 19–23)

Holland believes that these types are culture-specific. So, in Tolkien's Middle Earth, we would expect the typology of hobbits, ents, goblins, and trolls to involve different interests.

Holland further proposes that environments can be classified. Because the most important aspect of the environment is other people, this classification mirrors that of personality types. Accordingly, there are six environments: the realistic, the investigative, the artistic, the social, the enterprising, and the conventional. The "press" (see Murray, 1938) or "personality" (see Bem & Funder, 1978) of each environment is derived from the character of the people who congregate in it, and it demands certain behaviors on the part of the individual.

In a study of college teachers, John Smart (1982) found support for these ideas. Academic disciplines were classified as realistic, investigative, artistic, social, enterprising, or conventional (see Table 10-2), and instructors completed a questionnaire that assessed their teaching goals. The teachers in a particular discipline agreed among themselves about the importance of certain goals, and these goals in each case reflected their particular discipline. Instructors in realistic fields felt that education should prepare students for careers. Instructors in social fields believed that character development of students was important. And so on.

Holland's theory goes far beyond the modest intent of the SVIB and related questionnaires. His is a sophisticated vision of personality in keeping with the interactionist approach. A key postulate is that a match between the person and the setting is beneficial: the individual is satisfied and productive, and she has an identity and a circle of friends. The organization that serves as the setting is pleasant, stable, and successful.

Table 10-2

Typology of Academic Disciplines

Academic Environment	Representative Disciplines
Realistic	Agricultural Education Civil Engineering Forestry
Investigative	Economics Geology Mathematics
Artistic	Art English Music
Social	History Political Science Sociology
Enterprising	Law Marketing Personnel Management
Conventional	Accounting Business Education Finance

SOURCE: From Smart, 1982.

And a mismatch is not beneficial. Have any of you transferred from another college because it just wasn't you? Were you the only student there who listened to classical music—or the only one who didn't? Were you the only one who didn't think of the ERA as a measure of Tom Seaver's pitching ability? Holland's approach to person-environment fit explains your discomfort. If you feel like a square peg right now, find comfort in the possibility that there is a place for you elsewhere.

PERSONNEL SELECTION: CHOOSING PEOPLE FOR CAREERS

As you have just read, one application of the trait paradigm assists people in choosing occupations. Another application is involved with the other side of this process: helping business and industry choose employees. **Personnel selection** is concerned with individual differences leading to good and bad job performance. Accordingly, personnel psychologists often embrace the orientation of the trait paradigm.

Personnel tests are nothing new. Thousands of years ago, tests were used in Greece and China to select workers for particular jobs (Dunnette & Borman, 1979). The modern impetus for these tests began with World War I, when almost two million men were screened using group-administered intelligence tests. Similarly, Woodworth (1919) developed a test for identifying psychiatric disturbance among soldiers. His inventory was adapted for civilians and used by employers during the economically troubled 1930s to select "stable" and "cooperative" workers (Hogan, Carpenter, Briggs, & Hansson, 1984).

A second impetus came with World War II. Henry Murray went to work for the Office of Strategic Services (OSS), where he was charged with "judging the suitability of each candidate for a proposed assignment overseas" (Murray & MacKinnon, 1946, p. 76). Murray brought to bear his considerable assessment skills. The OSS wanted a simple "in" or "out" judgment to be made, but this was not the only decision required. Granted that a recruit was not grossly unfit, just how effective was he or she likely to be? Murray and MacKinnon fretted that "screening devices . . . efficient in distinguishing people . . . incapable of functioning effectively are not so successful in discriminating degrees of effectiveness among those whose test scores fall above the usual level of acceptability" (1946, p. 76).

Realize that the OSS was the forerunner of the CIA and that Murray was responsible for recommending people for particularly dangerous assignments, like being a spy or a resistance leader. He couldn't just rely on the

SVIB to pick men and women for these missions impossible. Instead, he developed a series of tests that mimicked situations likely to be confronted in the field. He inferred how a person would act in actual situations from how that person performed in mock situations. So, several decades prior to Mischel's (1968) critique of the trait paradigm, Murray devised two of the "contemporary" reactions to this critique: looking at actual behavior rather than questionnaire responses and taking the situation into account.

Here are two of the many tasks that Murray and his fellow psychologists developed. Imagine the situations that these tasks try to mimic:

Construction Test. The candidate was shown a glorified tinker-toy with which he was instructed to build a 5-foot cube with 7-foot diagonals in ten minutes with the aid of 2 helpers whom he was to direct. The "helpers" were members of the junior staff who soon turned the situation into a test of the candidate's frustration-tolerance by becoming increasingly lazy, recalcitrant, and insulting. No candidate ever finished the task, and there were those who became either markedly upset or enraged by the humiliations they suffered.

Stress Interview. The candidate was told to assume that he had just been caught going through a secret file in a government building in Washington, and, after ten minutes in which to think up an innocent and plausible explanation for his presence there, he reported to a basement room where, under the glare of a spotlight, he was given a grilling cross-examination on the details of his story in an attempt to confuse and disquiet him as much as possible. (Murray & MacKinnon, 1948, p. 78)

In yet another test, candidates were invited to a party and encouraged to get drunk: "the party which lasted usually long past midnight often revealed aspects of the candidates' personalities not seen in soberer states" (p. 79). *In vino veritas.*

Information from all these tests was collated by a diagnostic council, which characterized a candidate's traits and recommended assignments accordingly. We therefore see Murray's approach to assessment: a variety of tests and observations carried out by a variety of experts to describe the whole person. The specifics of Murray's recommendations are shrouded in military secrecy, but his program succeeded at a general level. Of the hundreds of men and women who passed through the diagnostic council, only a handful proved unsatisfactory in the eyes of their superiors or colleagues. When it was possible to calculate them, correlations between initial assessment and subsequent performance were positive, although modest (Office of Strategic Services, 1948).

After World War II, personnel selection exploded. Trait psychologists turned away from the situational tests favored by Murray and used the more efficient personality inventories being developed (like the MMPI and the 16PF) to predict subsequent job performance. Paralleling the history of trait research, enthusiasm for personality assessment in selection waned in the 1960s. The .30 "limit" was encountered in personnel selection, and some called for personnel psychologists to discard personality assessment (for example, Ghiselli, 1973; Guion & Gottier, 1965).

Hogan et al. (1984) suggest that several factors led to decreased enthusiasm. First, some of the popular personality inventories—like the MMPI— were best suited for predicting psychopathology. Scores were largely unrelated to job performance. Second, many personality scales were used to predict performance at jobs that had nothing to do with the traits being mea-

"Well, Mr. Cody, according to our questionnaire, you would probably excel in sales, advertising, slaughtering a few thousand buffalo, or market research."

SOURCE: "The Far Side" cartoon by Gary Larson is reproduced by permission of Chronicle Features, San Francisco.

sured. When the individual difference is pertinent to the job, successful prediction is possible. For instance, introversion-extraversion relates to the ability to work well in quiet or noisy settings (Hockey, 1972). Once again, the "problem" with personality questionnaires resides not in the measures themselves but in the purpose to which they are put.

Recent developments within personnel selection handle individual differences and their assessment with more sophistication (Dunnette & Borman, 1979). We see the realization that individual differences are better assessed by observing what people actually do as opposed to what they say they do. Simulations like those developed by Murray are popular once again, and aggregation is used to bolster the reliability of assessment. Personnel psychologists now define the specific requirements of jobs in behavioral terms, fitting people to these settings.

One of the notable success stories of personnel selection has been chronicled on the sports pages. In conducting its annual draft of college athletes, the National Football League straightforwardly applies the trait paradigm. Which individual differences lead to good or poor adaptation (that is, victories or losses)? How can these individual differences best be measured?

The Dallas Cowboys are the acknowledged innovators here (Furlong, 1971; Maule, 1968). In the early 1960s, Tex Schramm approached IBM about the possibility of using computers to assist in scouting the hundreds of college players he might use on his football team. IBM assigned Salam Qureishi (from Aligarh, India) to work with Schramm, and what ensued was a profitable collaboration between a Cowboy who knew nothing about computers and an Indian who knew nothing about football.

What are the qualities that make for a good football player? Qureishi talked to numerous coaches and distilled their answers down to eight individual differences: character; quickness and body control; competitiveness; mental alertness; strength and explosiveness; weight; height; and speed. Scouts rated prospects on 9-point scales corresponding to these categories. Recognizing potential problems in subjective ratings, the Cowboys developed objective measures of these qualities. This is where the now-familiar statistics on the 40-yard dash, the bench press, and hang time came from. Believe it or not, even IQ is figured into the formula. Character is harder to quantify, of course, but the Cowboys inferred it from lack of drug use (a prophetic operationalization, granted current scandals in sports).

A player's scores on the different scales are summed, and those with higher scores are drafted sooner. Does the system work? In 1964, the procedure produced this order of players: (1) Joe Namath; (2) Dick Butkus; (3) Gale Sayers; and (4) Fred Biletnikoff. Although none of these players played for the Dallas Cowboys, they all had successful careers in professional football. And the Cowboys have traditionally identified future stars overlooked by other football teams, like Calvin Hill. Who would have thought a halfback from Yale could be so good—isn't Yale the school for movie stars?

Over the years, other football teams have caught up with Dallas in personnel selection (and victories). The newest horizon is the use of similar techniques to select adaptive versus maladaptive plays. The San Francisco 49ers, for instance, have given computers to their assistant coaches (Compton, 1984). The success or failure of particular plays in particular circumstances is constantly monitored, and Coach Bill Walsh acts on this information throughout the game. In my reading, I haven't encountered the exact correlation coefficients involved, but I bet they exceed the .30 limit because they are based on aggregated information obtained from actual situations. The only thing missing to maximize the predictability of outcomes is the Bem and Allen procedure of distinguishing consistency versus inconsistency. But maybe the 49ers achieve consistency by playing Joe Montana as their quarterback.

PREDICTING PREFERENCES

What do Coca-Cola, Ronald Reagan, "M∗A∗S∗H," and people accused of crimes ranging from murder to conspiracy share in common? (This is my favorite rhetorical question in the entire book.) All of them have benefitted from an application of the trait paradigm. Just as the Dallas Cowboys predict the success of football players from individual differences, these people and groups predict their own success (that is, popularity) from individual differences. The techniques of opinion polling have become highly refined and are used in marketing products, charting political careers, selecting television shows, and even choosing sympathetic jurors. But at the bottom, they all embrace a similar logic stemming from the trait approach to personality.

It is assumed that people's likes and dislikes are stable and general individual differences. Much of society rises and falls according to preferences of the citizens, so information about predisposing individual differences is powerful indeed. In this section, I'll describe some representative investigations of public preference.

Political Polls

Polling is a way to gauge public opinion. The best-known polls predict the outcomes of elections for public office. As early as 1824, newspapers tried to forecast the presidential election by surveying a sample of voters (Gallup, 1972). And in 1883, the *Boston Globe* sent reporters into specially selected precincts the night of an election. This system is still used to project final returns. (With 2 percent of the precincts reporting, we give New Jersey to Smith.)

With a few famous exceptions (like the Dewey–Truman presidential race in 1948), modern political polling has been highly accurate in its forecasts. Accuracy results from randomly selecting respondents. Early polls were based on **convenience samples:** people on the street corner, people who mail back a postcard, people who answer the telephone. But, since the 1930s, it has become clear that such samples are confounded because political leanings tend to correlate with socioeconomic class. Any convenience sample which disproportionately samples rich people or poor people introduces a political bias as well. And most convenience samples do precisely this.

Modern polling began with George Gallup's random samples in the 1930s. Imagine a list of all 250 million people in the United States. If you want to know what presidential candidate was favored by these millions of people, you can get a highly accurate estimate by interviewing no more than 1,500 of them—so long as they were chosen at random, which means that every one of the 250 million has an equal chance of being included in the sample.

How does this work? It may not be intuitive, but the random sample guarantees accuracy. Gallup (1972) compares the process to a cook making soup. He wants to know how it tastes, so he stirs it a bit and sips a small spoonful. The spoonful tastes fine, so he assumes that the whole kettle of soup does. He does not worry that he has sampled only a small fraction of the soup, since his stirring "randomized" the potential spoonfuls. Had he not stirred the soup, his spoonful would have been a convenience sample, perhaps unrepresentative of the soup as a whole.

Would more than 1,500 people in a sample of the United States population improve accuracy? Of course, but not enough to warrant the increase in time and energy. Gallup (1972) reports that such a sample yields estimates that are accurate within 3 percent. (Most of us would be thrilled if our checkbook balance were that close to reality).

National polls do not start with a list of 250 million names and then randomly choose 1,500. That would be too unwieldy. Instead, they use a simpler procedure that yields essentially the same representative group of respondents. One variant starts by selecting at random a small number of precincts within the country. Then residences within these precincts are selected at random. And finally people within these are selected at random.

So far, I've described polls that ignore individual differences among respondents, since polls are only interested in overall national opinion. But many polls subdivide their sample by individual differences and make separate projections within groups defined by age, sex, race, religion, amount of education, type of employment, and place of residence.

Information about preferences due to individual differences allows political candidates to chart their campaigns, and here polling changes from a
means of estimating opinion to a strategy of capitalizing on opinion or even
creating it. Suppose a candidate for governor of your state finds that she is
extremely popular with affluent college graduates and extremely unpopular
with poor people of limited education. She might decide to direct her time,
energy, and money toward swaying the opinions of the people in between.
There's no need to visit the fancy suburbs or the inner cities, since those
people have already made up their minds.

Suppose the candidate finds out from polls that uncommitted voters are
particularly concerned with law and order, or with possible threats to the
nuclear family, or with economic issues. She can tailor her campaign speeches
accordingly, just as a psychotherapist tailors her treatment to a patient's illness. It's the exact same strategy, one that has been so refined in the United
States that no serious candidate is without polling experts on her campaign
staff. Remember the 1984 Presidential election? Both the Democratic and
Republican candidates embraced the family and patriotism. Both solicited
the support of Bruce Springsteen. (He wisely declined to take a stand.)

Consumer Behavior

Cynics have noted that candidates for political office are products to be sold
to the public. Once upon a time, this was not as insulting as it is today, since
marketing was product-oriented. Advertisements stressed the qualities of a
particular product, and it was assumed that good products sold better than
poor products.

But, by the 1950s, marketing had become consumer-oriented. There
were so many products available, and they were so similar, that advertisements began to stress the qualities of the *consumer*. It was assumed that
people bought products for reasons other than the nature of the product itself.
To the degree that a product touched on these reasons, it would sell.

The trait paradigm provided a number of ideas here, and the psychology
of consumer behavior is thus an application of this paradigm (McNeal, 1982).
In particular, the need theories of Murray and Maslow are used to predict,
understand, and manipulate the buying of products. When you go to the 7-
11 to get a six-pack of beer, you may regard this as a simple act to prepare
for watching TV that evening. But Big Business, from the viewpoint of the trait
paradigm, sees you as satisfying a number of needs, none of which have
anything to do with beer or television.

Let's consider Murray's theory. Remember how it catalogues needs that
people have to varying degrees? Some people have a high need for play,
while other people have a high need for achievement. Think about beer

commercials. They can be classified as appeals to play versus appeals to achievement. "Play" beers are used to have a good time: Miller Lite for example, while "achievement" beers are used to reward yourself for meritorious actions: Löwenbräu for example. These types of beer are marketed to appeal to different groups of people, in accordance with their dominant needs.

Sometimes beers change their image (though not their taste) to capture a larger market. Are you old enough to remember that Miller used to be the "champagne of bottled beer" and Michelob reserved "for special occasions"? These former achievement beers have become play beers. Indeed, with Michelob, you can have it all, which makes it a self-actualization beer. (Does one get a hangover from a peak experience?)

These are not silly examples. I've taken them all from a standard textbook of *Consumer Behavior* by James McNeal (1982). Any of you who take courses in marketing know the great extent that this field is influenced by the trait paradigm. The need profiles of different markets are carefully ascertained by businessmen, and products are advertised to appeal to prevailing needs. This is called **segmentation of the market.**

Why settle for champagne?

Although a person's needs are assumed to be stable and general, they can also wax and wane. So, advertising tries to arouse needs. You saw examples in Chapter 7 of how products may be linked to sexual needs. Sex sells, but so does play, achievement, power, affiliation, nurturance, and so on. Different advertisements try to tickle these different needs. And, although we are not always fully aware of the process, sometimes we are. A few months ago, I bought new Michelin tires for my car in direct response to television commercials showing an infant crawling through tires while her mother and father talked off-camera about the merits of cheap versus expensive tires. Whoever designed that commercial is a genius!

Television Polls

TV shows are a different sort of product, but network executives are similarly interested in the results of polls. Two specific matters concern them. First, which shows should make it onto television in the first place? Second, of those shows which do premier, which should be kept, and which scrapped? To answer these questions and related ones (like the particular time slot in which a show will be most successful), preference polls are taken.

The three major networks use slightly different procedures to choose among pilots (Gitlin, 1983). CBS passes out free tickets to tourists in Los Angeles and New York. The ticket entitles the holder to view pilot shows in special studios equipped with chairs having two buttons: if you like what you see, you press the green button; if you don't like what you see, you press the red button. After a show is seen, viewers complete questionnaires asking for more specific reactions to the show. ABC has its pilots screened through Preview House, an independent firm specializing in market research. Preview House contacts potential viewers by phone and invites them to come in and rate shows. NBC uses yet another procedure. It shows pilots on cable television in certain areas, and then phones viewers to ask their opinion.

None of these samples are chosen randomly, and so the networks try to achieve representativeness by weighting responses according to sex, race, and age. Problems nevertheless remain. It is frequently charged that racial minorities do not appreciably enter into this process. Bias may also be introduced by response sets and considerations of social desirability. For instance, respondents said that they would be interested in a mini-series based on the life of Martin Luther King (because this seems like the appropriate thing to say), but the series itself was unsuccessful (Gitlin, 1983).

Still, the system is reasonably accurate in predicting which shows will be popular or unpopular once they make it on the air. Testing figures from CBS for the years 1957 through 1980 show that whether or not a show ends up in the top half of all shows can be predicted from initial piloting over 80 percent of the time (Gitlin, 1983). However, spectacular exceptions are well-known.

"All in the Family" screened to below average ratings, but "clinical intuition" prevailed, and the show became a great success. Still, screening is successful enough that almost all shows that wind up on television have to survive the process.

Sometimes screening is used to fine-tune a show. The name "Dynasty" was chosen over the initially favored "Oil" by using a phone survey. Testing showed that American audiences preferred "M*A*S*H" with a superimposed laugh track, while British audiences preferred it without. (That gives rise to some interesting conclusions about national differences.) Preview House tried out new Angels for Charlie, and found a replacement for Suzanne Somers when "Three's Company" shrank to two.

Preference polls are refined to take into account individual differences among viewers. Different sorts of people watch television at different times and on different days, and networks try to tailor their shows to the available market. So, according to Gitlin (1983), shows like "Happy Days" are planned for eight o'clock slots, and shows like "Hill Street Blues" for ten o'clock slots. Advertisers are particularly interested in audience composition, since—as we have seen—different products are packaged to appeal to different groups of people.

Once shows are on the air, the Nielsen Company informs us about which shows are most watched. Recording devices are attached to television sets in several thousand homes across the country. They keep track of whether the set is on or off, and if on, what channel is being watched. This information is collated every two weeks to give network television a report card based on the absolute and relative popularity of different shows.

Like the use of screening polls, the Nielsen ratings are criticized for non-representative samples and for possible distortion. But, when checked by other procedures, like telephone questionnaires or viewer diaries, essentially the same ranking of shows results (Gitlin, 1983). So, we may conclude that the Nielsen Company will be an important part of television for the forseeable future.

Jury Selection

By now you are familiar with the way applications of the trait paradigm are carried out. If preferences of a group of people can be ascertained and related to individual differences, then one can predict future preferences from information about these individual differences. One of the most controversial forms of this application is in choosing members of a jury.

Juries are usually chosen by a procedure known as **voir dire.** Prosecution and defense lawyers interview prospective jurors, and each is allowed to dismiss a certain number on suspicion of bias. In practice, of course, the lawyers not only dismiss jurors who are biased against them but also select those who are biased in favor.

The lawyer cannot simply ask a potential juror if he is favorably biased. Justice is supposed to be blind, but this is a naive assumption. Because of individual differences brought into the courtroom, jurors differ markedly in the degree to which they are predisposed to reach a given verdict. If one has a handle on these predispositions, then one can "stack" the jury.

Knowing this, some lawyers have enlisted the help of some psychologists to conduct the *voir dire*. Since jurors for any given trial are drawn from a specific place, the psychologist may interview a random sample of individuals living there. Following the procedure of the political pollsters, he asks their opinion of the pending court case. And he asks a number of other questions as well, often about demographic and socioeconomic matters. He then determines which of these answers to these latter questions predict predisposition to convict or acquit.

During the examination of prospective jurors, a lawyer informed by these patterns of correlations asks these same "other questions," not because answers to them are interesting in their own right, but because they predict strict or lenient predisposition (bias). Jurors are dismissed or accepted accordingly. This procedure may sound a bit like science fiction, but it has been used in a number of cases with success (Brigham & Wrightsman, 1982).

Is this ethical? So far, jury surveys have been conducted only by defense lawyers, and some therefore argue that they serve to protect the accused's presumption of innocence. This argument would evaporate if prosecutors made use of the strategy. Others argue that lawyers have always attempted to stack the jury; surveys just help them do it a little better. I'm not impressed with any of these arguments, but the procedure of *voir dire* leads almost inevitably to jury surveys. For a number of reasons—and jury selection is but one—our justice system deserves scrutiny and change.

SHORT-CIRCUITING THE SYSTEM: CAN YOU BEAT THE SAT?

Since important decisions are based on the results of psychological tests, the question arises whether people can short-circuit the process. Granted that a high score on a test can lead to fame and fortune, is there a way to achieve these scores without possessing the attribute the test tries to assess? The answer is obviously yes, although it takes many forms—from downright cheating (stealing the answer key to a personnel selection test) to practicing (working sample items from the law boards) to being coached (taking a course in preparation for the SAT) to beating the system (figuring out the rationale of a test's right or wrong answers).

Disagreement exists concerning the ethics of these various strategies for scoring well on a test. It is predictable that the powers-that-be who create, administer, and use tests for important decisions wish that people would just take them and receive scores reflecting their "true" aptitude or interest. It is also predictable that the people whose lives hang on the results of tests do not always comply with this wish. They seek every advantage.

Claims and counter-claims about "getting a leg up on" the trait paradigm are most numerous with respect to tests of academic ability, in particular the SAT, used by almost all colleges and universities to make admission decisions. So I'll focus on the SAT.

All of you probably took the SAT, and you may remember that the test booklet advised you not to do so repeatedly, since scores are highly stable. Although the test booklet did not elaborate, do you see how this advice follows directly from a bedrock assumption of the trait paradigm? Individual differences are regarded as fixed characteristics, like eye color or height, since they have a genetic underpinning.

By this logic, repeatedly taking the SAT results in essentially the same scores, within the limits of reliability. Also by this logic, a student cannot prepare for the SAT, since scores cannot be shoved around at the last minute. And in particular by this logic, a student cannot be coached to do well on the SAT anymore than someone can be coached to have blue eyes or a tall stature.

So why is the SAT coaching business a thriving endeavor? Try this answer on: because coaching improves scores! Oh my. If you are from a small town, or if your family lacks the money to tune you up for the SAT, then you don't have the same opportunity to improve your SAT scores that someone from an affluent urban environment has. And you may not get into a highly selective university. And you may miss out on a good-looking husband or wife, a Winnebago, a summer home on the Cape, and the ability to guarantee the same for your daughter or son.

Am I being cynical here? Perhaps. SAT scores do matter, but SAT scores are not quite as fixed as higher education would like to believe. Although estimates about the degree to which coaching can improve scores vary, recent reviews of studies assessing the effects of testing agree that scores do improve following coaching (for example, Kulik, Bangert-Drowns, & Kulik, 1984; Messick & Jungeblut, 1981). And some methods of coaching are more effective than others. As a rule, the more contact time between the test taker and the coach, the greater the improvement.

Some argue that the SAT remains a valid way of assessing academic aptitude, since extensive coaching in effect changes the exact quality (intelligence) that the test purports to measure. This may be, but the argument is at odds with the typical interpretation of intelligence as a relatively fixed individual difference. It is also at odds with the procedures used in coaching, like memorizing lists of vocabulary words. That ain't intelligence.

Probably the most controversial attempt to coach SAT scores is reported by David Owen (1985) in his recent book *None of the Above,* in which he describes a plan for beating the system altogether, a way to get high scores while knowing nothing except how the SAT is put together.

Most of us know that if we eliminate a few answers on the SAT as obviously wrong, it is to our advantage to choose randomly among those that remain. Odds are that we'll get some of these right. The SAT instruction booklet gives this same advice.

Owen goes one step further by explaining how to guess among answers. Although his strategy has not been proven effective, it is based on sound reasoning. Questions on the SAT are there because they discriminate between respondents. Questions that are so easy that everyone gets them right do not exist, nor do questions that are so hard that everyone gets them wrong. So, the SAT taker is faced with the task of guessing correctly answers that other people guess incorrectly.

He or she can be taught to recognize so-called distractor answers—those that seem plausible to Joe or Josephine Sweathog, but not to Brad or Buffy Ivyleague. Owen catalogues a number of recognition strategies. One is to eliminate "obvious" answers. Here's an example:

> A literary agency's editors read 4 out of every 20 scripts submitted. What is the ratio of unread to read scripts?

The answer here is 4 to 1, since there are 16 unread scripts to every 4 that are read. But one of the alternatives is 5 to 1, which snares some respondents since it is an obvious (although wrong) answer: 20 divided by 4 equals 5. The general strategy here is to add, subtract, divide, and multiply the numbers contained in a problem, and then *eliminate* the answers to these permutations. Look elsewhere for the answer.

Another strategy recommended in *None of the Above* is to know the location within the SAT of sections that are experimental and thus unscored. The Educational Testing Services includes these sections for the purpose of developing new items for subsequent tests. If experimental items correlate well with other items on the SAT, they are kept for future versions of the test. But Owen tells test takers to skip these experimental items and spend their time on the parts of the test that count for them. (By the way, the experimental section can be recognized because its items are particularly ambiguous and difficult.)

Owen claims that such strategies can improve SAT scores by several hundred points. This claim is disputed by spokesmen of the Educational

Testing Service (Bowen, 1985), and I have no way of knowing who is right. However, I do know that Owen's logic is sound. All tests and measures have confounds—factors that produce high (or low) scores that have nothing to do with the quality ostensibly being measured. To the degree that these confounds can be imparted to a test taker, the system can be beat.

This is simply one more example of an enlightenment effect. Knowledge of the trait paradigm can be used to defeat the purpose of its applications. Realize that the dynamic I've just described plays itself out as well in other domains where the trait paradigm is applied. Consider disability pensions based on psychiatric illness. If a person manifests the "right" set of symptoms, then he can retire from the work force and receive a monthly stipend. While many disability decisions reflect the facts of the matter, it's not bizarre to suggest that at least some decisions reflect instead a strategic presentation of symptoms. When working as a clinician, I always got a kick out of the handful of patients who answered the question "How are you feeling?" with a list of symptoms *in the exact order* listed in DSM-III. These patients were invariably looking for some redress from the system, and they knew the rules well.

Similarly, producers of television shows sometimes try to take advantage of the way that pilots are evaluated (Gitlin, 1983). It is believed, for instance, that comedies preview particularly well, since laughter in a large audience is contagious. A pilot show contains more jokes than the actual series that comes from it, since a humorous pilot should test high: do you remember that even early episodes of "Miami Vice" contained a lot of gags?

Students often complete teacher evaluation forms at the end of a course. On the face of it, these forms measure teaching ability, and school administrations use them to make personnel decisions. Teachers keep the importance of evaluation forms in mind, passing them out under circumstances which create high instead of low ratings by students. Distribute them the day that you cancel the final examination, or the day you finally deliver a good lecture, or the day that your young children and aging parents visit the class and sit in front of the room. Beat the system.

AN ALTERNATIVE ROLE MODEL: MULTIPLE INTELLIGENCES

I might have ended the chapter with the previous section, but it contains too pessimistic a message about people and the world. Thus, I'll consider one more topic, and it points toward a more upbeat future for applications within the trait paradigm. Remember that I keep saying that this paradigm shows the influence of the intelligence testing tradition. It reflects the assumption that intelligence is fixed, unitary, and measurable with a test.

But what would the trait paradigm be like if influenced by a different conception of intelligence? A recent book by psychologist Howard Gardner (1983) describes a different way to think about intelligence. The subtitle of the book is *The Theory of Multiple Intelligences.* In it, Gardner criticizes the assumption that intelligence is a single entity, captured by a single score on an IQ test.

Instead, Gardner proposes that there are several intelligences, *largely independent of each other.* Intelligence measured by an IQ test is but one of these. An individual may be endowed with more versus less of each of the intelligences discussed by Gardner, so she must be described with a *profile.*

Let me give you some background. Alfred Binet originally devised intelligence tests to distinguish retarded children from those who did poorly at school for other reasons. There is nothing inherent in Binet's tests to suggest that they can make subtle distinctions along a continuum. And there is nothing inherent in the tests to suggest that the continuum they define captures the whole of what we ordinarily mean by intelligence.

These extrapolations of Binet's tests were brought about by the social and intellectual context in which they first appeared. Intelligence tests were rapidly assimilated to the newly provided viewpoint of Darwinian thought. The theory of evolution might seem to imply that all species can be arranged in order from most primitive to most advanced, and that all individuals within a species can be similarly arrayed. But this is *not* what the theory of evolution says. All species currently existing are as advanced (or as primitive) as any others. People are *not* more advanced than gorillas, or chimpanzees, or kangaroo rats, or cockroaches, or creeping bent grass; merely different. According to the theory of evolution, these are our cousins, not our ancestors.

Further, fitness is *not* an across-the-board characteristic which some people possess more of than others. Fitness must be specified with respect to a particular environmental niche. Some characteristics render an individual fit in one setting but not in another. And fitness means the capacity to reproduce. Oversimplified versions of the theory of evolution overlook these distinctions.

These are not difficult ideas, but psychologists concerned with intelligence have often misinterpreted them. "Intelligence" has been used as a synonym for fitness, although its criterion has been success in school and not reproductive capacity. (That's a topic for discussion: what do school success and procreation have in common?) Intelligence tests are used to arrange all people in rank order according to their presumed fitness.

Steven Gould (1981) observes that people are tempted to create over and over again what is called **The Great Chain of Being:** the ultimate rank order.

One of the many misuses of intelligence testing took place in the screening of immigrants at Ellis Island.

We see this in the handicapping of tennis players, in *The Book of Lists,* in record countdowns on Top 40 radio stations, in class ranks. Darwin's theory was made palatable, perhaps, by using it to create yet another chain, one with people at the top end (and with Englishmen as the epitome of the epitome). And intelligence tests fit nicely into this distortion of Darwinian thought, because they confirmed the assumptions by English and American psychologists about the relative standing of different ethnic groups. Intelligence was seen as unitary, since there is only one line in which to stand, and intelligence is biologically based, since—after all—fitness and worth run in families (and races).

Howard Gardner disagrees with almost all of these ideas about intelligence. In particular, he criticizes the assumption that intelligence is unitary. Other critics have also suggested that there are several independent human capacities, but their efforts have foundered because they relied on a single line of evidence to identify what these might be. In contrast, Gardner looks for convergence among several sources of evidence:

> Studies of prodigies, gifted individuals, brain-damaged individuals, *idiot savants,* normal children, normal adults, experts in different lines of work, and individuals from different cultures. (1983, p. 9)

What does Gardner look for to identify an intelligence, which he regards as a relatively autonomous human competence? He looks for its isolation in special populations (like individuals with brain damage). He looks for its development in specific individuals (like prodigies) or cultures. And he looks for agreement among experts about the core abilities involved in a particular skill.

Gardner takes a good scientific tack, looking for evidence in areas which have proven difficult for previous theories. No better example of such a troublesome area from the perspective of typical views of intelligence exists than that of idiot savants: individuals who possess an extraordinary ability that stands out against mediocrity or even deficiency in all other areas. The fact that a person who is "retarded" by the measure of a typical intelligence test is capable of creating a beautiful sculpture, or playing flawless music, or performing lightning-fast calculations is impossible to explain if intelligence is regarded as unitary. But, if independent intelligences exist, such striking individuals are no longer anomalous.

Similarly, Gardner looks for evidence of precocious accomplishment. Thanks to *Amadeus,* we are all familiar with Mozart's musical feats at an early age. Gardner cites other examples from different domains. Jean-Paul Sartre was a thoroughly fluent speaker and writer by age five. Saul Kripke worked through algebra on his own by the time he was in fourth grade. Other than their singular skills, each of these prodigies was otherwise a child, and this is precisely Gardner's point when he argues that people have multiple intelligences. One intelligence may far outstrip all others.

He requires that an ability be plausibly linked to the evolutionary history of our species. Can a case be made that a particular competence has been adaptive, granted what we know about the niche of our ancestors? Does linguistic skill, for instance, confer an advantage on a population of early hominids? Notice that Gardner does *not* use circular reasoning to argue that intelligence has an inherited basis.

From the convergence of the various lines of evidence, Gardner identifies these intelligences:

- Linguistic
- Musical

- Logical-Mathematical
- Spatial
- Bodily-Kinesthetic
- Personal

All of these are self-explanatory except the last intelligence, by which Gardner means the ability to have access to one's own feelings and the ability to make distinctions among others.

Gardner admits that his particular scheme of multiple intelligence is tentative. The evidence he cites was not gathered for the purpose of testing his theory, and, to date, no full-blown investigation of the theory has occurred. Measures for all the intelligences do not yet exist.

Still, I think Gardner's theory is important enough to be included here. It is important because it is a sophisticated application of the theory of evolution to individual differences. It shows that a biologically based scheme of human capacities need not be simplistic. It need not assume The Great Chain of Being. It need not be circular, since it starts with the capacity of concern, not an ambiguous measure.

Suppose trait theorists had followed this example rather than the one they did? Gardner *starts* with the capacities he wants to explain. He proceeds by taking into account findings from biology, neurology, anthropology, and so on. In short, he is concerned with behavior. Contrast this with personality psychologists who start with a trait and then search for the behaviors to which it might apply. Gardner gives examples of how people differ in terms of a particular intelligence: what they concretely do or do not do that shows a given level of intelligence. He shows how intelligences determine adaptation, not just for contemporary people, but for our ancestors.

Gardner's approach contrasts with typical theories of intelligence because it is hopeful. It does not reduce all ability to a single number; instead, it allows for variety in the way that people combine their different intelligences. Consider someone who is a government leader. She can do her job well in any of a number of ways: with linguistic intelligence (making speeches), with mathematical intelligence (planning budgets), with personal intelligence (telling citizens what they need to hear). Imagine the numerous ways these skills can be meshed.

Gardner takes great pains to explain that these intelligences are not immutable. In fact, his ultimate goal for the theory of multiple intelligences is to speak to educators about the ways that these different abilities can be cultivated. In particular, he hopes that his theory will bring about an end to the Western tendency to devalue all intelligences except the logical-mathematical.

Imagine the trait paradigm had it been modelled on the theory of multiple intelligences. First, *trait theorists would start with specific behaviors in particular settings, rather than broad traits.* Second, *attention to a single dimension of personality would be secondary to consideration of profiles of traits.* Third, *applications would cultivate traits.* As you saw in Chapter 9, contemporary trait psychologists are now doing such things, but it took decades of "false starts."

SUMMARY

Applications within the trait paradigm are numerous and controversial. Individual differences are assessed in a variety of domains and used to predict people's successes and failures. In this chapter, I described several such applications of the trait paradigm: **psychodiagnosis, personality disorders,** criminality, career counselling, **personnel selection,** political polls, consumer preferences, television polls, and jury selection. These applications are controversial because they may not accomplish their stated purpose. In some cases, assessment procedures give the wrong answer. I described how individuals may deliberately confound applications of the trait paradigm, creating for themselves high scores on tests and measures used to make important decisions. I concluded the chapter by considering how these applications would differ if the trait paradigm had once upon a time been influenced by a different conception of intelligence. To this end, I described Howard Gardner's theory of multiple intelligences, which proposes that "intelligence" is not a single entity.

11

COGNITIVE PARADIGM: THEORY

The last of the personality paradigms that I want to consider accords importance to the individual's thoughts and beliefs—the cognitive paradigm. After a discussion of common theoretical emphases, I will discuss the origins of the cognitive paradigm in the work of the gestalt psychologists. In particular, I will highlight the early contributions of Kurt Lewin and Fritz Heider, two psychologists who took ideas from gestalt approaches to perception and learning and applied them to complex behavior. Then I'll consider George Kelly's personal construct theory, an account of personality based on an elaboration of the person-as-scientist metaphor. (If you are looking for a giant figure in this chapter, a counterpart to Freud and Allport, then Kelly fits the role.) Next comes the self-theory of Carl Rogers, which stresses the individual's perception of his or her own self. After that, we'll look at Harvey, Hunt, and Schroder's approach to personality which is phrased in information processing language. Next is a discussion of cognitive social learning theory, the perspective shared by Albert Bandura and Walter Mischel. To conclude the chapter, we'll cover two contemporary cognitive approaches to personality: personal control and schemata.

THE FAMILY RESEMBLANCE OF COGNITIVE THEORIES

The basic premise of the cognitive paradigm is that we are what we think and how we think. Other theories so far described are cognitive in that they recognize the importance of a person's mental life. Psychoanalysis can be regarded as a cognitive theory (Erdelyi, 1985), and so can Allport's approach. However, what sets cognitive theories apart from related explanations of personality is their assumption that thoughts are the primary characteristic of personality. How we feel and how we act derive from how we think, not vice versa.

Also critical in defining the cognitive paradigm is the root metaphor of contextualism, which explains a phenomenon in terms of how it is interdependent with its context. Personality is the phenomenon, and the actual world is the context. The two determine each other. Indeed, in a number of cognitive theories, it is impossible to separate the person from the world. Kurt Lewin (1951), for instance, starts with the simple statement that:

$$B = f(P, E)$$

Behavior (B) is a function (f) of the person (P) and the environment (E). This is an instance of contextualism because Lewin defines the environment as **perceived reality.** It can only be understood from the viewpoint of the individual. And the individual in turn is defined by his perceptions of the *relationship between himself and the world.* He can only be understood by taking into account his setting. (And here we enter a hall of mirrors, since the world reflects the person, the person reflects the world, and so on and so forth.)

The distinction between physical reality and perceived reality is critical to the cognitive paradigm. For instance, environmental psychologists speak of **density** on the one hand (how many people are packed into a particular space) and **crowding** on the other (the experience of density). Sharing the backseat of a Volkswagen Bug is usually an unpleasant experience, unless the person shoved up against you is your sweetheart. Then you feel warm all over (except your left leg, which is numb). How you interpret the situation dictates your reactions to it. And your reactions in turn determine future interpretations. Suppose you find that you don't like sharing a backseat with someone? You will probably not fantasize about spending the rest of your life with that person.

Another expression of contextualism is psychologist Albert Bandura's (1978) notion of **reciprocal determinism,** the assumption that thoughts, behaviors, and situational factors mutually affect each other. At any point in time, any of these may be a "cause" and any may be an "effect." Bandura (1986) uses the example of television viewing. Your personal preferences lead you to watch certain shows instead of others. What you watch in turn affects programs available in the future. And the shows available in the future will influence your personal preferences.

There is a danger in reciprocal determinism and contextualism. It is reasonable to state that "people and their worlds can influence each other," which cautions theorists and researchers to approach personality expecting complexity. But it is fuzzy to assert that "everything is related to everything." This only invites muddling. Not knowing where to start, theorists and researchers can only throw up their hands.

The cognitive paradigm does at times get muddled. Problems can be avoided, however, when one's focus is concrete. Let me explain. Cognitive theories pay attention to one's thoughts and beliefs *about the world:* not a general world but a particular one. Although cognitions may be located "within" the person, they additionally reach "without" to reflect the specific world where she lives. Any particular transaction between the person and the world therefore has a particular causal structure (Bandura, 1986). In the abstract, everything is potentially related to everything else, but in the concrete, relations are much more simple, since causes work over time. For instance, when you watch the Saturday night movie because the star is your favorite actor, causality flows in one direction—from your interest to your behavior.

According to the cognitive paradigm, a person's personality is more in flux than implied by the psychoanalytic or trait paradigms. Situations are as important in explaining behavior as are a person's own characteristics. Theorists within the cognitive paradigm are therefore interested in explaining how and why personality changes. Sometimes this interest shows up in discussions of personality development and sometimes in statements about the process of psychotherapy. In either case, the interplay between the person and the world is stressed.

Besides the root metaphor of contextualism, cognitive theories share an additional family resemblance:

- Cognitive theories embrace the person-as-scientist metaphor.

- Cognitive theories regard people as active agents—not passive organisms. By this view, people do more than react to stimuli. They additionally attempt to understand the world in which they live.

- Cognitive theories assume that people are driven to make their understanding more accurate, more precise, or more consistent.

- Cognitive theories stress a give-and-take between the person and the world.

- Cognitive theories take self-report seriously. They assume that people can convey much of what is pertinent about their thoughts and beliefs.

The various cognitive theories differ in the particular cognitive constructs employed. Like the debate within the trait paradigm about which theoretical terms best describe individual differences, there is a debate within the cognitive paradigm about which units of analysis should be used to depict a person's view of the world.

Here is a rough classification of terms used by cognitive theorists. **Cognitive content** refers to a person's particular beliefs, attitudes, and values: "The Soviet Union is an evil empire." "My telephone number is 476-0013." "I detest cabbage and all things made with cabbage." "The grade I will get in this course has nothing to do with how hard I work." "The most important goal for mankind is the continuation of mankind." Note that each statement contains a specific item of information.

Cognitive style (or **structure**) describes the interrelations among a person's beliefs. So, in thinking about political events, you might have a simple view of matters: "My political party is composed of good people who favor good policies, while other political parties are composed of scoundrels who are trying to get rich." Or you might have a complex view of yourself: "I'm not a good student, but I'm an excellent athlete; as a friend, I'm getting more and more conscientious, but I'm not where I want to be yet." Note how specific items of information are related to each other.

Cognitive process refers to the ways that a person arrives at his beliefs or changes them. Some theorists suggest that our beliefs are characterized by harmony or balance. We therefore admit new information readily if it confirms already-held beliefs. In contrast, we resist new information to the degree that it contradicts what we already think. By this view, first impressions can be highly influential, since they provide the framework for understanding second impressions. I remember a "Peanuts" cartoon in which Linus explained that he only shined the front halves of his shoes, since it didn't matter what people thought of him when he left the room!

More exactly, perhaps, people interpret future experience in light of past experience. Beliefs have inertia, and theories of cognitive change must acknowledge this aspect of the process.

The distinctions among content, style, and process are not always easy to draw, so you should regard these categories as rough. They help me decide what about cognition I can ascertain by simply asking someone questions, and what about cognition I should assess in other ways. Content—but not process—is usually available to a person's awareness.

Let me make two general points about this subject. First, cognitive theories can be difficult to understand. Most of us do not think too much about thought. When we do, we usually regard thoughts and beliefs as accurate reflections of the world: "I saw it with my own two eyes." On rare occasion, we may regard thoughts and beliefs as complete hallucinations having nothing to do with the world: "I must have been blind." In contrast, cognitive theories treat thoughts and beliefs as reflecting both the way the world is and the biases we bring to the world. This can be confusing the first time you encounter it.

Second, my own work as a personality psychologist falls within the cognitive paradigm. I have thought a great deal about cognitive theories, and sometimes I am quite critical of them. This may show through in the present chapter, and you might think that I am less enchanted with the cognitive approach than with the other paradigms. Please don't think this. Appreciate that my criticism is born from familiarity with these theories, and the familiarity stems from fascination with them (I think).

GESTALT PSYCHOLOGY AND COGNITIVE APPROACHES

In Chapter 3, I sketched several key assumptions of the gestalt approach. First, the basic stuff of psychology is not elements but relationships. (The word **gestalt** means pattern or configuration.) Second, some relationships are more psychologically basic than others, so we have an automatic tendency to move toward these **good gestalts.** Third, psychology should be phrased in the language of **field theory,** since fields are *self-regulating systems defined by the interrelations among their parts.*

Although the original gestalt psychologists were concerned with molecular activities like perception and learning, other theorists applied these basic assumptions to complex behavior, including what we mean by personality. Notable here are Kurt Lewin (1951) and Fritz Heider (1958). Both were immigrants to the United States, where their influence on psychology has been immense. In particular, the cognitive paradigm of personality shows the effect of Lewin and Heider's earlier theorizing. (And so does social psychology, as one might expect granted the contextualism they embraced.)

Kurt Lewin: Concern with the Life Space

Lewin called the psychological field where behavior occurs the **life space,** and defined it as the sum of all forces acting upon a person at a particular time. By forces he means both internal and external factors that can potentially influence behavior, everything from biological needs to environmental stimuli. Note the use of the qualifier "potentially"; whether a particular factor indeed affects what someone does depends on the other forces present and their particular mesh. He depicted the life space in diagrams like those in Figure 11-1. You should note several things about these diagrams. For one thing, they represent only contemporary forces, not influences from the past or the future. Lewin's emphasis on the here-and-now was an important aspect

---

Figure 11-1
Sample Life Spaces

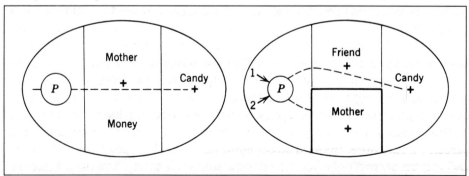

SOURCE: From C. S. Hall & G. Lindzey. *Theories of personality.* Copyright © 1978. Reprinted by permission of John Wiley & Sons, Inc., New York.

of his approach to personality, one that still characterizes cognitive theories in general. The past and the future affect behavior only to the degree that representations of them appear in the present life space.

The life space is divided into regions or sections. Lewin stresses that people are not perfectly unified; to varying degrees, personality is segmented. Each region has a particular **valence;** that is, it may be positive or negative for the individual, depending on whatever needs are operating at that particular moment. If you are hungry, then a bag of Fritos probably has a positive valence for you. If you are feeling discouraged, then a difficult school assignment probably has a negative valence.

Lewin reveals his gestalt background by his interest in *states of equilibrium:* conditions where forces are perfectly balanced. What happens when disequilibrium prevails? The pattern of needs and valences present at a given moment sets into motion activities aimed at reducing the tension that an individual is experiencing. This process restores equilibrium to the life space and allows the individual to attain a good gestalt.

Equilibrium can be restored in any of a number of ways. The hungry person can eat the Fritos, for instance, and thereby reduce his hunger. Or he can count the money in his pocket and realize that he doesn't have enough to buy Fritos and must buy a candy bar instead. Or he can think of the inches around his waist that he wants to lose and see the Fritos as threatening his goal, thereby changing their valence from positive to negative.

Much more so than the cognitive theorists who followed, Lewin was interested in motivation. Indeed, sometimes Lewin is classified with Freud and with Murray. Do you see the basis for this? All are concerned with needs or drives or motives; hence, each can be described as a **psychodynamic theorist,** since each points to the forces moving behavior. In this book, I have located these three theorists in different paradigms for reasons that I hope are evident. Appreciate nevertheless what they have in common.

Lewin described various properties of the life space, one important characteristic being the number of regions present. A life space with numerous regions is more **differentiated,** so we can expect behavior within it to be more complex in the sense that it is influenced by more forces. In contrast, a life space with few regions is undifferentiated. In discussing this aspect of Lewin's theory, Hall and Lindzey (1978) use terror as an example. Suppose you hear a bump in the night while walking down a dark street, and you are overcome with fright. At that moment, the noise is the only "fact" in your psychological reality, and you respond to it (and nothing else). You freak out! As time passes, we hope your life space becomes more differentiated. You perceive a safe area, under a street light. Now your life space has two "facts" and you act accordingly: you flee danger and seek safety. You may, however, dart across the street and into the path of a passing car, which has a tangible existence in physical reality but not in your psychological reality.

One of Lewin's most famous experiments demonstrates that four-year-old children when frustrated behave like two-year-old children (Barker, Dembo, & Lewin, 1941). This experimental study of *regression* shows that frustration can simplify an individual's life space. Behavior becomes more primitive because there are fewer regions in the life space.

More generally, Lewin conceived personality development in terms of differentiation of the life space. Although regression may occur, as just described, people on the whole develop an increasing number of regions (Hall & Lindzey, 1978). So, consider how distinctions along the dimension of time (past, present, and future) allow someone to view herself and the world differently: "That was yesterday!" Similarly, distinctions along the dimension of reality lead to a more differentiated life space: "You're dreaming!"

Organization is another key concept for understanding development in Lewin's terms. Not only do the regions of a life space become more numerous over the life-span, they also become more interdependent, coordinated, and integrated—adults are more able than children to combine separate activities into a whole. What makes this possible is an organization of life space regions into a hierarchy. Children's regions exist at the same level; influence among them is a simple give-and-take. Adults' regions exist at different levels; influence is thus more complex. A five-year-old girl fingerpaints because she loves it; her thirty-year-old father paints the outside of their house *in order to* improve its appearance, *in order to* increase its value, *in order to* sell it at a profit, *in*

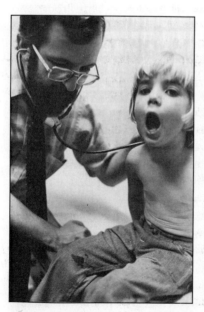

Adults and children may have different motives for performing the same behavior.

order to move to a neighborhood with better schools, *in order to* educate the little girl as well as possible because he loves her and her fingerpainting.

Another important characteristic of the life space describes the nature of the connections among its regions. In Lewin's diagrams, regions have varying degrees of influence on each other. He called this influence **accessibility**, and proposed that the more accessible two regions were, the more they could mutually influence each other. Accessibility is a direct function of the number of barriers between two regions. Suppose you still have a hankering for Fritos, and they are on sale at the local convenience store. But suppose further that you have no money on hand, that the only place to cash a check is on the other side of town, that your car has a flat tire, that it is freezing cold outside, and that you don't have a heavy coat. You can surmount all of these problems, I would think, but the number of intermediate steps between you and the Fritos makes it unlikely that they will influence you to get them. (If they do, then you probably have a profound problem with corn chips.)

Yet another characteristic of the life space is the **rigidity** versus **fluidity** of boundaries between regions. In some life spaces, regions respond slowly and inflexibly to the influence of other regions. These are *rigid* boundaries, and may be illustrated by an individual whose political beliefs (in Region A) are unswayed by available information to the contrary (in Region B). In contrast, other regions have *fluid* boundaries. Influence occurs across them suddenly.

Lewin articulated numerous properties of the life space, borrowing concepts from physics and topology to do so. His motivation for using terms from these disciplines is understandable. Field theories developed first in physics, which needed sophisticated equations and constructs to describe the operation of mutually determining forces. Topology is the branch of mathematics concerned with shapes and how they are maintained in the face of forces. Taken together, physics and topology promise the conceptual tools for understanding the life space and how it changes. Unfortunately, Lewin's mathematical representation of his theory proved to be its least accepted aspect. Other psychologists did not embrace his mathematical approach (for example, Cantril, 1935; London, 1944), in part because it was too metaphorical and in part because psychological methods could not produce precise enough data to make his equations worthwhile.

Nevertheless, Lewin's general approach to personality has been influential. His view of human nature still characterizes theories within the cognitive paradigm. People are conceived as complex systems acting in accordance with their view of things and seeking equilibrium within themselves and the world. The characteristics of each individual's life space are different, and these particular characteristics define the individual's personality. Theoretical terms used by later theorists have their counterparts among terms first introduced by Lewin. However, these constructs, like their forerunners, should not be confused with traits, since they change across time and situation.

Fritz Heider: Attention to Naive Psychology

One of the psychologists greatly influenced by Lewin's field theory is Fritz Heider, whose 1958 book *The Psychology of Interpersonal Relations* examines an important aspect of the life space: the way in which a person makes sense of her own behavior and that of others. Remember Lewin's emphasis on the life space as a psychological reality—reality as the individual perceives it. An immediate conclusion from this emphasis is that the psychologist who wants to understand an individual's behavior has to appreciate how that individual sees things. Fritz Heider called the everyday person's interpretation of behavior **naive psychology** and argued that psychologists must study it.

How is naive psychology different from scientific psychology? Scientific psychology is the proposal of tentative theories and their systematic testing against the evidence. Naive psychology is the commonsense approach to explaining behavior used by the person on the street. Its "theories" may not be tentative, and the evidence may be quite irrelevant to their presumed validity. In fact, naive psychology can be quite wrongheaded.

By suggesting that scientific psychologists study naive psychology, Heider is not proposing that naive psychology be substituted for actual psychology. He is making a more subtle point that captures the essence of the cognitive paradigm. Scientific psychology must take into account naive psychology, since a person's behavior can best be understood by taking into account his thoughts and beliefs—even if they may be "wrong" in a scientific sense.

So, a teacher might believe that students from the lower class who fail in school do so because they are lazy. Although one can argue persuasively from research that "laziness" is not a good explanation of school failure in this case, one still needs to know about the teacher's (mistaken) belief in order to have a full picture of how students behave in his class. Or consider a teacher who believes that doodling is a sign of moral degeneracy. Again, this is a mistaken belief (I hope), but one needs to know that the teacher embraces this idea if one is to understand why he assaults certain students and not others.

Heider describes how people make sense of behavior. He assumes that everyday people are like scientists in their attempt to understand the world. As argued above, however, he does not believe that naive psychology is necessarily valid. The points of agreement and disagreement between naive theories and actual theories are a thriving area of psychological research which can be traced directly to Heider's distinction between the two.

Heider believes that people seek to understand the causes of behavior. A fundamental distinction they make is between *internal* causes and *external* causes—between causes within a person (like traits, needs, or intentions) and causes within a situation (like norms, physical factors, or other people). In social psychology, this distinction is studied under the rubric of **attribution theory,** and there is great interest in how internal versus external attributions affect social behavior.

For example, imagine that you are on a date. Would it make any difference to you if your partner were moody and quarrelsome because of your Frito breath (internal attribution) or because of a pending sex-change operation (external attribution)? Depending on your explanation, regardless of its accuracy, you would most likely behave very differently.

In personality psychology, a host of theories are concerned with individual differences in how events are explained. In Chapter 2, you encountered Julian Rotter's (1966) notion of locus of control. Do people tend to believe that events follow their actions, or not? Rotter's theory and similar approaches will be considered in detail toward the end of this chapter, but in the present context, appreciate that these individual differences may be traced to Heider, Lewin, and then to gestalt psychology. Concern with how people see the world defines the cognitive paradigm.

Remember that the gestalt psychologists were concerned with visual illusions, since these showed how people sought good gestalts, even in the face of facts to the contrary. Heider argues that similar illusions may occur in naive psychology. The most important of these is the **fundamental attribution error** (Ross, 1977). This idea suggests that people show a strong tendency to explain someone's behavior with personal dispositions. They overlook the possible role of situational factors, even when a more careful consideration shows these factors to be critical.

Heider gives the fundamental attribution error a perceptual interpretation, arguing that a person's attention is usually drawn to salient objects in his visual field—in this case, other people. This attention encourages him to explain behavior with personality traits. As you recall, Mischel (1968) argued that our sense of trait consistency is partly an illusion, created and maintained by the fundamental attribution error.

At any rate, contemporary personality psychologists have become interested in such biases in their own right. In the course of understanding themselves and the world, people show individual differences in how they seek good gestalts. If a person takes a consistent shortcut toward this understanding, she has a **schema.** Schema theories of personality are currently being developed, and they will be reviewed toward the end of this chapter. Like theories of personal control, they can be traced directly to gestalt psychology.

GEORGE KELLY'S PERSONAL CONSTRUCT THEORY

The intellectual history of George Kelly is difficult to uncover. Who and what influenced his personal construct theory? Unlike other major personality theorists, who can be readily placed in historical and cultural contexts that explain why their theories took the form that they did, Kelly seems to be a natural. He did not grow up in a cosmopolitan city like Vienna. He did not attend a famous school like Harvard University or the University of London. He did not have a famous mentor like Galton or Freud or Jung. Instead, he worked largely on his own, publishing his personality theory in two volumes in 1955, to the literal astonishment of the academic community. In a review of the work, Jerome Bruner (1956) termed it "a genuine new departure and spirited contribution to the psychology of personality" (p. 356). George Kelly, in a very real sense, is the Rocky Balboa of personality psychology.

Kelly's Life

The details of Kelly's life are certainly no mystery, and they do shed some light on the origins of his personal construct theory. And many who review these facts locate Kelly's theory in his life experiences—not in his formal education.

Kelly lived from 1905 to 1967. Among other activities, like studying physics and mathematics, Kelly was a self-taught clinician. He worked in Kansas during the Great Depression, trying out a variety of approaches, keeping those that worked and discarding those that did not. There he began to develop a system of therapy that focused on a client's interpretation of events. He saw that a variety of interpretations were always possible, and that some were more functional than others. The seeds of his personal construct theory were planted by these insights. Indeed, in the preface to his 1955 books, Kelly describes how the theory originated in a handbook of clinical procedures.

After World War II, Kelly was appointed the director of the clinical psychology program at Ohio State University. It was here that he formally developed his theory, attracting students who have since done much to make his personal construct theory popular. One of his students was Walter Mischel, and you will see later in this chapter how Mischel's cognitive person variables bear a strong resemblance to Kelly's personal constructs.

I have asserted that cognitive theories have been influenced by gestalt psychology. Is this true of personal construct theory? Sort of, but it's hard to tell since Kelly was not one to reference the work of other psychologists (Neimeyer, 1985). He was clearly familiar with gestalt psychology; one of his earliest publications (1933) was concerned with the relationship between brain structure and perception. And in his 1955 books, Kelly says that his theory is concerned with what Lewin calls the life space (p. 279).

But most people believe that Kelly arrived at his cognitive theory largely through his clinical experiences on the plains of Kansas. So, although personal construct theory is consistent with many of the tenets of other cognitive approaches to personality psychology, it is not derived from them in any direct fashion.

Kelly's Theory

Personal construct theory is based on a single philosophical assumption, a position Kelly terms **constructive alternativism.** According to this bedrock notion, all present interpretations of the world are subject to revision or replacement: people can always change their minds. Is this a radical idea? In the abstract, most of us would agree that one can look at events in different ways. But in the concrete, most of us have trouble doing so. We assume that our views of the world reflect the way the world really is. Views other than our own are confused, wrong, or even bad (Berger & Luckmann, 1966).

I remember vividly the first time I visited San Francisco. A friend somewhat familiar with the city gave me a tour in his car, and he kept getting lost. Time after time we'd take a wrong turn and go over the Golden Gate Bridge. I became increasingly upset as I envisioned running out of gas, falling through the bridge, having the bridge collapse, straying into a dangerous neighborhood, and worst of all, not finding a place to go to the bathroom. The third time across the bridge, my friend turned to me and said, "Isn't this fun? I love driving across the Golden Gate Bridge."

I looked at him like he was crazy, but then I realized that it was possible to view our excursion as fun. We weren't trying to go anyplace—we were just cruising San Francisco. And the bridge is one of the highlights of the city. By this time, I knew more about the Golden Gate Bridge than many San Francisco natives.

This is what Kelly means by constructive alternativism. I changed my interpretation of the car trip from disaster to delight, and these different interpretations had profoundly different emotional consequences (although I still had to go to the bathroom).

Embedded here is a statement about human nature and its relationship to the world. People do not simply respond to an objective environment. Rather, they creatively represent the environment and then respond to their representations. If you see the world as an adventure, then you embark on life with vigor and excitement. If you see the world as an obstacle course, then you run through it with fear. In other words, Kelly echoes Lewin's earlier emphasis on perceived reality. He captures it in what he calls the **fundamental postulate** of personal construct theory: "A person's

Lodge owner Harold Shuffle saw only the negative
side of things.

SOURCE: "The Neighborhood" cartoon by Jerry Amerongen is reproduced with special permission of King Features Syndicate, Inc.

processes are psychologically channelized by the ways in which he anticipates events" (Kelly, 1955, p. 46). Kelly elaborates this postulate with a number of corollaries. Together, these proposals constitute personal construct theory.

Unlike Lewin, Kelly is not interested in motives and needs. In Kelly's view of things, people seek to predict and control the world, which is not necessarily the same thing as achieving equilibrium with it. So, in Kelly's theory we find an explicit statement of the person-as-scientist metaphor. Just as scientific theories are regarded as tentative, so too are the "theories" of everyday people. They hold onto their views of the world as scientists do—because these views are useful in predicting and controlling events.

Sometimes people's theories get them into trouble, but they still don't discard them. For instance, consider how many problems result from our assumption that others are mind readers. We may eventually discover that they were not so good at telepathy as we had assumed for so long: "Didn't you know that I hated that restaurant?" "How could you forget our anniversary?" "Wasn't it obvious that I didn't like that purple and orange dress?" "You

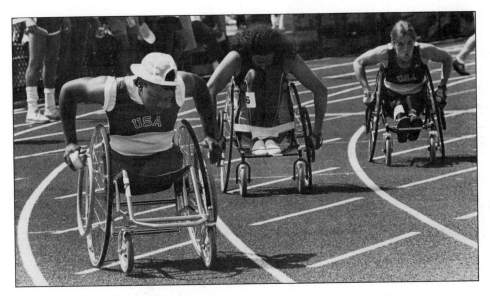

Some people approach life with vigor and excitement.

surely know I hate burned toast and raw eggs more than anything in the world!"

Do examples like this invalidate the person-as-scientist metaphor? Not at all, since scientists can be as wrongheaded as everyday people. You can conduct an experiment that cannot possibly prove a particular theory wrong. We've seen this as a charge against psychoanalytic research, for instance, when all possible evidence is consistent with "theoretical" prediction. When everyday people metaphorically conduct such nonfalsifiable experiments with the world, we say that they are setting into operation **self-fulfilling proph-ecies,** acting in such a way that their beliefs cannot be proven wrong.

Imagine someone who thinks he is a social loser. Because of this belief, he doesn't speak to others, doesn't go to parties, doesn't pursue friendships. And as a result, all the evidence he confronts about himself points to the conclusion that he is indeed a loser. But this is not an objective and unchang-ing fact. It is the product of a particular interpretation of the world. Kelly's techniques of psychotherapy, which we will consider in Chapter 13, aim at breaking a person out of these circular interpretations.

So far I've been referring to a person's interpretations of the world in general terms. Let's get more specific. Just how does a person frame her understanding of things? According to Kelly, the basic unit of a person's cog-nitive activity is the **personal construct.** In terming it personal, he stresses that cognitive activity belongs to a particular person. There are no interpre-tations without people, and all people have their own interpretations. In terming it a construct, he emphasizes that the individual actively builds (constructs) his or her view of the world. Personal constructs are not imposed on a person; they are chosen.

A personal construct is a category of experience, a way to sort ongoing life into bundles. So, we have another statement about human nature: *people are classifiers.* Kelly feels that constructs are *bipolar,* which means that they exist only when a person classifies some experiences as *similar* and others as *dissimilar.* Here is an example of the simplest case of a personal construct: "I live with three roommates. Two of them are college students, and the other dropped out last year."

A person makes sense of her experiences by assigning recurrent events to different categories. To the degree that this process helps her predict and control future events, the current system of categories is kept. To the degree that errors occur, her personal constructs are revised. Back in the 1960s, when I was in college, a female friend of mine always had crushes on men with long hair and beards. She explained to me that her brother had long hair and a beard, and he was a wonderful person, so she assumed that other men with these characteristics would also be wonderful. She eventually discarded this assumption, since it brought her more heartbreak than not. Would-be boyfriends were no longer categorized in terms of whether or not they were hairy.

People have many constructs, but it is the total of these, what Kelly calls one's **construct system,** that defines one's personality. Perhaps you are now shaking your head (don't let your constructs fall out!) and thinking that personal construct theory is hopelessly complex. Don't people have an infinite number of constructs? After all, more than 18,000 words can be used to describe personality traits (Chapter 1), and what happens when distinctions are made using "kind of . . . ," "sort of . . . ," "extremely . . . ," and "never on Sunday"?

Actually, a personal construct system is not as complicated as you might think. People do not have an infinite number of personal constructs, since their constructs are not equivalent to their vocabulary. Consider someone who thinks that all his friends are thrifty, reverent, courteous, and brave; he regards his enemies as wasteful, blasphemous, rude, and cowardly. How many personal constructs does he have? Only one, since he categories people—friends and enemies—redundantly with respect to thrift, reverence, courtesy, and courage. He can have an extremely rich vocabulary but a highly simple construct system. Even though he sorts his experiences into only a few categories, he uses several labels to describe these categories.

Kelly developed a procedure for measuring personal constructs, the **Role Constructs Repertory Test,** usually referred to as the **REP Test.** In one of its typical forms, the REP Test gives people the names of twenty social roles: mother, father, brother, sister, employer, friend, acquaintance, and so on. For each role, the respondent is asked to think of someone who fills it in his life. Then the person is asked to consider a particular triad of these people: for instance, brother, employer, friend. The subject then writes down how two of these people are alike yet different from the third. Then the respondent is given another particular triad, and the procedure is repeated fifteen, twenty, even thirty times.

Kelly assumes that the REP Test gives an insight into the constructs that a person uses in thinking about other people. From our earlier look at questionnaires, you know that this assumption warrants close examination. Indeed, the adequacy of the REP Test is hotly debated. Let me just note one obvious shortcoming of the typical form of this test: it relies on a respondent's verbalization.

As I've already pointed out, personal constructs are not the same thing as words. In many cases, of course, we use verbal labels to tag our personal constructs. But we can imagine "categories" of experience that are nonverbal, that channel our behavior yet elude our labels. Clinical psychologists are usually interested in precisely these kinds of constructs.

For instance, suppose a husband is extremely resistant when his wife asks for help with the chores and errands. He suddenly remembers that he has to do work at the office, call a friend on the phone, or write a letter to his brother. He never gets around to helping his wife. To the outside observer (and to his wife), it is obvious that this man has a personal construct making "requests from wife" equal to "imposition → ignore." But he is unable to verbalize this category. Indeed, he may even call himself a conscientious spouse.

Assuming that the comparisons and contrasts elicited by the REP Test bear a resemblance to someone's personal constructs, how is the test scored? Unlike the questionnaires I've described elsewhere, the REP Test does not yield a single score. Instead, a subject's responses can be used to assess a variety of cognitive characteristics.

The simplest thing you can do is to look at the substance (or meaning) of the constructs that a person uses. Do any particular constructs show up repeatedly? A person might categorize others mainly by their gender, or age, or friendliness. A frequently used construct is similar to a favorite shirt or pair of shoes. You bring it into many situations, and it is an important aspect of your personality.

You may also examine more abstract properties of the constructs. Kelly proposes that a construct's **range of convenience** is the set of events that it can be applied to. Not all of our constructs are used to make sense of all the experiences we have. We may think of our family members in terms of their generosity (or not), but never use this category when thinking about people outside our family.

A construct's **focus of convenience** is the set of events where it does its best job, allowing the person to make highly accurate predictions about the world. Consider someone who spends many hours every day working in a restaurant. She has a number of personal constructs that help her understand customers and her fellow employees. What happens when these constructs are applied outside that circle? They probably don't "work" as well, because she is attempting to understand events that fall outside the focus of convenience of her constructs. A fish out of water tries to swim, but it doesn't do too well. Similarly, a person who is using the wrong set of cognitive categories to understand events does a lot of gasping and flopping about.

Another important property of a personal construct is its **permeability:** the degree that it can be applied to new events. A person with a permeable construct readily interprets new experiences with it. In contrast, an impermeable construct is of no use to someone who encounters different events. So, a person who likes to travel to new places and eat in strange restaurants has permeable constructs (and an iron stomach). In contrast, someone else who shows little tolerance for the unusual or the irregular has impermeable constructs. This person has trouble switching from an automatic transmission to a manual, from a microwave oven to a campfire, or from a day job to a night job.

You can also score the REP Test for the entire construct system it reveals. How is one's construct system structured and organized? One important property is the **differentiation** of the construct system, sometimes called **cognitive complexity** (Bieri, 1955). Remember the earlier example about the man who regards his friends as good people and his enemies as bad people? Contrast him with a woman who believes some of her friends are bad people, while some of her enemies are good people. She uses the constructs of friend-enemy and good-bad independently, not redundantly, and thus her construct system is more differentiated than that of the man, who uses the constructs redundantly.

Kelly argues that a construct system is organized in a **hierarchical** fashion, since some constructs are more important than others. This way a person is able to choose among constructs when they lead him to contradictory predictions. When in conflict, he uses his **superordinate** construct to anticipate events. Think of the superordinate constructs your different friends use. For one, it is religion. For another, it is family. For still others, it may be whether objects come from England or not, their proximity to a vending machine, or their cost below retail.

Kelly views personality development simply as the elaboration of personal constructs. A person tries out different worldviews, keeping those that help her anticipate events and discarding those that do not. On the whole, she comes to possess an increasingly complex and accurate set of constructs. However, development may go awry. Particular constructs may be impermeable, or they may be nonverbal, which can preclude examination.

Evaluation: Popularity and Problems

Since his death in 1967, Kelly has become increasingly popular. Psychology in general and personality psychology in particular have become more cognitive in orientation, and Kelly's use of the person-as-scientist metaphor is now seen as ahead of its time. The theorists I discuss in the remainder of this chapter all acknowledge Kelly's influence on their own cognitive views of personality.

Nevertheless, personal construct theory has some problems. I have already mentioned the first one: personal construct properties are difficult to assess. Despite obvious questions about its validity, researchers tend to rely almost exclusively on the REP Test, which means that support of Kelly's theory is not as solid as one would expect given the popularity of the approach.

A second problem with personal construct theory involves Kelly's rather glib dismissal of motivation. Kelly argues that a psychological theory requires motivational constructs—needs, drives, instincts, and so on—only if you assume that the natural state of a person is at rest. Then you have to explain activity. In contrast, if you assume that a person is inherently active, then motivation is superfluous. Well, yes and no. Much of what Kelly says about motivation is reasonable, particularly when psychoanalytic theory shows us that excessive concern with drives can produce an unwieldy account of personality. At the same time, though, some notion of motivation is necessary. Not all people are active all of the time. What about depression, apathy, and procrastination, occasional friends to us all?

Here's another difficulty: do all people attempt to predict and control the events in the world? Again, we know of instances where people do not. Remember Erich Fromm's argument that people sometimes "escape from freedom" by aligning themselves with totalitarian political groups? Remember Zuckerman's trait of sensation seeking, which impels people to jump out of airplanes or ski recklessly—activities marked by lack of predictability and elusiveness of control? Personal construct theory is silent on such topics.

And another problem common to most cognitive theories is that passion and emotion are given "intellectual" interpretations, which means that their essence is overlooked. In his recent overview of cognitive approaches,

Gardner (1985) introduces the **computational paradox:** the more scientists attempt to describe the mind by stressing reason and rationality, the more clear it becomes that people do not work this way. As these terms are used, emotions and cognitions are different, and cognitive theories like Kelly's subsume the former under the latter. There is considerable debate about the wisdom of reducing emotions to cognitions.

A final problem with personal construct theory takes issue with the scientist metaphor. There is an important limitation here, which may have occurred to you as you read about Kelly's ideas. Science is basically an *inter*personal endeavor, but Kelly and other cognitive theorists usually apply it *intra*personally. What does this mean? Actual scientists typically work by proposing theories and conducting research to support their predictions. Other scientists attack these theories and try to falsify them. The generation and modification of scientific theories is a social process.

In contrast, personal construct theory argues that this process also occurs within each person. People change their minds about things, and they benefit by so doing. But is the process of change within an individual strictly analogous to the process of change within a science? When change occurs, is it for the same reasons? Personal construct theory does not explore such questions.

These problems with personal construct theory are not fatal flaws. The theory is quite flexible, and there is no reason why it can't be modified to more satisfactorily address motivation, emotion, and belief change.

CARL ROGERS'S SELF-THEORY

In his cognitive approach to personality, psychologist Carl Rogers stresses the way that a person views him- or herself. He regards one's self-perception as the critical characteristic of personality. His theory is therefore called **self-theory.** Like the approaches of Allport and Maslow, his is a humanistic account of personality, since it holds that people are inherently good. They strive to make the most of their potential. They strive to have a self-concept that is positive and consistent with their experience. The perspective championed by Rogers is upbeat and optimistic; many are drawn to the theory and to the theorist for these reasons.

Rogers's Life

Carl Rogers (1902–1987) was born in Oak Park, Illinois. He attended seminary to become a minister, but when his interests changed, he transferred to Teachers College of Columbia where he completed his clinical psychology degree in 1931. For the next ten years, Rogers worked as a clinician in Rochester, New York, at a predominantly psychoanalytic clinic.

Rogers at first tried to work within the Freudian system of psychotherapy, but became disenchanted with the results, feeling that when a clinician imposes an "insight" on the client, it does not lead to a miraculous cure. Rogers began to rely more and more on the client's own definition of his problem and view of how to solve it.

In 1940, Rogers took an academic position at Ohio State University. (This is the same school where Kelly taught, but their time there did not overlap.) In 1942, Rogers published *Counseling and Psychotherapy: Newer Concepts in Practice* as an alternative to psychoanalysis. In 1945, he went to the University of Chicago, where six years later he published his most famous book: *Client-Centered Therapy*. In this book, he described a different approach to psychotherapy and a different vision of personality.

In subsequent years, Rogers elaborated his ideas and applied them broadly. The titles of some of his books give a flavor of the breadth of these applications: *On Becoming A Person* (1961), *Freedom to Learn* (1969), *On Encounter Groups* (1970), *Becoming Partners* (1972), *Carl Rogers on Personal Power* (1977), and *A Way of Being* (1980). Rogers was always willing to present and argue for his view of human nature. His point-counterpoint with behaviorist B. F. Skinner is well-known and makes for intriguing reading (see, for example, Rogers & Skinner, 1956). Rogers also made a number of films in which he demonstrates his therapy and discusses his ideas. Perhaps your instructor can show one of these films to your class.

Rogers's Theory

Central to Rogers's theory of personality is the motive toward **actualization** that is also important to Maslow's view of human nature. People have an inherent need to survive, grow, and enhance themselves, even in the face of frustration and difficulty. The term **self-actualization** was first introduced to psychology by Kurt Goldstein (1939), who studied brain-damaged soldiers following World War I. Goldstein was struck that these individuals—despite an injured nervous system—still had an integrity and wholeness about their personalities. They were still intact.

Goldstein used gestalt ideas to explain the tendency of a person to crystallize his personality into a coherent and meaningful whole, even when injuries caused profound problems with memory, perception, and orientation. He termed this "property" of human nature self-actualization, and subsequent theorists who wished to emphasize the unity of the human spirit found it a powerful notion.

Rogers contends that people drive toward actualization, pushing themselves to increased complexity, independence, and social responsibility. The individual phrases these goals in cognitive terms, and they are thus best understood from the individual's own point of view: what Rogers calls their **phenomenological reality.** (Again, appreciate the similarity between this concept and Lewin's life space.)

People interpret ongoing experiences by reference to their actualizing tendency. Is self-actualization hindered or fostered by a particular experience? The answer depends upon whether a person regards the experience as positive or negative. Rogers believes that an **organismic valuing process** is inherent within each person. We do not have to learn what is good or bad for ourselves. We simply know it. He uses as an example a study of infants given the opportunity to choose their own diet; by and large, their choices were nutritious, and they were healthy (Davis, 1928). Contrast this view with that of other personality theories. They seem to predict that we'd all die by overdosing on Hershey Bars if given the opportunity.

Carl Rogers makes an important distinction between experience and awareness. **Experience** includes everything that is happening to a person at a given moment. In contrast, **awareness** is that part of an experience which we symbolize, usually in words. This distinction is important because we may erroneously symbolize our experience, leaving our awareness at odds with the rest of our experience. When this happens, the valuing process is bypassed, and we stop doing what is good for us.

The paradigm case for this discrepancy is when a person's symbolic view of his own characteristics and their worth is at odds with his view of what is good and desirable. Crucial here are the concepts of **self** and **ideal self.** Rogers defines the self as *an organized gestalt composed of a person's view of his own characteristics, his evaluation of these, and his perception of how he relates to others.* The ideal self is *what a person wishes to be.* The valuing process should lead people to a congruence between self and ideal self, but as noted, this does not always occur. What goes wrong? To Rogers, the culprit is other people who convey negative opinions and evaluations about the person.

So, to understand personality development, one must look at how someone is treated by others. You saw in Chapter 6 how warm and supportive parents tend to raise happy and adjusted children, and studies of self-esteem, like those mentioned in Chapter 9, show that children who value themselves succeed in a variety of domains (Coopersmith, 1967, 1968). From the viewpoint of self-theory, these findings are to be expected. When parents make their child feel worthy, he experiences no major discrepancy between experience and awareness, between his self and his ideal self. His valuing process is not subverted. He knows what is good for himself, he pursues it, and he benefits.

In contrast, consider the child raised in a negative atmosphere. The critical views of her parents are assimilated and become a part of her awareness. Particularly damaging is when the parents provide **conditional love:** "We love and value you to the extent that you conform to our wishes; if you fail to do so, then you suck toads." Since the most important part of the child's experience is how her parents treat her, conditional love takes a severe toll. Since she relies on someone else's rules for self-definition rather than on her own valuing process, self-actualization is thwarted. She is crippled.

As an academic advisor, I sometimes talk with students who are pursuing a particular course of studies because their family expects them to. Any attempt on their part to change their major is met with a great hue and cry from home. This is conditional love, and you can see why the students are miserable. They can't win. If they seek their own goals, their parents disown them. If they seek the goals of their parents, they disown themselves.

Rogers's **client-centered therapy** consists of techniques to heal the damage done by conditional love. It gives the individual **unconditional positive regard,** the polar opposite to the conditions that created the problem in the first place. The client-centered therapist accepts the statements of the client, and gives the sincere impression that the client is a person of worth and value. Explicit directions and exhortations—the rule of thumb for all other forms of psychotherapy—are avoided, since they send the message that the client is a screwup (because he is not already doing these things).

The goal of client-centered therapy is to bring experience and awareness back into congruence. Once this occurs, a person can correctly symbolize his experience. The valuing process is back on center stage. Self-actualization is again the central motive. In Lewin's terms, the person has achieved equilibrium with the world. In Kelly's terms, the person's construct system is accurately predicting and controlling events.

Humanistic psychologists are not always strong advocates of research; Rogers was different. He was always interested in the empirical investigation of his personality theory and approach to therapy (see, for example, Rogers & Dymond, 1954; Rogers, Gendlin, Kiesler, & Truax, 1967). He uses a Q-sort procedure to measure the person's self-concept. (Remember from Chapter 9 that a Q-sort is a set of trait adjectives that are sorted into piles according to the degree that they characterize a person.) Rogers asks a subject to describe herself with regard to the adjectives. Which are most characteristic? Which are least? Two sorts are typically made, one with respect to the self as the subject sees it, and one with respect to the self that the subject wishes to be.

The similarity of the two sorts is ascertained by correlating the different trait terms. To what degree do they fall in the same positions: like me or unlike me? Consistent with Rogers's ideas, psychological distress is marked by low or negative correlations between one's self and ideal self. Psychological health is associated with a high correlation between the two sorts.

Rogers has also taken a close look at the psychotherapy process. Again, his basic premises seem to be supported (for example, Gurman, 1977). Successful psychotherapy is conducted by therapists who are warm, sincere, and accepting. In the course of successful therapy, a client's self and ideal self converge. (I'll describe client-centered therapy in more detail in Chapter 13.)

Evaluation: Popularity and Problems

What should we make of Carl Rogers and his theory of self? Like Freud, his popularity transcends the realm of personality psychology and psychotherapy. His humanistic perspective is a correction to other views of human nature that downplay our positive aspects. So, Rogers's ideas are widely applied: to education, politics, administration, leadership, race relations, and so on (Levant & Schlien, 1984). In recent years, Rogers himself was drawn increasingly to social and societal applications. This trend makes sense granted the importance accorded other people in personality development and functioning.

All of us are "other people" to those whom we know, just as they are "other people" to us. The processes that Rogers describes occur within social systems. Happy people should cluster together, since they mutually bolster each other's sense of worth. And unhappy people should also feed into each other. (Should I say "feed on" each other?) This is an apt example of how people produce balance or harmony, not just *within* themselves but also *between* themselves.

In a fascinating essay, Carl Rogers and David Ryback (1984) extrapolate self-theory to a global level, using it to explain how international conflict might be avoided. For instance, Rogers conducted an encounter group with Protestants and Catholics in Belfast, Northern Ireland. These individuals, whose bloody feuds are well-known, were removed from their respective constituencies and met in an isolated retreat. In just sixteen hours of meetings, once open expression began to occur, the participants drastically modified their prejudices. Consider this exchange between Dennis, a Protestant, and Becky, a Catholic:

Becky: Words couldn't describe what I feel towards Dennis from the discussion we had at dinner time. We spoke quietly for about ten minutes and I felt that here I have got a friend and that was it.

Dennis: We sat here at dinner time and had a wee bit of a yarn quietly when you were all away for your dinner—

Becky: I think he fully understands me as a person.

Dennis: I do, there is no question about that—

Becky: And for that reason I am very grateful and I think I have found a friend. (p. 406)

What's going on? Presumably, when people are open with each other, they come to value themselves. And when they value themselves, there is no place for hatred and prejudice. Rogers and Ryback (1984) recommend that wide-scale encounter groups might go a long way toward easing world tensions. They admit that it sounds simplistic and utopian, but they observe that the individuals just described continued to meet after the encounter group was over. Might the billions of dollars spent on weapons and armies be more profitably spent on facilitating communication? Rogers and Ryback say yes.

At the same time, one can easily be critical of self-theory. It rests on some assumptions that are overly simple—if not simply incorrect. The valuing process is plausible to explain certain biological tendencies, but I'm not convinced that we have an internal barometer that helps us navigate the complex social world of values, morals, and politics. Answers to questions about what is good and bad for ourselves must be partly a social convention, since different societies value different practices. Rogers seems to overlook this possibility.

In some cases, therapy works precisely because it is nondirective. But in other cases, advice and recommendations are critical in psychotherapy. For instance, therapy for sexual difficulties often involves giving information. There are some matters that a person simply cannot figure out for him or herself, regardless of an accepting context.

Finally, a world of unconditional positive regard might be a confusing world, a caricature of the "I do my thing—you do your thing—and it's beautiful" worldview that was tried and discarded by the 1960s counterculture. Some people's "thing" invariably impinges on others, and these people should be called to task for their actions. Still, if Rogers's notion is revised to mean regard for people per se and appropriate reactions to what they do, then he is probably right about the conditions that help us to be all that we can be.

CONCEPTUAL SYSTEMS THEORY: CONCRETENESS VERSUS ABSTRACTNESS

In the last thirty years, the information-processing approach has become extremely popular within psychology (Gardner, 1985). Every field has been touched by the concern for how people identify useful stimuli in the environment, translate them into meaningful patterns, and base responses on these patterns: perception, learning, memory, cognition, physiology, social psychology, and so on (Suedfeld, 1971). Personality psychology is no exception. In 1961, psychologists O. J. Harvey, David Hunt, and Harold Schroder were among the first to propose a personality theory stressing individual differences in how people acquire, represent, and use information. Their approach is called **conceptual systems theory.**

Like other cognitive theories of personality, this information-processing approach looks to a person's cognition as the key to understanding personality. What makes it different from the approaches of Lewin, Kelly, and Rogers is its greater emphasis on the *structure* of thought. Harvey, Hunt, and Schroder follow the information-processing tradition, placing little emphasis on the specific contents of thought (Gardner, 1985). Like computers, people are thought to process all information in the same way, regardless of the particular meaning.

Concept is the key notion, defined by Harvey, Hunt, and Schroder (1961) as the link between input (stimuli) and output (responses). They refer to concepts as experiential filters. We can think of concepts as programs, as plans for how to react to information.

People are distinguished from each other by the characteristics of their concepts, and the most important characteristic is whether a concept is **concrete** or **abstract.** Concrete concepts are stimulus-bound, allowing little variation in the response to particular environmental inputs. Imagine a child's wind-up car. Its wheels turn whenever it is wound up. It runs even if it's near the edge of a table, upside down, or in your suitcase. The car's "program" is concrete.

In contrast, abstract concepts are not as bound by particular stimuli; they allow flexible responses to environmental inputs. If the toy car takes into account not only whether it's wound up, but whether it's on a level surface, then its "program" is more abstract. I've recently seen toy robots that can walk around your apartment, avoid children and pets, and seek out electrical outlets and lights. These toys are more abstract than many people!

According to Harvey, Hunt, and Schroder, people can be characterized by their overall concreteness or abstractness. People who think abstractly are capable of the following:

- differentiating between the outer and inner worlds (for example, distinguishing between one's desires and what actually is, or should be)
- assuming a mental set willfully and consciously
- accounting for one's acts to oneself or to others
- shifting reflectively from one aspect of a situation to another
- simultaneously holding in the mind various aspects of the same situation
- grasping the essentials of a given whole, breaking it up into parts, isolating and synthesizing them
- abstracting common properties and forming hierarchic concepts
- planning ahead and assuming the attitude of "the mere possible"

Concrete people cannot think in "what-if" terms. They'd never get a job at Hewlett-Packard. They are absolutists and maintain only the starkest of categories that represent the world. "All I know is that I don't like him." There is never a distinction between rules and the purpose of rules. Concrete people cruise at fifty-three miles per hour in the passing lane and leave the "do not remove" tags on pillows and mattresses.

Authoritarians are good examples of concrete thinkers, but it is important to stress that Harvey, Hunt, and Schroder conceive the abstractness or concreteness of concepts independently of content. So, an authoritarian has a characteristic style of thinking about particular matters, but it is his rigidity that makes him concrete, not his political and moral beliefs.

If someone holds liberal and permissive attitudes in an inflexible manner, then she is just as concrete as the person who believes that people on welfare should be executed simply for being poor. I'm sure you've encountered the sort of person I dub an authoritarian-libertarian, someone vehemently dedicated to principles of freedom—as he defines them. This person is as concrete (and perhaps as dangerous to the world) as the fascist.

Harvey, Hunt, and Schroder were influenced by Lewin's work on life spaces, particularly his concepts of differentiation and fluidity. A differentiated life space with fluid boundaries between its regions lets the person be flexible with the environment, and the world is a richer place when one's representation of it is more complex. Because of the advantages of abstract thinking, people naturally develop increasingly abstract concepts.

Harvey, Hunt, and Schroder were also influenced by developmental psychologists like Piaget (1932) and Werner (1957). Following their lead, Harvey and his colleagues proposed that in the course of development, people pass through stages defined by the abstractness of concepts. We develop in leaps and bounds, and therefore can be categorized depending on our stage of cognitive development. So, conceptual systems theory is both a theory of personality development and a typology.

Conceptual systems theory is highly similar to the perspective on moral reasoning proposed by Lawrence Kohlberg (1963, 1981, 1984), which I mentioned briefly in Chapter 6. As you may remember, Kohlberg suggests that children's moral reasoning develops through stages that are increasingly complex. In Harvey, Hunt, and Schroder's terms, children come to think about right and wrong in more-and-more abstract terms. This has been demonstrated by posing to children moral dilemmas like the following:

> In Europe, a woman was near death from a special kind of cancer. There was one drug that the doctors thought might save her. It was a form of radium that a druggist in the same town had recently discovered. The drug was expensive to make, but the druggist was charging ten times what the drug cost him to make. He paid $200 for the radium and charged $2000 for a small dose of the drug. The sick woman's husband, Heinz, went to everyone he knew to borrow the money, but he could only get together about $1000 which is half of what it cost. He told the druggist that his wife was dying and asked him to sell it cheaper

or let him pay later. But the druggist said, "No, I discovered the drug, and I'm going to make money from it." So Heinz got desperate and broke into the man's store to steal the drug for his wife. Should the husband have done that? (Kohlberg, 1963, pp. 18–19)

Children are asked to answer this question and to justify their answer.

Kohlberg argues that only a few types of justification occur, and that they appear in an invariant sequence as the child gets older, moving from concrete and egocentric justifications to those that are abstract and flexible. A young child might say, "It was alright to do this because he didn't want to lose his wife. Who would cook his meals or take out the garbage?" In contrast, an older child might respond to this dilemma more abstractly: "It was wrong because you just can't go around breaking laws like that." But the highest moral reasoning is thought to occur when reference is made to ethical principles, which are distinct from laws: "If the laws allow the druggist to do what he is doing, then the laws should be discarded. Human life is more important than profits."

The highest stage of moral reasoning appears to be rare. I read the sports pages for a number of reasons, one of which is to marvel at the way in which fines and punishments are meted out by the commissioners of the professional leagues. More often than not, they embody a primitive stage of moral reasoning, one that takes into account the magnitude of a transgression more than its intent. Some seasons ago in the National Basketball Association, Kermit Washington punched Rudy Tomjanovich in the face, while in a separate fight, Kareem Abdul-Jabbar did the same to Kent Benson. Kermit was thrown out of the league for the remainder of the season because Rudy was seriously injured, while Kareem was punished to a much lesser degree because the only harm done was to his own fist. According to Kohlberg, the highest level of moral reasoning would demand that these two cases be treated in the same way.

At any rate, how do individual differences in moral reasoning develop? The particular demands of the environment are important. Research shows that college students show more egocentric moral justification than do high school students, presumably because the larger and more impersonal college environment allows such reasoning considerable utility. (Are you reading this paragraph in a book you intend to return to the bookstore just prior to the midterm? Shame on you: your egocentrism is infringing on my royalties.)

Back to Harvey, Hunt, and Schroder, whose intent is the same as Kohlberg's, only broader. They propose four types of people characterized by how they typically process information. To identify a person's stage of development, Harvey, Hunt, and Schroder developed the **"This I Believe" Test** (also called the **TIB**), an open-ended questionnaire that gives respondents a series of statements beginning with "This I believe about . . ."; the statements end with various topics, and people complete them in their own words under a time constraint.

The time constraint is important because it forces people to rely on their characteristic way of thinking about things. The statements refer to topics of social concern, like gun control, abortion, nuclear war, and so on. Scoring is based not on what the person says about the social issue, but in the way she says it: is the response concrete or abstract?

Four conceptual system types are identified. Here are brief characterizations of each:

System One: the person is subject to external controls, is absolutist in character, regards rules as ends in their own right.

System Two: the person attempts to be free from external control, shows an undifferentiated tendency toward self-assertion, opposes all external constraints, desires "freedom from" rather than "freedom to."

System Three: the person is aware that others have intentions and motives and that these can be manipulated to achieve what one wants.

System Four: the person resolves the conflict between achieving independence, and satisfying others, is maximally abstract, is self-aware.

System One is any true believer with a lock on the truth. System Two is the prototypic rebellious teenager, what some people call an *anticonformist.* System Three is the stereotype of a Jewish mother: "It's okay; I'll sit in the dark." And System Four is the rare individual who sees all sides, the person who should be a United Nations delegate but all too seldom is.

Some years ago, I used the TIB in a study I conducted (Joffe & Peterson, 1981). Here is a response to the statement: "This I believe about Richard Nixon."

A sadly flawed human being, having taken on the flaws of most of us, and shown them to us, and thrown them back on us, and somehow taking our punishment as well as punishing us.

Appreciate that the research subject who wrote this did so off the top of her (considerably abstract) head in less than thirty seconds! Woodward and Bernstein never said it so well, and they worked overtime. The ability to see such nuances and intricacies epitomizes the System Four individual.

The four systems are arranged in their particular order for a reason; with each increase in stage, the person is capable of a further distinction. The System One person sees things only one way. The System Two person, although still stimulus bound, sees things in two ways: what "they" want me to do, and what I'm gonna do. The System Three person understands that other people

The "System One" individual is a "true believer."

have needs and wants. The System Four person is capable of satisfying both self and others, a feat that clearly involves abstract thinking.

As we develop, we move through the stages in order. Most of us do not arrive at the final destination, just as most of us fail to achieve self-actualization, maximal prediction and understanding, or total equilibrium with the world. Although there is an inherent push toward increasing abstractness, particular environments can resist it.

Harvey, Hunt, and Schroder argue that different methods of child-rearing set upper limits on the level of abstractness that a person can be expected to attain. The child who has rigid rules and regulations imposed on him is usually a System One, who returns the favor to his children. ("Why? Because I said so, that's why!") Capricious and arbitrary child-rearing sets the stage for a System Two. Parents who overindulge and overprotect their child, acting as buffers between the child and the world, teach tactics of manipulation. They raise a System Three. And System Four comes from a family that encourages the child to explore and inquire, and exposes him to diversity.

How do contemporary personality psychologists evaluate conceptual systems theory? First, it is not as popular now as it once was. As you have seen throughout the book, personality typologies—even those phrased with a computer metaphor—are considered too simple an approach to personality. Second, conceptual systems theory assumes that people think about all

While the "System Two" is the prototypical rebellious teenager.

environmental settings with essentially the same abstractness or concreteness. This assumption is wrong, and the theory has been modified to stress the interaction between a person's cognitive complexity and the complexity of her environment (for example, Driver & Streufert, 1969; Schroder, Driver, & Streufert, 1967; Streufert & Streufert, 1978). Third, the most popular application of the theory was to education, but the recent "back to basics" trend has dampened enthusiasm for the innovations suggested by the approach. Fourth, the developmental claims of conceptual systems theory have not been supported.

Still, we must regard the personality theory of Harvey, Hunt, and Schroder as an important part of the cognitive paradigm. It was the first sustained attempt to apply the person-as-computer metaphor to personality. It is therefore an important adjunct to theories like Kelly's which use the related person-as-scientist metaphor. Later, when we look at schema theories of personality, we will see these two metaphors productively combined.

COGNITIVE SOCIAL LEARNING THEORY

Some have decided that the era of great personality theories is over, since no theory to rival in scope those of Freud, Allport, and Kelly has been proposed for several decades (Sanford, 1976). Indeed, most of the theories covered in this and other personality textbooks date back fifty years or more. However, a striking exception has taken form in the past few years. A new theory of personality has emerged from the writings of Walter Mischel and Albert Bandura. And, by all signs, this approach to personality will grow in importance in the coming years.

I borrow Mischel's (1973, 1986) term and dub this approach **cognitive social learning theory,** although my intent is to include under this theory not only Mischel's ideas but also those of Bandura (1986), who calls his highly similar formulation **social cognitive theory.** These two psychologists were colleagues together for years at Stanford University. (Mischel has recently moved to Columbia University in New York, while Bandura remains in Palo Alto.) Although they started out as very different psychologists, their theories and research eventually brought them to the same conclusions about personality. No doubt they influenced each other along the way.

Their current perspective is very much in the cognitive tradition as discussed in this chapter. They emphasize the give-and-take between the person and the environment. More so than other cognitive theorists, they focus on particular types of learning. But they join rank with Lewin, Heider, Kelly, Rogers, and the others by stressing the importance of people's mental representations of themselves, the environment, and the transaction between the two.

Walter Mischel: Person Variables

Mischel was a student of George Kelly's at Ohio State University and was originally trained as a clinical psychologist. You know him so far in this book as the critic of trait psychology whose 1968 *Personality and Assessment* argued against the notion that people behave consistently across different situations. In the present context, let's phrase his thesis in a different way: according to Mischel, *people are highly sensitive to the particular settings in which they find themselves.*

Remember also that Mischel argued in his 1968 book that people go beyond the information given to "see" personality consistency that may not be there. Again, in the present context, let's say this differently: according to Mischel, *people have theories about themselves and the world that affect how they interact with the world.*

Taken together, these two restatements endorse the root metaphor of contextualism and reveal Mischel in 1968 as a cognitive theorist waiting in the wings. In the years since *Personality and Assessment,* Mischel (1973, 1979, 1984, 1986) indeed made his implicit cognitive theory an explicit one. Mischel proposes that the appropriate units of personality are cognitive **person variables,** so termed to distinguish them from traits. To Mischel, a person variable is an individual difference that is produced by one's interaction with past environments and influences one's interaction with future environments. Person variables thus span the person and the world, are accordingly circumscribed, and are in constant flux. (See the similarity to personal constructs?)

Here are the person variables that Mischel regards as important:

- *Competencies:* the individual's ability to use information.
- *Encoding Strategies:* the individual's style of representing information.
- *Expectancies:* the individual's beliefs about the consequences of actions.
- *Subjective Values:* the individual's assignment of worth to outcomes in the world.
- *Self-regulatory Systems:* the individual's plans, goals, and strategies for changing the environment (from Mischel, 1986, pp. 308–313).

The influence of previous cognitive theorists can be seen in Mischel's catalogue of person variables. So too can the influence of learning theorists, since all these person variables come together in the person's interaction with particular environments.

Albert Bandura: Cognition and Learning

Bandura was a student of Kenneth Spence's at the University of Iowa in the 1950s, and Spence earlier was a student of the behaviorist Clark Hull at Yale. So, in contrast to Mischel, Bandura has intellectual roots clearly and deeply embedded in the learning theory tradition.

However, as Bandura's thinking evolved, he introduced a number of ideas that took him ever further from traditional learning theory and closer to cognitive theory (which we'll discuss in Chapter 14). Here are some of the most important of his concepts. First, Bandura believes that most learning occurs through observation. By watching **models** perform actions, we vicariously acquire behaviors. When models are rewarded, we do what they do. When they are punished, we don't follow their example. Second, Bandura regards the essence of behavior change as the strengthening of one's **self-efficacy,** the belief that one can perform a particular behavior. Third, Bandura introduces **reciprocal determinism,** the notion that cognition, behavior, and the environment mutually influence each other.

Bandura (1986) also endorses a **microanalytic strategy,** limiting his analyses to particular behaviors in particular settings. In contrast to psychoanalytic and trait theories, all cognitive theories locate personality in a particular context. But Bandura takes this to an extreme, even among cognitive theories. He regards all his constructs as highly specific. For instance, there is no such thing as general self-efficacy.

As noted, Mischel and Bandura are greatly interested in particular types of learning. This allows them to give a fine-grained view of personality development in terms of particular interactions between the person and the world. For instance, Bandura has studied aggression among children, while Mischel has studied delay of gratification. Both topics have attracted the attention of other personality theorists. Recall how psychoanalytic theories invoke instincts to explain aggression and the ego to explain postponement of pleasure. Trait theorists point to biologically based individual differences. In contrast, Mischel and Bandura argue that aggression and delay of gratification are behaviors that are learned in particular environments where specific patterns of rewards and punishments prevail.

An intriguing aspect of learning as viewed from the vantage of cognitive social learning theory is that people differ with respect to their knowledge of learning principles. Some people know how to arrange rewards and punishments so they produce desired behaviors on their own part. They do the dishes prior to watching television, so that the latter activity reinforces the former. They succeed at their diets because they put Dove bars down the garbage disposal. (It's harder to raid the sewer than the freezer.) This is called **self-regulation.** What an intriguing twist; people both administer and receive reinforcement! Other people are less sophisticated in what they know about themselves and the world. They are victims of the principles of learning, not masters.

Throughout his career, Bandura has added to the therapy strategies of behavior modification. Chief among the techniques he has pioneered are those that rely on modelling to change undesired behavior. To learn new behaviors or extinguish old ones, it is not necessary to perform them. You can watch someone handle snakes on a videotape, for instance, and later be able to handle them yourself (Bandura, Blanchard, & Ritter, 1969).

Bandura (1986) has recently examined a client's self-efficacy with respect to a desired behavior. He has become interested, for instance, in how people can best recover from a heart attack. A significant component of recovery is psychological: does the person feel capable of resuming a physically active life? Fear of another heart attack will reduce someone's activity, but reduced activity only makes another heart attack more likely, since it limits cardiovascular capacity. The goal of the rehabilitation counselor is to convince the heart attack patient that he is quite capable of physical activity.

Bandura conceptualizes rehabilitation as a social matter, and involves a patient's spouse. A wife's perception of her husband's physical efficacy is as related to his efforts to be active as his own perception. So, Bandura increases a wife's belief in her husband's efficacy, thereby increasing the husband's actual activity and his eventual health. He does this first by putting the husband on a treadmill and having his wife watch the strain he can endure. Then the wife gets on the treadmill herself, and comes away with an appreciation of how robust her husband actually is. If he can do the treadmill, then he can do the activities required in the course of mundane life. If she believes, then he believes.

In sum, cognitive social learning theory looms as the next great theory of personality. Because this point of view is just now taking form, perhaps it is unfair to criticize it yet. Still, two pitfalls seem possible. The first is a danger in pushing the microanalytic strategy too far. Remember that "personality" includes those aspects of behavior that are stable, general, and integrated. Too narrow a focus precludes understanding the whole of what we mean by personality. The second danger is the generic problem of cognitive theories. With the exception of Lewin, cognitive theories ignore the motives and needs that drive behavior. They attribute too much rationality to people, ignoring their dark and passionate sides. A full account of personality must acknowledge not only when people are like scientists and computers, but also when they are like animals or actors (see, for example, Gardner, 1985).

CONTEMPORARY COGNITIVE TOPICS

What's hot and what's not? In this section, I will describe two lines of work that dominate the scene today within the cognitive paradigm. Both have evolved from the theories I've already sketched, so expect them to be concerned with individual differences in cognition, with the interplay between the person and the world, and with the movement toward greater understanding. The two areas differ in that the first line of work concerns itself with a particular cognitive *content*, while the second concerns itself with a particular cognitive *structure*.

Personal Control

A host of theories within psychology talk about an individual's sense of **personal control:** beliefs about how well he or she can bring about good events and avoid bad events. These theories stress that such beliefs do more than reflect one's past competence; they also determine a person's future actions with respect to events. A heightened sense of personal control is associated with emotional, behavioral, and even physiological vigor in the face of challenge. A diminished sense of control accompanies helplessness, apathy, and illness.

For instance, if you are well-prepared and confident about a test you are to take, you will approach the exam in a forthright fashion. You'll arrive on time, your pencils will be sharp, and you'll chuckle at the teacher's bad jokes. If your exam is missing a page, you'll notice it immediately and tell the proctor. And you'll enjoy the whole endeavor, not simply because you expect a good grade, but because you are interacting effectively with the situation. You are in charge.

But if you are poorly prepared for a test, you will take the exam as a wimp would. You'll arrive late, and you'll bring a pencil when you need a pen—or vice versa. The teacher's jokes will annoy you. And it's only as you hand in the exam that you realize that it was missing an entire page. Oh no! You will be depressed and anxious about the test, not simply because you expect a poor grade, but because you are acting like an utter and total boob. You are not in charge: the exam is.

These extremes capture the endpoints of personal control. Although a person's sense of control is shaped by the facts of the matter, it is not identical to them. So, the confident student high on personal control may be overestimating her mastery of the material, while the unconfident student low on personal control may be underestimating his knowledge. What is intriguing and important about personal control is that these beliefs have effects on subsequent coping above-and-beyond the facts. All things being equal, the individual with a sense of control outperforms the individual without a sense of control. This happens even when all things are not equal.

The roots of contemporary theories of personal control go back to Alfred Adler and the neoFreudians, who proposed that people are driven to interact effectively with their environment. And, as you recall, Henry Murray introduced the achievement motive. In an important paper, Robert White (1959) drew these early ideas together and labelled the motivation to be competent **effectance motivation.** He called the experience of effective interaction with the environment a feeling of **efficacy.** Remember learning to catch a baseball, thread a needle, or choose a course schedule that let you sleep until noon? The exhilaration you felt as you mastered these activities is what White means by efficacy. Even today, you are impelled to do these things well, for no other reason than the pleasure that comes from doing something in a competent way.

The work of Adler, Murray, and White does not fall directly within the cognitive paradigm, since their constructs stressed the motivational aspects of a person's sense of control. But the cognitive revolution of the 1960s transformed these motivational theories by rephrasing them in the new language of information processing. Effectance changed from a motive, with biological connotations, to an idea (belief, expectation, attribution, or perception). Where the early theorists emphasized one's drive to master the environment, the new generation of theorists spoke instead of one's beliefs about whether or not this could be done.

Recasting effectance motivation as beliefs has two important implications. First, the attention of researchers is directed toward specific aspects of the person, since beliefs are always about something. Motivation can be general, but beliefs are always specific. The specificity of beliefs about personal control distinguishes them from traits (Chapter 8) and improves our ability to predict future behavior from them. Second, the cognitive transformation of personal control encourages researchers to look to the environment and the way that a person interacts with it. Where motives reside within a person, beliefs refer to both the person and her world. Again, since beliefs in personal control span the person, the environment, and their interaction, one's ability to predict future behavior is enhanced.

The consequences of people's beliefs about control were examined in a variety of studies in the 1960s. "Control" was operationalized in different ways: as ability to choose, as ability to predict, and so on. Regardless, research results converged to show that control is usually beneficial (Janis, 1983). Further, people do not need to exercise control in order to benefit from it (Averill, 1973; Miller, 1979; Thompson, 1981). The mere perception of control is sufficient to reduce stress, increase motivation, and encourage performance.

For instance, Glass and Singer (1972) exposed research subjects to bursts of an unpleasant noise. Half the subjects were told that they could shut off the noise by pushing a button; the other subjects were not given the option. All were then given a proofreading task. The subjects who believed they had control over the original noise (even though they never pushed the button) made fewer proofreading errors than the other subjects. What a striking illustration of the notion that behavior occurs in a psychological environment sometimes at odds with the physical world!

As noted, numerous theories of personal control compete in the professional literature. I'll describe some of the more important of these that emphasize individual differences. Then I'll propose a generic theory of personal control.

Locus of Control   Psychologist Julian B. Rotter (1954, 1966, 1975) introduced his popular **locus of control** construct within his social learning theory (see Chapter 14). Rotter was a student of both Adler and Lewin, and his theory of learning reflects the influence of both. Rotter believes that reinforcement strengthens a person's responses only when she expects the response to lead to further rewards. This expectation, in turn, is determined first by task-specific characteristics and second by generalized expectations about the nature of reward, which Rotter terms locus of control.

Locus of control is an individual difference, ranging from an *internal* orientation on the one hand (when the person believes that rewards are brought about by his own actions) to an *external* orientation on the other (when the individual believes that rewards are due to chance factors, fate, or powerful others). Locus of control is measured by a questionnaire Rotter (1966) devised. This questionnaire shows respondents pairs of sentences, one reflecting internality and the other externality. The subject chooses the sentence from each pair that she agrees with more:

a. No matter how hard you try some people just don't like you.
b. People who can't get others to like them just don't understand how to get along with others.

a. What happens is my own doing.
b. Sometimes I feel that I don't have enough control over the direction that my life is taking.

Internals go for internal statements, while externals agree mostly with external statements.

So what? Well, literally thousands of investigations have looked at locus of control. Phares (1978) summarizes the thrust of these investigations by noting that

our survey . . . has revealed the typical internal to be one who actively comes to grips with the world. Compared to the external, the internal is resistant to social pressure and dedicated to the pursuit of excellence. (p. 295)

In a responsive environment—and this qualification is critical—individuals with an internal locus of control receive all sorts of benefits that elude those with an external locus of control.

Learned Helplessness and Explanatory Style   Helplessness theory is an account of why people (and animals) act in an inappropriately passive way and fail to cope with demands fully within their competence. Psychologists Steve Maier and Martin Seligman (1976) suggest that individuals act helplessly because they have learned to be helpless. The critical determinant of such helplessness is experience with uncontrollable events. What happens when someone repeatedly encounters bad outcomes, regardless of what he does or does not do?

According to Maier and Seligman, he learns that the bad outcomes are indeed uncontrollable. This learning leads to a general expectation that future outcomes will be uncontrollable. The diminished sense of personal control thereby produces ineffective behavior.

Learned helplessness was first investigated in dogs and rats. Maier and Seligman exposed animals to a series of uncontrollable shocks. Twenty-four hours later, the animals were tested in a shuttlebox. In a shuttlebox an animal receives a shock that it can turn off by moving from one end of the box to the other (that is, by shuttling). Most animals learn to shuttle with no difficulty.

Beliefs about control can determine your behavior.

In striking contrast, though, the animal previously exposed to uncontrollable shocks fails to learn how to escape. It sits there and passively absorbs the shocks. In a word, the animal is *helpless.* You might be thinking that the helpless animal was traumatized by the shocks the day before, but this is not the case. Dogs or rats exposed to physically identical shocks that they can control have no trouble learning to escape in the shuttlebox.

Seligman (1975) argues that learned helplessness occurs among people as well as animals. Research shows that a host of psychological and physical difficulties follow bad life events outside a person's control—like unemployment, death of a spouse, or victimization. The generalization of helplessness theory from animals to people was far from perfect, though, since research also shows that people exhibit a variety of responses to the same life events.

What determines people's helplessness versus vigor in the face of uncontrollability? In a refinement of helplessness theory, Lyn Abramson, John Teasdale, and Martin Seligman (1978) argued that one important influence on reactions to uncontrollability is a person's causal interpretation of the original bad events. So, Heider's (1958) naive psychology was invoked to provide insight into human helplessness.

When people encounter an uncontrollable event, they ask why it happened. Their answer channels their particular response to the event. Three aspects of causal explanation are important. An *internal* explanation ("It's me") makes self-esteem loss more likely than an *external* explanation ("It's the economy"). A *stable* explanation ("It's going to last forever") leads to more prolonged helplessness than an *unstable* explanation ("It's the glare from Haley's comet"). A *global* explanation ("It's going to screw up everything that I do") produces more pervasive deficits than a *specific* explanation ("It's the heat in that place").

Individuals show a characteristic style of offering causal explanations for bad events, habitually favoring certain explanations instead of others. They have an **explanatory style,** which can be measured with a questionnaire that I helped develop (Peterson, Semmel, von Baeyer, Abramson, Metalsky, & Seligman, 1982). This **Attributional Style Questionnaire** (or **ASQ**) presents research subjects with hypothetical events for them to explain. To the degree that an individual offers internal, stable, and global explanations for bad events, he responds poorly to such events when they occur. In contrast, the individual who construes the causes of bad events in external, unstable, and specific terms is robust (Peterson & Seligman, 1984).

The helplessness model and its refinement in terms of explanatory style has been applied widely to human ills. Depression, academic failure, bureaucratic apathy, response to child abuse, and even infectious illness have been viewed from the helplessness model. I'll describe some of these applications in Chapter 13. In the present context, what is important about learned helplessness and explanatory style is that they exemplify psychology's concern with personal control.

They also fit nicely within the cognitive paradigm. The original helplessness experiments with animals show the basic gestalt concern with relationships, in this case between behaviors and outcomes. Applied to people, learned helplessness theory assumes first that a person's perception of reality is critical, and second that a person acts "logically" in keeping with this perception. Learned helplessness is striking because the perception ends up being wrong.

Self-efficacy   As previously described, Albert Bandura (1977a, 1978, 1986) proposes a personal control cognate in the context of his cognitive theory. Much of Bandura's research is in the area of behavior modification. He tries to change phobic responses and to isolate the critical element responsible. Bandura has demonstrated that phobias can be alleviated through **vicarious learning.** Someone afraid of spiders may stop avoiding them and even be able to handle them without fear if she watches another person do it.

Bandura believes that at the heart of a phobia (or other maladaptive response) is the belief that you cannot cope with objects and events in the world. If you are phobic, you believe that you cannot master the situation presented by the spider, the wide-open space, the speech to be given, and so on. Modelling is effective if it strengthens an individual's personal control, which Bandura terms self-efficacy. A heightened sense of self-efficacy leads to changes in behaviors that are not specifically modelled, to a decrease in emotionality, and to a normalization of physiological functioning.

Bandura's research demonstrates that an individual's self-efficacy for a given response ("I am certain that I can let the spider walk up my arm") is a better predictor of whether he performs this response than his past success or failure in performing it. One of psychology's few truisms is that past behavior predicts future behavior; Bandura's research shows that attention to personal control improves upon it. And, in contrast to the other approaches to personal control, Bandura restricts his construct to specific contexts. He always specifies self-efficacy for some particular situation and some particular response.

A Generic Theory of Personal Control   I've written a paper with psychiatrist Albert Stunkard arguing that the different theories of personal control are more alike than different (Peterson & Stunkard, 1986). We combined locus of control, learned helplessness, self-efficacy, and another dozen or so similar theories. Here is the composite we created:

1. Personal control is one of the important ways in which people differ from each other.
2. Personal control resides in the transaction between the person and the world; it is neither just a disposition nor just a characteristic of the environment.
3. Personal control may take the form of believing that one can effect actual outcomes, choose among them, cope with their consequences, and/or understand them.
4. In a responsive environment, personal control is desirable; it encourages emotional, behavioral, and physiological vigor in the face of challenge.
5. Personal control may be thwarted by failure and encouraged by success, although it does not bear a one-to-one relationship to past patterns of success and failure.

So, personal control is both a cause and a consequence of the way people respond to their environment.

Stunkard and I believe that theories of personal control are popular today because personal control is a salient matter in the world. Perhaps it is *the* salient issue of the times, in a way that it has never been before. Several historical factors combine to make the 1980s the age of personal control.

First is the unlimited number of choices that we face among material goods: What kind of car? What color refrigerator? What brand of running shoes? What kind of personal computer? Which hunger relief campaign? These choices may sometimes overwhelm us (don't we all wish that AT&T again headed a telephone monopoly), but they underscore the control we have over the trappings of the material world.

Second is the series of assassinations of charismatic American leaders: John F. Kennedy, Martin Luther King, and Robert Kennedy; and the rash of terrorism and highjacking. The fact that a lone gunman can bring about profound changes in the course of world events is an unparalleled realization. Assassins and terrorists have control, and in the face of their deeds, everyday people have no control.

Third is the Vietnam War and the generation that protested against it. Raised in accordance with Dr. Spock, who counselled parents to follow their children's lead in choosing when and where to eat, sleep, and be toilet trained, the young people of the 1960s exercised the personal control encouraged within them. However murky the Vietnam era may be, it is clear that millions of individuals decided against all precedent *not* to participate in a war. And they didn't. Personal control became the badge of this generation, whose members are now leading figures in the social sciences.

Fourth, and perhaps most importantly, since Hiroshima, we have been faced with the possibility that a single individual can end life for all of us simply by pushing a button, regardless of anything the rest of us might do.

Personal control is a critical issue in a world that can be destroyed by a single individual.

Again: personal control ranging from total to nil is illustrated in a way never so clear to previous generations. Is it surprising that psychologists within the cognitive paradigm accord such importance to one's belief in personal control?

Schemata

The other topic of current interest within the cognitive paradigm is the **schema** (plural: schemata), defined as "a cognitive structure that represents one's general knowledge about a given concept or concept domain" (Fiske & Taylor, 1984, p. 13). Think of a schema as a filter or template: *a structure for making sense of the world, a way of going beyond actual information to make inferences.* Whether or not a person has a schema for a certain domain is a critical individual difference affecting attention, recall, and the use of information within that domain.

Suppose you have a schema about sororities and their members. One of your classmates wears a sweatshirt emblazoned with Greek letters, so you assume that she is a member of a sorority. She mentions that she will be busy the next weekend, so you assume that she is involved in the whirl of parties planned for the school's homecoming. In class the next Monday she looks tired, and her eyes are red, so you assume she stayed up late drinking too much.

Your assumptions may be correct, but notice that you did not directly observe any of the events and behaviors that seem plausible to you. Your schema gives rise to your assumptions, and in this example, you can see some of the beliefs that make it up:

- Young women who wear sweatshirts with Greek letters on them are sorority members.
- Sorority members go to parties on homecoming weekend.
- At parties, sorority members drink too much.

Notice that these beliefs are associated with each other. One leads to another. Given certain information, certain beliefs are entertained—given those beliefs, other beliefs are entertained—and so on.

But suppose your classmate is an exchange student from Athens. Suppose her family visited her in the United States for the first time in several years. Early Monday morning she bid them a tearful farewell at the airport. Your sorority schema, although sometimes quite useful in making sense of the world, has steered you wrong.

The notion of a schema should sound much like some of the other cognitive constructs mentioned in this chapter—like Kelly's personal construct or Harvey, Hunt, and Schroder's conceptual systems theory. It shares much in common with them, including a direct ancestry in gestalt psychology. Schema notions have long been popular in experimental psychology's study of cognition, where they are used to explain the organization inherent in memory (Bartlett, 1932). By this view, a person's memory is an active process of interpretation.

Contrast this with another view of memory that sees the process as essentially passive, as making a carbon copy of the sensations and perceptions we experience and retrieving the copy whenever we remember anything. This is a commonsense perspective, but experimental psychologists have proven it wrong (Neisser, 1967). Memory instead involves the interpretation of events through their assimilation to existing knowledge. The notion that memory is active has been shown in numerous experiments that find that people "remember" events that never occurred if these events are congruent with other beliefs and experiences. So, in the earlier example of the Greek student, you are positive that she told you she was in a sorority because all of your other ideas lead you to this (mistaken) memory.

On the other hand, experiments have also shown that people fail to remember events that actually did occur if these events are incongruent with their general knowledge. Again, the Greek student may have once mentioned that she was familiar with the Parthenon, but this fact did not stay with you, since it didn't jibe with your view of her.

More generally, people may not know that they go beyond the information available. Because one's inferences are often correct, there is a fuzzy line between them and actual facts about the world. This is an example of contextualism and the essence of the cognitive paradigm. One's schema is the meeting point of the person and the world; it refers to both.

So far, I have not explicitly applied the schema notion to personality. The original proponents of schemata were interested in molecular activities like learning and memory. Schema ideas began to be applied to personality when gestalt psychologists like Kurt Lewin, Solomon Asch, and Fritz Heider transported gestalt ideas to complex behaviors. All argued that social behavior needs to be understood by attending to the individual's interpretations, and further that these interpretations have a particular structure or pattern—what is now called a schema.

An early application of the schema idea to personality was **implicit personality theory** (Schneider, 1973), another instance of the person-as-scientist metaphor. Most people have a "theory" about personality: about which traits go with each other. They use these theories to make sense of themselves and others. Like all cognitive strategies, sometimes these theories prove useful in predicting, understanding, and even controlling what happens. Other times, these theories get the person into trouble.

Psychologist Daryl Bem gives us insight into the implicit personality theories of students who take one of his large classes and find him "open, personable, and friendly before a sea of 300 faces" (Bem & Allen, 1974, p. 509). Their "theory" about personality leads them to assume that Professor Bem will be even more outgoing when they visit him in his office. Instead, he is "rather formal" in this different setting, and they become confused. He appears "blatantly inconsistent" (p. 509). The careful way of describing his inconsistency is *not* to attribute it to the discrepancy between what he does in one setting versus another so much as to say that it occurs between what he does and what his students believe he should do.

You saw in Chapter 9 how Walter Mischel (1968) used schemata to criticize trait theories of personality. According to Mischel, people "see" consistency that isn't really present because their schemata concerning personality traits includes the assumption of consistency. They fill in the blanks and make consistency out of nothing at all.

Nancy Cantor and Walter Mischel (1977, 1979) argue that the trait terms popular in personality psychology are really ideal categories (or **prototypes**) used by people to make sense of themselves and others. These categories reflect on the one hand actual characteristics of people and on the other hand implicit "theories" about people. In their research, Cantor and Mischel demonstrate how prototypes affect what we perceive and remember about a person. So, if we are told that someone we are to meet is an extravert, we tend to notice their outgoing behaviors and recall them later. By using such schemata to understand other people, we exaggerate the consistencies they show.

However, an interesting thing happened to this criticism of personality consistency: theorists became interested in schemata as personality characteristics in their own right. Implicit in all the examples in this section is the possibility that people differ in the content and/or structure of their schemata for a given domain.

But to decide if schemata are good examples of personality characteristics, we need to know if they are general and enduring. You know from Chapter 9 that this question is much more subtle than it first seems. Taking into account the subtleties, the answer is a qualified yes. A schema is a way of making sense of the world, which means that one interprets events with the schema. We must stand somewhere to paint a floor. Similarly, we must have a particular vantage to understand the world. That is the schema; it must precede what we do with it. This guarantees that our schemata have a degree of consistency and continuity.

At the same time, let me emphasize that a schema is not a trait. First, by definition, a schema is tied to a particular domain. It refers to a subset of the world. The situational specificity of a schema is part of its meaning. A person's schema for sports cars, let us say, is mostly irrelevant to the way she thinks about her family members. (Unless little sister happens to be low-slung, and dear old Dad runs best on premium.)

Second, a schema is not fixed. We use it to interpret events we encounter, but at the same time, a schema changes as we use it. Schemata have inertia; they do not always change rapidly in the face of contrary facts, and sometimes they do not change at all. But schemata do not blind us completely to information inconsistent with them. I've been known to misread the thermometer outside my window and leave my apartment without bringing a coat. Despite my belief that it is warm outside, my chattering teeth and blue fingers soon persuade me that I am wrong. The same happens with respect to any schemata, although individual differences exist in the responsiveness of schemata to contrary information.

A full-blown schema theory of personality has yet to be proposed. However, it will incorporate the different schemata of interest to current investigators (Fiske & Taylor, 1984). **Person schemata** refer to someone's implicit personality theory. **Self-schemata** are systems of belief about one's own characteristics and behavior. (Self-schemata dovetail with the self as Rogers conceives it; Cartwright & Graham, 1984.) **Role schemata** describe norms and beliefs for broad social categories—like teacher or student, and **event schemata** pertain to the standard sequence of events for social occasions—like asking someone for a date or a ride to the airport.

Depicting someone's personality with these various schemata would require characterization of both their content and their structure. Psychologist Anthony Greenwald (1980) has made a start toward this goal by arguing that the typical "self" is characterized by information–control strategies (that is, schemata) akin to those used by totalitarian political regimes. Greenwald argues that people continually fabricate and revise their personal history so that their own role in events is highlighted and aggrandized. And what happens if a person does not have a totalitarian ego? They become depressed (Alloy & Abramson, 1979)!

An intriguing possibility of a schema theory of personality is that traits may be recast in schema language. Remember Sandra Bem's (1974) work on androgyny described in Chapter 9? In her recent work, she interprets one's sex-role orientation with what she calls a **gender schema:** beliefs about appropriate characteristics and behaviors of males and females (Bem, 1981). Many people in our society assimilate their self-concept to their gender schema, resulting in sex-typed individuals who regard social interaction in terms of gender.

Just yesterday I was at a restaurant sitting next to four middle-aged men. Their waitress was a young woman. The men joked and teased her throughout the meal. Without exception, every comment they made to her referred to her appearance and her sexuality. I've probably "genderized" such interactions myself, but to see it done by someone else was sobering.

Where do androgynous individuals fit into this theory? I think you can anticipate how androgyny is interpreted. Bem suggests that androgynous individuals do not view the world through the framework of a gender schemata, and so they are different from "traditional" masculine and feminine individuals.

This new view is more powerful than Bem's previous interpretation of androgyny as a trait. Gender schema theory encompasses the person and the world, and so it explains where androgyny is adaptive (that is, situations not divided into pink and blue) and where it is not. The theory explains how androgyny originates and changes. Perhaps most importantly, it has just as much to say about traditional individuals as it does about androgynous individuals.

If other trait theorists follow Bem's example, I'll have to change the organization of this book in future editions. Schema approaches to personality may lead to a genuine integration of the different personality psychology paradigms. Perhaps we will someday define a trait as a schema. Consistent with the research reviewed in Chapter 9, we will be forced to attend to person-environment interactions. We will not just acknowledge consistency or inconsistency with respect to particular characteristics, but be able to explain them as well: by the presence or absence of a schema.

Needless to say, this vision is far in the future, and several shortcomings work against the early attainment of a schema theory of personality. First, the schema notion is criticized as "mushy" (Fiske & Linville, 1980). Because it is not embedded in a general theory, its meaning is not clear. Second, schemata are seen as "nothing new" (Fiske & Linville, 1980). Is a schema different than a system of personal constructs? At a conceptual level, I think not. However, at a research level, they are quite different, and schema research promises to surmount certain problems with personal construct research. (In the next chapter, I'll explain what this means.) Third, in common with other cognitive theories of personality, the schema approach pays more attention to "cold" activities like perception and memory than to "hot" activities like motivation and passion. Fourth, theorists have little interest in the physiological underpinnings—if any—of schemata.

SUMMARY

The cognitive paradigm of personality psychology looks to an individual's thoughts and beliefs as the essence of her personality. Since thoughts are always about something, cognitive theories are concerned with the interplay between the person and the world. The contents of a person's thoughts, their organization or structure, or the process by which they change are emphasized.

In this chapter I sketched the origins of the cognitive paradigm in gestalt psychology, particularly the work of Kurt Lewin and Fritz Heider. Both of these theorists stressed the importance of understanding reality as the individual perceives it. And both believed that behavior is best described in **field** terms.

Next I described George Kelly's **personal construct** theory, an extended elaboration of the person-as-scientist metaphor. According to Kelly, people seek to predict and control events in the world by using categories—personal constructs—to interpret them. Although proposed in 1955, Kelly's theory continues to be the most impressive cognitive statement regarding personality.

Then I reviewed three other cognitive approaches to personality: the **self-theory** of Carl Rogers (concerned with the agreement or disagreement between a person's perceived self and his ideal self), the **conceptual systems theory** of O. J. Harvey, David Hunt, and Harold Schroder (based on a view of people as information processors), and the more recent **cognitive social learning theory** of Walter Mischel and Albert Bandura (interested in how thought mediates a person's learning). I concluded the chapter by considering two topics of considerable contemporary interest: **personal control** and **schemata**.

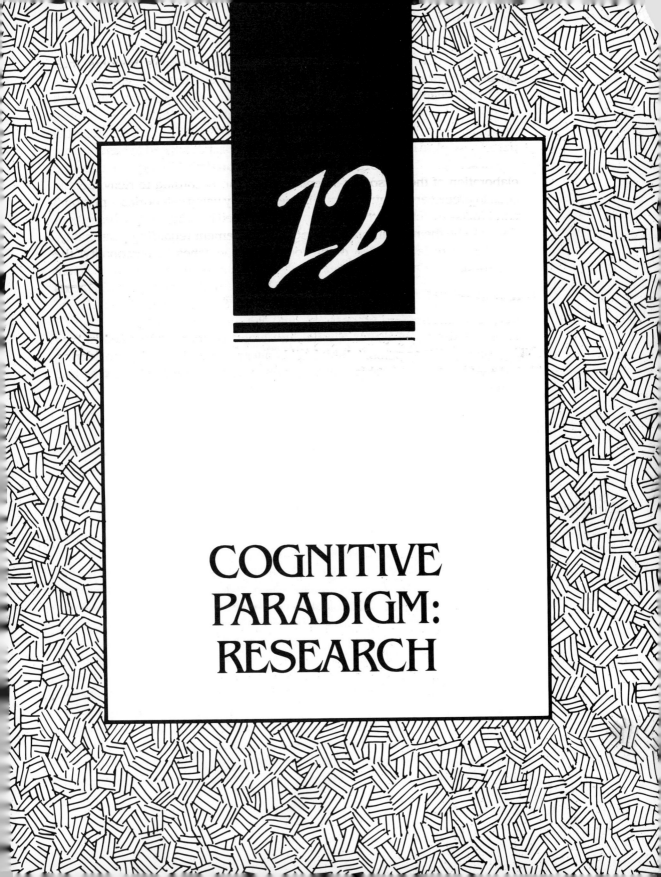

12

COGNITIVE PARADIGM: RESEARCH

The psychoanalytic paradigm is dominated by the case history approach. The trait paradigm frequently uses questionnaires. What is the favorite research technique of the cognitive paradigm? There is no simple answer. Various strategies for "getting inside the head" have been employed, with no single procedure being the overwhelming favorite of cognitive researchers (Taylor & Fiske, 1982). Indeed, research strategies are among the weakest links of this approach to personality.

Thoughts and beliefs—the subject matter of the cognitive paradigm—create the problem. Cognition is not observable in the same sense that we can see smiles or frowns. Instead, a person's thoughts and thought processes must be inferred from what he or she does. So far, this is no different than the psychoanalytic paradigm, in which the researcher makes inferences from what can be observed to what cannot be observed. But the cognitive paradigm is more complicated because of its assumption that people are conscious, active, and rational agents. These assumptions assign great importance to self-report in assessing an individual's cognitions.

But as you can imagine, self-report about cognitive matters may be suspect, regardless of how conscious, active, or rational someone might be. Even Mr. Spock is occasionally stumped. We have seen that cognitions are not the same thing as vocabulary. Stated another way, *cognitions are not the same thing as reports on cognitions.* Although most researchers subscribe to this truism, it's not clear what one should do with it.

Let's distinguish two general approaches. The first asks for a person's self-report on beliefs, attitudes, and the like. This approach shares much in common with questionnaire approaches in the trait paradigm except that the person reports his thoughts instead of his behaviors. To the degree that these thoughts are available to awareness and not distorted by confounds like social desirability, then self-report is a valid strategy. So, investigators concerned with personal control typically ask subjects about their control-relevant beliefs: "How confident are you that you can let the spider crawl up your arm?"

The other strategy popular in studying cognition borrows from experimental psychology. For instance, subjects may be given reaction-time tasks or memory tasks. At first glance these procedures seem identical to those used for one hundred years by experimental psychologists interested in molecular processes. But when personality psychologists use these procedures, it is not to study recall or reaction time per se but to make inferences about the underlying structures and processes that characterize personality. So researchers interested in depression look at how well depressed individuals recall their good versus bad experiences. Someone who is depressed is apt to remember bad events more accurately than good events; someone who is not depressed exhibits the opposite pattern of recall (Blaney, 1986).

Like self-report measures of cognition, these experimental probes are problematic. It is time-consuming to use these procedures. Subjects must be studied one at a time, sometimes for several hours, and even with such an extensive period of study, only a handful of cognitive domains can be investigated. While this is in keeping with the cognitive paradigm's distrust of broad dispositions and concern with specific cognitions, it interferes with a goal of all personality psychologists—to study what is *general* about an individual's behavior.

To help me decide which general approach (questionnaires or experimental tasks) is better for studying cognition, I distinguish between cognitive content and cognitive process. My rule of thumb is that cognitive content is studied through self-report, while cognitive process is studied with the complicated laboratory procedures pioneered by experimental psychologists. (Cognitive style can be studied with either approach.)

Nevertheless, here are some qualifications. As I mentioned in Chapter 11, it is not always clear where content ends and structure and process begin. Those cognitions in awareness are not always easy to identify. More basically, cognitions are not necessarily "real." They do not refer to entities that literally exist in a person's mind. When I've talked about cognition so far, I've used a casual way of speaking, one that treats cognitive contents, structures, and processes as if they pertain to real things.

But when the subject is examined carefully, such usage is impossible to justify. English philosopher Gilbert Ryle (1949), in his book *The Concept of Mind*, reminds us that "things" of the mind are not identical to "things" of the physical world. Ryle coins the term **category mistake** to explain the dangers of metaphorical speaking that does not recognize the metaphor. So, both everyday people and cognitive theorists speak of the mind in metaphorical terms, using expressions from the physical world. Consider these examples:

I see what you mean.

My thoughts are jumbled.

I crammed for the examination.

That information is at my fingertips.

Then again, perhaps it's not so clear.

I lost my way.

Let's go over that again.

It is a category mistake to forget that these expressions, though applied to cognition, are really taken from physical objects. Indeed, the basic distinctions I make among cognitive content, structure, and dynamics should sound

[handwritten margin note: They might not pertain to real things its hard to justify]

familiar to those who have studied physics. Over the years, cognitive theorists have explicitly borrowed these terms.

Are cognitions real? The answer is no, at least in the way we speak about them. Cognitive terms are best regarded as **hypothetical constructs,** as notions that the theorist devises to account for what she observes (Mac-Corquodale & Meehl, 1948). However, she should not go one step further and regard these terms as referring to something tangible.

Essentially *all* cognitive variables—at least at this time—are best thought of as hypothetical constructs. And hypothetical constructs should be measured with more than one operation. As hypothetical entities in a conceptual domain, their meaning can only be captured with a host of measures that presumably triangulate and converge. Unfortunately, this is not frequently done.

When cognitive researchers stay with one procedure, it can be frustrating to those of us who study their work. Cognitive theories have considerable overlap and are readily translatable, from one to another. For instance, Kelly's personal construct theory can be used to give an account of Rogers's self-theory. Conceptual systems theory can be used to express schema theory. But none of this is ever done! We are left with researchers interested in personal construct theory who use the REP Test exclusively, researchers interested in conceptual systems theory who use the TIB exclusively, researchers interested in self-theory who use Q-sorts exclusively, researchers interested in locus of control who use Rotter's scale exclusively. And so on. The relationships among these measures are simply not known.

Is all dark? Not really, because within each line of work there are solid and interesting empirical findings. (These were sketched in Chapter 11 as I described each theory.) My point here is to describe the bigger picture, however diffuse it may be. As you read the present chapter, you may suspect that you are missing something. Don't worry. Links among the different theories and lines of research within the cognitive paradigm are indeed missing. Among the three paradigms of personality, the cognitive paradigm is the most recent to take form. At the present time, it is also a hotly researched area. We can expect, therefore, that these links will soon be forged.

ASSESSING COGNITION WITH QUESTIONNAIRES

As you've just seen, many of the important cognitive theorists favor a particular questionnaire to assess an individual's cognition. Within each line of research, these questionnaires have been elevated to a rather sacred status, hampering methodological refinement. In this section, I'll describe a notable exception to this trend: the efforts of psychologist William A. Scott (1969, 1974). First at the University of Colorado (where he was my professor) and then at Australian National University, Scott developed a number of questionnaires for measuring individual differences in cognition. He has investigated important issues within the cognitive paradigm that other approaches—with their undue reliance on single procedures—have not been able to address. I'll first describe Scott's procedures in detail. Then I'll compare them to other questionnaire approaches within the cognitive paradigm.

Scott starts not with a particular theory of personality but rather with a general view of cognition as *the ascription of attributes to objects* (Scott, Osgood, & Peterson, 1979). An **attribute** is any basis a person uses to group or distinguish objects. So, my class roll is a list of my students ("objects") followed by their class level and major field of study ("attributes"). You think about your friends ("objects") in terms of their characteristics ("attributes").

One of the most important attributes that a person ascribes to objects is an evaluation: good, bad, ugly, or indifferent. If you like tutti-frutti ice cream, is your liking a reflection of you or of this particular dessert? Obviously both, and we see once again the central tenet of the cognitive approach to personality: cognitions span the transaction between the person and the world.

Perhaps you meditate, or know something about meditation. If so, consider this possibility. The goal of meditation is to think about events *without* ascribing attributes to them. One concentrates on breathing, for instance, as breathing—not in terms of whether it is labored or easy, louder or softer than someone else's, or good or bad. Meditation is difficult for most of us to do, which leads me to my main point: *in the course of everyday life, the ascription of attributes to objects is a natural and automatic activity.* It may lead to suffering, but it sure is easy.

Scott also introduces the notion of a **cognitive domain,** defined as a single set of cognitions: *a group of objects to which the same attributes can be meaningfully applied.* In limiting his attention to particular cognitive domains, Scott avoids the assumption that people have highly consistent ways of thinking about disparate topics. This may prove true, but we can investigate the possibility directly by comparing the way people think about different domains.

Cognitive domains are idiosyncratic. Different people group objects in different ways. For instance, compare a student at a commuting college with one at a school where most students live on campus. The first student is apt to regard the activities of "what I do where I live" and "what I do where I go to school" in different terms, while the second is less likely to make this distinction. In Scott's terms, the first student has two cognitive domains, while the second student has but one.

In practice, Scott takes a nomothetic approach to defining cognitive domains. He uses the conventions of a particular culture or language to identify

One goal of meditation is to think about events without ascribing attributes to them.

particular domains: for example, self-roles, nations, family activities, and so on. This means that for any given person, a nomothetic cognitive domain is more versus less coherent, and more versus less central. Think about the cognitive domain of women's clothing. On the whole, this is a more coherent and central domain for women than for men. But if a designer or a salesperson of women's clothing is a male, the domain coheres for him as well. He knows the language of 5's and 9's, juniors and petites, winters and springs.

Scott's view of cognition is implicit in many of the theories described in Chapter 11. Although Scott acknowledges that his object-attribute approach is awkward in describing certain aspects of cognition (like the rules of chess, for instance), he argues that it applies straightforwardly to most topics of concern within the cognitive paradigm. Note the similarity between Scott's cognitive domain and Lewin's life space, Kelly's construct system, Rogers's phenomenological reality, and so on.

How does Scott's formulation differ from that of Kelly or other theorists? Most importantly, he does not go much beyond his description of cognition in object-attribute terms. He takes no prior stance that the attributes a person uses are necessarily bipolar (as does Kelly). He does not assume that one is driven to assign the same attributes to the self as to the ideal self (as does

Rogers). And he does not propose that a person assigns attributes to objects in different domains in a similar fashion (as do Harvey, Hunt, and Schroder).

In short, Scott is not committed to particular theoretical stances, which is why his approach was not described in Chapter 11. He gives himself considerable latitude as a researcher, and has developed an array of techniques for assessing the ways people assign attributes to objects, using these to investigate the claims of a variety of cognitive theories.

Granted that an important aspect of cognition is the way that people assign attributes to objects, how do we depict this? Scott specifies properties of objects and attributes and the relationship between the two. Among the properties of an object are its **complexity** (the number of attributes assigned to it), its **valence** (the overall liking or disliking assigned to it), and its **ambivalence** (the relative mix of desirable and undesirable attributes used to describe it). I'm writing this paragraph shortly after the tragedy of the Space Shuttle Challenger. At this moment, I would imagine that most Americans have a complex, positive, yet highly ambivalent view of the shuttle program. You're reading this paragraph some time later. How would you characterize current opinions?

Cognitive attributes also have various properties. The **ordinality** of an attribute refers to whether its categories fall along a continuum, or whether they are simply different. Your college grade point average is ordinal, while

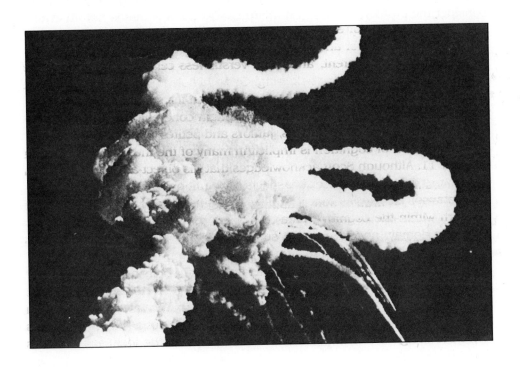

your major field of study is not. Personality traits are ordinal, but personality types are not. The salaries of major league baseball players are ordinal, but the positions they play (for example, defendant or witness for the prosecution) are not.

An attribute is **evaluative** to the degree that its categories are desirable or undesirable characteristics. The **precision** of an attribute is the number of distinctions it allows a person to make. A highly precise attribute is made up of many categories. Perhaps you have had the same experience that I have in the presence of a wine connoisseur: no idea what they're talking about when they appraise a particular wine with terms like woody, brittle, dry, subtle, or delightful. Though esoteric, their attributes are nevertheless precise. In contrast, mine extend to red versus white, cork versus no cork, cheap versus forget it.

The **centrality** of an attribute is the frequency that it is applied to objects in the domain. This is essentially what Kelly means by a construct's range of convenience. Remember Sandra Bem's notion of gender schema? She believes that for most people in our society, gender is a highly central attribute in the domains of self and others.

Finally, Scott also describes ways in which objects and attributes are related to each other, collectively called an individual's **cognitive structure.** One of the important properties is the **evaluative centrality** of a domain. To what degree are evaluative attributes more central than nonevaluative attributes? Consider the prototypic gossip: nothing passes his lips that is not an evaluation. Contrast what you hear from him with the error messages of a typical computer program, which patiently tell you that ERROR 237 was made 453 TIMES. There is no evaluation here, just a description. (I think of this example because when I was in college, a friend of mine had a job programming the error messages for the university computer. He decided to increase the evaluative centrality of the messages by following each description with a brief HA HA—YOU ****ED UP AGAIN! He was fired from his job, not simply for the "obscenity," but because he made the computer sound emotionally involved.)

Another property of cognitive structure is **image comparability:** the degree that all objects in a domain are described with the same set of attributes. Using my earlier point about (nomothetically defined) domains being more versus less coherent, you should see image comparability as an index of a domain's coherence. For an example of a domain with a high degree of image comparability, consider how physicists view the world. They use a scheme to describe the entire physical universe with respect to the same basic properties: mass, space, time, and whether it can be deducted on a 1040 tax form. For an example of a domain with a low degree of image comparability, consider Allport's vision of personality psychology as idiographic, describing each person with a unique set of traits. Since many consider high image comparability a prerequisite for science, you can see why Allport's approach has bothered many personality psychologists.

Another property of cognitive structure is **affective-evaluative consistency:** the degree that someone assigns favorable characteristics to liked objects and unfavorable characteristics to disliked objects. Consider Festinger's (1957) cognitive dissonance theory, which proposes that any form of inconsistency (such as, among the attributes one ascribes to the same object) is aversive to the individual and motivates her to change her evaluations. In contrast, Scott suggests that this "universal" tendency might be an individual difference. Some people only have friends who are saints and enemies who are dirtbags, but other people have friends with drawbacks and enemies with virtues. The former individuals are high on affective-evaluative consistency, while the latter individuals are low on this property of cognitive structure.

Finally, a cognitive domain has a characteristic level of **dimensionality,** what other cognitive theorists refer to as cognitive complexity (for example, Bieri, 1955). Does a person bring a variety of perspectives to bear on a particular topic? Does she have numerous personal constructs? When ascribing attributes to objects, does she use them independently or redundantly? A person with high dimensionality makes numerous distinctions among objects. Imagine Julia Child talking to you about food. A person with low dimensionality makes few distinctions. (Pass the ketchup, please.)

Scott's object-attribute model of cognition has two important implications. First, each of the properties it describes is an individual difference. Second, because these individual differences are explicitly defined, one can score them from responses to any task, procedure, or questionnaire that involves a person describing objects with attributes. Any time a person couples adjectives and nouns, he provides the necessary data for describing his cognition in Scott's terms.

Thus, the researcher has innumerable opportunities to assess individual differences in cognition and avoid undue reliance on a single questionnaire. Researchers might look at someone's letters, school essays, or diaries. They might listen to someone's casual conversations, formal speeches, or interview responses. They might even observe someone's overt behavior and infer the underlying attributes he uses to "classify" his actions. What actions does a person undertake at the same time or at different times? Which does he do with a smile or frown on his face? When is he energetic, and when is he sluggish?

Scott limits his assessment of individual differences in cognition to questionnaire responses. Here are descriptions of some of the questionnaires which ask respondents to describe objects with attributes:

Listing and Comparing Objects: The respondent generates twenty objects in a particular domain. Then he groups those objects together that are similar in an important way. He identifies the way they are similar. Finally, he groups those objects together that are different in this respect.

Free Description of Objects: The respondent is provided with twenty objects in a particular domain. Then she describes each in terms of its important characteristics. Finally, she rates each characteristic on a 7-point scale corresponding to how pleasant versus unpleasant it is.

Checklist Description of Objects: Respondents indicate whether each of seventy-two adjectives (representing thirty-six synonyms, half evaluative and half neutral) applies to each of twenty objects in a particular domain. They also indicate the degree to which they like or dislike each object.

Rating of Objects: The respondent uses ten bipolar rating scales to describe each of ten objects in a particular domain.

Most properties can be scored from most questionnaires. Think for a minute how this might be done. For instance, affective-evaluative consistency can be assessed from the *Checklist Description* questionnaire by calculating how frequently one assigns favorable characteristics to liked objects and unfavorable characteristics to disliked objects. And so forth.

Let's take stock. Scott defines many individual differences in cognition and provides many measures of them. So what? Well, the value of Scott's procedure can best be seen by comparing it to other questionnaire approaches within the cognitive paradigm. As noted earlier, each of the dominant theories tends to rely on a single questionnaire measure: the REP Test, the TIB, whatever.

You know from the discussion of trait research in Chapter 9 that there is considerable risk when one relies on a single questionnaire. A confound may distort a respondent's answers, but in the absence of a converging measure against which to validate the questionnaire, the confound remains undetected. Consider the REP Test as described in the last chapter. Research shows that cognitive complexity is sometimes correlated with general intelligence (for example, Vannoy, 1965) and with social desirability (Goldstein & Blackman, 1976). Do high cognitive complexity scores reflect the independent use of constructs, as personal construct theorists intend? Or do they instead reflect intelligence and/or acquiescence to social conventions? If the latter is at all true, interpretation of findings involving the REP Test must be drastically revised.

The REP Test is often administered to individuals with profound problems like depression or schizophrenia. Their responses invariably differ from those of people without such difficulties. Do these differences reside in the use of constructs per se (which are accurately reflected in REP Test responses), or do they reflect more general states like confusion, apathy, or suspicion? To repeat the point: sole reliance on one operationalization precludes the disentangling of such possibilities.

My purpose here is not to pick on the REP Test. Let me qualify my criticisms. First, I'm suggesting skepticism about questionnaire measures of cognition, not dismissal of the approach altogether. Second, I'm using the REP Test as a representative example. In a general review of questionnaire assessment of cognitive variables, Goldstein and Blackman (1978) criticize virtually all these tests. Third, researchers are well aware of the questions I raise, and they are trying to develop alternative questionnaire measures. Indeed, personal construct researchers are in the forefront of this attempt to broaden assessment (for example, Collett, 1979; Neimeyer & Neimeyer, 1981; Slater, 1976, 1977).

Still, I have highlighted the work of William Scott in this section because he has long recognized the difficulty of using questionnaires in cognitive research. His approach has not yet infiltrated the whole of the paradigm, but it represents a notable improvement over other questionnaire strategies. One reason why many researchers have yet to discover his questionnaires is ironic: his methodological focus! Scott has devoted much of his research program to developing his measures, so his substantive investigations are still very much in progress. Researchers in the cognitive paradigm are attracted to innovative ideas and findings, not to innovative procedures per se.

Scott has more recently used his multi-method strategy to investigate particular questions about the role of cognition in personality. Let me describe some of his findings. Keep in mind that these bear on most of the cognitive theories described in Chapter 11.

Do Different Measures of the Same Characteristics Agree? Appreciate that this is an extremely important question for personality psychologists interested in cognition. Yes, measures correlate, but the magnitude of these correlations is often close to the familiar .30 limit (Scott, Osgood, & Peterson, 1979). This means that even with respect to our thoughts about the same topic, we are far from showing perfect consistency. As Epstein recommends for measures of overt behavior, these results imply that cognitive researchers should aggregate as many measures of individual differences as possible.

Are Cognitive Properties General across Domains or Topic Specific? Again, appreciate that this is important to know. Theorists like Harvey, Hunt, and Schroder (1961) speak of abstractness versus concreteness regardless of content, while Mischel (1986) and especially Bandura (1986) prefer a much more circumscribed view. The answer is complex: there is evidence for consistency across different domains, but there is also evidence for topic specificity (Peterson & Scott, 1975). Depending on one's purpose, the researcher can speak about cognition in general or with respect to a particular topic.

What Is the Effect of Increased Experience and Information on Cognitive Structure? A variety of studies indicate that the more familiar you are with a cognitive domain, the greater your dimensionality with respect to it (Scott, Osgood, & Peterson, 1979). These findings support the general assumption by cognitive theorists that our thoughts and beliefs move toward increased sophistication and accuracy (at least if we assume that the world itself is a complicated state of affairs best understood in complicated terms).

What Is the Principle That Describes Cognitive Organization? The cognitive theories described in Chapter 11 propose that in the course of development, cognitions become more complex and at the same time more interconnected. The different theories hypothesize that various principles dictate this latter process. Rogers nominates congruence, for instance, while Kelly suggests that constructs become arranged in a hierarchy. Note that several of Scott's variables describe modes of integration among cognitions: evaluative centrality, image comparability, and affective-evaluative consistency. Are any of these predominant? The answer is no (Scott, 1974). Different people show different types of integration, and the type favored by the same individual may well vary across cognitive domains. This should give pause to theorists seeking a single tendency guiding cognitive development.

How Does Cognitive Structure Pertain to Psychological Well-being? Scott and Peterson (1975) found that well-adjusted college students (as judged by themselves and their friends) think about self and others as positive, univalent, and high in affective-evaluative consistency. These results are consistent with Rogers's view of mental health, as well as with that of the neo-Freudians (Chapter 5) who link personal adjustment with harmonious social relations.

Evaluation I've described Scott's method in detail because it stands in contrast to other cognitive approaches that use questionnaires. These other approaches rarely assess cognitive characteristics in more than one way, so there is no way of telling if scores reflect the characteristic of theoretical concern or some confound. When researchers occasionally create converging measures, their results are disappointing (for example, Goldstein & Blackman, 1978; Streufert & Streufert, 1978). Scott has been more successful in devising satisfactory measures, but even his successes are modest.

Several drawbacks to Scott's approach are evident. First, research subjects completing the measures must expend an inordinate amount of time and effort to complete them. Not all potential subjects have the inclination or ability to answer questionnaires for eight to ten hours. Second, Scott's lack of a theoretical stance cuts both ways. While it frees him from certain assumptions that may prove limiting, it also cuts the methods adrift. Theories tell researchers what to do with their techniques. Scott doesn't have a theory, so his substantive research proceeds quite slowly. Third, and relatedly, Scott has tended not to investigate how overt behaviors relate to his properties of cognitive structure.

ASSESSING COGNITION WITH PROCESS ANALYSIS

In contrasting measures of cognitive content with measures of cognitive process, Susan Fiske and Shelley Taylor (1984) ask their readers to compare a snapshot to a movie. What information does each convey? More importantly, what information does each fail to convey?

Like a photograph, questionnaires can freeze cognition for a moment and give a detailed look at content. William Scott's questionnaires represent the state of the art in capturing content. But whether a questionnaire resembles a Nikon or an Instamatic, it cannot capture cognition in use. How does cognitive structure develop? How does it shape behavior? How does it change in response to the world? These are questions about our thought processes, and they require assessment procedures that are sensitive to time.

Like a movie, these procedures follow the action over a period and depict the sequence of cognitive events. What complicates matters for cognitive psychologists (making them envious of those who make real movies for a living) is that cognitive events can never be literally glimpsed. Their presence or absence can only be inferred from observable actions of research subjects. How many words are remembered? In what order are items recalled? How quickly is a decision made?

Answers to these questions can give insights into cognitive processes when coupled with a theoretical statement about how we make sense of the world (Fiske & Taylor, 1984). However, in the absence of hypotheses, data about recall and reaction time are just numbers that are of no interest whatsoever to the personality psychologist. Contrast this with the approach of William Scott, where descriptions can be important in their own right.

Perhaps you are wondering why researchers don't use questionnaires to measure process, since they can give researchers considerable latitude. Remember my familiar warning: *cognitive processes are not typically available to someone's awareness.* Go back and read the preceding sentence carefully. It does *not* say that people are unaware of what they are thinking. It merely says that people cannot report on how they arrived at their thoughts, on why their beliefs change, or on what determines their beliefs.

I've mentioned several times Richard Nisbett and Timothy Wilson's (1977) argument that respondents to a questionnaire will "tell more than they can know" if posed questions about cognitive processes. If asked what factors influenced their preference among a series of consumer goods placed on a table, subjects will give an elaborate account of how they arrived at their decision. No one mentions the possibility that they were influenced by the location of the goods on the table, although subjects clearly prefer whatever item is on the far right.

The Nisbett and Wilson (1977) argument is an important caution to cognitive researchers: *don't confuse one's reports on a cognitive process with the process itself.* But some hear their argument as saying more than it really does, as arguing against self-report altogether in studying cognition, since people don't know what they're talking about. This is an unwarranted generalization.

First, this extreme version of Nisbett and Wilson's conclusion ignores the useful distinction between content and process. The experiments reported by Nisbett and Wilson ask a person to give his preference, for instance, with no second-guessing of the validity of *this* self-report. Second, even if a person is wrong about what determines her thoughts and beliefs, a psychologist trying to understand her personality is interested in this information. The central tenet of the cognitive paradigm is that one's thoughts and beliefs lie at the center of feelings and actions. This is true whether one's thoughts are reasonable or unreasonable.

But if the researcher wishes to understand cognitive process, then she must go beyond self-report questionnaires and study cognition across time. Fiske and Taylor (1984) provide a useful catalogue of techniques to do this. All start with a hypothesis about the presumed process, and then gather information to decide if the hypothesis is plausible or implausible.

Measures of Attention   We've seen that cognitive theories of personality liken cognitive structures to filters. They determine what we pay attention to in the world, and what we ignore. Following this logic, the researcher can work backwards from information about someone's attention (or inattention) to make conclusions about the person's cognition. Various strategies for assessing attention have thus been developed, ranging from technologically sophisticated videotapes of eye movements (where are one's eyeballs directed, and for how long) to primitive measures of how long someone stares at different items on a bulletin board.

For instance, Mischel, Ebbesen, and Zeiss (1973) had college students take a battery of personality tests. Then they prepared two notebooks for each student, one containing information about the supposed positive aspects of his or her personality and the other containing information about the supposed negative aspects. Next, each subject took a bogus intelligence test.

The researchers told half of the subjects that they had scored particularly well and the other half that they had scored particularly poorly. (Whether a given subject "succeeded" or "failed" was determined randomly.) After hearing about their intelligence test performance, the subjects were left alone with their "personality profile" notebooks for ten minutes.

The experimenters were curious about the amount of time subjects spent looking at positive information about themselves versus the amount of time spent looking at negative information. Success on the intelligence test led to greater attention to one's assets, while failure led to greater attention to one's liabilities, supporting the idea that people's thoughts and experiences seek congruence. When I was little and moped around, my mother would ask me if I wanted to go and eat some worms. Why not give myself an experience fully as wretched as my attitude? My mother was teasing, of course, but the experiment I've just described shows that people will do something analogous. In this case, a measure of attention leads to this conclusion.

Measures of Memory   Researchers interested in cognitive schemata are particularly fond of studying an individual's memory. Remember that a schema is a cognitive structure that represents what a person knows about some aspect of the world. In our transactions with the world, we use our schemata to go beyond the information given. An excellent way to understand someone's schema, therefore, is to see how and what a person remembers about a particular experience that's under the researcher's control.

Since the researcher knows what the facts actually are, any departures evident in a subject's recall or recognition suggest that a schema is operating. Suppose a subject is given a list of words that describe personality traits, some positive (for example, bright-eyed and bushy-tailed) and some negative (for example, dazed and confused). Ten minutes later he is asked to recall as many of these words as possible. What does it mean if he comes up with most of the negative traits and none of the positive ones? Some conclude that he has a "depressive" schema organized around negative views of himself and the world (for example, Derry & Kuiper, 1981). Most people remember more of the positive traits.

Do you see the interplay between the person and the world, and how the schema is the locus for this transaction? If the depressed person is attuned to bad things by virtue of his depressive schema, he will become more and more depressed as he thinks about his life, since he remembers what is bad. And if the nondepressed person is attuned to good things, she will be robust in the face of disappointments, since she remembers what is good about her life.

In her investigations of gender schema theory, Sandra Bem (1981) uses memory measures to support her argument that sex-typed individuals think in terms of gender. Subjects in one of her experiments completed her Sex

Role Inventory (Chapter 9). Then they were given a list of words in random order. Some of the words were considered masculine, since previous subjects had consistently rated them so (for example: gorilla, trousers); other words were considered feminine, again because of ratings by previous subjects (for example: butterfly, bikini); still other words were neutral (for example: ant, sweater).

After seeing the list of words, Bem gave her subjects a sheet of paper and asked them to write down as many of the words as they could remember, in any order. The critical measure is not the number of words that the subject remembers, but rather the order of recall. Experimental psychologists call this **clustering.** If words are clustered together in recall, when they were not clustered together in the first place (on the list originally presented), then one can draw conclusions about how these words are represented in the mind.

Suppose someone writes down words clustered according to their masculine or feminine connotations. It follows that he or she thinks about matters in these terms. A gender schema is arguably present. And this is exactly what Bem (1981) finds for subjects with a traditional sex-role orientation. Androgynous subjects do not cluster words according to gender connotations.

What a person does or does not remember is important to personality psychology not just because the content of memory is an intriguing individual difference (which it is) but because it channels the way we interact with the world. One of my male colleagues seems to remember the names of all the female students in his undergraduate classes but not the names of the male students—not even one. You don't need to be a cognitive theorist to see what this reveals about the workings of his mind, but appreciate that this mental bias also affects his behavior and in turn the world in which he lives.

How do *you* react to a teacher who knows your name versus one who does not? Odds are that you are friendlier in the former case; you are more likely to attend class and sit in the front row; and you may even try harder to do well in the course. It is not surprising that my colleague believes that female undergraduates are excellent students but that male undergraduates are idiots. (And he has more reason than ever to remember the names of the females but not the males!) So, memory pertains to more than isolated facts about the world; it is an important meeting ground between the person and the environment.

Measures of Decision-making   A final set of measures used by cognitive researchers to understand underlying processes looks at the ways people make decisions based on the information they receive. A favorite parameter here is the speed with which someone makes a decision: in other words, their **reaction time.** You saw in earlier chapters how Galton used reaction-time measures in an attempt to gauge intelligence, and how Jung used them to map out unconscious complexes.

The use of such measures by cognitive researchers is similar in spirit to that of Jung, although they prefer a markedly different interpretation of why a particular reaction is made quickly or slowly. Suppose your roommate badly cuts his finger. Through the window you see a car with lights on the roof. You run out and flag it down. The policewoman behind the wheel administers emergency first aid and then takes your roommate to the hospital. When you later visit the hospital, you remark to your roommate how lucky he was that a police car was passing by. You might also thank the schema that helped you decide—quickly and accurately—that a car with lights on the roof was a police car.

This is the logic behind using reaction-time measures to assess cognition. If someone has a particular schema, she recognizes and uses information relevant to it in an efficient (and usually rapid) manner. Hence, rapid reaction times for decisions or judgments about a given topic suggest that a schema is present.

Psychologist Hazel Markus (1977, 1980) uses reaction-time measures to study self-schemata. In one experiment, she had female subjects respond to several questionnaires measuring whether they were independent or dependent. She assumed that subjects who scored in an extreme direction (independent or dependent) had a self-schema incorporating this personality characteristic. Subjects scoring in the middle of these scales were termed **aschematic,** the assumption being that their self-schema did not include the dimension of independence or dependence.

Markus then asked the subjects to perform a variety of tasks. One involved presenting subjects a list of personality trait terms, one at a time with a slide projector, and asking them to push a button in each case indicating whether it was "like me" or "unlike me." The terms included synonyms of "independent" (such as, individualistic, outspoken, and assertive), synonyms of "dependent" (such as, conforming, submissive, and timid), and neutral words. She measured the speed with which subjects made the "like me" or "unlike me" decision for each type of word.

Granted the meaning of self-schemata, what results do you expect? Markus found that independent subjects more rapidly judged whether independent traits characterized them than did dependent subjects or aschematic subjects. She also found that dependent subjects more rapidly judged whether dependent traits characterized them. These results nicely support the existence of self-schemata, since they demonstrate that people differ in the efficiency with which they process certain classes of information.

Markus has since investigated the role of gender in self-schemata. Her approach is similar to Bem's (1981) investigations, although Markus favors a different view of androgyny. Where Bem argues that androgynous subjects lack a gender schema, Markus believes that these individuals do indeed think about themselves in terms of gender. Their schemata combine both masculine and feminine roles.

This argument is supported by a reaction-time experiment conducted by Markus, Crane, Bernstein, and Siladi (1982). Subjects completed the Bem Sex Role Inventory and were classified as masculine, feminine, or androgynous. They were then shown a list of trait words (one at a time) and asked to make a "like me" or "unlike me" decision in each case. Words were masculine, feminine, or neutral in connotation.

Masculine subjects made quicker decisions about masculine words than did feminine subjects. Feminine subjects in turn made quicker decisions about feminine words than did masculine subjects. What about the androgynous subjects? Bem (1981) believes that these individuals are aschematic with respect to gender, and so would predict their reaction times to be slower than sex-typed subjects for both masculine and feminine words. But this was not the case. Instead, androgynous subjects reacted as quickly to masculine words as did masculine subjects and as quickly to feminine words as did feminine subjects.

These findings imply that androgynous individuals are *not* blind to gender stereotypes. Rather, they think about themselves in terms that blend masculine and feminine characteristics. They interpret information to fit their multiple-gender self-schemata. *The Left Hand of Darkness* is a science fiction novel by Ursula K. LeGuin set on a planet where the residents do not have a fixed gender. Sometimes they are men, sometimes women, and sometimes they are in a state of transition. Needless to say, these people have complex gender schemata. Like androgynous individuals on our planet, "they are sensitive to and importantly concerned with both masculine and feminine aspects of their self-concepts" (Markus et al., 1982, p. 50).

Evaluation Measures of attention, memory, and decision-making have recently been adopted by personality researchers, and results to date are promising but incomplete. Not everyone familiar with these approaches is convinced that they are the techniques of the future, and several criticisms have been raised.

First, as I noted in Chapter 11, the schema concept used to make sense of most of these experimental approaches strikes many as fuzzy. Perhaps "schemata" are overly complicated ways of explaining research findings. For instance, need we invoke a depressive schema to explain why a depressed person says negative things about herself? After all, this is what depression means, and it may have a biological basis. What does a hypothesized cognitive structure add to our understanding of depression?

Further research is needed, and I suspect that the schema concept will be vindicated. Markus, Smith, and Moreland (1985), for instance, have demonstrated that all sorts of experimental measures converge with each other. In a particular cognitive domain, people recognize, organize, remember, and employ information in characteristic ways. Schemata cease being fuzzy and start being parsimonious when they help the theorist make sense of disparate findings.

Second, researchers fond of these experimental techniques have failed to explore exactly how individual differences in memory and reaction time relate to other aspects of someone's behavior (Markus & Zajonc, 1985). So, both Bem and Markus argue that schemata pertain to sex-role orientation as measured by the BSRI. Wouldn't we be more impressed with research demonstrating further that individuals with masculine or feminine schemata dress their babies in blue and pink, pursue traditionally sex-typed careers, and joke about members of NOW?

Third, you may have noticed that these techniques rely excessively on words. Although our understanding of the world is often phrased verbally, cognition is not the same thing as vocabulary. One of the most serious criticisms raised against the research techniques borrowed from experimental psychology is that they still are used to study how words are recognized and recalled. Subjects are now shown words like "ambitious" or "introverted" instead of words like "horse" or "dog." But is this enough of a change to say that researchers are studying the whole of personality? I think not, since personality refers to what is general, characteristic, enduring, integrated, and functional about a person.

To date, the validity of these experimental approaches to personality is unclear. It is ironic that cognitive schemata and the use of experimental probes to assess them received a big boost from Mischel's (1968) criticism of trait research as making infrequent contact with "real" behavior. Experimental techniques were an alternative to mindless investigations correlating one questionnaire with another. Yet schema research is subject to much the same criticism as past trait research! It's removed from "real" behavior.

In light of my criticisms, I have some suggestions for cognitive researchers. Let's admit that advice is easy to give, and so I advise researchers within the cognitive paradigm not to forget the hard-won realizations of the trait researchers. Studies of how people respond to abstract stimuli (be they questions on a questionnaire or trait words flashed on a screen) cannot substitute for studies of how people respond to the real world.

I recommend that researchers study attention by watching people as they mingle at a cocktail party or shop in a mall, for instance. Who and what is noticed? Maybe researchers could study memory by assessing what people remember and forget in the course of their everyday life. Why do some people remember to buy postage stamps but not diapers? Why do other people know what's on television but not in the newspaper? Finally, I suggest that researchers study decision-making by interviewing parole officers, abortion counselors, or car salesmen.

Actually, psychology researchers study behavior in all of these settings, which is why I chose them as examples. What has yet to be done is for personality researchers interested in the schema approach to venture into these arenas. For the time being, researchers using experimental techniques to study personality are staying close to their laboratories. While they gain control and reliability in their research, they sacrifice generality and validity.

CROSSCUTTING RESEARCH QUESTIONS

The cognitive paradigm is the most recent of the three personality paradigms to take form. Perhaps as a result, the lines of research are more independent than those within the psychoanalytic or trait paradigms. Questions posed by particular researchers tend to have significance within the context of a particular theory but not necessarily within the paradigm as a whole. Compare questionnaire studies with those employing process analysis. By and large, they are concerned with different aspects of cognition. Links certainly exist, but they have yet to be forged. I suspect, for instance, that schemata can be described as high or low in dimensionality. This distinction should affect how a person recognizes, remembers, and utilizes pertinent information. So, a cognitive researcher might someday arm herself with both Scott's questionnaires *and* a stopwatch.

At the present, this is not the case. But is it possible to identify questions that cut across the entire cognitive paradigm? The effort is hampered not only by the relative isolation of the different theories and the disagreement over appropriate research strategies, but also by the somewhat tautological nature of the entire paradigm. Cognitive theories are reasonable—perhaps too reasonable, according to some critics. Theories are often difficult to falsify. Once you accept the premise of a particular theory, the truth of its specific "predictions" is almost required.

Consider self-theory. Its central claim is that people are happy and adjusted to the degree that their view of themselves corresponds with their view of what is good and desirable. Well, sure. Could anyone even entertain the possibility that the opposite might be true, that happiness and adjustment go hand in hand with a view of the self as bad?

Or consider learned helplessness theory, which proposes that people and animals don't try to control outcomes when they expect to fail. Again, this is hard to argue with. Does anyone care to support the opposite position, that organisms expend effort precisely when tasks are seen as futile?

Matters are clarified by recalling the distinction from Chapter 6 between *clinical propositions* and *metapsychological propositions.* Some cognitive claims cannot sensibly be put to empirical test, but others certainly can. So, self-theory predicts that acceptance of the self should lead to acceptance by others. This prediction is not "obviously" true, and an investigation to test it would be worthwhile (see Shrauger & Shoeneman, 1979). And learned help-lessness theory predicts that one's expectation of response-outcome inde-pendence interferes with the recognition that outcomes really can be con-trolled. Again, this is not tautological (see Alloy & Seligman, 1979).

What clinical propositions are of concern to the cognitive paradigm as a whole? Several can be identified. First, individual differences in cognitive content, style, and dynamics exist, and have a degree of stability and gen-erality. Second, these cognitive characteristics reflect the influence of partic-ular environments as well as an inherent drive toward accuracy, congruence, complexity, and/or abstractness. Third, "higher" levels of these characteris-tics are associated with better adjustment.

Together, these claims can be subsumed under the general statement that cognition is important because it is the meeting place between the person and the world. In the remainder of this chapter, I'll describe a variety of studies that investigate this general statement about personality.

THE IMPORTANCE OF COGNITION

The most basic claim of the cognitive paradigm is that thoughts and beliefs are the essence of a person. They affect, in a critical way, everything else about a person. Perhaps this strikes you as extremely plausible: "I think; therefore I am." But not all individuals who address the matter agree about the primacy of cognition.

Behaviorism was ushered into psychology by John Watson's (1913) dis-missal of mental life as an appropriate or important topic for psychology. More recently, noted psychologist B. F. Skinner (1971) has echoed this asser-tion. Cognition, if not an outright myth, is no more than an **epiphenomenon,** an irrelevant derivation of the real essence of a person. Perhaps cognition is like exhaust coming from a car's tailpipe. It accompanies the movement of the car but does not make the car run.

The best way to answer these criticisms is with research demonstrating that thoughts and beliefs do indeed lie at the center of human activity. How would you show that someone's thoughts determine what she does? At first this question seems to have an obvious answer. You simply assess thoughts and actions, and prove that there is a substantial link between the two. But a closer examination reveals that this procedure is not foolproof, since it relies on a correlation between thought and deed. Correlations do not always reflect a direct causal sequence. Perhaps the behavior in question led to the particular thought. Perhaps both thought and behavior reflect some third variable.

For instance, consider a study that asks whether students who believe a particular instructor is an effective teacher will do well in this instructor's class. This hypothesis is consistent with the central claim of the cognitive paradigm that thoughts (for example, beliefs about an instructor) determine actions (for example, class performance). But it is also consistent with other possibilities. Maybe students decide after they've received grades whether a teacher did a good job or not: "That creep—look at how he marked me down!" Or maybe the students' beliefs and performance result from something the teacher does, like grading leniently or harshly. Beliefs and performance end up being correlated with each other—but not because there is a direct link between them.

These pitfalls are generic problems for researchers within the cognitive paradigm. They must be surmounted if one is to argue that thoughts and beliefs are primary characteristics of personality. Researchers buttress their cognitive arguments in various ways.

One obvious strategy is to assess cognition *prior* to assessing behavior. Causes don't work backwards in time. If you still find a link between thoughts and actions, then you've eliminated the argument that cognition is the effect rather than the cause. Consider the earlier example. If students give their opinions about their teacher's effectiveness before they write any papers or take any exams, and there is a correlation between their beliefs and their eventual achievement, one cannot argue that their performance led to their belief.

Eliminating third-variable arguments is not as easy. Researchers usually get rid of such confounds by conducting experiments, holding constant extraneous factors while manipulating the potential "cause" and measuring the consequence of this manipulation on the "effect" of interest. Cognitive researchers attempt to do this by manipulating cognitions and assessing behaviors. So, we might tell students in one class that their teacher is effective and students in a second class just the opposite. What is the effect on student performance?

Unfortunately, researchers cannot directly manipulate cognitions. Remember that thoughts are not literal "things" with a tangible existence. They can only be shoved around metaphorically, and our shoves will inevitably affect other aspects of a person. Any experimental study of cognition has only the guise of an experiment. In actuality, all such studies yield correlational data, and we must be continually alert for third variables.

Since experimentation doesn't automatically relieve the cognitive researcher from the threat of third variables, what is she to do? She employs two further strategies, usually in conjunction. The first involves so-called **manipulation checks:** measures of the hypothesized cognition and attempts to demonstrate that the manipulations correlate with these measures and that these measures in turn correlate with the effects being studied. If cognition is indeed involved, then both these correlations will be significant, and manipulations will not correlate with effects except insofar as the cognitive measures mediate this link. The logic here is diagrammed in Figure 12-1. (This strategy is brought to a high degree of mathematical sophistication in the statistical technique of **path analysis** which uses patterns of correlation coefficients to trace the path of causal influence among variables; Kenny, 1979.)

In our classroom example, we'd want to measure whether the students thought the teacher effective or ineffective. Is there an overall difference between the two classes? If so, we conclude that the instruction manipulation "took." Do the students who believe the teacher is effective do better than those who believe he is ineffective? If so, we conclude that beliefs mediate the link between the instruction and the performance.

The second strategy involves formulating likely third variables and then eliminating them by explicit test. To the degree that we test for plausible confounds and find them unlikely, we conclude that our original hypothesis is correct.

Let's return once more to the classroom example. We unobtrusively observe the students in the two classes and count the number of smiling versus frowning faces we see at any point in time. Maybe we calculate attendance. Or suppose we count how many students in the two classes are listening to Run DMC on their headphones. If none of these measures bear any relationship

Figure 12-1
Possible Relations among Variables

If cognition links *A* and *C,* then the correlations between *A* and *B and* between *B* and *C* will be significant.

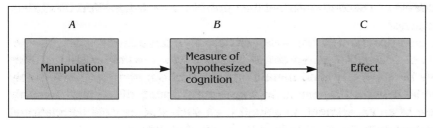

to the manipulated cause or the measured effect, then we can be confident that thoughts indeed affect behavior.

So much for the commonsense notion: "I think; therefore I am." To this maxim, we have to add temporal considerations, experimental manipulations, internal checks, and scrutiny of third variables. Descartes had an easier time than the researcher working within the cognitive paradigm!

Conclusions from cognitive research rest ultimately on a plausiblity judgment. Someone can always think of a possible third variable, of a way to argue that thoughts and beliefs do not play an important role in personality. The bottom line is slippery: does the third variable strike one as more or less plausible than an appeal to cognition? (Acceptance or rejection of psychoanalytic and trait research also rests on judgments of plausibility.) In the remainder of this section, I'll describe some of the more convincing cases that researchers have made for the importance of cognition.

Cognition Influences Behavior

The cognitive theories described in Chapter 11 have each inspired a line of research indicating that cognitions lie behind overt behavior. In this section, I sample from these lines of work. I'm going to start with learned helplessness research because it has been particularly attentive to the possible role of third variables. This work originated in studies of animals, and many psychologists resist explaining animal behavior with thoughts and beliefs. Following Watson, Skinner, and common sense (after all, anybody who's been in New York City doesn't want to accept that rats and pigeons can think), they prefer to explain animal behavior as an automatic (that is, noncognitive) conditioning process. The efforts of learned helplessness researchers in maintaining their cognitive emphasis illustrate the care that all cognitive researchers must take in building their case.

Learned Helplessness   When Steve Maier and Martin Seligman first described their helpless dogs, other researchers proposed explanations unrelated to cognition. Some argued that the animals were physiologically traumatized by their exposure to uncontrollable shock. Others argued that the animals had learned to hold still during the initial shocks, thereby decreasing the intensity. And still others suggested (tongue in cheek, I hope) that Maier and Seligman were using dead animals in their studies! Physiological trauma, holding still, and death do not involve beliefs in response-outcome independence or expectations of uncontrollability.

Maier and Seligman (1976) conducted a series of studies to rule out these alternative explanations and support their cognitive hypothesis. Central to these studies was the **triadic design,** a procedure using three different groups of animals. Animals in Group One are exposed to shocks that can be terminated by some response, like pushing a lever. Animals in Group Two are **yoked** to those in Group One, which means that they are given the exact same shocks with the critical difference that no control over their offset is allowed. Animals in Group Three receive no shock whatsoever, controllable or uncontrollable.

All three groups are then tested at the same task. What does it mean when animals in Group Two act passively in comparison to those in Groups One and Three? Obviously, they are helpless. More interesting, though, is that one cannot plausibly attribute their passivity to trauma, since Group One animals experienced the same physical events.

What about the argument that "helpless" animals have learned to hold still, and that their inactivity produces helplessness in the later situation? In an ingenious experiment, Maier (1970) ruled out this possibility by arranging matters so that animals in Group One could control shock *by doing nothing*. If they made a movement, shock would continue. If they held still, shock would cease. If the argument that learned helplessness involves learning to hold still is a good one, then Group One animals should be impaired at the test task. This was not the case, so Maier concluded that helplessness was mediated by a belief in uncontrollability.

Research to date has not ruled out the possibility that helpless animals are in actuality dead. Some evidence suggests that many of these dogs and rats still receive pension checks, but there is reason to be skeptical about this as an index of "life." I've recently read that our government still pays survivor benefits to widows of Civil War soldiers!

At any rate, when learned helplessness was first studied in people, researchers borrowed the triadic design to support the inference that cognitive factors are involved. Consistent with the animal studies, human studies found that people exposed to uncontrollable bad events behaved differently than those exposed to controllable bad events (or to no events at all). Perseverance, problem-solving, aggression, and sense of humor are just some of the activities affected by uncontrollable bad events (for example, Seligman, 1975).

These studies suggest that cognitions are responsible for the observed behaviors. This conclusion is further supported when manipulation checks (questions about perceived control) distinguish among groups in the triadic design and map into the particular deficits that comprise learned helplessness. Interestingly, manipulation checks don't always work out (Tennen, 1982). Whether a subject reports that he has control or not may have little to do with whether he acts helpless. This may mean that subjects cannot report with validity on their "control," or it may mean that helplessness theory is wrong in its cognitive emphasis. I find it ironic that the case for cognition's involvement seems stronger for animal helplessness than for human helplessness!

Lack of control over bad events is often distressing

Illusion of Control   Learned helplessness is induced in a person or an animal by exposure to uncontrollable events. However, other research cautions us not to expect helplessness to be easily created in all circumstances involving uncontrollability. Most people have a robust tendency to assume that events and outcomes fall within their influence. Sometimes this shows up even when the events are in actuality independent of anything the person does.

This phenomenon is termed the **illusion of control** and has been studied by a number of cognitive researchers (for example, Alloy & Abramson, 1979; Langer, 1975; Wortman, 1975). Here is what they have discovered: *people perceive control over events and outcomes to the degree that these are expected, familiar, pleasant, and/or associated with effort.* So, Langer (1975) conducted a series of experiments where subjects participated in a lottery: an objectively uncontrollable event. Subjects were more willing to hold onto their tickets if they had chosen their own three-digit number as opposed to having it assigned to them, if the digits were given to them one at a time as opposed to all at once, if the stakes were high versus low, and so on.

In another series of experiments, Alloy and Abramson (1979) compared the illusion of control experienced by depressed and nondepressed college students. Their findings are intriguing. Only the nondepressed incorrectly assumed control when none existed. Common sense and psychological theory usually assume that "illusion" is associated with psychopathology. The present results imply that illusions can also bolster psychological health. Shelley

Taylor (1983) makes the same point in her studies of cancer patients. Good adjustment to the aftermath of surgery is predicted by the perception of control over the future course of the cancer, even when this perception is at odds with medical knowledge.

The illusion of control is intriguing, but it is also theoretically important. It illustrates how people seek to master the world, and how cognitions are deployed toward this goal. Considerable benefits may accrue from this illusion, which is precisely the central claim of the cognitive paradigm.

Explanatory Style   Developmental psychologist Carol Dweck (1975) measures the beliefs of children about "responsibility" for academic outcomes. Following the example of Heider, Rotter, Seligman, and other cognitive theorists, she calls children who take responsibility for success and failure **mastery-oriented** and children who eschew responsibility **helplessness-oriented.** When given difficult problems to solve, mastery-oriented children approach them with gusto and use effective strategies for solving them. They enjoy themselves and regard the whole matter as an intriguing challenge. In contrast, helplessness-oriented children perform poorly and lethargically. They don't enjoy what they are doing.

In a study similar in spirit, Alloy, Peterson, Abramson, and Seligman (1984) determined whether a group of research subjects typically explained bad events with global causes (factors present in a range of situations) or with specific causes (factors present only in a particular situation). The subjects then participated in a learned helplessness experiment. (I discussed this type of experiment in Chapter 11.) Consistent with predictions from the helplessness model, subjects with global explanatory style exhibited a variety of problem-solving deficits following exposure to uncontrollable bursts of noise, while subjects with specific explanatory style had difficulty only when the test task involved learning to control noise.

In generalizations of these laboratory studies, Nolen-Hoeksema, Girgus, and Seligman (1986), Kamen and Seligman (1986), and Peterson and Barrett (1986) showed that explanatory style predicts the actual grades that students receive, both in grade school and in college. Individuals who explain bad events with internal, stable, and global causes tend to receive low grades. Individuals who invoke external, unstable, and specific causes tend to do well. Presumably, the pessimistic students give up in the face of failure, while the optimistic students keep trying. Again, the central claim of the cognitive paradigm seems to be supported, since behavior is under the sway of particular beliefs.

Stop and think about the most likely confound in these studies. How about a student's actual ability? Maybe the correlation between explanatory style and grade point average is really the result of the fact that both reflect ability. These researchers worried about this confound and ruled it out. They obtained scores for each subject on standard "intelligence" tests (California Achievement Test for the grade school students and Scholastic Aptitude Test for the college students) and showed that the link between grades and explanatory style still holds even when these scores are taken into account.

Personal Constructs   Other research linking cognition to behavior comes from the personal construct tradition (Bonarius, 1965). For instance, Hayden, Nasby, and Davids (1977) found that emotionally disturbed boys make relatively few distinctions among personal constructs they apply to other people. The lack of complexity is associated with the degree to which each child is socially impaired. Do you see how this follows from Kelly's characterization of personal constructs as tools for anticipating events? If your roadmap lacks details, you're going to lose your way more often than not.

Self-theory   From the Rogerian tradition comes another example of how cognition affects behavior. Chodorkoff (1954) ascertained the degree to which a person's self-description agreed with the description given by observers. (The greater the agreement, the greater the congruence between the person's awareness and experience.) Subjects were then tested at a perceptual defense task. Taboo and mundane words were flashed quickly on a screen, and subjects indicated when they could make them out. When recognition of taboo words is slow relative to recognition of mundane words, perceptual defense is present (Chapter 6). Consistent with prediction, the more congruent a subject's beliefs were with "reality" (judgments by other people), the *less* perceptual defense was observed.

Self-schemata   The growing popularity of schema approaches has breathed new life into the psychology of the self (for example, Schlenker, 1985; Suls & Greenwald, 1983). As explained in the last chapter, it is possible to regard the self as a schema: a theory about one's own characteristics (see Epstein, 1973). William Swann (1983) uses this perspective to explain the stability of a person's self-concept. He argues that people do things to verify the theory they hold about themselves, whether good, bad, or ugly.

For instance, Swann and Hill (1982) conducted an experiment in which they first ascertained whether subjects regarded themselves as dominant or submissive. Subjects were then placed in a situation where they interacted with another person, following which they were given a bogus evaluation telling them they were either dominant or submissive during the interaction. This information was either consistent or inconsistent with their own opinion. Subjects then returned to the interaction. Those given consistent information did not act differently, but those given inconsistent information did their utmost to contradict it. Self-defined dominant individuals acted as dominantly as

Negative behavior may be a means of verifying a negative self-image.

possible, while self-defined submissive individuals rolled over and played dead.

The point of course is that the individual's self-schema gives rise to behavior that ends up verifying its content. Suppose the schema is negative? The prediction still is that the person will try to verify his self-concept. He may deliberately fail or otherwise foul up. Students may get drunk the night before an examination. Teenagers may leave drug paraphernalia lying around for Mother to find. Job prospects may arrive late to an interview wearing a leather jacket over a Hawaiian shirt. This strategy has been termed **self-handicapping** (Berglas & Jones, 1978). (Freud calls it the death instinct, if you recall!) People may value consistency more than actualization.

Conceptual Systems Theory   Abstractness and concreteness as measured by the TIB relate to a variety of behaviors. Harvey (1966) reports that in comparison to concrete individuals, those with an abstract conceptual system are particularly creative, able to integrate contradictory information, and resistant to persuasive attempts by others. Hunt (1966) administered a variant of the TIB to ninth grade students, and then grouped them into three classes based on their concreteness-abstractness scores. The "concrete" class was the noisiest and most difficult to discipline. The "abstract" class was the most self-directed and spontaneous. As expected, the "middle" class fell between the other classes on most measures of behavior. Interestingly, Hunt (1966) found that different teaching strategies were effective for the different classes. The concrete class responded best to rote learning, the middle class to competition, and the abstract class to individualized instruction.

In an imaginative study of how abstractness and concreteness relate to behavior, Suedfeld and Rank (1976) obtained letters and diaries written by such revolutionary leaders as Oliver Cromwell, Patrick Henry, Leon Trotsky, Mao Ze-dong, Fidel Castro, and Che Guevera. Material was scored by the researchers for conceptual complexity (akin to cognitive complexity or abstractness). The revolutionaries were then classified as successful versus unsuccessful according to whether they held office in the new government that followed their revolution. The researchers predicted that conceptual complexity is associated with postrevolution success, since the "complex" individual is better able to shift from the demands of a revolution to those of ruling than the "simple" individual. And this is precisely what they found. This study is important not just because it proves that cognition is important in determining behavior, but because it demonstrates a novel procedure.

Other studies of cognitive complexity indicate that this characteristic of a person interacts with the complexity of a particular environment to determine his performance (Schroder, Driver, & Streufert, 1966). So, a task which makes few information-processing requirements is performed equally well by the cognitively simple and the cognitively complex. But if a task calls upon someone to integrate disparate items of information and/or large amounts of information, then cognitive complexity benefits a person. For instance, cognitive complexity is unrelated to how well students answer multiple-choice questions, but it is positively associated with how well they answer essay questions.

Delay of Gratification   Over the years, Walter Mischel (1986) has studied how people tolerate **delay of gratification:** the self-imposed postponement of rewards. The ability to delay immediate gratification makes possible a host of important human activities: higher education, arts and crafts, healthy living, marital fidelity, obeying laws against theft and assault—in short, any activity that extends over time, where long-term benefits outweigh short-term benefits, if one can resist the quick fix. Temptation is not always easy to ignore; we all know why grocery stores display candy bars, cigarettes, and sleazy tabloids next to the checkout line.

Everyday people explain delay of gratification in terms of willpower, whereas psychoanalytic theorists talk about ego strength. Mischel takes a closer look at the topic, investigating what people actually do in the course of resisting temptation. Much of what he has discovered lends itself to a cognitive interpretation.

The delay of gratification makes important achievements possible.

He studies preschool children who are shown objects, like toys or snacks, one being more desirable than the other. If a child can sit alone in a room until the experimenter returns, he gets the more desirable object. If a child is unable to sit and wait, and instead calls for the experimenter to return, he gets the less desirable object. (Sounds to me like the difference between buying a car off the lot versus ordering one *without* chartreuse racing stripes.) Mischel is interested in what makes waiting more versus less likely.

One of the most effective strategies used by the children who successfully delay gratification is to distract themselves from the objects. They sing or talk out loud, inspect their feet, or even cover their eyes with their hands. In short, they think about things other than the reward that awaits them.

Another strategy that works well is to think about the reward in ways that make it less tasty and tantalizing. It is easier to delay one's lunging at marshmallows if they are cognitively transformed into clouds or cotton balls or worse. Thinking about them as mouth-watering delicacies doesn't help you resist them.

Mischel's research is a good example of the interplay between the person and the environment so important to the cognitive paradigm. The child who effectively delays gratification changes the world in which she lives. She experiences greater rewards and opportunities, and these in turn affect her ability to master the world. Mischel (1984) reports that children who can delay eating pretzels for a few minutes end up a decade later to be more socially competent! My goodness.

Locus of Control   Literally thousands of studies have looked at the behaviors related to locus of control. These studies usually focus on behaviors in settings where people can act forthrightly versus passively: achievement, health care, interpersonal influence, social activism, helping, and so on (Phares, 1984). For instance, Prociuk and Breen (1977) found that students with an internal locus of control are more likely to consult with their teachers about how to prepare for an upcoming test than are students with an external locus of control.

The apparent conclusion that internality is desirable while externality is not must be qualified. Internality leads to beneficial consequences for a person only insofar as she finds herself in a situation that is responsive (Rotter, 1975). If situations truly elude her control, then it is more sensible for her to resign herself to this fact, rather than beating her head into an unyielding wall (Janoff-Bulman & Brickman, 1980). Indeed, a study of internal versus external students found them to be more satisfied with unstructured versus structured instruction, respectively (Forward, Wells, Canter, & Waggoner, 1975). Similarly, the finding that ethnic minorities, women, students, prisoners, paraplegics, and other groups with restricted control over the goodies in the world usually score in the external direction of Rotter's (1966) scale seems to reflect an accurate (though lamentable) view of current affairs. This interactionism with respect to an individual's locus of control and the actual causal structure of the world is yet another instance of contextualism. It is the *fit* between the person and the world that explains behavior.

Cognition Influences Mood

Another class of studies demonstrating the primacy of cognition in personality looks at how a person's beliefs affect subsequent feelings and emotions. I'll just touch on these studies here. You may have encountered in your general psychology course the famous Schacter and Singer (1962) experiment in which research subjects were injected with adrenaline (identified to them as a vitamin), creating heightened physiological arousal. Different subjects were then placed in different situations, designed to produce varying interpretations of why they felt as they did. In one condition, for instance, subjects were left with a goofy individual, who cracked jokes and did silly things. In another condition, subjects were insulted and treated rudely by another person. When asked to report the emotion they were experiencing, subjects reported feelings appropriate to the situation: happiness versus anger, respectively.

According to Schacter and Singer (1962) people used the information present in their particular social situation to make sense of their arousal. The cognitive label they gave their arousal defined the nature of the emotion they experienced. Have you ever felt attracted to someone in the course of some exciting activity you were sharing: like skiing, attending a rock concert, or working for a political cause? Perhaps you were interpreting arousal induced by the activity as love. Schacter and Singer believe your emotion is genuine, though, since cognition is considered the primary determinant of what we feel. If you think you are in love, then you are in love.

The Schacter and Singer study demonstrates that situational manipulations of one's thoughts affect mood. Other studies indicate that individual differences in cognition measured with a questionnaire also predict a person's mood. When researchers correlate locus of control scores with measures of anxiety, they find that increased externality is associated with increased anxiety (Lefcourt, 1976). This makes perfect sense. If a person feels that most events are beyond his control, he is apt to feel fearful about things in general.

In a series of studies, psychologist Bernard Weiner (1974, 1979; Weiner & Litman-Adizes, 1980) has shown that people's attributions for success and failure influence their emotional response to these outcomes. Although failure makes everyone feel bad, if it is explained internally, failure may produce shame and guilt. If it is explained externally, failure may lead to anger.

Dozens of studies have linked explanatory style with depressed mood (Sweeney, Anderson, & Bailey, 1986). For instance, Metalsky, Abramson, Seligman, Semmel, and Peterson (1982) conducted an investigation by studying how students reacted to a low midterm examination grade. Early in a school term, they assessed the explanatory style of college students in a particular course. The students then took the midterm exam and received grades. Some students were pleased, and others were not. Then all students completed a self-report measure of depressed mood. As predicted, students who explained bad events with internal, stable, and global causes *and* who received a low grade were most likely to be depressed. Neither explanatory style by itself nor a low grade by itself led to depression. It was the combination of the two.

Cognition Influences Physiology

Recent research suggests that cognition also plays an important role in affecting an individual's bodily processes. Some of the most interesting studies in the whole of personality psychology look at how a person's thoughts and beliefs affect her physical well-being. Much of this research comes out of the personal control tradition and implies that people with an enhanced sense of control over events in the world are less likely to fall ill than those with a diminished sense of control. Indeed, they may even live longer!

Psychologists Ellen Langer and Judith Rodin (1976) performed an experiment in a nursing home. Half of the elderly residents were assigned to an experimental condition where their sense of personal control was enhanced. They were told by the nursing home personnel that taking care of themselves was their own responsibility and that changing things was within their power. They were given choices to make: which plant to choose for their room, when to see a movie, and so on. The other half of the nursing home residents were assigned to a comparison condition with none of these interventions. Instead, these individuals were told that they would be well-treated and they should be happy.

Several weeks later, individuals in the two groups were compared with respect to happiness, activity, alertness, and health. On all of these measures, subjects who had experienced enhanced personal control scored higher, even though there had been no differences between these groups before the interventions.

Eighteen months later, Rodin and Langer (1977) found an even more startling difference between the two groups. While 15 percent of the nursing home residents in the enhanced personal control condition had died, 30 percent of the residents in the comparison condition had! So, personal control manifests itself not just in activity and alertness, but also in longevity.

The way in which personal control leads to long life is not clear (Rodin, Timko, & Anderson, 1985), but research suggests that susceptibility to illness may be one factor. Psychologist Suzanne Kobasa (1979) investigates an individual difference she calls **hardiness.** An important component of hardiness is the person's sense of personal control. The more control a person believes he has over events, the more hardy he is. In several studies, Kobasa has found that hardy individuals are less likely to fall ill in the face of stress than are nonhardy individuals (for example, Kobasa, Maddi, & Kahn, 1982).

We are all familiar with the notion that stressful events are likely to precede illness. Holmes and Rahe (1967) argue that **life changes** requiring adjustment on the part of the individual increase the likelihood of poor health. In their research, they give subjects a questionnaire asking about the frequency of occurrence of events like those in Table 12-1. The more events a person reports, the more likely he is to fall ill during the following year. I'm sure you know that many college freshmen suffer one cold after another throughout their first year at college. Think of all the changes and transitions involved in going away to school.

More recent research has refined the link between life change and illness, and this refinement takes the form of looking at how someone thinks about

Table 12-1
Stressful Life Events

Death of spouse	Marital reconciliation
Divorce	Retirement
Marital separation	Sex difficulties
Jail term	Change in residence
Death of close family member	Change in schools
Personal injury or illness	Vacation
Marriage	Minor violations of the law
Fired at work	

SOURCE: Holmes & Rahe, 1967.

life events. For instance, Suls and Mullen (1981) demonstrated that events make illness more likely only insofar as the individual perceives little control over them. Again, we see the importance of personal control for physical well-being. More generally, we see that someone's thoughts and beliefs affect the entire person.

Along with Martin Seligman and George Vaillant, I've ascertained the explanatory style of Vaillant's research subjects described in detail in Chapter 6 (Peterson, Seligman, & Vaillant, 1986). We looked at questionnaires completed by these men in 1946 at age twenty-five where they described their most difficult experiences during World War II. When they offered causal explanations, we pulled these out and rated them for internality, stability, and globality. So, in effect we scored their explanatory style. Also available to us were the results of physical examinations conducted by physicians every five years thereafter. Internal, stable, and global explanations for bad events at age twenty-five predicted poor physical health thirty-five years later, at age sixty. This held even when health at age twenty-five was taken into account. The moral of these findings: be pessimistic at risk to your health.

Several other studies convey this lesson as well. Here's their design. Research participants were given thorough medical examinations, and their health status was described in objective terms. They were then asked to rate how good or bad they perceived their own health to be. Finally, they were tracked for years, to the point where a number of them had died. Results are striking. "Objective health status" as originally measured is related to eventual mortality. But so too are self-ratings of health, even when at odds with the objective measures (Kaplan & Camacho, 1983; Mossey & Shapiro, 1982). In other words, perceived health may prove more important than actual health.

As you might imagine, the possibility that health and illness are not just states of the body but also states of the mind is controversial. In fact, an editorial in *The New England Journal of Medicine* has called for an end to explanations of illness in psychological terms (Angell, 1985). The editorial called such explanations "folklore" and blamed them for saddling the patient with guilt. Isn't it bad enough to be sick; do you also have to blame yourself?

In light of the studies I've described in this section, let me respond to this editorial. I strongly disagree with it. First, it doesn't mention the sorts of investigations conducted by Langer and Rodin, by Kobasa, or by Suls and Mullen.

Second, the editorial misinterprets what it means to explain illness in psychological terms. Psychological explanation is not the same thing as "blame" anymore than is biological explanation. What and how a patient thinks is determined just as surely as the effectiveness of his immunological system is determined. The fact that a person can change her beliefs does not mean she is to blame for what she thinks. In my experience with patients, I have found them excited by the possibility that an optimistic viewpoint will speed recovery (see also, Taylor, 1983).

Third, to say that thoughts and beliefs reflect health and illness is not to say that germs and smoking and diet do not. Psychological factors are but one of several determinants of physical well-being (Engel, 1980). Some proponents of psychological explanation make overly zealous claims, and I agree that these should be tempered. But an account of illness that includes psychological factors strikes me as reasonable.

Fourth, the editorial prematurely dismisses psychologists and psychology in the treatment and prevention of illness. At the present time, the field of health psychology is a bright and booming endeavor. Future psychologists may be able to help people lead healthier lives. Among the ideas that these psychologists will probably use are those from the cognitive paradigm. That's not folklore.

What Influences Cognition?

Despite findings arguing in favor of the primacy of cognition, there are other points of view about what constitutes the bottom line of a person. You have encountered some of these alternatives already in this book. Psychoanalytic theories conceive people in terms of underlying energy. Thoughts and beliefs are an important part of the psychoanalytic vision of human nature, but they are shaped by the individual's needs and drives. In themselves, they are not primary characteristics. Trait theories regard people in terms of biologically based individual differences. Again, thoughts and beliefs are part of this view of human nature, but like psychoanalytic theories, trait theories treat cognition as secondary.

Some researchers have argued directly against the central tenet of the cognitive paradigm. They do so by demonstrating that behavior, or mood, or physiology determine what and how a person thinks. These demonstrations are potentially powerful. If successful, the researcher can take all the research findings described so far in this chapter and subsume them under his or her favored perspective. "Yes, thoughts may determine a person's actions, feelings, and bodily processes, *but* thoughts in turn are determined by _____" (fill in the blank with whatever).

Before he became interested in issues of personality consistency, Daryl Bem was a social psychologist and a self-proclaimed radical behaviorist. In a series of intriguing papers, Bem (1965, 1967, 1972) argued against one of the most cherished notions in social psychology—that attitudes cause behaviors. Instead, suggested Bem, behaviors cause attitudes.

Here is how this presumably happens. The person behaves according to prevailing rewards and punishments in the environment. When asked about his attitude toward some object or event, the person stops and thinks about how he has behaved with respect to it: "Gee, I eat pistachio ice cream. I must like it." The person (and the social psychologist) mistakenly believe that the "attitude" so elicited existed all along, and that it led to the eating of the ice cream. But Bem contends that attitudes are an after-the-fact interpretation of one's behavior. By this view, cognition is not primary. Behavior is.

Other researchers argue that feelings are more basic than thoughts and beliefs. Psychologist Robert Zajonc (1980), for instance, suggests that cognitive theorists who believe feelings are derived from thoughts are mistaken. Instead, he concludes that an individual's *affective reaction* (like or dislike) to an object or event occurs independently of thoughts and beliefs. Studies conducted by Richard Moreland and Robert Zajonc (1977, 1979) indicate that people develop a liking for visual stimuli flashed on a tachistoscope even though they do *not* recognize these shapes and forms. At least in this situation, cognition is not primary. Affect is.

And still other researchers argue that physiological processes determine thoughts and beliefs. Much of psychiatry is based on this premise. The medical model holds that defects, injuries, or illnesses of the body affect everything about a person, including how and what he thinks. Consider schizophrenia, typically described as a thought disorder. Schizophrenics often believe that they are persecuted: that someone is out to get them. They may believe that television performers are speaking directly to them. They may have profound difficulties with attention and memory. Their interpretations of themselves and others can be inconsistent and idiosyncratic (Bannister, 1963, 1965).

One theory of schizophrenia popular among psychiatrists is the **dopamine hypothesis,** which proposes that schizophrenic symptoms are caused

"I paint what I see, child."

by an excess of this neurotransmitter in the brain (Snyder, 1980). Several lines of research support this interpretation. What is important here is that the dopamine hypothesis and similar biological theories stand in contrast to the cognitive theories we reviewed in Chapter 11. According to the biological theories, cognition is not primary. Physiology is.

What's the point? Research demonstrates that cognition affects behavior, mood, and bodily processes. But research also shows that these in turn affect cognition. Taken together, do these studies make us say that everything affects everything? Remember the muddle I mentioned in the previous chapter, where the cognitive paradigm courts explanatory disaster by implying that personality is hopelessly complex? The way to sidestep this muddle is to be specific and determine *in a given instance* which aspect of a person is determining which other aspects. In many of these cases, cognition gets the nod.

The cognitive paradigm accommodates the arguments of Bem, Zajonc, and others who claim that a person's thoughts and beliefs are sometimes determined by other factors (so long as sometimes doesn't mean always). In fact, such effects are expected from the perspective of field theory. The various aspects of a person and her world mutually determine each other. In arguing that cognition is important, theorists believe that thoughts and beliefs affect the other aspects just as much as these other aspects determine thoughts and beliefs. Most of my work as a personality researcher has been within the cognitive paradigm, so perhaps I'm biased. But my reading of the research literature supports this argument.

CONCLUSIONS: COGNITIVE THEORIES IN LIGHT OF THE RESEARCH

Of the three paradigms of personality psychology covered in this book, the cognitive paradigm is the newest. Not surprisingly, then, cognitive research is at an uncertain stage. This fact helps to explain why the field has yet to agree on a particular research strategy. Both questionnaires and experimental probes are employed, but rarely by the same researcher or even within the same research tradition.

Nevertheless, I'll draw some conclusions about cognitive theories. First, as illustrated by the studies reviewed in the previous section, the central premise of the cognitive paradigm appears quite reasonable. In a number of important instances, cognitive content, structure, and dynamics determine one's adjustment to the world. Someone's thoughts and beliefs affect behavior, mood, and even physical well-being.

At the same time, cognitive research hasn't gone much further than documenting the premise that cognition is important. Why has research been stuck at this point? I think because of the central role behaviorism has played in American psychology. Throughout much of this century, *mind* has been a semi-dirty word in many psychological circles. Cognitive researchers respond to the skepticism of their colleagues by repeatedly demonstrating the utility of looking at what and how a person thinks. I believe the case has been well made, but the inevitable cost has been a lack of progress elsewhere.

Second, just as I concluded about psychoanalytic and trait research, cognitive research supports the gist of all the theories within the paradigm without supporting any particular theory above any other. Maybe this is to be expected. Since the theories seem so similar to each other, it may be impossible to distinguish among them empirically.

Different cognitive theories do make different claims with respect to one idea. All propose that cognition changes, and that it does so according to an overarching principle or tendency. But the principle varies from theory to theory. Lewin argues for increased homeostasis; Kelly for increased prediction and control; Rogers for increased accuracy; Harvey, Hunt, and Schroder for increased abstractness; and so on. Are these different? If so, what happens when these principles come into conflict? Research findings to date fail to answer these questions, although Scott's work cautions us to expect no simple solution.

Third, personality psychologists who work within the cognitive paradigm should consider integrating the different theories. As I described in Chapter 11, a strong family resemblance characterizes the approaches of Lewin, Kelly, Rogers, and others. Perhaps the features that cut across these theories can be used to create a generic cognitive theory. With such a theory, researchers can move beyond merely documenting the importance of thoughts and beliefs.

Some critics have suggested that cognitive theories are not really theories of personality so much as perspectives. Some go further to argue that cognitive accounts of personality are tautologies: necessarily true—impossible to falsify. These may be extreme criticisms, and they apply to some cognitive claims but not others. Still, they are apt in the sense that research findings have rarely been used to refine the theories. Theoretical claims made decades ago by Lewin or Kelly or Rogers have not been tested against the evidence in the way that claims by psychoanalytic or trait theorists have been tested.

Fourth, a number of areas need further investigation. For instance, cognitive researchers tend to neglect so-called "hot" cognition: the passionate and emotional aspects of thought. People are conceived as cool, calm, and collected processors of information—even when this information is noncool, noncalm, and noncollected. In light of the strong possibility that memory and other cognitive processes are entwined with one's feelings (for example, Bower, 1981), this neglect is a serious shortcoming of the cognitive paradigm.

Relatedly, cognitive theorists need a better vocabulary for describing the whats and hows of the mind. Current terms force them to juxtapose thought and feeling and ask which is primary. Maybe such contrasts are strained, if not downright stupid. Is there a better way to describe cognition?

Also, we don't know enough about the origins of cognitive characteristics. How does a person choose one personal construct instead of another? Where do schemata originate? Cognitive theories are able to explain how cognitive contents and structures change, but give a less satisfactory account of their beginnings.

Finally, most cognitive theorists and researchers have devoted little attention to the physiological basis of cognition. In other fields of psychology, a great deal has been learned about how the brain and the nervous system work. Much of this knowledge should also be of interest to cognitive theorists and researchers. Consider the differences in information processing believed to characterize the left versus right hemispheres of the brain (Springer & Deutsch, 1985). If left-brain people are verbal and logical, while right-brain people are musical and intuitive, then personality psychologists have an intriguing individual difference to investigate.

Researchers are beginning to look at personality differences as a function of hemisphere dominance (Singer, 1984), but their work has yet to be assimilated into the cognitive paradigm. The traditional opposition between mind and body works against this assimilation. Maybe it's time to banish this *dualism* and speak of people as integrated entities, not as cognitive ghosts residing in a physiological machine. If nothing else, health psychologists and physicians might see that they have the same goal.

SUMMARY

The subject of this chapter was research conducted within the cognitive paradigm. Critical in understanding the current state of research is the fact that no single procedure is generally accepted: some researchers favor questionnaires for assessing cognition, while others prefer experimental techniques originally developed to study attention and memory. In the first part of the chapter, I described the questionnaire approach of William Scott, who has developed a variety of procedures for measuring individual differences in cognition. Then I described some of the techniques borrowed from experimental psychology and how they have been adopted by personality researchers.

For the most part, research within the cognitive paradigm stays in seg-regated areas, with particular investigators pursuing particular questions with particular techniques. As a whole, though, this research converges to support the central premise of the cognitive paradigm: a person's thoughts and beliefs affect his entire being—behavior, mood, and physiology. Challenges to the claim that cognition is primary were also discussed.

Finally, I evaluated cognitive theories of personality in light of the research evidence. I concluded that the gist of the theories is supported, but there is no basis for choosing one cognitive account of personality over another. Areas for future investigation by cognitive theorists were sketched, including the role of emotion in thought, the origins of cognitive characteristics, and the relation of cognition to physiology.

13

COGNITIVE
PARADIGM:
APPLICATIONS

"Let us reason together."

"It's all in your mind."

"Take another look at it."

"Try to picture it this way."

"It all depends on how you choose to see it."

"With an attitude like that, no wonder you're unhappy."

n everyday conversation, we endorse the main premise of the cognitive paradigm: *people are moved not simply by the events in the world but also by their views of those events.* Accordingly, if thoughts and beliefs about these matters are changed, people and their worlds will also change.

Over the years, a number of applications of the cognitive paradigm have developed. They share in common an attempt to explain matters by looking to a person's thoughts and beliefs. Like applications within the trait paradigm, individual differences are important. These are assessed by questionnaires and other procedures, and are used to make decisions about people in the clinic, the classroom, or the workplace. And like applications within the psychoanalytic paradigm, those within the cognitive paradigm focus on change. Techniques for altering someone's thoughts are used in various settings to help people adjust to difficulties there.

To date, cognitive applications to clinical topics like psychopathology and psychotherapy have predominated, so I'll concentrate on them in this chapter. But first, I'll discuss the common pitfalls of cognitive applications.

Two pitfalls are particularly hazardous. The first is inherent in the entire cognitive paradigm: the short shrift of feelings and emotions. Some of the most intriguing work by cognitive psychologists *derives* particular feelings from particular ways of thinking. But as we saw in Chapter 12, we can also make the case that emotions determine thoughts. Applications that ignore the possibility of a bidirectional influence often fail.

For instance, psychologists argue that conflict between people and groups may result from cognitive factors (for example, Balke, Hammond, & Meyer, 1973). The two sides don't understand each other; they have mistaken beliefs; they don't appreciate that their opponents see things differently. Techniques for resolving conflict have made it possible for ideological opponents to walk a mile in each other's shoes, so to speak. And this is often highly successful, but, at other times, it simply doesn't work. Individuals and groups may hate each other for any of a number of reasons that have nothing to do with cognition—historical events, religious differences, economic competition, and so on. Their hatred in turn leads to cognitive conflict, but resolving their differences in opinion doesn't change their hatred.

The second problem found in some applications is not an inherent one. Instead, it results from an oversimplification of the cognitive approach to personality. Problems are located *solely* between someone's ears, and the possibility that the world also determines the nature of things is overlooked. Just because "it's all in your mind" is frequently said by everyday people as well as psychologists doesn't make it so.

This phrase additionally means that "it's also not in the real world." This implicit message removes the E from Lewin's equation that $B = f(P, E)$, and pries us loose from the root metaphor of contextualism. Problems are reduced to hallucinations or projections, and they are attacked without reference to their context.

This is a conservative view that may lead us to blame the victim for whatever misfortune has befallen him. Indeed, there is a well-documented phenomenon in the social psychology literature showing that people assign responsibility even to those who suffer a clearly capricious bad event—like a rape, or a car accident, or a serious injury. This tendency is another instance of the fundamental attribution error: looking within the person for the source of occurrences rather than without.

Relatedly, psychologist Melvin Lerner (1971) argues that most of us need to believe in a **just world** where good and bad events are meted out according to our virtues or sins. Belief in a just world is a good gestalt since it allows us a harmonious perspective. But sometimes the world isn't just. Innocent people suffer. And the good die young.

We tend to overlook the evidence otherwise to endorse the notion that the world is just and harmonious. We assume, for instance, that someone is on welfare because he is lazy, that someone was raped because she asked for it, that someone is ill because he is dirty, that someone is unhappy because she is looking at things the wrong way. We ignore the possibility that the world has as much to do with these matters (including our thoughts and beliefs about it) as people themselves do.

So, in reading about applications within the cognitive paradigm, be wary of these two shortcomings. Is the cognitive practitioner justified in looking mainly to thoughts and beliefs to explain behavior and determine the best intervention? And in looking to cognition, is the practitioner neglecting the fact that the real world plays a role in shaping these cognitions?

PSYCHOPATHOLOGY AND PSYCHOTHERAPY

Synonyms for the problems suffered by people who seek out psychiatrists and clinical psychologists usually stress the physical or emotional aspects of their difficulties: mental illness, emotional disturbance, nervous breakdown, and so on. But in recent years, a new synonym has been introduced: **cognitive disorder.** This term implies that a person's thoughts and beliefs lie at the center of his problems in life. The growing popularity of this approach to psychopathology can be traced directly to the growing popularity of the cognitive perspective within personality psychology as a whole.

Contemporary psychologists are additionally excited about the cognitive approach to psychopathology because it leads naturally to another application: psychotherapy techniques deployed against a client's harmful way of viewing matters. Granted that thoughts and beliefs lie at the center of one's problems, and granted that thoughts and beliefs are somewhat malleable, cognitions are a natural target for the therapist. To the degree that people are like computers, they can be reprogrammed. To the degree that people are like scientists, they can be given new theories.

For many years, psychotherapy meant psychoanalysis in one form or another. But with the recent popularity of the cognitive paradigm, there is now an alternative. Techniques of **cognitive psychotherapy** provide the clinical psychologist with different ways of going about her work. In this section, I'll describe some of the cognitive approaches to psychopathology and psychotherapy.

George Kelly's Approach

George Kelly (1955) has made the most thorough attempt to explain psychopathology in cognitive terms. Using the language of personal constructs, he redefines the traditional emotional disorders in cognitive terms. For instance, *anxiety* is defined as an individual's awareness that the events in his life are outside the range of convenience of available constructs. Consider your fear when driving along a remote stretch of a Nebraska interstate and seeing that the fuel gauge needle is quivering on empty. Something bad is happening, and we may not have the wherewithal to construe it. Do we have to stay stranded on the side of I-80 for the rest of our lives? Will we turn into a Cornhusker? (What is a Cornhusker, anyway?) If we know that the state police patrol the highway regularly, on the lookout for fools like us, then we have a construct to make sense of our experience. We'll be angry, or humiliated, or even amused. (I wouldn't be amused.) But we won't be anxious. Kelly believes that anxiety results only when we are aware that our cognitive map doesn't correspond to the territory we are traversing.

A related emotion with a related cognitive interpretation is *threat,* which someone experiences when she realizes that her construct system is about to be shaken up. In other words, she is about to confront a massive invalidation of the way she views the world. Maybe the letter from the graduate school admissions committee has just been delivered. Is it a rejection? Her blind date is knocking on the front door. Is he a rejection? Her fiancé is late to the church. Is she a rejection? In each case, assuming that the possible event becomes a real event, she must change her constructs. The more central the construct involved, the more threatened she feels when it is attacked.

We do more than sit and quake in response to the world. Sometimes we do battle. So, Kelly interprets *hostility* as a person's effort to extort validation from the world for a prediction that has already been proven wrong. Some people are bullies not because they are inherently mean but because they have made incorrect predictions about the way things are. Rather than change their constructs, they try to change the world. As adolescents, haven't we all been on one side or the other of unrequited love? At first, it is paradoxical that one human being will beat up another human being for the "offense" of not reciprocating a crush. But by Kelly's view, this hostility makes perfect sense. Love is never having to say you're wrong.

Depression is interpreted as constructs that are constricted. Their range of convenience has shrunk to the point where they apply to almost nothing. The depressed person therefore experiences almost nothing. Symptoms that reflect constricted constructs predominate among the DSM-III diagnostic criteria for depression: loss of pleasure and interest in usual activities, decreased sex drive, decreased appetite for food, difficulty in concentrating, increased sleep. If you are depressed, you avoid everything. From the viewpoint of personal construct theory, you do so because your constructs are not sufficient for everyday life. Taking constricted constructs into the complex world is like taking a skateboard onto the Long Island Expressway.

The opposite of depression is *mania,* usually regarded as excessive and inappropriate elation. Kelly's cognitive rendering of mania points to dilated constructs, constructs stretched and expanded to the point that they fit everything. The manic individual is grandiose and expansive. Nothing gets him down or counts against his plans. He undertakes reckless activities in apparent disregard of their bad consequences. Why? Because his constructs have no room for disaster.

Neither the depressed person, with her constricted constructs, nor the manic person, with his dilated constructs, can ever be proven wrong. Remember the scientist metaphor? Imagine a scientist whose theories are so circumscribed that the right conditions for testing them can never be arranged.

Imagine a scientist whose theories are so general that they can encompass all possible evidence. These caricatures are the respective analogues of depression and mania.

Real science as well as real people must walk the line between the constriction and the dilation of theories. In order to refine our prediction and understanding of the world, we must dare to be wrong about things. By this view, both depression and mania reflect a lack of explanatory derring-do.

A final example of how psychopathology can be explained with personal constructs is Donald Bannister's (1963) interpretation of schizophrenia. Bannister administered REP Tests to schizophrenic patients. As noted in the last chapter, he found that these patients applied constructs to themselves and others in ways that were idiosyncratic and inconsistent. Bannister then asked what could give rise to this particular use of personal constructs.

The answer to this question is his **serial invalidation hypothesis,** which states that schizophrenics live in a world that continually invalidates their constructs. In other words, their experience contradicts their predictions. As a response to continual invalidation, the schizophrenic metaphorically loosens his constructs. He applies them differently than other people (that is, idiosyncratically), and he applies them differently from one moment to the next (that is, inconsistently). The result is two-fold. The good news is that invalidation is avoided. The bad news is that this worldview literally makes no sense.

Bannister hypothesizes that the schizophrenic randomly organizes her personal construct system. Experience is *kaleidoscopic* (Adams-Webber, 1979, p. 66). Imagine all AMTRAK passengers with different train schedules. Imagine that each schedule changes from minute to minute. (If you've ever ridden AMTRAK, this is easy to imagine.) Suppose your entire experience was this disordered! According to Bannister, this is the essence of schizophrenia.

In support of his theory of schizophrenic thought disorder, Bannister conducted laboratory experiments with normal individuals, asking them to make predictions about hypothetical people. Subjects were then told that their predictions were wrong. This process was repeated several times. Consistent with his prediction, Bannister found that serial invalidation does indeed lead subjects to make inconsistent predictions. Over time, subjects flip-flop between opposite poles of an invalidated construct, sometimes choosing one and sometimes another, suggesting the inconsistency of actual schizophrenic patients.

You have seen how Kelly explains psychopathology. As you might therefore imagine, he tries to undo problems by targeting a client's personal constructs for change. **Fixed-role therapy** uses role-playing to alter someone's construct system. The client quite literally is given the script of someone with a different personality and is asked to play it. The therapist designs this script so that the client ends up trying out new constructs while following it.

The ultimate goal of fixed-role therapy is for the client to see that her "personality" is just as much a fiction as that of the character she has played. This brings home *constructive alternativism,* demonstrating to the client that she is able to pick and choose the terms of her personality. *All* theories can be revised, even the near and dear belief that personality is fixed. Since we are what we think, and we choose our categories of thought, then it follows that we can choose who we are. (I choose to be a billionaire!)

Jack Adams-Webber (1981) provides a concrete description of fixed-role therapy. A client "Joan" is asked to write a character sketch of herself from the viewpoint of someone who knows her well. The purpose of the sketch is to provide the therapist with the constructs that Joan uses to understand herself. With this sketch as a reference, the therapist then writes another sketch of a different person, "Nancy." The second sketch emphasizes the constructs that Nancy uses to predict and understand events in the world. These are quite different than Joan's favored constructs.

Joan (the client) is given the sketch of Nancy (the role) and asked to play it. She is instructed to interact with other people in such a way that they leave with an impression of Nancy—not Joan. So, although Joan sees herself as cautious, Nancy sees herself as assertive. In following the script, the client must use a different personal construct. As she labors to interact with the world in different terms, the new construct becomes part of her worldview. If it leads to more accurate appraisals, this is not lost on her.

The therapist and the client meet frequently to plan how she is to enact the role. The therapist takes on the role of director, treating the client as if she were "in character." If the client acts like Joan, the therapist acts surprised. (You may recognize this as one of the strategies of method acting, where the actor immerses himself in the role he is playing, temporarily becoming his character.)

In fixed-role therapy, the therapist plays the parts of important people in the client's life, so she can practice her new role. They also change parts, which means that the therapist becomes Nancy, while the client becomes Joan's father, mother, husband, or employer. Switching roles accomplishes yet another change in perspective: the client comes to see that other people construe her just as she construes them.

At the end of therapy, Joan returns, presumably enlightened by the experience of seeing the world through Nancy's eyes. The therapist suggests that Nancy go into retirement, no matter how exciting she may have been. The important point is not the particular role that one plays, but that one can choose a role, revise it, and discard it, again and again. The client is left with the injunction to create a new Joan.

Role-playing is also used in other systems of psychotherapy to help people express their repressed emotions or perfect the skill with which they perform particular behaviors. These purposes are not the major concern of fixed-role therapy because Kelly's therapy tries to effect cognitive change. The skill with which the person plays a role is not crucial, and neither are the role's emotional aspects. Indeed, the client who feels awkward and uncomfortable with a particular role is apt to benefit most from the role-playing, since it provides a particularly different construct system.

Aaron Beck's Approach

Psychiatrist Aaron T. Beck presents another cognitive interpretation of psychopathology. Although he is best known for his theory of depression (Beck, 1967), he has also looked at how thoughts and beliefs produce anxiety (Beck & Emery, 1985). In contrast to the typical treatments of these psychopathologies, which regard them as emotional disorders, Beck believes that cognition is the primary characteristic and determinant of each.

Depression   Depressed people are characterized by both the content and the process of their thoughts. In contrast to the nondepressed, a depressed person has an excessively negative view of himself, his world, and his experience. (That doesn't leave much out, does it?) Further, he thinks about matters in such a way that his pessimism and hopelessness are perpetuated.

Consider this brief case history of a man whose wife has unexpectedly left him:

> The deserting wife has been the hub of shared experiences, fantasies, and expectations. The deserted husband . . . has built a network of positive ideas around his wife, such as "she is part of me"; "she is everything to me"; "I enjoy life because of her". . . . The more extreme and rigid these positive concepts, the greater the impact of the loss. . . .

> If the damage . . . is great enough, it sets off a chain reaction. . . . The deserted husband draws extreme, negative conclusions that parallel the extreme positive associations to his wife. He interprets the consequences of the loss as "I am nothing without her"; "I can never be happy again"; "I can't go on without her". . . .

> As the chain reaction progresses to a full-blown depression, his self-doubts and gloomy predictions expand into negative generalizations about himself, his world, and his future. He starts to see himself as permanently impoverished in terms of emotional satisfactions, as well as financially. In addition, he exacerbates his suffering by overly dramatizing the event: "It is too much for a person to bear". . . .

> The husband divorces himself from activities and goals that formerly gave him satisfaction. . . . His distress is aggravated by the physiological concomitants of depression, such as loss of appetite and sleep disturbance. Finally, he thinks of suicide as an escape ("because life is too painful").

> Since the chain reaction is circular, the depression becomes progressively worse. (Beck, 1976, pp. 109–111)

This case nicely illustrates the basics of the cognitive approach to personality. The deserted husband is depressed not simply because his wife left him but because of how he has interpreted the event. His interpretation sets into operation all sorts of processes which in turn feed back to his views of himself and the world.

Beck emphasizes that depression is *not* an inevitable consequence of a serious loss. Many men and women whose spouses leave them get on with their life in a satisfactory fashion. The difference between them and the depressed husband lies in how they look at their loss: as a lesson, as good riddance, as something outside of their control, and so on.

While most of us can place bad experiences within a cognitive context that minimizes their depressing consequences, the depressed individual employs **errors in logic** when thinking about these bad experiences. Their conclusions are always disastrous. Here are some of the errors that Beck has identified.

Arbitrary inference is a conclusion drawn in the absence of any evidence to support it. Suppose you want to get to know someone better, so you suggest a cup of coffee and a dash of conversation. However, the person says, "No, thank you, not today." What do you make of all this? The reasonable answer is nothing, since it is an isolated incident involving someone you do not know. But the depression-prone individual doesn't just shrug his shoulders and put the incident out of his mind. He'll draw an inference from it: "She hates me because I'm a boring person. No one wants to be my friend. I'm going to die a lonely old man."

A related error is **selective abstraction,** taking a detail out of context and focusing on it rather than on more general aspects of an experience. One Monday morning, a friend of mine was horribly depressed. I asked her what had happened, and she told me that she'd gone to a party that weekend and spent some time with an attractive man. So? According to her, "I was at the party for five hours, and for three of those hours, he didn't say a word to me!" When I remarked that it sounded like he had talked to her for two hours, which seemed like a long time, she stared at me with a puzzled look on her face. "That never occurred to me," she finally said.

Depressed people often **magnify** the impact of bad experiences. I usually get worked up when I can't find a parking place on a crowded street. I automatically assume that my failure foretells doom in all domains of my life! This is what Beck means by magnification. The other side of the coin is **minimization,** when we dismiss or trivialize good experiences. Modesty may be a virtue, but if taken to an extreme, it sets a person up for depression. "Oh, it's nothing. Anybody could have won the Olympic Gold Medal that day. The wind was blowing right."

Finally, **personalization** is another depressive error in logic: taking responsibility for bad events in the world that you are not connected with at all. Have you caught yourself apologizing for turmoil in the Phillipines because you once bought a Manila envelope? If so, you were probably personalizing matters.

Anxiety   Let's turn from Beck's explanation of depression to his explanation of anxiety. He starts by underscoring the importance of the **emergency response** that all living beings, from paramecium to people, show in response to threat. We (and they) have guaranteed our survival because we can rapidly mobilize our body's resources for fight or flight.

In people the emergency reaction is directed by our thoughts. We recognize danger, we judge our ability to cope with it, and we decide among response alternatives. Are you amazed that we can merge onto high-speed expressways with only occasional accidents? We do this so well because we are mindful of the potential dangers.

Anxiety disorders (like panic attacks or phobias) occur when we treat nonemergency situations as if they were emergencies. A racing heart, rapid breathing, tremors, and flushed skin are "natural" responses to a giant truck or a saber-toothed tiger closing in on us. These become symptoms of anxiety in the absence of any objective threat, when our appraisal of a situation is at odds with the facts of the matter. We get in trouble when we confuse a classroom examination, a date, or a shopping mall with an eighteen-wheeler run amok.

What leads to misappraisal? Similar to his explanation of depression, Beck argues that cognitive biases lead someone "logically" to anxiety. These tendencies conspire to make the person view herself as exceedingly vulnerable. If you regard yourself as made of spun glass, then you're going to be a timid and fearful person. Vulnerability can also be produced by a perception of *skill deficits* ("I've never taken a course in public speaking"), by *self-doubt* ("I'll forget to bring my notes"), and by *catastrophizing* ("They'll laugh at me and then walk out"). Needless to say, anxiety interferes with the performance of many activities, so the person's sense of vulnerability is vindicated. Like the depressed person who creates a depressing world for himself, the anxious person does her part in creating a world of threat and danger.

Cognitive Therapy   Beck developed his cognitive explanation of depression in conjunction with a treatment known as **cognitive therapy** (Beck, Rush, Shaw, & Emery, 1979). The therapist helps the depressed client identify the thoughts that produce depression, challenge them, and eventually replace them with a more productive view of matters. Beck calls his approach **collaborative empiricism,** since the therapist and the client work together to test the client's beliefs against the facts.

The central tenet of cognitive therapy is that depression is the result of an unduly pessimistic view of the self and the world, maintained by slipshod thinking. The depressive is not motivated to be unhappy (as psychoanalytic theories hold) or rewarded for displaying depressive symptoms (as learning theories suggest). Instead, she has a mistaken view. When her erroneous beliefs change, her depression goes away.

In the initial stages of cognitive therapy, the client learns the basics of Beck's theory of depression. The therapist emphasizes the possibility that thoughts produce emotions, urging the client to examine her own emotions to see the particular thoughts that precede them. At first, this is difficult for the client to do, since these thoughts may be highly routinized, a bad cognitive habit that occurs with little awareness.

These bad habits are called **automatic thoughts,** a running commentary on a person's experience that occurs so readily that the person is not conscious of it. What is apparent, however, is the depression it produces. Imagine Howard Cosell doing the play-by-play of your life! After years of hearing putdowns, you turn down the voice in your head. But the depressing effects remain. The cognitive therapist helps her client become aware of automatic thoughts. Once an automatic thought is out in the open and scrutinized as a hypothesis, it is often found to be lacking.

Suppose someone gets depressed at work when given an assignment. The automatic thought that produces depression may be: "I'll never finish things by the deadline, and my boss will think I'm incompetent." As long as this thought occurs automatically, it is naturally depressing. Once he identifies the thought, though, it can be evaluated in light of the fact that he has received steady raises and promotions ever since he began working. It seems implausible that he is incompetent.

If any doubts linger, the worker might be encouraged to ask his boss about the significance of the deadline. Suppose his boss says, "Oh, that's just a guess on my part. You know the work better than I do, so I figure you'll tell me if my deadline is off-base." See how much anguish and misery could be avoided if we simply asked people what *they* think about things, rather than basing what *we* think on clairvoyance.

Through exercises like this, the cognitive therapist helps the depressed client draw better conclusions about his experiences using the available evidence. Most of these cast the client in a better light, and his depression will lift. But, perhaps in some cases the negative inference is justified. Maybe the client's boss is indeed firm on deadlines and gets annoyed when her employees take too long to finish assignments. If this is ascertained, the worker still need not conclude that he is incompetent. Rather, he sees that he needs to change things. He can learn to manage his time better, stand up to the boss when her deadlines are unreasonable, or shrug off her fussing as a small price to pay for raises and promotions. The cognitive therapist is prepared to help the client do one or all of these things. Keep in mind that the important goal of cognitive therapy is to lead the depressed individual to a positive point of view.

Learned Helplessness Approach

Martin Seligman (1974, 1975) has suggested that learned helplessness is a model of depression. What does this mean? Remember the general discussion of models in Chapter 2. A model is metaphor for understanding some complex phenomenon. If learned helplessness is to be a model for depression, then parallels should exist between the two at a number of points: causes, symptoms, cures, and so on. For more than a decade, Seligman and his colleagues have explored these parallels. The concept of explanatory style was added to the learned helplessness theory largely to strengthen the link between learned helplessness and depression (Abramson et al., 1978).

How does learned helplessness fare as a model of depression? I think pretty well. Table 13-1 summarizes some of the parallels established between helplessness and depression with respect to symptoms, causes, therapy, prevention, and predisposition.

Much of my own work as a researcher has been in collaboration with Seligman testing the hypothesis that explanatory style is a risk factor for depression. On the basis of a number of studies, we conclude that people who typically offer internal, stable, and global explanations for bad events become depressed when such events occur (Peterson & Seligman, 1984). For instance, we've shown that adult men entering a prison are apt to become depressed while serving their time if they have a "depressive" explanatory style. We've also found that elementary school children become depressed over a six-month period if they make internal, stable, and global explanations for bad events. The same appears true for college students.

The learned helplessness theory of depression suggests several therapeutic strategies (Abramson et al., 1978; Seligman, 1981). All attempt to prevent or undo the particular thoughts that produce and maintain helplessness. They should therefore be effective in treating depression once it exists as well as in preventing it in the first place. So, depression can be combatted by *environmental enrichment*. With desirable outcomes more likely, and undesirable ones less likely, the individual can avoid the circumstances that produce helplessness altogether.

If bad events cannot be eradicated, then the individual can undergo *personal control training* that changes expectations from uncontrollability to controllability. As with Beck's approach, the therapist must be aware of the facts of the matter. If a person indeed has the ability to control outcomes but

Table 13-1
Similarity of Learned Helplessness and Depression

	Learned Helplessness	Depression
Symptoms	Passivity	Passivity
	Cognitive deficits	Negative cognitions
	Self-esteem deficits	Low self-esteem
	Sadness, hostility, anxiety	Sadness, hostility, anxiety
	Loss of appetite	Loss of appetite
	Loss of aggression	Loss of aggression
	Norepinephrine depletion	NE Depletion
Cause	Learned belief that responding is independent of important outcomes (plus attributions to internal, global, and stable factors)	Generalized belief that responding will be ineffective
Therapy	Change belief in response futility to belief in response effectiveness	Cognitive and behavioral antidepressant therapy
	ECT, MAO-I, Tricyclics	ECT, MAO-I, Tricyclics
	REM deprivation	REM deprivation
	Time	Time
Prevention	Immunization	Invulnerability factors
Predisposition	Insidious explanatory style	Insidious explanatory style

SOURCE: D. L. Rosenhan & M. E. P. Seligman (1984), p. 340.

believes otherwise, then personal control training challenges her erroneous expectation. But if the person indeed lacks the ability to bring about desired events, then the therapist must impart new skills.

Sometimes control remains elusive, and *resignation training* must be undertaken. In other words, a person must reduce the attractiveness of nice things that remain beyond her grasp. ("There are drawbacks to medical school.") And she must similarly reduce the aversiveness of crummy things that are inevitable. ("God has a plan for everyone.")

Finally, explanatory style provides a convenient target for therapy. *Attribution retraining* attempts to change someone's explanations of failure from internal, stable, and global causes to external, unstable, and specific causes, and to do the opposite for his explanations of success. What does this accomplish? Remember that helplessness theory assigns particular roles to each of these three dimensions of explanatory style. If success is explained internally and failure externally, then his self-esteem is bolstered. If success is explained stably and globally and failure unstably and specifically, then his triumphs are savored and his setbacks are dismissed.

These therapeutic strategies have yet to be explicitly packaged and deployed against depression. Seligman (1981) argues that cognitive psychotherapies like those of Beck (already discussed) and Ellis (to be discussed) are in effect using these tactics already in their treatment of depression. He further states that psychotherapy of depression is effective to the degree that it specifically changes the cognitions deemed important by helplessness theory. In his present research, Seligman is investigating this hypothesis.

The idea that helplessness is analogous to depression has been controversial and is far from generally accepted (for example, Arieti & Bemporad, 1978; Brewin, 1985; Buchwald, Coyne, & Cole, 1978; Costello, 1978; Depue & Monroe, 1978). Many critics argue that depression involves much more than passivity in the face of uncontrollability. If you recall the definition of a model, this is a somewhat misguided criticism. From the start, we should expect learned helplessness to fall short of capturing the whole of depression. Shortcomings are inherent in any model. The important question is whether a model includes the important aspects of a phenomenon. If so, then it is useful.

The parallels in Table 13-1 are generalizations: summaries of how most helpless people (or dogs or rats) behave and summaries of how most depressed people behave. Not all instances of helplessness and not all instances of depression fall into lockstep. Nevertheless, in a number of cases, helpless individuals act depressed, and depressed individuals act helpless. Indeed, Seligman (1978) has wondered if future diagnostic systems will include a category for **helplessness depression,** a disorder that helplessness theory describes particularly well.

Suppose some bad event over which you had no control occurred. It is obvious that you were unable to do anything about the event or its consequences. You began to feel hopeless about the future. And you became despondent, sluggish, and slow. If this sounds familiar, you've experienced a helplessness depression.

The first college where I taught went bankrupt six months after I arrived on campus! Following the announcement that the college would cease operations in the near future, most of the students and faculty members walked around like zombies. If I'd been thinking clearly at the time, I might have seized the opportunity to study learned helplessness in a natural setting. But I wasn't thinking clearly, which is expected from the helplessness model. I was sad and passive and inattentive.

Granted that there are good examples of depression as learned helplessness, another matter must be addressed in judging whether or not the analogy is worthwhile. As a metaphor of human ills, learned helplessness is

Helplessness may lie at the core of depression.

rich indeed. It can be applied to a wide variety of failures at adaptation, so long as they are marked by passivity and preceded by uncontrollable events. So, some theorists suggest that helplessness is involved not only in depression, but also in academic failure, child abuse, test anxiety, drug use, epilepsy, physical illness, loneliness, voodoo death, and problems of the lower class. Learned helplessness has even been linked by some writers to the escalation of the Vietnam War, to the plight of the New York Knicks basketball team, to the crises of faith described by Paul in the New Testament, and to the woes of the third world!

Does learned helplessness play a role in all of these problems? If so, then its specificity with respect to any one of them is nil. In particular, one is led to question whether it applies in particular to depression. To establish specificity, the researcher must do more than document analogies like those depicted in Table 13-1. In addition, he must demonstrate that these parallels do not hold true for other cases. (You should recognize this as a version of discriminant validity; see Chapter 2.) The surface has only been scratched here.

Researchers have mainly looked at the distinction between depression and schizophrenia with respect to helplessness. It appears that helplessness better captures depression than it does schizophrenia. Bad events are more likely to precede depression than schizophrenia (Thoits, 1983), and depressed individuals are more likely to offer internal, stable, and global explanations for such events than schizophrenic individuals (Raps, Peterson, Reinhard, Abramson, & Seligman, 1982). But the issue of specificity is still very much up in the air.

Several other cognitive approaches to psychotherapy are also well-known, and all assume that people's difficulties are produced by particular ways of thinking. Each therefore tries to change a client's cognitions to reduce distress and enhance adjustment.

Client-centered Therapy

This is the approach that Carl Rogers (1942, 1951) developed, basing it on his self-theory. As you remember, Rogers believes that people have an inherent drive to actualize themselves: to bring their perceived selves into congruence with their ideal selves. Actualization can be thwarted when people find that the love and acceptance of others is conditional. **Client-centered therapy** arranges the opposite conditions, allowing the client to achieve a more healthy view of himself.

Several strategies define client-centered therapy (Prochaska, 1984). First is the basic assumption that gives the therapy its name. Rogers and his followers maintain that the individual knows what is good for himself and how to achieve it, as long as he is in a setting where this is possible. Hence, the therapy centers on the client and is *nondirective,* keeping the therapist from steering it in a particular direction.

Second is the establishment of a good *therapeutic relationship* between the client and the therapist. The therapist must be genuine and concerned. Perhaps it is misleading for me to call this a strategy, since authenticity on the part of the therapist is not something she puts on and takes off like a pair of gloves.

Third is the *accurate empathic understanding* by the therapist of the client's inner world. How does the client see things? How does he symbolize his experience? The client-centered therapist must do a lot of listening to her client, and she must communicate that she has understood what she has heard. She walks a mile in his shoes, and lets the client know that it was done with empathy—not with anger, confusion, fear, or blisters.

Fourth is the *unconditional positive regard* by the therapist for the client. Granted that the other three conditions for client-centered therapy are present, unconditional acceptance of what the client says and does will right the wrongs that brought him to therapy in the first place. When the client begins to feel that he is valued, he will start to value himself. As his self-regard increases, his perceptions become more accurate. Awareness and experience coincide. Why are puppies so popular? They don't care that you are a wretched student, friend, and lover. They've mastered the art of unconditional acceptance.

Some theorists believe that client-centered therapy works because its techniques bring about more efficient information processing (Wexler, 1974). Erroneous beliefs are corrected because the person starts examining them. To this end, client-centered therapists frequently reflect back to a client his thoughts and feelings:

Client: I feel discouraged about the future. I'll never get a good job.

Therapist: You seem pessimistic about things. Does that include your present job?

As the client talks about his thoughts and feelings, perhaps for the first time to a person who isn't harsh or critical, he begins to judge them more accurately against the evidence of the world.

Psychiatrist Kenneth Colby has developed a variant of client-centered therapy: a computer program that conducts interviews with patients! The strategy of reflecting the client's thoughts and feelings is an important aspect of the program, which occasionally produces quite a credible exchange:

Person: I seem to have lost interest in everything.

Program: Tell me more about such feelings.

Person: I have some idea why I feel this way too.

Program: You have.

Person: It seems that I miss having a family.

Program: What makes you feel you miss having a family?

Person: There is a challenge about it.

Program: Why is that important to you? (Colby, Watt, & Gilbert, 1966, p. 150)

I'm not suggesting that computers will someday replace therapists. Rather, Colby's program illustrates how unconditionally accepting what a person says can evoke a significant emotional response (Loehlin, 1968). If unconditional regard on the part of a computer program is beneficial, what happens when acceptance comes from another person?

Victor Raimy (1976)—a student of Carl Rogers—has developed another version of client-centered therapy that specifically targets one's **misconceptions** about the self. According to Raimy, common to all troubled individuals are false ideas; common to all effective therapies are techniques to identify and change these false ideas. Although misconceptions span a dazzling range (there are more ways to be inaccurate than accurate), several are particularly common.

Phrenophobia is *one's belief that he or she is going insane.* This is a misconception because it confuses neurosis with psychosis. People with various worries, fears, and phobias have definite problems, but the possibility of a breakdown followed by a long hospitalization is not one of them. But many neurotics make more of their anxiety than they should, causing them to become even more anxious!

Raimy terms a second common misunderstanding the **special-person misconception:** *the belief that one has a unique status in the world.* In contrast to others, the special person feels superior and powerful. She never gives in to others. She strives for perfection. She feels that her frustrations are more intense than those experienced by "lesser" beings. Needless to say, these beliefs get her into trouble.

Adolescents in particular suffer the special-person misconception. They aggrandize themselves, and turn their back on friends and family, since "no one understands." The sexual stirrings brought on by puberty may be the source of the special-person misconception among adolescents. If the teenager bothered to ask others about these stirrings, he would find that *everyone* understands them, particularly his parents.

Adolescents in particular may believe they have a unique status in the world.

Rational-Emotive Therapy

One of the earliest cognitive approaches to therapy was introduced by Albert Ellis (1962, 1973). **Rational-emotive therapy** is as simple as ABC (Prochaska, 1984). According to Ellis, personality can be understood in terms of Activating events, Beliefs used to interpret these events, and emotional Consequences of these beliefs. This formula nicely summarizes the cognitive perspective, regarding beliefs as central in determining people's response to the world.

Beliefs are rational or irrational. Rational beliefs produce pleasant or productive consequences for the person, while irrational beliefs lead to misery and warts. The rational-emotive therapist assumes that her client is troubled because he entertains irrational beliefs. Therapy thus tries to identify these beliefs and eradicate them.

Ellis identifies several irrational beliefs commonly held by members of our society. How many of these strike you as familiar? How many of these have produced anger, guilt, or frustration in you?

- The basic human desires are needs.
- Certain events, like standing in line or being rejected by a lover, are intolerable.
- Our worth as human beings is determined by our material success.
- The world should treat us fairly.
- I can't live without love.
- We cannot be happy unless people approve of everything we do.
- Things must turn out as we plan them.
- We can't go without cigarettes, or beer, or bon-bons.

Characteristic of irrational beliefs are their absolute nature and the fervor that they inspire. In Kelly's terms, irrational beliefs are superordinate. Despite the hassles they produce, we cling to them because it is inconceivable to us that we can (or may) let them go.

Ellis criticizes other forms of therapy that focus on the A's or C's of personality and ignore the B's. In particular, he lambasts psychoanalysis, arguing that insight into the past (the A's) and recognition of one's feelings (the C's) don't solve a client's problems. The client's crooked thinking (the B's) must be changed, and this is done by Disputing his beliefs. "Where is it written down that life is fair?" "Who says that you'll die if your marriage ends?" "What evidence do you have that being promoted will make you happy?"

Rational-emotive therapy has been compared to an educational process (Prochaska, 1984), an apt analogy, since this form of therapy strives to change one's beliefs. To this end, clients are given homework assignments to test for themselves the consequences of their particular beliefs. Suppose a student believes that she cannot speak up in class because she will be laughed at. The therapist may ask her to find out if this will really happen. So she speaks up in class. And no one laughs; they don't even wake up. Her irrational belief has been challenged.

Reattribution Therapy

In Chapter 12, I described Schacter and Singer's (1962) classic experiment demonstrating that people's interpretation of physiological arousal determined the emotion they experienced. How do I know if he really loves me? The answer depends on what he thinks about his feelings when in your presence.

Once Schacter and Singer reported their results, clinical psychologists quickly seized on an intriguing implication of this research. A client's negative emotions, particularly fear and anxiety, could be changed into positive emotions if the client could be induced to reattribute their source. So, several psychologists described techniques for doing this, and **reattribution therapy** was born (Harvey & Galvin, 1984).

The general strategy of reattribution therapy requires the client to switch from internal attributions for negative emotions and behaviors to external attributions. (Note the similarity to Seligman's, 1981, proposed reattribution training.) An experiment by Michael Storms and Richard Nisbett (1970) illustrates the benefits of reattribution. Insomniacs were recruited and given a pill to take before they went to bed. Although the pill was a *placebo*, half the subjects were told that it would increase their arousal, while the other half were told that it would relax them. The results may surprise you. Insomniacs given the "arousing" pill reported that they fell asleep more quickly than usual, and insomniacs given the "relaxing" pill found it harder to fall asleep than ever.

These results are consistent with Schacter and Singer's theory. Think through the logic. Insomniacs have trouble sleeping because they are aroused, and they attribute this arousal to some defect in themselves: "Here I go again. I'll never be able to fall asleep." This self-attribution only increases their arousal. Suppose that they have a plausible source for their arousal that has nothing to do with themselves. Then they can attribute their nervousness elsewhere and relax. The "arousing" pill provides precisely this external source of arousal. In contrast, the "relaxing" pill only compounds the worries of the insomniac. The pressure of having to relax only heightens arousal further: "My goodness. I've taken a tranquilizer, and I'm still not sleepy. This is going to be one of those nights."

Reattribution therapy has been used to treat problems such as fear of public speaking, shyness, and cigarette smoking (Harvey & Galvin, 1984).

But it has not always worked, and the current opinion about reattribution therapy is that it must be integrated into a more complete strategy of psychotherapy.

Perhaps clinical psychologists were naive to think that a single instruction about the source of negative emotions could overturn long-standing cognitive and emotional habits, particularly when the instruction is at odds with the facts. So, insomniacs really do have trouble falling asleep, cigarette smokers really do experience cravings during withdrawal, and shy people really do feel nervous around others. The therapist who tells these people that they are wrong about these matters risks her credibility.

One area where I think the reattribution approach has considerable promise is in the treatment of sexual dysfunctions. Here, misinformation abounds. For all the importance of sex and sexuality, many people don't even know the basics about how their bodies work. For instance, occasional impotence is common among men and has little significance—unless someone draws a conclusion to the contrary. Such a conclusion may create anxiety which leads to further sexual difficulty. Information about the frequency of impotence can head all this off at the pass.

In this case, reattribution doesn't try to change a plausible interpretation into an implausible one. Instead, it moves toward increasing plausibility. If a person finds that a new point of view leads not only to decreased anxiety, but also to more accurate predictions and successful control of events, then the person will seize upon this perspective.

Here is an example from a case study I once read. A man sought out therapy because of long-standing impotence (so to speak). He couldn't get an erection, and this sexual problem was leading to all sorts of other problems in his marriage. He viewed himself as less than a man. His wife viewed herself as less than a woman. Needless to say, these attributions did not create an atmosphere conducive to sexual arousal, trapping the couple in a vicious circle.

After talking to the man and achieving rapport, the therapist asked to see a picture of his wife. The client pulled a photo out of his wallet, and watched as the therapist studied it carefully. "What a beautiful woman!" the therapist finally said. "Any man would be spellbound in her presence."

And what a beautiful intervention by the therapist! Do you see how this new perspective liberates the client and his wife from their damaging self-attributions. "I'm anxious around my wife because she's so attractive." Fear turns into desire. The long-standing problem is no more (as it were).

Another area where reattribution therapy has promise is academic counselling. Again, misinformation may lead students to self-damaging attributions. If these can be changed, then their morale and grade point average will rise. Wilson and Linville (1982, 1985), for instance, note that college freshmen tend to get particularly low grades. Various factors are responsible for this, and many have nothing to do with a particular student's intellectual ability. Consider what freshmen confront as they start college: harsh grading curves in introductory courses, no curfew, noisy dormitories, no curfew, bizarre roommates, no curfew, mysterious study habits, no curfew, and so on. Yet freshmen with a report card full of C's and D's and F's may look past these plausible explanations for their poor performance and attribute it instead to deficient ability.

And then they give up. In subsequent years, their grades continue to be low, even though renewed effort would pay off. Suppose students were encouraged to attribute low grades during their first year to external and unstable factors. Wilson and Linville (1982, 1985) make precisely this intervention. Guess what? Grades indeed go up following a brief message like that in the preceding paragraph. Students who do not receive this message improve their grades less.

Cognitive-Behavioral Therapy

Rational-emotive therapy and reattribution techniques can be criticized for neglecting the real world. I'm troubled by some of the beliefs that Ellis terms irrational, because these beliefs sometimes mirror the way things really work. Consider the belief that the world treats good-looking, wealthy, and successful people nicer than it treats the rest of us. Is this an irrational belief? Ellis would say it is, but any social psychology textbook describes research proving that this is *exactly* the case. ("I learned the truth at seventeen, that love is meant for beauty queens.") The fact that the world works this way is lamentable, but the person who recognizes it is hardly irrational.

As I mentioned in connection with reattribution therapy, cognitive interventions are apt to succeed to the degree that they are consistent with the events that the person is likely to experience. In some cases, as with the case of impotence just described, a new perspective doesn't get the person in trouble at all, and therapy can be "purely" cognitive. In many other cases, though, the person's thoughts—despite their association with misery—bear some resemblance to reality. Therapy must then address not only cognitions but also the world.

In recent years, cognitive strategies have been combined with those of behavior modification to yield a new approach to help people with their problems: **cognitive-behavioral therapy** (for example, Kendall & Hollon, 1979; Mahoney, 1974; Meichenbaum, 1977). This form of therapy tries to change both the thoughts of the client and the world in which he lives. As such, cognitive-behavioral therapy is a contextual therapy, recognizing the interdependence of the person and the environment.

Suppose someone is afraid of cats. This fear creates serious problems, since she avoids places where she might come across a cat. She doesn't go to the zoo, and she won't even watch Saturday morning cartoons. Albert Bandura (1986) has a procedure for treating such phobias, attacking the problem at both its cognitive and behavioral levels. The woman afraid of cats is asked to watch another person handle a kitten. Then she is encouraged to handle the kitten. Through **observational learning** in the first case and **enactive learning** in the second case, the woman develops a new ability: how to hold a cat without being bitten or scratched. This new ability literally changes her world. If she is at a friend's house, and a cat enters the room, she is now able to pick up the cat and toss him out the front door, along with any lingering fears.

But this therapy has done more than just change the woman's behavior. It has also changed the way she thinks about herself. Specifically, her self-efficacy with respect to cats has been altered. She now regards herself as a master of the little beasts, and her enhanced sense of personal control further

This year's Irrational Fears Grand Champion worries, from her home in Madison, Wisconsin, about being caught up in a deadly lava flow.

SOURCE: "The Neighborhood" cartoon by Jerry Van Amerongen is reproduced with special permission of King Features Syndicate, Inc.

reduces her fear. She may even get a kitten of her own, since cats now remind her of her competence in confronting the world.

In the next chapter, I'll briefly describe some of the techniques of behavior modification. Bandura and other cognitive theorists believe that these therapy techniques work because they change a person's cognitions. So, **systematic desensitization** at first seems to be a simple application of Pavlovian conditioning. A person is taught to relax and imagine a feared object (like a snake or a roach) while relaxed. Fear decreases as the object is paired with the relaxation. Although systematic desensitization is highly effective in decreasing fears, its success may not be due to the "automatic" (noncognitive) process of conditioning as much as the way it changes thoughts and beliefs.

Conclusion: Cognitive Therapy

As you read about the different psychotherapies within the cognitive paradigm, you may have been struck by their similarities. Indeed, a strong family resemblance holds them together, one derived from the common features of the cognitive paradigm itself. Here are some generic statements about cognitive psychotherapy:

- Emotional distress and maladaptive behaviors stem from a person's way of thinking about himself and the world.

- These thoughts reflect characteristics of the person as well as characteristics of the world.

- Therapeutic intervention targets thoughts for change.

- Thoughts may be changed by several techniques, including deductive strategies (appeals to logic) and inductive strategies (changes in the world).

- As thoughts become more accurate, harmonious, and/or precise, emotional distress is alleviated, and the person engages the world more forthrightly.

The goal of cognitive psychotherapy is to make the person and the world fit together nicely.

Theories of cognitive disorders and the therapies based on these theories are also subject to the same pitfalls: reducing all behavior to thoughts and beliefs and ignoring the real world where behavior occurs. I once talked to a young therapist about a client he was seeing. She suffered from severe attacks of anxiety, and he was undertaking a standard treatment for the problem. First, he taught her some techniques of relaxation, so that she could cool out whenever she felt the anxiety rise. Second, he suggested that she use a thought-stopping strategy: whenever her mind would turn to anxiety-arousing topics, she would banish them. No thoughts—no anxiety.

What the therapist told me made sense, but I wanted to hear more about his client, so I asked him what sorts of thoughts made the woman anxious. His answer almost made me fall out of my chair. "Oh," he said, "She believes her son-in-law is molesting her grandchild. Whenever she thinks about it, she gets really upset." I started yelling. The gist of what I said, although not in these exact words, was "Hey, maybe she's right about that. Regardless, as a therapist you have a legal and ethical responsibility to check out that fear."

My point here is that the young therapist made a serious mistake by overlooking how reality (that is, the son-in-law) contributes to the client's thoughts and eventually to her anxiety. He was treating her obvious symptom, but failing to address the more serious problem. (This incident led to a good resolution, as the therapist ascertained the facts of the matter and acted on them. His client then had no cause for anxiety.)

James Coyne and Ian Gotlib (1983) argue that Beck and Seligman (and other cognitive theorists) overlook the role of the world in producing and maintaining distress. Cognitive theorists are charged with locating psychopathology too much inside the person and not enough outside. Is this fair? Yes and no. As I've described theories for you, I've emphasized the give-and-take between the person and the world. In principle, Beck and Seligman certainly recognize the importance of the world in determining a person's behavior. But much of the research conducted in support of these cognitive theories doesn't really look at the facts of the matter.

For instance, I've done a study from which I concluded that depressed people magnify their bad experiences (Cook & Peterson, 1986). What I did was ask people, depressed and nondepressed, to describe events in their lives. In the judgment of raters recruited for the research, the depressed subjects seemed to make more of bad events than the nondepressed subjects. However, maybe what struck the judges as magnification on the part of the depressives was in reality accurate. I didn't check with the friends and relatives of my research subjects to see if a particular failed examination or unpleasant date really had catastrophic consequences or not. In retrospect, I see that I should have.

A second, related criticism of cognitive interpretations of psychopathology takes issue with the characterization of depressed and anxious individuals as irrational and out of touch with the real world. As described in Chapter 12, Lauren Alloy and Lyn Abramson (1979) suggest that "normal" people can be estranged from reality. In their laboratory experiments, these researchers demonstrate that depressed college students more accurately judge the relationships between their responses and actual outcomes than do nondepressed students. "Normal" individuals consistently overestimate the effect they have on events.

Consider the implications of these findings. First, seeing the world the way it is may be dangerous. Second, therapists should create illusions in their clients rather than dispel them. Do I agree with these implications? Not exactly, since they seem to claim that unhappy people have special access to the real world. In keeping with the general thrust of the cognitive paradigm, I believe that *all* people (miserable and sublime) see the world in terms of their characteristic thoughts and beliefs. Still, the research of Alloy and Abramson reminds cognitive theorists not to assume automatically that unhappy individuals are illogical or irrational.

Causal priority of cognitive variables can also be criticized. If a given way of thinking about events foreshadows psychopathology, one must demonstrate that the sequence runs from a person's constructs to her problems. A contemporaneous correlation between cognitive characteristics and DSM-III diagnosis does not demonstrate that thoughts are causal. To date, psychopathologists working within the cognitive paradigm have relied too much on cross-sectional correlations to argue their case.

With regard to learned helplessness, we know that bad events precede bouts of depression (Lloyd, 1980). But we are not sure that it is the uncontrollability of these events that leads to the depression. Perhaps their other traumatizing properties are responsible. Since the triadic design does not lend itself to field research, it is hard to tease out the uncontrollability of bad events from their other characteristics.

Researchers typically ask subjects to rate events that have occurred in terms of uncontrollability. Or the researchers themselves rate the events. Do these ratings predict the depressing effect of bad events? The answer is yes (for example, Paykel, 1973), but you can see that this correlation does not establish a definite causal link.

Again we see cognitive psychologists cautioned not to locate matters solely in one's head. Thoughts and beliefs affect how we behave, but these thoughts and beliefs are not randomly held. They reflect the world as much as the person. In applying the cognitive theories to psychopathology and psychotherapy, the psychologist must remember that thoughts and beliefs pertain to actual events.

Is cognitive psychotherapy effective? The answer seems to be yes for the approach of Rogers (for example, Gurman, 1977), Beck (for example, Rush, Beck, Kovacs, & Hollon, 1977), and cognitive-behavior modification (for example, Bandura, 1986). Well-controlled investigations of the other strategies of cognitive psychotherapy still need to be conducted. In all cases, though, research has yet to show that changed cognitions are the active ingredient in successful therapy.

To close, let's compare cognitive psychotherapy with psychoanalytic therapy as described in Chapter 7. The client is seen as in error, not in conflict. Therapy is akin to education, not energy release. When progress is slow, this is due to inertia, not resistance. Perhaps most importantly, the cognitive approach is much more optimistic about the prospects for improvement than is psychoanalysis. Eventual harmony is expected between the person and the world, not inherent antagonism.

Cognitive psychotherapy is not diametrically opposed to psychoanalytic therapy at all points. Remember, psychoanalysis provided the example for all other talking therapies. Kelly, Rogers, Ellis, and Beck at one time all conducted therapy from a psychoanalytic perspective and then developed their own strategy.

A psychoanalytic flavor still remains. Cognitive psychotherapists accord great importance to the therapist-client relationship. Also, they sometimes blame the external world for the problems their clients face. Finally, they usually adopt a weak version of the unconscious. People's thoughts and beliefs may work below the level of full awareness. Cognitive therapists do not join with the Freudians in attributing this lack of awareness to motivation, but they do agree that what people don't know can hurt them.

PERSONAL CONTROL AND HEALTH PROMOTION

Health psychologists are interested in the psychological factors that lead to good versus poor health. Personal control is widely believed to be among the most important of these factors. As described in Chapter 12, people with an enhanced sense of control are healthier than those with a diminished sense; they may even live longer.

Just how personal control leads to good health is not clear. In all likelihood, there are several complex links (Rodin, Timko, & Anderson, 1985). Personal control is thought to underlie coping in the broadest sense. So, people with high personal control are more likely to have a healthy lifestyle, to seek and follow professional advice when ill, to avoid life crises to a greater degree than those with low personal control, to defuse crises that do occur, and to garner more social support, which in turn buffers them against illness (see Cobb, 1976). Finally, and perhaps most intriguingly, they may have more competent immune systems.

A historical view suggests three stages in health care. From the time of the earliest healers to the 1800s, the focus was on the *treatment* of a disease. But Jenner's discovery of vaccination in 1796 introduced the era of disease *prevention,* leading to a drastic reduction or eradication of such ills as smallpox, malaria, poliomyelitis, and diphtheria. Today, we are on the verge of a third stage in health care: the active *promotion* of healthy lifestyles. As we enter this era, personal control will prove important to the health-care field.

The most basic difference between health promotion and disease treatment and prevention lies in what is required of those who will benefit from health-care strategies. Disease can be successfully treated if patients passively comply with physicians. Disease can be successfully prevented if citizens passively comply with public health officials. Health cannot be promoted, however, unless the individual actively participates in the effort.

The concrete problem faced by health psychologists is how to induce someone to take the long view, to sacrifice immediate pleasures for the promise of increased quantity and quality of life in the there and then. To date, this problem has not been fully solved. Let me offer two generalizations about health promotion programs (for example, Kasl, 1978). First, all are somewhat successful: in reducing obesity, cigarette smoking, use of salt, and so on. Second, none are completely successful. Programs always fail to reach some substantial segment of the intended population. Notoriously unresponsive to health promotion programs are lower-class males and members of minority groups.

Why aren't programs more successful than they have been? The glib answer is that they are bucking human nature. It's hard for people to change. My view is a bit more specific. I think that today's health-promotion programs have not fully taken into account individual differences in personal control (Peterson & Stunkard, 1986). Surely it is no coincidence that the groups most unresponsive to health promotion are precisely the groups which rank lowest in the belief that they can bring about important events. Fatalism and pessimism do not psych someone up to go jogging or eat sprouts.

Health promotion starts with epidemiological findings. What factors have researchers linked with subsequent illness? Here are some of the most common: poor nutrition; obesity; lack of exercise; immoderate use of alcohol; smoking; and stress (Taylor, Denham, & Ureda, 1982). Notice that every one of these risk factors involves behavior. Unlike earlier eras, where people were more likely to die from accidents and plagues that they had no control over, in our era, Americans are apt to die from their own bad habits!

Accordingly, health promoters are attempting to change these risk factors, which means that psychologists are called upon to help individuals and groups change their unhealthy habits into healthy ones. Psychologists have expertise in changing behavior, and health promotion is analogous to psychotherapy. In the one case, the goal of therapy is to alleviate misery, and in the other case, the goal is to promote health and longevity.

Health Promotion Programs

Health promotion programs are going on all around you. If you listen to the radio or watch television, you are constantly reminded that you should curtail drinking and driving, that only dopes use dope, that high blood pressure has no overt symptoms, that you shouldn't salt your food before tasting it. If you buy a GM car, the company makes a wager with you. They bet that if you wear your seat belt, you can't die in an accident! The stakes are $10,000 versus your life. The grocery store where I shop has a video monitor in the produce section that constantly runs brief clips on how to prepare vegetables without losing vitamins. If you live in Palo Alto (CA), or Pawtucket (RI), or Minneapolis (MN), or Lycoming County (PA), or North Korelia (Finland), then you know that teams of health professionals have worked for years to help you reduce the risk of coronary disease. Pamphlets, public service announcements, phone calls, and volunteer groups have all been deployed toward this goal.

Psychotherapy and health promotion differ in one critical way. A neurotic lifestyle makes one unhappy: depressed, anxious, and unproductive. But an unhealthy lifestyle makes one happy (in the short run): fat, sassy, and complacent. Exercise hurts. Saying no to gooey deserts, aromatic cigars, and exotic liqueurs is a drag. To the degree that someone lives in the here and now, health promotion is impossible.

Health promotion programs must do more than provide information and moral exhortation. They must also change a person's beliefs about what he can or cannot do. Before embarking on a long trip, someone has to believe that the directions they will follow are correct, and they also have to believe that they are capable of following these directions. Bandura (1986) calls these beliefs **outcome expectancies** and **efficacy expectancies,** respectively. Someone must feel confident about both before she will change her behavior. So far, health promotion has emphasized the former (yes, good nutrition leads to longer life) but ignored the latter (and yes, you can do what is required to achieve good nutrition).

Health promotion programs have been instituted in businesses around the world.

Preliminary evidence suggests that health promotion that targets personal control over specific behaviors can be highly successful. So, Condiotte and Lichtenstein (1981) demonstrated that self-efficacy with respect to not smoking predicted who would or would not relapse following a smoking cessation program. As you may know, it is easy to give up smoking. Mark Twain supposedly remarked that it was so easy that he had done it dozens of times. The real trick is not to backslide. The same is true for losing weight, eating right, exercising, and so on. Good intentions carry a person through an initial flurry of beneficial activity, but they do not sustain permanent changes in behavior.

Perhaps those small numbers of people who successfully alter their unhealthy habits are those with an enhanced sense of personal control. In a recent review of research on risk-factor reduction, Anne O'Leary (1985) concludes that personal control is undoubtedly important:

> The evidence taken as a whole is consistent in showing that people's perceptions of their efficacy are related to different forms of health behavior. In the realm of substance abuse, perceived self-regulatory efficacy is a reliable predictor of who will relapse and the circumstances of each person's first slip. Strong percepts of efficacy to manage pain increase pain tolerance. . . . [Personal control over] eating and weight predicts who will succeed in overcoming eating disorders. Recovery from the severe trauma of myocardial infarction is tremendously facilitated by the enhancement of the patients' and their spouses' judgments of their physical and cardiac capabilities. And self-efficacy to affect one's own health increases adherence to medical regimens. . . .
>
> While specific strategies may differ for different domains, the general strategy of assessing and enhancing self-percepts of efficacy to affect health . . . has substantial general utility. (pp. 448–449)

In the future, health-promotion programs need to assess the personal control of the targeted population. Different strategies would unfold depending on the level of control. Those with a mastery orientation toward their health need little more than information about what's healthy and what's not. Those with a helplessness orientation need their personal control bolstered before information per se will have any effect on their behavior. To this end, some of the techniques of cognitive psychotherapy may be useful.

In closing this section, I'd like to touch on two intriguing suggestions about how to enhance health. Both have received a great deal of popular attention, and both have generated controversy. Although neither has been explicitly discussed in terms of the cognitive paradigm of personality, I think they fit here nicely. The first topic is the personal account of author Norman Cousins (1979) about how he laughed himself out of his death bed, vanquishing a critical illness with good humor and optimism. The second topic is Carl and Stephanie Simonton's (1975) radical therapy for cancer that tries to help patients destroy their own tumors through visual imagery.

Laughing One's Way to Health

In his book *Anatomy of an Illness,* Cousins (1979) describes how he fell ill in 1964 with a collagen disease: a disease of the connective tissue of the body. Cousins was able to move only with great difficulty, and nodules appeared under his skin. One specialist gave him one chance in 500 of recovering.

Cousins decided that the one person out of 500 who could recover from such an illness must do more than wait passively to see what would happen. So he decided to take control of his illness as best he could. His reading convinced him that he had fallen ill in part because his adrenal glands were exhausted from too much stress.

How do you recharge your adrenal system? Cousins chose a two-pronged approach. First, he stopped taking the aspirin prescribed for his pain (under

Testing whether laughter IS the best medicine

SOURCE:"The Far Side" cartoon by Gary Larson is reproduced by permission of Chronicle Features, San Francisco.

the assumption that aspirin further taxes the adrenals) and substituted instead massive amounts of Vitamin C (under the assumption that ascorbic acid combats collagen breakdown). Second, he mobilized his positive emotions—love, hope, faith, confidence, and laughter. Research has repeatedly shown that negative emotions have harmful effects on the body's biochemistry. Does it follow that positive emotions have beneficial effects?

Norman Cousins explored the possibility. Because he found his hospital room a depressing place, he left the hospital and checked into a hotel. He read humor books. Cousins obtained some of the classic "Candid Camera" episodes from Allen Funt, watching them for hours at a time. (By the way, if you like interesting facts, consider this one: as a college boy, Allen Funt worked as a research assistant for . . . Kurt Lewin! Isn't the basic premise of "Candid Camera" that people will do the darnedest things to restore equilibrium to their life space?)

Cousins recovered fully from his illness. On the one hand, this was a miracle. On the other hand, Cousins prefers to view it as a concrete example of the will to live:

> I have learned never to underestimate the capacity of the human mind and body to regenerate—even when the prospects seem most wretched. The life-force may be the least understood force on earth. William James said that human beings tend to live too far within self-imposed limits. It is possible that these limits will recede when we respect more fully the natural drive of the human mind and body toward perfectibility and regeneration. Protecting and cherishing that natural drive may well represent the finest exercise of human freedom. (Cousins, 1977, p. 51)

I can easily imagine Lewin and Kelly and Rogers and the cognitive theorists nodding in agreement.

Fighting Cancer with Visual Images

Carl and Stephanie Simonton (1975) also believe that a person's thoughts and beliefs determine her physical well-being. In particular, they believe that cancer is a psychological phenomenon, brought about by a particular way of viewing the world, which can be successfully treated by changing this worldview. An important aspect of the so-called Simonton method is mental imagery of the "battle" between the body's defenses and the cancer cells that threaten life.

Links between cancer and personality have been suggested by many who've examined the subject. Many theorists believe that cancer-prone individuals have a poor self-image and a hopeless outlook on matters, although there is no good research evidence for this hypothesized correlation (Fox, 1978). Nevertheless, the Simontons are convinced that cancer has psychological roots:

> Malignancy is . . . despair that has been experienced biologically, despair at the level of the cell. In this sense, suggest the Simontons, none of us *gets* cancer; we reach a point at which our deepest need and wish is to withdraw from life, and we therefore "choose" to develop cancer. . . . In the Simontons' view, the illness is a defective coping strategy used by someone who was not able to meet an adaptive demand. (Scarf, 1980, pp. 37–39)

Here we see constructive alternativism extended beyond points of view to encompass ways of life or death.

Because the Simontons equate cancer with despair, they have been severely criticized for saddling the cancer patient with guilt (for example, Kolata, 1980). The Simontons, in turn, argue that their theory instills hope, since it promises that the patient has power over his illness. What the mind can do, the mind can undo.

So, treatment for cancer takes the form of psychotherapy. The patient/client is taught how to deal with problems that otherwise seem insurmountable (and presumably have caused the malignancy). He is taught how to derive the benefits of illness, like getting attention or concern from others, without having to be ill. And he learns about mental imagery.

Carl Simonton first hit upon mental imagery while treating a sixty-one-year-old man with advanced throat cancer. Simonton is a physician trained in radiology, and he was giving his patient daily radiation treatments. He asked the man to imagine how the radiation was affecting his cancer:

> The radiation therapy was to be visualized as a stream of tiny bullets of energy that struck all body cells, normal and abnormal, but destroyed only the weaker, aberrant, "confused" ones—the cancer cells. The patient was instructed to imagine his body's white blood cells coming in, swarming over the dead and dying cancer cells, and flushing them off (via the liver and kidneys) as one might remove the dead and dying enemy from the field of lost battle. Each imaging session was to close with the patient's visualizing his tumor as decreasing in size and his health as returning to normal. (Scarf, 1980, p. 37)

This particular patient recovered fully, and from there the Simonton method took form. The cancer victim fights cancer on a mental battlefield, willing himself to health by using his thoughts and images. A newly developed video game, "Killer T Cell" assists this struggle by allowing cancer patients to zap cancer cells, depicted on a television screen (Jaret, 1986). Who said video games have no saving grace.

Figure 13-1

Example of Cancer Imagery

A patient has drawn a knight (a white blood cell) stabbing an armadillo (a cancer cell).

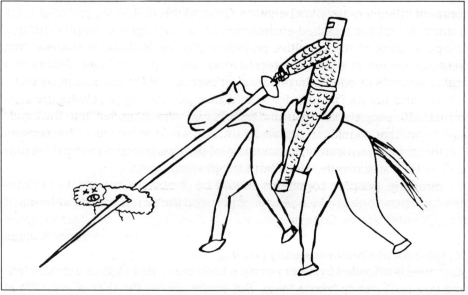

SOURCE: Taken from Jeanne Achterberg and G. Frank Lawlis, *Imagery and disease*, copyright © 1978, 1984 by the Institute for Personality and Ability Testing, Inc. Reproduced by permission.

Some researchers even claim that a correlation exists between a cancer patient's imagery and his eventual success or failure in conquering the illness (Lenard, 1981). When the body's defenses are pictured in strong terms, and the cancer in weak terms, prognosis is good (See Figure 13-1). In the opposite case, prognosis is poor.

How do I evaluate all of this? As you know from Chapter 12, I believe that psychological factors play a role in our susceptibility to disease as well as our recovery from it. Whether the specific role is that described by the Simontons or by Norman Cousins is not yet known. The strongest evidence in support of their claims is isolated case histories. More extensive research is needed.

I wish to emphasize that neither the Simontons nor Norman Cousins recommends that patients avoid traditional medical care. Psychological treatments, particularly right now, are best pursued as adjuncts to medical treatments. The best way to insure the hope that is so important to sustaining life is to cover all the bases, and this means the traditional ones as well as the innovative ones.

ENVIRONMENTAL PSYCHOLOGY

Environmental psychology is concerned with how and why the physical environment influences people's behavior. Granted this definition, you might find it unusual that I've included environmental psychology in a chapter devoted to applications of the cognitive paradigm. Cognitive theories contend that behavior occurs in a psychological world, not a physical one. Meaningful reality consists of one's interpretation of events, not the events themselves.

Yes and no. As I've noted several times, personality psychologists concerned with people's thoughts and beliefs may retreat too far "into the head" and forget that cognitions pertain to the real world as well as to the person. But the physical environment should be of obvious concern to cognitive psychologists, since people think about the physical world.

Similarly, people's cognitions should be of obvious concern to environmental psychologists, since people apprehend the physical world in terms of thoughts and beliefs. Compare attending a standing-room-only concert given by Bruce Springsteen to waiting in the back of a crowded elevator as it stops at each floor of a twenty-one-story building. In each case, your toes are crushed, your nose is offended by other people's body odor, your clothes are rumpled, and you can't see or hear a thing. But you're having the time of your life at the concert, while you're feeling incredibly angry in the elevator. The physical stimulation in both cases is essentially the same, so we must look to your interpretations to understand your differing reactions.

Environmental psychologists agree that cognitions mediate people's response to crowding, to aversive noise, and even to pollution. I'll describe some of this work in the present section. Then I'll conclude by considering **cognitive maps,** an intriguing research area that applies Lewin's idea of the life space to the physical environment.

Crowding

Since the early 1960s, when fears of overpopulation became widespread, literally hundreds of researchers have looked at the psychological consequences of crowding. You may have heard about James Calhoun's (1962) experimental study of overcrowded rats. He confined rats to a room of fixed size, providing them with ample food and water. The rats reproduced freely, increasing the population size, and social pathology was the eventual result. As the rats became more densely packed in the room, they acted in negative ways. They fought with each other. They cannibalized their young. They became physically ill. They let their voter registrations lapse. They stopped supporting public television. The male rats even pierced their ears!

So, crowding can be harmful. Studies with human subjects support this conclusion (Baron & Byrne, 1984). As population density goes up in a town, so too does the crime rate. In a college dormitory, crowded conditions lead to interpersonal friction, low grades, and even illness. (And you thought that living with three other roommates would be fun!)

But not all research concludes that crowded conditions are harmful. Perhaps this shouldn't surprise you. Many of our fellow citizens love to live in cities, and those of us who do not, often visit shopping malls just to rub shoulders with the milling masses. What's going on here?

People appear less affected by overcrowded conditions than animals. People can mitigate the harmful effects of physical crowding with cognitive strategies. For instance, we can limit our attention to external stimuli. Occasional visitors to large cities are aghast when they see residents walk down a sidewalk oblivious to unconscious bodies. The fundamental attribution error is often invoked: "New Yorkers don't care about people." This is probably an unfair criticism. Instead, city dwellers have learned to shut such unpleasant stimuli out of their awareness (Milgram, 1970). Calhoun's rats exhibited pathology in part because of physiological changes brought about by too much stimulation. City residents protect themselves against **stimulus overload** by walking fast, by looking the other way, and by avoiding eye contact. (They also avoid being shot.)

Relatedly, our perceived control over crowding determines its effect. Remember my earlier example about the difference between a rock concert

Crowding is not always aversive—it often depends on the individual's interpretation of the situation.

and a slow elevator? In both cases, aversive stimuli are present. But the person at the concert chose to go and feels free to leave, while the person in the elevator is literally trapped. Indeed, in a study of elevator passengers, Rodin, Solomon, and Metcalf (1979) found that people standing near the control panel felt less crowded than those standing far away from it.

According to laboratory studies, control over crowding mitigates its negative consequences. For instance, Dru Sherrod (1974) crowded subjects into a laboratory room. Some subjects had access to a button that they could push to summon Sherrod to remove them from the room. Although these subjects did not exercise this option, they were less distressed by the crowding than other subjects who didn't have access to an escape button.

These cognitive insights into the effects of crowding have been used by architects and urban planners to design environments so that personal control is enhanced (and perceived crowding is decreased). One strategy is to arrange settings so that interactions are more predictable (Zimring, 1981). For instance, houses built on cul-de-sacs tend to keep strangers away. You are more apt to encounter people familiar to you, enhancing your control over ensuing events. Similarly, college dormitories arranged with rooms on short hallways or in suites minimize uncontrollable interactions; students in these dorms are happier and healthier than their counterparts in rooms on long hallways. If school administrators believed that suite residents make more money once they graduated (which they of course would donate to the school), you better believe that there would be dormitory renovations on every campus!

Sometimes settings are designed to be unpleasant, so that people won't feel comfortable and settle into them. Waiting rooms at bus and train stations are intentionally miserable, and the more modern they are, the more misery they cause. There is no way to escape from the gaze of others; there is no place to put your feet up; there is no way to control the events that occur. Do these designs keep out panhandlers and bums? Maybe so. On the other hand, they might add to the ranks of the undesirable. Craig Zimring (1981) describes reports that the Dallas–Fort Worth Airport, which is laid out in a vast circle, is so disorienting that it sometimes precipitates psychiatric disturbances!

Noise and Pollution

The conclusions that environmental psychologists make about crowding are the same they make about noise. In broad terms, noise has negative consequences. Unwanted noise can mask what we want to hear; it can lead to auditory damage; and it can make us irritable and inattentive (Cohen & Weinstein, 1981). But if we take a closer "look" at noise, we find that how a person interprets it determines her psychological reactions. So, listen up.

Context is important in determining whether noise is unpleasant or not. Crashing surf on the beach at Malibu is exhilarating, while whispers in the back of Carnegie Hall are intolerable! When my friend Lisa and I take turns driving a car, whoever rides shotgun is in charge of the radio. Invariably, the driver finds the radio too loud because the doo-wops interfere with passing and merging.

Also, the control we perceive over noise is important. When Lisa and I are travelling, at least some of the driver's annoyance stems from not being able to choose the song currently blasting through the speakers. Or consider a dormitory where everybody has to ask everybody else to turn down their stereo. No one finds their own tunes annoying. Personal control has something to do with this form of hypocrisy.

Psychologist Sheldon Cohen and his colleagues (1980) conducted an important study which found that children whose school was under the flight paths of an airport solved problems more poorly than other children who were not subject to uncontrollable noise. Further, Cohen and his fellow researchers (1981) later found that these effects could be reversed (though not totally) by reducing classroom noise (see also, Bronzaft, 1981).

These studies are correlational. That is, it is not clear whether these harmful consequences were due to physical trauma, to uncontrollability, or to some unknown third variable. However, laboratory studies suggest uncontrollability is a possible mechanism.

David Glass and Jerome Singer (1972) ran a series of experiments exposing subjects to aversive noise. Half the subjects were led to believe that they could terminate the noise if they wished. The other half were given no such instruction. Although subjects with control did not exercise it, they still outperformed the other subjects on problem-solving measures. Interestingly, performance differences were only evident after subjects were exposed to the noise, suggesting that the noise produced learned helplessness. (Notice the similarity to the studies done on the effects of crowding?)

In other words, a person's interpretation of noise affects not only her immediate reaction but also her long-term reaction. Maybe this is why airplane pilots show no harmful effects from hearing jet engines, while the school children they fly their airplanes over fall victim. Indeed, some research even implies that people living close to airports are at increased risk for psychiatric illness (Cohen & Weinstein, 1981). Other studies challenge these findings, and I wonder if the debate could be resolved by comparing psychiatric admissions of those who lived in an area *before* an airport was built versus those who moved there *after* it was operating. If personal control is critical, I'd expect the former group to be more at risk than the latter group, who presumably chose to expose themselves to the noise.

Let me change the topic from noise to air pollution. Again, we have an example of the physical environment impinging on the individual. The effects

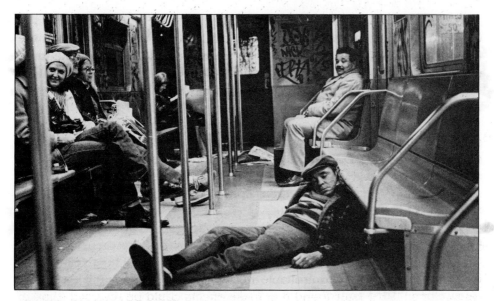

People shut out annoying stimuli by ignoring them.

of air pollution (by definition) are harmful: illness, death, irritability, aggression, lack of altruism, sleep disturbance, auto accidents, and so on. But above and beyond the physical consequences of air pollution, one's interpretation of it channels one's exact reaction. Once again, a person's perceived control is important. Evans and Jacobs (1981) describe research modeled on Glass and Singer's investigations of uncontrollable noise: bad odors that are seen as uncontrollable disrupt performance to a greater degree than the same odors believed to be controllable.

In this context, realize that most Americans regard pollution as here to stay (for example, Swan, 1972). Perhaps this fatalism will exacerbate the negative consequences of pollution. On the other hand, some researchers believe that people can accommodate pollution, at least in a psychological sense. When new versus old residents of smog-ridden Los Angeles were compared, the long-term residents reported better health, less concern with smog, and decreased likelihood of curtailing activities in the face of pollution alerts (Evans & Jacobs, 1981). In other words, air pollution had ceased to be an important aspect of their life space! Whether this is foolish or brave is a matter for debate; it proves, however, that people will keep on keeping on in the face of physical reality, with particular ways of thinking making this possible.

Cognitive Maps

The life space depicts the person's view of his environment. For the most part, psychologists in the cognitive tradition construe "environment" in the broadest sense, including other people, goals, paths, ghosts, goblins, squeezable toilet paper, and the military-industrial complex. But some environmental psychologists look specifically at how people view the physical layout of their neighborhood, their town, or their nation. Striking individual differences in these cognitive maps have been discovered, and further research finds that these individual differences relate to other characteristics of people.

I sometimes demonstrate cognitive maps with a classroom exercise. I ask my students to draw a map of the building where our class meets: "Put in as much detail as you can." The male students draw a building with several restrooms for men, but none for the women. And the female students draw a building with several women's restrooms, but none for the men.

What's my point? Our cognitive maps are practical creations. They contain features that are meaningful in our day-to-day transactions with the real world. They don't contain features that are personally irrelevant. The student in a wheelchair knows where all of the ramps and elevators are in a building, while students without the need to know this don't. Left-handed students know where "left-handed" desks are located in a classroom. The rest of us may not even know that these desks exist.

In a similar exercise, I've asked my students to draw a map of our town. I can interpret the people by looking at their maps. I usually know who is of legal drinking age, because they locate all seventeen of the town's bars on their maps. I usually know who has children, because their maps contain the local hospital, the preschool, and the convenience stores that sell Pampers twenty-four hours a day. I usually know who drives a car, because parking lots and stoplights abound. And I usually know who is a pedestrian, because alleys and paths connect the different parts of the town, while streets hardly exist.

Geographers Peter Gould and Rodney White (1974) describe systematic investigations of people's cognitive maps that support these informal conclusions. Techniques exist for creating composite cognitive maps for a group of individuals. Look at the maps in Figure 13-2. All depict Los Angeles, but notice the vast contrast in detail as you move from the left map to the right maps. The left map shows the rich knowledge of the city possessed by upper-class, white residents of Westwood. The top right map shows the more restricted view of black residents in Avalon (near Watts). And the bottom right map shows the extremely circumscribed sense of Los Angeles possessed by Spanish-speaking residents in Boyle Heights. As Gould and White note, "Their collective map includes only the immediate area, the City Hall, and, pathetically, the bus depot—the major entrance and exit to their tiny urban world" (1974, p. 37).

Don't misinterpret what Gould and White mean by pathetic. They are commenting not on the cognitive maps of a particular urban group so much as on our stratified society. It's obvious to us all that people have different amounts of money, but it's cause for alarm when we see so graphically how money translates itself into access to the world. Access in turn leads to a rich and differentiated worldview, which can only make the world more accessible. And so it goes.

Gould and White have also asked Americans in different parts of the country about where they prefer to live and how much they know about different areas. Preference and knowledge go together, and are inversely related to what is called the **confusion matrix:** the tendency to confuse adjacent states with each other. Most Americans show a regional bias, preferring their own state and knowing a great deal about it. If they don't live near the following sets of states, they tend to confuse Vermont with New Hampshire, Mississippi with Alabama, and Illinois with Indiana. Hmmm. Students in at least six states should now be reflecting on the fact that most Americans don't even know where their state is located!

We don't need to be social scientists to see that ignorance is a potential breeding ground for all sorts of problems. No wonder Americans favor locating nuclear waste dumps someplace, as long as it is over there in Utah, or Iowa, or New Jersey, or wherever they don't know anything about. Regional prejudices make more sense once we see (literally) how people in one part of the country ignore the other parts.

However, cognitive maps need not be depressing. They provide information that can be used to change the physical environment so that people can interact more forthrightly with it. So, Gould and White describe several lines of research that can lead to practical interventions. What do people view as the central landmarks of their city? Skyscrapers are not usually depicted as such, which makes sense when you think about it. People can't see skyscrapers. Instead, buildings and places at street level are much more frequently included in cognitive maps. To me, this means that city planners should worry less about how a city looks from a helicopter or airplane and more about how it looks from a car or on foot.

How do people draw neighborhood boundaries? Again, research results are at odds with "theories" of certain urban experts. Everyday people mark out their neighborhood area by its physical area, not on the density of its population. To me, this suggests a need for drastic revision in the way buildings, neighborhoods, and towns are designed.

Finally, where do people feel at danger? Research finds consensus among neighborhood residents about safe versus dangerous places. Maybe street lights and police patrols should be concentrated where cognitive maps indicate fear. And, on the other hand, research also suggests that people are sometimes completely oblivious to environmental hazards. Although geologists are certain that the West Coast will experience a cataclysmic earthquake

Figure 13-2

Cognitive Maps of Los Angeles

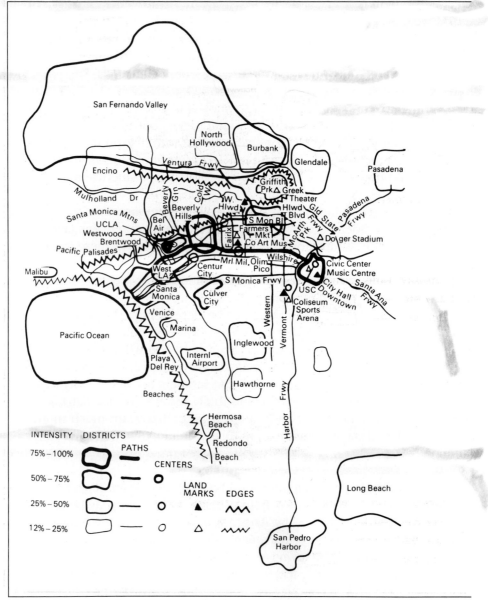

SOURCE: P. Gould & R. White (1974). *Mental maps*. New York: Penguin, p. 36.

sometime in this century, this fact is not represented in people's cognitive maps. The Far West is one of the few parts of the country that almost all Americans regard as highly desirable. To me, the West would be even more

Figure 13-2
(Continued)

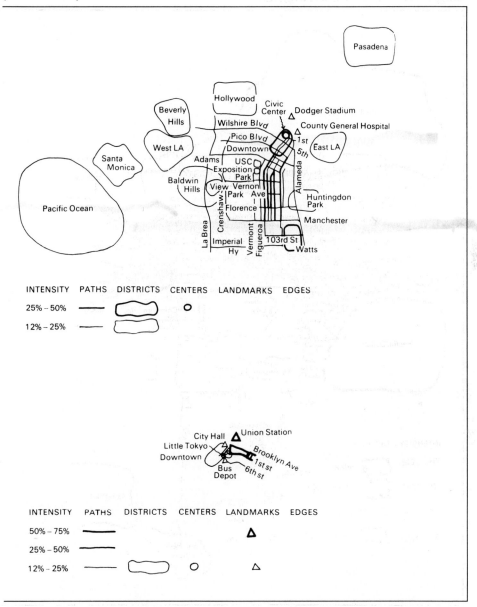

desirable if concrete plans for coping with the aftermath of an earthquake
were in place. This won't happen as long as the possibility of an earthquake
is not represented in people's cognitive maps.

FREEDOM TO LEARN (REVISITED)

One of the most influential applications of the cognitive paradigm to education is that of Carl Rogers. In his 1969 book, *Freedom to Learn,* Rogers analyzes traditional education and finds it wanting. His self-theory suggests that the typical goals and strategies of higher education can only thwart a student's natural curiosity and deplete her self-regard. Rogers instead believes we should take a different approach to education, one that is student-centered.

According to Rogers, traditional education is objectionable for two reasons. First, it is teacher-centered. The teacher sets the agenda and makes sure that it is followed, deciding when the class will start and when it will end, what will be read and what will be skipped, which assignments will be completed and which will be scrapped.

Second, traditional education is evaluative. In fact, evaluation may be the most salient part of education for many students. Consider grade point averages, class ranks, honors, and probation. These are all explicit evaluations of someone's worth. It's good to have high grades, a decent class rank, all sorts of honors, and avoid probation. It's bad to have low grades, a poor class rank, no honors, and be on probation.

Traditional education is problematical for two reasons: it is teacher-centered, and it is evaluative.

Teachers, parents, and *Time* magazine may decry students' concern with grades, but grade-grubbers are more in touch with the real world than their critics. Higher education is evaluative, and rewards and punishments are handed out according to these evaluations. The tragedy is that but a handful of students can win the race. One student gets good grades only because other students do not. One student can feel good about herself only because other students feel crummy.

Rogers believes that traditional education therefore exacts a severe toll. Most students think poorly of themselves as a result of attending school. What should be the most exciting and important aspect of a young person's life becomes, all in all, just another brick in the wall.

Rogers suggests a radical solution. Education should pattern itself on client-centered therapy. Take the teacher off focus and let the student make decisions about what is to be learned and how best to go about this. The teacher switches her role from a drill sergeant to a resource, there to advise but not to direct. Students do not follow a syllabus handed to them the first day of class; rather, they design their own course of studies and make a contract with the teacher to follow it.

Just as importantly, grades are eliminated, since they are the academic equivalent of conditional love. And once you eliminate grades, tests become superfluous. Think about it. What is the purpose of the typical test, one that queries you about "all of the above" or "none of the above" or "can you guess what side of the bed I'll get up on the day I grade this"? Tests help the teacher to assign you a place in the Great Chain of Being. Rogers calls for open seating at a theater-in-the-round.

Let me put *Freedom to Learn* in context. I have used innovative techniques in my teaching. (My favorite is to break the class into study groups and assign grades to a particular student that reflect only how his or her fellow students do. Competition becomes downright hazardous!) I've even taught at a college without grades. The biggest problem with Rogers's proposal is that higher education can't achieve it all at once. Small steps in the direction of student-centered learning have trouble surviving in a larger world diametrically opposed to the idea.

Many of my classroom innovations fall flat because my students blow off my course to study for their traditional courses. My unconditional love, so to speak, is met with conditional love on their part. And I can't blame them. If they have a finite amount of time to do two assignments, and they will be punished severely for the lateness of one but not for the other, which one will they work on? Even a cockroach would make the same choice.

The innovative school where I taught was the one I mentioned earlier in this chapter that went bankrupt. Among the college's problems was an insufficient number of students. Everybody agreed that we were doing something good, but our graduates needed grades to get admitted to law school or to obtain a job. The larger society wasn't ready for college students without a class rank. Would-be applicants figured this out before we did, and the school's demise was inevitable.

Rogers's vision of education therefore strikes me as utopian. It would be wonderful to work in a place where the students felt free to learn, but I can't find it in Barron's *Guide.* Until I do, I'll remember what I said in Chapter 11 about self-theory: there is an important distinction between people and what they do. I try to value all of my students as people. I place grades on their papers and tests, and not on their foreheads. I suggest that you do the same, and speak of your academic successes and failures as behaviors instead of traits.

SUMMARY

The subject of this chapter was applications of cognitive approaches to personality. The most extensive of these have been to psychopathology and psychotherapy. Cognitive interpretations of problems-in-living abound, as psychopathologists have identified characteristic contents and processes of thinking at the base of problems like depression and anxiety. Cognitive psychotherapies also abound, all of which target maladaptive thoughts for change, under the assumption that a different perspective will alleviate suffering.

I also touched upon several other areas where the cognitive approach has been applied: health promotion, environmental psychology, and education. In each case, applied psychologists look at particular topics in terms of people's thoughts and beliefs. Specific cognitions create problems; changing them provides solutions.

Finally, I explained that the biggest danger in cognitive applications is adopting too mentalistic a view. I stressed that the cognitive paradigm explicitly endorses a give-and-take between the person and the world. Sometimes the "world" part of this process is neglected.

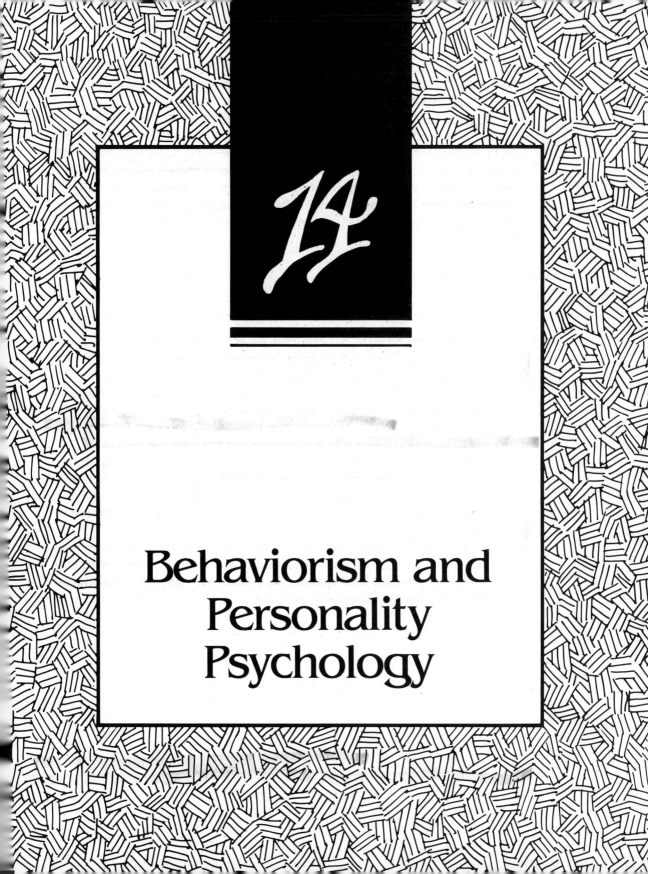

14

Behaviorism and
Personality
Psychology

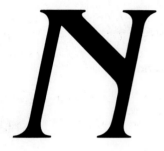

No psychologist would have any trouble choosing the right answer to the following multiple-choice question:

Which name does not belong?
  A. Freud
  B. Allport
  C. Kelly
  D. Skinner

I'm sure that you too know that the odd man out is Skinner, which explains why I'm describing the ideas of behaviorists like Skinner in this late chapter rather than in a section parallel to those on the psychoanalytic, trait, and cognitive paradigms.

Behaviorism provides a coherent paradigm for psychology, one based on a mechanistic metaphor. In my view this paradigm is, therefore, a challenge to personality psychology, not an alternative way of going about it. Obviously, a general theory of psychology need not be the same thing as a theory of personality; and in the case of behaviorism, its general stance takes issue with *all* of the personality theories I've described in this book.

In this chapter, I'll describe what behaviorism means and show how it challenges personality psychology. Then I'll describe the types of learning emphasized by behaviorists and sketch how each is important to our understanding of human behavior. Next, I'll describe two notable attempts to apply the behavioral approach to traditional personality psychology topics: the efforts of John Dollard and Neal Miller (1950) stressing drive reduction, and the work of Julian Rotter (1954) stressing social learning. Finally, I'll explain how contemporary personality psychology has benefitted from the challenge of behaviorism. In short, theories, research, and applications have become more sophisticated as a result of the continual reminder to locate behavior in its situational context.

THE FAMILY RESEMBLANCE OF BEHAVIORISM

Behaviorism didn't start out as an ordinary language term, but it became one after John Watson's (1913) manifesto called for psychology to concern itself with the overt actions of people and animals instead of unobservable mental events. From this beginning, the term behaviorism has evolved to include a broad set of emphases:

1. The explanation of observable behavior is the most important goal for psychology.
2. Behavior can be explained from the bottom up, by emphasizing what animals and people have in common.
3. The most basic explanations are those phrased in terms of the environment.
4. Learning is the most important psychological process.
5. The method of choice for psychology is laboratory experimentation, using animals as well as people for research subjects.

Not all behaviorists endorse all of these emphases. There is no single behaviorist camp, and any history lesson of psychology in the United States details the theoretical and empirical skirmishes between the different camps.

Radical behaviorists completely disavow all reference to unobservables. The mind and the characteristics we ascribe to it are regarded as epiphenomena that impede the progress of psychology. Other behaviorists introduce terms like drives that have clear biological connotations. And still others freely phrase their explanations in cognitive language.

Regardless, all behaviorists favor a reductionistic strategy for psychology: explaining what is complex in terms of what is simple. They all stress that the environment determines behavior. They are all concerned with one form of learning or another. And they are all experimentalists.

Most people—including myself—have a strong opinion about behaviorism. Sometimes the strength of their opinion has nothing to do with what they know about this approach to psychology. At one school where I taught, the students regarded certain psychology courses as behavioral and other psychology courses as nonbehavioral. They made the distinction solely upon whether the course had an accompanying lab or not, which led to the bizarre conclusion that a course in perception was behavioral, while a course in behavior modification was not!

Strong opinion aside, we recognize that behaviorism is very attractive because of its optimism about the human condition. Since the environment determines all, we need only manipulate it to bring about whatever behaviors we desire.

We also recognize that behaviorism is very unattractive because it smacks of Big Brother. Our freedom and dignity may be insulted by attempts to modify our behavior, however well intended. And suppose we disagree with the goals of behavior modification? We might envision insidious dictators turning us into unwilling robots through skillful coercion. (Put an orange M & M in my ear, and I'll do anything!)

Both of these are extreme views. If you want a cause to embrace or rebel against, then skip this paragraph. For the rest of you, let me put the promise and peril of behaviorism in context. First, every approach to psychology believes that a person's behavior has causes. Behaviorism disputes "free will" no more (or no less) than psychoanalytic, trait, or cognitive theories. Second, techniques of behavior modification are not as powerful as their advocates or opponents believe. Although situational factors like rewards and punishments are of course important influences on behavior, the simple fact is that they do not always change behavior in significant ways. If they did, dictators who control the circumstances of their "followers" would never fear revolt. Clearly they do. Even clients willing to be treated with behavior modification relapse. And animals trained with rewards and punishments can be quite obstinate about the whole matter (for example, Breland & Breland, 1961).

Good, bad, or indifferent, you can see why behaviorism is antagonistic to personality psychology. Someone's "personality" refers to his general, characteristic, enduring, and functional aspects. Most behavioral approaches do not believe that general, characteristic, and enduring aspects of people exist! Instead, all organisms are viewed as exquisitely responsive to their particular environment, shaped by the prevailing pattern of rewards and punishments.

When a person (or a rat or a pigeon) moves from one setting to another, behavior changes as the rewards and punishments change. Hence, there is *nothing general* for personality psychologists to explain. Since individual differences are arbitrarily produced by particular events, they can easily be changed. Hence, there is *nothing characteristic* for personality psychologists to explain. As a person moves through time, she continually adapts to existing conditions. Hence, there is *nothing enduring* for personality psychologists to explain.

The only place where behavioral approaches make contact with the goals of personality psychology is their concern with function and dysfunction. Here, learning theories provide persuasive explanations of how and why behavior goes awry. Although not miraculous, behavior modification techniques derived from these learning theories alleviate suffering and misery. Although I am not a behaviorist, I consider behavior modification one of the primary achievements of psychology as a whole, and I believe it has dramatically changed psychotherapy for the better.

But back to personality psychology: behaviorism essentially dismisses the very subject matter of this field. I believe there is something else going on after the psychologist takes into account rewards and punishments. Behaviorists do not. In fact, there is a fundamental split within psychology on precisely this issue.

Lee Cronbach (1957) describes the **two disciplines of scientific psychology.** On the one hand is the approach concerned with how situations impact on people, and on the other hand is the approach concerned with what people bring to situations. The first approach is exemplified by behaviorism and the research strategy of experimentation (that is, the manipulation of situations). The second approach is exemplified by personality psychology and the research strategy of correlation (that is, the description of individual differences). Cronbach calls for a merging of these two disciplines. At the present time, this merger appears to be occurring, but my point is that traditionally behaviorism and personality psychology have been no kind of bedfellows at all.

History casts behaviorism in the role of loyal (and sometimes not so loyal) opposition to personality psychology. So, it is important to consider behaviorism in a textbook on personality psychology *in these terms.* To highlight the contributions of behaviorism to personality psychology, I have contrasted the two in admittedly blunt terms. To do otherwise would be to obscure these contributions.

TYPES OF LEARNING

From its beginning, behaviorism has concerned itself with how we interact with the environment and how our behavior changes as a result of that interaction. These changes are called learning. As a sophomore in college, I took Psychology 248—Learning, and I expected the course to be devoted to what I did in the library Sunday through Thursday evenings: studying lecture notes, outlining book chapters, working problems, and so on. Instead, the course was devoted to how dogs came to salivate in the presence of Russian scientists, to how cats without hats learned to escape from boxes where they had been imprisoned by Ivy League professors, and to how lists of nonsense words like GLP, BZT, and XRM were memorized by German philosophers. This information was interesting enough, and I "learned" it pretty well. But I had trouble understanding why psychologists regarded these activities as instances of learning. I now understand. Maybe I can save you similar confusion.

Psychologists interested in learning take a broad view of their subject matter. They start by considering all possible changes in behavior, some of which can be attributed to biological processes like maturation or fatigue. The rest can only be due to one's interaction with the environment. From a broad view, these latter changes share more in common with each other than not. All are considered learning. (To reserve "learning" for changes in behavior resulting from higher education is overly restrictive and ultimately arbitrary.)

Behaviorists are interested in simple examples of learning precisely because of their simplicity. If one assumes that all forms of learning share a common essence, then why not study those forms that are easy to study? With hindsight, we can criticize this assumption made by the early learning psychologists (see, for example, Gardner, 1985). At the same time, we can see it as a reasonable strategy on their part. If physics and chemistry have profited greatly by studying pared down versions of their subject matter in the laboratory, then why not psychology?

Among learning theorists, there has been considerable debate about the best way to depict learning. Are there different types of learning, or is one type primary? If one form of learning is primary, which one is it? An overview of this debate is beyond the scope of this chapter. Instead, let me describe the major types of learning stressed by different behavioral theories. In each case, I'll try to sketch the role this type of learning plays in human behavior. Keep in mind that at least some behaviorists regard each type as a general explanation of behavior and behavior change.

Classical Conditioning

Classical conditioning is the form of learning first described by the Russian physiologist Ivan Pavlov at the turn of the century. You should be familiar with classical conditioning and its terminology from your introductory psychology course. An **unconditioned stimulus** that elicits some **unconditioned response** is repeatedly paired with some environmental event, like a sound. This event eventually becomes a **conditioned stimulus** and comes to elicit a version of the original behavior, now termed a **conditioned response.**

A familiar instance of classical conditioning is the phenomenon of taste aversion (Logue, 1979). Have you ever drank too much alcohol and become horribly ill? Suppose this happened, and the culprit was tequila. The alcohol in this liquor is the unconditioned stimulus, and your vomiting is the unconditioned response. (This is turning into a nasty example.) Anyway, the former led to the latter not through learning but through a biological reflex that protects you from poisoning yourself (although not, unfortunately, from making a fool of yourself).

When you later smell tequila and feel queasy as a result, the smell is the conditioned stimulus and your queasiness is the conditioned response. Note that alcohol was what made you sick, not the taste of tequila per se. But because of classical conditioning, you have learned to respond this way to tequila. Perhaps you have learned to be a wiser individual (at least for a day or two).

Classical conditioning was enthusiastically endorsed by John Watson as the key to understanding all of human learning. But a more circumscribed view is now in favor—classical conditioning is implicated mostly in our learning of emotional reactions (Schwartz, 1984). This is still an important aspect of the human condition.

Fears and phobias may arise through classical conditioning. I was once mugged on a dark street by a group of young men. For years afterward, my heart beat faster when I walked along a street at night and had to pass an alley. If I saw a group of fellows on the street, I came close to panicking. But, over the years, my fear has gradually **extinguished** itself, since dark streets and young men were never again paired with trauma. In other words, because the conditioned stimulus (dark street) no longer occurred with the unconditioned stimulus (mugging), the conditioned response (fear) went away.

Good emotions can also be interpreted in terms of classical conditioning. There is a television commercial for a perfume that captures this well. A young woman sees her lover on the other side of a crowded restaurant. She sprays her perfume on a piece of paper, and the waiter delivers the scent. The young man breathes deeply from the paper, becomes sexually aroused, and makes a pass at the waiter. (Well, not exactly, but you get the point.)

Some psychologists question whether these kinds of examples really reflect the operation of an automatic process of conditioning (Schwartz, 1984). Cognitive theorists, for instance, argue that emotional reactions cannot be imprinted upon us without accompanying mental activity. My being fearful on dark streets after I was mugged might have been due to an expectation of danger rather than to a pairing of a stimulus with a response. If I'd been mugged in broad daylight, I'd probably still be wary on dark streets, even more so than on well-lit streets.

Instrumental Learning

Shortly after Pavlov described classical conditioning, the American psychologist Edward Thorndike (1911) began to study how cats learned responses that allowed them to escape from boxes. Through trial-and-error, his animal subjects learned that some responses had desirable effects (allowing them to escape) while other responses did not. The cats repeated the former responses but not the latter. Thorndike summarized this type of learning with the **Law of Effect,** so termed because animals (and people) learn behaviors according to their effects on the environment.

This type of learning is called **instrumental** to stress the pragmatic (instrumental) nature of behavior. Animals and people do things that work—actions that lead to good things and avoid bad things. Another name for this is **operant conditioning,** which implies a similar point—that learning involves operations (movements) on the part of an animal or a person, followed by some consequence that determines whether or not the organism will repeat the operations in the future. In classical conditioning, environmental stimuli elicit particular responses from people or animals. In operant conditioning, the organism does something first, and then environmental stimuli follow.

This type of learning casts *hedonism* in psychological terms. Pleasure becomes positive reinforcement, while pain becomes punishment. Current learning psychologists use the terms reinforcement and punishment in a particular fashion, though, that cuts them loose from the mentalistic connotations of pleasure and pain. So, **positive reinforcement** is any stimulus that increases the frequency of a behavior that it follows. And **punishment** is any stimulus that decreases the frequency of a behavior that it follows. Note that one must see the consequences of a stimulus on behavior before one decides that it is reinforcement, punishment, or neither.

By the way, a frequently misused term is **negative reinforcement,** so be careful in reading this paragraph. Negative reinforcement is not the same as punishment. It is reinforcement because a person or animal—by definition—increases the frequency of the behavior that it follows. What they achieve, though, is relief from some stimulus. For instance, if you use the term negative reinforcement correctly, your teacher removes the threat of asking about it on your final examination. This is negative reinforcement!

In and of itself, the Law of Effect is somewhat limited in terms of what it can explain. However, as elaborated over the years by different theorists, most notably B. F. Skinner (1938), instrumental learning has become an extremely powerful explanation of human behavior. In fact, additional concepts have been introduced precisely to bolster the Law of Effect in the face of questions about its breadth.

For instance, if behaviors must be emitted before they can be reinforced, how can we learn to do things we've never done before? The idea of **shaping** answers this question. We learn new behaviors by having our past behaviors gradually shaped into them through reinforcement and punishment. A common example is teaching your dog to roll over. You don't sit around holding some treat in your hand waiting for Fido to flip. The treat will spoil before the dog performs the behavior you want to reward him for. Instead, you start by rewarding Fido first for holding still on command. When he starts to do that pretty well, you reward him for his occasional listing to one side. Eventually he'll fall on the ground. (Maybe because he's weighted down from the 10,000 treats you've given him.) You keep reinforcing him for **successive approximations** to the desired behavior. If the two of you are patient enough, he will learn to roll over. According to learning theorists, all complex behavior is learned in this way.

Relatedly, what accounts for the novelty of behavior? We don't always do things in exactly the same way or in exactly the same situation. Students don't have to be shaped from scratch each time they take a class. They know to raise their hands to be called on, to bring pencils and notebooks to class, to go to the bookstore for texts, and so on. What they are doing is termed **generalization** of past learning to new circumstances.

Instrumental learning provides a technology for training animals—and people.

And if generalization of instrumental learning occurs, why is it not rampant? Students learn to raise their hand to be called upon in class; however, they usually do not do so on a date or on the job. Generalization of learning is curbed by **discrimination.** What we learn is taken to new situations, but hardly to all of them. The more dissimilar two situations, the more likely we are to discriminate between them. When a light bulb burns out, you unscrew it and replace it; when a car engine breaks down, you don't approach it as you would the light bulb.

Why does behavior occur in the absence of obvious reinforcement? This is the biggest problem in using instrumental learning to explain the bulk of human behavior. Mundane reality presents us with neither pleasure nor pain; to encounter either one, we usually have to wait for Friday afternoon and Monday morning (respectively). But we keep on behaving at other times.

Here are several concepts that explain why we behave in the absence of obvious reinforcement. The first is **chaining.** Suppose we learn some response that leads to a reward. No problem. Well, we will also learn a second response that gives us the opportunity to perform the first response (that leads to the reward). And we will learn a third response that leads to the second that leads to the first that leads to the reward (to be found in the house that Jack built). In other words, we chain responses together. Responses at the beginning of the chain occur without obvious reward, but they ultimately lead to it. Consider grocery shopping. Early in our lives (or late at night), we learned that if we stood in front of the candy bars in aisle seven and pointed, someone would buy one for us. As we grew older, though, we learned a more complicated sequence of events: making a grocery list, clipping coupons, checking the time of day. And we still end up on aisle seven!

A second concept is that of **secondary reinforcement.** Some stimuli are reinforcing because of their biological character: food, water, safety, and so on. Other stimuli become reinforcing through association with these primary reinforcers. Social approval, for instance, is a secondary reinforcer for most of us, because we learned as infants that approval from our parents went hand-in-hand with attention to our basic biological needs.

A final way to explain behavior in the absence of obvious reinforcement is with the notion of **schedules of reinforcement** (Ferster & Skinner, 1957). People (and animals) need not be reinforced after every particular response in order to learn that response. Instead, reinforcement can be delivered on a variety of schedules: after every third response, after four minutes have elapsed, on alternate Fridays, and so on. These different patterns of rein-forcement all maintain behavior. In fact, under some circumstances, highly intermittent reinforcement can lead to a frenzy of responding. Some learning

Highly intermittent reinforcement can lead to a frenzy of response.

theorists cite gambling as an example of behavior reinforced by the most infrequent of rewards.

With concepts like shaping, generalization, discrimination, chaining, secondary reinforcement, and so on, instrumental learning has a wide range of convenience. I sometimes ask my students to think of an example of some behavior or response that appears *not* to be the product of operant conditioning. They have a lot of trouble doing this. Try it yourself; you'll find it's not a rewarding activity.

Prepared Learning

Some things are easier to learn than other things. Everybody knows this, but appreciate that this truism is not included in traditional accounts of classical conditioning and instrumental learning. Instead, learning theorists have assumed that all learning occurs in the same fashion. In light of this assumption, any differences among learning are dismissed as unimportant. However, this simplifying assumption has been successfully challenged in the last decade or so. Some theorists argue that learning can be difficult or easy according to an organism's biological predispositions (for example, Revusky & Garcia, 1970; Rozin & Kalat, 1971).

Think back to my example of taste aversion. This phenomenon is so common that we overlook one of its striking characteristics. When we drink too much tequila and get sick, what is it that later makes us nauseous? Classical conditioning predicts that we should be conditioned to all stimuli associated with the experience. But this doesn't happen. We are nauseated by the smell and taste of the liquor—not by bottles, or glasses, or salt, or lemons, or bars, or bullfight songs. Taste aversion is highly specific. We associate illness with tastes and smells, not other stimuli.

This observation has been confirmed in studies with rats (for example, Garcia & Koelling, 1966). The association between illnesses and tastes is easy for rats to learn. But even when sights or sounds are repeatedly paired with illness, no conditioning occurs. Martin Seligman (1970) suggests that the ease versus difficulty of learning such associations can be explained by considering the evolutionary significance of the learning.

An animal that readily associates particular tastes or smells with gastric disturbance has a survival advantage over other animals, since it will therefore learn to avoid foods that will make it sick. Over the eons, animals that learn this link quickly will survive and pass on their predisposition. Seligman calls this predisposition **prepared learning.**

In contrast, an animal that readily associates sights or sounds with gastric disturbance is a confused creature, since that's not the way its body works. Through evolution, this tendency has therefore been selected against. What results, in Seligman's terminology, is **contraprepared learning.**

Placing learning in an evolutionary context goes against typical behaviorism and its emphasis on the particular environment in the here and now. And while the full implications of prepared learning are still being explored, there is some agreement that human phobias can be explained in these terms (for example, Ohman, Fredrickson, Hugdahl, & Rimmo, 1976; Seligman, 1971). More speculatively, perhaps fetishes reflect evolutionary considerations (Rosenhan & Seligman, 1984). Striking about phobias and fetishes is how narrow a range of objects fall (respectively) into these categories. People develop phobias to spiders and snakes, not to electric outlets and guns. People develop fetishes to objects that in particular tickle the senses of touch and smell. Are these arbitrary facts, or do they reveal something about the evolution of our species? And what are we to make of the fact that women have more phobias than men, while men have more fetishes than women?

Insight Learning

Classical conditioning and operant conditioning share the assumption that learning is a gradual process, built up by repeated pairings of stimuli and responses. Prepared learning suggests that this process can be speeded up if it involves a biologically predisposed link, but it still emphasizes that learning results from an accumulation of associations.

Some psychologists disagree that learning is a gradual process. They argue that learning can occur in leaps and bounds, that people have "Aha" experiences. As you might imagine, these psychologists invoke cognitive language to explain learning. We don't learn associations between stimuli and responses through some automatic process; instead, we learn relationships, solutions, plans, and schemes through an active process of problem solving and hypothesis testing. Learning occurs when we see the answer.

There is a drastic difference between learning achieved through associations and learning achieved through insights. Both interpretations of learning attribute changes in our behavior to our interactions with the environment. But, where conditioning stresses the responses that are learned, **insight learning** stresses cognitions. What happens when a rat learns to run through a maze in order to gain a Cheeto? A conditioning explanation would say that he has learned to run twenty paces forward, turn left, run ten more paces, and turn right. Then he is rewarded by the food. A cognitive explanation would say that he has learned a map of the maze.

In support of cognitive learning, psychologist Edward Tolman (1948) has argued that rats (and people) learn by forming mental representations. In his experiments, he tested his explanation against the alternative notion that learning involves only responses. Take, for example, the rat who learned to run the maze. Suppose we flood the maze, so that the rat must swim through it to get the Cheeto, soggy though it may be. If all the rat had learned to do was chain together different responses, then he should not be able to find the treat. These responses are irrelevant in a flooded maze. But if he has a cognitive map, he can successfully traverse the maze, even though the required responses are now entirely different. And the rat is actually able to swim the maze, illustrating Tolman's argument.

Another example of insight learning comes from the research of Wolfgang Kohler (1924), whom I mentioned in Chapter 2. Kohler was one of the founders of gestalt psychology, and so he was interested in relations. According to Kohler, learning consisted of seeing how one's means could lead to one's ends. He studied problem solving among chimpanzees, placing them in situations where trial-and-error learning was not possible. If a banana is hanging from the ceiling beyond one's reach, and there is a stick in the room, then "insight" leads to the use of the stick to reach the banana. Learning occurs all at once.

Who is right—those who emphasize conditioning or those who emphasize insight? In my view, both emphases are warranted, depending on the particular behavior that is learned. As I mentioned earlier, learning theorists have argued long and hard about which type of learning is primary. A more profitable strategy might instead be to ask which type of learning is implicated in which type of behavior.

Insight learning is clearly an important component of so-called intelligent behavior. If I've locked the keys inside my car, I don't start emitting behaviors at random. Instead, I study the situation and consider various ways to gain entry. Are any windows open? Have I left spare keys anyplace? Can I force the door? Where can I get a coat hanger? Do I have the money for a locksmith?

Trial-and-error learning also has its place. If I've found a coat hanger to open the door, I have to fish around with it before I master the process. I have to experiment with bending little hooks at its end. And if I do open the door this way, it wasn't because I achieved insight into the way to manipulate the coat hanger. I was lucky, just like Thorndike's cats, and the next time I lock my keys in the car, I'll again have to go through a number of failed responses before one works. (I would hope that my behavior has been shaped by the prior experience and that I can thus unlock the door more quickly the second time.)

Observational Learning

The final form of learning is **observational learning**, which describes changes in behavior that result from watching what other people do and how they are reinforced or punished. Unlike other forms of learning that interest behaviorists, observational learning does not require that the learner do anything overt. Rather, to use Albert Bandura's (1977b) language, learning occurs vicariously.

"Listen... You've got to relax... The more you think about changing colors, the less chance you'll succeed... Shall we try the green background again?"

SOURCE: "The Far Side" cartoon by Gary Larson is reproduced by permission of Chronicle Features, San Francisco.

Observational learning explains why complex and novel behavior often appears out of the blue, when it is implausible that shaping played any role at all. We learn where to mail letters, how to order meals at a restaurant, how to dissect a frog, when to say please and thank you, and all sorts of behaviors by watching others perform them. These people are our **models,** and we pay attention to the consequences of their actions. If they are rewarded for doing something, then we are apt to do the same. If they are punished, then we are apt to restrain ourselves.

Bandura (1974) feels that classical conditioning and operant conditioning exist, but he further believes that these types of learning don't have nearly

Much of what we learn (which affects our personality) comes from observing others.

the applicability to complex human behavior that observational learning has. Observational learning is responsible not just for isolated behaviors, but also for complex actions like creativity and sex roles (Bandura, 1986). Indeed, our very "personality" can be viewed as a product of social learning (Bandura & Walters, 1963).

As I mentioned in Chapter 11, Bandura's interest in observational learning developed through his studies of aggression. In a series of studies, Bandura (1973) investigated whether a child exposed to a violent model would later act violently himself. His results are consistent with the perspective sketched here. If the model is rewarded, the child is likely to act in an aggressive way. If the model is eventually punished, the child is less likely to be aggressive. Further qualifications exist as well. For instance, the status of the model and the relationship of the model to the child influence the course of observational learning (Bandura, 1986).

Such research is behind the attempts to limit violence in the movies and on television, or at least to ensure that violence is ultimately punished. Arnold Schwarzenegger's character in *The Terminator* wreaks havoc on the world, but is eventually dispatched. This may satisfy the letter of Bandura's theory, but hardly its spirit; regardless, censors to date seem satisfied to see that villains eventually fail, no matter how much fun they have first.

As I described in previous chapters, Bandura (1986) presently regards observational learning in cognitive terms. In particular, vicarious learning involves learning how the world works (outcome expectations) and how one's self works (efficacy expectations). Both forms of expectancy are regarded as hypotheses that guide problem solving. Accordingly, Bandura's observational learning overlaps considerably with insight learning.

DOLLARD AND MILLER: PSYCHOANALYSIS AND BEHAVIORISM

Perhaps the most important attempt on the part of behaviorists to apply learning concepts to "traditional" personality psychology is that of John Dollard and Neal Miller. Their 1950 book *Personality and Psychotherapy,* which draws on both psychoanalytic theory and learning theory, is sometimes regarded as a translation of psychoanalytic thought into learning terms, but this description oversimplifies what Dollard and Miller achieved. Their work goes a long way toward explaining the sometimes exotic and puzzling topics of clinical psychology in the simpler terms of stimulus and response.

Background: Clark Hull's Behaviorism

To explain Dollard and Miller's work, I must first give you some background on their Yale University colleague, Clark Hull, since Hull's version of behaviorism provided them with their basic learning concepts. At one time, it was one of the most influential of the behavioral theories. Skinner's version of behaviorism may be better known today, but Hull's (1943) system has influenced personality psychology to a much greater degree.

There are several reasons for his influence. First, while Skinner (1950) downplays theory in favor of documenting empirical relationships among stimuli and responses, Hull's theory is phrased as a formal theoretical model, replete with postulates, equations, and the like. As you have seen throughout this book, one of the common threads in personality psychology is theory. Hull's approach to psychology, however divergent its details, represents a strategy of science that personality psychologists understand.

Second, Hull's behaviorism does not disavow unobservables. Indeed, one of his central theoretical notions is the **drive,** defined as *any stimulus that impels action.* A drive originates in the environment (as when we step on the hot sand at the beach and are motivated to dash furiously into the water), or it originates inside the person (as when we get the munchies and are motivated to dash to the refreshment stand at the end of the beach). Behaviors are reinforced to the degree that drives are reduced.

Third, Hull has had an impact on personality psychology because he worked with an interdisciplinary group at Yale University, whose interests extended to the sorts of topics that interest personality psychologists. Hull's behaviorism was one of the guiding frameworks for his colleagues, including sociologist John Dollard and psychologist Neal Miller.

Application to Personality

After accepting positions at Yale's Institute of Social Relations, Dollard and Miller collaborated on several important books. One of these projects proposed the well-known **frustration-aggression hypothesis** (Dollard, Doob, Miller, Mowrer, & Sears, 1939), stating that *frustration is a necessary and sufficient condition for aggression.* Frustration is viewed in broad terms as the interruption of any goal-directed activity. Almost everyone knows not to pet a dog while it is eating—even Lassie might bite you if you get between her and her Purina. And almost everyone knows not to change the television channel when someone is watching his favorite show—even a good ol' friend might bite you if you get between him and his "Dukes of Hazzard." (I sympathize more with Lassie than with your friend who likes the Dukes, but that's just an opinion.)

The strong statement that the frustration-aggression hypothesis makes is no longer accepted today, but it has survived in a weaker form (Baron & Byrne, 1984). Frustration that is intense or arbitrarily imposed indeed leads to aggression. So, your friend might not bite you if you just flipped the channel during the commercials, or if there was a hurricane threatening and you switched to the twenty-four-hour weather channel. At any rate, the frustration-aggression hypothesis well exemplifies the Hullian approach to psychology. It is phrased in strong theoretical language; it lends itself to empirical test; and it stresses drives (that is, frustration) as causes of behaviors (that is, aggression).

Similar emphases are evident in Dollard and Miller's (1950) treatment of personality and psychotherapy. Someone's "personality" is viewed in terms of specific **habits:** links between stimuli and responses established by learning. They believe that all behavior—normal and abnormal—is established in the same way by the same process of drive reduction. Habits may produce anxiety and misery, but they are nonetheless learned.

So, you may learn to fear cats because you were scratched by one as an infant. Your fear response is established by classical conditioning. This fear then functions as a drive itself. Whenever you see a cat, you experience fear, and you leave the situation. Your fear is therefore reduced, and you continue to leave situations where you encounter cats. What may seem a puzzling phobia to someone who only sees the measures you take to avoid cats is easily understood by someone else who knows your learning history.

By this view, psychotherapy involves learning new habits to replace old habits. Your fear of cats can be overcome if you lock yourself in a room where several kittens are frolicking about. You will be overcome with fear and try to escape, probably to the great amusement of the kittens, who will (we hope) start to lick your quivering fingers and purr into your pounding ears. After some time, your fear will extinguish itself, since you are finally in a situation where you will confront the fact that cats will not harm you.

Dollard and Miller similarly interpret a variety of clinical phenomena. Consider repression, which plays a key role in psychoanalytic formulations of abnormality (Chapter 5). These theorists explain repression in an elegant fashion, defining it as *not* thinking, and then arguing that a person is reinforced for not thinking about a topic because anxiety is thereby reduced. Remember what you did at the party last week? Not exactly, because every time you thought about the nasty comments you made, you grew anxious. And every time you stopped thinking, the anxiety went away. Voilà: repression.

Contrast this with Freud's view of repression. In both cases, repression is viewed as a motivated activity. But while Freud regards repression as the person banishing a particular cognitive content to a place called the unconscious, Dollard and Miller see it simply in terms of the person not thinking about those contents. The unconscious is not a place but a deficit.

Another example of their theorizing is regression, also an important Freudian concept (Chapter 5). As you remember, regression is when a person faced with stress retreats to an earlier mode of behaving. Do you ever curl up in the fetal position while taking a final exam? That's regression. Less extreme examples include pouting, sucking your thumb, or sticking out your tongue when you feel at a loss.

Freud interprets regression as a defense mechanism, as a return to a more primitive way of acting in response to an overwhelming situation. In contrast, Dollard and Miller explain it more simply by citing animal research demonstrating that conditions of high drive disrupt poorly learned responses while facilitating those that are well learned. This phenomenon is familiar to any of you who have sung, danced, or acted in front of an audience. The audience arouses you. If you have practiced your performance, you do well with the audience; if you have not practiced, you bomb out (Zajonc, 1965).

Habits acquired early in life are apt to be much better learned than those acquired later in life. So, anxiety has the dual effect of disrupting new habits and rekindling old habits. This is exactly what happens in regression.

I saw a good example of regression in these terms when I worked as a psychologist on a psychiatric ward. One of our patients suffered from post-traumatic stress disorder, which means that he would sometimes vividly relive a traumatic event from his past. In this case, he had flashbacks to a terrible battle in Vietnam where many of his buddies were killed. The patient also had a seizure disorder, so he periodically passed out.

One day, this patient passed out and slid to the floor. A physician not regularly assigned to our ward happened to be present, and he rushed to him, bending over him just as he regained consciousness. By coincidence, the doctor was an Asian-American, and when the patient saw his face peering at him, he literally believed himself under attack in Vietnam. He grabbed the doctor by the throat and started to choke him.

As the two men rolled around on the floor, the ward erupted. Actually, the other patients were cool about the whole thing, moving away, expecting the doctors and nurses to separate the two men. But the staff was so upset by what was going on that nobody made that move. As the poor doctor choked, the staff started to do things that were well-learned. The head nurse called a meeting. The head psychiatrist started to lecture the doctor being choked about the folly of rushing into an unknown situation. A hospital policeman arrived on the scene, and put his gloves on, and took them off, and put them on again, and took them off. What did I do? I started to apologize to everyone who would listen. (If you knew me better, you'd recognize this as the thing I do better than anything else in the world. I'm sorry if the point was lost on you.)

The situation resolved itself nicely, though, when the patient stopped choking the doctor and fell asleep. Whether this was a well-learned response, a variant of a seizure, or just a graceful way to exit an embarrassing situation, I don't know. I do know that the rest of us had called upon our well-learned habits, even though they were inappropriate for the situation. To complete this honest-to-goodness example, the doctor who'd been choked went around asking all of us how *we* felt. I told him that I was breathing easier than I had a minute ago. He didn't see my bad joke (another well-learned habit of mine). At any rate, now you have a flavor of how Dollard and Miller use learning theory to explain clinical phenomena.

Like Freud, Dollard and Miller sketch development in terms of an interplay between one's biological drives and one's social setting. Parents can produce conflicts in their children in the domains of hunger, elimination, sexuality, or aggression by punishing attempts to reduce drives. If the child learns to deal with anxiety through repression, the pattern is set for neurotic behavior later in life.

Suppose parents punish their young child severely for touching his genitals while at the local McDonalds. (That would make an interesting theme for a commercial: Mc-no-no!) The parents' intention may be simply to curtail masturbation in public. However, the child may generalize the punishment to include all behaviors associated with pleasure and his body. As an adolescent and adult, he fails to recognize his sexuality. He experiences severe anxiety in sexual situations. And who knows what he associates with McDonalds? Notice how Dollard and Miller end up with the same predictions as Freud by taking a behavioral route.

These theorists were greatly interested in how individuals resolve conflicts. Their paradigm case is the **approach-avoidance conflict** that is now a part of everyday language. You want to eat a Twinkie because you are hungry, but the snack will make you fat. What do you do? The conflict is resolved by the relative strengths of your drive to approach it versus your drive to avoid it, by how close or far you find yourself from the Twinkie, by whether this is a Twinkie par excellence or one that's seen better days, and so on. Neurotic individuals experience particular difficulty resolving their approach-avoidance conflicts, hovering in the vicinity of whatever plays the part of a Twinkie in their life, neither eating it nor leaving it.

Like all behaviorists trying to explain "personality" topics, Dollard and Miller run into trouble. Habits are too small to account for the generality attributed to personality, and too fragile to account for its stability. Dollard and Miller are aware of these problems and attempt to deal with them.

So, they accord great importance to language, an unusual emphasis among behaviorists. To them, words arouse drives, playing the role of sticks and stones. Words also reduce drives, smoothing ruffled feathers. Language is also critical in determining the generalization and discrimination of our learning. By introducing language into their learning theory, Dollard and Miller make their approach more applicable to personality.

Dollard and Miller also propose that potential responses exist in a hierarchy. For a particular person, some responses are consistently more likely than other responses. Again, this notion helps them explain the consistent and stable aspects of human behavior, since it explains why a particular behavior is chosen over other behaviors time and again.

How well do Dollard and Miller succeed in explaining personality and psychotherapy? Their effort is heroic, and many of their particular interpretations are ingenious; however, the bulk of the research supporting their claims about personality is indirect. They derive their ideas from carefully conducted experiments with animal subjects and extrapolate them to people, sometimes without further testing (Hall & Lindzey, 1957).

In my view, Dollard and Miller's biggest shortcoming is that their use of learning theory sometimes is metaphorical. Although thoughts and beliefs can be spoken of as "covert" stimuli and responses, this stretches what these terms actually mean. Perhaps Dollard and Miller would be better off using cognitive terms in the first place, rather than appropriating notions from animal learning experiments and forcing them inside the head. But then they wouldn't be behaviorists.

JULIAN ROTTER'S SOCIAL LEARNING THEORY

Clark Hull also influenced a second generation of behavioral theorists interested in clinical topics. Among these, Julian Rotter deserves special mention. I've already discussed some of his ideas in Chapter 11, and you know that he uses cognitive terms much more freely than his predecessors.

Rotter calls his approach **social learning theory.** (Don't be confused by the fact that Bandura used the same label to describe earlier versions of what is now his social cognitive theory.) Dollard and Miller introduced the term social learning to stress the importance of the social context in which learning occurs. Rotter goes further and makes social learning the cornerstone of his theory, proposing that people learn mainly through interaction with others.

Reinforcement plays an important role in Rotter's view of learning. All things being equal, people are more likely to act in ways that have been rewarded than punished. However, reinforcement by itself does not allow accurate predictions of what someone will do in a complex situation. The choices faced by a person are obviously more numerous than those faced by a rat or pigeon in an experimental laboratory. The hungry animal can either push a lever for food or starve to death. That's pretty stark. The hungry person can invite himself next door for dinner, or heat up leftovers from his roommate's dinner, or order a pizza to be delivered, or walk to a restaurant, or drive to a grocery store, or feed spare change into a vending machine. That's a lot of choices, all of which have rewarding consequences. Which one is the hungry person apt to do?

To answer questions like this, Rotter (1954) introduces additional concepts. People can respond in a variety of ways to a particular situation. This is the idea of **behavior potential:** each behavior has a certain likelihood of occurrence (or potential) in a certain situation. The greater the likelihood, the more apt the person is to perform that behavior rather than another. Behavior potential in turn is determined by the person's **expectancy** that the behavior will lead to a given goal and by the **reinforcement value** of that goal (its valance). All of these must be specified with respect to a particular **psychological situation,** since Rotter recognizes the importance of the setting in determining someone's particular expectancies and reinforcement values.

Back to the hungry fellow in the above example. How he chooses to respond to his growling stomach can be predicted if we know what he believes about the alternatives available to him. Suppose he has a low expectation that some of the ways to get fed will succeed. The vending machine he has in mind tends to keep his money and chuckle. The pizza place may not deliver after midnight, and it's already 11:55 P.M. His neighbor may be away, having placed a padlock on the refrigerator. At the same time, suppose he also has a poor opinion of the cooks at the local restaurants; they're almost as inept as he is! So, all things considered, there is only one choice with both high expectancy and high reward value: heat up the remains of his roommate's dinner.

Like Dollard and Miller, Rotter must grapple with the stability and consistency of human behavior. Part of the burden for explaining why people act in a similar fashion can be placed on the environment; people act the same to the degree they find themselves in the same psychological situation. How many times has our friend raided the refrigerator for his roommate's leftovers? More than once, we can be sure.

But stability and consistency are also explained by Rotter in terms of **generalized expectancies,** *beliefs of the person that transcend particular settings.* In Chapter 11, we encountered one of these generalized expectancies: locus of control. Whether or not a person generally believes that reinforcement follows her own responses is an important individual difference (Rotter, 1966). Another generalized expectancy is Rotter's (1971) **interpersonal trust,** defined as *the extent that someone relies on the word of others.* Trust is measured by a questionnaire posing questions like these:

> In dealing with strangers one is better off to be cautious until they have provided evidence that they are trustworthy.

> Parents can usually be relied upon to keep promises.

> Most elected officials are really sincere in their campaign promises. (Rotter, 1967)

Research shows that people high in trust act as we would expect (Phares, 1984). They are less likely to lie, they respect the rights of others, and they give people a second chance.

What does interpersonal trust have to do with learning? Take my word that it does. Rotter believes that learning occurs in a social context. People high in trust rely on what other people say about the world. They allow others to shape their expectancies ("You'll never finish that assignment in an hour") and define their reinforcement values ("That's a great record album"). People low in trust are suspicious of others and as a result may be less "social" in their learning.

I can't resist proposing a personality typology that combines Rotter's internal versus external distinction with his high versus low interpersonal trust distinction. Here are examples for each type:

- Internal-Trusting: Charlie Brown
- Internal-Nontrusting: Rambo
- External-Trusting: Bambi
- External-Untrusting: Chicken Little

Imagine each of these characters as your roommate; how would they respond if you ate *their* dinner?

BEHAVIOR MODIFICATION

According to some who have commented on the recent history of psychology, behaviorism has lost its grip on the discipline, and may even have become extinct (for example, Gardner, 1985). I'm not sure whether this is generally true or not, but in the specific domain of therapy, behaviorism is alive and well in the form of **behavior modification.** B-mod, as it is sometimes called, is an arsenal of strategies for changing troubled behavior. A recently published *Dictionary of Behavior Therapy Techniques* lists 158 different procedures, from "anger control therapy" through "dry pants training" to "respiratory relief" (Bellack & Hersen, 1985).

All these strategies are derived from traditional learning theories and reflect the assumption that behaviors—normal or abnormal—are learned in the same fashion. Hence, they can be relearned or unlearned. From the very start, behaviorism has been optimistic about the ease and success of changing behavior through environmental manipulation. Watson, Hull, Skinner, Dollard and Miller, Rotter, and others in this tradition have been concerned with how best to alleviate people's pain and suffering. To a large degree, b-mod is the proof of their concern. These techniques are demonstrably effective for a variety of problems, including some highly resistant to other forms of therapy.

In this section, I'll describe some of the more common of the behavior modification techniques based on classical and operant conditioning. Appreciate that a number of other b-mod techniques also exist, including many derived from Bandura's (1969) notions of observational learning (Chapters 11 and 13). Even if behaviorism may not explain the whole of what is meant by personality, it certainly has succeeded in giving therapists a handle on problematic behavior and how to change it.

Classical Conditioning Techniques

These therapeutic strategies attempt to change our emotional reaction to objects by pairing these objects with stimuli that elicit a different emotional reaction. After repeated pairings, through classical conditioning, the objects will eventually give rise to the new emotion. Classical conditioning techniques are most successful when consistent with prepared learning and are least successful when they push against biologically predisposed associations.

One of the best-known of the classical conditioning techniques is **systematic desensitization,** originally developed by psychiatrist Joseph Wolpe (1958). Systematic desensitization is deployed against fears and phobias. The therapist first shows the client how to relax thoroughly, since relaxation is incompatible with anxiety. Then the therapist and the client devise a hierarchy of scenes and situations reflecting the client's particular fear. Suppose the person is scared to death of speaking in class. An item low in the hierarchy might involve the client nodding her agreement to a professor's rhetorical question. An item intermediate in the hierarchy may have the client asking the teacher to repeat a definition. Finally, an item high in the hierarchy would be the client standing up and disputing her instructor's conclusion.

Therapy proceeds by having the client relax and visualize the scene lowest in the hierarchy. As long as the imagery is tolerated without anxiety, the client holds on to it. If and when anxiety occurs, the client again relaxes until she can imagine the scene comfortably. Gradually, the client works her way up the hierarchy, so that the feared scenes are repeatedly paired with relaxation instead of anxiety. In this way, fears and phobias are vanquished. Success rates have been reported as high as 80 to 90 percent, and success is maintained years later (for example, Paul, 1967).

Systematic desensitization has been deployed against an incredible variety of fears. Bernstein and Nietzel report that it has been used to treat "fear of balloons, wind, the year 1952, feathers, violins, dirty shirts, and short people" (1980, p. 368). (I assume they mean in different clients; regardless, the generality of the technique is clear.)

Sex therapists William Masters and Virginia Johnson (1970) use an analogous procedure in their treatment of sexual dysfunctions occasioned by excessive anxiety (like impotence or inhibited orgasm). In **sensate focus,** couples kiss and caress with the goal of giving pleasure to their partner, not as a prerequisite for intercourse. Performance anxiety is reduced, and relaxation is increased, with both emotional states becoming associated with caressing. Eventually, their lovemaking progresses to intercourse and orgasm, but the path leads through classical conditioning.

Another b-mod technique of this type is **flooding** (Marshall, Gauthier, & Gordon, 1979), which I've used as an example in several earlier contexts. (It is not an adjunct to dry pants training, in case you were curious.) In flooding, the person is exposed to the object or situation that he fears, and is not allowed to flee from it. (We assume that the therapist has not miscalculated, that there is no objective danger in the confrontation.) The fear eventually extinguishes. (Maybe this is the way you learned to swim—head-first into the deep end. You survived, and any fears you had about the water were conquered.) Needless to say, flooding must be used with caution. If the person leaves the situation before fear is alleviated, there is good reason to think that the fear will be exacerbated!

In **aversion therapy,** a therapist tries to induce his client's avoidance of some object by pairing that object with a negative experience. Alcoholics and drug users may be given a particular chemical that reacts violently with the abused substance, making them deathly ill. The hope is that some variant of taste aversion will be conditioned, and the clients will avoid alcohol or drugs. Similarly, child molesters may be shown pictures of children at the same time as they are given painful electric shocks. The hope again is that their initial positive response will be changed to a negative one through classical conditioning.

Perhaps you've seen the movie *A Clockwork Orange*, set in a futuristic Great Britain where the police treat violent criminals with classical conditioning, pairing scenes of violence with illness and pain, so that the criminals are later repulsed by opportunities to commit crimes. The basic strategy is not science fiction. Only the effectiveness of the procedure is exaggerated in the movie.

Aversion therapy seems to work in the short run, but a determined individual can undo the conditioning by playing b-mod therapist himself (Bernstein & Nietzel, 1980). Someone determined to drink will go ahead and drink in the face of conditioned nausea. Eventually, this learning will be extinguished, and the person can drink without feeling queasy. I believe that the lesson here is the same one learned by practitioners of all forms of psychotherapy. There are no miracle treatments; success must involve hard work by the client. This includes the need for "booster" sessions with the behavior therapist, where the original learning is repeated.

Instrumental Learning Techniques

An equally impressive array of techniques is based on the Law of Effect and its current descendants. All of them try to increase the frequency of desired behaviors by **selective reward** and/or to decrease the frequency of undesired behaviors by **selective punishment.** The rationale behind these operant conditioning strategies is that once the person is engaging in positive behaviors while refraining from negative ones, her natural environment will take over and maintain this style of behaving. Accordingly, the therapist who uses these techniques carefully studies the actual settings to which the person will take her new skills. If these settings are not conducive to the new skills, if the desired behaviors will not be rewarded in them, then the therapist must change the situation. There's no point in teaching people to say please and thank you if they live in a hostile and rude environment.

So, b-mod sometimes need not involve the "client" at all. A therapist can deal with a child's noncompliance by instituting **parent training,** teaching parents to be behavior therapists for their child. Perhaps they have been unwittingly rewarding the child's outbursts while ignoring or even punishing his occasional moments of calm. When parents start to pay more attention to how they respond to what their child does, his behavior changes for the better.

One effective technique for curbing a child's undesirable activities is called **time out** (Leitenberg, 1976). When the kid bounces off the walls, he is removed from the situation for a short period of time and placed in a quiet and isolated room. If time out follows every attempt on his part to imitate a Superball, then he will spend more time acting like a little boy.

An operant therapy for depression is **social skills training.** A popular theory of depression sees the problem as resulting from inadequate levels of reward (Lewinsohn, 1974), and one reason that the person may not be getting enough goodies from the environment is that he lacks the skills to earn them. In social skills training, he is taught what many people learned on their own as children, that one catches more flies (and good grades, and promotions, and compliments, and friends, and lovers) with honey than with vinegar. So specific techniques of positive social interaction are taught.

A **token economy** is operant therapy implemented on a large scale, often on an entire hospital ward (Kazdin, 1977). Patients earn tokens for positive behaviors like staying awake, making eye contact, initiating conversations, keeping clean, and so on. They lose tokens for negative behaviors, like acting bizarre, picking fights, or shirking assigned duties. Tokens can be used to "purchase" desired commodities—cigarettes, candy, weekend passes, movie tickets, whatever. Token economies represent the behaviorist view of the way the world really runs, except that the system of rewards and punishments in the token economy is explicit and coherent.

A final b-mod technique based on instrumental learning is **biofeedback.** Most biofeedback applications stem from Neal Miller's (1969) suggestion that physiological responses like one's heart rate, glandular secretions, skin temperature, or brain waves can be altered through reward and punishment just like overt responses. People have difficulty identifying these responses because they are covert. Biofeedback solves this problem by monitoring bodily responses with an appropriate machine and providing the person with the information (or feedback). Then, a person can change her bodily responses.

The basic premise of biofeedback has been questioned because researchers find it difficult to replicate Miller's original studies showing that the autonomic nervous system could be conditioned. Nevertheless, biofeedback is a thriving enterprise, used to combat migraine headaches, insomnia, pain, and high blood pressure. (I'm using it, so far without much success, to cultivate dimples and a twinkle in my eyes.) If nothing else, biofeedback shows the far-flung domains that behaviorism has ventured into.

A behavior therapist doesn't believe there is any real line between traditional therapy and other types of behavior change. All are attributed to learning. Strategies based on instrumental learning (and occasionally on classical conditioning) have therefore been implemented in every conceivable setting.

For instance, educational psychologists have used behavior modification to control disruptive students, to bolster attendance, and to increase the

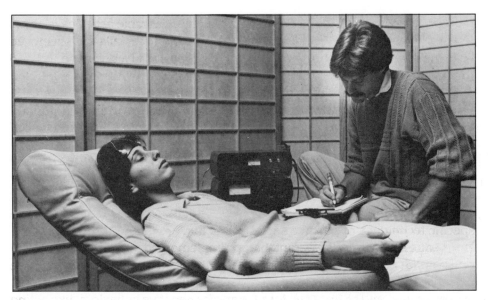

Biofeedback makes covert responses overt—giving a person greater control over her bodily responses.

quantity and quality of academic work (Lahey & Rubinoff, 1981). Some of these interventions have aroused controversy (Winett & Winkler, 1972), but they have, nevertheless, proven effective.

Behavior modification has also altered educational material and the very nature of a class. Fred Keller (1969) bases his popular **Personalized Self Instruction** (or **PSI**) explicitly on principles of operant conditioning. Perhaps you have taken a PSI course, which is usually broken into a series of small units you work through at your own pace. The units may be contained in a book or—more recently—in an interactive computer program. Testing is extremely frequent, yet conventional grades are not given. Instead, a student is told whether or not she has mastered the material. Mastery of one unit occurs before she moves on to the next. If lectures occur at all, they are regarded as "reinforcement" for mastering units of the course.

Other psychologists have used behavior modification techniques in the workplace. Collectively, their interventions are termed **organizational behavior management**. Productivity can be increased with the appropriate use of positive reinforcement (for example, Andrasik, 1979). At the same time, absenteeism can be decreased (for example, Kempen & Hall, 1977). Training of new skills is an obvious area where b-mod has been used. Less obvious, perhaps, is that industries and organizations are becoming interested in how to promote the health of their employees. The motive here is not completely altruistic. Appreciate how much money a business can save if sick leave, disability pensions, and inefficiency due to illness can be reduced.

(Maybe these savings might even trickle down to the consumer someday!) For this reason, health promotion at the worksite is increasingly popular (Nathan, 1984). Programs to reduce smoking, hypertension, cholesterol, alcohol use, obesity, and so on rely on behavior modification techniques generalized from individual therapy to the work setting.

A final example of how broadly b-mod has been applied is its use by environmental psychologists to encourage people to take better care of our planet. So, Burgess, Clark, and Handee (1971) reinforced movie patrons for disposing of trash (no, silly, not the movie they had seen . . . candy wrappers and paper cups). Giving away money and free movie tickets proved highly effective. Other researchers have been able to increase such important behaviors as gasoline conservation and recycling (Hake, 1981).

CONCLUSIONS: BEHAVIORISM AND PERSONALITY IN THE PAST, PRESENT, AND FUTURE

I've only sketched the basics of behaviorism and theories of learning, concentrating on their relevance to what we mean by personality. As you study psychology further, you will encounter behaviorism again. It has colored the whole of American psychology, since its pragmatic and optimistic bent has fit well with the spirit of our country during the twentieth century.

Think of the major types of learning of interest to behaviorists. Separately and together, they sit on top of what it means to be a person. One of our most notable characteristics as a species is our malleability, our ability to change, adapt, accommodate, and create. In short, men and women can and do learn new ways of behaving. So perhaps the best way to describe human nature is to say that there is no single nature (see Chapter 2).

Granted all this, learning theories powerfully explain human behavior. Behaviorism is a coherent paradigm for the whole of psychology. Some psychologists feel that behaviorism can even explain those topics of interest to personality psychology. By this view, everything that can be attributed to unconscious conflicts, or to the self, or to schemata, or to any of the other theoretical constructs introduced by personality psychologists can be explained in terms of transactions with a particular environment.

Learning theory stresses that the environment determines what we are all about. In this mechanistic view, stimuli are causes and our behaviors are effects. To most learning theorists, we *are* our behaviors, and our behaviors are responses. If we know the system of rewards and punishments prevailing in a particular setting, and if we know an individual's reinforcement history, then we know everything necessary to predict, control, and understand what he does. Reference to "personality" is therefore unnecessary at best and misleading at worst.

What's the behavioral beef with the three personality paradigms? Generic criticisms include their penchant for unobservables and lack of experimental studies. More specifically, the psychoanalytic paradigm is suspect because its terms are difficult to operationalize and test; the trait paradigm is dubious because it ignores situations; and the cognitive paradigm is unacceptable because its language is mentalistic. Now that you've studied these three paradigms, try to think of how proponents of each would rebut these criticisms. Keep in mind, however, that behavioral psychologists are raising legitimate questions about these approaches.

I have two general conclusions about the relationship between behaviorism and personality psychology. The first looks back in time. As I stressed at the beginning of this chapter, the general thrust of behaviorism has challenged personality psychology as it is conducted within the psychoanalytic, trait, and cognitive paradigms. In the face of this challenge, personality psychologists have felt obliged to define their terms better, to make their theories more parsimonious, to subject claims to empirical testing, and to take explicit recognition of the situation in which personality metaphorically resides. But personality psychology is not the only field to have changed; learning theory has also evolved in response to criticisms of its behavioral approach.

The shortcomings of behaviorism are myriad. In its boldest form, it is too simple and cannot readily account for complex behavior. The failure of traditional learning theory to explain language, for instance, is well known (for example, Chomsky, 1959). Relatedly, behaviorism has relied too much on studies of animals in artificial situations. While it would be foolish to dismiss any analogy between rats and people, neither is the overlap of these two species perfect. After all, it is us studying them, not vice versa. A psychology that ignores or minimizes the mental life of people is open to severe criticism (Gardner, 1985).

But learning theorists have not been blind to these shortcomings. Their conceptualizations move steadily toward greater sophistication and complexity: learning theory gives way to social learning theory which in turn gives way to cognitive social learning theory which (I think) will eventually give way to cognitive theory. In other words, learning theory has become more suitable for explaining what is meant by personality.

My second conclusion looks ahead in time. I suspect that in the future, learning theory will be regarded as an important strand in the cognitive paradigm of personality. In light of past history, this is ironic. But after all, cognitive theories of personality are concerned with the environment as much as with the person. Learning theories deal explicitly with the environment. In recent years, theorists like Rotter, Bandura, and Mischel have stressed that the human environment is not a collection of physical stimuli so much as a structure of meaningful symbols. This change in how the environment is conceived is not trivial. It moves learning theory out of the tradition of behaviorism and fully into the tradition of personality psychology. Welcome!

SUMMARY

Behaviorism is a group of approaches to psychology that emphasizes observable behavior, reductionistic explanation, the environment, learning, and laboratory experimentation. In this chapter, I described behaviorism and how it relates to personality psychology. For the most part, behaviorism has challenged personality theories, taking issue with the possibility that there is anything general, characteristic, or enduring about people's behavior once you take into account the rewards and punishments that prevail in a particular setting.

I described five types of learning—**classical conditioning, instrumental learning, prepared learning, insight learning, and observational learning**—and explained their relevance to human behavior. Then I described two important attempts to apply learning concepts to the traditional topics of personality psychology—the **drive-reduction** approach of Dollard and Miller and the **social-learning** approach of Rotter. Techniques of behavior modification are the crowning achievement of behavioral psychology, and I sketched the most common of these therapeutic strategies, which help troubled individuals learn more productive ways of behaving.

I drew two conclusions. First, in the role of critic, behaviorism has forced personality psychology to become more sophisticated theoretically and methodologically. Second, behaviorism itself has evolved over the years, introducing concepts that nudge learning theories ever closer to the personality tradition. To judge by the work of Bandura and Mischel, the journey may be almost complete. The past relationship between learning theory and personality psychology has been antagonistic; the future relationship will be harmonious.

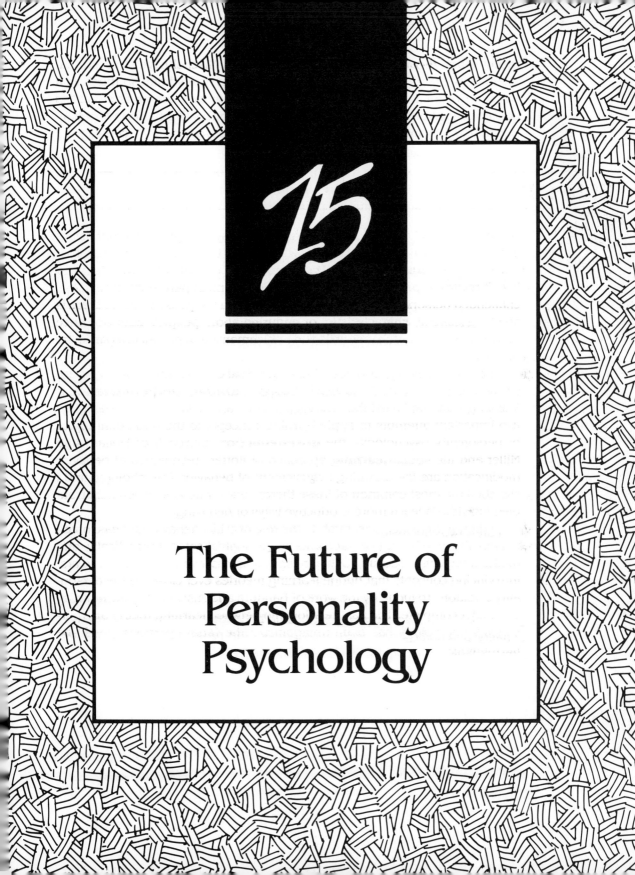

15

The Future of
Personality
Psychology

*I*n one sense, I'm done with my purpose here, having described personality psychology to you. In another sense, though, I'm not at all finished. Like any science, personality psychology is not static. Just as surely as personality psychology has extended from the past into the present, so too will it extend from the present into the future. So, in this brief concluding chapter, I want to speculate about the future of personality psychology. My conclusion is also an introduction.

Looking back, over the decades since psychology first took form, certain trends are apparent. These will continue, and we can expect psychology to become more specialized, to rely more on sophisticated methods, to become less an ivory tower endeavor, and to become more enmeshed in the complex world in which we live. Psychologists won't stay in their traditional haunts—the clinic and the university—but will move further into industry, hospitals, and the campaign staffs of politicians. We may even see a psychologist, well-trained in statistical inference, appointed to the Supreme Court, since so many matters of justice and injustice rest nowadays on the ability to discern patterns among complex data.

But these are my predictions about psychology as a whole. And since our particular interest is in personality psychology, what specific predictions can I make about this field? I'll make a bold one. My prediction comes from considering what the three major personality paradigms have in common. Although these paradigms (by definition) have very different flavors, I nevertheless see changes in each that are nudging them toward a consensus.

I predict that in the not-so-distant future, a new paradigm of personality psychology will emerge, a single point of view about the best way to study personality. The seeds of this new paradigm have already sprouted in each of the contemporary paradigms. But will it be a combination of the three? Nothing so simple.

The overarching conclusion in each paradigm is that *people are best described in complex terms that take into explicit account their transactions with the world.* We've seen this point of view numerous times. This is the neo-Freudian perspective; this is interactionism; this is field theory; and this is reciprocal determinism.

A TRANSACTIONAL PERSPECTIVE ON PERSONALITY

Let me term this new approach to personality psychology **transactional theory** to capture its emphasis on the give-and-take between the person and the world. This approach is impatient with the dichotomies that clutter the history of psychology and continue to polarize the current personality paradigms. Remember the fundamental issues that I described in Chapter 4? They are useful for understanding the way psychology has been, but not so useful for charting the future direction of the field.

Within each of the personality paradigms, we've seen theorists and researchers come to the conclusion that a number of these fundamental issues are phrased too simply in either-or terms. Both ends need to be integrated. Consider biology and psychology; cognitions and feelings; conscious and unconscious; consistency and inconsistency; instincts and learning; maturation and development; minds and bodies; nature and nurture; observables and unobservables; person and society; rationality and irrationality; selfish versus social nature of people; and stimuli and responses. Personality psychology cannot emphasize one end to the exclusion of the other. Too much that is important in understanding what we are all about lives on the other side.

A similar argument can be made with respect to research methods. We've noticed, for instance, that each paradigm favors one particular research strategy or another. Sometimes, the researchers within a paradigm embrace one tactic and completely ignore all the others. At a methodological level, these preferences are dichotomies that are no longer productive.

Finally, what about the applications of personality psychology? They go awry to the degree that they stress one aspect of human nature to the exclusion of others. Psychoanalytic applications become strained when they overemphasize sex; trait applications become strained when they overemphasize stability and consistency; and cognitive applications become strained when they overemphasize rationality.

However, a transactional approach to personality recognizes both sides of theory, research, and application. Even more critically, a transactional approach recognizes that the ends of these dichotomies must be integrated. Personality theorists, researchers, and practitioners have recognized the problem of narrow perspectives, but they remain unsure as to how to broaden their view.

I am not calling for a mushy combination of personality approaches. Instead, I am suggesting a common ground from which to view them all. Even the craziest of quilts is stitched onto a backing. I'm predicting that in the short run, a transactional perspective can serve as this backing. And in the long run, as genuinely transactional concepts and methods are developed, personality psychologists will produce more than "quilts." Right now we do not have such concepts. We struggle with traditional terms and traditional methods, knowing that we cannot reach our goals by using them. We need a new vocabulary, one that refers to different transactions between and within people.

I wish I could give you some simple examples of transactional concepts that apply to personality. But as I keep emphasizing, we have few of them as yet, although psychologists have the mindset to use these concepts. Let me instead draw on some other disciplines and perspectives based on a transactional vision. When you get a feel for what I mean by a transaction, I'll turn to the work of the handful of personality psychologists who have already grappled with the future as I see it.

SOME EXAMPLES OF TRANSACTIONS

Ecology

Ecology is a branch of biology that has lately come into its own as a science. Its central concern is how species and their environments mesh. The ecologist does not examine a particular organism or a particular setting in isolation; rather, she conceptualizes the entire system as an integrated whole.

What makes ecology a coherent approach are transactional concepts that explicitly capture the fit between a species and its environment. A **niche,** for instance, is one such transactional concept because it refers neither to a species by itself nor to an environment by itself. Rather, a niche is the role played by a particular species in a particular environment.

Family Systems

The family systems approach to therapy is a social science discipline that provides additional transactional concepts. According to this view of people's problems, no one has difficulty independently of his or her social context. Indeed, problems are not even attributed to individual people (except insofar as insurance companies require that a "client" be identified). Problems are viewed instead as a manifestation of social processes within a family.

Suppose a first-grader has become withdrawn at school and started to wet his bed at night. The typical psychotherapist would say that the child has a problem, and would conceptualize the problem in terms of individual characteristics, be they inner conflicts, erroneous thoughts, or faulty learning. But a family systems therapist would conceptualize the withdrawn behavior and wet sheets as symptoms of a family problem and would look for recent changes in the family makeup. Maybe Mom and Dad have started to fight about finances. Perhaps a little sister just arrived on the scene.

The first-grader is showing symptoms of the disturbed family, but he is not the problem. When we have intestinal flu, we do not say that our intestine is sick. We say that *we* are feeling lousy and have a bug. Similarly, the family systems therapist says that the first-grader's family has a problem.

Like ecology, family systems therapy is a coherent discipline, having a vocabulary that describes different modes of family interaction, that refers to the family as a whole. For example, a **schismatic family** is one in which the parents are caught up in personal problems and have grown contemptuous of each other; children are treated as pawns in a battle between the two (Lidz, 1975). Notice that this term refers not simply to the individuals in the family but to the transactions among them.

Eastern Philosophies

For a final example of a transactional discipline, I turn to Eastern philosophies. Zen Buddhism and Taoism take issue with all dichotomies, branding them illusions. Chief among these illusions is the belief that we have a "self" somehow separate from the rest of the world. Enlightenment occurs when one sees that there is no one to be enlightened, conceiving the human enterprise in transactional terms.

In *Zen in the Art of Archery*, Eugen Herrigel (1971) conveys the essence of this approach with a parable. He seeks out a master teacher to learn about Zen. The teacher is not at all interested in teaching Zen; rather, he instructs Herrigel in how to use a bow and arrows. This strikes Herrigel as rather unusual, but he complies with the master. (Haven't we all taken a college course that doesn't have much to do with the syllabus?)

However, Herrigel learns about Zen while learning the best way to shoot an arrow, by *not* conceptualizing archery as something he does with the bow. Rather, archery is something that happens, and the archer is no more important than the bow. The arrow shoots itself just as much as it is shot.

Let me stress that this is not word magic. If any of you have used a bow and arrow, you know that the only way to hit the target is to ever so gently release the taut string and let the arrow fly. The best archer is one who literally does not know when he lets go of the string. Letting go all at once results in a flinch, and the arrow does not fly true.

Maybe you haven't used a bow and arrow, but you're into photography. Good, that's nonviolent. You know that you squeeze the shutter, not push it. Or maybe you're into kissing. (Finally, an example that will make sense!) When kisses are good and right, they are not assaults. They simply happen. You don't start the kiss, carry it through, and break it off; neither does your partner. Any attempt to regard you or your partner as the primary kisser would be bizarre.

I hope that my examples convey the idea that activity spans the person and the world. Despite our tendency to conceptualize activity as "us" doing "it" to "them" or whatever, the Zen Buddhist or Taoist prefers to look at activity in less discrete terms. The word **tao** means "the way of all life" and conveys the notion that life flows, regardless of the interpretations we place upon it.

The personality psychologist of the future must devise notions like that of niche or schismatic family or tao that specifically pertain to personality.

Transactional terms will make personality psychology a transactional field, rather than three paradigms wanting such a field but not knowing how to go about it. They will unite psychoanalytic, trait, and cognitive theories by depicting the ways in which the factors of one mesh with those of the others. Following this unified theory will be methods and applications quite unlike those that psychologists have so far developed.

THEORISTS AHEAD OF THEIR TIMES

Almost all personality psychologists, past and present, can be fit into one of the three paradigms I've used to structure this book. That's why I chose these paradigms as a means of organization. But as I wrote, I felt occasional misgivings when I encountered a particular personality psychologist whose work defied my system. What did I do with these contrary individuals? I ignored them. (I'm only human.) But then my thoughts turned to the future of personality psychology and the transactional paradigm that it seems to hold. I realized what these neglected theorists had in common (other than making me feel uncomfortable)—all were ahead of their time in stressing concepts that span the different paradigms. On the one hand, they resist simple categorization. On the other hand, they give us a glimpse into the future.

Joseph Conrad wrote in *Heart of Darkness* that the mind is "capable of anything—because everything is in it, all the past as well as all the future." I'd like to qualify this adage and say that some minds have more of the future in them than do other minds. It is to three such minds that I now turn: those of Gardner Murphy (1947), Silvan Tomkins (1962, 1963), and Robert Hogan (1982). Each proposes a theory of personality that takes issue with one or more of the traditional dichotomies of personality psychology. Their work foreshadows the transactional paradigm that I see as the future of the field.

Gardner Murphy: Biosocial Theory

Murphy's (1947) approach to personality is called **biosocial theory,** and it represents self-conscious eclecticism. He was well-suited to weave together disparate strands of psychology since he was familiar with almost all of them (Hilgard, 1987). During Murphy's career, he wrote influential books not only about personality psychology but also about general psychology, social psychology, and the history of psychology. He was also interested in "psychology" as studied in different cultures.

Murphy chose to call his theory biosocial because he maintains that the most important aspect of personality is the reciprocal relationship between the person as a biological being and the social and material environment. He uses the language of field theory to define personality:

> A personality is a structured organism-environment field, each aspect of which stands in dynamic relation to each other aspect. There is organization within the organism and organization within the environment, but it is the cross organization of the two that is investigated in personality psychology. (Murphy, 1947, p. 8)

He further notes that his perspective does not disagree with other views of personality (like those of the psychoanalytic, trait, and cognitive paradigms). Instead, it subsumes them, preserving their individual insights while achieving new ones by integrating them.

Since Murphy wishes in particular to integrate biological and social views, he finds notions of development useful. We enter the world as biological beings, with physiological dispositions termed **organic traits.** In the course of our socialization, these organic traits become **symbolic traits** through processes of learning. Thus, we learn socially approved ways of satisfying biologically based needs. This is **canalization,** and it is responsible for making us social beings.

So, the newborn infant is hungry. Her hunger is a drive that can be satisfied in any of a number of ways. Depending on the circumstances of her upbringing, though, she soon comes to demand not food in general but food in particular: cookies and milk; tofu; whale blubber; raw eggs; Whopper and fries. Taste in food becomes specific (Murphy, 1947, p. 161). Do you see that food preference is a transactional concept? It is obviously biological; it is obviously social; but it is most obviously *both.*

During development, the person's needs and drives become more differentiated. Read the last sentence again. It is not just behavior or cognition that becomes more complex as our personality takes shape; rather, our biological drives become more complex as well through canalization. Other personality psychologists derive the range of thoughts, feelings, and actions from a few underlying drives or motives. Personality development is seen as making the links between overt behavior and underlying drives more complicated, but the drives stay the same. Murphy argues instead that *the drives themselves change.* To believe otherwise is to sacrifice the transactional vision by implying that drives are primary.

Murphy was also interested in **parapsychology** (that is, the scientific study of telekinesis, clairvoyance, telepathy, and so on). This interest follows from his transactional orientation. If personality does not stop at the skin, it must extend beyond. To date, we know not where. Since other researchers look mainly at the person *or* at the situation to understand personality, they may be oblivious to "broader" personality dimensions, those that possibly link the person to the physical world (telekinesis), to the future (clairvoyance),

Food preference is transactional—both biological *and* social.

or to another person (telepathy). Please note, Murphy is not interested in the **occult** with its connotations of spookiness and evil; rather, he suggests that important personality phenomena and principles remain to be discovered.

Finally, let me add that Hall and Lindzey (1957) give biosocial theory a prominent position in the first edition of their textbook. They call it a "wide-screen production of tremendous scope and deep perspectives" (p. 535). But in subsequent editions, it is mentioned fewer and fewer times, which seems to reflect how the larger field has reacted to Murphy's ideas. Although many of his particular notions have been assimilated by other theorists (which shows their appeal), his overall vision has not taken root. I think this is because he was ahead of his time. Perhaps future personality psychologists will again highlight the work of Gardner Murphy.

Silvan Tomkins: Cognitive-Affective Theory

In discussing the cognitive paradigm, I brought out the criticism that its theories neglect *hot cognition*: the emotions and feelings that are part of us as people, but not the part clarified by computer or scientist metaphors. A notable exception is the **cognitive-affective theory** of Silvan Tomkins (1962, 1963).

Tomkins (1979) stresses cognition and favors an information-processing approach to personality. But at the same time, he emphasizes biologically based emotions like fear and anger and surprise (Tomkins, 1981). Most importantly, he addresses how cognitions and emotions mutually affect each other. This marks his approach as transactional and shows Tomkins leading personality psychology into its future.

Like Murphy, Tomkins emphasizes the mutual influence of systems usually studied in isolation. In particular, Tomkins views personality in terms of five sets of influences: *homeostatic or regulating mechanisms; drives; emotions; the motor apparatus;* and *cognitions.* People's behavior reflects how these systems respond to internal and external conditions (Singer, 1984). Since the systems are highly entwined and integrated with each other, one's personality can be described as the particular mesh among them.

Tomkins devotes much of his attention to the interaction between emotions and cognitions, so let me describe this in more detail. Emotions reflect motivational states, since they amplify biological needs and drives. Tomkins hypothesizes that people are genetically programmed with a limited number of basic emotions (and therefore a limited number of basic motives). This is an intriguing idea that goes against the typical cognitive assumption that particular beliefs dictate particular emotions (Schacter & Singer, 1962). One might therefore assume that basic emotions do not exist, since people experience all those feelings and only those feelings recognized in their particular culture.

However, researchers give us good reason to question this assumption concerning the cultural relativism of emotions. Individuals in a variety of societies seem to experience the same types of emotions, notably enjoyment, interest, fear, surprise, distress, disgust, anger, shame, and contempt (for example, Darwin, 1872; Ekman, 1971; Izard, 1977). Even more intriguingly, studies that focus on facial expression indicate that people *show* emotions in the same way and *recognize* emotions in others without difficulty, even if the people are from places as different as the United States and New Guinea (see Figure 15-1).

Findings like this led Tomkins to emphasize the role of the face in communicating our emotions (and hence our motivations) to others. Indeed, he seems to favor an evolutionary argument that natural selection produced our face as it is because of the considerable advantage that accrues to people who understand each other's internal states.

However, understanding is phrased in cognitive language, and so Tomkins additionally concerns himself with how people interpret the information they receive. Interpretation is imperative. Although the world can be confusing, a person must react to it in an integrated fashion. Somehow, disparate items of information must be combined and assimilated into someone's overall

Figure 15-1

Facial Expression of Emotion

In literate cultures, the expressions in these photos have been judged to be sadness (A), anger (B), and surprise (C). When 189 New Guinea adults were shown these photos and asked to choose the one in which "his child died and he felt sad," 79 percent chose photo A, convincing evidence that the facial expression of emotion is the same in literate and preliterate cultures.

 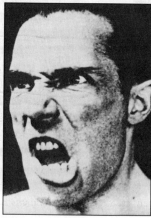 

A   B   C

SOURCE: Ekman, P. (Ed.). (1982). *Emotion in the human face,* (2nd ed.). New York: Cambridge University Press.

plan of action in a specific setting. We all want to increase our positive emotions and decrease our negative ones, but this goal is impossible without sophisticated cognitive styles and strategies for processing information.

Chief among these cognitive strategies are general plans called **scripts.** Scripts tell a person how to act in a given situation to achieve a given aim. Most of us have scripts for how to use a VISA card, make a collect call, board an airplane, apply for a job, park a car, start a fight, end a fight, write a letter, and make love out of nothing at all. Scripts are analogous to computer programs (see, Schank & Abelson, 1977) or the event schemata that I described in Chapter 11. Remember, though, that scripts are called upon for a purpose. Accordingly, positive or negative emotions are an inherent aspect of them.

Remember the *concept* notion introduced by Harvey, Hunt, and Schroder (1961)? Tomkins would agree that someone's script can be described as abstract or concrete, but he goes further in saying that concepts are used for a reason: to moderate our emotions. Harvey, Hunt, and Schroder, along with other cognitive theorists, explain *how* we think but not really *why*. A transactional perspective explains both.

The relationship between emotions and cognitions goes both ways. I've described how a particular emotion can lead a person to call up a particular

Scripts tell us how to act in a given situation (like a business lunch) to achieve a given aim.

script. He hopes that the script is adequate to the need (as in the television commercial where the stomach mutters "thank you . . . thank you . . . thank you . . ." following a fast-food fix). But cognitions can also affect emotions. Consider the different scripts written for us by our family or by society. We are socialized to emphasize either positive or negative emotions. We are taught to express or inhibit certain emotions in particular circumstances. We are encouraged to create and follow different scripts.

A transactional view like that of Tomkins shows what can be gained by taking issue with the dichotomy between "thoughts versus feelings." What might be discovered if personality psychology tried to integrate the opposite ends of *all* traditional dichotomies?

Robert Hogan: Socioanalytic Theory

A third theory that hints at a transactional future is the **socioanalytic theory** of psychologist Robert Hogan (1982). He draws upon several disparate traditions to give a unified view of human nature: psychoanalytic theory, evolutionary biology, and symbolic interactionism. Note that he is weaving together ideas from all three major personality paradigms.

According to Hogan, there are two striking aspects of human evolution. First, we have always lived in groups, even before we were people. Second, these groups have always been organized in terms of a status hierarchy. But personality theories to date have not incorporated these conclusions, now generally accepted among anthropologists and evolutionary theorists. The major implication here is that drives for **status** and **popularity** are important human motives, since they make life in a stratified group possible. Status causes us to climb the ladder as high as we can, even at the expense of others. Popularity protects us from the wrath of those we step on during the climb. Hogan accords these drives preeminence in human motivation and proposes that they have a biological basis.

Contrast this view with those of the psychoanalytic theorists that I discussed in Chapter 5. Freud assumes that people are inherently selfish. Whatever tendencies we have to cultivate approval and avoid criticism develop in the course of socialization, imposed from without by the process of defensive identification. NeoFreudians assume that people are social, but they make this move by disavowing any strong role of biology. Hogan has it both ways, which is why I consider his theory transactional. People are genetically predisposed to be social. They are impelled to interact with each other and to achieve and maintain a status hierarchy.

Hogan borrows the notion of the unconscious from the psychoanalytic paradigm, chiding trait and cognitive theorists for neglecting this insight into human behavior. People are self-deceived, Hogan proposes, and they are in particular self-deceived about their motives. But unlike Freud, he goes on to say that people blind themselves not to their sexual motives but to their social ones. A status hierarchy requires that we behave in a ritualized way. In other words, we must play out roles, as friends and lovers, leaders and followers, parents and children, students and teachers. The more central we find a role, the less willing we become to acknowledge its ritualized nature: "Oh no, this is the way I *really* am."

According to Hogan, "sincerity" must accompany our role-playing. Other people resent being used as mere props in our striving for status and popularity. The best way to be sincere is through a self-presentation where we deny that we strive for these goals: "I'd be your friend under any circumstances; it's just the craziest of coincidences that you have looks and a whole lot of money, that your parents own the company where I've applied for a job, and that you've got season tickets to the Bears." And the best way to deceive others is to deceive ourselves: "What a great guy he is!"

In this context, Hogan offers an interesting contrast between *cheaters* and *spoilsports.* A cheater is someone who fails to be what she claims to be: a good person, a college graduate, a size 7, or a close friend. A spoilsport is someone who points out the inconsistencies in how others play their roles. He tells us that what we said on Thursday is not how we acted on Friday, that we keep few of our promises, or that we wrap cheap presents in boxes from expensive stores. Here's an intriguing fact: we like cheaters much better than we like spoilsports! With a cheater, the social game is still possible. With a spoilsport, it all comes to a screeching halt.

Like the symbolic interactionists, Hogan emphasizes the importance of self-presentation and the social construction of meaning. What we do reflects strategic consideration of who is to see it. Unlike these sociologists, though, Hogan believes there is a real self behind the roles. Our behavior originates not in response to environmental demands but instead from our biologically based social motives. So, people are consistent (in their motives) as well as inconsistent (in their performance to different audiences). They are social beings as well as biological creatures. The capacity of socioanalytic theory to integrate such traditional dichotomies stamps it as a transactional perspective on personality.

A CONCLUSION AND FAREWELL

How does the transactional paradigm I envision differ from the three examples that I just described? On the one hand, the difference is one of degree. Murphy, Tomkins, and Hogan show how polarized concepts can be productively combined. Each theorist does this for a single or a few sets of notions. A fully transactional approach to personality will do this for all notions. On the other hand, if a personality psychologist were to achieve an across-the-board transactional theory, the difference would be one of kind as well. Workers within the individual paradigms are creeping toward a transactional perspective; and Murphy, Tomkins, and Hogan have taken the first toddling steps. No particular theorist has yet followed through to the inevitable conclusion that his or her own approach to personality *cannot* serve as the foundation of the new paradigm.

A transactional paradigm cannot emphasize one class of variables over another. This is still happening within the psychoanalytic, trait, and cognitive paradigms, which is why they are still separate from each other. Even though the neoFreudians infuse needs and drives with a social flavor, they still emphasize these internal characteristics. Even though trait theorists acknowledge the importance of the situation, they still locate individual differences "within" the person. And even though cognitive theorists endorse contextualism, they still place cognitions in the foreground against the backdrop of the world.

To a lesser degree, the emphasis of one class of variables over another still happens within the theories of Murphy, Tomkins, and Hogan. Here the emphasis takes the form of casting some ideas in transactional terms while leaving others in their traditional polarized state.

I wish I could be more specific about how a fully transactional perspective will look, but if I knew the future, it wouldn't be the future. All I know is that personality psychologists are trying to build a starship with hammers and saws. Are we fools? I think not. Look at the science that our intellectual ancestors built with their bare hands.

SUMMARY

I speculated in this chapter about the future of personality psychology, concluding that we may see a single paradigm come to dominate the field. I called this as-yet-nonexistent paradigm a transactional approach, since it will integrate the dichotomies that polarize the current personality paradigms. I described ecology, family therapy, and Eastern philosophy as fields with transactional concepts. I also sketched three theories of personality which seem to me ahead of their time in their combination of concepts from different paradigms: Gardner Murphy's **biosocial theory,** Silvan Tomkins's **cognitive-affective theory,** and Robert Hogan's **socioanalytic theory.** I concluded on an optimistic note and a challenge: the future awaits us. It promises to be even more interesting than the past.

SOURCE: *Never Eat Anything Bigger Than Your Head & Other Drawings,* published by Workman Publishing Company. Copyright © 1976 by B. Kliban. Used with permission.

GLOSSARY

Boldface numbers represent the chapter(s) where the term is discussed.

A

abstractness (versus concreteness) Flexibility of a person's concepts; degree to which they are not stimulus-bound. **11**

accessibility Degree that two cognitive regions influence each other. **11**

achievement motivation Need or drive to excel in situations that are characterized by a standard of excellence. **3, 9**

act-frequency approach Procedure developed by Buss and Craik for deciding which behaviors reflect which dispositions. **9**

action research Research aimed at solving social problems. **3**

actualization Individual's drive to realize all of one's potential. **11**

adoption study Research technique for disentangling nature and nurture by comparing the characteristics of adopted children with the characteristics of their biological and foster parents. **8**

affective-evaluative consistency Congruence between one's liking for objects and one's evaluation of them. **12**

aggregation Measurement strategy in which multiple assessments are made and then combined. **9**

ambivalence Assignment of both positive and negative attributes to the same object. **12**

androgyny Combination of stereotypically masculine and feminine characteristics in the same person. **9**

anthropomorphic model Metaphor for human nature that stresses people's uniquely human characteristics. **2**

approach-avoidance conflict Situation possessing both desirable and undesirable aspects, which simultaneously draws and repels the individual. **14**

archetype Structures that are part of Jung's collective unconscious; inherited tendencies to pattern experience. **5**

anima A particular archetype: the female side of a male.

animus A particular archetype: the male side of a female.

mandala Magic circle; symbol of unity and balance among the components of personality.

self A particular archetype: the part of personality that strives for balance and unity.

shadow A particular archetype: the inferior and evil part of personality.

aschematic Not having a particular schema. **12**

attitudes Basic orientations to our experience. **5**

extraversion Outward attitude.

introversion Inward attitude.

attribute Any property of an object. **12**

attribution theory Social psychology approach concerned with how people explain their own behavior and that of others. **11**

Attributional Style Questionnaire Measure of a person's habitual way of explaining good and bad events. **11**

authoritarianism Rigid conventionality, submission to authority, and degradation of minorities. **3, 9**

automatic thoughts Unbidden and habitual thoughts, usually self-critical, which Beck believes can cause depression. **13**

awareness Symbolized experience. **11**

B

basic anxiety Feelings of isolation and loneliness caused by disturbed relationships between people. **5**

behavior modification Psychotherapy based on principles of learning. **3, 14**

aversion therapy Classical conditioning technique used to induce avoidance; client confronts object to be avoided along with some aversive experience like pain or nausea.

biofeedback Operant conditioning technique in which people learn to modify bodily responses by attending to information about these responses, usually provided by a machine.

flooding Classical conditioning technique used to treat fears and phobias; client is exposed to feared object until fear extinguishes.

parent training Therapy approach in which parents are instructed in behavior modification techniques which they then use with their children.

selective punishment Operant conditioning technique for decreasing frequency of some behavior by punishing it.

selective reward Operant conditioning technique for increasing frequency of some behavior by reinforcing it.

sensate focus Classical conditioning technique used to treat sexual dysfunctions; client and partner kiss and caress to feel pleasure instead of to prepare for intercourse.

social skills training Therapy approach in which client is taught how to gain rewards from others.

systematic desensitization Classical conditioning technique used to treat fears and phobias; client relaxes while imagining feared object.

time out Operant conditioning technique for decreasing frequency of some behavior by removing the individual from an ongoing situation for a period of time whenever he or she performs the behavior.

token economy Operant therapy on a large scale; clients earn tokens for positive behaviors and lose them for negative behaviors; tokens in turn are exchanged for desired commodities.

behavior potential Likelihood that a particular behavior will occur in a particular situation. **14**

behaviorism General psychology approach that concerns itself with the overt actions of people and animals, usually in terms of how these behaviors are learned in particular settings. **3, 14**

biosocial theory Murphy's personality theory, which stresses both the biological and social aspects of people. **15**

Blacky Test Projective test for assessing psychosexual conflicts. **6**

body build basic physique category. **8**
asthenic Frail, linear body build.
athletic Muscular body build.
dysplastic Rare and "ugly" body build; mixture of several basic types.
pyknic Plump body build.

C

canalization Process where needs become more easily met by specific satisfiers than by others of the same class. **15**

case history Research strategy where one individual (or group) is studied in great detail. **4**

castration anxiety Fear by young boys that their father will castrate them. **5**

category mistake A metaphor taken concretely. **12**

catharsis Outpouring of emotion following an expression of unconscious conflict. **5**

centrality Frequency that an attribute is applied to objects. **12**

character armor Notion that a person's psychological conflicts are expressed in posture. **7**

character type Basic category of people, usually associated with fixation at a particular stage of psychosexual development. **5**
anal character type Person preoccupied with elimination.
anal compulsive stingy, fastidious, stubborn person.
anal expulsive Sloppy, disorganized person.
biophilous character type Person attracted to life and other people.
exploitative character type Person who takes what is wanted from others by force or guile.
hoarding character type Stingy and withdrawn person.
marketing character type Person keenly interested in maintaining appearances and self-presentation.
necrophilous character type Person attracted to death and destruction.
oral character type Person concerned with activities of the mouth.
oral eroticism Licking and sucking.
oral sadism Biting and chewing.
phallic character type Person preoccupied with self.
receptive character type Dependent and passive person.

classical conditioning Form of learning where responses come to be associated with particular stimuli through repeated associations of unconditioned stimuli with conditioned stimuli (see terms below); Pavlovian conditioning. **14**

conditioned response Behavior elicited by *conditioned stimulus.*

conditioned stimulus Originally neutral stimulus paired with *unconditioned stimulus,* which comes to itself elicit behavior.

unconditioned response Behavior elicited by *unconditioned stimulus.*

unconditioned stimulus Stimulus that can elicit particular behavior as a reflex, without learning.

client-centered therapy Psychotherapy approach developed by Carl Rogers, based on assumption that the client best knows how to solve his or her own problems, so long as a supportive environment is provided. **13**

clinical proposition Psychoanalytic claim that can be tested by research (see *metapsychological proposition*). **6**

clustering Simultaneous recall of items. **12**

cognitive complexity Number of perspectives, constructs, attributes, and so on that someone brings to bear on topics (see *dimensionality*). **11**

cognitive content Particular thoughts and beliefs. **11**

cognitive disorder Psychopathology caused and/or characterized chiefly by particular ways of thinking. **13**

cognitive domain Set of objects and attributes usually considered together. **12**

cognitive dynamics Processes by which thoughts originate and/or change. **11**

cognitive map Mental representation of a physical place. **13**

cognitive paradigm General personality approach that stresses a person's thoughts. **4**

cognitive social learning theory Bandura and Mischel's account of personality that draws on both cognitive theories and learning theories. **11**

cognitive style (structure) Interrelationships among thoughts and beliefs. **11, 12**

cognitive psychotherapy Psychotherapy approach that targets a client's thoughts for change. **13**

cognitive therapy Beck's therapy for depression. **13**

cognitive-affective theory Tomkin's personality theory stressing emotions and cognitions. **15**

cognitive-behavioral therapy Psychotherapy approach that blends techniques of cognitive therapy and behavior modification. **13**

collaborative empiricism Beck's notion that therapists and clients should work together to test the client's assumptions against the facts. **13**

collective unconscious Memories and tendencies inherited from our ancestors (see *archetypes*). **5**

common trait Trait used to describe all people (see *personal trait*). **8**

complex Cluster of unconscious ideas that function autonomously of the rest of our personality. **5**

complexity Number of attributes assigned to an object. **12**

compulsion to repeat Freud's notion that people are driven to recreate painful experiences. **5**

computational paradox The more psychologists study the mind as if it were a computer, the more it becomes clear it is not. **11**

concept Program or plan for reacting to information. **11**

conceptual systems theory Harvey, Hunt, and Schroder's approach to personality that stresses the characteristic abstractness or concreteness of a person's thoughts. **11**

conditional love Acceptance and concern for people only when they perform particular behaviors (see *unconditional positive regard*). **11**

confluence model Theory of how the mutual influence among family members can affect the intellectual development of each. **6**

confound Third variable actually responsible for an apparent association between two other variables. **4**

confusion matrix Tendency of people to mix up adjacent states of the nation, like Vermont and New Hampshire. **13**

conscious Thoughts and feelings in awareness (see also *preconscious; unconscious*). **5**

construct system An individual's personal constructs considered together. **11**

constructive alternativism Kelly's assumption that all present interpretations of the universe are subject to revision or replacement. **11**

contextualism Root metaphor for explanation: one that points to interdependence of phenomenon and context. **4**

contraprepared learning Particularly difficult learning selected against by evolution (see also *prepared learning*). **14**

contrast effect   Tendency of fraternal twins to show opposite characteristics. **8**

convenience sample   Group of people chosen for opinion poll because they are at hand; not a random sample. **10**

conversion disorder   New term for *hysteria*. **7**

cookbook approach   Strategy of psychodiagnosis in which one predicts that a person will behave like those with similar test scores have behaved in the past. **10**

core conflictual relationship theme method (CCRT)   Luborsky's research method for studying transference in psychotherapy. **6**

correlation coefficient   Measure of linear association between two variables. **2, 3**

   independent (zero)   No association between two variables.

   negative   Relation between two variables in which high values of one variable go together with low values of the other.

   positive   Relation between two variables in which high values of one variable go together with high values of the other variable.

correlational study   Research strategy that describes how variables covary with each other. **4**

crowding   The experience of density. **11**

D

death instinct   Freud's idea that people are driven toward destruction and death (see also *life instinct*). **5**

defense mechanism   Technique of the ego that protects the conscious mind from unconscious thoughts and impulses. **5**

defensive identification   Fear-driven process by which children come to identify with same-sex parent. **5**

deficiency needs   Biological needs that require "filling up" (see also *metaneeds*). **8**

delay of gratification   Ability to postpone reward. **12**

demand characteristic   Subtle clue in a psychology experiment that conveys to the research subject the behavior the experimenter wants to observe. **4**

density   Number of people in a fixed area. **11**

depth interview   Marketing research technique which determines people's motives for buying products. **7**

diagnostic council   Henry Murray's approach to making judgments about personality; experts from different fields test an individual and pool their results and conclusions in a group meeting. **8**

differentiation   Division of life space into numerous regions. **11**

diffusion of responsibility   Social psychology notion that people in a group feel less responsibility than people alone. **7**

dimensionality   Complexity with which people assign attributes to objects (see also *cognitive complexity*). **12**

dopamine hypothesis   Theory that schizophrenia is caused by too much of the neurotransmitter dopamine. **12**

dreamwork   Techniques used in dreams to disguise their meaning. **5**

   condensation   Combination of dream elements.

   displacement   Transfer of emotional significance from the actual source to an unrelated one.

   symbolism   Representation of thoughts in similes, metaphors, and/or images.

drive   Biologically based motive. **6, 14**

dynamism   Transformation of energy. **5**

E

econetics   Cattell's proposed study of environments. **8**

effectance motivation   Drive to be competent. **11**

efficacy   Experience of effective interaction with the environment. **11**

efficacy expectancy   Belief that a particular behavior can be performed (see also *outcome expectancy*). **13**

ego   Part of personality that mediates conflicts between id and superego. **5**

ego psychology   Form of psychoanalytic theory that stresses the role of the ego in adaptation. **5**

ego-control   Ability to control impulses. **9**

ego-resiliency   Flexibility in response to environmental demands. **9**

embedding   Advertising technique in which messages are hidden in ads. **7**

emergency response   Mustering of the body's resources in the face of threat. **13**

emergent property   Characteristic of a complex system not present in or derived from any of its parts. **4**

enactive learning   Learning by active doing. **13**

enlightenment effect Invalidation of a scientific finding as people learn of the finding and act contrary to it. **7**

epiphenomenon Secondary phenomenon accompanying and caused by some primary phenomenon. **12**

errors in logic Beck's term for ways of thinking that cause depression. **13**

arbitrary inference Drawing a conclusion in the absence of evidence.

catastrophizing Assuming bad events are worse than they actually are.

magnification and minimization Exaggerating bad events and dismissing good events.

personalization Taking bad events personally.

selective abstraction Pulling a detail from its appropriate context.

eugenics "Science" concerned with improvement of the hereditary qualities of the human species. **3**

evaluation apprehension Anxiety experienced by subject in psychology experiment due to expectation that his or her competence is being judged. **4**

evaluative attribute Attribute with desirable and/or undesirable characteristics as categories. **12**

evaluative centrality Preponderance of evaluative attributes in a cognitive domain. **12**

expectancy Belief that behavior will lead to a particular outcome. **14**

experience Everything that happens to a person at any given moment. **11**

experiment Research strategy that manipulates situational factors and assesses the effects. **4**

experimental artifacts Confounds in laboratory experiments. **4**

experimenter bias Unintentional influence of experimenter's wishes and expectations on the results of the experiment. **4**

explanatory style Habitual manner of explaining good and bad events. **11**

extinction In classical conditioning, not pairing unconditioned stimulus and conditioned stimulus; in operant conditioning, not following behavior with reward or punishment. **14**

F

factor Abstract dimension underlying observed correlations. **2**

factor analysis Statistical technique for discerning factors among set of correlations. **2, 3, 8**

factor structure Set of factors underlying set of correlations. **8**

family resemblance Characteristics common to many (but not necessarily all) members of some group. **1**

family study Research technique for disentangling nature and nurture by comparing characteristics of family members who have different degrees of relatedness. **8**

field Self-regulating system where changes in one part affect all other parts (see also *machine*). **2**

field dependence/independence Personality dimension ranging from the use of external frames of reference to interpret incoming information (field dependence) to the use of internal frames of reference (field independence). **9**

field theory Theory that conceives phenomena as *fields*. **11**

fields of applied psychology 4

aesthetics and criticism Use of psychology to explain creation and appreciation of artistic and literary works.

clinical psychology Use of psychology to diagnose and treat the problems of troubled individuals.

community psychology Use of psychology to prevent difficulties by intervening at the community level.

consumer psychology Use of psychology to predict and influence the buying of products.

counselling psychology Use of psychology to help individuals use skills to solve particular problems.

educational psychology Use of psychology to assist teaching and learning.

engineering psychology Use of psychology to optimize work methods, equipment, and environments.

environmental psychology Use of psychology to explain the relationship between people and their physical environment.

health psychology Use of psychology to promote and maintain physical well-being.

industrial psychology Use of psychology in business and industry.

organizational psychology Use of psychology to increase effectiveness and satisfaction of members in a complex organization, usually workers in a work setting.

psychohistory Use of psychology, usually psychoanalytic theory, to explain historical figures and events.

figure and ground In perception: object (figure) and backdrop (ground) against which it is perceived. **3**

fixation Tying up of libidinal energy at a particular stage of psychosexual development, due to frustration or indulgence. **5**

fixed-role therapy Psychotherapy approach developed by George Kelly, where client tries out different roles and their associated personal constructs. **13**

focus of convenience Topics to which a personal construct best applies (see also *range of convenience*). **11**

formism Root metaphor for explanation: one that assigns phenomena to categories. **4**

free association Technique for investigating the unconscious; individual is encouraged to associate one idea with another without censorship. **5**

frustration-aggression hypothesis Theory that frustration is a necessary and sufficient condition for aggression. **14**

functional autonomy of motives Allport's idea that behavior undertaken to satisfy one motive may be continued in the service of another motive. **8**

functional explanation Explanation in terms of consequences. **8**

functionalism General approach within psychology that emphasizes the consequences of mind in use (see also *pragmatism*). **3**

functions Basic psychological processes proposed by Jung. **5**

feeling Function characterized by emotions.

intuiting Function characterized by intuitions.

sensing Function characterized by sensations.

thinking Function characterized by thoughts.

fundamental attribution error Tendency to explain behavior in terms of characteristics of the person and not characteristics of the situation. **11**

fundamental postulate Kelly's basic assumption about personality: "a person's processes are psychologically channelized by the ways in which he anticipates events." **11**

G

g Factor underlying correlations among different measures of ability; interpreted by some as general intelligence. **3**

generality Degree to which psychological findings and/or theories apply broadly. **4**

generalized expectancies For Rotter, beliefs that transcend particular settings. **14**

germ model Theory that diseases are caused by germs. **3**

gestalt Pattern; configuration. **3, 11**

gestalt psychology General approach within psychology that concerns itself with the organization and homeostasis of psychological systems. **3**

good gestalt Psychologically fundamental organization. **3, 11**

Great Chain of Being Pervasive belief that all entities can be placed in an invariant order. **10**

H

habit Link between stimulus and response established by learning. **14**

hardiness Personality characteristic that renders person resistant to illness. **12**

helping alliance Relationship between therapist and client where both work to solve client's problems. **7**

helplessness depression Form of depressive disorder characterized by passivity and well-explained by the learned helplessness model. **13**

helplessness orientation Predisposition to respond to frustration and failure by giving up (see also *mastery orientation*). **12**

hierarchical organization Kelly's term for the manner in which construct systems are organized: *superordinate constructs* subsume subordinate constructs. **11**

hierarchy of needs Maslow's idea that needs can be arrayed from deficiency needs to growth needs; deficiency needs require satisfaction before growth needs can be satisfied. **8**

humanistic psychology General psychology approach that stresses human goodness, health, and growth. **8**

humour Bodily fluid, a preponderance of which is thought to produce a basic personality type. **8**

choleric type Excessively excitable person, presumably with too much yellow bile.

melancholic type Excessively sad person, presumably with too much black bile.

phlegmatic type Excessively calm person, presumably with too much phlegm.

sanguine type Excessively outgoing person, presumably with too much blood.

hypothetical construct Scientific term with no literal counterpart in reality. **12**

hysteria Psychopathology characterized by the failure of a body part or system, with no physical reason. **3**

I

id Freud's term for the instinctive, animalistic aspect of personality. **5**

ideal self Our view of the good and desirable characteristics for ourselves. **11**

idiographic-nomothetic debate Disagreement over the goals of personality psychology: to speak about the specific person (idiographic emphasis) or about people in general (nomothetic emphasis). **3, 8**

illusion of control Mistaken belief that one influences the occurrence of good and bad outcomes. **13**

illusory correlation Mistaken belief that variables correlate with each other. **9**

image comparability Use of the same attributes to describe a set of objects. **12**

implicit personality theory Beliefs about the covariation of traits. **11**

inferiority complex Person's sense that he or she is weak and inadequate in some respect. **5**

insight learning Learning characterized by sudden appreciation of relationships, solutions, or plans. **14**

instinct Inherited behavior. **6**

instrumental learning Change in behavior caused by response-contingent rewards and punishments; trial-and-error learning; operant conditioning. **14**

discrimination Nonperformance of behavior in situations different from where the behavior was originally learned.

generalization Performance of behavior in situations different from where the behavior was originally learned.

negative reinforcement Stimulus that increases frequency of a particular behavior when taken away immediately after the behavior.

positive reinforcement Stimulus that increases frequency of a particular behavior when presented immediately after the behavior.

punishment Stimulus that decreases frequency of a particular behavior when presented immediately after the behavior.

schedules of reinforcement Pattern by which reinforcement occurs: after every behavior, after every tenth behavior, and so on.

secondary reinforcement Stimuli that come to reinforce behavior following a pairing with reinforcing stimuli.

shaping through successive approximations Process for learning complex behavior; forms of the desired behavior are gradually reinforced as they come to resemble the target behavior.

intelligence quotient (IQ) Ratio of mental age to chronological age, multiplied by 100 (see *mental age*). **3**

interactionist approach Personality approach that stresses the importance of both individual differences and situational factors. **9**

interest inventory Questionnaire for assessing vocational interests. **10**

interpersonal trust Person's tendency to believe what others say about the way the world works. **14**

introspection Research technique of early psychologists; "looking in" and reporting on mental contents and processes. **3**

introversion-extraversion Basic orientation to experience, either inward (introversion) or outward (extraversion) (see *attitudes*). **8, 9**

J

just world Belief that people deserve the fortunes or misfortunes that befall them. **13**

L

L-data Cattell's term for information from life records. **8**

Law of Effect Thorndike's statement that reward strengthens behavior, while punishment weakens it. **14**

learned helplessness Maladaptive passivity following experiences with uncontrollability. **11**

libido Sexual energy. **5**

life changes Stressful events requiring people to make adjustments in their lives. **12**

life instinct Freud's idea that people are

driven toward self-preservation and sexual gratification (see also *death instinct*). **5**

life space According to Lewin, all the forces acting on a person at one time; also, a person's mental representation of the relationship between the self and world. **3, 11**

locus of control Personality dimension ranging from belief that rewards come from within a person (internal locus) to belief that rewards come from without (external locus). **11**

M

Machiavellianism Personality dimension; degree that one believes that ends justify means. **8**

machine Static system where changes in one part affect only adjacent parts (see also *field*). **2**

macho personality constellation Hypermasculinity. **6**

manipulation check Assessment in an experiment whether an independent variable was manipulated in the desired way. **12**

masculine protest Compensation for feelings of inferiority. **5**

mastery orientation Predisposition to respond to frustration and failure by renewed effort (see also *helplessness orientation*). **12**

mechanism Root metaphor for explanation; one that centers on causes and effects. **4**

medical model Theory that diseases are caused by physical problems: germs, injuries, or defects. **3**

mental age Performance on an intelligence test that corresponds to the average performance of individuals of a particular age (for example, a mental age of eight means that someone performs as well as the average eight-year-old). **3**

mental test Procedure for assessing an individual's mental abilities, characterized by brevity and emphasis on performance. **3**

mesmerism Old term for hypnotism, from Franz Anton Mesmer, who developed the technique. **3**

meta-analysis Statistical technique for summarizing the results of different studies in quantitative terms. **3**

metaneeds Maslow's terms for higher, nonbiological needs; growth needs (see also *deficiency needs*). **8**

metapsychological proposition psychoanalytic claim that cannot be tested by research (see also *clinical proposition*). **6**

microanalytic strategy Bandura's highly focused approach to research; examination of particular beliefs and behaviors in specific situations. **11**

misconceptions Raimy's term for mistaken beliefs that produce emotional distress. **13**

model Metaphor for understanding some phenomenon. **2**

model Person observed in modelling (see *modelling*). **11**

modelling Idea that we learn behavior by watching another person perform it; vicarious learning. **6, 14**

modified idiographic approach Bem and Allen's procedure of dividing subjects into (relatively) consistent versus (relatively) inconsistent groups with respect to a particular trait (see also *idiographic-nomothetic debate*). **9**

multiple abstract variance analysis (MAVA) Cattell's statistical technique for estimating relative contributions of nature and nurture to personality traits. **8**

multiple intelligences Gardner's idea that human intelligence is not singular but instead composed of several abilities and capacities. **10**

Myers-Briggs Type Indicator Questionnaire that describes people in terms of Jung's attitudes and functions. **6**

N

naive psychology Beliefs of everyday people about the causes of behavior. **11**

natural attitude Unquestioned assumptions about the way the world really is. **6**

natural history method Research approach where the lives of individuals are described in great detail over a significant period of time. **6**

necessary condition Characteristic that all members of some class possess (see also *sufficient condition*). **1**

need Impulse motivating behavior that is aimed at achieving some satisfaction. **8**

neoFreudians Psychoanalytic theorists who emphasize the importance of the environment and de-emphasize the importance of instincts; most notably: Karen Horney, Erich Fromm, and Harry Stack Sullivan. **5**

neurosis Psychopathology characterized by excessive guilt and anxiety. **5**

neurotic need Insatiable, unhealthy need that results in conflict. **5**

neuroticism One of Eysenck's basic dimensions of personality; strong emotionality. **8**

niche Ecology term describing the fit between a particular species and a particular environment. **15**

O

observational learning Notion that we learn behaviors by watching someone else perform them; vicarious learning (see *modelling*). **13, 14**

occult Supernatural phenomena. **15**

Oedipus complex Freud's idea that young children experience sexual desire for their opposite-sex parent and resentment against their same-sex parent. **5**

operant conditioning Trial-and-error learning (see *instrumental learning*). **3, 14**

operational definition Definition that specifies necessary and sufficient conditions for identifying (that is, measuring) a concept. **1**

ordinality Term for whether or not categories of an attribute fall along a continuum. **12**

ordinary language philosophy Branch of philosophy concerned with the meaning of concepts as used in everyday conversation. **1**

organ inferiority Idea that some organs of the body are weaker than others; these may be susceptible to disease or injury, but they may also lead to compensation and strengthening. **5**

organic trait Biologically based individual difference (see also *symbolic trait*). **15**

organicism Root metaphor for explanation; one that describes the unfolding of an inherent nature. **4**

organismic valuing process Rogers's notion that people intuitively know what is good for them. **11**

organization Interdependence, coordination, and integration of a *life space*. **11**

organizational behavior management Use of behavior modification techniques in work organizations. **14**

orgone Reich's term for the presumed physical counterpart of libido. **7**

Ortgeist Intellectual spirit of a particular place. **3**

ostensive definition Definition that points to a striking instance of a concept. **1**

outcome expectancy Belief that a particular behavior will lead to a particular outcome (see also *efficacy expectancy*). **13**

over-determined behavior Psychoanalytic assumption that even the most trivial behavior has numerous causes. **5**

P

paradigm Scientific worldview. **4**

parapraxes Slips of the tongue or pen; Freudian slips. **5**

parapsychology Science that studies telepathy, clairvoyance, and telekinesis. **15**

parsimony Brevity; simplicity. **4**

path analysis Statistical technique for tentatively identifying causal links among nonmanipulated variables. **12**

peak experience Feelings of intense enjoyment where sense of self is lost. **8**

penis envy Freud's term suggesting that girls and women wish to have male genitals. **5**

perceived reality Notion that people behave in response to the world as they perceive and interpret it. **11**

perceptual defense Tendency to recognize threatening stimuli less readily than neutral stimuli. **6**

perceptual vigilance Tendency to recognize threatening stimuli more readily than neutral stimuli. **6**

permeability Degree to which a personal construct can be applied to new events. **11**

person variable Mischel's phrase for an individual difference tied to a particular situation. **3, 11**

personal construct Category of experience. **11**

personal control Belief that one can influence the occurrence of events. **11**

personal trait Trait with which only some people can be described; individual disposition (see also *common trait*). **8**

  cardinal disposition Personal trait so pervasive as to characterize someone's entire personality.

  central disposition Personal trait that importantly characterizes someone's personality.

  secondary disposition Personal trait that

characterizes a circumscribed aspect of someone's personality.

personality Fuzzy term that encompasses psychological characteristics of the individual that are general, characteristic, enduring, integrated, and/or functional. **1**

personality disorder Inherently dysfunctional type of person. **10**

antisocial personality disorder Dysfunction characterized by an inability to get along with others or with society.

avoidant personality disorder Dysfunction characterized by sensitivity to rejection.

borderline personality disorder Dysfunction characterized by unpredictability, instability, and intensity.

compulsive personality disorder Dysfunction characterized by perfectionism.

dependent personality disorder Dysfunction characterized by subordination of needs and abdication of decision-making to others.

histrionic personality disorder Dysfunction characterized by melodramatic self-presentation.

narcissistic personality disorder Dysfunction characterized by overblown self-worth.

paranoid personality disorder Dysfunction characterized by suspicion and distrust.

passive-aggressive personality disorder Dysfunction characterized by indirect resistance to demands.

schizoid personality disorder Dysfunction characterized by emotional indifference and aloofness.

schizotypal personality disorder Dysfunction characterized by social anxiety coupled with eccentricities.

personality questionnaire Written measure completed by individual that provides a score with respect to one or more personality characteristics. **3**

personality test Any measure that scores individuals with respect to one or more personality characteristics. **3**

Personalized Self Instruction (PSI) Programmed instruction based on operant conditioning principles. **14**

personification Person's symbolization of self. **5**

personnel selection Procedure for choosing particular workers for particular jobs. **10**

personology Murray's term for personality psychology; the science of the individual person. **3, 8**

phenomenological reality Rogers's term for a person's subjective view of reality. **11**

phenotype-genotype problem Notion that overt behavior (phenotype) does not directly reflect underlying states or traits (genotype). **6**

phi phenomenon Illusion that an object is moving when in actuality its background is moving. **3**

phrenology Pseudo-science that identified mental and personality characteristics from bumps on the head. **8**

phrenophobia Fear of a mental breakdown. **13**

pleasure principle Freud's idea that the id is motivated solely to achieve pleasure and avoid pain (see also *reality principle*). **5**

positive denial Denial of negative occurrences and possibilities, leading to healthy consequences. **9**

postdiction Explanation after-the-fact. **5**

postFreudian Erikson's preferred term for himself (see also *neoFreudians*). **5**

power motivation Need or drive to have impact on others. **9**

pragmatism Philosophy that stresses practical consequences (see also *functionalism*). **3**

precision Number of categories of an attribute. **12**

preconscious Thoughts and feelings that are not part of our awareness but are potentially available to it (see also *conscious; unconscious*). **5**

prepared learning Particularly easy learning selected for by evolution (see also *contraprepared learning*). **14**

press Murray's term for environmental determinant of behavior. **8**

alpha press Objective characteristics of press.

beta press Perceived characteristics of press.

primary process Thinking dominated by wishes and impulses (see also *secondary process*). **5**

projection Attribution of one's own undesirable characteristics to others. **5**

projective test Personality test that presents individuals with ambiguous stimuli onto which they "project" their personality as they respond. **3**

proprium Word coined by Allport for the functions typically ascribed to the self. **8**

prototype Particularly good example of some concept or category; ideal category. **1, 11**

psychoanalysis Approach to general psychology, personality, abnormality, and psychotherapy associated with Freud and his followers. **5**

psychoanalytic paradigm Approach to personality that stresses transformations of a person's energy (see *psychoanalysis*). **4**

psychodiagnosis Procedure of describing a person's psychological problems. **10**

   behavioral assessment Psychodiagnosis emphasizing overt behavior.

   personological assessment Psychodiagnosis emphasizing rich description.

   psychometric assessment Psychodiagnosis emphasizing psychological test scores.

psychodynamic theory Theory that stresses mental or emotional motives and needs. **11**

psychohistory Use of psychology, usually psychoanalytic theory, to explain historical figures and events. **7**

psychological situation Rotter's term for the setting in which behavior occurs. **14**

psychological testing Use of tests to describe individual differences in performance, ability, personality, and so on. **3**

psychosexual development Freud's idea that children in the course of development pass through stages that are defined by the part of the body that provides sexual gratification (see order below). **5**

   oral stage Gratification centers on nursing and feeding.

   anal stage Gratification centers on retention and elimination of feces.

   phallic stage Gratification centers on manipulation of genitals.

   latency period Temporary cessation of sexual gratification.

   genital stage Gratification centers on intercourse with partner.

psychosocial development Erikson's idea that children in the course of development pass through stages defined by a particular social conflict to be resolved. **5**

psychosomatic disorder Physical problem with a psychological cause. **7**

psychosomatic medicine Branch of medicine concerned with psychosomatic disorders. **7**

psychoticism One of Eysenck's basic dimensions of personality: insensitivity, aloofness, hostility, aggressiveness. **8**

Q

Q-data Cattell's term for information from questionnaires. **8**

Q-Sort Procedure for describing someone's personality by sorting a set of trait labels into piles ranging from "unlike" the person to "like" the person. **9**

quasi-experiment Research strategy that uses correlational data to draw causal conclusions. **4**

R

range of convenience Topics to which a personal construct applies (see also *focus of convenience*). **4, 11**

rational-emotive therapy Psychotherapy approach developed by Albert Ellis, based on assumption that problems are caused by irrational thinking. **13**

reaction formation Replacement of an impulse or emotion with its opposite. **5**

reaction time Speed of response to a stimulus. **12**

readymade Art technique pioneered by the Dadaists; the exhibition of everyday objects as works of art. **7**

reality principle Freud's idea that the ego takes into account the real world: constraints of time and space (see also *pleasure principle*). **5**

reattribution therapy Psychotherapy technique in which people are encouraged to explain events or behaviors in a way that will minimize distress. **13**

reciprocal determinism Bandura's notion that thoughts, behaviors, and situations mutually affect each other. **11**

reductionism Explanation of the complex in terms of the simple. **2**

regression Retreat to an earlier or more primitive way of acting in the face of anxiety. **5**

regression in the service of the ego Ability of creative individuals to gain access to primary process thinking for insights and inspirations. **7**

reinforcement value Degree to which a goal is reinforcing. **14**

reliability Consistency with which a psychological measure provides the same result. **2**

internal consistency   Agreement of different items on a test or questionnaire.

test-retest reliability   Agreement across time.

replication   Repetition of a scientific investigation. **4**

conceptual replication   Investigation repeated with different procedures.

exact replication   Investigation repeated with identical procedures.

repression   Removal of threatening material from consciousness; motivated forgetting. **5**

repression-sensitization   Personality dimension ranging from habitual ignoring of threatening stimuli (*repression*) to habitual attention (*sensitization*). **8, 9**

resistance   Unwillingness of psychotherapy client to comply with therapy. **7**

response set   Characteristic way of completing personality questionnaires, regardless of the content of the questions. **9**

rigidity   (versus fluidity)   Degree to which a region of the life space is unresponsive (versus responsive) to other regions. **11**

ritualism   Overly rigid and subverted ritualization (see *ritualization*). **5**

ritualization   Erikson's concept of socially provided aid for resolving psychosocial conflicts. **5**

role   Part that society assigns to a person. **2**

role appropriateness   Correct role for an individual granted the setting.

role propriety   Skill with which an individual plays a role.

Role Constructs Repertory Test (REP Test)   Procedure for assessing an individual's personal constructs: person is presented with triads of objects and asked to specify how two of them are alike and different from the third. **11**

S

satisfaction   Sullivan's term for a biological drive. **5**

schema   Organized knowledge about some domain. **11**

event schema   Schema about standard sequence of events for social occasions.

gender schema   Schema about appropriate characteristics and behaviors of males and females.

person schema   Schema about personality traits (see *implicit personality theory*).

role schema   Schema about broad social categories.

self-schema   Schema about one's own characteristics and behavior.

schismatic family   Family where parents are caught up in personal problems and use children as pawns. **15**

script   General plan for how to act in a given situation to achieve a given aim. **15**

second-order factor   Factor that emerges from a factor analysis of correlations among factors. **8**

secondary process   Thinking dominated by logic and order (see also *primary process*). **5**

security   Sullivan's term for a social need. **5**

see-through illusion   According to Wilson Key, advertising technique in which pictures are placed on the back of a page to show through and alter the meaning of pictures on the front of the page. **7**

segmentation of the market   Marketing term: distinctions among consumers in terms of needs and motives for buying products. **10**

self   Hypothetical construct that refers to the entity behind personal identity, agency, goals, purpose, and so on. **2, 11**

self-actualization   (see *actualization*). **3, 8, 11**

self-deception   Motivated lying to oneself. **6**

self-efficacy   Belief that one can perform a particular behavior. **11**

self-esteem   Liking and valuing of oneself. **9**

self-fulfilling prophecy   A belief that initiates a process that will make the belief come true. **11**

self-handicapping   Process of intentionally interfering with one's own best performance. **12**

self-monitoring   Personality dimension: degree to which a person (a) pays attention to how particular situations respond to particular behaviors and (b) modifies his or her actions accordingly. **9**

self-regulation   Modification of one's own behavior through deliberate manipulation of rewards and punishments. **11**

self-theory   Rogers's personality theory, which stresses how people think about themselves, as they are and as they wish to be. **11**

sensation-seeking   Personality dimension: degree to which a person seeks out (or avoids) novel and/or exciting stimuli. **9**

sensory deprivation Situation characterized by marked reduction of all stimulation. **9**

serial invalidation hypothesis Bannister's theory that schizophrenia results from repeated contradiction of personal contructs. **13**

Sixteen Personality Factor Test (16PF) Cattell's personality questionnaire for measuring his sixteen source traits. **8**

social cognitive theory Bandura's term for his version of cognitive social learning theory. **11**

social desirability Tendency to respond to questionnaires in a socially acceptable way. **9**

social interest Adler's notion that people are motivated to be of service to others. **5**

social learning theory (1) Rotter's learning theory that stresses the importance of expectancy; (2) Bandura's former term for his learning theory that stresses the importance of modelling (see *social cognitive theory*). **14**

socioanalytic theory Hogan's personality theory that stresses evolution, symbolic interactionism, and psychoanalysis. **15**

sociobiology Field of biology that interprets social behavior in evolutionary terms. **2**

somatotype Sheldon's description of physique in terms of three dimensions. **8**

    ectomorphy Degree to which physique is slender and angular.

    endomorphy Degree to which physique is round.

    mesomorphy Degree to which physique is muscular.

source trait Cattell's term for factors underlying observed traits (see also *surface trait*). **8**

special person misconception Raimy's idea that some people suffer from the mistaken belief that they share nothing in common with others. **13**

specification equation Cattell's formula predicting how a person will behave. **8**

spontaneous remission Cure or recovery without treatment. **7**

statistical significance Judgment that a research finding did not arise by chance. **2**

status Social rank. **15**

stimulus error Confusing sensation with the responsible stimulus. **3**

stimulus overload State where the individual receives too much stimulation to respond effectively. **13**

striving for superiority Adler's idea that people are driven to overcome inferiority. **3**

Strong Vocational Interest Blank (SVIB) Widely used questionnaire for determining vocational preferences. **10**

structural theory of the mind Freud's theory that the mind is divided into the id, ego, and superego. **5**

structuralism General approach within psychology concerned with the elements of consciousness. **3**

sublimation Channeling of undesirable impulses into valued activities. **5**

subliminal stimulation Stimulation below a person's awareness that nevertheless affects behavior. **6**

sufficient condition Characteristic that only members of some class possess (see also *necessary condition*). **1**

superego Freud's term for the conscience. **5**

superordinate construct Personal construct that subsumes other personal constructs. **11**

surface trait Cattell's term for observed individual traits (see also *source trait*). **8**

symbolic interactionism Sociology approach that looks at how symbols are involved in social interaction. **5**

symbolic trait Socially based individual difference (see also *organic trait*). **15**

symptom-context method Luborsky's research approach for studying psychoanalytic phenomena (symptoms) as they naturally occur (in context) during psychotherapy sessions. **6**

systematic desensitization Behavior modification technique based on classical conditioning that is used to treat fears and phobias; client relaxes while imagining feared object. **13, 14**

T

T-data Cattell's term for information from objective tests. **8**

tao "The way of all life"; the notion that life is unified and whole regardless of the interpretations that people may place on it. **15**

teleology Explanation in terms of goals or purposes. **5**

temperament Biologically based style of behaving. **8**

tendentious humor Humor with a purpose (or tendency); sexual and/or aggressive humor. **5**

thema Murray's term for the combination of a *need* and a *press*. **8**

Thematic Apperception Test (TAT) Projective test for assessing needs. **8**

"This I Believe" Test (TIB) Test for assessing conceptual systems. **11**

time-limited psychoanalysis Psychoanalytic therapy conducted within a set period of time. **7**

topographical theory of the mind Freud's theory dividing the mind into conscious, unconscious, and preconscious. **5**

trait Stable and pervasive individual difference. **1, 2, 8**

  common trait Trait with which all people can be described.

  personal trait Trait with which only some people can be described.

trait anxiety Personality dimension; degree of chronic anxiety. **9**

trait paradigm General approach to personality that stresses individual differences. **4**

transactional theory Approach to personality that stresses mutual influence among factors. **15**

transference Tendency of psychotherapy client to transfer emotions from past relationships to the present relationship with therapist. **5**

triadic design Experimental design used in learned helplessness research to separate the effects of uncontrollability and trauma (see *yoking*). **12**

twin method Research technique for disentangling nature and nurture by comparing the resemblances of identical twins with those of fraternal twins. **8**

two disciplines of scientific psychology Lee Cronbach's distinction between correlational research traditions and experimental research traditions. **14**

type Basic category of personality (see *typology*). **2**

Type A coronary-prone behavior pattern Behavioral style linked to coronary disease, characterized by incessant striving, time urgency, and hostility. **7, 9**

typology Set of categories for describing basic personality types. **8**

U

unconditional positive regard Acceptance and concern for people regardless of what they do (see also *conditional love*). **11**

unconscious Thoughts and feelings unavailable to awareness because of their threatening nature (see also *conscious; preconscious*). **5**

V

valence Degree of attractiveness. **11, 12**

validity Degree to which a psychological test or questionnaire accomplishes its intended purpose; whether it measures what it claims to measure. **2**

  construct validity Degree to which a test relates to other tests of theoretically related characteristics.

  content validity Degree to which a test samples what it tries to measure.

  convergent and discriminant validity Degree to which a test correlates with other tests of the same characteristic (convergent validity) and not with other tests of different characteristic (discriminant validity).

  criterion validity Degree to which a test predicts some index of what it tries to measure.

  face validity Degree to which a test appears valid on the face of it.

  known-group validity Degree to which a test distinguishes between groups of individuals known to differ on the characteristic it tries to measure.

vicarious learning Learning through observation, without performance (see *modelling*). **14**

voir dire Procedure by which lawyers evaluate the suitability of prospective jurors. **10**

Y

yoking Procedure in learned helplessness experiments: two subjects are exposed to the identical events, except that one has control over them while the other does not (see *triadic design*). **12**

Z

Zeitgeist Intellectual spirit of a particular historical era. **3**

REFERENCES

Abelson, R. P. (1963). Computer simulation of "hot" cognition. In S. S. Tomkins & S. Messick (Eds.), *Computer simulation of personality.* New York: Wiley.

Abraham, K. (1927). *Selected papers.* London: Hogarth.

Abrahamsen, D. (1978). *Nixon vs. Nixon: An emotional tragedy.* New York: New American Library.

Abramson, L. Y., Seligman, M. E. P., & Teasdale, J. D. (1978). Learned helplessness in humans: Critique and reformulation. *Journal of Abormal Psychology, 87,* 49–74.

Adams-Webber, J. R. (1979). *Personal construct theory: Concepts and applications.* Chichester: Wiley.

Adams-Webber, J. R. (1981). Fixed role therapy. In R. J. Corsini (Ed.), *Handbook of innovative psychotherapies.* New York: Wiley.

Adelson, J., & Redmond, J. (1958). Personality differences in the capacity for verbal recall. *Journal of Abnormal and Social Psychology, 57,* 244–248.

Ades, D. (1978). *Dada and surrealism.* Woodbury, NY: Barron's.

Adler, A. (1907). Organic inferiority and its compensation. In H. L. Ansbacher & R. R. Ansbacher (Eds.), *The individual psychology of Alfred Adler.* New York: Harper, 1964.

Adler, A. (1910). Inferiority feeling and defiance and obedience. In H. L. Ansbacher & R. R. Ansbacher (Eds.), *The individual psychology of Alfred Adler.* New York: Harper, 1964.

Adler, A. (1927). *The theory and practice of individual psychology.* New York: Harcourt, Brace & World.

Adler, A. (1931). *What life should mean to you.* Boston: Little, Brown.

Adorno, T. W., Frenkel-Brunswik, E., Levinson, D., & Sanford, N. (1950). *The authoritarian personality.* New York: Harper.

Akiskal, H. S., & McKinney, W. T. (1975). Overview of recent research in depression. *Archives of General Psychiatry, 32,* 285–305.

Alexander, F. (1939). Emotional factors in essential hypertension. *Psychosomatic Medicine, 1,* 139–152.

Alexander, F. (1950). *Psychosomatic medicine: Its principles and applications.* New York: Norton.

Allen, W. (1975). *Without feathers.* New York: Random House.

Alloy, L. B., & Abramson, L. Y. (1979). Judgment of contingency in depressed and nondepressed college students: Sadder but wiser? *Journal of Experimental Psychology: General, 108,* 441–487.

Alloy, L. B., & Seligman, M. E. P. (1979). On the cognitive components of learned helplessness and depression. In G. H. Bower (Ed.), *Psychology of learning and motivation (Vol. 13).* New York: Academic Press.

Alloy, L. B., Peterson, C., Abramson, L. Y., & Seligman, M. E. P. (1984). Attributional style and the generality of learned helplessness. *Journal of Personality and Social Psychology, 46,* 681–687.

Allport, G. W. (1937). *Personality: A psychological interpretation.* New York: Holt.

Allport, G. W. (1961). *Pattern and growth in personality.* New York: Holt, Rinehart & Winston.

Allport, G. W. (Ed.). (1965). *Letters from Jenny.* New York: Harcourt Brace Jovanovich.

Allport, G. W. (1968). The historical background of modern social psychology. In G. Lindzey & E. Aronson (Eds.), *The handbook of social psychology (2nd ed., Vol. 1).* Reading, MA: Addison-Wesley. (a)

Allport, G. W. (1968). *The person in psychology: Selected essays.* Boston: Beacon. (b)

Allport, G. W., & Allport, F. H. (1921). Personality traits: Their classification and measurement. *Journal of Abnormal and Social Psychology, 16,* 6–40.

Allport, G. W., & Odbert, H. S. (1936). Trait-names: A psycho-lexical study. *Psychological Monographs: General and Applied, 47,* 171–220. (1, Whole No. 211).

Allport, G. W., & Vernon, P. E. (1931). *A study of values.* Boston: Houghton Mifflin.

Allport, G. W., & Vernon, P. E. (1933). *Studies in expressive movement.* New York: Macmillan.

Allport, G. W., Vernon, P. E., & Lindzey, G. (1960). *A study of values (Rev. ed.).* Boston: Houghton Mifflin.

Altman, I. (1975). *The environment and social behavior: Privacy, personal space, territory, and crowding.* Monterey, CA: Brooks/Cole.

Amabile, T. M., & Kabat, L. G. (1982). When self-descriptions contradict behavior: Actions do speak louder than words. *Social Cognition, 1,* 311–325.

American Psychiatric Association (1980). *Diagnostic and statistical manual of mental disorders (3rd ed.).* Washington, D.C.: author.

American Psychological Association (1981). *Ethical principles of psychologists.* Washington, D.C.: author.

Anastasi, A. (1979). *Fields of applied psychology (2nd ed.).* New York: McGraw-Hill.

Anastasi, A. (1982). *Psychological testing (5th ed.).* New York: Macmillan.

Anderson, T. H. (1978). Becoming sane with psychohistory. *The Historian, 41,* 1–20.

Andrasik, F. (1979). Organizational behavior modification: A methodological and content review. *Journal of Organizational Behavior Management, 2,* 85–102.

Angell, M. (1985). Disease as reflection of the psyche. *The New England Journal of Medicine, 312,* 1570–1572.

Ardrey, R. (1966). *The territorial imperative.* New York: Atheneum.

Argyris, C. (1969). Some unintended consequences of rigorous research. *Psychological Bulletin, 70,* 185–197.

Arieti, S., & Bemporad, J. (1978). *Severe and mild depression.* New York: Basic Books.

Averill, J. R. (1973). Personal control over aversive stimuli and its relationship to stress. *Psychological Bulletin, 80,* 286–303.

Balke, W. M., Hammond, K. R., & Meyer, G. D. (1973). An alternate approach to labor-management relations; *Administrative Science Quarterly, 18,* 311–327.

Bandura, A. (1969). *Principles of behavior modification.* New York: Holt, Rinehart & Winston.

Bandura, A. (1973). *Aggression: A social learning analysis.* Englewood Cliffs, NJ: Prentice-Hall.

Bandura, A. (1974). Behavior theories and the models of man. *American Psychologist, 29,* 859–869.

Bandura, A. (1977). Self-efficacy: Toward a unifying theory of behavioral change. *Psychological Review, 84,* 191–215. (a)

Bandura, A. (1977). *Social learning theory.* Englewood Cliffs, NJ: Prentice-Hall. (b)

Bandura, A. (1978). The self system in reciprocal determinism. *American Psychologist, 33,* 344–358.

Bandura, A. (1986). *Social foundations of thought and action.* Englewood Cliffs, NJ: Prentice-Hall.

Bandura, A., Blanchard, E. B., & Ritter, B. (1969). Relative efficacy of desensitization and modeling approaches for inducing behavioral, affective, and attitudinal changes. *Journal of Personality and Social Psychology, 13,* 173–199.

Bandura, A., & Walters, R. (1963). *Social learning and personality development.* New York: Holt, Rinehart & Winston.

Bannister, D. (1963). The genesis of schizophrenic thought disorder: A serial invalidation hypothesis. *British Journal of Psychiatry, 109,* 680–686.

Bannister, D. (1965). The genesis of schizophrenic thought disorder: Re-test of the serial invalidation hypothesis. *British Journal of Psychiatry, 111,* 377–382.

Barker, R. G., Dembo, T., & Lewin, K. (1941). Frustration and regression: An experiment with young children. *University of Iowa Studies in Child Welfare, 18* (1). Described in C. S. Hall & G. Lindzey (1970). *Theories of personality (2nd ed.).* New York: Wiley.

Baron, R. A., & Byrne, D. (1984). *Social psychology: Understanding human interaction (4th ed.).* Boston: Allyn & Bacon.

Barry, H., & Blane, H. T. (1977). Birth order of alcoholics. *Journal of Individual Psychology, 33,* 62–69.

Bartlett, F. (1932). *A study in experimental and social psychology.* New York: Cambridge University.

Bateson, G., Jackson, D. D., Haley, J., & Weakland, J. (1956). Toward a theory of schizophrenia. *Behavioral Science, 1,* 251–264.

Beck, A. T. (1967). *Depression: Clinical, experimental, and theoretical aspects.* New York: Hoeber.

Beck, A. T. (1976). *Cognitive therapy and the emotional disorders.* New York: International Universities Press.

Beck, A. T., & Emery, G. (1985). *Anxiety disorders and phobias: A cognitive perspective.* New York: Basic Books.

Beck, A. T., Rush, A. J., Shaw, B. F., & Emery, G. (1979). *Cognitive therapy of depression.* New York: Guilford.

Becker, H. (1953). Becoming a marijuana user. *American Journal of Sociology, 59,* 235–242,

Becker, H. (1982). *Art worlds.* Berkeley: University of California Press.

Bell, P. A., & Byrne, D. (1978). Repression-sensitization. In H. London & J. E. Exner (Eds.), *Dimensions of personality.* New York: Wiley.

Bellack, A. S., & Hersen, M. (Eds.). (1985). *Dictionary of behavior therapy techniques.* New York: Pergamon.

Belmont, L., & Marolla, F. A. (1973). Birth order, family size, and intelligence. *Science, 182,* 1096–1101.

Bem, D. J. (1965). An experimental analysis of self-persuasion. *Journal of Experimental Social Psychology, 1,* 199–218.

Bem, D. J. (1967). Self-perception: An alternative interpretation of cognitive dissonance phenomena. *Psychological Review, 74,* 183–200.

Bem, D. J. (1972). Self-perception theory. In L. Berkowitz (Ed.), *Advances in experimental social psychology (Vol. 6).* New York: Academic Press.

Bem, D. J. (1983). Further deja-vu in the search for cross-situational consistency: A response to Mischel and Peake. *Psychological Review, 90,* 390–393.

Bem, D. J., & Allen, A. (1974). On predicting some of the people some of the time: The search for cross-situational consistencies in behavior. *Psychological Review, 81,* 506–520.

Bem, D. J., & Funder, D. C. (1978). Predicting more of the people more of the time: Assessing the personality of situations. *Psychological Review, 85,* 485–501.

Bem, S. L. (1974). The measurement of psychological androgyny. *Journal of Consulting and Clinical Psychology, 42,* 155–162.

Bem, S. L. (1975). Sex role adaptability: One consequence of psychological androgyny. *Journal of Personality and Social Psychology, 31,* 634–643.

Bem, S. L. (1981). Gender schema theory: A cognitive account of sex-typing. *Psychological Review, 88,* 354–364.

Berger, P. L., & Luckmann, T. (1966). *The social construction of reality.* New York: Doubleday.

Berglas, S., & Jones, E. E. (1978). Drug choice as a self-handicapping strategy in response to noncontingent success. *Journal of Personality and Social Psychology, 36,* 405–417.

Berkowitz, L. (1974). Some determinants of impulsive aggression: Role of mediated associations with reinforcements for aggression. *Psychological Review, 81,* 165–176.

Bernstein, D. A., & Nietzel, M. T. (1980). *Introduction to clinical psychology.* New York: McGraw-Hill.

Berry, J. W. (1966). Temne and Eskimo perceptual skills. *International Journal of Psychology, 1,* 207–229.

Berry, J. W., & Annis, R. C. (1974). Ecology, culture, and psychological differentiation. *International Journal of Psychology, 9,* 173–193.

Bersoff, D. N. (1981). Testing and the law. *American Psychologist, 36,* 1047–1056.

Bevan, W. (1964). Subliminal stimulation: A pervasive problem for psychology. *Psychological Bulletin, 61,* 81–99.

Bieri, J. (1955). Cognitive complexity-simplicity and predictive behavior. *Journal of Abnormal and Social Psychology, 51,* 263–268.

Binet, A., & Simon, T. (1913). *A method of measuring the development of the intelligence of young children (3rd ed.).* Chicago: Chicago Medical Books.

Blaney, P. H. (1986). Affect and memory: A review. *Psychological Bulletin, 99,* 229–246.

Blatt, S. J. (1964). An attempt to define mental health. *Journal of Consulting Psychology, 28,* 146–153.

Block, J. (1971). *Lives through time.* Berkeley: Bancroft Books.

Blum, G. S. (1949). A study of the psychoanalytic theory of psychosexual development. *Genetic Psychology Monographs, 39,* 3–99.

Blum, G. S. (1962). A guide for the research use of the Blacky pictures. *Journal of Projective Techniques, 26,* 3–29.

Blum, G. S., & Hunt, H. F. (1952). The validity of the Blacky Pictures. *Psychological Bulletin, 49,* 238–250.

Bobko, P., & Schwartz, J. P. (1984). A metric for combining theoretically related but statistically uncorrelated constructs. *Journal of Personality Assessment, 48,* 11–16.

Bonarius, J. C. J. (1965). Research in the personal construct theory of George A. Kelly: Role construct repertory test and basic theory. In B. A. Maher (Ed.), *Progress in experimental personality research (pp. 1–46).* New York: Academic Press.

Boring, E. G. (1950). *A history of experimental psychology (2nd ed.).* New York: Appleton-Century-Crofts.

Bowen, E. (1985). Cracking the SAT code. *Time,* April 22, p. 61.

Bower, G. H. (1981). Mood and memory. *American Psychologist, 36,* 129–148.

Bowers, K. S. (1973). Situationism in psychology: An analysis and critique. *Psychological Review, 80,* 307–336.

Breland, H. M. (1974). Birth order, family constellation, and verbal achievement. *Child Development, 45,* 1011–1019.

Breland, K., & Breland, M. (1961). The misbehavior of organisms. *American Psychologist, 16,* 681–684.

Breuer, J., & Freud, S. (1895). Studies on hysteria. *Collected works (Vol. II)* London: Hogarth.

Brewin, C. R. (1985). Depression and causal attribution: What is their relation? *Psychological Bulletin, 98,* 297–309.

Brigham, J. C., & Wrightsman, L. S. (1982). *Contemporary issues in social psychology (4th ed.).* Monterey, CA: Brooks/Cole.

Brody, B. (1970). Freud's case load. *Psychotherapy: Theory, Research, and Practice, 7,* 8–12.

Bromberg, W. (1959). *The mind of man: A history of psychotherapy and psychoanalysis.* New York: Harper & Row.

Bronzaft, A. L. (1981). The effect of a noise abatement program on reading ability. *Journal of Environmental Psychology, 1,* 215–222.

Broverman, I. K., Vogel, S. R., Broverman, D. M., Clarkson, F. E., & Rosenkrantz, P. S. (1972). Sex-role stereotypes: A current appraisal. *Journal of Social Issues, 28,* 59–78.

Brown, J. A. C. (1964). *Freud and the post-Freudians.* New York: Penguin.

Brown, N. O. (1959). *Life against death.* Middletown, CN: Wesleyan University Press.

Bruner, J. S. (1956). You are your constructs. *Contemporary Psychology, 1,* 355–357.

Buchwald, A. M., Coyne, J. C., & Cole, C. S. (1978). A critical evaluation of the learned helplessness model of depression. *Journal of Abnormal Psychology, 87,* 180–193.

Burgess, R. L., Clark, R. N., & Handee, J. C. (1971). An experimental analysis of anti-litter procedures. *Journal of Applied Behavior Analysis, 4,* 71–75.

Bursten, B. (1979). Psychiatry and the rhetoric of models. *American Journal of Psychiatry, 136,* 661–666.

Burton, R. V. (1963). Generality of honesty reconsidered. *Psychological Review, 70,* 481–499.

Buss, A. H., & Plomin, R. (1975). *A temperament theory of personality.* New York: Wiley.

Buss, A. H., & Plomin, R. (1984). *Temperament: Early developing personality traits.* Hillsdale, NJ: Erlbaum.

Buss, D. M. (1984). Toward a psychology of person-environment (PE) correlation: The role of spouse selection. *Journal of Personality and Social Psychology, 47,* 361–377.

Buss, D. M., & Craik, K. H. (1984). Acts, dispositions, and personality. In B. A. Maher (Ed.), *Progress in experimental personality research (Vol. 13).* New York: Academic Press.

Butcher, J. N., & Keller, L. S. (1984). Objective personality assessment. In G. Goldstein & M. Hersen (Eds.), *Handbook of psychological assessment.* New York: Pergamon.

Byrne, D. (1961). The Repression-sensitization scale: Rationale, reliability, and validity. *Journal of Personality, 29,* 334–349.

Byrne, D. (1964). Repression-sensitization as a dimension of personality. In B. A. Maher (Ed.), *Progress in experimental personality research (Vol. 1).* New York: Academic Press.

Byrne, D., Cherry, J., Lamberth, J., & Mitchell, H. E. (1973). Husband-wife similarity in response to erotic stimuli. *Journal of Personality, 41,* 385–394.

Calhoun, J. B. (1962). Population density and social pathology. *Scientific American, 206*(3), 139–148.

Campbell, D. P. (1971). *Manual for the Strong Vocational Interest Blank.* Stanford: Stanford University Press.

Campbell, D. T., & Fiske, D. W. (1959). Convergent and discriminant validity by the multitrait-multimethod matrix. *Psychological Bulletin, 56,* 81–105.

Campbell, D. T., & Stanley, J. C. (1966). *Experimental and quasi-experimental designs for research.* Chicago: Rand McNally.

Cantor, N., & Mischel, W. (1977). Traits as prototypes: Effects on recognition memory. *Personality and Social Psychology: 37,* 337–344.

Cantor, N., & Mischel, W. (1979). Prototypes in person perception. In L. Berkowitz (Ed.), *Advances in experimental social psychology (Vol. 12).* New York: Academic Press.

Cantril, H. (1935). Review of Lewin's *A dynamic theory of personality. Journal of Abnormal and Social Psychology, 30,* 534–537.

Carlson, R. (1971). Where is the person in personality research? *Psychological Bulletin, 75,* 203–219.

Carlyn, M. (1977). An assessment of the Myers-Briggs Type Indicator. *Journal of Personality Assessment, 41,* 461–473.

Cartwright, D. S., & Graham, M. J. (1984). Self-concept and identity: Overlapping portions of a cognitive structure of self. In R. F. Levant & J. M. Shlien (Eds.), *Client-centered therapy and the person-centered approach: New directions in theory, research, and practice.* New York: Praeger.

Cattell, J. M. (1890). Mental tests and measurements. *Mind, 15,* 373–380.

Cattell, R. B. (1950). *Personality: A systematic, theoretical, and factual study.* New York: McGraw-Hill.

Cattell, R. B. (1972). *A new morality from science: Beyondism.* New York: Pergamon.

Cattell, R. B. (1979). *Personality and learning theory: The structure of personality in its environment (Vol. 1).* New York: Springer.

Cattell, R. B. (1984). The voyage of a laboratory, 1928–1984. *Multivariate Behavioral Research, 19,* 121–174.

Cattell, R. B., Blewett, D. B., & Beloff, J. R. (1955). The inheritance of personality: A multiple variance analysis determination of approximate nature-nurture ratios for primary personality ratios in Q data. *American Journal of Human Genetics, 7,* 122–146.

Cattell, R. B., Stice, G. F., & Kristy, N. F. (1957). A first approximation to nature-nurture ratios for eleven primary personality factors in objective tests. *Journal of Abnormal and Social Psychology, 54,* 143–159.

Cattell, R. B., & Scheier, I. H. (1961). *The meaning and measurement of neuroticism and anxiety.* New York: Ronald.

Chaplin, W. F., & Goldberg, L. R. (1984). A failure to replicate the Bem and Allen study of individual differences in cross-situational consistency. *Journal of Personality and Social Psychology, 47,* 1074–1090.

Chapman, L. J., & Chapman, J. P. (1969). Illusory correlation as an obstacle to the use of valid psychodiagnostic signs. *Journal of Abnormal Psychology, 74,* 271–280.

Child, D. (1970). *The essentials of factor analysis.* London: Holt, Rinehart & Winston.

Child, I. L. (1968). Personality in culture. In E. F. Borgatta & W. W. Lambert (Eds.), *Handbook of personality theory and research.* Chicago: Rand McNally.

Chodorkoff, B. (1954). Self-perception, perceptual defense, and adjustment. *Journal of Abnormal and Social Psychology, 49,* 508–512.

Chomsky, N. (1959). A review of B. F. Skinner's *Verbal behavior. Language, 35,* 26–58.

Christie, R., & Geis, F. L. (1970). *Studies in Machiavellianism.* New York: Academic Press.

Coates, D., & Wortman, C. B. (1980). Depression maintenance and interpersonal control. In A. Baum & J. E. Singer (Eds.), *Advances in environmental psychology: Applications of personal control (Vol. 2).* Hillsdale, NJ: Erlbaum.

Cobb, S. (1976). Social support as a moderator of life stress. *Psychosomatic Medicine, 38,* 300–314.

Cohen, S., Evans, G. W., Krantz, D. S., & Stokols, D. (1980). Physiological, motivational, and cognitive effects of aircraft noise on children: Moving from the laboratory to the field. *American Psychologist, 35,* 231–243.

Cohen, S., Evans, G. W., Krantz, D. S., Stokols, D., & Kelly, S. (1981). Aircraft noise and children: Longitudinal and cross-sectional evidence on adaptation to noise and the effectiveness of noise abatement. *Journal of Personality and Social Psychology, 40,* 331–345.

Cohen, S., & Weinstein, N. (1981). Nonauditory effects of noise on behavior and health. *Journal of Social Issues, 37*(1), 36–70.

Cohn, T. S. (1956). Relation of the F Scale to a response set to answer positively. *Journal of Social Psychology, 44,* 129–133.

Colby, K. M., Watt, J. B., & Gilbert, J. P. (1966). A computer method of psychotherapy. *Journal of Nervous and Mental Disease, 142,* 148–152.

Collett, P. (1979). The repertory grid in psychological research. In G. P. Ginsburg (Ed.), *Emerging strategies in social psychological research.* Chichester: Wiley.

Compton, M. (1984). Sideline computing in the NFL. *Personal Computing,* January, pp. 29; 32.

Condiotte, M. M., & Lichtenstein, E. (1981). Self-efficacy and relapse in smoking cessation programs. *Journal of Consulting and Clinical Psychology, 49,* 648–658.

Conley, J. J. (1984). Longitudinal consistency of adult personality: Self-reported psychological characteristics across 45 years. *Journal of Personality and Social Psychology, 47,* 1325–1333. (a)

Conley, J. J. (1984). Relation of temporal stability and cross-situational consistency in personality: Comment on the Mischel-Epstein debate. *Psychological Review, 91,* 491–496. (b)

Cook, M. L., & Peterson, C. (1986). Depressive irrationality. *Cognitive Therapy and Research, 10,* 293–298.

Cook, S. W. (1969). Motives in a conceptual analysis of attitude-related behaviors. In W. J. Arnold & D. Levine (Eds.), *Nebraska symposium on motivation (Vol. 17).* Lincoln: University of Nebraska Press.

Coopersmith, S. (1967). *The antecedents of self-esteem.* San Francisco: Freeman.

Coopersmith, S. (1968). Studies in self-esteem. *Scientific American, 218*(2), 96–106.

Costello, C. G. (1978). A critical review of Seligman's laboratory experiments on learned helplessness and depression in humans. *Journal of Abnormal Psychology, 87,* 21–31.

Cousins, N. (1977). Anatomy of an illness (as perceived by the patient). *Saturday Review,* May 28, pp. 4–6; 48–51.

Cousins, N. (1979). *The anatomy of an illness.* New York: Norton.

Coyne, J. C. (1976). Toward an interactional description of depression. *Psychiatry, 39,* 28–40.

Coyne, J. C., & Gotlib, I. H. (1983). The role of cognition in depression: A critical appraisal. *Psychological Bulletin, 94,* 472–505.

Cronbach, L. J. (1946). Response sets and test validity. *Educational and Psychological Measurement, 6,* 475–494.

Cronbach, L. J. (1957). The two disciplines of scientific psychology. *American Psychologist, 12,* 671–684.

Cronbach, L. J., & Meehl, P. E. (1955). Construct validity in psychological tests. *Psychological Bulletin, 52,* 281–302.

Crosby, F., & Crosby, T. L. (1981). Psychobiography and psychohistory. In S. Long (Ed.), *Handbook of political behavior (Vol. 1).* New York: Plenum.

Culver, C. M., Cohen, S. I., Silverman, A. J., Shmavonian, B. M. (1964). Cognitive restructuring, field dependence-independence, and the psychophysiological response to perceptual isolation. In J. Wortis (Ed.), *Recent advances in biological psychiatry (Vol. VI).* New York: Plenum.

Darley, J. M., & Latané, B. (1968). Bystander intervention in emergencies: Diffusion of responsibility. *Journal of Personality and Social Psychology, 8,* 377–383.

Darwin, C. R. (1859). *The origin of species.* London: Murray.

Darwin, C. R. (1872). *The expression of emotions in man and animals.* London: Murray.

Davis, C. M. (1928). Self-selection of diet by newly weaned infants. *American Journal of Diseases of Children, 36,* 651–679.

Depue, R. A., & Monroe, S. M. (1978). Learned helplessness in the perspective of the depressive disorders. *Journal of Abnormal Psychology, 87,* 3–20.

Derry, P. A., & Kuiper, N. A. (1981). Schematic processing and self-reference in clinical depression. *Journal of Abnormal Psychology, 90,* 286–297.

Deutsch, M. (1968). Field theory in social psychology. In G. Lindzey & E. Aronson (Eds.), *The handbook of social psychology (2nd ed., Vol. 1).* Reading, MA: Addison-Wesley.

Dewey, J. (1896). The reflex arc concept in psychology. *Psychological Review, 3,* 357–370.

Diamond, S. (1957). *Personality and temperament.* New York: Harper.

Dillehay, R. C. (1978). Authoritarianism. In H. London & J. E. Exner (Eds.), *Dimensions of personality.* New York: Wiley.

Dollard, J., Doob, L. W., Miller, N. E., Mowrer, O. H., & Sears, R. R. (1939). *Frustration and aggression.* New Haven: Yale University Press.

Dollard, J., & Miller, N. E. (1950). *Personality and psychotherapy: An analysis in terms of learning, thinking, and culture.* New York: McGraw-Hill.

Dor-Shav, N. K. (1978). On the long-range effects of concentration camp internment on Nazi victims: 25 years later. *Journal of Consulting and Clinical Psychology, 46,* 1–11.

Downey, J. E. (1923). *The will temperament and its testing.* New York: World Book.

Driver, M. J., & Streufert, S. (1969). Integrative complexity: An approach to individuals and groups as information processing systems. *Administrative Science Quarterly, 14,* 272–285.

Dunnette, M. D. (Ed.). (1976). *Handbook of industrial and organizational psychology.* Chicago: Rand McNally.

Dunnette, M. D., & Borman, W. C. (1979). Personnel selection and classification systems. *Annual Review of Psychology, 30,* 477–525.

Dweck, C. S. (1975). The role of expectations and attributions in the alleviation of learned helplessness. *Journal of Personality and Social Psychology, 31,* 674–685.

Edwards, A. L. (1957). *The social desirability variable in personality assessment and research.* New York: Dryden.

Ekehammar, B. (1974). Interactionism in psychology from a historical perspective. *Psychological Bulletin, 81,* 1026–1048.

Ekman, P. (1984). Expression and the nature of emotion. In K. Scherer & P. Ekman (Eds.), *Approaches to emotions.* Hillsdale, N.J.: Erlbaum.

Ellis, A. (1962). *Reason and emotion in psychotherapy.* New York: Stuart.

Ellis, A. (1973). *Humanistic psychotherapy: The rational-emotive approach.* New York: Julian.

Elms, A. C., & Milgram, S. (1966). Personality characteristics associated with obedience and defiance toward authoritative command. *Journal of Experimental Research in Personality, 1,* 282–289.

Endler, N. S., & Magnusson, D. (Eds.) (1976). *Interactional psychology and personality.* Washington, D.C.: Hemisphere. (a)

Endler, N. S., & Magnusson, D. (1976). Toward an interactional theory of personality. *Psychological Bulletin, 83,* 956–974. (b)

Engel, G. L. (1971). Sudden and rapid death during psychological stress: Folklore or folkwisdom? *Annals of Internal Medicine, 74,* 771–782.

Engel, G. L. (1980). The clinical application of the biopsychosocial model. *American Journal of Psychiatry, 137,* 535–544.

Epstein, R. (1966). Aggression toward outgroups as a function of authoritarianism and imitation of aggressive models. *Journal of Personality and Social Psychology, 3,* 574–579.

Epstein, S. (1973). The self-concept revisited: Or a theory of a theory. *American Psychologist, 28,* 404–416.

Epstein, S. (1979). The stability of behavior: I. On predicting most of the people much of the time. *Journal of Personality and Social Psychology, 37,* 1097–1126.

Epstein, S. (1980). The stability of behavior: II. Implications for psychological research. *American Psychologist, 35,* 790–806.

Epstein, S. (1983). Aggregation and beyond: Some basic issues on the prediction of behavior. *Journal of Personality, 51,* 360–392. (a)

Epstein, S. (1983). The stability of confusion: A reply to Mischel and Peake. *Psychological Review, 90,* 179–184. (b)

Epstein, S. (1984). The stability of behavior across time and situations. In R. A. Zucker, J. Aronoff, & A. I. Rabin (Eds.), *Personality and the prediction of behavior.* Orlando, FL: Academic Press.

Erdelyi, M. H. (1974). A new look at the new look: Perceptual defense and vigilance. *Psychological Review, 81,* 1–25.

Erdelyi, M. H. (1985). *Psychoanalysis: Freud's cognitive psychology.* New York: Freeman.

Erikson, E. H. (1950). *Childhood and society.* New York: Norton.

Erikson, E. H. (1958). *Young man Luther.* New York: Norton.

Erikson, E. H. (1968). *Identity: Youth and crisis.* New York: Norton.

Erikson, E. H. (1969). *Ghandi's truth.* New York: Norton.

Erikson, E. H. (1974). *Dimensions of a new identity.* New York: Norton.

Ernst, C., & Angst, J. (1983). *Birth order: Its influence on personality.* Berlin: Springer-Verlag.

Evans, G. W., & Jacobs, S. V. (1981). Air pollution and human behavior. *Journal of Social Issues, 37*(1), 95–125.

Eysenck, H. J. (1947). *Dimensions of personality.* London: Routledge & Kegan Paul.

Eysenck, H. J. (1952). The effects of psychotherapy: An evaluation. *Journal of Consulting Psychology, 16,* 319–324. (a)

Eysenck, H. J. (1952). *The scientific study of personality.* London: Routledge & Kegan Paul. (b)

Eysenck, H. J. (1953). *Uses and abuses of psychology.* Harmondsworth, England: Penguin.

Eysenck, H. J. (1954). The science of psychology: Nomothetic! *Psychological Review, 61,* 339–342.

Eysenck, H. J. (Ed.) (1961). *The handbook of abnormal psychology: An experimental approach.* New York: Basic Books.

Eysenck, H. J. (1967). *The biological basis of personality.* Springfield, MA: Thomas.

Eysenck, H. J. (1971). *Readings in extraversion-introversion. II. Fields of application.* London: Staples.

Eysenck, H. J. (1973). *The inequality of man.* London: Temple Smith.

Eysenck, H. J. (1976). *Sex and personality.* Austin: University of Texas Press.

Eysenck, H. J. (1982). *Personality, genetics, and behavior.* New York: Praeger.

Eysenck, H. J., & Wilson, G. D. (1973). *The experimental study of Freudian theories.* London: Methuen.

Fancher, R. E. (1973). *Psychoanalytic psychology: The development of Freud's thought.* New York: Norton.

Farrell, B. A. (1981). *The standing of psychoanalysis.* Oxford: Oxford University Press.

Fernald, G. G. (1912). The defective-delinquent class differentiating tests. *American Journal of Insanity, 68,* 524–594.

Ferster, C. B., & Skinner, B. F. (1957). *Schedules of reinforcement.* New York: Appleton-Century-Crofts.

Festinger, L. (1957). *A theory of cognitive dissonance.* Evanston: Row, Peterson.

Fisher, S., & Greenberg, R. P. (1977). *The scientific credibility of Freud's theories and therapy.* New York: Basic Books.

Fiske, D. W. (1971). *Measuring the concepts of personality.* Chicago: Aldine.

Fiske, D. W. (1973). Can a personality construct be validated empirically? *Psychological Bulletin, 80,* 89–92.

Fiske, S. T., & Linville, P. W. (1980). What does the schema concept buy us? *Personality and Social Psychology Bulletin, 6,* 543–557.

Fiske, S. T., & Taylor, S. E. (1984). *Social cognition.* Reading, MA: Addison-Wesley.

Flaherty, J. E., & Dusek, J. B. (1980). An investigation of the relationship between psychological androgyny and components of self-concept. *Journal of Personality and Social Psychology, 38,* 984–992.

Forward, J. R., Wells, K., Canter, R., & Waggoner, M. (1975). Teacher control strategies and choice of educational objectives among college students. *Journal of Educational Psychology, 67,* 757–763.

Fox, B. H. (1978). Premorbid psychological factors as related to cancer incidence. *Journal of Behavioral Medicine, 1,* 45–133.

Freedman, J. L. (1982). *Introductory psychology (2nd ed.).* Reading, MA: Addison-Wesley.

Freeman, F. N. (1926). *Mental tests: Their history, principles, and applications.* Boston: Houghton Mifflin.

Freeman, F. S. (1962). *Theory and practice of psychological testing (3rd ed.).* New York: Holt, Rinehart & Winston.

Freud, A. (1937). *The ego and the mechanisms of defense.* London: Hogarth.

Freud, S. (1900). The interpretation of dreams. *Collected works (Vol. IV).* London: Hogarth.

Freud, S. (1901). On dreams. *Collected works (Vol. V).* London: Hogarth. (a)

Freud, S. (1901). The psychopathology of everyday life. *Collected works (Vol. VI).* London: Hogarth. (b)

Freud, S. (1905). Fragment of an analysis of a case of hysteria. *Collected works (Vol. VII).* London: Hogarth (a)

Freud, S. (1905). Humor and its relation to the unconscious. *Collected works (Vol. VIII).* London: Hogarth. (b)

Freud, S. (1905). Three essays on the theory of sexuality. *Collected works (Vol. VII).* London: Hogarth. (c)

Freud, S. (1908). Character and anal eroticism. *Collected works (Vol. IX).* London: Hogarth. (a)

Freud, S. (1908). Creative writers and day-dreaming. *Collected works (Vol. IX).* London: Hogarth. (b)

Freud, S. (1909). Analysis of a phobia in a five-year-old boy. *Collected works (Vol. X).* London: Hogarth. (a)

Freud, S. (1909). Notes upon a case of obsessional neurosis. *Collected works (Vol. X).* London: Hogarth. (b)

Freud, S. (1910). Leonardo da Vinci and a memory of his childhood. *Collected works (Vol. XI).* London: Hogarth.

Freud, S. (1911). Psycho-analytic notes on an autobiographical account of a case of paranoia (dementia paranoides). *Collected works (Vol. XII).* London: Hogarth.

Freud, S. (1912). Papers on technique: The dynamics of transference. *Collected works (Vol. XII).* London: Hogarth.

Freud, S. (1917). Mourning and melancholia. *Collected works (Vol. XIV).* London: Hogarth.

Freud, S. (1920). Beyond the pleasure principle. *Collected works (Vol. XVIII).* London: Hogarth.

Freud, S. (1925). An autobiographical study. *Collected works (Vol. XX).* London: Hogarth.

Freud, S. (1928). Dostoevsky and parricide. *Collected works (Vol. XXI).* London: Hogarth.

Freud, S. (1930). Civilization and its discontents. *Collected works (Vol. XXI).* London: Hogarth.

Freud, S. (1939). Moses and monotheism. *Collected works (Vol. XXIII).* London: Hogarth.

Freud, S. (1950). Project for a scientific psychology. *Collected works (Vol. I).* London: Hogarth.

Friedlander, S. (1978). *History and psychoanalysis: An inquiry into the possibilities and limits of psychohistory.* New York: Holmes & Meier.

Friedman, J. (1959). Weight problems and psychological factors. *Journal of Consulting Psychology, 23,* 524–527.

Friedman, M., & Rosenman, R. H. (1974). *Type A behavior and your heart.* New York: Knopf.

Friedman, S. M. (1952). An empirical study of the castration and Oedipus complexes. *Genetic Psychology Monographs, 46,* 61–130.

Fromm, E. (1941). *Escape from freedom.* New York: Rinehart.

Fromm, E. (1947). *Man for himself.* New York: Rinehart.

Fromm, E. (1955). *The sane society.* New York: Rinehart.

Fromm, E. (1968). *The revolution of hope.* New York: Harper & Row.

Fromm, E. (1973). *The anatomy of human destructiveness.* New York: Fawcett Crest.

Fromm, E., & Maccoby, M. (1970). *Social character in a Mexican village.* Englewood Cliffs, NJ: Prentice-Hall.

Fulker, D. W., Eysenck, S. B. G., & Zuckerman, M. (1980). A genetic and environmental analysis of sensation seeking. *Journal of Research in Personality, 14,* 261–281.

Funder, D. C. (1983). The "consistency" controversy and the accuracy of personality judgments. *Journal of Personality, 48,* 473–493.

Funder, D. C., Block, J. H., & Block, J. (1983). Delay of gratification: Some longitudinal personality correlates. *Journal of Personality and Social Psychology, 44,* 1198–1213.

Funder, D. C., & Ozer, D. J. (1983). Behavior as a function of the situation. *Journal of Personality and Social Psychology, 44,* 107–112.

Furlong, W. B. (1971). What is a punter's 'hang time'? *New York Times Magazine,* January 10, pp. 30–32+.

Gallup, G. (1972). *The sophisticated poll watcher's guide.* Princeton, NJ: Princeton Opinion Press.

Galton, F. (1869). *Hereditary genius.* London: Macmillan.

Galton, F. (1874). *English men of science: Their nature and nurture.* London: Macmillan.

Galton, F. (1876). The history of twins, as a criterion of the relative powers of nature and nurture. *Journal of the Anthropological Institute, 5,* 324–329.

Galton, F. (1883). *Inquiries into human faculty and development.* London: Macmillan.

Galton, F. (1888). Co-relations and their measurement. *Proceedings of the Royal Society, 45,* 135–145.

Galton, F. (1889). *Natural inheritance.* London: Macmillan.

Garcia, J., & Koelling, R. A. (1966). Relation of cue to consequence in avoidance learning. *Psychonomic Science, 4,* 123–124.

Gardner, H. (1983). *Frames of mind: The theory of multiple intelligence.* New York: Basic Books.

Gardner, H. (1985). *The mind's new science: A history of the cognitive revolution.* New York: Basic Books.

Geen, R. G. (1984). Preferred stimulation levels in introverts and extraverts: Effects on arousal and performance. *Journal of Personality and Social Psychology, 46,* 1303–1312.

Geller, E. S. (1983). Rewarding safety belt usage at an industrial setting: Tests of treatment generality and response maintenance. *Journal of Applied Behavioral Analysis, 16,* 189–202.

Gergen, K. J. (1973). Social psychology as history. *Journal of Personality and Social Psychology, 26,* 309–320.

Ghiselli, E. E. (1973). The validity of aptitude tests in personnel selection. *Personnel Psychology, 26,* 461–477.

Gibson, H. B. (1981). *Hans Eysenck: The man and his work.* London: Peter Owen.

Gilligan, C. (1982). *In a different voice.* Cambridge, MA: Harvard University Press.

Gitlin, T. (1983). *Inside prime time.* New York: Pantheon.

Glass, D. C. (1977). *Behavior patterns, stress, and coronary disease.* Hillsdale, NJ: Erlbaum.

Glass, D. C., & Singer, J. E. (1972). *Urban stress: Experiments on noise and social stressors.* New York: Academic Press.

Glueck, S., & Glueck, E. T. (1950). *Unraveling juvenile delinquency.* Cambridge, MA: Harvard University Press.

Glueck, S., & Glueck, E. T. (1968). *Delinquents and nondelinquents in perspective.* Cambridge, MA: Harvard University Press.

Goffman, E. (1959). *The presentation of self in everyday life.* Garden City, NY: Doubleday.

Goldfried, M. R., & Kent, R. N. (1972). Traditional versus behavioral personality assessment: A comparison of methodological and theoretical assumptions. *Psychological Bulletin, 77,* 409–420.

Goldstein, K. M., & Blackman, S. (1976). Cognitive complexity, maternal child rearing, and acquiescence. *Social Behavior and Personality, 4,* 97–103.

Goldstein, K. M., & Blackman, S. (1978). *Cognitive style: Five approaches and relevant research.* New York: Wiley.

Goldstein, K. (1939). *The organism.* New York: American Book Company.

Goleman, D. (1986). Major personality study finds that traits are mostly inherited. *New York Times,* December 2, pp. 17–18.

Goodenough, D. R. (1978). Field dependence. In H. London & J. E. Exner (Eds.), *Dimensions of personality.* New York: Wiley.

Gorsuch, R. L. (1974). *Factor analysis.* Philadelphia: Saunders.

Goshen, C. E. (1952). The original case material of psychoanalysis. *American Journal of Psychiatry, 108,* 829–834.

Gould, P., & White, R. (1974). *Mental maps.* New York: Penguin.

Gould, S. J. (1981). *The mismeasure of man.* New York: Norton.

Grace, W. J., & Graham, D. T. (1952). Relationship of specific attitudes and emotions to certain bodily diseases. *Psychosomatic Medicine, 14,* 243–251.

Greenwald, A. G. (1976). An editorial. *Journal of Personality and Social Psychology, 33,* 1–7.

Greenwald, A. G. (1980). The totalitarian ego: Fabrication and revision of personal history. *American Psychologist, 35,* 603–618.

Guilford, J. P. (1975). Factors and factors of personality. *Psychological Bulletin, 82,* 802–814.

Guion, R. M., & Gottier, R. J. (1965). Validity of personality measures in personnel selection. *Personnel Psychology, 18,* 135–164.

Gunderson, J. G., & Singer, M. T. (1975). Defining borderline patients: An overview. *American Journal of Psychiatry, 132,* 1–10.

Gur, R. C., & Sackeim, H. A. (1979). Self-deception: A concept in search of a phenomenon. *Journal of Personality and Social Psychology, 37,* 147–169.

Gurman, A. S. (1977). The patient's perception of the therapeutic relationship. In A. S. Gurman & A. M. Razin (Eds.), *Effective psychotherapy: A handbook of research.* New York: Pergamon.

Hackett, T. P., & Cassem, N. H. (1974). Development of a quantitative rating scale to assess denial. *Journal of Psychosomatic Research, 18,* 93–100.

Hackman, J. R., Lawler, E. E., & Porter, L. W. (Eds.). (1977). *Perspectives on behavior in organizations.* New York: McGraw-Hill.

Hake, D. F. (1981). Behavioral ecology: A social systems approach to environmental problems. In L. Michelson, M. Hersen, & S. M. Turner (Eds.), *Future perspectives in behavior therapy.* New York: Plenum.

Hall, C. S. (1963). Strangers in dreams: An empirical confirmation of the Oedipus complex. *Journal of Personality. 31,* 336–345.

Hall, C. S., & Lindzey, G. (1957). *Theories of personality.* New York: Wiley.

Hall, C. S., & Lindzey, G. (1970). *Theories of personality (2nd ed.).* New York: Wiley.

Hall, C. S., & Lindzey, G. (1978). *Theories of personality (3rd ed.).* New York: Wiley.

Hall, C. S., Lindzey, G., Loehlin, J. C., & Manosevitz, M. (1985). *Introduction to theories of personality.* New York: Wiley.

Hall, C. S., & Nordby, V. J. (1973). *A primer of Jungian psychology.* New York: Mentor.

Hall, J. A., & Taylor, M. C. (1985). Psychological androgyny and the masculinity $\times$ femininity interaction. *Journal of Personality and Social Psychology, 49,* 429–435.

Hall, M. H. (1968). Abraham H. Maslow. *Psychology Today, 2*(2), 35–37; 54–57.

Hamilton, D. L., & Gifford, R. K. (1976). Illusory correlation in interpersonal perception: A cognitive basis of stereotypic judgments. *Journal of Experimental Social Psychology, 12,* 392–407.

Hansen, J. C. (1984). Interest inventories. In G. Goldstein & M. Hersen (Eds.), *Handbook of psychological assessment.* New York: Pergamon.

Hare, R. D. (1970). *Psychopathy: Theory and research.* New York: Wiley.

Harlow, H. F. (1958). The nature of love. *American Psychologist, 13,* 673–685.

Harré, R., & Secord, P. F. (1973). *The explanation of social behaviour.* Totowa, NJ: Littlefield-Adams.

Hartmann, H. (1939). *Ego psychology and the problem of adaptation.* New York: International Universities Press.

Hartshorne, H., & May, M. A. (1928). *Studies in deceit.* New York: Macmillan.

Harvey, J. H., & Galvin, K. S. (1984). Clinical implications of attribution theory and research. *Clinical Psychology Review, 4,* 15–33.

Harvey, O. J. (1966). System structure, flexibility, and creativity. In O. J. Harvey (Ed.), *Experience, structure, and adaptability.* New York: Springer.

Harvey, O. J., Hunt, D. E., & Schroder, H. M. (1961). *Conceptual systems and personality organization.* New York: Wiley.

Hathaway, S. R., & McKinley, J. C. (1943). *The Minnesota Multiphasic Personality Inventory.* Minneapolis: University of Minnesota Press.

Hayden, B., Nasby, W., & Davids, A. (1977). Interpersonal conceptual structures, predictive accuracy, and social adjustment of emotionally disturbed boys. *Journal of Abnormal Psychology, 86,* 315–320.

Heider, F. (1958). *The psychology of interpersonal relations.* New York: Wiley.

Heinstein, M. I. (1963). Behavioral correlates of breast-bottle regimes under varying parent-infant relationships. *Monographs of the Society for Research in Child Development, 28,* No. 88.

Hemmings, R. (1972). *Fifty years of freedom: A study of the development of the ideas of A. S. Neill.* London: George Allen & Unwin.

Hendry, L. B., & Gillies, P. (1978). Body type, body esteem, school, and leisure: A study of overweight, average, and underweight adolescents. *Journal of Youth and Adolescence, 7,* 181–194.

Herrigel, E. (1971). *Zen in the art of archery.* New York: Vintage.

Hilgard, E. R. (1987). *Psychology in America: A historical survey.* San Diego: Harcourt Brace Jovanovich.

Hirt, E. (1902). *Die Temperamente.* Leipzig: Barth.

Hockey, G. R. J. (1972). Effects of noise on human efficiency and some individual differences. *Journal of Sound Vibrations, 20,* 299–304.

Hoffman, M. L. (1963). Childrearing practices and moral development: Generalizations from empirical research. *Child Development, 34,* 295–318.

Hogan, R. (1982). A socioanalytic theory of personality. In M. Page (Ed.), *Nebraska symposium on motivation (Vol. 30).* Lincoln: University of Nebraska Press.

Hogan, R., Carpenter, B. N., Briggs, S. R., & Hansson, R. O. (1984). Personality assessment and personnel selection. In H. J. Bernardin & D. A. Bownas (Eds.), *Personality assessment in organizations.* New York: Praeger.

Hogan, R., deSoto, C. N., & Solano, C. (1977). Traits, tests, and personality research. *American Psychologist, 32,* 255–264.

Holland, J. L. (1966). *The psychology of vocational choice: A theory of personality types and model environments.* Waltham, MA: Blaisdell.

Holland, J. L. (1985). *Making vocational choices: A theory of vocational personalities and work environments (2nd ed.).* Englewood Cliffs, NJ: Prentice-Hall.

Holmes, T. H., & Rahe, R. H. (1967). The social readjustment scale. *Journal of Psychosomatic Research, 11,* 213–218.

Holt, R. R. (1970). Yet another look at clinical and statistical prediction: Or, is clinical psychology worthwhile? *American Psychologist, 25,* 337–349.

Horney, K. (1937). *Neurotic personality of our times.* New York: Norton.

Horney, K. (1945). *Our inner conflicts.* New York: Norton.

Howes, D., & Solomon, R. L. (1950). A note on McGinnies' emotionality and perceptual defense. *Psychological Review, 57,* 229–234.

Hoyt, M. F., & Raven, B. H. (1973). Birth order and the 1971 Los Angeles earthquake. *Journal of Personality and Social Psychology, 28,* 123–128.

Hull, C. L. (1943). *Principles of behavior.* New York: Appleton-Century-Crofts.

Hunt, D. E. (1966). A conceptual systems change model and its application in education. In O. J. Harvey (Ed.), *Experience, structure, and adaptability.* New York: Springer.

Izard, C. E. (1977). *Human emotions.* New York: Plenum.

Jaccard, J. J. (1974). Predicting social behavior from personality traits. *Journal of Research in Personality, 7,* 358–367.

Jackson, D. N., & Paunonen, S. V. (1985). Construct validity and the predictability of behavior. *Journal of Personality and Social Psychology, 49,* 554–570.

Jacoby, J. (1976). Consumer psychology: An octennium. *Annual Review of Psychology, 27,* 331–358.

James, W. (1890). *Principles of psychology (2 vols.).* New York: Holt.

Janis, I. L. (1983). Foreword. In E. J. Langer, *The psychology of control.* Beverly Hills, CA: Sage.

Janoff-Bulman, R., & Brickman, P. (1980). Expectations and what people learn from failure. In N. T. Feather (Ed.), *Expectancy, incentive, and failure.* Hillsdale, NJ: Erlbaum.

Jaret, P. (1986). Our immune systems: The wars within. *National Geographic, 169*(6), 702–735.

Jastrow, J. (1915). The antecedents of the study of character and temperament. *The Popular Science Monthly, 86,* 590–613.

Jemmott, J. B., & Locke, S. E. (1984). Psychosocial factors, immunologic mediation, and human susceptibility to infectious diseases: How much do we know? *Psychological Bulletin, 95,* 78–108.

Jenkins, C. D., Rosenman, R. H., & Zyzanski, S. J. (1974). Prediction of clinical coronary heart disease by a test for the coronary-prone behavior pattern. *The New England Journal of Medicine, 23,* 1271–1275.

Jenkins, C. D., Zyzanski, S. J., & Rosenman, R. H. (1976). Risk of new myocardial infarction in middle age men with manifest coronary heart disease. *Circulation, 53,* 342–347.

Joffe, J. A., & Peterson, C. (1981). Cognitive style and literary regression. *Journal of Personality, 49,* 337–348.

Johansson, C. B., & Campbell, D. P. (1971). Stability of the Strong Vocational Interest Blank for Men. *Journal of Applied Psychology, 55,* 24–26.

Jones, E. (1910). The Oedipus complex as an explanation of Hamlet's mystery. *American Journal of Psychiatry, 67,* 279–286.

Jones, E. (1923). *Papers on psychoanalysis.* London: Bailliere Tindall.

Jones, H. E. (1931). Order of birth in relation to the development of the child. In C. Murchinson (Ed.), *Handbook of child psychology.* Worcester, MA: Clark University Press.

Jones, R. G. (1968). *A factored measure of Ellis' irrational belief systems.* Wichita, KA: Test Systems.

Jung, C. G. (1907). The psychology of dementia praecox. *Collected works (Vol. 3).* New York: Pantheon.

Jung, C. G. (1912). Symbols of transformation. Part II. *Collected works (Vol. 5).* New York: Pantheon.

Jung, C. G. (1924). *Psychological types.* New York: Random House.

Kamen, L. P., & Seligman, M. E. P. (1986). *Explanatory style predicts college grade point average.* Unpublished manuscript, University of Pennsylvania.

Kaplan, G. A., & Camacho, T. (1983). Perceived health and mortality: A nine-year follow-up of the human population laboratory cohort. *American Journal of Epidemiology, 117,* 292–304.

Kaplan, M. (1983). A woman's view of DSM-III. *American Psychologist, 38,* 786–792.

Kasl, S. V. (1978). A social-psychological perspective on successful community control of high blood pressure: A review. *Journal of Behavioral Medicine, 1,* 347–381.

Kazdin, A. E. (1977). *The token economy.* New York: Plenum.

Keller, F. S. (1969). A programmed system of instruction. *Educational Technology Monographs, 2,* 1–27.

Kellogg, M. A. (1976). Updating Dr. Spock. *Newsweek,* May 3, p. 86.

Kelly, G. A. (1933). Some observations on the relation of cerebral dominance to the perception of symbols. *Psychological Bulletin, 30,* 583–584.

Kelly, G. A. (1955). *The psychology of personal constructs (2 vols.).* New York: Norton.

Kelly, J., & Worrell, L. (1976). Parent behaviors related to masculine, feminine, and androgynous sex role orientations. *Journal of Consulting and Clinical Psychology, 44,* 843–851.

Kempen, R. W., & Hall, R. V. (1977). Reduction of industrial absenteeism: Results of a behavioral approach. *Journal of Organizational Behavior Management, 1,* 1–21.

Kendall, P. C., & Hollon, S. D. (1979). *Cognitive-behavioral interventions: Theory, research, and procedures.* New York: Academic Press.

Kenny, D. A. (1979). *Correlation and causality.* New York: Wiley.

Kenrick, D. T., & Stringfield, D. O. (1980). Personality traits and the eye of the beholder: Crossing some traditional philosophical boundaries in the search for consistency in all of the people. *Psychological Review, 87,* 88–104.

Kernberg, O. F. (1975). *Borderline condition and pathological narcissism.* New York: Jason Aronson.

Key, W. B. (1973). *Subliminal seduction.* Englewood Cliffs, NJ: Prentice-Hall.

Key, W. B. (1976). *Media sexploitation.* Englewood Cliffs, NJ: Prentice-Hall.

Kimeldorf, C., & Geiwitz, P. J. (1966). Smoking and the Blacky orality factors. *Journal of Projective Techniques and Personality Assessment, 30,* 167–168.

Kinsey, A. C., Pomeroy, W. D., & Martin, C. E. (1948). *Sexual behavior in the human male.* Philadelphia: Saunders.

Kinsey, A. C., Pomeroy, W. D., Martin, C. E., & Gebhard, P. H. (1953). *Sexual behavior in the human female.* Philadelphia: Saunders.

Kline, P. (1968). Obsessional traits, obsessional symptoms, and anal eroticism. *British Journal of Medical Psychology, 41,* 299–305.

Kline, P. (1972). *Fact and fantasy in Freudian theory.* London: Methuen.

Kline, P. (1984). *Psychology and Freudian theory.* London: Methuen.

Kobasa, S. C. (1979). Stressful life events, personality, and health: An inquiry into hardiness. *Journal of Personality and Social Psychology, 37,* 1–11.

Kobasa, S. C., Maddi, S. R., & Kahn, S. (1982). Hardiness and health: A prospective study. *Journal of Personality and Social Psychology, 42,* 168–177.

Kohlberg, L. (1963). The development of children's orientations toward a moral order: I. Sequence in the development of human thought. *Vita Humana, 6,* 11–33.

Kohlberg, L. (1966). A cognitive-developmental analysis of children's sex-role concepts and attitudes. In E. Maccoby (Ed.), *The development of sex differences.* Stanford: Stanford University Press.

Kohlberg, L. (1981). *Essays on moral development (Vol. 1).* New York: Harper & Row.

Kohlberg, L. (1984). *Essays on moral development (Vol. 2).* New York: Harper & Row.

Kohler, W. (1924). *The mentality of apes.* London: Kegan Paul.

Kolata, G. (1980). Texas counselors use psychology in cancer therapy. *Smithsonian,* August, pp. 48–57.

Korchin, S. J. (1983). The history of clinical psychology: A personal view. In M. Hersen, A. E. Kazdin, & A. S. Bellack (Eds.), *The clinical psychology handbook.* New York: Pergamon.

Korchin, S. J., & Schuldberg, D. (1981). The future of clinical assessment. *American Psychologist, 36,* 1147–1158.

Kretschmer, E. (1921). *Korperbau und Charakter.* Berlin: Springer.

Kris, E. (1952). *Psychoanalytic explorations in art.* New York: International Universities Press.

Kuhn, T. S. (1970). *The structure of scientific revolutions (2nd ed.).* Chicago: University of Chicago Press.

Kulik, J. A., Bangert-Drowns, R. L., & Kulik, C. C. (1984). Effectiveness of coaching for aptitude tests. *Psychological Bulletin, 95,* 179–188.

Lahey, B. B., & Rubinoff, A. (1981). Behavior therapy in education. In L. Michelson, M. Hersen, & S. M. Turner (Eds.), *Future perspectives in behavior therapy.* New York: Plenum.

Laing, R. D. (1965). *The divided self.* Baltimore: Penguin.

Lamb, D. H. (1978). Anxiety. In H. London & J. E. Exner (Eds.), *Dimensions of personality.* New York: Wiley.

Langer, E. J. (1975). The illusion of control. *Journal of Personality and Social Psychology, 32,* 311–328.

Langer, E. J., & Rodin, J. (1976). The effects of choice and enhanced personal responsibility for the aged: A field experiment in an institutional setting. *Journal of Personality and Social Psychology, 34,* 191–198.

Langer, E. J., & Saegert, S. (1977). Crowding and cognitive control. *Journal of Personality and Social Psychology, 35,* 175–182.

Lashley, K. (1929). *Brain mechanisms and intelligence.* Chicago: University of Chicago Press.

Lazarus, R. S. (1979). Positive denial: The case of not facing reality. *Psychology Today, 13*(6), 44–60.

Lefcourt, H. M. (1976). *Locus of control: Current trends in theory and research.* Hillsdale, NJ: Erlbaum.

Lehmann, H. E. (1980). Schizophrenia: Clinical features. In H. I. Kaplan, A. M. Freedman, & B. J. Sadock (Eds.), *Comprehensive textbook of psychiatry* (3rd ed., Vol. 2). Baltimore: Williams and Wilkins.

Leitenberg, H. (1976). *Handbook of behavior modification and behavior therapy.* Englewood Cliffs, NJ: Prentice-Hall.

Lenard, L. (1981). Visions that vanquish cancer. *Science Digest,* April, pp. 58–62; 110–111.

Leo, J. (1985). Are criminals born, not made? *Time,* October 21, p. 94.

Lerner, M. J. (1971). Observers' evaluation of a victim: Justice, guilt, and veridical perception. *Journal of Personality and Social Psychology, 20,* 127–135.

Levant, R. F., & Schlien, J. M. (Eds.). (1984). *Client-centered therapy and the person-centered approach: New directions in theory, research, and practice.* New York: Praeger.

Lewin, K. (1935). *A dynamic theory of personality.* New York: McGraw-Hill.

Lewin, K. (1951). *Field theory in social science: Selected theoretical papers.* New York: Harper.

Lewinsohn, P. M. (1974). A behavioral approach to depression. In R. J. Friedman & M. M. Katz (Eds.), *The psychology of depression: Contemporary theory and research.* Washington, D.C.: Winston-Wiley.

Lewis, C. S. (1941). Psycho-analysis and literary criticism. *Essays and Studies by Members of the English Association, 27,* 7–21.

Lewis, H. B. (1981). *Freud and modern psychology: The emotional basis of mental illness (Vol. 1).* New York: Plenum.

Lewontin, R. C., Rose, S., & Kamin, L. (1984). *Not in our genes: Biology: ideology, and human nature.* New York: Pantheon.

Lidz, T. (1975). *The origin and treatment of schizophrenic disorders.* London: Hutchinson.

Lloyd, C. (1980). Life events and depressive disorders reviewed. I. Events as predisposing factors. II. Events as precipitating factors. *Archives of General Psychiatry, 37,* 529–548.

Loeb, R. (1975). Content-concomitants of boys' locus of control examined in parent-child interactions. *Developmental Psychology, 11,* 353–359.

Loehlin, J. C. (1968). *Computer models of personality.* New York: Random House.

Loehlin, J. C. (1984). R. B. Cattell and behavior genetics. *Multivariate Behavioral Research, 19,* 310–321.

Loehlin, J. C., & Nichols, R. C. (1976). *Heredity, environment, and personality.* Austin: University of Texas Press.

Loevinger, J. (1976). *Ego development.* San Francisco: Jossey-Bass.

Loewenberg, P. (1983). *Decoding the past: The psychohistorical approach.* New York: Knopf.

Logue, A. W. (1979). Taste aversion and the generality of the laws of learning. *Psychological Bulletin, 86,* 276–296.

London, H., & Exner, J. E. (Eds.). (1978). *Dimensions of personality.* New York: Wiley.

London, I. D. (1944). Psychologists' misuse of the auxiliary concepts of physics and mathematics. *Psychological Review, 51,* 266–291.

London: M., & Bray, D. W. (1980). Ethical issues in testing and evaluation for personnel decisions. *American Psychologist, 35,* 890–901.

Lord, C. G. (1982). Predicting behavioral consistency from an individual's perception of situational similarities. *Journal of Personality and Social Psychology, 42,* 1076–1088.

Lorenz, K. S. (1966). *On aggression.* New York: Harcourt Brace Jovanovich.

Luborsky, L. (1964). A psychoanalytic research on momentary forgetting during free association. *Bulletin of the Philadelphia Association for Psycholoanalysis, 14,* 119–137.

Luborsky, L. (1970). New directions in research on neurotic and psychosomatic symptoms. *American Scientist, 58,* 661–668.

Luborsky, L. (1976). Helping alliance in psychotherapy: The groundwork for a study of their relationship to its outcome. In J. L. Claghorn (Ed.), *Successful psychotherapy.* New York: Brunner/Mazel.

Luborsky, L. (1977). Measuring a pervasive psychic structure in psychotherapy: The core conflictual relationship theme. In N. Freedman & S. Grand (Eds.), *Communicative structures and psychic structures.* New York: Plenum.

Luborsky, L. (1984). *Principles of psychoanalytic psychotherapy.* New York: Basic Books.

Luborsky, L., Crits-Christoph, P., & Mellon, J. (1986). Advent of objective measures of the transference concept. *Journal of Consulting and Clinical Psychology, 54,* 39–47.

Luborsky, L., Sackeim, H., & Christoph, P. (1979). The state conducive to momentary forgetting. In J. F. Kihlstom & F. J. Evans (Eds.), *Functional disorders of memory.* Hillsdale, NJ: Erlbaum.

Lykken, D. T. (1957). A study of anxiety in the sociopathic personality. *Journal of Abnormal and Social Psychology, 55,* 6–10.

Lyle, W. H., & Levitt, E. E. (1955). Punitiveness, authoritarianism, and parental discipline of grade school children. *Journal of Abnormal and Social Psychology, 51,* 42–46.

MacCorquodale, K., & Meehl, P. E. (1948). On a distinction between hypothetical constructs and intervening variables. *Psychological Review, 55,* 95–107.

Maddi, S. R. (1980). *Personality theories: A comparative analysis.* Homewood, IL: Dorsey.

Maddi, S. R. (1984). Personology for the 1980's. In R. A. Zucker, J. Aronoff, & A. I. Rabin (Eds.), *Personality and the prediction of behavior.* New York: Academic Press.

Magnusson, D., & Endler, N. S. (Eds.). (1977). *Personality at the crossroads: Current issues in interactional psychology.* Hillsdale, NJ: Erlbaum.

Maher, B. A., & Maher, W. B. (1979). Psychopathology. In E. Hearst (Ed.), *The first century of experimental psychology.* Hillsdale, NJ: Erlbaum.

Mahoney, M. J. (1974). *Cognition and behavior modification.* Cambridge, MA: Ballinger.

Maier, S. F. (1970). Failure to escape traumatic shock: Incompatible skeletal motor responses or learned helplessness? *Learning and Motivation, 1,* 157–170.

Maier, S. F., & Seligman, M. E. P. (1976). Learned helplessness: Theory and evidence. *Journal of Experimental Psychology: General, 105,* 3–46.

Marcuse, H. (1962). *Eros and civilization.* New York: Vintage.

Marks, I. M. (1969). *Fears and phobias.* New York: Academic Press.

Markus, H. (1977). Self-schemas and processing information about the self. *Journal of Personality and Social Psychology, 35,* 63–78.

Markus, H. (1980). The self in thought and memory. In D. M. Wegner & R. R. Vallacher (Eds.), *The self in social psychology.* New York: Oxford.

Markus, H., Crane, M., Bernstein, S., & Siladi, M. (1982). Self-schemas and gender. *Journal of Personality and Social Psychology, 42,* 38–50.

Markus, H., Smith, J., & Moreland, R. L. (1985). Role of the self-concept in the perception of others. *Journal of Personality and Social Psychology, 49,* 1494–1512.

Markus, H., & Zajonc, R. B. (1985). The cognitive perspective in social psychology. In G. Lindzey & E. Aronson (Eds.), *The handbook of social psychology (3rd ed., Vol. 1).* New York: Random House.

Marsh, H. W., & Parker, J. W. (1984). Determinants of student self-concept: Is it better to be a relatively large fish in a small pond even if you don't learn to swim as well? *Journal of Personality and Social Psychology, 47,* 213–231.

Marshall, W. L., Gauthier, J., & Gordon, A. (1979). The current status of flooding therapy. In M. Hersen, R. M. Eisler, & P. M. Miller (Eds.), *Progress in behavior modification (Vol. 7).* New York: Academic Press.

Maslow, A. H. (1966). *The psychology of science: A reconnaissance.* New York: Harper & Row.

Maslow, A. H. (1970). *Motivation and personality (2nd ed.).* New York: Harper & Row.

Masters, W. H., & Johnson, V. E. (1970). *Human sexual inadequacy.* Boston: Little, Brown.

Matthews, K. A. (1982). Psychological perspectives on the Type A behavior pattern. *Psychological Bulletin, 91,* 293–323.

Maule, T. (1968). Make no mistakes about it. *Sports Illustrated,* January 29, pp. 24–26+.

Mazur, A., & Robertson, L. S. (1972). *Biology and social behavior.* New York: Macmillan.

McCain, G., & Segal, E. M. (1973). *The game of science (2nd ed.).* Monterey, CA: Brooks/Cole.

McClelland, D. C. (1961). *The achieving society.* Princeton, NJ: Van Nostrand.

McClelland, D. C. (1965). Toward a theory of motive acquisition. *American Psychologist, 20,* 321–333.

McClelland, D. C. (1971). *Assessing human motivation.* Morristown, NJ: General Learning Press.

McClelland, D. C. (1975). *Power: The inner experience.* New York: Wiley.

McClelland, D. C. (1980). Motive dispositions: The merits of operant and respondent measures. In L. Wheeler (Ed.), *Review of personality and social psychology (Vol. I).* Beverly Hills, CA: Sage.

McClelland, D. C., Atkinson, J. W., Clark, R. A., & Lowell, E. I. (1953). *The achievement motive.* New York: Appleton-Century-Crofts.

McClelland, D. C., & Winter, D. G. (1969). *Motivating economic achievement.* New York: Free Press.

McCormick, E. J. (1976). *Human factors in engineering and design* (4th ed.). New York: McGraw-Hill.

McGinnies, E. (1949). Emotionality and perceptual defense. *Psychological Review, 56,* 244–251.

McGuire, W. J., & McGuire, C. V. (1981). The spontaneous self-concept as affected by personal distinctiveness. In M. D. Lynch, A. A. Norem-Hebeisen, & K. J. Gergen (Eds.), *Self-concept: Advances in theory and research.* Cambridge, MA: Ballinger.

McNeal, J. U. (1982). *Consumer behavior: An integrative approach.* Boston: Little, Brown.

Mead, M. (1928). *Coming of age in Samoa.* New York: Morrow.

Mednick, S. A., Gabrielli, W. F., & Hutchings, B. (1984). Genetic influences in criminal convictions: Evidence from an adoption cohort. *Science, 224,* 891–894.

Meehl, P. E. (1954). *Clinical versus statistical prediction.* Minneapolis: University of Minnesota Press.

Meehl, P. E. (1957). When shall we use our heads instead of the formula? *Journal of Counseling Psychology, 4,* 268–273.

Meer, J. (1984). The winter of schizophrenia. *Psychology Today, 18*(8), 14.

Meichenbaum, D. (1977). *Cognitive behavior-modification: An integrative approach.* New York: Plenum.

Meissner, W. W. (1980). Theories of personality and psychopathology: Classical psychoanalysis. In H. I. Kaplan, A. M. Freedman, & B. J. Sadock (Eds.), *Comprehensive textbook of psychiatry* (3rd ed., Vol. 1). Baltimore: Williams & Wilkins.

Mellstrom, M., Cicala, G. A., & Zuckerman, M. (1976). General versus specific trait anxiety measures in the prediction of fear of snakes, heights, and darkness. *Journal of Consulting and Clinical Psychology, 44,* 83–91.

Mendelsohn, G. A. (1983). What should we tell students about theories of personality? *Contemporary Psychology, 28,* 435–437.

Messick, S., & Jungeblut, A. (1981). Time and method of coaching for the SAT. *Psychological Bulletin, 89,* 191–216.

Metalsky, G. I., Abramson, L. Y., Seligman, M. E. P., Semmel, A., & Peterson, C. (1982). Attributional styles and life events in the classroom: Vulnerability and invulnerability to depressive mood reactions. *Journal of Personality and Social Psychology, 43,* 612–617.

Metzner, R. (1979). *Know your type: Maps of identity.* Garden City, NY: Anchor Press.

Milgram, S. (1963). Behavioral study of obedience. *Journal of Abnormal and Social Psychology, 67,* 371–378.

Milgram, S. (1970). The experience of living in cities. *Science, 167,* 1461–1468.

Milgram, S. (1974). *Obedience to authority.* New York: Harper & Row.

Miller, G. A. (1969). Psychology as a means of promoting human welfare. *American Psychologist, 24,* 1063–1075.

Miller, N. E. (1969). Learning of visceral and glandular responses. *Science, 163,* 434–445.

Miller, N. E., & Dworkin, B. R. (1974). Visceral learning: Recent difficulties with curarized rats and significant problems for human research. In P. A. Obrist, A. H. Black, J. Brener, & L. V. DiCara (Eds.), *Cardiovascular psychophysiology.* Chicago: Aldine.

Miller, S. M. (1979). Controllability and human stress: Method, evidence, and theory. *Behaviour Research and Therapy, 17,* 287–304.

Millon, T. (1981). *Disorders of personality.* New York: Wiley.

Mineka, S., & Kihlstrom, J. F. (1978). Unpredictable and uncontrollable events: A new perspective on experimental neurosis. *Journal of Abnormal Psychology, 87,* 256–271.

Mischel, W. (1968). *Personality and assessment.* New York: Wiley.

Mischel, W. (1971). *Introduction to personality.* New York: Holt, Rinehart & Winston.

Mischel, W. (1973). Toward a cognitive social learning theory reconceptualization of personality. *Psychological Review, 80,* 252–283.

Mischel, W. (1977). On the future of personality assessment. *American Psychologist, 32,* 246–254.

Mischel, W. (1979). On the interface of cognition and personality: Beyond the person-situation debate. *American Psychologist, 34,* 740–754.

Mischel, W. (1984). On the predictability of behavior and the structure of personality. In R. A. Zucker, J. Aronoff, & A. I. Rabin (Eds.), *Personality and the prediction of behavior.* New York: Academic Press.

Mischel, W. (1986). *Introduction to personality (4th ed.).* New York: Holt, Rinehart & Winston.

Mischel, W., Ebbesen, E. B., & Zeiss, A. R. (1973). Selective attention to the self: Situational and dispositional determinants. *Journal of Personality and Social Psychology, 27,* 129–142.

Mischel, W., & Peake, P. K. (1982). Beyond deja-vu in the search for cross-situational consistency. *Psychological Review, 89,* 730–755.

Mischler, E. G., & Waxler, N. (1968). *Interaction in families: An experimental study of family processes and schizophrenia.* New York: Wiley.

Mixon, D. (1971). Behavior analysis treating subjects as actors rather than organisms. *Journal for the Theory of Social Behaviour, 1,* 19–32.

Mollinger, R. N. (1981). *Psychoanalysis and literature: An introduction.* Chicago: Nelson-Hall.

Monson, T. C., Hesley, J. W., & Chernick, L. (1982). Specifying when personality traits can and cannot predict behavior: An alternative to abandoning the attempt to predict single-act criteria. *Journal of Personality and Social Psychology, 43,* 385–399.

Moreland, R. L., & Zajonc, R. B. (1977). Is stimulus recognition a necessary condition for the occurrence of exposure effects? *Journal of Personality and Social Psychology, 35,* 191–199.

Moreland, R. L., & Zajonc, R. B. (1979). Exposure effects may not depend on stimulus recognition. *Journal of Personality and Social Psychology, 37,* 1085–1089.

Morgan, C. D., & Murray, H. A. (1935). A method for investigating fantasies. *Archives of Neurology and Psychiatry, 34,* 289–306.

Morgan, E., Mull, H. K., & Wasburn, M. F. (1919). An attempt to test the moods or temperament of cheerfulness and depression by directed recall of emotionally toned experiences. *American Journal of Psychology, 30,* 302–304.

Mosher, D. L., & Sirkin, M. (1984). Measuring a macho personality constellation. *Journal of Research in Personality, 18,* 150–163.

Moskowitz, D. S., & Schwarz, J. C. (1982). Validity comparison of behavior counts and ratings by knowledgeable informants. *Journal of Personality and Social Psychology, 42,* 518–528.

Mossey, J. M., & Shapiro, E. (1982). Self-rated health: A prediction of mortality among the elderly. *American Journal of Public Health, 72,* 800–808.

Munsterberg, H. (1913). *Psychology and industrial efficiency.* Boston: Houghton Mifflin.

Murphy, G. (1947). *Personality: A biosocial approach to origins and structure.* New York: Harper.

Murphy, G. (1949). Psychical research and personality. *Proceedings of the Society for Psychical Research, 49,* 1–15.

Murphy, G., & Kovach, J. K. (1972). *Historical introduction to modern psychology (3rd ed.).* New York: Harcourt Brace Jovanovich.

Murray, H. A. (1938). *Explorations in personality.* New York: Oxford.

Murray, H. A. (1951). Toward a classification of interaction. In T. Parsons & E. A. Shils (Eds.), *Toward a general theory of action.* Cambridge, MA: Harvard University Press.

Murray, H. A., & MacKinnon, D. W. (1946). Assessment of OSS personnel. *Journal of Consulting Psychology, 10,* 76–80.

Myer, I. B. (1962). *Manual: Myers-Briggs Type Indicator.* Palo Alto, CA: Consulting Psychologists Press.

Nathan, P. E. (1984). The worksite as a setting for health promotion and positive lifestyle change. In J. D. Matarazzo et al. (Eds.), *Behavioral health: A handbook of health enhancement and disease prevention.* New York: Wiley.

Neill, A. S. (1960). *Summerhill: A radical approach to child rearing.* New York: Hart.

Neimeyer, G. J., & Neimeyer, R. A. (1981). Personal construct perspectives on cognitive assessment. In T. Merluzzi, C. Glass, & M. Genest (Eds.), *Cognitive assessment.* New York: Guilford.

Neimeyer, R. A. (1985). *The development of personal construct psychology.* Lincoln: University of Nebraska Press.

Neisser, U. (1967). *Cognitive psychology.* Englewood Cliffs, NJ: Prentice-Hall.

Nemiah, J. C. (1980). Obsessive-compulsive disorder (obsessive-compulsive neurosis). In H. I. Kaplan, A. M. Freedman, & B. J. Sadock (Eds.), *Comprehensive textbook of psychiatry (3rd ed., Vol. 2).* Baltimore: Williams & Wilkins. (a)

Nemiah, J. C. (1980). Phobic disorder (phonic neurosis). In H. I. Kaplan, A. M. Freedman, & B. J. Sadock (Eds.), *Comprehensive textbook of psychiatry (3rd ed., Vol. 2).* Baltimore: Williams & Wilkins. (b)

Nemiah, J. C. (1980). Somatoform disorders. In H. I. Kaplan, A. M. Freedman, & B. J. Sadock (Eds.), *Comprehensive textbook of psychiatry (3rd ed., Vol. 2).* Baltimore: Williams & Wilkins. (c)

Nevill, D. (1974). Experimental manipulation of dependency motivation and its effects on eye contact and measures of field dependency. *Journal of Personality and Social Psychology, 29,* 72–79.

Newsweek. (1968, September 23). Talk with Dr. Spock: In praise of the younger generation. pp. 70–71.

Nicholls, J. G., Licht, B. G., & Pearl, R. A. (1982). Some dangers of using personality questionnaires to study personality. *Psychological Bulletin, 92,* 572–580.

Niederland, W. (1959). The "miracled-up" world of Schreber's childhood. *Psychoanalytic Study of the Child, 14,* 383–413.

Nisbett, R. E., & Wilson, T. W. (1977). Telling more than we can know: Verbal reports on mental processes. *Psychological Review, 84,* 231–259.

Noblin, C. D. (1962). *Experimental analysis of psychoanalytic character types through the operant conditioning of verbal responses.* Unpublished doctoral dissertation, Louisiana State University.

Noblin, C. D., Timmons, E. O., & Kael, H. C. (1966). Differential effects of positive and negative verbal reinforcement on psychoanalytic character types. *Journal of Personality and Social Psychology, 4,* 224–228.

Nolen-Hoeksema, S., Girgus, J. S., & Seligman, M. E. P. (1986). Learned helplessness in children: A longitudinal study of depression, achievement, and explanatory style. *Journal of Personality and Social Psychology, 51,* 435–442.

Office of Strategic Services Assessment Staff. (1948). *Assessment of men.* New York: Rinehart.

Ohman, A., Fredrickson, M., Hugdahl, K., & Rimmo, P. (1976). The premise of equipotentiality in human classical conditioning: Conditioned electrodermal responses to potentially phobic stimuli. *Journal of Experimental Psychology: General, 105,* 313–337.

O'Leary, A. (1985). Self-efficacy and health. *Behaviour Research and Therapy, 23,* 437–451.

Oltman, P. K., Goodenough, D. R., Witkin, H. A., Freedman, N., & Friedman, F. (1975). Psychological differentiation as a factor in conflict resolution. *Journal of Personality and Social Psychology, 32,* 730–736.

Orne, M. T. (1962). On the social psychology of the psychology experiment: With particular reference to demand characteristics and their implications. *American Psychologist, 17,* 776–783.

Owen, D. (1985). *None of the above.* Boston: Houghton Mifflin.

Packard, V. (1957). *The hidden persuaders.* New York: David McKay.

Paul, G. L. (1967). Insight vs. desensitization in psychotherapy two years after termination. *Journal of Consulting Psychology, 31,* 333–348.

Paykel, E. S. (1974). Life stress and psychiatric disorder: Applications of the clinical approach. In B. S. Dowrenwend & B. P. Dowrenwend (Eds.), *Stressful life events: Their nature and effects.* New York: Wiley.

Pearson, K. (1896). Mathematical contributions to the theory of evolution. *Philosophical Transactions, 187,* 253–318.

Pedhazur, E. J., & Tetenbaum, T. J. (1979). Bem Sex Role Inventory: A theoretical and methodological critique. *Journal of Personality and Social Psychology, 37,* 996–1016.

Pepper, S. C. (1942). *World hypotheses.* Berkeley: University of California Press.

Pervin, L. A. (1985). Personality: Current controversies, issues, and directions. *Annual Review of Psychology, 36,* 83–114.

Peterson, C. (1986). *Explanatory style as a risk factor for illness.* Unpublished manuscript, Virginia Polytechnic Institute and State University.

Peterson, C., & Barrett, L. C. (1986). *Explanatory style and academic performance among university freshmen.* Unpublished manuscript, Virginia Polytechnic Institute and State University.

Peterson, C., Schwartz, S. M., & Seligman, M. E. P. (1981). Self-blame and depressive symptoms. *Journal of Personality and Social Psychology, 49,* 337–348.

Peterson, C., & Scott, W. A. (1975). Generality and topic specificity of cognitive styles. *Journal of Research in Personality, 9,* 366–374.

Peterson, C., & Seligman, M. E. P. (1984). Causal explanations as a risk factor for depression: Theory and evidence. *Psychological Review, 91,* 347–374.

Peterson, C., Seligman, M. E. P., & Vaillant, G. E. (1986). *Explanatory style is a risk factor for physical illness.* Unpublished manuscript, University of Michigan.

Peterson, C., Semmel, A., von Baeyer, C., Abramson, L. Y., Metalsky, G. I., & Seligman, M. E. P. (1982). The Attributional Style Questionnaire. *Cognitive Therapy and Research, 6,* 287–299.

Peterson, C., & Stunkard, A. J. (1986). *Personal control and health promotion.* Unpublished manuscript, Virginia Polytechnic Institute and State University.

Peterson, D. R. (1968). *The clinical study of social behavior.* New York: Appleton.

Phares, E. J. (1978). Locus of control. In H. London & J. E. Exner (Eds.), *Dimensions of personality.* New York: Wiley.

Phares, E. J. (1984). *Introduction to personality.* Columbus, OH: Merrill.

Phillips, B. N., Martin, R. P., & Meyers, J. (1972). Interventions in relation to anxiety in school. In C. D. Spielberger (Ed.), *Anxiety: Current trends in theory and research (Vol. II).* New York: Academic Press.

Piaget, J. (1932). *Moral judgment of the child.* New York: Harcourt Brace.

Plomin, R., DeFries, J. C., & McClearn, G. E. (1980). *Behavioral genetics: A primer.* San Francisco: Freeman.

Popper, K. R. (1959). *The logic of discovery.* London: Hutchinson.

Porter, N., Geis, F. L., Cooper, E., & Newman, E. (1985). Androgyny and leadership in mixed-sex groups. *Journal of Personality and Social Psychology, 49,* 808–823.

Portis, S. A. (1949). Idiopathic ulcerative colitis: Newer concepts concerning its cause and management. *JAMA, 139,* 208–214.

Premack, D. (1971). Language in the chimpanzee? *Science, 172,* 808–822.

Pressey, S. L. (1921). A group scale for investigating the emotions. *Journal of Abnormal Psychology, 16,* 55–64.

Price, R. H., & Bouffard, D. L. (1974). Behavioral appropriateness and situational constraints as dimensions of social behavior. *Journal of Personality and Social Psychology, 30,* 579–586.

Prichard, J. C. (1837). *Treatise on insanity and other disorders affecting the mind.* Philadelphia: Haswell, Barrington, & Haswell.

Prochaska, J. O. (1984). *Systems of psychotherapy: A transhistorical analysis (2nd ed.).* Homewood, IL: Dorsey.

Prociuk, T. J., & Breen, L. J. (1977). Internal-external locus of control and information-seeking in a college academic situation. *Journal of Social Psychology, 101,* 309–310.

Quine, W. V., & Ullian, J. S. (1978). *The web of belief (2nd ed.).* New York: Random House.

Rachman, S. J. (1978). *Fear and courage.* New York: Freeman.

Raimy, V. (1976). *Misunderstandings of the self: Cognitive psychotherapy and the misconception hypothesis.* San Francisco: Jossey-Bass.

Rapaport, D. (1959). The structure of psychoanalytic theory: A systematizing attempt. In S. Koch (Ed.), *Psychology: A study of a science (Vol. 1).* New York: McGraw-Hill.

Raps, C. S., Peterson, C., Reinhard, K. E., Abramson, L. Y., & Seligman, M. E. P. (1982). Attributional style among depressed patients. *Journal of Abnormal Psychology, 91,* 102–108.

Raynor, J. O. (1970). Relationships between achievement-related motives, future orientation, and academic performance. *Journal of Personality and Social Psychology, 15,* 28–33.

Reeves, D. J., & Booth, R. F. (1979). Expressed versus inventoried interests as predictors of paramedic effectiveness. *Journal of Vocational Behavior, 15,* 155–163.

Reich, W. (1933). *Charakteranalyse.* Berlin: Selbstverlag des Verfassers.

Revusky, S. H., & Garcia, J. (1970). Learned associations over long delays. In G. H. Bower & J. T. Spence (Eds.), *Psychology of learning and motivation (Vol. 4).* New York: Academic Press.

Riddle, M., & Roberts, A. H. (1977). Delinquency, delay of gratification, recidivism, and the Porteus maze tests. *Psychological Bulletin, 84,* 417–425.

Roazen, P. (1975). *Freud and his followers.* New York: Knopf.

Rodin, J., & Langer, E. J. (1977). Long-term effects of a control-relevant intervention with the institutionalized aged. *Journal of Personality and Social Psychology, 35,* 897–902.

Rodin, J., Solomon, S., & Metcalf, J. (1978). Role of control in mediating perceptions of density. *Journal of Personality and Social Psychology, 36,* 988–999.

Rodin, J., Timko, C., & Anderson, S. (1985). The construct of control. In P. Lawton & G. Maddox (Eds.), *Annual review of gerontology and geriatrics (Vol. 5).* New York: Springer.

Rogers, C. R. (1942). *Counseling and psychotherapy: Newer concepts in practice.* Boston: Houghton Mifflin.

Rogers, C. R. (1951). *Client-centered therapy: Its current practices, implications, and theory.* Boston: Houghton Mifflin.

Rogers, C. R. (1961). *On becoming a person.* Boston: Houghton Mifflin.

Rogers, C. R. (1969). *Freedom to learn.* Columbus, OH: Merrill.

Rogers, C. R. (1970). *On encounter groups.* New York: Harper & Row.

Rogers, C. R. (1972). *Becoming partners.* New York: Dell.

Rogers, C. R. (1977). *Carl Rogers on personal power: Inner strength and its revolutionary impact.* New York: Delacorte.

Rogers, C. R. (1980). *A way of being.* Boston: Houghton Mifflin.

Rogers, C. R., & Dymond, R. F. (Eds.). (1954). *Psychotherapy and personality change.* Chicago: University of Chicago Press.

Rogers, C. R., Gendlin, E. T., Kiesler, D. J., & Truax, C. B. (1967). *The therapeutic relationship and its impact: A study of psychotherapy with schizophrenics.* Madison: University of Wisconsin Press.

Rogers, C. R., & Ryback, D. (1984). One alternative to nuclear planetary suicide. In R. F. Levant & J. M. Shlien (Eds.), *Client-centered therapy and the person-centered approach: New directions in theory, research, and practice.* New York: Praeger.

Rogers, C. R., & Skinner, B. F. (1956). Some issues concerning the control of human behavior. *Science, 124,* 1057–1066.

Rorschach, H. (1942). *Psychodiagnostics: A diagnostic test based on perception.* Berne: Huber.

Rosch, E., & Mervis, C. B. (1975). Family resemblances: Studies in the internal structure of categories. *Cognitive Psychology, 7,* 573–605.

Rosenbaum, M. (1984). Anna O. (Bertha Pappenheim): Her history. In M. Rosenbaum & M. Muroff (Eds.), *Anna O.: Fourteen contemporary interpretations.* New York: Free Press.

Rosenberg, M. J. (1965). When dissonance fails: On eliminating evaluation apprehension from attitude measurement. *Journal of Personality and Social Psychology, 1,* 18–42.

Rosenhan, D. L., & Seligman, M. E. P. (1984). *Abnormal psychology.* New York: Norton.

Rosenthal, R. (1966). *Experimenter effects in behavioral research.* New York: Appleton-Century-Crofts.

Rosenthal, R., & Rosnow, R. L. (Eds.) (1969). *Artifact in behavioral research.* New York: Academic Press.

Rosenthal, R., & Rubin, D. B. (1982). A simple, general purpose display of magnitude of experimental effect. *Journal of Educational Psychology, 74,* 166–169.

Rosenzweig, S. (1954). A transvaluation of psychotherapy: A reply to Hans Eysenck. *Journal of Abnormal and Social Psychology, 49,* 298–304.

Ross, L. (1977). The intuitive psychologist and his shortcomings: Distortions in the attribution process. In L. Berkowitz (Ed.), *Advances in experimental social psychology (Vol. 10).* New York: Academic Press.

Rotter, J. B. (1954). *Social learning and clinical psychology.* Englewood Cliffs, NJ: Prentice-Hall.

Rotter, J. B. (1966). Generalized expectancies for internal versus external control of reinforcement. *Psychological Monographs, 81* (1, Whole No. 609).

Rotter, J. B. (1967). A new scale for the measurement of interpersonal trust. *Journal of Personality, 35,* 651–655.

Rotter, J. B. (1971). Generalized expectancies for interpersonal trust. *American Psychologist, 26,* 443–452.

Rotter, J. B. (1975). Some problems and misconceptions related to the construct of internal versus external reinforcement. *Journal of Consulting and Clinical Psychology, 43,* 56–67.

Roubertoux, P. (1985). Genetic correlates of personality and temperament: The origins of individual differences. In J. Strelau, F. H. Farley, & A. Gale (Eds.), *The biological bases of personality and behavior: Theories, measurement techniques, and development (Vol. 1).* Washington, D.C.: Hemisphere.

Rozin, P., & Kalat, J. W. (1971). Specific hungers and poison avoidance as adaptive specializations of learning. *Psychological Review, 78,* 459–486.

Runyan, W. M. (1981). Why did Van Gogh cut off his ear? The problem of alternative explanations in psychobiography. *Journal of Personality and Social Psychology, 40,* 1070–1077.

Runyan, W. M. (1982). *Life histories and psychobiography: Explorations in theory and method.* New York: Oxford.

Rush, A. J., Beck, A. T., Kovacs, M., & Hollon, S. D. (1977). Comparative efficacy of cognitive therapy and imipramine in the treatment of depressed outpatients. *Cognitive Therapy and Research, 1,* 17–37.

Rushton, J. P., Brainerd, C. J., & Pressley, M. (1983). Behavioral development and construct validity: The principle of aggregation. *Psychological Bulletin, 94,* 18–38.

Ryle, G. (1949). *The concept of mind.* London: Hutchinson.

Sackeim, H., Nordlie, J., & Gur, R. (1979). A model of hysterical and hypnotic blindness: Cognition, motivation, and awareness. *Journal of Abnormal Psychology, 88,* 474–489.

Sanford, N. (1976). Graduate education then and now. *American Psychologist, 31,* 756–764.

Sarason, I. G. (Ed.). (1980). *Test anxiety: Theory, research, and applications.* Hillsdale, NJ: Erlbaum.

Sarbin, T. R., & Allen, V. L. (1968). Role theory. In G. Lindzey & E. Aronson (Eds.), *The handbook of social psychology (2nd ed., Vol. 1).* Reading, MA: Addison-Wesley.

Scarf, M. (1980). Images that heal: A doubtful idea whose time has come. *Psychology Today,* September, pp. 32–46.

Scarr, S. (1968). Environmental bias in twin studies. *Eugenics Quarterly, 15,* 34–40.

Schacter, S. (1959). *The psychology of affiliation.* Stanford, CA: Stanford University Press.

Schacter, S. (1982). Recidivism and self-cure of smoking and obesity. *American Psychologist, 37,* 436–444.

Schacter, S., & Latané, B. T. (1964). Crime, cognition, and the autonomic nervous system. In D. Levine (Ed.), *Nebraska Symposium on Motivation (Vol. 12).* Lincoln: University of Nebraska Press.

Schacter, S., & Singer, J. E. (1962). Cognitive, social, and physiological determinants of emotional state. *Psychological Review, 65,* 379–399.

Schaffer, H. R., & Emerson, P. R. (1964). The development of social attachments in infancy. *Child Development Monographs, 29*(2).

Schank, R. R., & Abelson, R. P. (1977). *Scripts, plans, goals, and understanding*. New York: Halsted.

Schapiro, M. (1956). Leonardo and Freud: An art-historical study. *Journal of the History of Ideas, 17,* 147–178.

Scheier, M. F., & Carver, C. S. (1985). Optimism, coping, and health: Assessment and implications of generalized outcome expectancies. *Health Psychology, 4,* 219–247.

Schill, T. (1966). Sex differences in identification of the castrating agent on the Blacky Test. *Journal of Clinical Psychology, 22,* 324–325.

Schlenker, B. R. (Ed.). (1985). *The self and social life*. New York: McGraw-Hill.

Schmidt, D. E., & Keating, J. P. (1979). Human crowding and personal control: An integration of the research. *Psychological Bulletin, 86,* 680–700.

Schneider, D. J. (1973). Implicit personality theory: A review. *Psychological Bulletin, 79,* 294–309.

Schooler, C. (1972). Birth order effects: Not here, not now! *Psychological Bulletin, 78,* 161–175.

Schooler, C., Zahn, T. P., Murphy, D. L., & Buchsbaum, M. S. (1978). Psychological correlates of monoamine oxidase in normals. *Journal of Nervous and Mental Diseases, 166,* 177–186.

Schroder, H. M., Driver, M. J., & Streufert, S. (1967). *Human information processing: Individuals and groups functioning in complex social situations*. New York: Holt, Rinehart & Winston.

Schutte, N. S., Kenrick, D. T., & Sadalla, E. K. (1985). The search for predictable settings: Situational prototypes, constraint, and behavioral variation. *Journal of Personality and Social Psychology, 49,* 121–128.

Schwartz, B. (1984). *Psychology of learning and behavior (2nd ed.)*. New York: Norton.

Scott, J. P., & Fuller, J. L. (1965). *Genetics and the social behavior of the dog*. Chicago: University of Chicago Press.

Scott, W. A. (1969). Structure of natural cognitions. *Journal of Personality and Social Psychology, 12,* 261–278.

Scott, W. A. (1974). Varieties of cognitive integration. *Journal of Personality and Social Psychology, 30,* 563–578.

Scott, W. A., Osgood, D. W., & Peterson, C. (1979). *Cognitive structure: Theory and measurement of individual differences*. Washington, D.C.: Winston.

Scott, W. A., & Peterson, C. (1975). Adjustment, Pollyannaism, and attraction to close personal relationships. *Journal of Consulting and Clinical Psychology, 43,* 872–880.

Scott, W. D. (1908). *Psychology of advertising*. Boston: Small, Maynard.

Sears, P. S. (1953). Child-rearing factors related to playing of sex-typed roles. *American Psychologist, 8,* 431.

Sears, R. R. (1943). *Survey of objective studies of psychoanalytic concepts*. New York: Social Science Research Council.

Sears, R. R. (1970). Relation of early socialization experiences to self-concept and gender role in middle childhood. *Child Development, 41,* 267–289.

Sears, R. R., Rau, L., & Alpert, R. (1965). *Identification and childrearing*. Stanford, CA: Stanford University Press.

Seligman, M. E. P. (1970). On the generality of the laws of learning. *Psychological Review, 77,* 406–418.

Seligman, M. E. P. (1971). Phobias and preparedness. *Behavior Therapy, 2,* 307–321.

Seligman, M. E. P. (1974). Depression and learned helplessness. In R. J. Friedman & M. M. Katz (Eds.), *The psychology of depression: Contemporary theory and research*. Washington, D.C.: Winston.

Seligman, M. E. P. (1975). *Helplessness: On depression, development, and death*. San Francisco: Freeman.

Seligman, M. E. P. (1978). Comment and integration. *Journal of Abnormal Psychology, 87,* 165–179.

Seligman, M. E. P. (1981). A learned helplessness point of view. In L. P. Rehm (Ed.), *Behavior therapy for depression: Present status and future directions*. New York: Academic Press.

Shaw, J. S. (1982). Psychological androgyny and stressful life events. *Journal of Personality and Social Psychology, 43,* 145–153.

Sheldon, W. H. (1940). *The varieties of human physique.* New York: Harper.

Sheldon, W. H. (1942). *The varieties of temperament.* New York: Harper.

Sherrod, D. R. (1974). Crowding, perceived control, and behavioral after-effects. *Journal of Applied Social Psychology, 4,* 171–186.

Shields, J. (1976). Heredity and environment. In H. J. Eysenck & G. D. Wilson (Eds.), *A textbook of human psychology.* Baltimore: University Park Press.

Shrauger, J. S., & Shoeneman, T. J. (1979). Symbolic interactionist view of self-concept: Through the looking glass darkly. *Psychological Bulletin, 82,* 581–596.

Silverman, L. H. (1971). An experimental technique for the study of unconscious conflict. *British Journal of Medical Psychology, 44,* 17–25.

Silverman, L. H. (1976). Psychoanalytic theory: "The reports of my death are greatly exaggerated." *American Psychologist, 31,* 621–637.

Silverman, L. H., Bronstein, A., & Mendelsohn, E. (1976). The further use of the subliminal psychodynamic activation method for the experimental study of the clinical theory of psychoanalysis: On the specificity of relationships between manifest psychopathology and unconscious conflict. *Psychotherapy: Theory, Research, and Practice, 13,* 2–16.

Silverman, L. H., & Fishel, A. K. (1981). The Oedipus complex: Studies in adult male behavior. In L. Wheeler (Ed.), *Review of personality and social psychology (Vol. 2).* Beverly Hills, CA: Sage.

Silverman, M. A. (1980). A fresh look at the case of Little Hans. In M. Kanzer & J. Glenn (Eds.), *Freud and his patients.* New York: Aronson.

Simonton, O. C., & Simonton, S. (1975). Belief systems and management of the emotional aspects of malignancy. *Journal of Transpersonal Psychology, 7,* 29–48.

Singer, J. L. (1984). *The human personality.* San Diego: Harcourt Brace Jovanovich.

Skinner, B. F. (1938). *The behavior of organisms.* New York: Appleton-Century-Crofts.

Skinner, B. F. (1950). Are theories of learning necessary? *Psychological Review, 57,* 193–216.

Skinner, B. F. (1971). *Beyond freedom and dignity.* New York: Knopf.

Slater, P. (Ed.). (1976). *Explorations in intrapersonal space (Vol. 1).* London: Wiley.

Slater, P. (Ed.). (1977). *Explorations in intrapersonal space (Vol. 2).* London: Wiley.

Smart, J. C. (1982). Faculty teaching goals: A test of Holland's theory. *Journal of Educational Psychology, 74,* 180–188.

Smith, M. L., & Glass, G. V (1977). The meta-analysis of psychotherapy outcome studies. *American Psychologist, 32,* 752–760.

Snyder, M. (1983). The influence of individuals on situations: Implications for understanding the links between personality and social behavior. *Journal of Personality, 51,* 497–516.

Snyder, M., & Gangestad, S. (1982). Choosing social situations: Two investigations of self-monitoring processes. *Journal of Personality and Social Psychology, 43,* 123–135.

Snyder, S. H. (1980). *Biological aspects of mental disorder.* New York: Oxford.

Spearman, C. (1904). "General intelligence" objectively determined and measured. *American Journal of Psychology, 15,* 201–292.

Spence, K. W. (1960). *Behavior theory and learning.* Englewood Cliffs, NJ: Prentice-Hall.

Spielberger, C. D. (1966). *Anxiety and behavior.* New York: Academic Press.

Spock, B. (1946). *Common sense book of baby and child care.* New York: Duell, Sloane, & Pearce.

Spock, B. (1971). Don't blame me. *Look,* January 26, pp. 37–38.

Spock, B. (1984). Coercion in the classroom will not work. *The Education Digest,* October, pp. 28–31.

Springer, S. P., & Deutsch, G. (1985). *Left brain, right brain, (Rev. ed.).* New York: Freeman.

Stagner, R. (1936). *Psychology of personality.* New York: McGraw-Hill.

Stern, W. (1904). *The psychological methods of testing intelligence.* Baltimore: Warwick & York.

Storms, M. D., & Nisbett, R. E. (1970). Insomnia and the attribution process. *Journal of Personality and Social Psychology, 16,* 319–328.

Streufert, S., & Streufert, S. C. (1978). *Behavior in the complex environment.* Washington, D.C.: Winston.

Stricker, L. J., & Ross, J. (1964). Some correlates of a Jungian personality inventory. *Psychological Reports, 14*, 623–643.

Stross, L., & Shevrin, H. (1969). Hypnosis as a method for investigating unconscious thought processes: A review of research. *Journal of the American Psychoanalytic Association, 17*, 100–135.

Suedfeld, P. (1971). Information processing as a personality model. In H. M. Schroder & P. Suedfeld (Eds.), *Personality theory and information processing*. New York: Ronald.

Suedfeld, P., & Rank, A. D. (1976). Revolutionary leaders: Long-term success as a function of changes in cognitive complexity. *Journal of Personality and Social Psychology, 34*, 169–178.

Suler, J. R. (1980). Primary process thinking and creativity. *Psychological Bulletin, 88*, 144–165.

Sullivan, H. S. (1947). *Conceptions of modern psychiatry*. Washington, D.C.: William Alanson White Psychiatric Foundation.

Sullivan, H. S. (1953). *The interpersonal theory of psychiatry*. New York: Norton.

Sullivan, H. S. (1954). *The psychiatric interview*. New York: Norton.

Sullivan, H. S. (1956). *Clinical studies in psychiatry*. New York: Norton.

Sullivan, H. S. (1962). *Schizophrenia as a human process*. New York: Norton.

Sullivan, H. S. (1964). *The fusion of psychiatry and social science*. New York: Norton.

Sulloway, F. J. (1979). *Freud: Biologist of the mind*. New York: Basic Books.

Suls, J., & Greenwald, A. G. (Eds.). (1983). *Psychological perspectives on the self (Vol. 2)*. Hillsdale, NJ: Erlbaum.

Suls, J., & Mullen, B. (1981). Life events, perceived control, and illness: The role of uncertainty. *Journal of Human Stress, 7*, 30–34.

Swan, J. A. (1972). Public response to air pollution. In J. F. Wohlwill & D. H. Carson (Eds.), *Environment and the social sciences*. Washington, D.C.: American Psychological Association.

Swann, W. B. (1983). Self-verification: Bringing social reality into harmony with the self. In J. Suls & A. G. Greenwald (Eds.), *Psychological perspectives on the self (Vol. 2)*. Hillsdale, NJ: Erlbaum.

Swann, W. B., & Hill, C. A. (1982). When our identities are mistaken: Reaffirming self-conceptions through social interaction. *Journal of Personality and Social Psychology, 43*, 59–66.

Sweeney, P. D., Anderson, K., & Bailey, S. (1986). Attributional style in depression: A meta-analytic review. *Journal of Personality and Social Psychology, 50*, 974–991.

Ssasz, T. S. (1961). *The myth of mental illness*. New York: Hoeber.

Taylor, M. C., & Hall, J. A. (1982). Psychological androgyny: Theories, methods, and conclusions. *Psychological Bulletin, 92*, 347–366.

Taylor, R. B., Denham, J. R., & Ureda, J. W. (1982). *Health promotion: Principles and clinical applications*. Norwalk, CN: Appleton-Century-Crofts.

Taylor, S. E. (1983). Adjustment to threatening events: A theory of cognitive adaptation. *American Psychologist, 38*, 1161–1173.

Taylor, S. E., & Fiske, S. T. (1982). Getting inside the head: Methodologies for process analysis in attribution and social cognition. In J. Harvey, W. Ickes, & R. Kidd (Eds.), *New directions in attribution research (Vol. 3)*. Hillsdale, NJ: Erlbaum.

Tennen, H. (1982). A re-view of cognitive mediators of learned helplessness. *Journal of Personality, 50*, 526–541.

Terman, L. M., & Childs, H. G. (1912). A tentative revision and extension of the Binet-Simon measuring scale of intelligence. *Journal of Educational Psychology, 3*, 61–74, 133–143, 198–208, 277–289.

Thigpen, C. H., & Cleckley, H. (1954). A case of multiple personality. *Journal of Abnormal and Social Psychology, 49*, 135–151.

Thigpen, C. H., & Cleckley, H. (1957). *The three faces of Eve*. New York: McGraw-Hill.

Thoits, P. A. (1983). Dimensions of life events that influence psychological distress: An evaluation and synthesis of the literature. In H. Kaplan (Ed.), *Psychosocial stress: Trends in theory and research*. New York: Academic Press.

Thomas, A., & Chess, S. (1977). *Temperament and development*. New York: Bruner/Mazel.

Thomas, A., Chess, S., Birch, H., Hertzig, M., & Korn, S. (1963). *Behavioral individuality in early childhood*. New York: New York University Press.

Thompson, S. (1981). Will it hurt less if I can control it? A complex answer to a simple question. *Psychological Bulletin, 90,* 89–101.

Thorndike, E. L. (1911). *Animal intelligence: Experimental studies.* New York: Macmillan.

Thorndike, E. L. (1916). Tests of aesthetic appreciation. *Journal of Educational Psychology, 7,* 509–522.

Thorngate, W. (1976). Possible limits on a science of social behavior. In L. H. Strickland, F. E. Aboud, & K. J. Gergen (Eds.), *Social psychology in transition.* New York: Plenum.

Thurston, J. R., & Mussen, P. E. (1951). Infant feeding gratification and adult personality. *Journal of Personality, 19,* 449–458.

Tolman, E. C. (1932). *Purposive behavior in animals and man.* New York: Appleton-Century-Crofts.

Tolman, E. C. (1948). Cognitive maps in rats and men. *Psychological Review, 55,* 189–208.

Tomkins, S. S. (1962). *Affect, imagery, consciousness (Vol. 1).* New York: Springer.

Tomkins, S. S. (1963). *Affect, imagery, consciousness (Vol. 2).* New York: Springer.

Tomkins, S. S. (1979). Script theory: Differential magnification of affects. In H. E. Howe & R. A. Dienstbier (Eds.), *Nebraska symposium on motivation (Vol. 26).* Lincoln: University of Nebraska Press.

Tomkins, S. S. (1981). The quest for primary motives: Biography and autobiography of an idea. *Journal of Personality and Social Psychology, 41,* 306–329.

Tribich, D., & Messer, S. (1974). Psychoanalytic type and status of authority as determiners of suggestibility. *Journal of Consulting and Clinical Psychology, 42,* 842–848.

Trilling, L. (1977). Art and neurosis. In W. Anderson (Ed.), *Therapy and the arts.* New York: Harper & Row.

Ullmann, L. P., & Krasner, L. (1975). *A psychological approach to abnormal behavior (2nd ed.).* Englewood Cliffs, NJ: Prentice-Hall.

Vaihinger, H. (1911). *The psychology of "as if": A system of the theoretical, practical, and religious fictions of mankind.* New York: Harcourt, Brace & World.

Vaillant, G. E. (1971). Theoretical hierarchy of adaptive ego mechanisms. *Archives of General Psychiatry, 24,* 107–118.

Vaillant, G. E. (1977). *Adaptation to life.* Boston: Little, Brown.

Vaillant, G. E. (1983). *The natural history of alcoholism.* Cambridge, MA: Harvard University Press.

Vandenberg, S. G. (1962). The hereditary abilities study: Hereditary components in a psychological test battery. *American Journal of Human Genetics, 14,* 220–227.

Van Egeren, L. F. (1979). Social interactions, communications, and the coronary-prone behavior pattern: A psychophysiological study. *Psychosomatic Medicine, 41,* 2–18.

Vannoy, J. S. (1965). Generality of cognitive complexity-simplicity as a personality construct. *Journal of Personality and Social Psychology, 2,* 385–396.

Vernon, P. E. (1964). *Personality assessment: A critical survey.* New York: Wiley.

Viorst, M. (1972). Meet the People's Party Candidate. *New York Times Magazine,* June 4, pp. 42–58.

Wachtel, P. (1973). Psychodynamics, behavior therapy, and the implacable experimenter: An inquiry into the consistency of personality. *Journal of Abnormal Psychology, 82,* 323–334.

Wagner, M. E., & Schubert, H. J. P. (1977). Sibship variables and United States presidents. *Journal of Individual Psychology, 33,* 78–85.

Walker, J. I., & Brodie, H. K. H. (1980). Paranoid disorders. In H. I. Kaplan, A. M. Freedman, & B. J. Sadock (Eds.), *Comprehensive textbook of psychiatry (3rd ed., Vol. 2).* Baltimore: Williams & Wilkins.

Watson, J. B. (1913). Psychology as the behaviorist views it. *Psychological Review, 20,* 158–177.

Watson, J. B. (1930). *Behaviorism (Rev. ed.)* New York: Norton.

Watson, J. B., & Rayner, R. (1920). Conditioned emotional reactions. *Journal of Experimental Psychology, 3,* 1–14.

Webster's new collegiate dictionary. (1977). Springfield, MA: Merriam.

Weiner, B. (1974). *Achievement motivation and attribution theory.* Morristown, NJ: General Learning Press.

Weiner, B. (1978). Achievement strivings. In H. London & J. E. Exner (Eds.), *Dimensions of personality.* New York: Wiley.

Weiner, B. (1979). A theory of motivation for some classroom experiences. *Journal of Educational Psychology, 71,* 3–25.

Weiner, B., & Litman-Adizes, T. (1980). An attributional, expectancy-value analysis of learned helplessness and depression. In J. Garber & M. E. P. Seligman (Eds.), *Human helplessness.* New York: Academic Press.

Weiner, H. (1977). *Psychobiology and human disease.* New York: Elsevier.

Wells, B. W. P. (1983). *Body and personality.* London: Longman.

Werner, H. (1957). *Comparative psychology of mental development (Rev. ed.).* New York: International Universities Press.

Wertheimer, M. (1972). *Fundamental issues in psychology.* New York: Holt, Rinehart & Winston.

Wertheimer, M. (1979). *A brief history of psychology (Rev. ed.).* New York: Holt, Rinehart & Winston.

West, S. G. (1983). Personality and prediction: An introduction. *Journal of Personality, 51,* 275–285.

Wexler, D. (1974). A cognitive theory of experiencing, self-actualization, and therapeutic process. In D. Wexler & L. Rice (Eds.), *Innovations in client-centered therapy.* New York: Wiley.

White, R. W. (1959). Motivation reconsidered: The concept of competence. *Psychological Review, 66,* 297–333.

White, R. W. (1966). *Lives in progress (2nd ed.).* New York: Holt.

Whiting, J. W. M., & Child, I. L. (1953). *Child-training and personality.* New Haven: Yale University Press.

Wilhelm, R., & Jung, C. G. (1931). *The secret of the golden flower.* New York: Harcourt, Brace & World.

Willerman, L. (1979). *The psychology of group and individual differences.* San Francisco: Freeman.

Wilson, E. O. (1975). *Sociobiology: The new synthesis.* Cambridge, MA: Harvard University Press.

Wilson, G. D. (1978). Introversion/extraversion. In H. London & J. E. Exner (Eds.), *Dimensions of personality.* New York: Wiley.

Wilson, J. Q., & Herrnstein, R. J. (1985). *Crime and human nature.* New York: Simon & Schuster.

Wilson, T. D., & Linville, P. W. (1982). Improving the academic performance of college freshmen: Attribution therapy revisited. *Journal of Personality and Social Psychology, 42,* 367–376.

Wilson, T. D., & Linville, P. W. (1985). Improving the performance of college freshmen with attributional techniques. *Journal of Personality and Social Psychology, 49,* 287–293.

Winett, R. A., & Winkler, R. C. (1972). Current behavior modification in the classroom: Be still, be quiet, be docile. *Journal of Applied Behavior Analysis, 5,* 499–504.

Witkin, H. A. (1949). Perception of body position and of the position of the visual field. *Psychological Monographs, 63,* (7, Whole No. 302).

Witkin, H. A., Lewis, H. B., Hertzman, M., Machover, K., Meissner, P. B., & Wapner, S. (1954). *Personality through perception.* New York: Harper.

Wittgenstein, L. (1953). *Philosophical investigations.* New York: Macmillan.

Wolpe, J. (1958). *Psychotherapy by reciprocal inhibition.* Stanford: Stanford University Press.

Wolpe, J., & Rachman, S. J. (1960). Psychoanalytic "evidence": A critique based on Freud's case of Little Hans. *Journal of Nervous and Mental Disease, 131,* 135–147.

Wolpert, E. A. (1980). Major affective disorders. In H. I. Kaplan, A. M. Freedman, & B. J. Sadock (Eds.), *Comprehensive textbook of psychiatry (3rd ed., Vol. 2).* Baltimore: Williams & Wilkins.

Woodruffe, C. (1984). The consistency of presented personality: Additional evidence from aggregation. *Journal of Personality, 52,* 307–317.

Woodworth, R. S. (1918). *Dynamic psychology.* New York: Columbia University Press.

Woodworth, R. S. (1919). *Personal data sheet (Psychoneurotic inventory).* Chicago: Stoelting.

Wortman, C. B. (1975). Some determinants of perceived control. *Journal of Personality and Social Psychology, 31,* 282–294.

Wylie, R. C. (1968). The present status of self theory. In E. F. Borgatta & W. W. Lambert (Eds.), *Handbook of personality theory and research.* Chicago: Rand McNally.

Yerkes, R. M. (1943). *Chimpanzees.* New Haven: Yale University Press.

Zajonc, R. B. (1965). Social facilitation. *Science, 149,* 269–274.

Zajonc, R. B. (1980). Feeling and thinking. *American Psychologist, 35,* 151–175.

Zajonc, R. B., & Bargh, J. (1980). Birth order, family size, and decline of SAT scores. *American Psychologist, 35,* 662–668.

Zajonc, R. B., & Markus, G. B. (1975). Birth order and intellectual development. *Psychological Review, 82,* 74–88.

Zimring, C. M. (1981). Stress and the designed environment. *Journal of Social Issues, 37,* 145–171.

Zuckerman, M. (1969). Theoretical formulations. In J. P. Zubek (Ed.), *Sensory deprivation: Fifteen years of research.* New York: Appleton-Century-Crofts. (a)

Zuckerman, M. (1969). Variables affecting deprivation results. In J. P. Zubek (Ed.), *Sensory deprivation: Fifteen years of research.* New York: Appleton-Century-Crofts. (b)

Zuckerman, M. (1974). The sensation seeking motive. In B. A. Maher (Ed.), *Progress in experimental personality research (Vol. 7).* New York: Academic Press.

Zuckerman, M. (1978). Sensation seeking. In H. London & J. E. Exner (Eds.), *Dimensions of personality.* New York: Wiley.

Zuckerman, M. (1985). Biological foundations of the sensation-seeking temperament. In J. Strelau, F. H. Farley, & A. Gale (Eds.), *The biological bases of personality and behavior: Theories, measurement techniques, and development (Vol. 1).* Washington, D.C.: Hemisphere.

Zukav, G. (1979). *The dancing Wu Li masters: An overview of the new physics.* New York: Morrow.

Zytowski, D. G. (1973). Considerations in the selection and use of interest inventories. In D. G. Zytowski (Ed.), *Interest measurement.* Minneapolis: University of Minnesota Press.

AUTHOR INDEX

Gergen, K. J., 242
Ghiselli, E. E., 391
Gibson, H. B., 317
Gifford, R. K., 39
Gilbert, J. P., 515
Gillies, P., 297
Gilligan, C., 225–226
Girgus, J. S., 483
Gitlin, T., 397–398, 402
Glass, D. C., 146, 343, 445, 536, 537
Glass, G. V, 97
Glueck, E. T., 382
Glueck, S., 382
Goffman, E., 42
Goldberg, L. R., 357
Goldfried, M. R., 373
Goldstein, Kenneth M., 125, 126, 332, 466, 467, 468
Goldstein, Kurt, 92, 307, 429
Goodenough, D. R., 50, 334–335
Gordon, A., 568
Gorsuch, R. L., 311
Goshen, C. E., 197
Gotlib, I. H., 523
Gottier, R. J., 391
Gould, P., 538–540
Gould, S. J., 84, 285, 312, 403
Grace, W. J., 259–260
Graham, D. T., 259–260
Graham, M. J., 454
Greenberg, R. P., 128, 135, 212, 214, 222, 230–232, 234, 250, 251
Greenwald, A. G., 124, 454, 484
Guilford, J. P., 345
Guion, R. M., 391
Gunderson, J. G., 375
Gur, R. C., 220–221, 246
Gurman, A. S., 431, 524

H

Hackett, T. P., 339
Hackman, J. R., 143
Hake, D. F., 572
Haley, J., 133
Hall, C. S., 95, 98, 112, 175, 180, 181, 183, 184, 223, 288, 296, 306, 317, 414, 415, 416, 564, 582
Hall, J. A., 328, 329
Hall, M. H., 307
Hall, R. V., 571
Hamilton, D. L., 39
Hammond, K. R., 500
Handee, J. C., 572
Hansen, J. C., 385–386
Hansson, R. O., 389
Hare, R. D., 377

Harlow, H. F., 94
Harré, R., 46
Hartmann, H., 170
Hartshorne, H., 347, 349, 350
Harvey, J. H., 518
Harvey, O. J., 410, 433–436, 438, 451, 463, 467, 485, 496, 584
Hathaway, S. R., 90, 338
Hayden, B., 484
Heider, F., 410, 414, 418–419, 440, 447, 452, 483
Heinstein, M. I., 233
Hemmings, R., 266
Hendry, L. B., 297
Henri, V., 85
Herrigel, E., 579
Herrnstein, R. J., 379–384
Hersen, M., 567
Hertzig, M., 297
Hesley, J. W., 361
Hilgard, E. R., 580
Hill, C. A., 484
Hirt, E., 375
Hockey, G. R. J., 392
Hoffman, M. L., 225
Hogan, R., 350, 351, 364, 389, 391, 580, 585–587
Holland, J. L., 387–388
Hollon, S. D., 520, 524
Holmes, T. H., 260, 490–491
Holt, R. R., 373
Horney, K., 91, 175, 181–182, 185
Howes, D., 218
Hoyt, M. F., 229
Hugdahl, K., 556
Hull, C. L., 92, 94, 441, 560, 564
Hunt, D. E., 410, 433–436, 438, 451, 467, 485–486, 584
Hunt, H. F., 232, 463, 496
Hutchings, B., 381

I

Izard, C. E., 583

J

Jaccard, J. J., 97
Jackson, D. D., 133
Jackson, D. N., 357
Jacobs, S. V., 537
Jacoby, J., 145
James, W., 44, 71–72, 76, 307, 351
Janet, P., 531
Janis, I. L., 445
Janoff-Bulman, R., 488
Jaret, P., 531

Jastrow, J., 293
Jemmott, J. B., 146, 328
Jenkins, C. D., 260–261, 343
Joffe, J. A., 437
Johansson, C. B., 385
Johnson, V. E., 265, 568
Jones, Edward E., 485
Jones, Ernest, 147, 231, 278
Jones, H. E., 229
Jones, R. G., 149
Jung, C. G., 91, 153, 154, 166, 176–181, 182, 189, 203, 236–237, 278, 303, 420, 473
Jungeblut, A., 400

K

Kabat, L. G., 358
Kael, H. C., 233
Kahn, S., 490
Kalat, J. W., 555
Kamen, L., 483
Kamin, L., 118
Kaplan, G. A., 491
Kaplan, M., 378
Kasl, V., 526
Kazdin, A. E., 570
Keating, J. P., 144
Keller, F. S., 571
Keller, L. S., 372
Kellog, M. A., 263
Kelly, G. A., 41, 94, 97, 115, 128, 410, 420–428, 429, 431, 434, 439, 440, 451, 460, 462, 464, 484, 496, 502–504, 506, 525, 546
Kelly, J., 329
Kempen, R. W., 571
Kendall, P. C., 520
Kenny, D. A., 479
Kenrick, D. T., 356–357, 361
Kent, R. N., 373
Kernberg, O. F., 251
Key, W. B., 272–275
Kiesler, D. J., 431
Kihlstrom, J. F., 331
Kimeldorf, C., 232
Kinsey, A. C., 214
Kline, P., 212, 214, 230–232, 234, 251, 255
Kobasa, S. C., 490, 492
Koelling, R. A., 555
Koffka, K., 69
Kohlberg, L., 225, 226, 435–436
Kohler, W., 69, 557
Kolata, G., 531
Korchin, S. J., 89, 371, 373
Korn, S., 298
Kovach, J. K., 72, 85
Kovacs, M., 524

SUBJECT INDEX

ILLUSTRATION CREDITS

CHAPTER 1: **Page 8:** Brown Brothers; **9:** (left) UPI/Bettmann Newsphotos; (right) Reuters/Bettmann Newsphotos; **24:** © Bill Bachman/Photo Researchers; **25:** © Peter Vandermark/Stock, Boston.

CHAPTER 2: **Page 33:** Culver Pictures; **35:** (left) © Walter Chandoha; (right) AP/Wide World Photos; **43:** © Eric Kroll/Taurus Photos; **61:** © Shelly Rusten.

CHAPTER 3: **Page 73:** © Carol Palmer/The Picture Cube; **75:** Photo courtesy of Prof. Benjamin Harris, University of Wisconsin—Parkside. Taken from John Watson's 1919 film, *Experimental Investigation of Babies;* **80:** The Bettmann Archive; **87:** Signal Corps Photo/National Archives III-SC-386.

CHAPTER 4: **Page 106:** © Erika Stone/Photo Researchers; **107:** © Jeff Albertson; **108:** (bottom) © M. C. Escher Heirs, c/o Cordon Art BV, Baarn (Holland); **120:** Courtesy of Christopher Lofting; **144:** © Nancy J. Pierce/Photo Researchers.

CHAPTER 5: **Page 155:** AP/Wide World Photos; **163:** © Joel Gordon 1978; **164:** © Arthur Tress/Photo Researchers; **165:** © Cathy Cheney/EKM-Nepenthe; **172:** © Janice Rogovin/The Picture Cube; **180:** *The Collected Works of C.G. Jung,* trans. R.F.C. Hull, Bollingen Series XX, Vol. 9, I: *The Archetypes and the Collective Unconscious.* Copyright © 1959, 1969 by Princeton University Press. Figures 1 and 40 (between pp. 356 and 357) reprinted with permission of Princeton University Press; **185:** © Peter Vandermark/Stock, Boston; **189:** © Tim Davis/Photo Researchers.

CHAPTER 6: **Page 198:** UPI/Bettmann Newsphotos; **215:** © Jill Cannefax/EKM-Nepenthe; **224:** © Richard Younker, Click/Chicago; **227:** Movie Still Archives.

CHAPTER 7: **Page 243:** © Michael Weisbrot/Stock, Boston; **244:** © Polly Brown/The Picture Cube; **256:** © Tom Ballard/EKM-Nepenthe; **279:** Assemblage: metal wheel, 25 1/2" diameter, mounted on painted wood stool, 23 3/4" high; overall, 50 1/2" high. The Sidney and Harriet Janis Collection. Gift to the Museum of Modern Art; **280:** Courtesy Alexander Iolas Gallery, New York; **281:** (top) Oil and collage on composition board, 9 3/8 × 13 3/4". Sidney and Harriet Janis Collection. Gift to the Museum of Modern Art; (bottom) Courtesy Robert des Charnes.

CHAPTER 8: **Page 295:** The Bettmann Archive; **302:** © Harvey Stein; **310:** © Abraham Menashe/Photo Researchers.

CHAPTER 9: **Page 327:** © Andrew Sacks/Black Star; **329:** AP/Wide World Photos; **331:** © Carol Bernson/Black Star; **333:** © l'Illustration/Sygma; **335:** David Linton; **337:** (left) UPI/Bettmann Newsphotos; (right) UPI/Bettmann Newsphotos; **341:** © Stanley Rowin/The Picture Cube; **344:** © Rick Mansfield/The Image Works.

CHAPTER 10: **Page 369:** © Lynn McLaren/Photo Researchers; **380:** © David Woo/Stock, Boston; **386:** NASA; **396:** Courtesy of Doyle Dane Bernbach, Inc.; **404:** Brown Brothers.

CHAPTER 11: **Page 416:** (left) © Richard Wood/The Picture Cube; (right) © David S. Strickler/The Picture Cube; **423:** © Alan Carey/The Image Works; **438:** © Budd Gray/Stock, Boston; **439:** © Anestis Diakopolous/Stock, Boston; **447:** © Warren Uzzle/Photo Researchers; **450:** U.S. Air Force Photo.

CHAPTER 12: **Page 462:** © Jerry Howard/Stock, Boston; **463:** © Knott-Boston Globe/Sygma; **482:** © Michael Hayman/Stock, Boston; **485:** © Bob Combs/Photo Researchers; **487:** © Elizabeth Crews.

CHAPTER 13: **Page 513:** © Chester Higgins, Jr./Photo Researchers; **516:** © Shirley Zeiberg/Taurus Photos; **527:** © Paolo Koch/Photo Researchers; **534:** © Jan Lukas/Photo Researchers; **537:** © Irwin Karnick/Photo Researchers; **542:** Brown Brothers.

CHAPTER 14: **Page 553:** © Alan Carey/The Image Works; **554:** © Elizabeth Crews/Stock, Boston; **559:** © Suzanne Szasz/Photo Researchers; **571:** © Joel Gordon 1985.

CHAPTER 15: **Page 582:** © Andrew Brilliant/The Picture Cube; **584:** Photos used with permission of Paul Ekman, Edward Gallob, and Silvan Tomkins; **585:** © Chester Higgins, Jr./Photo Researchers.

COPYRIGHTS AND ACKNOWLEDGMENTS